Bharatanatyam

This volume illuminates the various forces that have
shaped Bharatanatyam over the past two centuries.
It brings into sharp focus the social, political, and aesthetic
transformations in the representation and practice of
the dance form in terms of its colonial and postcolonial
legacies. Exploring the historicity and aesthetic
development of Bharatanatyam, this volume questions the
assumption of its homogeneous past, maps its global steps,
and gauges its contemporary forays.

Bharatanatyam

A Reader

edited by

DAVESH SONEJI

OXFORD

UNIVERSITY PRESS

OXFORD
UNIVERSITY PRESS

Oxford University Press is a department of the University of Oxford.
It furthers the University's objective of excellence in research, scholarship,
and education by publishing worldwide. Oxford is a registered trademark of
Oxford University Press in the UK and in certain other countries

Published in India by
Oxford University Press
YMCA Library Building, 1 Jai Singh Road, New Delhi 110 001, India

© Oxford University Press 2010

The moral rights of the author have been asserted

First Edition published in 2010
Oxford India Paperbacks 2012
Second impression 2013

ISBN-13: 978-0-19-808377-1
ISBN-10: 0-19-808377-7

Typeset in Adobe Jenson Pro 10.5/12.6
by Le Studio Graphique, Gurgaon 122 001
Printed in India by Artxel, Noida 201 301

for
B.M. Sundaram

Contents

PART III

Contemporary Extensions

PART IV

Dancers Speak: Personal Journeys to and from Bharatanatyam

Davesh Soneji

Critical Steps

Thinking through Bharatanatyam
in the Twenty-first Century

The story of the transfiguration of Bharatanatyam dance and its emergence as a global cultural form over the last two centuries presents one of the most complex and compelling narratives about modern South Asia. The practice and politics of Bharatanatyam make palpable both realist and utopian visions of culture, nation, religion, and aesthetics. Despite its dynamic and highly visible presence in India's contemporary cultural scene, Bharatanatyam and the multiple narratives of its modern transformation remain highly understudied and underrepresented in scholarly works. This first-ever scholarly anthology on Bharatanatyam spans two hundred years of writing in English on the subject, and moves in the direction of a critical historicization and aesthetic analysis of the dance form.

Today Bharatanatyam is understood as a seamless and homogenous cultural artifact, comfortably reconciled with the logic and structures of global capitalism. At the heart of the celebration of Bharatanatyam dance is a story told of its 'revival' that began in Madras city in the 1930s. Indeed, elements of this tale of revival have become narratological conventions among practitioners and scholars of Bharatanatyam. Tropes such as the 'fall of the devadasis' and 'temple to theatre', for example, are consistently used to index idealized, nationalized, and easy claims to moments in Bharatanatyam's heterogeneous and ambiguous pasts. Embedded in these everyday statements are historical and aesthetic presumptions about both the dance's past and present. The mythopoeic 'histories' of Bharatanatyam, whether they make use of Sanskrit aesthetic and Puranic texts, or forge links between the contemporary dancer and the ancient 'dancing girl' figurines of Mohenjodaro, threaten to obfuscate the social history of the dance, largely in order to enable a continuous view of Indian culture.

Carefully etched into the urban memoryscapes of South India is this story of the invention of South Indian 'heritage' that can be both *told* and *seen* through today's Bharatanatyam. Indeed, embodied heritage—represented by Kanchipuram saris, Karnatak music, and Bharatanatyam dance—is at the heart of South India's urban, middle-class aspirations. In cities like Chennai and Bengaluru, Bharatanatyam powerfully mediates the tensions between strangeness and familiarity, tradition and modernity, past and present.

As a global cultural practice, Bharatanatyam flows from the illustrious state-supported auditoriums of New Delhi to Hare Krishna temples in Russia to the basements of suburban Toronto homes. Deeply embedded in a politics of national identity, global Bharatanatyam is a chequered site on which history, meaning, and power are repeatedly contested and negotiated. Bharatanatyam's transnational avatar indexes issues of representation, race, and identity. As Janet O'Shea notes,

... bharata natyam stands, on the one hand, in relation to social and political issues endemic to the Indian social landscape of the twentieth century. On the other hand, these concerns travel across the world's stages. The dance practice developed into a contemporary, urban, concert art informed by the investments of the nation, the region, and the urban center and expressed through notions of gendered reputability. This complex history has created a series of double binds in which dancers, instructors, writers, and viewers expect bharata natyam to be verifiably traditional yet creative, authentically Indian yet globally accessible, respectable yet commercially viable. (O'Shea 2007: 25)

In this volume I bring together a range of primary texts and secondary materials that address the complexity of Bharatanatyam's past, and speak to its future. One of the major aims of this anthology is to present historical documents that have hitherto remained inaccessible alongside some of the best critical analyses of the dance's social and aesthetic trajectories. The collection is capped by selections of writing by well-respected dance practitioners who speak about their experiences with the creative and affective vocabularies that Bharatanatyam affords the modern artist. The articles span a range of written media—from research essays to primary archival documents to personal narratives about the creative process. While the collection is by no means comprehensive, it offers some important points of departure for the serious study of Bharatanatyam.

In the interest of making the texts more accessible to the reader, I have grouped them into four sections: (1) Devadasi Dance: History and Representation; (2) Reinventing Dance in South India; (3) Contemporary Extensions; and (4) Dancers Speak: Personal Journeys to and from

Bharatanatyam. In the introduction that follows, I contextualize the essays in an effort to open doors for further conversation on these and other issues in the study of Bharatanatyam. Given the lack of critical historical writing on Bharatanatyam, much of this introduction is devoted to the essays that appear in the first half of the volume. The texts that appear in the second half are, for the most part, self-contained works. Together, they provide a window to the historical provenance, aesthetic and political debates, and personal journeys that have shaped one of the world's fastest growing art forms. The writings in this collection enable us take those critical steps that will move us forward in our articulations of the precedents and potential of Bharatanatyam dance.

DEVADASI DANCE: HISTORY AND REPRESENTATION

At the centre of Bharatanatyam's history stands the enigmatic figure of the devadasi. From the sixteenth to early twentieth century, devadasis have functioned as temple servants and secular courtesans, typically organized in guilds called *melams*. On the one hand, women in these communities possessed a degree of social agency, in that they were not restricted by the norms of patrifocal kinship. They lived in matrilineal homes, had sexual relationships with upper-caste men, and were literate at moments in history when most South Indian women were not. On the other hand, records from centres of political power such as the court at Tanjavur also describe a rigorous code of conduct for professional dancing women, enforced through punishment. These records document the fact that courtesans were commodities regularly bought and sold through the intercession of the court. In other contexts, as the mistresses or 'second wives' of South Indian elites, they were implicated in a larger world of servitude that focused on the fulfillment of male desires. Beginning in the mid-nineteenth century, vociferous social reform movements in South India aimed to dislodge communities of professional dancing women from their hereditary performance practices. Over the next hundred years, their lifestyles were criminalized on the basis of their non-conjugal sexuality, which reformers framed as prostitution. The Madras Devadasis (Prevention of Dedication) Act, implemented in 1947, officially outlawed the social, ritual, and aesthetic practices of devadasis.

Though many Indologists and nationalist historians advance the claim that Bharatanatyam is a direct descendant of the arts of the Tamil Cankam Age (*c.* 300 BCE to 300 CE), a critical reading of Bharatanatyam's history can only begin with the Telugu-speaking Nayaka court in South India in the late sixteenth and seventeenth century. To be sure, professional dancing women, courtesans, prostitutes, and temple women are found throughout South India's literary, epigraphic, and oral histories. The female bards (*virali*) of the ancient Tamil Cankam poems, the courtesan Matavi of the Tamil epic *Cilappatikaram*, the temple woman Paravaiyar of the Tamil Saiva Bhakti tradition, the 400 'women of the temple quarter' (*talicceri pentukal*) mentioned in King Rajaraja Cola's inscription at the Brhadisvara temple in Tanjavur—these could all be construed as predecessors of eighteenth and nineteenth century devadasi-courtesans.[1] But for our purposes, it is important that these scattered and fragmentary references to temple women, court dancers, and other 'public women' only coalesce in the Nayaka period, when these hitherto independent roles are fully collapsed, and the identity of the devadasi as we understand her in colonial South India—with simultaneous links to temple, courtly, and public cultures, complex dance and music practices, and a matrifocal kinship structure—emerges (Narayana Rao, Shulman, and Subrahmanyam 1992: 187). In the Nayaka period, the devadasi-courtesan appears as a distinct cultural presence, inextricably linked to sophisticated articulations of courtly eroticism. Narayana Rao, Shulman, and Subrahmanyam call this a 'telos with existential features, that is, "enjoyment" (*bhoga*)' (ibid.: 57). This culture of bhoga, of erotic longing and fulfillment, is one in which courtesans (*bhoga-stri, vesya*) and temple women have merged into a single universe. In their new role as artists who performed both in temple and courtly contexts, these women were also imaged as concubines, secondary wives, or even queens at the Nayaka court (ibid.: 187).

The court also supported creative writing by courtesans; works by Ramabhadramba and Rangajamma, for example, are considered among the crowning literary pieces from this period.[2] This is also the period when the erotic poems (*padams*) of Ksetrayya were composed, perhaps under the partial patronage of Vijayaraghava Nayaka (r. 1634–73). The padams of Ksetrayya, which continue to survive in the repertoire of the Telugu devadasi community today, reflect innovative images of womanhood and a unique world of fully eroticized aesthetic practices. Many of these songs express female desire and are completely unabashed in their representations of the corporeality of sexual experience. It is against this backdrop that we find the names of a number of professional dancing women at the Nayaka *darbar* in Tanjavur.[3] Most significantly, however, the *substance* of the surviving aesthetic practices of devadasis—the padams of Ksetrayya, a lineage of hereditary dance-masters (*nattuvanars*), and musical genres such as *sabdam* and *varnam*—can only be traced as far back as the Nayaka period. It is also largely in simulation of Nayaka courtly practices at Tanjavur and Madurai that courtesans and their arts moved into small zamindari kingdoms such as those at Pudukkottai and Ramanathapuram.

The Maratha presence in South India, which succeeded Nayaka rule in Tanjavur, augmented the patronage of devadasi-courtesans in this region. From the period of Sahaji Maharaja (1684–1712), court records provide meticulous details about professional dancing women. The Tanjavur Maratha court also produces an incredible amount of literary material meant specifically for interpretation through dance. A notable codification of dance practices—including a guide to the practice of *atavu*s or dance-steps—is found in a Sanskrit work entitled *Sangita Saramrta*, attributed to King Tulaja I (r. 1729–35).

Nearly all extant Bharatanatyam dance repertoire emerges from colonial Tanjavur, a fact obfuscated by contemporary nationalist claims for the dance's 'classical' heritage. The court produced a peculiar syncretic culture that integrated aspects of indigenous Tamil culture, Telugu literary material, the new Mughal-style courtly practices from Maharashtra, and the modernity of the European enlightenment. King Serfoji II (r. 1798–1832) and his heir Sivaji II (r. 1832–55) deployed courtesan dancers in their rituals of display, casting themselves as rulers who, though divested of political authority by successive British annexations, were nevertheless effective, modern patrons of culture. The events at the Tanjavur Maratha court thus exemplify the ways in which devadasis were instrumentalized as emblems of cultural capital in the context of an emergent colonial modernity. The presence of a Western-style band, North Indian (Hindustani) musicians of a high calibre, and the integration of western music into the dance repertoire, distinguished Serfoji's court as an early theatre of cultural experimentation. At the centre of Tanjavur's dance practices were a number of dance-masters (nattuvanars) including the famous *tanjai nalvar* ('Tanjore Quartet', c. 1802–1864, Fig. 1).[4] Under the patronage of Serfoji and Sivaji, Tanjavur nattuvanars are thought to have radically transformed the dance practices at the court through the creation of new compositions and genres that superseded nearly all existing dance repertoire in the region. According to oral traditions, the now well-known suite of a solo Bharatanatyam performance—consisting of the genres *alarippu*, *jatisvaram*, shabdam, varnam, padam, *tillana*, and *sloka*—is attributed to the creativity of the Quartet. The court records of Maratha Tanjavur, preserved in Modi script, furnish the names of several prominent devadasi-courtesans who performed at the *darbar* even

FIG. I   Maratha-style portraits of Cinnaiya (1802–1856) and Ponnaiya (1804–1864), the two elder brothers among the 'Tanjore Quartet'. This image is currently housed in the ancestral home of the brothers on West Main Street in Tanjavur. Photograph by Cylla von Tiedemann

after the annexation of Tanjavur to the British in 1856.[5] Archived in the minds and bodies of professional dancing women, the repertoire was incorporated into colonial ritual and travelled from Tanjavur to Madras when a major migration of artists occurred in the mid-nineteenth century. In Madras, these courtly aesthetic innovations had enduring effects, and would later be re-inscribed as 'classical' dance in the twentieth century.

The migration of devadasis into the new colonial civic centre of Madras began as early as 1857, and established the city as the emergent centre of cultural production in South India. As Lakshmi Subramanian (2006) has argued, this movement gave rise to the formation of a new system of patronage, in which Company dubashes and local zamindars funded and hosted professional performances of music and dance.[6] This new, competitive system was distinct from the traditional ritual- and honour-based modes of patronage (mariyatai), in which devadasis were guaranteed the opportunity to perform in temples and courtly settings by hereditary right. Velala dubashes and other native elites such as Smarta brahmins, Mudaliyars, Nayudus, and Chettiyars sponsored performances of vocal music and poetry in their homes at the time of calendrical festivals.

These included performances of dance, called *mejuvani* in Telugu, which were private displays of wealth and social prestige, and were also usually accompanied by elaborate dinners.[7] At the same time, the competitive artistic culture of the salon occasioned the creation of new literary and performance genres such as the Telugu *javali* that I discuss later in this volume. These 'salon' performances also engendered intimate relationships between devadasis and Madras's civil servants, sometimes composers and poets themselves. Devadasis and their upper-caste patrons composed and performed new songs that amplified the genres developed in Tanjavur; they experimented with new aesthetic modes, Western melodies, and even engaged the English language. It is these salon performances, defined by the presentation of erotic compositions, that ignited the anti-nautch movement in the Madras Presidency. Early print materials from this period such as Tamil and Telugu poems, tracts, and novels, perpetuated urban constructions of Madras devadasis as morally corrupt, diseased, and fallen. They facilitated new representations of dance and its practitioners as worthy targets of moral and aesthetic reform.

While devadasi performance culture continued to flourish in Madras in the nineteenth century, by the first decades of the twentieth century salon performances had nearly become obsolete. The disappearance of these venues gave rise to publicly funded institutions like the Madras Music Academy (estd. 1927) and several other cultural organizations calling themselves *sabha*s ('assemblies'). A handful of devadasis performed at these venues until the 1940s, perhaps in a final nod to the culture of the old-style salon, but this too was short-lived. Meanwhile, a small number of devadasis living in and around Madras became well-known as 'gramophone artists' and film actresses.[8] Devadasi dance was thus detached from the location of its emergence, only to be imported into diffuse systems of value, new media, and new technologies of knowledge.

Representations of Dance in Colonial South India

The first section of this anthology deals with knowledge about devadasi dance captured in print and visual media that traverses imperial circuits in the nineteenth century. Its aim is twofold: (1) to make evident the multiple voices (European and native) that produced colonial discourses on devadasis; and (2) to enable the reader to interrogate these textual representations not only for their well-known moralizing tendencies, but also for clues to the aesthetic lives of the devadasis they are describing.

The opening essay is the earliest writing on devadasis by an Indian written in the English language. Published in 1806—before the time of the famous 'Tanjore Quartet', and long before any anti-nautch discourse began in the Madras Presidency—the essay, 'A short account of the dancing girls, treating concisely on the general principles of dancing and singing, with the translations of two Hindo [sic] songs' offers many significant contributions to the historicization of Bharatanatyam. It is certainly the earliest description of a full-length performance by devadasis and also provides us with details and translations of the dances being performed. The sixteenth-century padams of Ksetrayya, masterpieces of Telugu poetry meant for courtesan performance, are translated into English for the first time in this document.[9] Significantly, it also uses the name Bharatanatyam ('Bharata Nateya') to refer to the dance, dispelling any doubts that the term was 'invented' in the 1930s by revivalists such as Rukmini Devi Arundale, E. Krishna Iyer, or V. Raghavan.

The author of the essay, a Telugu brahmin named Partheputt Ragaviah Charry, appears knowledgeable about the technique of devadasi dance, and notes that his primary aim is to enlighten European audiences about the dance.[10] He writes that those 'English gentlemen ... and more particularly the Ladies, who are not acquainted with the Poetical part of the Native languages in which the songs are composed, must remain contented with the information of the eye,' and his work is an attempt to make the poetic dimensions of the dance, namely *abhinaya*, intelligible to Europeans. The essay includes deliberations on aesthetics (*rasa* theory), the classification and names of hand gestures, and *tala* (rhythm). The latter half of the essay describes a performance of devadasi dance from beginning to end. It opens with the nattuvanar reciting the *melaprapti*, a rhythmic prelude, followed by the *todaya mangalam* (*jaya janaki ramana*, described and translated in the text as 'a Prayer to Rama'). This is followed by a 'Hymn of Salam' (the *salam daruvu*) dedicated to the King Pratapasimha of Tanjavur (r. 1740–63). P. Ragaviah Charry informs us that that the remainder of the performance consists of abhinaya in the form of varnams, padams, and *kirtana*s. This sequence for rendering a recital is still preserved in the Telugu-speaking *kalavantula* community in coastal Andhra Pradesh (Soneji 2008). P. Ragaviah Charry's essay is thus a document that provides us with remarkably sharp descriptions of devadasi performance in the Madras Presidency.

In the second essay in this section, 'Mamia, Ammani and other Bayaderes: Europe's Portrayal of India's Temple Dancers', Joep Bor provides a scholarly overview of European responses to devadasis from the time of Marco Polo to the end of the nineteenth century. These include analyses of print and visual materials in various European languages.

Specifically, Bor focuses on the troupe of devadasis who were brought from Tiruvendipuram (just outside Pondicherry) to perform in London and Paris in 1838. In this brilliant essay, Bor highlights the connections and dissonance between colonial and Orientalist formations of knowledge about professional dancing women from South India and the reception of real devadasis in Europe.

Community, Repertoire, and Aesthetics

The next cluster of essays foregrounds issues of aesthetics and community. Saskia Kersenboom's essay, 'The Traditional Repertoire of the Tiruttani Temple Dancers' examines a localized temple dance and music repertoire from the town of Tiruttani (Tiruvallur district, Tamilnadu). Based on her work with P. Ranganayaki (1914–2005), the last devadasi of the Subrahmanya Svami temple in Tiruttani, Kersenboom's essay carefully delineates the ritual tasks and privileges (mariyatai) afforded to devadasis, documents the daily and festival dance and music programs of the temple, and allows us to hear Ranganayaki's perspectives on these and other issues. Next is an essay by Hari Krishnan on the relationships between texts and devadasi repertoire. Krishnan convincingly demonstrates that 'textualizations' of dance repertoire occurred at the Tanjavur court, and with the advent of print culture, devadasi performance practices flowed through this medium as well. Citing important but understudied texts in Sanskrit, Marathi, Tamil, and Telugu, Krishnan reveals how documentation and creation of performance scripts foreshadowed the disappearance of dance practices within the devadasi community.

This section closes with my own essay that attempts to shift the focus away from the over-emphasized temple associations of devadasis, into a larger world of professional dancing women in colonial South India. 'Salon to Cinema: The Distinctively Modern Life of the Telugu Javali' maps the aesthetics and politics of salon performances in the Madras Presidency through the genre known as javali. In the essay I argue that the javali, as opposed to the earlier Telugu padam genre from which it draws its structure and poetics, can only be understood as a definitively modern genre. Tracing the javali's movement from the Mysore court to early print materials to the Telugu cinema of the 1950s, I interrogate its elusive, hybrid form. I demonstrate that a critical historicization of the genre must take salon performances and colonial modernity seriously, a proposition I extend to the critical study of devadasis and Bharatanatyam as well.

Anti-Nautch Revisited

The term 'reform' is ubiquitously found in scholarly and popular representations of Bharatanatyam's history. It refers to social purity movements that sought to *reform* devadasi-courtesans who had been legally and socially constructed as prostitutes.[11] It also indexes the oft-repeated argument that devadasi dance could thrive independently of devadasis themselves, but only after being *reformed* in order to suppress its supposedly licentious content. The 'double-reed' implications of reform thus stood at the complex intersections of morality, caste, national and regional concerns, and the politics of affect.

Devadasis always occupied an ambiguous social status in colonial South India, right from the time of their presence at the Nayaka and Maratha courts in Tanjavur. However, the efforts of reformers served to amplify the disquiet that attended devadasis' sexuality, their role in the economies of land, and the overall legitimacy of their profession. These were now legitimate topics for public debate. The doors of public debate were first opened in print by Kandukuri Viresalingam (1848–1919), a brahmin from Rajahmundry, who lived much of his early life in the Godavari delta. In 1874, Viresalingam began his post as the headmaster of the Anglo-Vernacular School and also started publishing his first Telugu journal, *Viveka Vardhani*. In 1875, the journal carried an article called 'Vesyalu.' In it, he posits his town of Rajahmundry, a stronghold of courtesan culture, as overrun by 'whorehouses.' Viresalingam also wrote a Telugu satire called *Vesyapriya Prahasanamu* ridiculing men who had relations with bhogam women, which he staged in Dowlaiswaram and the Rajahmundry region (Ramakrishna 1983: 139). In 1893, he encouraged public opinion in the Godavari delta in support of a memo sent to the Governor of Madras, from the newly-formed Madras Hindu Social Reform Association, an organization headed by Subramaniya Aiyer, editor of *The Hindu*. The Madras Association's memo requested that the government discourage the devadasi system, for that would 'strengthen the hands of those who are trying to purify the social life of their community.'[12] The efforts of Viresalingam functioned largely on rhetorical and discursive levels. It raised the stakes in terms of women's reforms in the Madras Presidency, and instilled a new moral consciousness among many urban men. But it was up to Dr S. Muthulakshmi Reddi (1866–1968) to make concrete legal interventions that would officially regulate the lives of women in devadasi communities.

Reddi was born to a woman named Chandrammal (who was related to the family of Sivarama Nattuvanar of Pudukkottai [1879–1945]), and

S. Narayanaswami Ayyar, a *smarta* brahmin who in Reddi's own words was 'a great patron of music, dance and drama' (Fig. 2). Reddi was the first female doctor in the Madras Presidency and was responsible for implementing a series of reforms related to women's physical and social health in her role as the first female legislator in pre-Independence India. Inspired by Gandhi and supportive of Periyar's Self-Respect Movement, Reddi was responsible for drafting 'A Bill to Prevent the Dedication of Women to Hindu Temples' in 1930 and later the 'Madras Devadasis (Prevention of Dedication) Act' in 1947. Reddi's initial engagements with the issue began in 1927 when she drafted a resolution for the Madras Legislative Council recommending that 'the Government of India ... undertake legislation at a very early date to put a stop to the practice of dedication of young girls and young women to Hindu temples for immoral purposes under the pretext of caste, custom or religion'. Devadasi communities responded to Reddi's resolution in a number of ways, both supporting and condemning it. Among those public figures who strongly supported the resolution was Muvalur Ramamirttammal (1883–1950), an outspoken member of Periyar's Self-Respect Movement.[13]

The ritual of *pottukkattutal* (the 'dedication' of a girl to the image of a deity or other object by tying a ritual emblem known as *pottu* around her neck) was criminalized in 1947 with the Madras Devadasis (Prevention of Dedication) Act. For reformers, the ritual of pottukkattutal enabled

F<small>IG</small>. 2 The natal family of Muthulakshmi Reddi (centre, standing), including her father Narayanaswami Ayyar and her mother Chandrammal (seated far right). Photo from Davesh Soneji's collection

prostitution and the abuse of women that resulted from relationships unsanctioned by marriage. The Act aimed to detach modern India from the archaic and patriarchal sign of temple dedication by instituting a new form of citizenship for devadasi women. The hundred years of debate that publicized and scrutinized the social customs and aesthetic practices of devadasis had already made a profound impact within their communities. By 1947, very few women from these communities were willing to identify as devadasis, and their aesthetic labour had already been discounted by temples, courts, zamindaris, and individual patrons. Reform activity also prompted men from devadasi communities to reinvent themselves as new caste-groups with titles such as 'Isai Velalar' in the Tamil-speaking regions, and 'Suryabalija' in the Telugu-speaking regions. Caste associations (with names such as 'Tanjai Jilla Isai Velalar Sangam' or 'Kalavantula Samskarana Sangham') universally joined the movement to outlaw professional dancing by women from their communities. Devadasi reform thus engendered serious deliberations on the forging of new masculinities, the control of women's sexuality, and the restoration of patriliny in these communities, even as devadasi women themselves remained largely absent from these debates.

'Why Should the Devadasi Institution in the Hindu Temples be Abolished?' is one of the earliest documents drafted by Reddi. In this paper, Reddi provides justification for the 1927 resolution that she proposed to the Madras Legislative Council, which would eventually lead to the Madras Devadasis (Prevention of Dedication) Act of 1947. She unequivocally equates the tying of the *pottu* with 'vice' and deploying the language of medical science, argues that the continued existence of devadasi culture will result in a drastic increase in venereal disease. Reddi calls for the permanent enfranchisement of the lands (*maniyams, manyalu*) traditionally given to devadasis, but 'without any expectation of service from them in return.' She also calls for an end to the ritual of tying the pottu. For Reddi, the issue of devadasi reform is unquestioningly guided by a nationalist imperative. In her words, devadasi reform in Madras is 'a question of national importance and interest.'

Devadasis responded directly to Reddi's arguments. In this anthology, Reddi's essay is thus juxtaposed with a document entitled 'The Humble Memorial of Devadasis of the Madras Presidency' (1929) signed by a number of devadasis from Madras who had just formed the 'Madras Devadasis Association' (known in Tamil as the 'Cennai Uruttirakanikai Cankam') to counter the Bill proposed by Reddi.[14] In this protest, we are confronted by an impassioned plea for the persistence of devadasi culture. Interestingly, the document speaks in the language of religious nationalism, projecting devadasis back into a glorious world of Tamil *Saiva* religion, and attempts to claim their rights from this space. Devadasis mobilized these rhetorical strategies in attempts to convince their audiences of their legitimate social location as rightful citizens of the emergent nation-state. The invocation of religion and religious history could have tactically opened up the spaces of nation and citizenship for these women. Locating themselves in a timeless distinctiveness, and foregrounding their links to the iconic institution of the temple, these devadasis traced a civilizational genealogy for themselves which was palatable to nationalist reformers and other native elites. But all these strategic manoeuvres affected no recognizable change in perceptions of devadasis in the twentieth century. The promises assured by early twentieth century reformers did not materialize for women in the devadasi communities, even after reform legislation was passed. As failed citizens of the modern nation-state, women in devadasi communities today have inherited only the subterfuges of respectability.

This section concludes with two scholarly essays that serve to put some of these debates into a broader framework. Amrit Srinivasan's pathfinding essay 'Reform or Conformity? Temple "Prostitution" and the Community in the Madras Presidency' foregrounds issues of caste, politics, and profession in the context of the anti-nautch debates. Among other things, Srinivasan highlights the kinship and economic structures of devadasi communities and historicizes reform debates by locating them in the wider context of non-brahmin assertion in Tamil-speaking South India.

Teresa Hubel's essay focuses on the ways in which the anti-nautch movement framed itself as a 'women's movement,' even as it idealized and valourized women's roles as wives and mothers. Hubel argues that the non-conjugal sexual lives of devadasis, combined with their ambiguous caste status made the pioneers of the Indian women's movement uncomfortable. She also speaks to the tensions and resonances between reform-related activities for brahmin women and devadasis. Ultimately, Hubel demonstrates the great irony that underpinned the anti-nautch movement, namely how 'the liberation of one female group at the expense of another undercuts the ideals that propel [the project of feminism].'

REINVENTING DANCE IN SOUTH INDIA
At the same time that public debates around the status of the devadasi communities were making headlines in the press, another issue—that of the aesthetic 'restoration' of the nation—was also brewing. An essential

part of reinventing the nation's artistic heritage was the grafting of 'classical' traditions of dance and music onto the bodies 'respectable' women. E. Krishna Iyer (1897–1968), a Tamil brahmin lawyer, launched what he called a 'pro art' stance on the issue of devadasi reform.[15] As Secretary of the newly created Madras Music Academy, Krishna Iyer was keen on presenting dance as part of its programmes. But in 1927, the same year that the Music Academy was established, the Madras Legislative Assembly, prompted by Reddi, unanimously passed a resolution to draft a bill to prevent the dedication of devadasis (this would eventually become the *Abolition Bill* of 1930). A few years later, on 15 March 1931, the Music Academy presented a dance performance by Rajalakshmi (1900–1969) and Jeevaratnam (1905–1933), the young daughters of Tiruvalapputtur Kalyani (1873–1958), a highly accomplished devadasi. The performance was appreciated by a small audience, and the Academy subsequently invited a few other women from devadasi backgrounds to perform under its aegis until 1939. Krishna Iyer would later reflect that even though the 'renaissance of Indian dance' was somewhat successful by the late 1930s,

Bharata Natya was still in the hands of exponents of the old professional class, with all its possible and lurking dangers as pointed out by social reformers. The efforts of the present writer were turned towards steadily taking it out of their hands and introducing it among cultured family women of respectable classes. (Krishna Iyer 1949: 24)

It was at the second performance of Rajalakshmi and Jeevaratnam at the Music Academy in January of 1933 that Rukmini Arundale (1904–1986), a young cosmopolitan Theosophist, saw a full public performance of Bharatanatyam for the first time (Fig. 3). Rukmini Arundale would have a profound and far-reaching effect on Bharatanatyam, and we shall return to her a little later.

The second section of this volume, 'Reinventing Dance in South India,' focuses on the complex historical process by which localized devadasi traditions were transfigured into the pan-Indian form of 'classical' dance. As Matthew Allen notes in his seminal work 'Re-writing the Script for South Indian Dance,' the process now coded as the dance revival involved not only a 're-vivification,' but also a re-population. re-construction, re-situation, and re-storation. This complex reinvention of the dance rested on the building-blocks of modernity in South Asia— colonialism, Orientalism, nationalism, redefinitions of womanhood and citizenship, religion, science, and aesthetic reform—which all had their parts to play in this project.

FIG. 3 Tiruvalapputtur Rajalakshmi and Jeevaratnam, flanked by Tiruvalapputtur Pakkirisvami, a clarionet player (left) and Tiruvalapputtur Svaminatha Nattuvanar (right) after their performance in Madras in January 1933. Photograph courtesy B.M. Sundaram

Orientalism, Religion, and Dance

Certainly, one of the most prominent elements in the project of 'revival' had to do with the retrieval of a textual antiquity for the dance. But unlike nineteenth-century non-brahmin nattuvanars who, for example, also wrote about the links of devadasi dance to the god Siva and to the 'Bharata Sastra', the invocation of texts in the dance revival had an altogether different aim.[16] The new interest in Sanskrit texts sought to recover a literal correspondence between living traditions and texts, and harnessed the authority of 'tradition' represented by the texts. The search for the antiquity of Bharatanatyam in Sanskrit texts in the twentieth century disassociated the dance from its social roots in highly localized non-brahmin communities, and universalized its aesthetics and history. It also enabled a nationalized 'pan-Indian' reading of aesthetic history, with the *Natyasastra* read as the 'common root' of all regional performance traditions.

'Discovered' in fragments by Orientalist scholars from France, England, and Germany between 1866 and 1888, the *Natyasastra*, in its present form, was pieced together by pandits named Shivadatta and Kashinath Pandurang Purab and published in India for the first time in 1894. This early, transnational project of recovering the antiquity of India's performing arts was, as Kapila Vatsyayan (1989) has pointed out, situated entirely in the method of textual analysis. It was only after the discovery of manuscripts of Abhinavagupta's commentary

Abhinavabharati in the 1930s that the text gained wider, interdisciplinary attention. The linkage of the text with sculptural representations of the dance movements (*karanas*) described in the fourth chapter of the text was of particular interest to textual scholars, art historians, and dance researchers.[17] But Vatsyayan also speaks to the methodological simplicity of this early interdisciplinary work: 'Here is a text, here are the sculptures, and all we have to do now is to identify them and proceed further.' The symbolic power that the *Natyasastra* has amassed since 1894 is startling to say the least, and embedded deep within the iconization of the text is its perceived link with Bharatanatyam in particular.

On the other hand, it is also clear that the idea of the figure of Bharata, the semi-divine author of the *Natyasastra*, had been cultivated among professional communities of dancing women and male nattuvanars. As we have already seen, for example, in the 1806 essay by P. Ragaviah Charry, one of the names by which dance was referred to in these communities in the nineteenth century was 'bharata natyam' or 'bharata sastram'. So attributing the 'Sanskritization' of the form to brahmin revivalists, as some scholars have suggested, denies hereditary performers and teachers a consciousness of Sanskrit aesthetics in the nineteenth century and creates the illusion that the relationship between Sanskrit language and devadasi dance is a novel contribution of the dance revival. What is 'new,' therefore, about the Orientalist discovery of the *Natyasastra* is the way in which it is read and mobilized to nationalist ends in the twentieth century.

Another crucial force in the reinvention of Bharatanatyam was the invocation of a nationalist-inspired religiosity, an emphasis on religion that was markedly 'middle-class.' Urban middle-class religion, as it emerged in the twentieth century, replicated upper-caste values, and could perhaps best be described as a 'repackaging of brahmanical religion in ways that would make it palatable to the middle and lower classes, especially women' (Hawley 2001: 224). Elite, neo-Vedantic philosophical and allegorical interpretations of the arts were among the strategies deployed by the middle-class to transform the cultural sphere in this period. Texts, icons, and a new discursive style comingled to produce Bharatanatyam's links with this modified upper-caste religion. As we shall see below, the religious symbology of the dance that was configured at this time has enduring, if not amplified resonances in today's Bharatanatyam.

In 1912, art historian and philosopher Ananda Kentish Coomaraswamy (1877–1947) composed an essay entitled 'The Dance of Siva.' As Avanthi Meduri (1996) and Matthew Allen (in this volume) point out, Coomaraswamy's essay revolutionized the ways in which the public understood the dance of South Indian devadasis. The essay created a consciousness about the metaphysics of dance in a manner that was palatable for Indian elites who were already involved with esoteric projects like the Theosophical Society. Though the essay itself mainly draws connections between Sanskrit and Tamil philosophical texts and the bronze image of Nataraja imagined in Chola-period Tamilnadu, it interestingly does *not* focus on aesthetic theory. In Coomaraswamy's interpretation, the theological significance of the icon trumps the importance of its aesthetic history. Coomaraswamy's emphasis on the religious dimensions of dance and music in India would have profound effects on the nationalist project of retrieving and 'classicizing' the arts. 'The Dance of Siva' represents a set of key metaphysical interpretations of dance (based loosely on an interpretation of the Tamil philosophical school of Saiva Siddhanta) that were harnessed and disseminated in the 1930s and beyond.

But Coomaraswamy also had a deep interest in the performing arts and their technical dimensions. He worked, for example, with Gopala Krishnayya Duggirala, a Telugu scholar, on retrieving the Sanskrit text *Abhinayadarpana*, published under the title *The Mirror of Gesture* by Harvard University Press in 1917. Most palm leaf manuscripts of the *Abhinayadarpana* were in Telugu script, and were likely found, like many manuscripts of *Bhamakalapam* and the *Gitagovinda*, in the homes of brahmin scholar-poets who interacted with Telugu-speaking devadasis.[18] As an appendix to their work, Coomaraswamy and Duggirala provide photos of a devadasi (likely Tiruvarur Jnanam, 1857–1927) demonstrating gestures from her practice, thereby clearly establishing the link between texts and living traditions. The content of the *Abhinayadarpana* itself focuses mainly on hand gestures and their meanings and applications. It was the *Abhinayadarpana* that subsequently functioned as the textbook for dance theory as it was taught at Kalakshetra and other urban institutions.[19]

It is significant that Coomaraswamy's work was not first published in South Asia. Some of the earliest non-hereditary performers of 'Indian dance' were in fact not Indian, nor did their performances necessarily take place in India. Esther Sherman (1893–1982), better known as Ragini Devi, for example, had an extraordinary career as an 'Indian dancer' in early twentieth-century America. Rachel Lindsay Mattson, who has written a brilliant dissertation on Ragini Devi, describes the complex interstices of race, religion, and aesthetics from which the figure of Ragini Devi must be read:

Replacing Minnesotan frocks with an Indian sari, she invented a series of dances, called them 'Hindu,' and danced her way into minor fame as Ragini Devi, 'dancer of Hindu Dances, player upon the Tambura and Sitar.' And for the better part of her American career (1922–1930, 1940–1947), she passed as a South Asian. Explaining that she was a Kashmiri Hindu from north India, she created a new identity for herself out of the cultural scraps that circulated into her orbit: stereotypes, historical information—and exotic fantasy (2004: 3–4).

Ragini Devi was not alone in her dramatization of 'Indianness' through dance. 'Oriental Dance,' enabled to a degree by the circulation of texts about Indian dance, had become very popular in America and Europe by the 1920s, and Ted Shawn, Ruth St Denis, La Meri, Uday Shankar, and even Rukmini Arundale experimented with this kind of dance that ubiquitously reified notions of an 'othered' India with its dual emphasis on the 'Oriental' dancing body and Hinduism.[20] Although Ragini Devi would later be celebrated in India owing largely to her daughter Indrani Rahman's accomplishments in Bharatanatyam and Odissi, *Nritanjali* (1928), her earliest work, composed before she ever visited India, picks up almost directly from the writings of Orientalist scholars such as Coomaraswamy.[21] In it, the Sanskrit textual tradition and Hindu gods and goddesses are identified with the history and technique of dance. In particular, Ragini Devi's writing makes it appear as if living dance forms from India are 'impersonal and animated by a sense of inner spirituality.' This transcendent nature of aesthetics becomes a major preoccupation of the later 'revivalists,' but it is important to recognize that these ideas about Indian dance were already circulating along imperial axes more than a decade before the work of the Madras revivalists begins.

New Beginnings? Voices from Twentieth-century Madras

This section traces key articulations of Bharatanatyam's pasts from within the discourse of 'revival' in twentieth-century Madras. It opens with a remarkable essay from 1933 by eminent Sanskritist Dr V. Raghavan who wrote it under the pseudonym 'Bhava Raga Tala.' This essay was composed two years before Rukmini Arundale's first public performance of Bharatanatyam in 1935, and at the height of public debates over Muthulakshmi Reddi's proposed abolition bill. Raghavan notes that, 'It is suggested that the [devadasi] community must first be done away with and that "respectable" family women must then take to the art.' He then proceeds to provide a long list of reasons why 'family women' will 'lower the standard of perfection' and transform the art into an amateur practice. Raghavan's essay, couched in the language of Gandhian nationalism, is

a plea to reconsider the disenfranchisement of the devadasi community
that was being proposed by the pro-abolition lobby. Raghavan's vision of
the dance 'renaissance,' unlike that of Krishna Iyer or Rukmini Arundale,
involves facilitating the art of the hereditary professional class of women
rather than displacing them.

Rukmini Arundale (Fig. 4), the daughter of Theosophist Nilakantha
Sastri, was married at the age of sixteen to George Arundale, protégé
of Annie Besant. In 1928, at the age of 24, she was declared 'World
Mother' by Annie Besant and the Theosophical Society, in a move
that permanently bestowed the title 'Devi' upon her.[22] In her role as a
key figure in the Theosophical Society, Rukmini was imbricated in the
transatlantic flows of this global organization, and had travelled around
the world before she was 30 years old. When she witnessed the dance
of the devadasis Rajalakshmi and Jeevaratnam at the Music Academy in
1933, she was already interested in dance, having met Anna Pavlova in
1928, and had studied Russian Ballet under Cleo Nordi of London.[23]
She first trained for a few months under the distinguished nattuvanar
Pandanallur Meenakshisundaram Pillai (1869–1954), the great great-
grandson of Ponnaiya of the 'Tanjore Quartet.' In 1935, after six months
of training, she decided to give a public debut performance for the
Diamond Jubilee Celebrations of the Theosophical Society in Madras,

FIG. 4   Rukmini Devi Arundale (1904–1986). Photo courtesy SAMUDRI
Archives, The Sruti Foundation, Chennai

much to the disappointment of Pillai, who refused to conduct the performance as nattuvanar (Arundale n.d.: 41; Allen, this volume). For her debut performance, among other 'reforms,' together with Alex and Mary Elmore, she designed a 'costume,' an altered version of which has become the standard dress for contemporary Bharatanatyam dancers.

Chennai elites admired Rukmini's performance, and this paved the road for vital developments in modern Bharatanatyam. In 1936, Rukmini Arundale established the International Academy for the Arts, later renamed Kalakshetra (Fig. 5). Initially, she included ballet classes as part of the training at Kalakshetra. She felt that this would render the 'adavus [dance steps] accurate in form.' In addition to Bharatanatyam, the institution also taught music, Kathakali, drama, painting, sculpture, crafts, and weaving. In 1942, Kalakshetra began to offer diplomas, and in 1944, its music courses were affiliated with the University of Madras. The student body always included foreign students from America, Europe, and Australia, and many of these students came via the Theosophical connection.

In 1944, Rukmini Arundale began to create 'dance-dramas,' which drew from a range of dance vocabularies including the Kuravanci dramas performed by devadasis, the Bhagavata Mela ritual theatre traditions of Tanjavur district, the Kathakali drama of Kerala, and of course, her own exposure to theatre in a range of global contexts. From 1949 until her death, she choreographed several dance-dramas based on literary texts in a variety of languages, including the Sanskrit Ramayana of Valmiki, the *Gitagovinda* of Jayadeva, and the devotional songs of Mirabai.

This dance-drama idiom radically altered the tradition of solo dance as well. It narrativized the abhinaya for solo dance, which had traditionally been associated with non-linear lyrical interpretation. The new narrativization of Bharatanatyam also shifted the content and genres of songs considered appropriate for interpretation through dance. The interpretation, through abhinaya, of devotional genres from the South Indian concert music repertoire such as *krti* or kirtana allowed dancers to introduce episodes from epic and Puranic narratives into the dance. Today, many of the traditional genres associated with devadasi dance practices, such as varnams, have been rewritten to suit the tastes and religious leanings of urban audiences who almost universally understand Bharatanatyam dance as 'storytelling.'

The new Bharatanatyam was read as a religious allegory thanks to the Orientalist discoveries of the *Natyasastra* and Nataraja on the one hand, and that of Rukmini Arundale and the Theosophical Society on

FIG 5   Bharatanatyam class at Kalakshetra, 2006. Photograph courtesy the author

the other (Meduri 2008). The essay by Rukmini Arundale in this volume, entitled 'The Spiritual Background of Indian Dance', reflects some of the ways in which religion, aesthetics, and nationalism came together in a seamless manner in these discourses on Bharatanatyam's pasts. Although this essay was composed later in Rukmini Arundale's life, it nonetheless speaks to the nationalization of Bharatanatyam, a task accomplished by the state in the 1950s, due in no small part to Rukmini Arundale's vision of the dance. The essay dwells on the failing standards of dance in the post-revival period, and harks back to a pan-Indian 'golden age' for dance. Arundale conceives of the dance revival as an 'awakening from forgetfulness', and urges contemporary Indian artists to proactively remember the past so that 'art will regain its original height and the dance will return to the people in all its pristine purity'. In the piece we also see traces of Coomaraswamy's writings on Nataraja, yogic allegories for dance, and a celebration of religious belief in the modern world.

This essay is followed by 'Bharata Natyam', the Presidential Address for the 33rd Annual Conference of the Tamil Isai Sangam delivered by Tanjavur Balasaraswati on 12 December 1975. Balasaraswati (Fig. 6), born into a family of devadasi dancers and musicians who moved from Tanjavur to Madras around 1857, has been universally appreciated as

FIG. 6   Tanjavur Balasaraswati (1918–1984). Photo courtesy SAMUDRI
Archives, The Sruti Foundation, Chennai

one of the foremost Bharatanatyam artists of the last century. As one of
the only hereditary voices in the dance 'revival,' Balasaraswati's own story
is one of resistance to upper-caste re-interpretations of Bharatanatyam.
Her performances dwelt on the traditional compositions of erotic longing
(varnams, padams, javalis), and provided a counterpoint to the new forms
of Bharatanatyam that emerged in Madras in the 1940s. Beginning in the
early sixties, Balasaraswati travelled to the United States and taught her
dance at a number of American universities, including Wesleyan University
in Connecticut, where her siblings also taught music. Balasaraswati's
daughter Lakshmi settled in the United States, and her son Aniruddha
continues to perform in his grandmother's unique style.

But as the essay by Balasaraswati demonstrates, she also played a
central role in the fashioning of a distinctly *religious* history for the dance.
Despite the fact that many of her own performances took place in the
homes of Chettiyars and other elites, nowhere does she speak publicly
about these, or about the 'salon-style' chamber performances for which
her family had become justly famous in colonial Madras. By shifting the
dance's location into the transcendent space of the temple, Balasaraswati

also framed devadasi dance along themes of spirituality and transcendence. Though I do not want to imply here that Balasaraswati's professional struggles were parallel to those of upper-caste 'dance revivalists'—for certainly they were not—I do want to highlight the parallel discursive constructions of Bharatanatyam's temple past that dominates historical and historiographic writing over the last fifty years. To be sure, Balasaraswati's voice, unlike that of upper-caste dance revivalists, *did* challenge the narrative of the 'fall' of devadasis, and clearly spoke with an agenda to restore respectability to traditional courtly dance repertoire, including some of its erotic dimensions. Dance, like Indian music, had already been grafted onto the frameworks of nation and religion, and it was impossible for women, especially those from devadasi backgrounds, to address dance from outside these epistemologies. Janet O'Shea notes how Balasaraswati's emphasis on the spiritual dimensions of the dance enabled her own professional life:

Like [Rukmini] Devi, she deployed an idea of spirituality, in addition to religiosity, abstracting bharata natyam from a relationship only to its immediate context. For Balasaraswati, however, this higher function came through emotionality and interiority, aspects that provided bharata natyam with regional, national, and global affiliations. Through this reference to universalism, Balasaraswati could bridge the gap between her valorization of the devadasi community and the realities of her instructional and patronage situation. This maneuver partially defused the tensions between her celebration of the devadasi legacy and her performing for and teaching Brahmans, non-Tamils, and non-Indians. (O'Shea 2007: 91)

The universalization of Bharatanatyam obfuscated the particularities of names, identities, and aesthetic practices of devadasi women. Indeed, the historical 'truth' of salon dance in South India was left out of the historical puzzle precisely because of these generalized, translocal, spiritualized tellings of the dance's past. Yet some women from devadasi backgrounds also saw the instrumental value of such discourses. Temple-based representations of devadasi pasts, such as those echoed by the Madras Devadasis Association or Balasaraswati, *might* have enabled a form of citizenship for devadasis on the eve of 'heritage building' for the nation.

Reading the history of the 'dance revival' through figures such as Rukmini Arundale, Balasaraswati, and E. Krishna Iyer only completes part of the picture. The dance revival has to be understood in the wider context of the democratization, domestication, and institutionalization of concert music in South India (Weidman 2006), and burgeoning popular representations of dance in Tamil and Telugu cinema, which enabled its respectability and popularity *c*. 1935–60.

This section ends with three analytical essays that help us contextualize the primary texts by Rukmini Arundale and Balasaraswati. The first reading, 'Rewriting the Script for South Indian Dance' foregrounds nearly all the key issues we have examined thus far. Allen's work masterfully weaves concerns around respectability, religion, caste, and performance practices together in a compelling critical examination of the dance revival. Allen's pathfinding essay makes the political complexities of the revival palpable.

Avanthi Meduri's 'Bharatanatyam as World Historical Form' argues that Rukmini Arundale theatricalized twentieth century historiography of the dance by visualizing it symbolically in a modern, allegorical stage setting amidst the three iconic signs of Nataraja, the *Natyasastra*, and the Guru. Meduri demonstrates that this tripartite symbolic order allowed Rukmini Devi to simultaneously articulate a metaphorization and historicization for Bharatanatyam in the 1930s. A key argument in this essay is the contrast Meduri posits between the two dance revivals of the 1930s—one sponsored by scholars in the Madras Music Academy, featuring traditional devadasi dancers and nattuvanars, and the other being Rukmini Arundale's transformation of a transnational revival sponsored by the Theosophical Society. The difference, Meduri says, lies in the semiotic-theatrical-performative nature of Devi's project. Unlike the devadasi dancers, and unlike the conceptualist historiographers of the dance, by theatricalizing the dance, Rukmini Arundale became the first urban South Indian 'dancer-historian' in the modern era.

The final essay by Anne-Marie Gaston entitled 'Dance and the Hindu Woman: Bharatanatyam Re-ritualized' takes us into contemporary discussions of religion, sexuality, and performance among upper-caste practitioners of Bharatanatyam. She examines the 're-ritualization' of Bharatanatyam by its contemporary middle-class practitioners, highlighting the iconic religious dimensions of dance performance, and the refashioning of the dance as a definitively 'spiritual exercise'. She notes how this leads to the recrafting of technique to make it speak to an imagined temple past. Gaston also illustrates how social practices associated with devadasi communities (such as the rites-of-passage known as *gajjai puja* and *arankerram*) take on new 'respectable' socio-cultural and religious meanings at the hands of the Indian middle-class.

CONTEMPORARY EXTENSIONS

Bharatanatyam's iconic status as both a marker of national and regional (Tamil) identity has enabled it to circulate in ever-expansive pathways.

Early in the history of its 'reconstructed' avatar, Bharatanatyam had already forged caste and class-based alliances. As a product of Madras's urban elites, it travelled throughout India as they relocated outside Tamilnadu, and quickly became lodged into the official, state-endorsed practices of culture in every region of the country. As anthropologist Mary Hancock has noted, the cultural production of modernity in South India, indexed by practices such as Bharatanatyam, is 'located in the space between domestic life and the projects of the nation-state' (Hancock 1999: 31). Today, capitalist flows of culture sweep across the globe, and Bharatanatyam floats proudly, if awkwardly, along these torrents.[24]

This section of the volume maps some of the key political and aesthetic strategies deployed by dancers of Bharatanatyam to both reify and resist the hegemonic pushes of culture in the context of the nation and beyond. The essays touch on themes that are timely and profoundly impact global Bharatanatyam, including strategies for the circumvention of Orientalist interpretations of Indian dance, the relationship between politicized religion and dance, and hybrid transnational identities.

This section opens with a pathfinding essay by Janet O'Shea that addresses the ways in which individual Bharatanatyam artists from around the world deploy radically innovative choreographic strategies to 'interpret' their dance for global audiences. The essay also investigates the tensions between 'tradition' and 'innovation' that have been endemic to the post-revival practice of Bharatanatyam. O'Shea offers an analysis of the choreographic strategies of several prominent dancers including Hari Krishnan (Fig. 7). Krishnan serves as an example of a choreographer and performer who eludes dichotomous constructions of tradition and innovation. Elsewhere, O'Shea has noted that Krishnan

... embraces experimentation for its own sake. He refers to history as a source of choreographic material but not as a standard that sets the parameters for innovation. In projecting both of these agendas in a single concert, he suggests that the two imperatives need not compete with one another or cancel each other out. He intertwines commitments to tradition and innovation without validating one through the other .... (O'Shea 2007: 63–4)

In this essay, O'Shea juxtaposes the work of Krishnan with that of other choreographers who 'subvert a tendency to place European thought systems as the primary framework of interpretation'. O'Shea skillfully demonstrates how these choreographers reify Bharatanatyam's transnational position and respond to their hybrid identities through original choreographic stances.

FIG. 7   Hari Krishnan in a contemporary abstraction of Bharatanatyam.
Photograph by Cylla von Tiedemann

The second essay tasks us deeper into the relationship between dance, religion, and the state. Andrée Grau's essay 'Political Activism and South Asian Dance' deals with what could be thought of as a logical end to the 'Hinduness' of Bharatanatyam that was forged during the days of the dance revival. Grau examines the case of Mallika Sarabhai, one of India's most prominent Bharatanatyam dancers and social activists, and her struggles with the oppressive regime of Hindutva politics that for sometime disabled her professional activities in the state of Gujarat.[25] The essay is a reminder of the ways in which contemporary discourses on Indian culture in general and Bharatanatyam in particular are moving in the direction of right-wing and fundamentalist politics.[26] Indeed, it is modern Bharatanatyam's peculiarly transnational, middle-class religious epistemologies that enable these dangerous yet very real connections between fundamentalisms, the state, and popular culture.

The following essay, 'What's the Matter? Shakti's Re-collection of Race, Nationhood and Gender' by Anita Kumar addresses Bharatanatyam in contemporary North America. Kumar addresses the inherited legacy of Indian nationalism in the diaspora that perpetuates tensions between 'India' and 'the West,' and the 'spiritual' and the 'material'.[27] In this context, Bharatanatyam is what Kumar characterizes as the 'quintessential rite-of-passage' among the South Asian bourgeoisie in America. The essay focuses on the Shakti Dance Company and its founder, Viji Prakash, in Los Angeles, California. As she notes, the construction of 'Indianness' in America is far from a tidy state-of-being. Rather, it rests on what Kumar calls 'the ephemeral boundaries of inclusion versus exclusion' that are negotiated on a daily basis by young women of South Asian origin. Kumar posits that Bharatanatyam offers these women 'another construction of femininity—poise, independence, assertiveness.' Kumar's discussions of the Shakti Dance Company and the students of Viji Prakash present an exceptional counterpoint to the 'mainstream' cultural, moral, and gendered pedagogy that appears to be inseparable from much of contemporary Bharatanatyam.

DANCERS SPEAK: PERSONAL JOURNEYS TO AND FROM BHARATANATYAM

The final section of this anthology focuses on the voices of dancer-writers who have practised Bharatanatyam, and have also made significant contributions to the form in the twentieth century. Spatial constraints have limited the number of dance professionals whose writings could be included in this category. I have therefore chosen to focus on dancer-scholars or dancer-writers who have made original contributions to our knowledge of Bharatanatyam through their own innovations in writing and performance.

Mrinalini Sarabhai, a pioneer choreographer, was born in Madras into a Nayar family from Palakkad district, Kerala. Educated at Santiniketan under the guidance of Rabindranath Tagore, she also trained in Bharatanatyam under Pandanallur Meenakshisundaram Pillai. In 1942, she married Vikram Sarabhai, a renowned physicist, and founded an arts institution known as Darpana in Ahmedabad, Gujarat in the year 1949. That same year, Sarabhai created one of the earliest works that in retrospect we may call 'contemporary dance.' This piece, *Manushya*, an abstract 'creation myth' narrative, arose out of Sarabhai's own reflections on metaphysics. Sarabhai went on to create several significant 'firsts' in Bharatanatyam, including *Memory is a Ragged Fragment of Eternity* (1971), a secular, socially-driven choreography about dowry deaths in Saurashtra, which was perhaps the earliest Bharatanatyam-based work in this genre. Sarabhai's meditations on these works were originally published as part of a collection of writings entitled *Creations* (1986). These writings open the fourth and last part of our anthology.

The anthology comes to a close with writings by two of Bharatanatyam's most avant-garde representatives, Shobana Jeyasingh and the late Chandralekha (1928–2006). The essay by UK-based choreographer Shobana Jeyasingh entitled 'Getting off the Orient Express', offers a world-class choreographer's perspective on issues of the relevance and importance of dance history, the necessity for Bharatanatyam performers to move beyond the presuppositions of Orientalism, and the need for cultivating virtuosity and excellence in performance. Jeyasingh, born in Chennai and trained under Valuvur Samaraj Pillai (1938–2004), founded the Shobana Jeyasingh Dance Company in London in 1988. Shobana's works are known for their celebrations of transnational, urban, hybrid identity and technical virtuosity. She deploys what Janet O'Shea calls 'a bharata natyam-based movement lexicon in order to create works within a highly modernist tradition that avoids both narrative and lyric dramatic modes' (O'Shea 2007: 65). Jeyasingh's recent work *Faultline* (Fig. 8), for example, is loosely inspired by Gautam Malkani's novel *Londonstani*. It brings multimedia into conversation with Shobana's mixed corporeal language, just as the characters in Malkani's novel speak a hybrid language that frames the conceptual and narrative dimensions of the book.

Chandralekha, born Chandralekha Prabhudas Patel, trained under Kanchipuram Ellappa Pillai (1908–1974), but by 1959, began to feel dissatisfied with the elements of spectacle and religiosity that appeared to be at the heart of post-revival Bharatanatyam. From that point onward, she choreographed a number of increasingly experimental and provocative works that self-consciously approached the body, sexuality, and dance in a new way. Chandralekha's choreography not only contravened prevailing aesthetic sensibilities in the world of 'classical' Indian dance, but also offered a radical political and intellectual alternative to commodified Bharatanatyam.[28] In some ways, it could be said that she also foreshadowed

FIG. 8   Saju Hari in Shobana Jeyasingh's *Faultline* (2007).
Photograph by Chris Nash

the mobilization of Bharatanatyam to fundamentalist religious ends
that we see today. Her bold re-interpretations and affectively-charged
presentations of dance created controversy but also enabled new
possibilities for dancers who were seeking something beyond the religious
and social spectacle that was urban Bharatanatyam. Ananya Chatterjea
notes that in the work of Chandralekha,

dance is reconceptualized as a practice that generates a particularly powerful
awareness of bodies and how they come to be produced. This is one of the
markers of the radical in Chandralekha's work: the relatively 'modern' idea of
a women's movement is revitalized through rearticulating ideas drawn from
older, traditional, and indigenous thought systems and cultural practices.
This alignment immediately challenges ... critiques that, ignoring historical
evidence, align notions of women's rights and demands for gender equality with

Westernization, and uphold notions of tradition that cancel the possibility of resistive and progressive thought in [the] past .... (Chatterjea 2004: 37)

The essay by Chandralekha entitled 'Reflections on New Directions in Indian Dance' is followed by dance scholar Ananya Chatterjea's 'text dances' (descriptive analyses) about two of Chandralekha's most important choreographic works, *Raga* (1998) and *Sloka* (1999). The insightful and riveting commentaries by Chatterjea bring Chandralekha's politics and aesthetics to life in vivid detail.

Many of the texts in this volume provide for a variety of potential connections between scholars, performers, and audiences. They represent creative interventions and illuminate, from a range of interpretative perspectives, the complexities of the social and aesthetic histories of Bharatanatyam. I have attempted to arrange this reader in a manner that captures multiple voices and charts alternative narrative paths through the field. While I urge readers to follow the suggestions for further reading below, the effort must be continually made to reassess received histories of dance in South Asia, and to identify missing links in the study of Bharatanatyam that merit systematic inquiry.

NOTES

1. Leslie Orr has recently commented on the problematic construction of the 'transhistorical devadasi' in scholarly works from the nineteenth and twentieth centuries. As she notes 'the devadasis' role has been interpreted almost entirely with reference to abstract, overarching conceptions such *sakti* or auspiciousness ... This approach obscures historical and regional variations in the activities and circumstances of [these] women, effaces the individuality of temple women, and conceals change.' (2000: 10).

2. Ramabhadramba, a highly learned courtesan and consort of King Raghunatha Nayaka (r. 1600–34), composed a Sanskrit literary masterpiece called *Raghunathabhyudaya*, valorizing the deeds of the king, and linking him explicitly to god by positing his royal career as a re-enactment of Rama's life. Rangajamma was the author of two *yakshagana* dramas, *Ushaparinayamu*, describing the love and eventual marriage of the demon Banasura's daughter Usha with Krishna's grandson Aniruddha; and *Mannarudasa Vilasamu*, celebrating the marriage of King Vijayaraghava Nayaka and the courtesan Kantimati.

3. For example, the Telugu literary work *Rajagopala Vilasamu* by Cengalvakalakavi composed during the reign of Vijayaraghava names several courtesans who dance, sing, and play instruments at the Tanjavur court (Seetha 1981: 52–7; Kusuma Bai 2000: 128–50). A serious study of dance at the Tanjavur Nayaka court is yet to be written.

4. Although the family of the 'Tanjore Quartet' has been afforded a significant place in histories of Bharatanatyam, it is important to remember that there were three nattuvanar families serving at the Tanjavur court in the early nineteenth

century. These included the family of the Quartet, that of Venkatakrishna Nattuvanar, and that of Ramu Nattuvanar. The current descendants of the Venkatakrishna family reside in Mumbai and run an organization called Sri Rajarajeswari Bharatha Natya Kala Mandir, while the last professional artist from Ramu Nattuvanar's family was the vocalist T.M. Thyagarajan (1923–2007). For more information on these figures and on the 'Tanjore Quartet' see Sundaram (1997; 2002a).

5. Unfortunately, the vast number of Maratha Tanjavur's court records in Modi script have not been transcribed or translated. A portion have been translated into Tamil and published in three volumes by Tamil University (Venkataramaiya and Vivekanandagopal 1984). Some of the records in this set related to dance have been discussed by Radhika (1996).

6. The term dubash or dubashi (> *dvibhasi*) refers to elite men who were interlocutors for the East India Company and later for the British Government in India. More on the cultural and political negotiations of Madras dubashes is found in Mukund (2005), Neild (1977), Neild-Basu (1984), and Waghorne (2004).

7. The Telugu word *mejuvani* comes from the Urdu *mezban* or *mezman*, referring to the host of a feast. Though I am using this word, which is still current in Telugu-speaking devadasi communities, salon dance itself was ubiquitous throughout the Tamil and Telugu speaking parts of the Madras Presidency in the nineteenth century.

8. This is complex yet highly understudied area. For more on devadasis and gramophone recordings, see Hughes (2002; 2007) and Weidman (2006). Hari Krishnan is currently working on a major project on devadasis, Bharatanatyam, and Tamil cinema.

9. Excellent contemporary translations of Ksetrayya's padams are found in Ramanujan, Narayana Rao, and Shulman (1997). This work also contains an introduction to the figure of Ksetrayya, and to the culture of salon performance by courtesans in South India.

10. P. Ragaviah Charry was a 'native informant' for Holt Mackenzie's Mysore Survey Project. Holt Mackenzie (1787–1876) is best remembered for drafting a memorandum on land revenue in northern India which became the template for the revenue systems that were implemented by the British in northern and central India. In addition, Mackenzie was also President of the Council of the College of Fort William in Calcutta. Ragaviah Charry, whose dates are unknown, was educated in mission schools and at the College of Fort William. A number of manuscripts attributed to him are preserved at the British Library in London. These include his polemics against Thomas Newnham's essay entitled 'The Character and Capacity of the Asiaticks' published in 1802. Ragaviah resisted Christian critiques of Hinduism as a religion of 'horrid' practices and beliefs. In one of this works, he advocates the formation of a literary association in Madras whose aim would be to facilitate dialogue between natives and Europeans.

11. Kunal Parker (1998) maps the long and complex process by which Anglo-Indian courts constructed professional dancing women as prostitutes in legal terms between 1800 and 1914. The Madras High Court already refused to

recognize devadasis as professional artists in the nineteenth century, and the legal debates consistently posited devadasis in contrast to legally married women.

12. Riding on the coattails of Viresalingam was Raghupati Venkataratnam Naidu (1862–1939), born in Machilipatnam and a member of the Brahmo Samaj in Madras. He was president of the Metropolitan Temperance and Purity Association in Madras, and it was in this capacity that he formally moved an 'anti-nautch' resolution at the eighth annual Indian Social Conference in 1895. At the end of his paper, Venkataratnam Naidu proposed a 'Purity Pledge' to be taken by upper-caste men in the region. Naidu felt that if such pledges, modeled after the purity pledges of Christian organizations such as the White Cross Societies of America, were adhered to by men and boys in South India, their patronage of 'nautch parties' (mejuvani, melam) would significantly decrease (Naidu 1901). Purity pledges in which men vowed not to support or watch dance were signed by many Madras elites including Neelakanta Sastri, father of Rukmini Arundale.

13. Ramamirttammal also wrote a Tamil novel entitled *Tasikal Mocavalai allatu Matiperra Mainar* (*The Dasis' Web of Deceit, or How the Minor Came to His Senses*), published in 1936. This novel provides a fictionalized account of what Ramamirttammal claims to see around her—unscrupulous, money-hungry devadasis who ensnare young men ('minors') into their deceitful world of pleasure. Ultimately, the dasis at centre of the narrative who initially resist the devadasi abolition movement later embrace it, having lost all their fortunes to the man who was their *mama* ('uncle,' pimp). Ramamirttammal began her career as an activist in the Congress party, and then quickly rose to the front ranks of the Self-Respect Movement founded by E.V. Ramasami Naicker (Periyar) and it was in this capacity that she wrote *Tasikal Mocavalai*. The work has been translated by Kannabiran and Kannabiran (2003). For an excellent analysis of devadasis and the Dravidian movement and translations of Periyar's writings on the issue of reform, see Srilata (2002; 2003).

14. One of the key architects of this document was Bangalore Nagaratnam (1878–1952), who herself never served in a temple, but nonetheless appropriated and mobilized religious enunciations of devadasi history. Nagaratnam is remembered among the urban middle-class today largely because of her philanthropic work in building the *samadhi* (commemorative shrine) of Tyagaraja (1767–1847), the famous composer of Karnatak concert music, in the town of Tiruvaiyaru in the year 1925. Susie Tharu and K. Lalita's work 'Empire, Nation, and the Literary Text' focuses on Nagaratnam's radical defiance of Madras' literati in the early twentieth century when she published the erotic Telugu work *Radhika Santvanamu* ('Appeasing Radha') in 1910. The work, a poem written by an eighteenth-century courtesan named Muddupalani who lived during the reign of the Maratha king Pratapasimha, focused on the passion between Krishna and his young new wife Iladevi, and was considered a masterpiece of Telugu literature. In 1911, the year after Nagaratnam's edition was released, police seized all copies in Madras city, and charged Vavilla Ramaswami Sastrulu and Sons, the publishers, with distributing a book that contravened obscenity laws. The controversy raged on for decades, and the book was banned by the colonial government until 1952, when the ban was finally lifted and the book was reprinted. Tharu and Lalita's

insightful analysis of the twentieth-century life of *Radhika Santvanamu* displays not only Nagaratnam's audacity in light of the anti-nautch movement, but also the ways in which devadasi culture itself, represented by *Radhika Santvanamu*, was considered unfit for the public sphere. Recent work on Bangalore Nagaratnam, in addition to the piece reproduced in this reader, includes William Jackson's chapter entitled 'Obeying the Dream: Bangalore Nagaratnammal and the Veneration of Sri Tyagaraja' in his book *Tyagaraja and the Renewal of Tradition* (1994) and a recent biography of Nagaratnam entitled *The Devadasi and the Saint: The Life and Times of Bangalore Nagarathnamma* (2007) by V. Sriram.

15. E. Krishna Iyer came to the study of dance because of his involvement in amateur theatre performances with a group called Suguna Vilas Sabha in Madras. He trained with Madhurantakam Jagadambal (1873–1943), a famous devadasi who lived in Madras until 1929 and was a disciple of the dance-master Valuvur Samu Nattuvanar (1844–1903). Later, Krishna Iyer trained with a brahmin dance-master named A.P. Natesa Ayyar, who practised a form of dance-theatre called Bhagavata Mela Nataka from the village of Melattur. Natesa Ayyar also taught abhinaya to several devadasis in Madras.

16. The popularity and accessibility of early print culture in colonial Tamilnadu enabled nattuvanars to compose texts that preserve dance repertoire in the form of affordable chapbooks. *Natanati Vattiya Rancanam*, composed in Tirunelveli in the year 1898, the text cited in the essay by Hari Krishnan, provides an excellent example. In the preface to this work, the author Pacuvantanai Kankaimuttu Pillai (1837–1920) links the practice of devadasi dance with Tamil Saiva metaphysics. He also speaks of the preservation of the art of 'Bharatasastram':

Bharatasastram, as I have noted, has been explained by various teachers in differing ways. It is boundless like a vast ocean. Only a few have mastered it in its entirety. Most have neither learnt it properly nor preserved the *sastras* [associated with it]. As a result, there have been many setbacks [to the art of dance]. If this great *sastra* has reached such a poor state even in these days of prosperity, nothing more needs to be said about its potentially deplorable state in the future. I believe that the preservation of this art has been the sole purpose of my education, and so I had been thinking about how such preservation could take place. The answer was to write a book in a simple style that could be understood by everyone, young and old alike. So I researched the Arya [Sanskrit], Dravida [Tamil], and Andhra [Telugu] Bharata-sastras, and composed this work *Natanati Vattiya Rancanam* ... (Kankaimuttu Pillai 1898: 9)

17. As Vatsyayan explains, this interest in the fourth chapter of *Natyasastra* was given a jumpstart by an early publication by Naidu, Naidu, and Pantulu (1936) entitled *Tandava Laksanam, or The Fundamentals of Ancient Hindu Dancing, being A Translation into English of the Fourth Chapter of the Natya Sastra*. This early work also contained woodblock prints of sculptural representations of the *karanas* from South Indian temples. The text played a major role in linking local South Indian temple traditions (and by extension, devadasi dance) with a pan-Indian, textual, Sanskrit dance tradition made accessible to urban elites through the English language.

18. South Indian brahmin males from both Smarta (Ayyar) and Srivaisnava (Ayyankar) backgrounds were involved in the production of devadasi dance

as composers, scholar-teachers, and interpreters. Some of the most well-known examples of brahmins as composers of songs meant for devadasi dance include Patnam Subrahmanya Ayyar (1845–1902), Dharmapuri Subbaraya Ayyar (c. 1864–1927), and Tirupanandal Pattabhiramayya (c. 1863–1924) who composed Telugu javalis (love lyrics) for devadasis in Madras city. Lesser-known examples come from coastal Andhra Pradesh, where brahmins such as and Gaddam Subbarayudu Sastri (d. 1940) composed librettos for devadasi performances of *Bhamakalapam*. Brahmin men were also involved as the scholarly collaborators of devadasis and nattuvanars in some parts of South India. Examples of these include Chetlur Narayana Ayyankar, who in 1886 co-authored the text *Abhinaya Navanitam* in Tamil with Panchapakesa Nattuvanar of Tanjavur (1842–1902), and Devulapalli Viraraghava Sastri who wrote the Telugu work *Abhinaya Svayambodhini* in 1915 (see Krishnan in this volume for details). Both of these texts represent the codification of devadasi dance repertoire by brahmin men. But the silence around much of this nineteenth-century inter-caste collaboration has to with the fact that brahmin men were also largely the sexual partners of devadasis. This, combined with political non-brahmin assertion and the appropriation of Bharatanatyam by brahmins in the middle of the twentieth century, has created serious, palpable caste-based tensions around music and dance in Tamilnadu.

19. The *Abhinayadarpana* was edited and translated again from five manuscripts (also transcribed from Telugu script) by Manomohan Ghosh in 1944. This version appears to have become more popular than *The Mirror of Gesture*, and is very commonly prescribed reading for students of Bharatanatyam.

20. As both Priya Srinivasan (2003; 2009) and Mattson (2004: 50–2) argue, early Amercian experiments with Indian dance must be understood in the context of India-themed shows—such as World's fairs, dime museums, and the 'Oriental India' show of Barnum and Bailey's circus (1896)—that had become staple events in late nineteenth and early twentieth century America. Representations of Indian 'nautch' dancers were ubiquitous in these kinds of spectacles, and as Srinivasan notes, the events 'simultaneously glorified and denigrated Asianness' (2003: 53). For an overview of many of these experiments, see Coorlawala (1994). For details on Uday Shankar, see Erdman (1996) and Vatsyayan (2003); on La Meri, see Venkateswaran (2005).

21. In 1972, Ragini Devi authored *Dance Dialects of India*, in which she describes the training she later received in Bharatanatyam under two women, Mylapore Gauri Ammal (1892–1971) a devadasi in Madras, and Jetti Tayamma (1855–1947), a palace dancer of Mysore, around the time that her daughter Indrani was born. In addition to the dissertation by Mattson, information on Ragini Devi is also found in *Dancing in the Family*, a biography of Ragini Devi and her daughter Indrani, written by Indrani's daughter Sukanya Rahman.

21. The concept of the 'World Mother' reflected a kind of apocalyptic vision in the Theosophical Society. Arundale's position was parallel to that of J. Krishnamurti (1895–1986) who was seen as the 'World Father'. C.W. Leadbeater (1854–1934), tutor of Rukmini's husband George Arundale, encoded the role of the 'World Mother' in the language of a universal domesticity,

and these concepts would later reverberate in Rukmini Arundale's constructions of Bharatanatyam:

From the occult standpoint the greatest glory of a woman is not to become a leader in society, nor is it to take a high university degree and live in a flat in scornful isolation, but to provide vehicles for the egos that are to come into incarnation, and to preside over a home in which her children can be properly and happily trained to live their life and to do their appointed work in the world … The World-Mother has at Her command vast hosts of Angelic beings, and at the birth of every child one of these is always present as Her representative; so that we may quite truly say that in and through that representative, the World-Mother Herself is present at the bedside of every suffering mother. What the World-Mother wishes is to achieve the spiritualization of the whole idea of motherhood and of marriage, and those of us who wish to serve Her must endeavour to use in that direction whatever influence we may have. Some of us perhaps can deliver lectures; others can write articles (Leadbeater 1928: 39–40)

For more on gender, Victorian morality, and role of domesticity in the works of Rukmini Arundale, see O'Shea (2005)

23.   As a child, Rukmini Arundale had also informally studied 'Greek dancing,' a reconstructed form taught at the Theosophical Society by a woman named Eleanor Elder, who wrote a book entitled *Dance: A National Art*, published by Theosophical Society in 1918. Elder, together with her sister Kathleen, used to stage plays for the Theosophical Society that enacted some of the occult beliefs of the organization. Rukmini herself created dramas for the annual Thesophical Conventions at Adyar, playing the roles of the Buddhist deity Kwan-yin and Queen Guinevere, consort of King Arthur, in these productions (Arundale n.d.: 8–13; 32–6). These activities no doubt shaped her vision of the religious 'dance drama' form that she conceived later in her life.

24.   Analyses of the transnational flows and politics of today's Bharatanatyam as seen from its 'hub' Chennai are found in Pillai (2002) and O'Shea (2007).

25.   In 2009, Mallika Sarabhai ran for a seat in the Lok Sabha as an independent candidate in the Gandhinagar constituency. She was running against L.K. Advani, the Bharatiya Janata Party's prime ministerial candidate. Though Sarabhai did not win the election, her agenda, which foregrounded sustainable rural development, women's rights, and funding for academic and cultural institutions, created considerable awareness about these issues throughout Gujarat.

26.   Prominent Bharatanatyam celebrities are routinely connected with the Hindu right wing, and the BJP and VHP in particular. Recently, for example, in a felicitation speech for BJP leader L.K. Advani, dancer Padma Subrahmanyam exclaimed '[I] pray to the Almighty and Bharat Mata to make our country and people deserve a Prime Minister in him.' http://www.lkadvani.in/eng/content/view/599/281/ (accessed on 10 April 2009). On the other hand, in 2007, Leela Samson, the present Director of Kalakshetra was accused of harbouring a 'visceral hatred for Hinduism' by an organization connected to the Sangh Parivar when she moved images of Ganesa on the Kalakshetra compound and redesigned the logo of the institution. The organization, based in Mumbai, urged that 'members of the Hindu community should initiate an action immediately to stop the planned

destruction of a glorious institution teaching and nurturing the ancient traditions of Sanatana Dharma.'
http://www.organiser.org/dynamic/modules.php?name=Content&pa=showpage&pid=181&page=10 (accessed on 10 April 2009).

27. Other excellent analyses of the relationship between dance, diasporic identity and Indian nationalism are found in two of anthropologist Kalpana Ram's essays (2000 and 2005).

28. A fascinating account of Chandralekha's life and work is found in Rustom Bharucha's biography, *Chandralekha: Dance, Woman, Resistance* (1995).

REFERENCES AND FURTHER READING

Allen, Matthew Harp, 1992, 'The Tamil Padam: A Dance Music Genre of South India', PhD Dissertation, Department of Ethnomusicology, Wesleyan University.

Anandhi, S., 1991, 'Representing Devadasis: "Dasigal Mosavalai" as a Radical Text', *Economic and Political Weekly*, 26 (11/12), pp. 739–46.

Arundale, Rukmini Devi, n.d., 'Rukmini on Herself', in Shakuntala Ramani (ed.), 2003, *Rukmini Devi Arundale Birth Centenary Volume*, Chennai: The Kalakshetra Foundation.

Bharucha, Rustom, 1995, *Chandralekha: Woman, Dance, Resistance*, Delhi: Harper-Collins.

———, 2000, *The Politics of Cultural Practice: Thinking through Theatre in an Age of Globalization*, Middletown, CT: Wesleyan University Press and New Delhi: Oxford University Press.

Chatterjea, Ananya, 2004, *Butting Out: Reading Resistive Choreographies Through Works by Jawole Willa Jo Zollar and Chandralekha*, Middletown, CT: Wesleyan University Press.

Coomaraswamy, Ananda K. and Gopala Krishnayya Duggirala, 1917, *Mirror of Gesture: Being the Abhinayadarpana of Nandikesvara*, Cambridge, MA: Harvard University Press.

Coorlawala, Uttara Asha, 1994, 'Classical and Contemporary Indian Dance: Overview, Criteria, and a Choreographic Analysis', PhD dissertation, Department of Dance, New York University.

David, Ann R., 2005, 'Performing Faith: Dance, Identity and Religion in Hindu Communities in Leicester and London', PhD dissertation, DeMontfort University.

Devi, Ragini, 1928 [rpt. 1982], *Nritanjali: An Introduction to Hindu Dancing*, Delhi: Sumit Publications.

———, 1972, *Dance Dialects of India*, New Delhi: Vikas Publishing House.

Erdman, Joan L., 1996, 'Dance Discourses: Rethinking the History of the Oriental Dance', in Gay Morris (ed.), *Moving Words: Re-writing Dance*, London: Routledge.

Gaston, Anne-Marie, 1996, *Bharata Natyam: From Temple to Theatre*, Delhi: Manohar.

Ghosh, Manomohan, 1944 [3rd edn 1975], *Nandikesvara's Abhinayadarpanam*, Calcutta: Manisha Granthalaya.

Hancock, Mary, 1999, *Womanhood in the Making: Domestic Ritual and Public Culture in Urban South India*, Boulder, CO: Westview Press.

_____, 2008, *The Politics of Heritage from Madras to Chennai*, Bloomington: Indiana University Press.

Hawley, John Stratton, 2001, 'Modern India and the Question of Middle-Class Religion', *International Journal of Hindu Studies*, 5 (3), pp. 217–25.

Higgins, Jon, 1993, *The Music of Bharata Natyam*, New Delhi: ARCE-AIIS/ Oxford and IBH.

Inoue, Takako, 2005, 'La réforme de la tradition des devadasi: Danse et musique dans les temples hindous', *Cahiers de Musiques Traditionnelles: Entre Femmes* (18), Genève: Ateliers d'ethnomusicologie.

_____, 2008, 'Between Art and Religion: Bhagavata Mela in Thanjavur', in Yoshitaka Terada (ed.), *Music and Society in South Asia: Perspectives from Japan*, Osaka: National Museum of Ethnology.

Jackson, William J., 1994, *Tyagaraja and the Renewal of Tradition*, Delhi: Motilal Banarsidass.

Jordan, Kay Kirkpatrick, 1993, 'Devadasi Reform: Driving the Priestesses or the Prostitutes Out of Hindu Temples?' in Robert D. Baird (ed.), *Religion and Law in Independent India*, Delhi: Manohar.

_____, 2003, *From Sacred Servant to Profane Prostitute: A History of the Changing Legal Status of the Devadasis, 1857–1947*, Delhi: Manohar.

Kannabiran, Kalpana, 1995, 'Judiciary, Social Reform and Debate on "Religious Prostitution" in Colonial India', *Economic and Political Weekly*, 30 (43), WS 59–65.

Kannabiran, Kalpana and Vasanth Kannabiran, 2003, *Muvalur Ramamirthammal's Web of Deceit: Devadasi Reform in Colonial India*, Delhi: Kali for Women.

Kankaimuttu Pillai, Pacuvantanai, 1898, *Natanati Vattiya Rancanam*, Tirunelveli: Union Central Press.

Katrak, Ketu H., 2004, 'Cultural Translation of Bharata Natyam into "Contemporary Indian Dance": Second-generation South Asian Americans and Cultural Politics in Diasporic Locations', *South Asian Popular Culture*, 2 (2), pp. 79–102.

_____, 2008, 'The Gestures of Bharata Natyam: Migrating into Diasporic Contemporary Indian Dance', in Carrie Noland and Sally Ann Ness (eds), *Migrations of Gesture*, Minneapolis: University of Minnesota Press.

Kersenboom, Saskia, 1981, 'Virali: Possible Sources of the Devadasi Tradition in the Tamil Bardic Period', *Journal of Tamil Studies*, 19, pp. 19–41.

_____, 1987, *Nityasumangali: Devadasi Tradition in South India*, Delhi: Motilal Banarsidass.

_____, 1988, 'Cinna Melam or Dasi Attam: Songs and Dances of the Devadasis of Tamilnadu', in S.S. Janaki (ed.), *Siva Temple and Temple Rituals*, Madras: Kuppuswami Research Institute.

_____, 1995, *Word, Sound, Image: The Life of the Tamil Text*, Oxford: Berg Publishers.

Krishna Iyer, E., 1948, 'Renaissance of Indian Dance and its Architects', *Souvenir of the Sixteenth South Indian Music Conference*, Madras: The Indian Fine Arts Society.

Krishnan, Hari, 2009, 'From Gynemimesis to Hyper-Masculinity: The Shifting Orientations of Male Performers of South Indian Court Dance', in Jennifer Fisher and Anthony Shay (eds), *When Men Dance: Choreographing Masculinities Across Borders*, New York: Oxford University Press.

Kusuma Bai, K., 2000, *Music, Dance, and Musical Instruments during the Period of the Nayakas (1673–1732)*, Varanasi: Chaukhambha Sanskrit Bhawan.

Leadbeater, C.W., 1928, *The World Mother as Symbol and Fact*, Adyar, Madras: Theosophical Publishing House.

Levine, Philippa, 2003, *Prostitution, Race and Politics: Policing Venereal Disease in the British Empire*, New York and London: Routledge.

Mattson, Rachel Lindsay, 2004, 'The Seductions of Dissonance: Ragini Devi and the Idea of India in the US, 1893–1965', PhD dissertation, New York University.

McClintock, Anne, 1995, *Imperial Leather: Race, Gender and Sexuality in the Colonial Contest*, New York and London: Routledge.

Meduri, Avanthi, 1988, 'Bharata Natyam: What Are You?' in *Asian Theatre Journal*, 5 (1), pp. 1–22.

_____, 1996, 'Nation, Woman, Representation: The Sutured History of the Devadasi and Her Dance', PhD dissertation, New York University.

_____, 2008a, 'Temple-Stage as Historical Allegory in Bharatanatyam: Rukmini Devi as Dancer-Historian', in Indira Viswanathan Peterson and Davesh Soneji (eds), *Performing Pasts: Reinventing the Arts in Modern South India*, Delhi: Oxford University Press.

_____, 2008b, 'Labels, Histories, Politics: Indian/South Asian Dance on the Global Stage', *Dance Research*, 26(2), pp. 223–43.

Mukund, Kanakalatha, 2005, *The View from Below: Indigenous Society, Temples and the Early Colonial State in Tamilnadu, 1700–1835*, New Delhi: Orient Longman.

Naidu, Bijayeti Venkata Narayanaswami, Pasupuleti Srinivasulu Naidu, and Ongole Venkata Rangayya Pantulu, 1936 [rpt. 1971], *Tandava Laksanam or The Fundamentals of Ancient Hindu Dancing, being a Translation into English of the Fourth Chapter of the Natya Sastra*, New Delhi: Munshiram Manoharlal.

Naidu, Venkataratnam R., 1901, 'Social Purity and the Anti-Nautch Movement', in C. Yajneswara Chintaman (ed.), *Indian Social Reform*, Madras: Thompson & Co.

Nair, Janaki, 1994, 'The Devadasi, Dharma, and the State', *Economic and Political Weekly*, 10 December, pp. 3157–67.

Narayana Rao, Velcheru, David Shulman, and Sanjay Subrahmanyam, 1992, *Symbols of Substance: Court and State in Nayaka Period Tamilnadu*, Delhi: Oxford University Press.

Natarajan, Srividya, 1994, 'Another Stage in the Life of the Nation: Sadir, Bharatanatyam, Feminist Theory', PhD dissertation, Department of English, University of Hyderabad.

Neild, Susan Margaret, 1977, 'Madras: The Growth of a Colonial City, 1780–1840', PhD dissertation, Department of History, University of Chicago.

Neild-Basu, Susan, 1984, 'The Dubashes of Madras', *Modern Asian Studies*, 18 (1), pp. 1–31.

Orr, Leslie C., 2000, *Donors, Devotees, and Daughters of God: Temple Women in Medieval Tamilnadu*, New York: Oxford University Press.

O'Shea, Janet, 2005, 'Rukmini Devi: Rethinking the Classical', in Avanthi Meduri (ed.), *Rukmini Devi Arundale: A Visionary Architect of Indian Culture and the Performing Arts*, Delhi: Motilal Banarsidass.

_____, 2006a, 'Dancing through History and Ethnography: Indian Classical Dance the Performance of the Past', in Theresa Jill Buckland (ed.), *Dancing from Past to Present: Nation, Culture, Identities*, Madison: University of Wisconsin Press.

_____, 2006b, 'From Temple to Battlefield: Dance in Sri Lanka', *Pulse*, 13 (Spring), pp. 33–5.

_____, 2007, *At Home in the World: Bharata Natyam on the Global Stage*, Middletown, CT: Wesleyan University Press.

_____, 2008, 'Serving Two Masters? Bharatanatyam and Tamil Cultural Production', in Indira Viswanathan Peterson and Davesh Soneji (eds), *Performing Pasts: Reinventing the Arts in Modern South India*, Delhi: Oxford University Press.

Parker, Kunal M., 1998, 'A Corporation of Superior Prostitutes: Anglo-Indian Legal Conceptions of Temple Dancing Girls, 1800–1914', *Modern Asian Studies*, 32 (3), pp. 559–633.

Pillai, Shanti, 2002, 'Rethinking Global Indian Dance through Local Eyes: The Contemporary Bharatanatyam Scene in Chennai', *Dance Research Journal*, 34 (2), pp. 14–29.

Radhika, V.S., 1996, 'Development of Sadir in the Court of King Serfoji II (1798–1832) of Tanjore', PhD dissertation, Department of Dance, University of Hyderabad.

Rahman, Sukanya, 2004, *Dancing in the Family: An Unconventional Memoir of Three Women*, Delhi: Rupa and Co.

Ram, Kalpana, 2004, 'Dancing the Past into Life: The Rasa, Nrtta and Raga of Immigrant Experience', *The Australian Journal of Anthropology*, 11 (3), pp. 261–73.

_____, 2005, 'Phantom Limbs: South Indian Dance and Immigrant Reifications of the Female Body', *Journal of Intercultural Studies*, 26 (1), pp. 121–37.

Ramakrishna, V., 1983, *Social Reform in Andhra (1848–1919)*, Delhi: Vikas Publishing House Pvt. Ltd.

Ramanujan, A.K., Velcheru Narayana Rao, and David Shulman, 1994, *When God is a Customer: Telugu Courtesan Songs by Ksetrayya and Others*, Berkeley: University of California Press.

Reddi, S. Muthulakshmi, 1928, *The Awakening: Demand for Devadasi Legislation*. Madras: Madras Printing Co.

_____, 1964, *My Experience as a Legislator*, Triplicane, Madras: Current Thought Press.

_____, 1964, *Autobiography of Dr (Mrs) S. Muthulakshmi Reddi*, Madras: Author.

Sastri, S. Subrahmanya (ed.), 1942, *Sangita Saramrta*, Madas: The Music Academy.

Seetha, S., 1981, *Tanjore as a Seat of Music (During the 17th, 18th and 19th Centuries)*, Madras: University of Madras.

Shortt, John, 1869, 'The Bayadère; or, Dancing Girls of Southern India', in *Memoirs Read Before the Anthropological Society of London* (Vol. 3), pp. 182–94.

Srinivasan, Amrit, 1984, 'Temple "Prostitution" and Community Reform: An Examination of the Ethnographic, Historical and Textual Context of the Devadasi of Tamil Nadu, South India', PhD dissertation, Cambridge University.

_____, 1985, 'Reform and Revival: The Devadasi and Her Dance', *Economic and Political Weekly*, 20 (44), pp. 1869–76.

_____, 1998a, 'Far from Over: Some Reflections on the Devadasi and Her Discourse', in Ashish Khokar (ed.), *Attendance: The Dance Annual of India 1998*, New Delhi: The Mohan Khokar Dance Foundation.

_____, 1998b, 'Culture, Community, Cosmos: Two Temple Orchestras of Tamil Nadu', *Sangeet Natak*, 129–30, pp. 3–15.

Srinivasan, Priya, 2003, 'Performing Indian Dance in America: Interrogating Modernity, Tradition, and the Myth of Cultural Purity', PhD dissertation, Northwestern University.

_____, 2009, 'The Nautch Women Dancers of the 1880s: Corporeality, US Orientalism, and Anti-Asian Immigration Laws', *Women and Performance*, 19 (1), pp. 3–22.

Srilata, K., 2002, 'Looking for Other Stories: Women's Writing, Self-Respect Movement and the Politics of Feminist Translations', *Inter-Asia Cultural Studies*, 3 (3), pp. 437–48.

_____, 2003, *The Other Half of the Coconut: Women Writing Self-Respect History*, New Delhi: Zubaan-Kali for Women.

Sriram, V., 2007, *The Devadasi and the Saint: The Life and Times of Bangalore Nagarathnamma*, Chennai: East-West Books (Madras) Pvt. Ltd.

Subramanian, Lakshmi, 2006, *From the Tanjore Court to the Madras Music Academy: A Social History of Music in South India*, Delhi: Oxford University Press.

Sundaram, B.M., 1997, 'Towards a Genealogy of Some Tanjavur Natyacharyas and their Kinsfolk', *Sangeet Natak*, 124, pp. 30–41.

_____, 2002a, *Marapu Vali Paratap Peracankal* [Tamil], Citamparam: Meyyappan Tamilaylakam.

_____, 2002b, *Varna Svara Jati*, Thanjavur: Sarasvati Mahal Library.

_____, 2003, *Marapu Tanta Manikkankal* [Tamil], Chennai: V. Raghavan Centre for the Performing Arts.

Terada, Yoshitaka, 1992, 'Multiple Interpretations of a Charismatic Individual: The Case of the Great Nagasvaram Musician, T.N. Rajarattinam Pillai', PhD dissertation, University of Washington.

_____, 2008, 'Temple Music Traditions in Hindu South India: Periya Melam and its Performance Practice', *Asian Music*, 39 (2), pp. 108–51.

Tharu, Susie and K. Lalita, 1993, 'Empire, Nation, and the Literary Text', in Tejaswini Niranjana et al. (eds), *Interrogating Modernity: Culture and Colonialism in India*, Calcutta: Seagull Books.

Vatsyayan, Kapila, 1989, 'The Natyasastra: A History of Criticism', in Anna Libera Dallapiccola (ed.), *Shastric Traditions in Indian Arts* (Vol. 1), Stuttgart: Steiner Verlag Wiesbaden GMBH.

_____, 2003, 'Modern Dance: The Contribution of Uday Shankar and his Associates', in Sunil Kothari (ed.), *New Directions in Indian Dance*, Mumbai: Marg Publications.

Venkataramaiya, K.M., 1985, *Tancai Marattiya Mannarkal Araciyalum Camutaya Varalkkaiyum: Administration and Social Life under the Maratha Rules of Thanjavur*, Thanjavur: Tamil University.

Venkataramaiya, K.M. and S. Vivekanandagopal, 1984, *Tancai Marattiya Mannar Moti Avant Tamilakkamum Kurippuraiyum*, Thanjavur: Tamil University.

Venkateswaran, Usha, 2005, *The Life and Times of La Meri: The Queen of Ethnic Dance*, Delhi: IGNCA and Aryan Books.

Vijaisri, Priyadarshini, 2004, *Recasting the Devadasi: Patterns of Sacred Prostitution in Colonial South India*, Delhi: Kanishka Publishers.

Viswanathan, Gauri, 1998, *Outside the Fold: Conversion, Modernity, and Belief*, Princeton, NJ: Princeton University Press.

Viswanathan, T. and Matthew Harp Allen, 2004, *Music in South India*, New York: Oxford University Press.

Waghorne, Joanne, 2004, *Diaspora of the Gods: Modern Hindu Temples in an Urban Middle-Class World*, New York: Oxford University Press.

Weidman, Amanda J., 2006, *Singing the Classical, Voicing the Modern: The Postcolonial Politics of Music in South India*, Durham, NC: Duke University Press.

Whitehead, Judith, 1998, 'Community Honor/Sexual Boundaries: A Discursive Analysis of Devadasi Criminalization in Madras, India, 1920–1947', in James E. Elias et al. (eds), *Prostitution: On Whores, Hustlers, and Johns*, New York: Prometheus Books.

_____, 2001, 'Measuring Women's Value: Continuity and Change in the Regulation of Prostitution in Madras Presidency, 1860–1947', in Himani Bannerji et al. (eds), *Of Property and Propriety: The Role of Gender and Class in Imperialism and Nationalism*, Toronto: University of Toronto Press.

Zubko, Katherine C., 2008, 'Embodying Bhakti Rasa: Dancing across Religious Boundaries in Bharata Natyam', PhD dissertation, Graduate Division of Religion, Emory University.

PART I

Devadasi Dance: History and Representation

Representations of Dance in
Colonial South India

Part I

P. Ragaviah Charry

A Short account of the Dancing Girls, treating concisely on the general principles of Dancing and Singing, with the translations of two Hindo Songs

The habitual politeness of English Gentlemen ever induces them to accept the attentive invitations of the Natives, to partake the pleasures of a *natch*, or the feats of Dancing Girls; an entertainment common throughout Hindostan, nay India; but I am inclined to think that many of the Gentlemen, and more particularly Ladies, who are not acquainted with the Poetical part of the Native languages, in which the Songs are composed, must remain contented with the information of the eye; without that more rational relish of which the understanding is susceptible—this is the case even with many natives.

It may therefore be useful to have translations of Songs, the meaning of which are represented by the dancing women, in various motions; at the same time adding a short Sketch of the general principles on which they are founded.

Without involving myself in the scientific and technical system of Hindoo music, which would render what I propose abstruse and comparatively useless to the purpose, I intend this as a sort of *hand bill* for the respectable persons whose affability and natural goodness has given a ready acceptance to my request of witnessing a *Tamasha*.

Men are inquisitive in the first instance and that very properly, to know the history and character of the objects presented to their view, before other considerations which may lead to an enquiry into their accomplishments and profession.

I therefore proceed to relate an account of the origin of the Dancing Girls, a race of public women in all parts of India, regularly bred up for dancing and singing—Why the like does not exist in Europe, may be easily accounted for—The Ladies of all ranks and families in Europe, are indiscriminately taught to read and write, and initiated in the art of music and dancing.

But the customs and manners of modern eastern nations in general, allow their women no education or liberty—this circumstance necessarily renders a particular set of women useful for pubic diversion and entertainment.

In former days, we had certainly some established rules to regulate their conduct, for as public women they were not destitute of fidelity and attachment—at present the case is otherwise, and needs no explanation, from the miserable objects we often see in the public bazars.

This race of women in this part of the country is formed into three grand divisions—

1st—A particular set employed in the service of our Temples, where dancing is performed at regulated hours—They are not remarkable for their beauty, because they are the refuse of the following Class; and their *Masters*, (the images in the *Temple*) are not nice upon this point.

2nd—The fashionable set—the women under this Class, carry the prize of the day, for they are accomplished to a certain degree in music, they profess the trade of dancing, and are initiated in the bewitching arts or Harlotry—they are pretty, not without exception, and live decent and in good circumstances.

3rd—A shameless race, the common women—they have no pretensions to any sort of acquirements, and wholly depend for the necessaries of life on the common trade to which they became devoted.

The fashionable class with whose theatrical representations the public is entertained, are originally descended from the tribe of *Kicolas* or weavers, who from immemorial usage dedicated one of the female offspring of each family to the service of the Temples and Public—this custom is not in much practice now; for the uninterrupted employment the weavers find under auspices of the Honourable Company, together with their circumstances, has improved their feelings of honor and virtue.

The deficiency arising from the above cause, is made up by purchases of Girls, from different parts of the country, where the calamities of famine and war, domestic misfortunes and peculiar religious customs, drive the parents to the necessity of disposing of their Children.

An elderly woman, and one or two Girls form a *set*, which is distinguished after the young or old Lady's name, as fortune or fame may render either of them conspicuous.

The young Girls are sent to the dancing school at about 5 or 6 years of age, and at 8, they begin learning music; either vocal or instrumental—some attain a great proficiency in dancing, or others in singing; but the first art is limited to a certain period of life, for dancing in the Hindoo style requires great agility of constitution—thus, no women after the age of 25 years is reckoned competent to the task.

The expence attending the education of a Girl, and to render her accomplished will probably amount to between 300 and 400 Pagodas, this is either managed by contracts, or monthly payment to the *nativa*, the dancing master, and *Pataca* the singer.

When the Girl attains a certain degree of proficiency, the friends and the relations of the old Mother, are invited, and after observing certain formalities and ceremonies, the young student is introduced to the assembly and her merit is examined and assayed.

The expence of this first exhibition is great, including the presents to the dancing masters, and it is born either by the bethrothed gallant of the Girl, or the friend of her mother.—After this ceremony, and not until then, the set gain admittance to the favours of the Public, and are asked to attend marriages and other feasts.

With regard to their Revenues, the first source of emolument proceeds from their destination, as *public* women—When the young lady arrives at the age of Puberry, she is consigned to the protection of a man, who generally pays a large premium, besides a suitable monthly allowance—changes of men are made as often as it suits the conveniency and advantage of the old matron.

The second channel of benefit arises from the presents made to them for dancing or singing—unfortunately, no standard of hire was ever established, but it is entirely left to the arrangements of the parties—A *set*, will probably receive from 30 to 500 Rupees for the performance of 3 or 4 days as the circumstances and disposition of the person who requests their dance may admit;—The spectators, sometimes, give a few Rupees to them, either from liberality or vanity—The produce of this supply goes in shares to every individual forming the set, viz.

Five or 10 per cent on the whole is taken off for Charities. The residue is then divided into two shares, of which one is allowed to the dancing woman. The other subdivided into 6½ shares, of which 2½ to *Natuva* or the dancing master, 1½ to Pataca, singer, 1¾ to *Pillangolo* or the flute player, 1½ to *Maddalagar* or trumpeter, ½ to *Srutyman* or bellower, the dancing woman pay the latter ½ from her share.

It is but doing justice to say, that the arts of music and dancing are more perfect in and about Madras than in any part of Hindostan. The old Kings of Trichinopoly and Tanjore and the Rajahs of Pondeman and other Poliguery country, have for ages devoted their time and fortune to the culture and improvement of these entertaining arts—but since the empoverishment of these Princes, the seat of Musical learning was transferred to Madras where an encreasing Population and the introduction of lucary keep them in demand.

Bharata sastra or the art of dancing was originally invented by *Seva* or *Maha Dava*; and brought to perfection by the sage called *Bharata*, after whom the *Saster* was named—besides, the word *Bharata* is the compound of ideas, modes, or tunes, and time;—thus, *Bha* for *ideas*, *ra*, is meant for *Raga or modes*, or *ta* for *thàlum*, or the time.

It is related in the *Brummanda Poorana*, that *Mahadava* and Parvaty were enjoying the felicity of conjugal happiness on the sacred mountain *Kylàsa*, their established seat of Residence; but a misunderstanding having once taken place between this fond pair—it was the intention of *Sivan* to offer some entertainment to regain the favours of his spouse—he then began to dance, singing melodiously and keeping time with the movement of his feet; while he aptly expressed, the meaning of the Poems he sung by various appropriate motions.

This casual act of *Siva* established an art, which was taken up by 32 of our Gods, who wrote separate treatises each differing a little in details.

After this, Parvaty, in her incarnation of Bhudrabally, learned to dance, with the frailty of a woman, to excel her husband; for ladies are sometimes jealous—all discriptions of Gods assembled, and an examination was set on foot—The divine pair danced, but an indecent posture of *Iswara* induced *Bhudrabally* to give up the contest—*Maha Dava* then instructed Brumma with it, who communicated it to Indra, and by him it descended to divine Sages, who transferred it to *Apseharasas* or the heavenly nymphs, who stand in the same relation with our dancing women, in the upper Regions.

It is stated that *Bharata Nateya* or dancing should be composed of 5 *Angàs* or parts—1st *natá* (the Ticta man who regulates the time) 2nd Mindenga (a small drum) 3rd Pataca (the singer) sruty (the Bellows which blows the easy tunes) and *Patra* the actress.

An actress should be young and healthy—The females of *Sata Goharjara* and *Sourastra*, and said in the Porana's, to be beautiful.

The breed of *Carnata* and *virà ta*, are *pretty* and the girls of *Dravida* are of ordinary kind, we are unfortunately situated on the last division of the Country so that it is no wonder, our dancing Girls are not remarkable for personal beauty.

I premised that *Bharata Sasto* is composed of Ideas, mode, and time.

The ideas or feelings are nine in number, divided into three Classes, which relate to Love, Fear, and Hatred. viz:

Vearā Ràsa or the sense of honor and glory.
Dayà Ràsa of Compassion and Affection.
Carona Ràsa of Mercy.
Srungara Ràsa of Love and pleasure.
Haseya Ràsa of Mirth and sprightliness.
Bhayanaca Ràsa of Fear and terror.
Rowdra Ràsa of Rage, accompanied with tears.
Bhibhutcha Ràsa of Apprehension and confusion.
Adbhuta Ràsa of Excellence and wisdom.

All subjects, which relate to human nature, contain some one of these passions, and the whole is represented by 37 *hastas*, or as many different changes of hands, and thirteen of the head.

Of the 37 *hastas* and 13 heads, I give a few samples here.

1. *Pathaca hustra*, or Flag shaped hand; to denote excellence, approbation, friendship, and point out sides, comers, &c.
2. *Ardhapataco*, or half flag shaped; to point out females, the Ear rings, Mountains, Trident, &c.
3. *Tripathaca*, the same as the first, with the exception of the third finger folded, to express conjugal attachment, gallant intercourse and others, as *Ardhapataca*.
4. *Mayura*, or Peacock shaped; to mark Peacocks and other birds; saphire, garlands, and rows of pearls, &c.
5. *Ardhachundra*, or half Moon to signify, *Ancosa*, half Moon; the waist of a woman, to chastise, &c.
6. *Soocatundum*, or the beak of a bird, to denote Bows and Arrows, Elephant, several war implements and birds.
7. *Soochy Mookhum*, or the Needles end; expressing trifles, writing, pointing out objects, &c.
8. *Pudra Cosa*, or the bird of loters.
9. *Senha Moekhum*, or the head of a Lion.
10. *Moograshurshum*, or the head of an Antelope.

The remainder may be conjectured to be of the same kind. The Motions of the Heads are,

1. *Acompetum,* or the head in an erect position, very slightly shaken occasionally, to denote solemn expression; to make a demand, point out objects, expressive anger and to give a negative answer.
2. *Compitim,* heaving head, this marks approbation, contemplation, deep thought of a lover, and pleasing circumstances.
3. *Dhotem,* nodding head; expressing contempt, sorrow, surprise, &c.
4. *Vidhotum,* shaking head; to express indisposition, fever, terror, and the desire of driving away.
5. *Parivahacum,* leaning on one side; expressing surprise, satisfaction, recollection, &c.
6. *Anchitim,* learning on one side, but to shake often; feigning to be fainted, expressing indisposition, sorrow, &c.
7. *Oaeshiptem* to have the head up; on marking dust, in pointing objects above heaven, &c.

I forbear to proceed on these scientific atoms farther, for they will tire the Reader, and they rend to no great use—The changes of hands and heads, and whirling of the Eyes, with an appropriate attitude of the same, sufficiently explains the meaning of the Songs.

I think the Hindoos in this respect excel all other nations.

The *Ragas* or modes are many, but 32 principal ones, are much in use. Each of these *Ragas* has its peculiar property of pleasing the ear, and the difference is formed by variations of *Swaras* or notes, which are 8 in number.

Sà ri ga ma pa dà ni sa.

We have 7 *Talems,* or measures regulating the time.

1st—*Dhruva tala* measuring 14 syllables.
2nd—*Matteya* for 10 syllables.
3rd—*Aathala* for 14 syllables.
4th—*Rupaca* for 6 syllables.
5th—*Jumpa* for 10 syllables.
6th—*Triputa* for 7 syllables.
7th—*Yacathalum* for 4 syllables.
8th—*Aditalum* for 4 syllables.

In dancing, these syllables are formed of hard constructed *technical* language called *Sula* and this is pronounced with a loud, sometimes harsh voice by the Ticta fellow. viz.

Tha tha, Dindà thà, thé thà, thà thà, Dinda tha; are the *Soolas* for 12 instead of 10, but this encrease and decrease originates from the number of gooroo and lagho *Matras*, an explanation of which, like the rest, must be left to a large treatise on Music.

It is now time to begin with the proceedings of the Dancing set, when entered on the Court Yard.

With the Girl in front, the *Natuvas* (generally 2) one on each side, and the small drum with the sruti bellows, and the Singer together with the old mother on the rear, the scene commences.

Natuva expresses first of all the technical syllables of *Dim Dim* in honor of *Sambho*, the first inventor of the art, and commemorates *Brumma* with similar unmeaning sounds.

An invocation to *Venayaka* or Pelliar follow: 'O *Venaica*, the son of *Paravaty* and Elephant faced, than who dancest inemitably, let the *Natuva* or the *time beater* know him, and resound the technical syllable in *his praise* and attend particularly to the change of times.'

A Prayer to Rama is then offered.

Victory be to the favorite of *Janaky* (Ramah's affectionate Wife) or the Patron of Vibeeshana (the King of Lunka or Ceyloan) let happiness attend the Lotus footed, and the merciful towards the distressed. Let the Preserver of the World, and Saviour of his followers be crowned with happiness.—Grace be to his beautiful Mein, as he is an image of virtue. He is omnipotent, and *at the same time* an Inhabitant of *Ayadheya* or Oude. Glory be to the Spotless, who loves the truth, &c.

Rama, was the great hero who conquered the King of Giants. He is reckoned to be most valiant as well as a just Prince and hence he is invoked for the success of prosperity of all undertakings.

His spouse *Sitta* follows him in order.

After Complimenting the Gods; an Hymn of Salam is sung in honor of some one of our ancient or modern Kings.

Pratapa Rudra a famous King of Carnata, *Yova Runga*, and extravagant Poligar of fame and *Pratapa Sinha* and *Tolaja Rajas* of Tanjore, have been in their respective days, the Patrons of Music.

Song

'*Pratapa Sinha*, the valiant in war; You are exclusively endowed with the accomplishments of Music and Poetry, in the abstruse science of *Bharata Sasha*, and in the art of *Abinia* or counterfeited—you are well versed on all

subjects and your mind is liberal and you possess unbounded courage—
To you, O Maha Raja, I render Salam.'

Thus ending a bustling and noisy commencement, the dancing set
have a few minutes composure; and regulate harmony to commence on
Abhinia, representing the sense of a *Padà*.

Songs, among the Hindoos, are of three principal kinds—*Varna*,
Padà, and *Keertana*—the former is heavy, and the latter is dedicated to
religious and divine Themes.

Pada—or Songs of this discription contain every thing relating to
love—Yet, the religious principles of the Hindoo Poets are ever untainted,
for every *Padà* is stamped with the name of some or other of their Deities,
excepting those, which they dedicate to please their Masters—the
Rajahs; or others who hire their labour to transmit an individual name
to posterity,

Cashatreya, a modern Poet of first note, who composed innumerable
*Pada*s marked with the name of *Moova Gopala* (Kristna)—his style
is elegant and musical; his language is easy and clear, and his meaning
comprehensive.

From this Poet's productions, I have selected two Songs an indifferent
translation of which, (for to be literal and elegant it does not become me—I
am concerned to find, my poor abilities to attempt) I annex below.

The *Pallavy* or Chorus of every *Pada* is sung at the end of every
Charana or sentence.

Pada—first.

Panto rally Raga, Aditala} '*Naramá Commá, Vádandoka, Chára rá
Dumma.*'

'It is a crime, ah friend thy face is beautiful as the *blossoms* of Roses;
Why does he disdain to approach, or come near me.'

1st—'When *he*, the King of the world once was sporting with me, I left
the agreeable emotions of his repeated embraces, which tickled me, and
I blushed and remained smilingly *silent* with my head bashfully reclined;
but he wished me, *at the time* to speak, but I could not' 'Is it a *crime, oh*
friend, why does he disdain to *approach* or come near me.'

2nd—'At the time, that I was contemplating the pleasing occurrences
which his agreeable company and sweet embraces produced in me, I
laughed to myself and remained mute, without being able to acquaint him
the *value* of the present moment.'

'*Is it a crime, oh friend, &c.*'

3rd—'When his efforts to divert me succeeded to my hearts desire, and I was enjoying the bliss of his love in *his arms, is it possible*, that I could have expected *Toopacoola Krestnama Naik*, that I was not satisfied.'

'Is it a crime, oh friend, &c.'

Observation

The above *pada* contains the language of a woman, addressed to her female friend, acquainting how harmoniously she lived with her lover, and explains the cause of the present variance—the heroine, is called *Madheyama*, or the discreet woman, for she is, (as it is inferable from her sentiments in the song) perfectly accomplished in the gallantries of love, but circumspect and modest—the complains of her lover's mistake with regard to his idea of offence, which originates from her being modest, and not sprightly and gay.—The gallant is *Paty*, or man of fidelity, for he is not reproached with intriguing with other women, and his fault is a *mistake in judgment*.

Pada—second.

Asavary Raga.
Ata Thála.

'Màhà gàya, oh, *Moova Gopaula Nivagalallah, Màiàssàvà.*'

"Tis very surprising, O, *Movo Gopaula* all your gallantries, tis exceedingly pretty.'

1st—'To you I give the folded beetle, but you hand it over to that lotus Eyed' (a pretty woman;) with whom the world laughs at your intrigues.

"Tis very surprising, &c.

2nd—'I waste my intreaties on you; but you love her, whose eyes are beautiful as lotus: you freely express, a *contempt* of me, and the circumstance is rediculed at the houses of those *flowerlike framed* women of delicate and elegant constitutions.'

"Tis very surprising &c.

'Third throw myself into your arms and take an interest in your amusements, oh, *Mova Gopala*, but you listen to malicious reports and live at variance, you hold me in disdain, and esteem her that female friend.'

"Tis very surprising &c.'

Observation

It is almost needless to mention that the *Naiky* or heroine of the above song is a *jealous wife*.

She is termed *Sweya* and *Vipraluboha* or has the command of herself but was deceived, because she does not employ a third person to negotiate the return of her lover's affection and attachment; but she reproaches him, directly with bold language for his improper conduct.

The *Naika*, or the lover is *Ductshow* or a gallant of changeable attachment.

TRIPLICANE,
3rd December, 1806.

Joep Bor[1]

Mamia, Ammani and other *Bayadères*

Europe's Portrayal of India's Temple Dancers[2]

INTRODUCTION

On Monday 1 October 1838, Ammani, Rangam and Sundaram made history with their debut at the London Adelphi Theatre. Earlier they had baffled audiences at the Théâtre des Variétés in Paris. These young girls were the stars of the first professional Indian dance troupe to perform in Europe. Billed as the Bayadères, the group consisted of five temple dancers, known in Sanskrit as *devadasis* (lit. 'female servants of god'),[3] and three musicians. 'The public was in a state of great agitation,' according to the French writer Théophile Gautier, 'for at last they were going to see something strange, mysterious and charming, something completely unknown to Europe, something new!'[4]

In this chapter I will explore an aspect of the encounter with the Other that has not been dealt with by Gerry Farrell in his excellent study *Indian Music and the West*, and has also been ignored by writers on *bharata natyam*, the classical dance of Southern India.[5] First I will show that India's temple dancers and singers have a long history in European travel literature, giving a brief overview of the way they were portrayed. Next I will focus on Jacob Haafner's remarkable essay on the devadasis; published in his *Reize in eenen Palanquin* (1808), it was written in memory of his beloved, the young dancer Mamia.

After Goethe wrote his poem *Der Gott und die Bajadere* in 1797, nineteenth-century librettists metamorphosed the temple dancers into the fictitious *Bayadères* who became the heroines of various operas and ballets. These are briefly discussed in the section on the bayadère legend.[6] Examining dozens of articles and reviews, I will finally demonstrate that during the autumn of 1838 the 'real' Bayadères were 'the chief magnets of attraction' and 'greatest curiosities in London'.[7] In fact, part of the success of the 1838–39 season at the Adelphi Theatre could be attributed to the foreign dancers.[8]

TRAVELLERS' ACCOUNTS, c. 1298–1782

At the end of the thirteenth century, the famous Venetian traveller Marco Polo was the first European to provide a lengthy account of India's temple dancers.[9] After this it became somewhat of a convention to say something about them. Although many descriptions are superficial, biased and based on earlier reports, some travellers presented original and lively eyewitness accounts. These tell us a great deal about the Indian dancers and, perhaps more importantly, reveal the way they were perceived.

Marco Polo's Temple Maidens

Marco Polo tells his readers that many young girls (*donzelle*) of Malabar (on the Coromandel Coast in Southern India) were dedicated to the temples to entertain the deities with song and dance:

Their mother and father offer them to certain idols, whichever they please. Once they have been offered, then whenever the monks of these idol monasteries require them ... to entertain the idol, they come as they are bidden; and sing and afford a lively entertainment. And there are great numbers of these maidens, because they form large bevies. Several times a week in every month they bring food to the idols to which they are dedicated; and I will explain how they bring it and how they say that the idol has eaten ...[10]

And the reason why they are called on to amuse the idols is this. The priests of the idols very often declare: 'The god is estranged from the goddess. One will not cohabit with the other, nor will they hold speech together. Since they are thus estranged and angry with each other, unless they are reconciled and make their peace, all our affairs will miscarry and go from bad to worse, because they will not bestow their blessing and their favour'. So these maidens go to the monastery as I have said. And there, completely naked, except that they cover their private parts, they sing before the god and goddess.[11]

Polo also says that the young girls served the gods 'until they take husbands', but all research confirms that they were formally married to the deity of the temple to which they were attached. In other respects Polo's portrayal of the young dancers and the services they performed seems to be fairly accurate.[12]

Recent scholars have shown that temple women or devadasis had firmly established themselves as professional experts in the performing arts by the thirteenth century.[13] The importance of their services had developed to such an extent that in some large temples a special dance hall was built. The main duty of the devadasis was to sing and dance simultaneously with the food offerings to the gods, particularly the great gods Shiva and Vishnu. Their consorts were housed in shrines built within the temple compounds, precisely the way Marco Polo describes:

The god stands by himself on an altar under a canopy, the goddess by herself on another altar under another canopy. And the people say that he often dallies with her, and they have intercourse together; but when they are estranged they refrain from intercourse, and then these maidens come to placate them. When they are there, they devote themselves to singing, dancing, leaping, tumbling, and every sort of exercise to amuse the god and goddess and to reconcile them.[14]

Goddesses personify the divine female power or energy in Hindu religion. The devadasis were the living representatives of such goddesses. In other words, their female sexuality was essential to their ritual function, inasmuch as they acted as the 'wives' of the male deities enshrined in the temples.[15] Without their female power and the songs and dances they performed, there could be no food and no intercourse between the god and the goddess. And as Polo noted, without their presence evils and calamities could not be averted.[16]

At the beginning of the fifteenth century the devadasis were depicted in the illustrated manuscript *Le Livre des merveilles* that once belonged to Duke Jean de Berry. It contains early travel accounts in the East, including the short French version of Marco Polo's text of 1307. The temple maidens are portrayed here as stereotypical blond nuns! While six of them hold hands and dance in a circle, another girl offers food to a dark-skinned nun-like deity standing on an altar (Fig. 1).[17]

Bailadeiras and *Ballatrici*

In 1420 the well-known Italian explorer Nicolò dé Conti described a festival procession in Vijayanagar in which the 'idol is carried through the city, placed between two chariots, in which are young women richly adorned, who sing hymns to the god, and [are] accompanied by a great concourse of people'.[18] A hundred years later, the Portuguese trader Domingos Paes referred to the dancers of Vijayanagar as *baylhadeiras* (or *bailadeiras*, lit. female dancers). Like Polo, he noted that the main duty of the temple dancers was to 'feed the idol every day'.[19] Paes was greatly impressed by their prestige and says that they lived in grand style:

These women are of loose character, and live in the best streets that are in the city; it is the same in all their cities, their streets have the best rows of houses. They are very much esteemed, and are classed amongst those honoured ones who are the mistresses of the captains; any respectable man may go to their houses without any blame attaching thereto. These women are allowed even to enter the presence

FIG. 1   Boucicaut, 'Danse des servantes ou esclaves des dieux',
Le Livre des merveilles (c. 1413): fol. 80

of the wives of the king, and they stay with them and eat betel with them, a thing which no other person may do, no matter what his rank may be.[20]

Although the dancers were wealthy and respectable citizens, as mistresses of the elite they were 'of loose character', according to Paes. Several sixteenth-century travellers note that they provided sexual entertainment, but the moral condemnation of the dancers probably began at the end of the century.

The Venetian jeweller Gasparo Balbi (1590) may have been the first to use the derogatory term 'temple whores' (puttane del pagodo).[21] A few years later Jan Huygen van Linschoten refers to the dancers of Goa as 'heydensche lichte vrouwen, geheeten balliadera', or as his English translator puts it in 1598: 'the heathenish whore called Balliadera'.[22] Abraham Rogerius, a Dutch Calvinist minister, also calls them whores in his Open-Deure tot het Verborgen Heydendom (1651). He was shocked that brahman priests allowed such women to dance and sing in their sacred temples. In his own words: 'It seems a very strange affair, that while these Bramines regard the Pagodas as holy places, and the images are so holy that the Soudraes may not even touch them, that they also allow such lewd women to serve their gods. They let those women dance for them who are not only indecently clad, but whose lewdness is known to everyone.'[23]

Other well-known seventeenth-century travellers such as François Bernier, Jean-Baptiste Tavernier and Niccolò Manucci took it for granted that the temple women prostituted themselves. But according to the English sailor Thomas Bowrey, the dancers of the famous Jagannath temple (in Orissa) 'are wholly at theire own choice whether they will marry or noe, or live Subject to any one man, and have the liberty to be made use of by whom they please'.[24] Nevertheless, Bernier wrote in his widely read journal (published in Paris in 1670, and translated into English in 1671) that the *brahman* priests of the Jagannath temple 'raped' the young dancers after they were 'married' to the god:

These knaves select a beautiful young maiden to become ... the bride of *Jagannat*, who accompanies the god to the temple with all the pomp and ceremony which I have noticed, where she remains the whole night, having been made to believe that *Jagannat* will come and lie with her ... In the night one of these impostors enters the temple through a small back door, enjoys the unsuspecting damsel, [and] makes her believe whatever may be deemed necessary ...[25]

This depiction of the priests as evil, lustful characters and the dancing girls as their erotic victims would be repeated many times in travel literature. It also became a common theme of several eighteenth- and nineteenth-century plays, operas and ballets.

A different picture of the dancers was presented by Pietro della Valle. He also assumed that the 'public dancers' (*pubbliche ballatrici*) were prostitutes and that their songs and dances were lascivious, but this cultured nobleman of Rome did not dwell on the subject. Instead, he provided a long description of the dance that was part of a grand religious procession in which the two deities of the temple of Ikkeri were carried through the street. On 20 November 1623 he noted down:

First march'd the Trumpets and other instruments of divers sorts, continually sounding, then follow'd amongst many Torches a long train of Dancing-women, two and two, bareheaded, in their dancing dress and deck'd with many ornaments, of Gold and Jewels. After them came the *Palanchino* of the Idols ... In this order they came into the Piazza, and there, after they had made a large ring, the dancing began; first two Dancing-women, one from one side of the circle, and another from another, yet both with their Faces always turn'd towards the Idols, walk'd three steps forward and then three steps backward; and this they did innumerable times ... This Salutation, or Preamble of the Ballet, being many times repeated, they began to dance, namely two that danc'd better than the rest, one on the right side of the circle, and the other on the left ... Their dancing was high, with frequent leapings and odd motions, sometimes inclining their haunches as if they meant to sit down, sometimes rising very high and causing the skirt wherewith they are cover'd from the girdle downward to fly out, and always holding one Arm strech'd out before them ...[26]

Della Valle tells us that some of the dancers fanned the deities with flywhisks, and others were 'guided by a Man who danced with them and was their Master'.[27] His lively descriptions of Indian music and dance are the most informative of the period.[28]

Devadasis and Bayadères

The Sanskrit term devadasi appears for the first time in European literature in one of the Lettres édifiantes et curieuses (1713), in which a Jesuit missionary mentions that he baptized such a 'divine slave'.[29] The Dutch pastor François Valentyn (1726) uses the Tamil term devadasigal.[30] Like Rogerius, he was embarrassed by these 'dancing whores' (danshoeren). But, repeating the observations of Pietro della Valle, it is doubtful that he ever saw them perform.

An extensive account of South India's poetry, music and dance appears in Bartholomäus Ziegenbalg's Malabarisches Heidenthum, which was written in 1711 but not published until 1926.[31] The German author of this work was sent by the king of Denmark to Tranquebar, the base of the first Protestant mission in India. Ziegenbalg's knowledge of Tamil allowed him to consult authentic works—he had collected hundreds of them—and receive inside information from the local people. In a lengthy description of the temple he notes that among the 13 different types of servants the devadasigal sang and danced in a separate building.[32] These female servants of the gods (Götterdienerinnen) were listed as the eleventh category, before the musicians:

The Déwatáschigöl or servants of the gods whose duties consist in singing and dancing ... have to learn to read and write, and also understand something of poetry. For this purpose the cleverest and finest maidens are picked out. They should have flawless bodies, and are not allowed to get married. They are well adorned and can be immediately recognized by their external appearance for who they are. In the large pagodas there as a great number of them, in the small pagodas there are few, or even none at all ... But such singers and dancers are nothing more than everyone's whores, who have a privileged way of carrying out their business, and thus are called dancing whores by the Europeans.[33]

In a separate chapter on South Indian music Ziegenbalg says that the young devadasis performed daily for the deities, and describes the marriage ceremony to the god:

When they are taken on as servants to the gods in a pagoda, they have to become betrothed only to the god whom they serve. Then the priest of the gods carries out the full wedding ceremony with them, and binds them to the gods with a golden bridal necklace, which is the sign of all those who are married. Afterwards all the young maidens who have been married to the gods are given a marvellous procession around the streets, as happens at other weddings.[34]

Once again Ziegenbalg emphasizes that 'they are free to whore with whomever they like', and that their houses are 'public brothels'. He also says that Europeans enjoyed watching the devadasis sing and dance in the streets, and that many of them visited their houses. In his view this was a great shame and an insult to Christianity![35]

Other authors were less moralistic, but in eighteenth-century Europe it was somewhat of a platitude that India's courtesans 'have made vows of unchastity which they religiously keep'.[36] This was the opinion of John Henry Grose, who provides a ten-page description of the dancing girls of Surat in his *Voyage to the East-Indies* (1757). It contains little information about temple dancers, however. Grose's work was translated into French in 1758, and 15 years later part of his description of the dancers appeared in the *Histoire philosophique et politique des deux Indes* (1773), which strongly attacks colonialism and slavery.[37] In this widely read work of Abbé Guillaume-Thomas Raynal, the Indian temple dancers are referred to as *balladieres*.

The devadasis of Surat are also described and depicted (Fig. 2) in a *Voyage aux Indes orientales et à la Chine* (1782) of the scholarly traveller Pierre Sonnerat. Once again we are told: 'Les Brames cultivent leurs jeunesse, dont ils dérobent les prémices; elles finissent par devenir femmes publiques' (The Brahmins cherish their youthfulness and are the first to deprive them of it; the girls end up becoming public women). The description that follows does not contain new material, except that it mentions the cymbals *tala* (or *talam*) and barrel-shaped drum *mattalam*, the musical instruments that were used for dance performances.[38] More importantly, Sonnerat was probably the first author to change the commonly used Portuguese term *bailadeira* into the French word *bayadère*. His book was translated into German in 1785 and into English in 1788, and was so influential that many nineteenth-century authors thought that bayadère was an Indian word. In fact, in *Webster's Unabridged Dictionary* (1999) 'bayadere' is still described as 'a professional female dancer of India'![39]

FIG. 2   Pierre Sonnerat, 'Dance des Bayadères', *Voyage aux Indes orientales et à la Chine* (1782): vol. 1, opp. p. 41

JACOB HAAFNER'S *DEVADASIS*

By the end of the eighteenth century a picture had emerged of the devadasis as pretty temple servants who dressed conspicuously and were privileged in that they were taught reading, writing, singing and dancing. Their main duty was to worship the gods with songs and dances, but, according to most travellers, their gestures were lascivious and their songs obscene. And virtually all the travellers noted that the dancers were public prostitutes. Although some Europeans realized that devadasis were experts in singing and dancing, they could not (or refused to) understand that these temple servants sang devotional songs of an erotic nature, and that due to their marriage to the god they were 'auspicious' women. It was this very blend of eroticism and devotional worship that shocked the missionaries.

One writer presented a radically different view of the devadasis. This was the Dutchman Jacob Haafner (1754–1809), who lived more than 13 years in India and Sri Lanka. He spoke Tamil, was a staunch anti-colonialist, despised the British, and was convinced that Christian preachers wasted their time in India.[40] In his romantic masterpiece *Reize in eenen Palanquin* (1808), a lively and well-written account of his travels on the east coast of India, he describes how in 1786 he fell madly in love with the young dancer Mamia.

At first he refuses to accept the 'love betel' Mamia offers him after she and the dancers of her troupe entertain him. He is suspicious and wonders if the girl is sincere. As Haafner notes, it was common knowledge that Indian dancers were not honest to their lovers.[41] In spite of his doubts he realizes that he has lost his heart to Mamia, and that her love for him is reciprocal. For a short while she becomes his companion and Haafner describes at length how beautiful, devoted and faithful she is.

Mamia plays a central role in *Reize in eenen Palanquin*. Like Princess Khair un-Nissa, the beloved of James Kirkpatrick in William Dalrymple's *White Mughals*, she offers him a true and unselfish love.[42] And like Dalrymple's heartbreaking story, Haafner's *Reize* has a tragic end: Mamia dies an early death after saving him from a shipwreck. After this Haafner decides to return to Europe. Thanks to Mamia he devoted a separate chapter of his book to the devadasis.[43] This is the most detailed account I have come across in travel literature, and must have been based largely on what Mamia told Haafner about the dancers. For this reason I pay special attention to it.

Jacob Haafner begins his essay with a brief definition and says that the 'main duty of the devadasis is to dance in front of the image of the deity they serve ... and to sing in praise of the god, and about his deeds'.[44] He makes a distinction between temple dancers and troupes of independent dancers (such as Mamia) who moved from place to place and performed at public rest houses, weddings and festivals. Devadasis were divided into two ranks,[45] but the requirements for being dedicated to the temple were the same for all girls: they should not yet have reached puberty, should have nice features and supple limbs, and should be swift on their feet and well-formed.[46]

Dancers attached to the temples of the main gods Vishnu and Shiva belonged to the first order. They were recruited from the mercantile *vaisya* caste and entered the temple from childhood. Such devadasis lived within the walls surrounding the temple and were not allowed to leave the compound without permission from the main priest. They were the mistresses of Brahmins and other high caste men. If a devadasi of the first order had an affair with a low-caste man she was severely punished and excommunicated.[47] Haafner provides an interesting list of the tasks and duties of such devadasis. In addition to singing the praise of the gods and dancing in front of them—either in the temples or when the deities were carried through the streets in festival processions—devadasis carried out menial tasks. These included weaving the garlands of flowers with which the deities were adorned, binding the bouquets that were used at rituals or for the decoration of the 'altars', sweeping the temple courtyard and cells of the priests, preparing sandal paste for adornment of the deities, cleaning the lamps and supplying these with oil and wicks.[48]

Devadasis of the second rank served the less prominent gods. They were recruited from the low *sudra* caste, particularly the weaver community, but received the same training as the other devadasis. The lived in villages or towns, and were free to move about unless it was their turn to sing and dance in the temple. They were also obliged to perform at important rituals and processions. In addition to what they received from the temple and their admirers, they were richly rewarded with money, clothes and jewellery at the various venues where they performed. Such devadasis earned much money, and their lovers—banias and other businessmen—were wealthier and more generous than brahmins. Some dancers carried eight to ten thousand rupees' worth of gold and jewels on their bodies. Although they enjoyed complete freedom, they were not allowed to have liaisons with men from the untouchable *pariah* caste, nor with European or Muslims.[49]

Parents who wished to offer their daughter to the temple informed the main priest. If the girl was suitable the parents signed a written document in which they gave up the rights of the child. For the dedication ceremony an auspicious day was chosen. The young girl was led to the temple with pomp and ceremony, and the devadasis received her from the hands of her parents. They first made her bathe in the pond, dressed her with new linen clothes and decorated her with ornaments that belonged to the temple:

The main priest then leads her to the statue of the deity, and makes her repeat a vow in which she dedicates herself to the service of the god for her entire life. To reinforce her vow, he takes a garland of flowers that adorns the deity and puts it around her neck, and makes her drink the milk with which the statue has been washed. Next he takes a pick and pierces her earlobe, ending the ceremony, after which the girl is forever attached to the service of the god.[50]

After this her education began. She was taught everything she had to know for her profession: reading, writing, singing, dancing and the history of the gods, particularly of the god she worshipped. In addition, she had to learn auspicious songs (*mangalas*).

According to Haafner, it was incorrect that devadasis were 'obliged to offer themselves first to the main priest of the temple' after they reached puberty. 'The contrary is true, they can choose their paramours in and outside the temple, as long as the men belong to high castes'—that is, the priestly (brahman) or warrior (kshatriya) classes. 'They are also free to remain life-long virgins if they so desire.'[51] The Dutchman also gives a detailed description of their make-up, ornaments and dress (Fig. 3), including the Indian forerunner of the Western bra.[52] The he says that they 'are great admirers of flowers, and when they dance they are always covered with garlands of flowers. One rarely sees them without bouquets in their hands; they also love fragrant oils, mainly *attar* (rose oil).'[53] He summarizes the foregoing as follows:

A young and beautiful dancer, completely dressed up, with her natural and free attitude and graceful gait, is indeed an enchanting and tempting creature. Her simple head ornament, her moderately bare, beautiful bosom and full arms, the tightly fitting dress with artful neatness and pleats twisted around her high, well-formed hips, the graceful curves of the veil—in other words, the whole garment of these girls is completely calculated to emphasize and add to their natural

FIG. 3   Jacob Haafner, 'Devadaschie, of Indiasche Danseresse', *Reize in eenen Palanquin* (1808): vol. 1, opp. p. 224

beauty, and to radiate a certain gracefulness of her persona and gestures. Each movement of her limbs is shown at its best, and her figure can be perceived in the most enchanting and modest way.[54]

No doubt, Haafner was totally captivated by the grace and beauty of India's dancers. But it needed some explanation (I think he refers here to Rogerius's *Open-Deure tot het Verborgen Heydendom*) as to why the priests allowed women of the lower castes to perform before the deity in the inner portion of the temple. According to the brahmins he consulted, the dancers were only employed at 'ceremonies or festival days, suited and intended to rejoice and to thank, praise and exalt the deity'.[55] As this could not take place without singing and dancing, the priests were simply obliged to engage the devadasis! Finally, let us see what the Dutch author has to say about their dance:

Their dances are very different from ours. Some of them consist of supple and fast movements of the limbs, which are regulated and gracious; others of light and ingenious jumps and steps. They are excellent mime artists. With an amazing precision of attitude and gestures, while singing and dancing, they can portray a love story or any other theme, even a fight. Their art to express emotions has been developed to such a height that our dancers and showgirls on the stage, with their cold and meaningless gestures, contortions of the body and break-neck jumps, would compare poorly to an Indian dancer.

The young devadasis, with their faces veiled, stand together in a group ready to dance ... At once they uncover their faces and drop the veil. They now come forward and form rows; with an amazing agility and artfulness they whirl around each other or dance in groups or in pairs. Their eyes, arms, hands, and even their fingers—all their limbs—move with a wonderful expression, gracefulness and art. Meanwhile the *cilampukaran* [dance master], playing his cymbals and following them closely on their heels, encourages them with his voice and gestures, and the *tays*, or aged dancers, keep time with their hands and sing.[56]

Haafner mentions musical instruments such as the *tutti, nagasvaram, karna, talam, mattalam* and *dhol*, which were used for a dance performance. Earlier these were described and depicted in Pierre Sonnerat's well-known book, and it is clear that he consulted this and other works.[57] However, his lengthy essay on the devadasis contains information that is nowhere else to be found in European travel literature.

Reize in eenen Palanquin was translated into German in 1809, and two years later into French.[58] In 1814 Haafner's passion for Mamia was a source of inspiration for Gaetano Gioja's ballet *I Riti Indiani*, in which a Dutchman falls in love with an Indian temple dancer.[59] His work was the main source on Indian dance in the early nineteenth century. It was cited, for example, by Auguste-Alexis Baron in his *Lettres sur la danse*

(1825) and by Juste-Adrien de la Fage in his remarkable *Historie générale de la musique et de la danse*, which was published in 1844 and is entirely devoted to non-Western music and dance.[60] Haafner's chapter on the devadasis was an important source of information for Théophile Gautier and other French critics as well (see p. 59).

THE BAYADÈRE LEGEND

Jacob Haafner had good reason to tell his readers it was nonsense that the devadasis were sex objects of the brahman priests. He knew more about India's temple dancers than his precursors and was determined to show that their descriptions were biased, wrong or incomplete.[61] Clearly, he was referring to such influential writers as François Bernier, Abbé Raynal and Pierre Sonnerat, who assumed that the young girls were at the mercy of the brahmins. In 1817 the Baptist missionary William Ward repeated it once again: 'The officiating Brahmans there continually live in adulterous connection with them.'[62] And according to the oft-quoted Abbé Jean-Antoine Dubois (1816), who provides a fairly detailed description of the devadasis: 'All the time which they have to spare in the intervals of the various ceremonies is devoted to infinitely more shameful practices; and it is not an uncommon thing to see even sacred temples converted into mere brothels.'[63]

False or not, the picture travellers and missionaries had drawn of the temple dancers as victims of the priests suited the taste of European playwrights. The first play featuring such a wicked priest was *La Veuve du Malabar* (1770) by Antoine-Marin Lemierre. In this tragedy a young Hindu widow had fallen in love with a French general who arrives just in time to save her from burning to death. As Jackie Assayag notes, it was the first of many plays, operas and ballets that ended dramatically with the heroine, a devoted Indian widow, committing sati: sacrificing herself on the funeral pyre of her decreased husband.[64]

However, Johann Wolfgang von Goethe was responsible for the fact that librettists began introducing the bayadère as a recurring theme in operas and ballets. His 'Indian legend' *Der Gott und die Bajadere* (1797) narrates the story of 'Mahadöh' (in other words, Mahadeva, the common name of Lord Shiva) wandering the earth in human disguise. A dancing girl offers him shelter and hospitality, and a true and unselfish love. But in order to test her devotion and fidelity he feigns being dead, and is carried away to the funeral pile:

Bei der Bahre stürtzt sie nieder,
Ihr Geschrei durchdringt die Luft:

'Meinen Gatten will ich wieder!
Und ich such' ihn in der Gruft.
Soll zur Asche mir zerfallen
Dieser Glieder Götterpracht?
Mein! Er war es, mein vor allen!
Ach, nur eine süße Nacht!'[65]

Ignoring the remark of the priests that the young man is not her husband, the dancing girl casts herself on his pyre. But the divine lover rises from the flames and takes the girl with him to 'heaven' where she is liberated from her earthly ties and rewarded with immortality.

Several scholars have pointed out that Goethe borrowed the term *Bajadere* from the German translation of Pierre Sonnerat's *Voyage*.[66] But for his poem Goethe must have drawn inspiration from the German translation of the above-mentioned *Open-Deure tot het Verborgen Heydendom*.[67] It describes the love between 'Dewendre' (Goethe's 'Mahadöh') in his form as a god-lover and (what Rogerius calls) a whore:

It so happened ... that *Dewendre*, in human form, one time came upon a certain whore, and he wanted to test if she was loyal. He reached an agreement with her, and gave her a good whore-wage. Considering the payment, she served him very well that night, without going to sleep herself. And this night it happened that *Dewendre* let her think that he had died; and indeed she thought he had died. The whore wanted to be burned with him, and her friends could not dissuade her; they impressed upon her that he was not her husband. But after they had tried in vain to talk her out of it, she had the fire lit in order to jump into it. At the last possible moment *Dewendre* woke up, and said that he had only let her think he was dead in order to discover if she was faithful; and he told her, as a reward for her loyalty, that she could go with him to the *Dewendre-locon* (which is one of the places of bliss). And as the *Bramine* told, so did it happen.[68]

Abraham Rogerius claims that the Brahmin Padmanabha told the story to him. But it is possible that he concocted it himself, because he combined the two aspect of 'paganism' he despised most: the devadasi and sati. In the legend Rogerius cleverly transforms the 'licentious' dancer into a devoted wife who desires to immolate herself on her lover's funeral pyre, thus merging the two characters into one.

Carl Friedrich Zelter set *Der Gott und die Bajadere* to music in 1798, and Franz Schubert in 1815; many other composers followed suit. The first opera inspired by Goethe's 'Indian legend' was Charles-Simon Catel's *Les Bayadères*, which was first staged at the Paris Théâtre de l'Académie on 8 August 1810 and was frequently performed until 1828. The libretto was by the prolific writer Etienne de Jouy, who had spent several years in India serving in the French army.[69] In his *Notice historique sur les Bayadères* he present his own version of the bayadère legend. The god-lover 'Shirven' (Shiva) has disguised himself as King 'Devendren' (Rogerius's 'Dewendre') and passes a life of pleasure and bliss with twelve hundred beautiful courtesans. In order to test their sincerity and fidelity, he feigns being on the point of dying. He calls his mistresses together and promises to marry the one who is prepared to immolate herself after his death. Only one bayadère (in the opera she is called Laméa, and the king Demaly) wants to sacrifice her life for the honour of becoming his wife. But after she lies down beside his 'dead' body and lights the funeral pyre the god-king arises. Before taking his new bride to heaven, Shiva commands that the event should be commemorated by the dancers attached to the service of his temples, and that they should be called devadasis or 'favourites' of the deity![70]

The most successful rendition of Goethe's poem was the opera-ballet *Le Dieu et la* bayadère, which was known in England as *The Maid of Cashmere*. Created by composer Daniel Auber, librettist Eugène Scribe and choreographer Filippo Taglioni, the ballet was first performed at the Paris Opéra on 13 October 1830.[71] In Scribe's libretto the dumb bayadère Zoloé gives shelter to the mysterious god Brahma, rather than Shiva or Mahadeva. It was the fist triumph of Taglioni's daughter Marie (Fig. 4) and she performed it on and off for at least 14 years. Authenticity was not an issue of course. The ballet was specially designed for the ethereal Mlle Taglioni to display the spirituality of the heroine, a bayadère who was an exotic stereotype of the sensual and mysterious Oriental dancing girl.

THE PERFORMANCES OF THE 'REAL' BAYADÈRES[72]

As a result of the publications of great writers such as Victor Hugo and travellers such as Victor Jacquemont, the French became widely interested in the Orient. Hugo's poem *Les Orientales*, for example, went through 14 publications in a month in 1829. A year later Kalidasa's Sanskrit play *Sakuntala* was translated into French by Antoine-Leonard de Chézy, and Marie Taglioni attained fame as an Indian temple dancer in *Le Dieu et la bayadère*. In short, bohemian Paris was in the midst of an Oriental vogue in the 1830s, and for this reason the enterprising French impresario E.C. Tardivel must have thought that the Parisians were ready for the real thing. Some time in 1838 he signed an agreement in Pondicherry with four devadasis and three musicians.[73] The contract, published in the *Revue et gazette des théâtres* and the *Courrier des théâtres*, was for a term of 18 months and mentions the names and ages of the artists; their signatures (in Telugu) were reproduced in the *Magasin pittoresque*.[74]

FIG. 4   Mathieu Barathier, 'Le Dieu et la bayadère' portraying ballerina Marie
         Taglioni and tenor Adolphe Nouritt (1849)

In charge of the troupe was the senior dancer Tilammal who was
30 years old and belonged to the weaver community.[75] Several writers
point out that she looked much older and 'never smiles'.[76] Next came
Ammani, aged 18, and Rangam and Sundaram who were 14 and 13.[77] The
latter may have been Tilammal's daughter and Rangam her niece.[78] The
dancers were from Tiruvendipuram, a small town close to Pondicherry

that housed the temple of Lord Perumal to which the dancers were attached.[79] Not mentioned in the agreement is the youngest dancer, who was only 6 years old.[80] According to the *Magasin pittoresque*, she was the granddaughter of Ramalingam Mudali, the grey-bearded dance master or nattuvan who sang and kept time with a pair of cymbals (talam).[81] 'He leads the music—accompanies the dances of the Bayadères with his voice—laughs, weeps, and represents by his expressive face all the passions which they exhibit in the dance'.[82] The other two musicians played the barrel-shaped drum mattalam and the drone pipe *titti* (or tutti).

Bordeaux and Paris

This was the first professional Indian dance troupe to make the long journey to the West, and to ensure that the devadasis were not regarded as common dancing girls or public prostitutes they were presented as 'priestesses' and launched as the 'real' Bayadères. As soon as they arrived in Bordeaux on 24 July 1838, the novelty was widely announced in the French and British newspapers, and the 'interesting strangers' became the talk of the town.[83] A correspondent of the *Observer* describes the scene when the Bayadères gave their first private performance in Bordeaux:

Curiosity was at its highest pitch, when the door opened, and five women of a bright copper colour advanced with a regular step, gracefully covered with a thin robe of white muslin, which scarcely covered the bosom and shoulders. The five heads bent down simultaneously to the floor, and they made a *salam* with both hands ... The five Bayaderes remained for some time immovable in the middle of the room, as if to allow the company to inspect them fully.[84]

According to the *Courrier de Bordeaux*: 'They went to the theatre the other evening, when *Le Dieu et la bayadère* was given for their special entertainment, and where they excited the greatest attention ... The French dancing they look upon as being licentious; and as to a *pirouette*, they cannot bear it'![85]

The Bayadères arrived in Paris on 8 August, and a few days later long articles appeared in the *Journal des débats*, and other newspapers and magazines.[86] On 19 August they performed for two hours at the Tuileries before King Louis Philippe, receiving presents from the queen and princesses.[87] The next day the *Journal des débats* published another lengthy article about the dancers:

Their dances are like nothing that we have seen, or that can be imagined. The dancers of all Europe dance with their feet, but that is all. Examine them well. The body rests cold and constrained while the feet move. The movement of the arms is proverbially graceless. The head obeys with a mechanical precision, and the mouth wears an eternal smile. Thus, with some exceptions ... the dance of Europe is without style and expression. Taglioni invented a style, which no one can successfully imitate. Without her the ballet is insufferably tedious.

The Bayaderes dance in a different manner. They dance with their whole frame. Their heads dance, their arms dance—their eyes, above all, obey the movement and fury of the dance ... Their feet click against the floor—the arms and the hands flash in the air—the eyes sparkle—the bosom heaves—their mouths mutter—the whole body quivers ...

The dance of the Bayaderes is something strange, impetuous, passionate, and burlesque. It is a mixture of modesty and abandonment—of gentleness and fury. It is a species of poem which a Bacchante recites as she runs—a religious drama, which a young priestess delivers without pause—as if the god of the pagoda pursued her to the last.[88]

Two days before their debut at the Théâtre des Variétés on 22 August, the French poet novelist and dance critic Théophile Gautier published a long article about them in *La Presse*.[89] He had written essays about the famous ballerina Marie Taglioni, her rival Fanny Elssler, and several other dancers. Like so many of his contemporaries he was fascinated by the Orient and thrilled therefore to see the Indian dancers in a private display at their house in Paris. A large part of the article is devoted to Ammani, 'the prettiest and tallest of the troupe':

In colour her skin is like a Florentine bronze—a shade that is a mixture of olive-green and gold, very warm and very gentle ... To the touch [her] skin is silkier that rice paper and cooler than a lizard's underbelly. Amany has blue-black hair, long, fine and flowing like the hair of a dark European. Her hands and feet are extremely tiny and refined. Her ankles are slender and bare ... As for her eyes, they are incomparably beautiful and brilliant. They are like two jade suns revolving in a crystal sky.[90]

It is clear that Gautier was mesmerized by Ammani's delicate beauty; in more than one way she corresponded to the poetic image he had formed of India as a place that was ancient, mysterious, pure, wild, colourful and sensual. In the detailed account that follows he describes Ammani's make-up, jewellery, dress and some of the dances, similar to the way Jacob Haafner had portrayed the devadasis; no doubt, the French translation of Haafner's *Reize in eenen Palanquin* was Gautier's main source of information on the devadasis.[91] But while Haafner had had a passionate love affair with Mamia, Ammani and India were a distant dream to the poet, an unattainable romantic ideal. As Ivor Guest notes, it was to Ammani that he looked back 20 years later when he adapted Kalidasa's classic play *Sakuntala* for his grandiose ballet *Sacountalâ*.[92]

Between 22 August and 25 September the Bayadères performed 26 times at the Théâtre des Variétés, twice at the Tivoli and once in Versailles. Numerous articles about them were published in newspapers and magazines, and the portrait sculptor Jean-Auguste Barre made a lovely statuette of Ammani dancing 'The Malapou or Dance of Delight' (Fig. 5).[93] The Indian dancers attracted so much attention that according to a correspondent, they 'menace to eclipse Taglioni and her fairy train'.[94] But I will focus here on what was written in the British press after their arrival on 28 September at London Bridge.

FIG. 5   Auguste Barre, 'Amany' (1838)

London and Brighton

The Bayadères were received by the well-known comedian Frederick Yates.[95] This enterprising manager of the Adelphi Theatre was constantly in search of novelties to present to his audiences, and had leased the dancers from E.C. Tardivel 'for fourteen months, for the sum of £5,000 sterling'.[96] According to a sceptical columnist of the *Observer* of 30 September:

The question is, what will the Bayaderes do for the Adelphi? That they will draw crowds for some time there can be no doubt; but having seen them once, will anybody wish to see them again? We do not at all rely upon published representations of the disappointment of Parisian audiences. We have met several gentlemen who saw the Bayaderes in the French capital, and who say that there existed a very divided sentiment respecting them. We must say that we should much prefer Taglioni's or Duvernay's imitation to the original; and we advise all who go to the Adelphi next week to dismiss any such injurious reminiscences.[97]

A week later the columnist changed his mind. After their debut at the Adelphi Theatre on 1 October (Fig. 6) he must have realized that this was not just another foreign novelty or freak show but something of a different order, and wrote: 'The Bayaderes, at the Adelphi, have been

FIG. 6   Theatre Royal Adelphi, 'First Appearance of the Bayadères' (1 October 1838)

completely successful, and are drawing crowds of inquisitive spectators; not only, we are bound to say, from the novelty of the exhibition, but from the real excellence of the performance.'[98]

The Indian dancers showed up in the second piece, a one-act burletta called *The Law of Brahma* or *The Hindoo Widow*—an adapted and abridged version of Lemierre's well-known tragedy *The Widow of Malabar*—in which a Hindu widow is rescued from the funeral pyre by the intervention of British troops! They were drawn to the front of the stage 'upon a moving platform.'[99] Sitting with flywhisks in their hand 'around a statue of Vishnu, in the interior of a temple, they [were] performing the important duty of fanning the image.'[100] 'By the time these females were introduced upon the stage the curiosity of the audience had arrived at the highest point of excitement.'[101] First Sundaram and Rangam performed 'The Robing of Vishnu', 'a *pas de deux* with poniards, which received the loudly expressed approbation of the spectators'. After this the youngest girl danced 'The Salute to the Rajah', 'with a vivacity that promises much for her performance hereafter.'[102]

The 'Hindoo Lament' was danced by Amany, who is considered a Hindoo beauty. Her countenance is more aquiline than those of her companions, and the expression of her eye is very remarkable ... The dance was to a slower movement than the preceding, being expressive of deeper feeling and stronger excitement. 'The Dagger Dance' which followed was executed by the two girls who danced the 'Robing of Vishnu,' and was, perhaps, the most interesting of all ... The whole concluded with 'The Malapou, or Delightful Dance,' by the whole of the *corps de ballet*, the little Veydoun excepted. The movement was slow, but impassioned and peculiarly expressive.[103]

Although they had been advertised as 'auxiliaries', the Bayadères proved to be the main attraction. Virtually all newspapers carried raving reviews and reported that during the first few nights a host of fashionables (including Prince Esterhazy and Baron von Münchhausen) were present at the show.[104] A critic of the *Era* noted: 'We have scarcely ever witnessed a greater excitement than that produced by the appearance of these very extraordinary people ... and consequently, at a very early hour, the doors of the Adelphi were besieged by a numerous and impatient mob, that entirely filled the theatre the moment the doors opened.'[105] Another reviewer wrote:

We are in raptures with the BAYADERES. Until now 'the poetry of motion' has been a mere term, and 'grace', a *beau ideal*, existing only in the fancy. These Hindoo girls, however, embody and give life and portraiture to what has hitherto been but viewed with the mind's eye. Their forms are symmetrical to perfection. Every movement is exquisitely graceful, and the animation—the flash and soul which lights up the eyes of the dancers as they execute their fascinating evolutions, is absolutely magical.[106]

The French public had favoured Ammani, but the critic of the *Morning Post* was more impressed by Rangam and Sundaram. They 'are as light and as gentle as fawns', and looked so much alike that they could easily pass for twins.[107] Like the editor of the *Journal des débats*, he makes an interesting comparison with contemporary ballet:

They do not resemble in the least our European artists. All the extravagance of the French ballet is evidently unknown to them. They form no pirouettes, cut no entrechats, nor bound like TAGLIONI or FANNY ELSSLER ... The speak a language in their dance. Their animated countenances and expressive eyes respond to the magic of their gestures. The arms, feet, and every portion of the pliant frame undulate to the same idea ... They form ever varying groupes. They commence in languor and rise in animation as it proceeds. The whole frame appears convulsed, and they retire panting and exhausted.[108]

Another critic regarded 'the performance as peculiarly sensual, using that term at its best and highest sense ... The dancers of other countries *excite*—these *lull* the soul'.[109] However, almost all reporters agreed that their nose-rings were ugly, and that the music was 'monotonous, but ... not displeasing'.[110]

During October and November the Indian dancers remained the great attraction at the Adelphi, and the *Era* published three gossipy letters to their friends in Pondicherry.[111] Drawings of the Bayadères were published in several magazines—for example in the *Mirror* of 13 October (Fig. 7)—and lithographs were offered for sale.[112] According to the *Sunday Times*, the charming drawing by B. Johnston was 'the only good representation of the interesting strangers yet published'.[113] He must have been unaware of the beautiful statuette of Ammani made by the French sculptor Jean-Auguste Barre.

On 22 October the play *Arajoon* or *The Conquest of Mysore* was 'produced with the view of bringing the Bayaderes before the public in a new light'.[114] 'For each appearance they seem to make, if possible, a more lasting impression upon the public mind', wrote the *Mirror of the World*, and, according to the *Penny Satirist*, 'the house is nightly crammed'.[115] On 5 November the Bayadères also began performing (during the morning) at the Egyptian Hall in Piccadilly.[116] On the same day the French melodrama *Louise de Lignarolles* 'superseded the red and blue fire piece that introduced the Bayaderes' at the Adelphi.[117] But on 19 November, when the theatre opened with Edward Stirling's successful adaptation of

Fig. 7 N. Whittich, 'The Bayadères; or Dancing Girls of India', *Mirror of Literature, Amusement, and Instrument* (13 October 1838), vol. 32, 1

Charles Dickens's *Nicholas Nickleby*, their performance was downgraded to incidental dancing.

Although 'the all-enchanting Bayaderes' were still called 'the wonder and delight of London' on 24 November, a week later the *Mirror of the World* reported that their services 'are soon to be dispensed with [and] will not be missed'.[118] A critic who regarded 'the performance of the Bayaderes as the most interesting [he] ever saw', explains why they failed to attract large audiences any longer:

We suspect that there is something in the performance not exactly consistent with our English tastes and feelings. The dancing of the Bayaderes is altogether opposed to that of our English school—there is none of that lightness of step and motion which distinguishes the Elsslers' aerial flights ... These are sacred dances—of high antiquity, and embodying the religious feelings and passions of the Bayaderes. But they are not fitted for the mass ... People do not throng to see the Bayaderes because they do not comprehend their performance. The interesting dancers themselves may attract their notice—the curious tattoo of their hands—their jewels and dress—may be matters of wonders, but nine out of ten think nothing at all of the dances, and would much sooner see a bad *ballet* at Drury-lane. Their idea of dancing is different from this, and they can't tell what to make of it.[119]

The Bayadères performed 55 times at the Adelphi, and their last appearance (for their own benefit) was on 1 December.[120] After this they continued performing at the Egyptian Hall, and *The Times* announced that they danced 'upon an elevated stage' and had added the much-admired 'Formation of the Dove' to their programme.[121] In this dance Ammani stood between Rangam and Sundaram and 'took a scarf of cambric 40 feet in length, and having laid it in plaits across her arm commenced turning round and round upon one leg and so continued for a quarter of an hour. During this time she gradually formed out of the scarf a dove sitting upon a palm tree'.[122]

After their last show at the Egyptian Hall on 4 January 1839, the Bayadères performed in Brighton; first at the Devonshire Rooms, and on 21 and 22 January at the Theatre Royal where they 'attracted numerous visitors to box, pit, and gallery'.[123] Two days later they went to Antwerp and on 2 February they began performing at the Théâtre du Parc in Brussels.[124] After this they danced in other European cities, including Frankfurt, Berlin and Vienna.

The fate of the dancers from Tiruvendipuram is unknown.[125] But according to Théophile Gautier—in two other reviews of *Le Dieu et la bayadère* he compares ballerina Marie Taglioni to Ammani, Rangam and Sundaram—the public had become so accustomed to the fictitious Bayadères that the were unable to comprehend the genuine devadasis; only artists could appreciate their beauty and perfection.[126] Clearly, it was not the real Orient that appealed to audiences in nineteenth-century Europe but an imaginary Orient: a world composed of sylphs, nymphs, shades and other supernatural beings. In this illusionary world Marie Taglioni, Fanny Elssler and other well-known ballerinas and opera singers flourished in their roles of temple priestesses, slave girls and harem women.

POSTSCRIPT

Le Dieu et la bayadère was the forerunner of Marius Petipa's famous ballet *La Bayadère*, which was first staged at the Maryinsky Theatre in St Petersburg on 4 February 1877.[127] Although Bayadères remained an important theme in French literature throughout the nineteenth century, in British India a different picture emerged of the devadasis.[128] After the 1850s they became a topic for ethnographic research and public debate. An informative but biased paper called 'The Bayadère or Dancing Girls of Southern India' was presented before the Anthropological Society of London in 1868.[129] The author of this essay, John Shortt, was the Surgeon-General of Madras Presidency. He met several devadasis in his 'professional capacity while they lived as mistresses with European officers', and was 'greatly surprised at their lady-like manner, modesty and gentleness'.[130]

Shortt makes a distinction between 'pagoda dancers' or devadasis, who 'live in concubinage as a rule', and 'dancing prostitutes' or *dasis*, who 'belong for the most part to itinerant bands' and 'keep brothels in the several large towns'.[131] He describes six different types of dances, the dancer's dress, and musical instruments such as the dhol, mattalam, tutti and talam that were played during the performances. Although the doctor greatly admired the beauty and dances of the devadasis, he was of the opinion that 'they know but one form of pleasure, vice, in which their lives are spent'.[132] Dwelling on the exploitation of the girls, he says:

The money salary they receive is nominal—seldom exceeding a few annas, and sometimes a rupee or two a month. The chief object in being paid this sum as a salary is to indicate that they are servants of the temple; in addition to this one or more of them receive a meal a-day, consisting merely of boiled rice rolled into a ball ...

As soon as a girl attains maturity, her virginity, if not debauched by the pagoda brahmins, is sold to outsiders in proportion to the wealth of the party seeking the honour, if such it may be termed, after which she leads a continuous course of prostitution—prostituting her person at random, to all but outcasts, for any trifling sum. The practice of kidnapping for prostitution is not uncommon ...[133]

It was not the art of the devadasis, but this type of conflicting information that started a heated debate in India about those 'poor unfortunate women being the victims of such [an immoral] system'.[134] This led to detailed entries about them in ethnographic surveys and census reports, in which they were irrevocably branded as prostitutes, and ultimately to legislation banning the dedication of young girls as temple servants. But this story has been told many times and need not be repeated here.[135]

CONCLUSION

In order to keep the length of this chapter within limits. I have focused on the portrayal of the devadasis by Jacob Haafner and the reception of the Indian temple dances in London in 1838. However, devadasis have a long history in European travel writing, and the words travellers chose to call them give us an idea of how they were perceived.[136] Some travellers aptly referred to the dancers as servants of god; others called them simply dancing women, dancing girls or pagoda dancers; and others again— particularly missionaries—used derogatory terms such as temple whores or dancing whores. At the end of the eighteenth century the widely used Portuguese word bailadeira was substituted by the French term bayadère, which aroused the imagination of Goethe and many other writers in Europe, particularly in France. As Théophile Gautier put it: 'The very word bayadère evokes notions of sunshine, perfume and beauty even to the most prosaic and bourgeois minds'.[137]

Whether temple dancers were promiscuous or not remains a contentious issue and depends of course on how promiscuity is defined. According to Leslie Orr, in none of the medieval inscriptions are temple women referred to as prostitutes.[138] Marco Polo (c. 1298) also did not portray them as harlots but says: 'for a penny they will allow a man to pinch [the maidens] as hard as he can'.[139] And Domingos Paes (c. 1520) noted that the bailadeiras were highly respected but 'of loose character'; in other words, they had liaisons with upper-caste men. By the end of the sixteenth century European travellers began representing the temple dancers as public prostitutes. Nevertheless, Goethe and those who took inspiration from him—De Jouy, Scribe, Gautier and Petipa—created an image of the Bayadères as sophisticated, honest and faithful women, thereby rejecting (or ignoring) the biased opinion of most travellers and missionaries.

No traveller seems to have had access to the dancers who performed *inside* the temples. Their descriptions were either based on reports of local informants or on the public displays of the dancers *outside* the temples. It is likely therefore that travellers confused the devadasis, who performed in the inner part of the shrines, with 'dancing prostitutes' (dasis), who had no association with the temples whatsoever. Haafner emphasizes that, unlike ordinary dancers, devadasis had prestige and were treated with respect. They did not participate in the sex trade and could choose their own lovers, but he implies that devadasis of the second rank had more sexual freedom. In other words, their relationships were a private affair; as the *Journal des débats* put it:

From their birth they are destined to a religious life, and they are married, as it is called when they are consecrated to that god in whose Pagoda they serve. As to civil marriage the law forbids it, but each choses a Bramin and lives with him as long as fancy lasts. It is a *liaison* altogether sensual which religion does not prevent as a spiritual fidelity to their celestial husband is all that morality requires.[140]

In this chapter I have demonstrated that Haafner's description of the devadasis was far more informative than those of other travellers, including the lurid account of the Abbé Dubois. Although Haafner may be labelled as a typical romantic, he was an exceptionally sharp observer. What he wrote about the devadasis was original and, it seems, quite accurate. He admired the dancers, appreciated their art, and did not share the based views of earlier writers. In addition to the descriptions by Abbé Raynal and Etienne de Jouy, Haafner's chapter was an important source of information for French critics who reviewed the performances of the 'real' Bayadères in 1838. Indirectly, his essay also provided source material for British reviewers, who quoted or paraphrased the articles of their French colleagues.

There does not seem to be any evidence that these critics condemned the Indian dancers. Although they were at a loss to describe their dance, they wrote about it with an open mind. Several writers compared the dance of the Bayadères to that of the pioneering ballerinas Marie Taglioni (in Le Dieu et la bayadère) and Fanny Elssler, and as such put it on an equal footing with contemporary ballet. Unsurprisingly, the French and British public were not able to comprehend Indian dance; as a reviewer noted, this sacred dance was 'not fitted for the mass'.[141] Only in a few articles have I found an allusion to what Edward Said calls 'an almost uniform association between the Orient and [licentious] sex' in his famous book Orientalism.[142] But the authors emphasize that the devadasis were utterly modest and 'give offence of none'.[143] They were 'perfectly distinct from the Nautch girls of Northern India or the Almé of Egypt, the equivocal character of whose evolutions has excited so much horror in the mind of virtuous Europe'![144] And according to some critics, the Hindu dancers were 'the most respectable of their class' and 'infinitely to the ladies of the corps de ballet at home'.[145]

Haafner's Reize in eenen Palanquin was translated into French and German but not into English, and has therefore remained inaccessible to British and American scholars. Even if it had been known to Edward Said, it is doubtful whether he would have changed his view that the 'relationship between Occident and Orient is a relationship of power, of domination, of varying degrees of a complex hegemony ....'[146] To support the argument he writes:

There is very little consent to be found, for example, in the fact that Flaubert's encounter with an Egyptian courtesan produced a widely influential model of the Oriental women; she never spoke of herself, she never represented her emotions, presence, or history. He spoke for and represented her. He was foreign, comparatively wealthy, male, and these were historical facts of domination that allowed him not only to possess Kuchuk Hanem physically but to speak for her and tell his readers in what way she was 'typically Oriental'.[147]

But if Said had explored Jacob Haafner's passionate love affair with Mamia instead of Gustave Flaubert's one-night stand with Kuchuk Hanem, he might have been in trouble. Haafner truly adored and respected Mamia, and gave her a voice. Thanks to her he portrayed the devadasis not as perverse prostitutes, but as model women who were dedicated to their art and devoted to their god. Following in his footsteps, Théophile Gautier represented Ammani as a dancer of the same calibre as Marie Taglioni, creating in my opinion a far more powerful image of an 'Oriental women' than his compatriot Flaubert.

NOTES

1. I wish to thank Debby Korfmacher for digging up the press reviews of the Bayadères in various archives: the British Library (including the Newspaper Library), the Theatre Museum, the Westminster Reference Library, the Westminster Archives Centre and the Brighton History Centre. Tiziana Leucci has been very helpful in supplying French material and pointing out relevant details. My other dear friends Philippe Bruguière, Lodewijk Brunt, Roxanne Gupta, Jane Harvey, Saskia Kersenboom, Wim van der Meer, Suvarnalata Rao and Jetty Roels have given useful suggestions as well. I am very grateful to them. Most of the reviews taken from the above archives are cited without page numbers in this chapter.

2. For Durga.

3. The honorific term in Tamil is *tevaratiyal* (plural: *tevaratiyar*) or *devadasigal*.

4. T. Gautier, 1986, *La Presse* (27 August 1838), in I. Guest (trans. and ed.), London: Dance Books, pp. 48–9.

5. G. Farrell, 1997, *Indian Music and the West*, Oxford: Clarendon Press.

6. For an extensive analysis of such 'Indian' plays, operas and ballets, see T. Leucci, 2005, *Devadasi e Bayadères: tra storia e leggenda; Le danzatrici indiane nei racconti di viaggio a nell'immaginario teatrale occidentale (XIII–XX secolo*, Bologna: CLUEB).

7. 'Theatricals: Adelphi', *Penny Satirist*, 20 October 1838, p. 2.

8. See A.L. Nelson and G.B. Cross (eds), 1998, *The Adelphi Theatre 1806–1900*, Ypsilanti: Eastern Michigan University, www.emich.edu/public/english/adelphi_calendar/m38d.htm

9. M. Polo, 1958, rpt. 1976, *The Travels of Marco Polo*, translated by R. Latham, Middlesex and New York: Penguin Books, pp. 270–1; also quoted in N.M. Penzer, 1952, 'Sacred Prostitution', in *Poison-Damsels and Other Essays in Folklore and Anthropology*, London: Chas. J. Sawyer, pp. 147–8.

10. Here Polo says that the damsels prepare dishes of meat! As Tiziana Leucci pointed out to me, the word 'meat' may be a wrong translation of the old French word *mets* which meant 'food' or 'meal'. In old English 'meat' had the same meaning.

11. Polo, *The Travels*, pp. 270–1.

12. Marco Polo's observation that the temple dancers were practically naked is probably accurate as well, although Penzer ('Sacred Prostitution', pp. 148–9)

noted that in virtually all accounts that come later the devadasis are described as being clothed. According to Polo (*The Travels*, p. 262), the people of Malabar 'go stark naked all the year round ... except that they cover their private parts with a scrap of cloth'. And from the eleventh to thirteenth centuries there is an abundance of temple sculptures in which the dancers are portrayed bare breasted, clad in a thin transparent garment from the waist down, or sometimes wearing no garment at all.

13. See, for example, F. Appfel Marglin, 1985, *Wives of the God-King: The Rituals of the Devadasis of Puri*, Delhi: Oxford University Press; S.C. Kersenboom, 1987, *Nityasumangali: Devadasi Tradition in South India*, Delhi: Motilal Banarsidass; K. Sadasivan, 1993, *Devadasi System in Medieval Tamil Nadu*, Trivandrum: CHB Publications; L.C. Orr, 2000, *Donors, Devotees, and Daughters of God: Temple Women in Tamilnadu*, New York and Oxford: Oxford University Press.

14. Polo, *The Travels*, p. 271.

15. Marglin, *Wives of the God-King*, p. 76.

16. Saskia Kersenboom (*Nityasumangali*, pp. 60–1, 112–13, 119) has shown that removing evil and protecting against danger was indeed one the main functions of the devadasis.

17. See M. Meiss, 1968, *French Painting in the Time of Jean de Berry: The Boucicaut Master*, London: Phaidon, pp. ill, 38, 116–19, 85; P. Mitter, 1977, *Much Maligned Monsters: History of European Reactions to Indian Art*, Oxford: Clarendon Press, pp. 3–5.

18. R.H. Major (ed.), 1857, *India in the Fifteenth Century*, London: The Hakluyt Society, p. 28.

19. Cited in Penzer, 'Sacred Prostitution', p. 149.

20. Ibid., pp. 149–50.

21. Leucci, *Devadasi e Bayadères*, p. 37.

22. J.H. van Linschoten, 1956, *Itinerario: Voyage ofte Schipvaert van Jan Huygen van Linschoten near Oost ofte Portugaels Indien, 1579–1592*, edited by H. Kern, 's-Gravenhage: Martinus Nijhoff, 1956, vol. 2, 28; *The Voyage of John Huyghen van Linschoten to the East Indies*, trans. A.C. Burnell and P.A. Tiele (London: The Hakluyt Society, 1885): vol. 1, 264.

23. A. Rogerius, 1915, *De Open-Deure tot het Verborgen Heydendom*, edited by W. Caland, 's-Gravenhage: Martinus Nijhoff, p. 125; quote translated by Jane Harvey.

24. T. Bowrey, 1905, *A Geographical Account of Countries Round the Bay of Bengal, 1669 to 1679*, edited by R.C. Temple, Cambridge: The Hakluyt Society, p. 14.

25. F. Bernier, 1934, *Travels in the Mogul Empire AD 1656–1668*, translated by A. Constable and edited by V.A. Smith, London: Oxford University Press; rpt. New Delhi: Oriental Reprint, 1983, p. 305. To a certain extent Bernier was correct. In the Jagannath temple (in Puri) it was usually a *brahman* priest who first had sexual intercourse with the young *devadasi* after she was dedicated and married to the god; see Marglin, *Wives of the God-King*: 75–7.

26. P. della Valle, 1892, *The Travels of Pietro della Valle in India*, translated by G. Havers and edited by E. Grey, London: The Hakluyt Society, vol. 2, pp. 279–81.

27. Ibid., p. 282; on p. 273 he also refers to the 'Master of Ballet'.

28. For other descriptions of Indian dance see della Valle, *The Travels*, pp. 258, 261, 263, 269–70, 272–3; also see J. Bor, 'The Rise of Ethnomusicology: Sources on Indian Music *c.* 1780–*c.* 1890', *Yearbook for Traditional Music* 20(1988): 52; Leucci, *Devadasi e Bayadères*, pp. 40–5.

29. *Lettres édifiantes et curieuses écrites des missions étrangères* (Paris: Nicolas de Clerc, 1713): vol. 10, 245, cited in H. Yule and A.C. Burnell, 1903, *Hobson-Jobson: A Glossary of Anglo-Indian Colloquial Words and Phrases*, edited by W. Crooke, London: John Murray; rpt. New Delhi: Munshiram Manoharlal, 1979, p. 307; also see J. Assayag, *L'Inde fabuleuse: Le Charme discret de l'exoticisme français (XVIIe–XXe siècles)* (Paris: Editions Kimé, 1999): p. 70n20.

30. F. Valentyn, 1726, *Oud en Nieuw Oost-Indiën*, Dordrecht and Amsterdam: Joannes van Braam and Gerard Onder den Linden, vol. 5, p. 54.

31. See Bor, 'The Rise of Ethnomusicology', pp. 53–4.

32. W. Caland (trans. and ed.), 1926, *Ziegenbalg's Malabarisches Heidenthum*, Amsterdam: Koninklijke Akademie van Wetenschappen, p. 127.

33. Ibid., pp. 131–2; quotation translated by Jane Harvey.

34. Ibid., pp. 228–9; quotation translated by Jane Harvey.

35. Ibid., p. 229.

36. J.H. Grose, 1757, *A Voyage to the East-Indies with Observations on Various Parts There*, London: S. Hooper and A. Morley, p. 222.

37. G.T. Raynal, 1773, *Histoire philosophique et politique des établissements et du commerce des Européens dans les deux Indes*, Amsterdam, vol. 2, pp. 20–4.

38. P. Sonnerat, 1782, *Voyage aux Indes orientales et à la Chine*, Paris: Chez l'auteur, vol. 1, pp. 40–1.

39. *Random House Webster's Unabridged Dictionary* (New York: Random House, 1999), p. 179.

40. See his *Onderzoek naar het Nut van Zendelingen en Zendeling Genootschappen* (Haarlem: Teyler's Godgeleerd Genootschap, 1807), vol. 22.

41. J. Haafner, 1997, *De Werken van Jacob Haafner*, edited by J.A. de Moor and P.G.E.I.J. van der Velde, Zutphen: Walburg Pers, vol. 3, p. 191.

42. Haafner's love affair with an Indian girl was no exception at the time. According to William Dalrymple, between 1770 and 1830 'there was wholesale interracial exploration and surprisingly widespread cultural assimilation and hybridity ... Virtually all Englishmen in India at this period Indianised themselves to some extent'; see W. Dalrymple, 2002, *White Mughals: Love and Betrayal in Eighteenth-Century India*, New Delhi: Viking, p. 10.

43. It is called 'Van de Danseressen, of Devedaschies' (On the dancers or devadasis). See J. Haafner, 1808, *Reize in eenen Palanquin; of Lotgevallen en Merkwaardige Aanteekeningen op eene Reize langs de Kusten Orixa en Choromandel*, Amsterdam: Johannes Allart, vol. 1, pp. 194–225; *De Werken van Jacob Haafner*, pp. 111–25.

44. Haafner, *De Werken van Jacob Haafner*, p. 111.

45. According to F. Appfel Marglin (*Wives of the God-King*, p. 127), the women singers and dancers attached to the Jagannath temple in Puri were, depending on their ritual duties, divided into two groups: the *bhitar gauni* performed in the inner portion of the temple before the deity, and the *bahar gauni* performed only in the outer portion. E. Thurston and K. Rangachari, 1909, *Castes and Tribes of Southern India*, Madras: Government Press, vol. 2, p. 128, also refer to the two divisions of devadasis, called *velangai* (right-hand) and *idangai* (left-hand). In the Sucindram temple the women of the second category (*murakkudi*) attended to the daily routine work, and those of the first rank (*cirappukkudi*) served mainly on festive occasions; see K.K. Pillay, 1953, *The Sucindram Temple*, Madras: Kalakshetra Publications, p. 282.

46. Haafner, *De Werken van Jacob Haafner*, pp. 114–15.

47. Ibid., pp. 112–14.

48. Ibid., p. 113. Similar tasks are described in the Agamas, ritual handbooks that were written in Sanskrit between 500 and 1500, and in several medieval temple inscriptions in Southern India; see Kersenboom, *Nityasumangali*, pp. 104–51; Orr, *Donors, Devotees, and Daughters of God*, pp. 112–21.

49. Haafner, *De Werken van Jacob Haafner*, pp. 113, 115–17.

50. Ibid., p. 115. For the dedication and marriage ceremonies of the *maharis* attached to the temple of Jagannath, see Marglin, *Wives of the God-King*, pp. 67–72; for the initiation, marriage and dedication ceremonies of the devadasis in general, see Kersenboom, *Nityasumangali*, pp. 185–9.

51. Haafner, *De Werken van Jacob Haafner*, p. 115.

52. From Marco Polo (*The Travels*, p. 271) onwards travellers were fascinated by the 'hardness' of the breasts of the Indian dancers. Pietro della Valle (*The Travels*, p. 269) may have been the first to note that the dancers wore 'Pectorals, or Breast-plates, almost round, in the fashion of a Shield and butting out with a sharp ridge before, embroyder'd with Gold and stuck either with Jewels, or some such things, which reflected the Sun-beams with marvellous splendour'. John Henry Grose (*A Voyage to the East Indies*, p. 228) says about their breasts: 'They enclose them in a pair of hollow cups of cases, exactly fitted to them, made of a very light wood, linked together, and buckle at the back ... Then the outside of them is spread with a thin gold, or silver gilt plate, also set with gems according to their ability ... and they are easily laid aside, and resumed at pleasure.' And Haafner (*De Werken van Jacob Haafner*, p. 119) writes: 'To avoid the bosom, for as long as possible, from becoming larger or smaller, each breast is enclosed in a mould; these are connected to each other with strips, and tied at the back against the body. Since the moulds are extraordinarily thin, transparent and elastic, and have the same colour as the skin of those who wear them, it is hard to recognize this garment on the body.'

53. Haafner, *De Werken van Jacob Haafner*, p. 121.

54. Ibid.

55. Ibid.

56. Ibid., pp. 122–3. In a footnote Haafner explains that the cilampukaran plays a pair of hand cymbals and 'is similar to our ballet master. With his gestures, voice and these cymbals he keeps time, and regulates the dance and the steps of

the dancers.' Abbé Dubois uses the common Tamil term *nattuvan* for the dance master: '[He] is the most remarkable of all the musicians. In beating time he taps with his fingers on a narrow drum. As he beats, his head, shoulders, arms, thighs, and in fact all the parts of his body perform successive movements; and simultaneously he utters inarticulate cries, thus animating the musicians both by voice and gesture'; see Abbé J.A. Dubois, 1816, *Description of the Character, Manners, and Customs of the People of India*, London, *Hindu Manners, Customs and Ceremonies*, H.K. Beauchamp (trans. and ed.), Oxford: Clarendon Press rpt. Delhi: Oxford University Press, 1978, p. 588.

57. Sonnerat, *Voyage aux Indes orientales et à la Chine*, pp. 101–2.

58. J. Haafner, 1809, *Landreise längs der Küste Orixa und Koromandel auf der westlichen Indischen Halbinsel*, T.F. Ehrman (trans.), Weimer: Verlage des Landes-Industrie-Comptoirs; M. Jansen (trans.), 1811, *Voyages dans la pénninsule occidentale de l'Inde et dans l'île de Ceylan*, Paris: Arthus Bertrand.

59. Leucci, *Devadasi e Bayadères*, pp. 120–2.

60. A. Baron, 1825, *Lettres et entretiens sur la danse: Ancienne, moderne, religieuse, civile et théâtrale*, Paris: Dondey-Dupré Père et Fils, pp. 43–5; J.A. de la Fage, 1844, *Histoire générale de la musique et de la danse*, Paris: Au Comptoir des Imprimeurs Unis, vol. 1, pp. 574, 588. A summary of Haafner's chapter on the devadasis appeared in *Le Monde dramatique* (1835), vol. 1, pp. 161–2.

61. Haafner, *De Werken van Jacob Haafner*, p. 110.

62. Cited in Penzer, 'Sacred Prostitution', p. 141.

63. Dubois, *Hindu Manners, Customs and Ceremonies*, p. 585.

64. Assayag, *L'Inde fabuleuse*, pp. 43–5; also see B. Mehta, 2002, *Widows, Pariahs, and Bayadères: India as Spectacle*, London: Associated University Presses, pp. 57–67.

65. 'She falls down by the bier,/Her cries cutting through the air: "I want my husband again!/I seek for him in the crypt./Shall these limbs of such divine splendour/Fall into ash before my very eyes?/Mine! He was mine! I came before everyone else!/Ah, only one sweet night!"'; see R. Friedenthal (ed.), 1957, *Goethes Werke in Zwei Bänden*, München and Zürich: Droemerische Verlagsanstalt Th. Knaur, vol. 1, pp. 74–7.

66. See, for example, D. Figueira, 'Die Flambierte Frau: Sati in European Culture', in J.S. Hawley (ed.), 1994, *Sati, the Blessing and the Curse: The Burning Wives in India*, New York and Oxford: Oxford University Press, p. 59ff.

67. This was first noted by Willem Caland, the editor of this book; see Rogerius, *De Open-Deure tot het Verborgen Heydendom*, p. 125n2.

68. Ibid., pp. 125–6; quote translated by Jane Harvey.

69. Earlier he had written the libretto for Gaspare Spontini's successful opera *La Vestale* (1807) in which the heroine is a divine Roman priestess, and later he wrote the libretto for Rossini's masterpiece *Guillaume Tell* (1829). See Assayag, *L'Inde fabuleuse*, pp. 53–4; Leucci, *Devadasi e Bayadères*, pp. 101–13.

70. E. de Jouy, 1821, 'Notice historique sur les Bayadères', in *Les Bayadères: Opéra en trios actes*, Paris: Roullet, pp. 5–12. The opera ends happily with a magnificent celebration of the marriage of King Demaly and his new Queen Laméa. See Leucci, *Devadasi e Bayadères*, pp. 104–13.

71. The scenery was by Pierre Ciceri and the costumes by Hippolyte Lecomte; the famous tenor Adolphe Nourrit played the role of Lord Brahma.

72. Twenty-one years ago, the well-known dance scholar Ivor Guest paid attention to the performances of the devadasis in Paris in the summer of 1838, and their impact on Théophile Gautier; see I. Guest (trans. and ed.), 1986, *Gautier on Dance*, London: Dance Books, pp. xxv, 39–50, 135–6, 315–16.

73. See 'Les Bayadères par-devant notaire', *Revue et gazette des théâtres*, 13 August 1838, p. 226; 'Les Bayadères: Leur traité evec M. Tardivel', *Courrier des théâtres*, 15 September 1838, pp. 2–3; 'The Bayaderes', *The Morning Post*, 3 October 1838; also see Gautier, *Gautier on Dance*, p. 40n6; J.M. MacKenzie, 1995, *Orientalism; History and the Arts*, Manchester and New York: Manchester University Press, p. 193.

74. 'Les Bayadères', *Magasin pittoresque*, 1838, vol. 40, pp. 313–16.

75. In the agreement and reviews she is called Tillé Ammalle. Haafner (*De Werken van Jacob Haafner*, p. 114) says that families of the weaver community (called *tantiravayan*) dedicated one of their daughters to the service of the temples; and according to Thurston and Rangachari (*Castes and Tribes of Southern India*, p. 127), the two classes from which most of the devadasis were recruited were the *vellalas* (agriculturists and cultivators) and *kaikkolar* (weavers). A columnist also refers to the weavers, 'who, from immemorial usage, have dedicated the female offspring of each family to the service of the temples and the public'; see 'The Bayaderes, or Dancing Girls', *Sunday Times*, 23 September 1838.

76. See for example 'The Bayaderes', *Morning Post* (3 October 1838). 'She may be about thirty years of age, but the ardent sun of India has given her the appearance of being much older', wrote the *Mirror of the World* 1/1 (27 October 1838), p. 1.

77. In articles and reviews these girls are referred to as Amany or Ammany, Ranga, Rangom or Ramgoun, and Soundra, Soundirom, Soundiroun or Saundiroun.

78. 'Les Bayadères aux Tuileries', *Journal des débats* (20 August 1838); also see 'Adelphi Theatre', *The Times* 2 October 1838; 'Adelphi', *The Standard* (2 October 1838; 'The Bayaderes', *Morning Post* (3 October 1838); 'Adelphi', *Observer* (7 October 1838). However, the agreement says that Ammani, Rangam and Sundaram were sisters.

79. 'Les Bayadères aux Tuileries', *Journal des débats* (20 August 1838); 'The Bayaderes', *Morning Post* (3 October 1838).

80. She is called Veydoun or Veydon, but her real name was probably Vaidam.

81. 'Les Bayadères', *Magasin pittoresque*, 1838, vol. 40, p. 315.

82. 'The Bayaderes', *Morning Post* (3 October 1838).

83. See, for example, *Courrier des théâtres* (30 July 1838), p. 4; *Le Figaro* (30–31 July 1838), p. 3; *Revue et gazette musicale de Paris* 31 (5 August 1838), p. 318; *The Times* (9 August 1838), p. 5.

84. 'The Bayaderes', *Observer* (30 September 1838); also see 'Nouvelles de Paris', *Courrier des théâtres* (4 August 1838), pp. 4–5; 'Les Bayadères à Bordeaux', *Courrier français* (4 August 1838), p. 2; 'Variétés: Les Bayadères', *Revue et gazette des théâtres* (5 August 1838), pp. 181–2.

85. Quoted in *The Times* (9 August 1838), p. 5; also see *Courrier français* (4 August 1838), p. 3; 'Les Bayadères à Bordeaux', *Le Figaro* (7 August 1838), p. 2; *Courrier des théâtres* (10 August 1838), p. 4.

86. 'Les Bayadères', *Journal des débats* (13 August 1838); also see 'Variétés: Les Bayadères', *Revue et gazette des théâtres* (9 August 1838), p. 186; 'Les Bayadères à l'allée des Veuves', *Le Figaro* (13 August 1838), p. 3; 'Les Bayadères', *Courrier des théâtres* (16 August 1838), p. 3.

87. 'Les Bayadères aux Tuileries', *Journal des débats* (20 August 1838); mention of their performance at the Tuileries is also made in *Courrier français* (20 August 1838), p. 3; *The Times* (22 August 1838), p. 4; and the *Athenaeum* (1 September 1838).

88. 'Les Bayadères aux Tuileries', *Journal des débats* (20 August 1838); the quote is from the *Morning Post* (3 October 1838), which published part of the article. Interestingly, a Paris correspondent of *The Times* (23 August 1838) wrote: 'Do not believe a word put forth by the *Journal des débats*; do not credit the statement in that paper that the Bayaderes had the honour of dancing before the Royal Family at the Tuileries on Saturday night last'!

89. T. Gautier, 'Les Devadasis dites bayadères', *La Presse* (20 August 1838); *Gautier on Dance*, pp. 39–46.

90. Gautier, 'Les Devadasis dites bayadères'; *Gautier on Dance*, p. 41; Assayag, *L'Inde fabuleuse*, p. 129. Binita Mehta (*Widows, Pariahs, and Bayadères*, pp. 156–8) ridicules Gautier's depiction of Ammani 'as a sum of body parts'. I don't think she understands that this was the way Gautier described all dancers in his reviews. As Ivor Guest ('Introduction', in *Gautier on Dance*, p. xxvi) puts it: 'No other critic of his time had ... the poet's perception and the gift of verbal imagery that enabled him to convey the magic of a performance on the printed page.'

91. Gautier ('Les Devadasis dites bayadères') says: 'à l'exception de la ravissante histoire de Mamia recontée par Hummer [he means Haafner], nous ne savions rien sur les danseuses de l'Inde, pas même leur nom ...' (apart from [Haafner's] ravishing story of Mamia, we knew nothing of the dancers of India, not even their name).

92. Guest, 'Introduction', in *Gautier on Dance*, p. xxv.

93. See *Courrier français* (19 August 1838), p. 3; *La Presse* (27 August 1838); Gautier, *Gautier on Dance*, p. 49. A copy of Ammani's statuette was sold by Sotheby's on 27 April 2001. A drawing of it (also by Barre) appeared in the *Magasin pittoresque*, 1838, vol. 40, p. 313 and in La Fage's previously mentioned *Histoire générale de la musique et de la danse*, 1844, vol. 2, XIVbis. Barre is now remembered for his bronzes of the famous ballerinas Marie Taglioni, Fanny Elssler and Emma Livry.

94. 'The Bayaderes', *Observer* (30 September 1838).

95. In London the dancers were launched as the bayaderes or priestesses of Pondicherry (see Fig. 6), and in some articles they are referred to as the Hindoo Dancing-Girls, the Dancing-Girls of India or the dancing priestesses.

96. 'Arrival of the Bayaderes', *Morning Post* (29 September 1838). *The Times* (5 September 1838), p. 4 describes how Frederick Yates had 'secured the Bayaderes in spite of a host of competitors'.

97. 'Dramatic Intelligence', *Observer* (30 September 1838). Although he had not seen their performance, the Paris correspondent of the *Athenæum* (1 September 1838) was also prejudiced: 'Nothing ... can be more monotonous than their dancing; the inimitable rolling of their eyes, too, and the wave-like play of the figure, must be completely lost to a large audience ...'

98. 'Dramatic Intelligence', *Observer* (7 October 1838).

99. 'The Adelphi Theatre', *Era* (7 October 1838).

100. 'Adelphi', *Courier* (2 October 1838).

101. See 'Adelphi Theatre', *The Times* (2 October 1838); 'Adelphi', *Standard* (2 October 1838); 'Adelphi', *Observer* (7 October 1838); these newspapers have similar reviews.

102. 'Adelphi Theatre', *The Times* (2 October 1828).

103. 'Adelphi Theatre', *English Chronicle and Whitehall Evening Post* (2 October 1828); also see 'Adelphi Theatre', *The Times* (2 October 1838); 'Adelphi', *Standard* (2 October 1838); 'Adelphi', *Sun* (2 October 1838); 'Adelphi', *Observer* (7 October 1838).

104. See for example 'Theatrical Chit Chat', *Observer* (7 October 1838); 'Theatricals: Adelphi', *Penny Satirist* (13 October 1838), p. 2.

105. 'The Adelphi Theatre', *Era* (7 October 1838).

106. 'Theatricals: Adelphi', *Penny Satirist* (13 October 1838), p. 2.

107. 'Adelphi', *Morning Post* (2 October 1838); also see 'Adelphi Theatre', *The Times* (2 October 1838).

108. 'Adelphi', *Morning Post* (2 October 1838).

109. 'Adelphi', *Sunday Times* (7 October 1838).

110. 'Adelphi', *Morning Post* (2 October 1838).

111. The letters were probably written on their behalf and 'contain a most dispassionate account of the government and state of England'; they were 'translated' by one Mrs Trollope with the assistance of a familiar character of the Cheapside of London, 'the turbaned vendor of the very best rhubarb'! See 'Billets Doux of the Bayaderes', *Era* (28 October 1838, p. 53; also see the *Era* of 4 and 11 November 1838).

112. *Penny Satirist* (20 October 1838, p. 2) announces that 'an accurate representation of THE BAYADERES; or, DANCING-GIRLS OF INDIA' was published on that day. Other pictures of the bayadères can be found in *Theatrical Register* 3 (15 October 1838), p. 1; *Mirror of the World* 1/1 (27 October 1838), p. 1.

113. 'Engravings', *Sunday Times* (18 November 1838); this drawing has not yet been found.

114. 'Things Theatrical', *Weekly Dispatch* (28 October 1838).

115. 'Bayaderes, or Devadasis of Hindoo', *Mirror of the World* 1/1 (27 October 1838), p. 7; 'Theatricals: Adelphi', *Penny Satirist* (3 November 1838), p. 2.

116. See the announcement in *The Times* (3 November 1838), p. 4.

117. 'Music and the Drama', *Athenæum* (10 November 1838), p. 812.

118. 'Theatricals: Adelphi', *Penny Satirist* (24 November 1838), p. 2; 'The Drama: Adelphi', *Mirror of the World* 1/6 (1 December 1838), p. 47.

119. 'The Bayaderes', *Brighton Herald* (19 January 1839). Much later, Frederick Yates's son wrote that the venture had been a commercial flop: 'On one occasion

a rumour reached London that a great success had been achieved in Paris by the performance of a set of Hindoo dancers, called *Les Bayadères*, who were supposed to be priestesses of a certain sect; and the London theatrical managers were at once on the *qui vive* to secure the new attraction ... My father had concluded the arrangement with the *Bayadères* before his brother managers arrived in Paris. Shortly afterwards, the Hindoo priestesses appeared at the Adelphi. They were utterly uninteresting, wholly unattractive. My father lost 2000l. by the speculation; and in the family they were known as the "Buy-em-dears" even after'; see E. Yates, 1884, *Edmund Yates: His Recollections and Experiences*, London: Richard Bentley and Son, vol. 1, pp. 29–30.

120. *The Times* (1 December 1838).

121. *The Times* (22 November 1838). The last advertisement in *The Times* (2 January 1839) says that the Bayadères 'will positively leave London for Brighton at the end of this week'. According to the *Observer* (11 November 1838), a description of the Bayadères could be purchased at the doors of the Egyptian Hall. Unfortunately, this description has not yet been found.

122. 'The Bayaderes', *Brighton Guardian* (16 January 1839); also see Gautier, *Gautier on Dance*, p. 45, and *L'Entr'acte* (16 August 1838), which printed the poem on which the dance was based.

123. 'Brighton Theatre', *Brighton Herald* (26 January 1839).

124. 'Fashionable News', *Brighton Herald* (9 February 1839).

125. Gautier writes in *La Presse* (10 June 1844) that 'on one of those days of yellow fog when one cannot see the candle in one's hand', Ammani went into a depression in London and committed suicide by hanging herself. Ivor Guest doubts that she committed suicide: 'There seems to be no report of Amany's death in the London press of the time, nor does any record of her death appear in the General Register of Deaths'; see Gautier, *Gautier on Dance*, p. 136n5.

126. *La Presse* (10 June 1844); *Le Moniteur universel* (29 January 1866); see Gautier, *Gautier on Dance*, pp. 134–7, 315–16.

127. Ludwig (or Léon) Minkus set it to music, and Ekaterina Vazem performed the role of the temple dancer Nikiya.

128. For example, Louis Jacolliot devoted a whole section to the Indian dancers in his *Voyage au pays des bayadères*, 1877, Paris: E. Dentu, pp. 243–81, and also translated a Tamil play into French, called *La Devadassi*, 1868, Paris, pp. 1–46. Pierre Loti wrote about the 'Danse de bayadère' in his well-known book *L'Inde (sans les Anglais)*, 1934, Paris: Calmann-Lévy; first published in 1903, pp. 217–23. In Gustave Flaubert's *Dictionnaire des idées reçues*, 1881, Paris: Garnier-Flammarion), 'bayadère' is ironically described as: 'Mot qui entraîne l'imagination. Toutes les femmes de l'Orient sont des bayadères (v. Odalisques)' (A word that arouses the imagination. All women of the Orient are bayadères [see Odalisques]). And Odalisques are described as: 'Toutes les femmes de l'Orient sont des odalisques (v. Bayadères)' (All women of the Orient are Odalisques [see Bayadères]); see Assayag, *L'Inde fabuleuse*, p. 40.

129. J. Shortt, 1870, 'The Bayadère; or, Dancing Girls of Southern India', *Memoirs Read Before the Anthropological Society of London* 1867–8–93, pp. 182–94.

130. Ibid., pp. 191–2.

131. Ibid., p. 187.

132. Ibid., p. 191.

133. Ibid., pp. 183–5.

134. Ibid., p. 194.

135. See, for example, A. Srinivasan, 1983, 'The Hindu Temple-Dancer: Prostitute or Nun?', *Cambridge Anthropology* 8/1, pp. 73–99; K.M. Parker, 1998, 'A Corporation of Superior Prostitutes: Anglo-Indian Legal Conceptions of Temple Dancing Girls, 1800–1914', *Modern Asian Studies* 32/3, pp. 559–633; K.K. Jordan, 2003, *From Servant to Profane Prostitute: A History of the Changing Legal Status of the Devadasis in India, 1857–1947*, New Delhi: Manohar; also see Orr, *Donors, Devotees, and Daughters of God*, pp. 12–16, 197–9, nn.21, 22, and 27.

136. For the complexities involved in interpreting travel writing, see, for example, K. Teltscher, 1995, *India Inscribed: European and British Writing on India 1600–1800*, Delhi: Oxford University Press; K. Brown, 2000, 'Reading Indian Music: The Interpretation of Seventeenth-Century European Travel-Writing in the (Re)construction of Indian Music History', *British Journal of Ethnomusicology* 9/2, pp. 1–34.

137. Gautier, 'Les Devadasis dites bayadères'; *Gautier on Dance*, p. 39.

138. Orr, *Donors, Devotees, and Daughters of God*, p. 50.

139. Polo, *The Travels*, p. 271.

140. 'Les Bayadères aux Tuileries', *Journal des débats* (20 August 1838); the quote is from the *Morning Post* (3 October 1838), which published part of the article. Frédérique Marglin (*Wives of the God-King*, p. 90) also came to the conclusion that most devadasis had long-term relationships with high-caste men of their own choice.

141. 'The Bayaderes', *Brighton Herald* (19 January 1839).

142. E.W. Said, 1991, *Orientalism: Western Conceptions of the Orient*, London: Penguin Books, p. 188. Rana Kabbani, 1986, devotes a large part of her *Europe's Myths of Orient*, Bloomington: Indiana University Press, to the portrayal of Oriental women but is more radical than Said.

143. See, for example, 'Adelphi Theatre', *The Times* (2 October 1838); 'Adelphi', *Standard* (2 October 1838).

144. 'Adelphi Theatre', *Morning Chronicle* (2 October 1838); also see 'The Bayaderes, or Dancing Girls', *Sunday Times* (23 September 1838); 'Theatres Adelphi', *Penny Satirist* (29 September 1838), p. 2.

145. 'The Bayaderes', *Era* (14 October 1838); also see 'Theatricals: Adelphi', *Penny Satirist* (20 October 1838), p. 2.

146. Said, *Orientalism*, p. 5.

147. Ibid., p. 6; also see pp. 186–8.

Community, Repertoire, and Aesthetics

Saskia C. Kersenboom

The Traditional Repertoire of the Tiruttani Temple Dancers[*]

INTRODUCTION

On Sunday 19 January 1986, Smt P. Ranganayaki, a temple dancer or *devadasi* of the Sri Subrahmanyasvami Temple in Tiruttani prepared a wedding necklace (*tali*) for me in her prayer- (or *puja-*) room.[1] She tied the necklace, blessed me, and pronounced me the successor of her family line. She then gave me a manuscript[2] written by her grandmother, Smt Subburatnamma (1871–1950). Smt Subburatnamma had served as a devadasi in the same Sri Subrahmanyasvami Temple in Tiruttani. In that manuscript, she has noted down her entire repertoire of songs and dances as performed within the context of temple ritual (*arcana*), rites of passage (*samskara*), and concert practice.[3] In this way, I became the heir to a devadasi family tradition that goes back four generations.

Smt P. Ranganayaki was trained by her grandmother, Smt Subburatnamma. In 1931 she was dedicated to the Sri Subrahmanyasvami Temple as a devadasi in the rite called 'branding'.[4] Her tali was tied by her grandmother's sister, Smt Jayaratnamma. This practice of dedicating women to temples, images and religious objects became illegal with the Devadasi Act of 26 November 1947.[5]

THE LINE OF SUCCESSION

What did it mean, in traditional terms, to succeed in a line (*parampara*) of generations of devadasis? Who were the devadasis? What was their function within the accepted practice of Hinduism and its meaning? How was succession validated?

---

* The fieldwork for this study was conducted in Tiruttani (in Tamilnadu, South India) in 1985–6 with the generous help of the Netherlands Foundation for the Advancement of Tropical Research (WOTRO).

Fig. 8   The author with P. Ranganayaki

The Devadasi Community

The term devadasi is frequently misunderstood. The misuse of the term and the social stigma that became attached to it have caused many misrepresentations. One of the most basic errors is the reference to a devadasi and her family as members of the 'devadasi caste'. According to several devadasi informants, there is a devadasi 'life' (*vrtti*), and a devadasi 'order or traditional right' (*murai*, Tamil), but not a devadasi 'caste' (*jati*). It seems probable that the right to become a devadasi was hereditary, although not exclusively so since girls could be adopted and made eligible for the position. However, whether this right was exercised or not depended on many factors: the explicit wish of her parents, the behaviour of the girl in question, and the consent of the relevant authorities. There was a case in Tiruttani, for example, of a girl who was refused admission to the devadasi initiation ceremony in spite of the fact that she was well trained in song and dance, beautiful to look at, and of a good personal reputation. The authorities justified their decision on the grounds that her mother had gone astray before obtaining admission to the initiation ceremony. Her family was therefore no longer considered respectable and hence was unfit to offer a daughter to the temple. The unfortunate girl finally obtained permission to be dedicated to a shrine in Kancipuram where the rules of ritual purity were less strictly observed.

The Function of the Devadasi

In Tiruttani, the right to be dedicated to the temple was attributed to nine families. The members of these nine families were given nine houses in

Mele ('Upper') Tiruttani, a small settlement behind the temple inhabited by the families of devadasis and temple priests (*gurukkal*, Tamil). The nine houses corresponded to a cycle of nine years. Each year, one house was responsible for the most characteristic task of the devadasi: the obligatory performance of waving the pot-lamp (*kumbhadipa*) in front of the god (*kumbharati*). This task rotated among the nine families. Smt P. Ranganayaki belonged to the fifth house and thus to the fifth year in the cycle of attendance. During a year of service, the house had to be kept in a ritually pure state (*mati*, Telugu). Any individuals who were ritually unclean had to stay elsewhere during their period of impurity.[6] These restrictions notwithstanding, the house responsible had to provide a devadasi for the daily performance of waving the pot-lamp.

According to data gathered among devadasis during the period 1977–83, the task of waving the pot-lamp in front of a god, goddess, king or patron, was the most characteristic feature of the position of devadasi. Although European sources (both travelogues and missionary reports) usually depict devadasis as 'sacred courtesans' who excel in the various performing arts (including the art of love), none of these

FIG. 9   Kumbha dipa. Photograph courtesy the author

artistic skills received much attention in the last decades of this age-old tradition (Kersenboom-Story 1987: 207). Few devadasis who had served in temples before 1947 could remember more than a handful of songs. However, they all remembered clearly the task of waving the pot-lamp during daily rituals and at the conclusion of a procession. For them, being a devadasi was synonymous with waving the pot-lamp. Why?

In the ritual action of waving the pot-lamp, we are confronted with a complex weave of symbols. The aim of the action is to ward off the jealous 'evil eye' (drsti, literally 'glance') that may have been cast on the object of worship. The method is a triple clock-wise rotation, concluded by a sweeping gesture from the head of the image to its foot. These movements are performed with implements that are considered to be powerful antidotes to the vicious energy of the evil eye. First and foremost among them are lamps (dipa), of which the pot-lamp is held to be the most effective. In addition, the same movements may be performed with plates (tattu, Tamil) containing substances believed to absorb or counteract evil influence; substances such as solutions of charcoal powder, red kumkum powder, yellow turmeric powder,[7] or lemons.

This rite should be understood as arising from a notion of the divine as eternally ambivalent and omnipresent, one that expresses itself incessantly in the dynamic tension of creation and destruction, of balance and imbalance, of the auspicious and the inauspicious. In the earliest period of indigenous South Indian literature available to us, we find this divine force referred to as ananku (Tamil), a term that suggests an awe-inspiring, fear-provoking and oppressive power.[8] In later times, we are confronted with complementary oppositions such as 'auspicious-inauspicious', 'heating-cooling', 'pure-impure', augmentation and merit (punya) versus the jealous evil eye that consumes everything. The ambivalent tension of the divine has evidently been felt throughout human history; although an exact pattern of dynamic change could not be constructed, the diagnostic features of the two basic forces were distinguished and the attempt was made to regulate their cause and effect for the benefit (subham) of mankind.

The opposition in question is that between the dynamic, creative principle associated with the goddess, and the more abstract, quiescent principle associated with the god. The dynamic principle can be both destructive and protective. An excess of dynamism destroys; properly harmonized, however, it creates, nourishes, and protects. A method was devised for controlling this dynamism from within: the creation of female ritualist whose power (sakti) could be ritually merged with that of the great goddess (*Sakti*). As we shall see, the devadasi was such a ritualist. Her waving of the pot-lamp was doubly effective: both her person and the implement of the pot (*kumbha*) were synonymous with the goddess. Only in this way could the removal of the evil eye be ensured.

The Validation of the Devadasi

The transformation of an ordinary girl into a devadasi is marked by three important rites:

1. Initiation (*gajjai puja*, literally 'worship of the ankle-bells' worn by the dancer; *gajjai*, Tamil). This rite concludes the dance training (see Kersenboom-Story 1987: 185–6).

2. Marriage (*kalyanam*). With this rite, the female power (sakti) of the devadasi becomes merged with the god's sakti, that is, with the goddess (Sakti). In the case of Smt P. Ranganayaki, this meant a full-scale wedding ceremony with the spear (*vel*, Tamil) representing the sakti of Sri Subrahmanyasvami. Consequently, her marriage partner is not a part of the god standing for the whole but a manifestation of the goddess (see Kersenboom-Story 1987: 186).

3. Dedication (literally 'branding'; see note 4). This ceremony concludes the first concert given by the girl before the main deity in the temple. On the occasion, she is branded with the sign of the trident (*trisula*) on her right upper arm. This painful procedure was considered both an ordeal and an ultimate test of the girl's purity: if the application were granted to an undeserving girl, then she would suffer severely from a wound that refused to heal. After the branding, the newly ordained devadasi performs the ritual waving of the pot-lamp for the first time for her husband and patron, Sri Subrahmanyasvami (see Kersenboom-Story 1987: 188–9).

After this triple validation, the girl is considered 'an ever-auspicious woman' (*nityasumangali*). This term needs further elucidation.

The traditional view holds that all women, by their very nature, share in the power of the goddess. In the imagined continuum of auspiciousness (*mangalam*), individual women are placed at one end of the scale or the other according to their status. At the top is the married woman whose husband is alive and who has borne several children: she is called 'auspicious woman' (*sumangali*). At the bottom of the scale is the widow for she is considered highly inauspicious. In ritual terms, however, the devadasi exceeds even the sumangali in auspiciousness. Two reasons are given for this. First, her individual female powers are merged with those of the goddess. Second, she is dedicated to a divine husband who can never die. Since she can never lose her (double) auspiciousness, she is called 'ever auspicious' (nityasumangali).

HER TRADITION

The quality of 'eternal auspiciousness' that characterizes the devadasi is the key to both her tradition (sampradaya) and all that that implies: ritual objects, implements, jewellery, costumes, make-up, ritual actions, and the ritual repertoire of songs and dances.

As indicated above, human beings sought to construct a pattern of dynamic change as well as to manipulate it for their own benefit. This was attempted in various ways: by regular communication with the divine through traditional (agamic) temple worship; by occasional propitiation, as in village sacrifices; by giving nourishment to the living proofs of prosperity and vitality in the form of service to the king; and by the ubiquitous preventive, propitiating, and purifying measures taken at every step in daily life as well as during important events. The traditional expertise of the devadasi covered all these spheres of divine influence: the personal, especially during rites of passage; the political, through attendance on the king; and the purely ritual, in the performance of temple worship. In fact, none of these spheres of contact with the divine can be called exclusively social, political, or ritual. For the element of manipulating and influencing the divine energies that they all share is strongly reminiscent of the activities of the medieval alchemist. Song and dance are primarily instruments to this end; the aesthetic quality and effect comes second.

Before giving examples of compositions that operate in these three different spheres—the personal, the political, and the ritual—it is useful to analyse the character of ritual attendance. Bearing in mind the risks of oversimplification, I should like to suggest two basic categories (Fig. 10).

The traditional repertoire of the devadasis provides songs and dances for both categories and for their subdivisions. The richest offering is to be found in the temple repertoire which includes compositions to serve all these aims. The king's court requires more artistic sophistication and entertainment than is usually found in the temple. In the private, social sphere, however, the emphasis is on the removal of, or protection against, the evil eye.

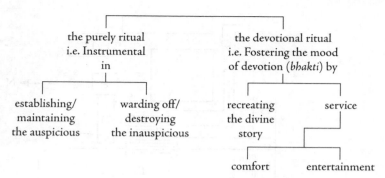

FIG. 10   The character of the ritual attendance of the *devadasi*

The Repertoire for Temple Ritual

As indicated above, it is in the temple that the devadasi repertoire is displayed in its full scope. Both the daily ritual and the festival ritual feature a variety of compositions.

The daily ritual

In the days when Smt P. Ranganayaki was an active devadasi, regular attendance began at 11.00 a.m. with the singing of praise-poems (*stotra*) for several gods and goddesses residing in the temple grounds. An alternative name for these compositions is *sobhana* (*copanam*, Tamil), meaning 'happy event, auspiciousness, congratulations'. These fall into the category of ritual songs intended to establish or maintain the auspicious state of the divine.

The next ritual attendance (puja) which required devadasi participation was that of twilight worship held at sunset.[9] The 'junction' of 6.00 p.m. is considered extremely dangerous and so, as day slips away into night, the gods need all the support and attendance mankind can give. The ritual waving of the pot-lamp by a devadasi was considered the most effective method of warding off an inauspicious state of the divine. During the year in which the fifth house was responsible for the waving of the pot-lamp, Smt P. Ranganayaki would observe the rules of ritual purity very strictly. At such times, she would wear the long nine-yard sari fastened in the brahmin style (*matisar*, Tamil). She would arrange her hair in a loose knot, put an auspicious round red powder mark (*kumkumanpottu*, Tamil; see n. 7) and sacred ash (*vibhuti*) on her forehead, and wear a necklace of black beads. She would then embark on the ritual programme for the puja, given here in full (for the locations indicated, see Fig. 11):

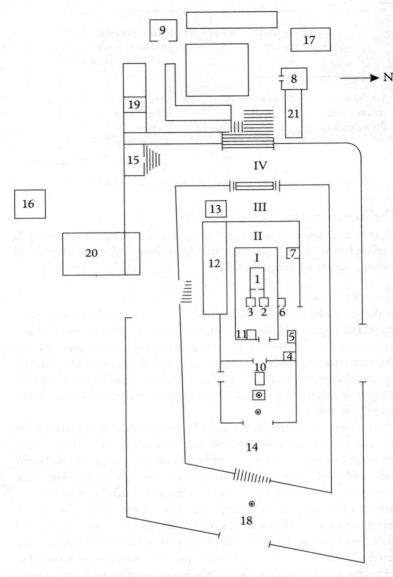

FIG. 11   Plan of the Sri Subrahmanyasvami Temple, Tiruttani

1. The main shrine (*mulavar*, Tamil) of Sri Subrahmanyasvami
2. The shrine of Sri Devasena
3. The shrine of Sri Valliyamma
4. The shrine of Sri Apatsakaya Vinayaka
5. The festival image of Sri Sanmukhasvami
6. The large processional image of Sri Subrahmanyasvami
7. The small processional image of Sri Subrahmanyasvami
8. The shrine of Sri Brahmanavidhi Vinayaka
9. The Shrine of Sri Sarasvati
10. The main Shrine of Sri Subrahmanyasvami (*Puspanjalimandapa*)
11. The shrine where the bedroom images are kept (see note 10)
12. The spring pavilion (*vasantamandapa*)
13. The pavilion in which the instruments are sounded for the entertainment of the god (*sarvavadyamandapa*)
14. The pavilion by the main gates (*mahadvaramandapa*)
15. The pavilion of the 'mounts' or 'vehicles' of the deities (*vahanamandapa*)
16. Sri Valliyamma's wedding pavilion
17. Sri Devasena's wedding pavilion
18. The pedestal for camphor (*karpura akantam*)
19. The houses of the *devadasis* (no. V)
20. The king's palace
21. The houses of the priests
   I. The first or inner circuit
  II. The second circuit
 III. The third circuit
 IV. The fourth circuit

Fig. 11 (contd)   Key to Figure 11

1. A composite offering of song, dance, (imaginary) flowers, and the waving of the pot-lamp at the main shrine of Sri Subrahmanyasvami (*svamipuspanjali*, locus 10):
   - pure dance (*nrtta*);
   - a verse accompanying the offering of imaginary flowers (*puspanjalisloka*);
   - danced mime (*nrtta*, *nrtya*);
   - an auspicious verse (*mangalam*);
   - a laudatory verse (*sobhana*);
   - cooling the image by waving a fly-whisk (*camara*);

- an auspicious verse acclaiming victory (*svamijayamangalam*), accompanied by the waving of lamps on plates (*tattudipa*, Tamil and Sanskrit).

2. A verse accompanying the offering of imaginary flowers and an auspicious verse for Sri Apatsakaya Vinayaka (*vinayakapuspanjali*; locus 4).
3. As 2, for Sri Devasena (*devasenapuspanjali*; locus 2).
4. As 2, for Sri Valliyamma (*valliyammapuspanjali*; locus 3).
5. An auspicious verse for the small processional image of Sri Subrahmanyasvami (*cinnotsavamurtimangalam*; locus 7).
6. An auspicious verse for the large processional image of Sri Subrahmanyasvami (*peddotsavamurtimangalam*; locus 6).

This concludes the sunset ritual.

At 9.00 p.m., the rituals of the early evening hour (*ardhayama*) and the daily procession (*nityotsava*) were perfomed. Devadasis played their part in the daily procession of a small image of Sri Subrahmanyasvami by accompanying the processional group and singing devotional songs (such as 'daily songs' *praharilu*, Telugu), or simple songs about the Lord in order to foster the mood of devotion.

Around 10.00 p.m., the divine pair would be seated on a swing in the bedroom. Here the devadasis took part in the 'service in the bedroom' (*palliyarai seva*, Tamil, Sanskrit) by singing lullabies (*lali*, Tamil etc.) and swing songs (*uncal*, Tamil), while the priests offered a tasty evening snack and rocked god and goddess to sleep.[10] The devadasis concluded their attendance for the day by singing an auspicious song to ensure that all was safe until the following morning.

The festival ritual

We have seen how the categories of establishing auspiciousness (mangalam), warding off inauspiciousness (*amangalam*, *drsti*), creating the mood of devotion (bhakti), and offering service (*seva*) in the form of comfort were expressed in the repertoire of songs and dances performed by the devadasis in the course of the daily ritual. The categories of 'recreating the divine story' and 'entertainment' seem to be more pronounced in the programmes of festival worship.

The most characteristic feature of festival worship is the procession (*pradaksina*) of the god, the goddess, or both. Such a procession is part of a larger unit called a 'festival' (*utsava*). A festival may last as little as a few hours or as long as twenty-seven days. The power of the god or goddess, the local version of the divine story, and the time of the year are important criteria for determining the length, elaboration, mood, and sophistication of a festival.

Examples of the story-telling part of a festival are the small dance-drama (*Kaman kuttu*, Tamil), and the quarrel-dialogue between the god and his first wife, both found in the manuscript of Smt Subburatnamma and taught to me by Smt P. Ranganayaki.

In the dance drama, performed on the sixth day of the great festival (*brahmotsava*) held in January or February (*maci macam*, Tamil), Sri Subrahmanyasvami is depicted as Kaman, the god of love. First, a devadasi appears dressed as Kaman, complete with bow and arrows (here in the shape of a fruit). Naturally, the god of love tries to lure young girls into his game; so, after an introductory verse announcing the arrival of some beautiful girls (also played by devadasis), a dialogue ensues between the god and the girls. The latter complain about his treacherous behaviour while Kaman expresses his longing for love. This dialogue is conveyed in mime to the accompaniment of a (Telugu) text sung by the devadasis. The merriment increases with the throwing of turmeric water.

The ninth day of the same festival featured the wedding of Sri Subrahmanyasvami and his second wife, Sri Valliyamma. On that day, the devadasis were busy from morning till evening recreating the divine love story: the abduction of Sri Valli (cf. Zvelebil 1977, 1980), the wedding, the quarrel between the god and his first wife, Sri Devasena, and their reconciliation. Serving as bridesmaids, the devadasis carried the wedding presents and sang swing songs and wedding songs (*nalanku*, Tamil) in the wedding pavilion (*kalyanamandapa*). To conclude the festivities, they performed a grand, purificatory waving of lamps (including the powerful pot-lamp) in order to absorb and counteract the cumulative effects of the evil eye accrued during the long day.

An interesting moment during this festival day occurs around 6.00 p.m. when Sri Subrahmanyasvami returns with his new wife to the temple only to find the door of the shrine of Sri Devasena locked. The goddess is furious with her husband for his unpardonable behaviour. She seems determined not to see him again. Lord Subrahmanyasvami begs her understanding and forgiveness. Their spicy quarrel was impersonated by devadasis singing along the following lines (in Telugu):

S: 'Quickly open the door, dear Devasena!'
D: 'Go away! Do not come here publicly!'
S: 'I have come to your street full of love, Devasena!'

D: 'Tender love and sweet repentance do not affect me! Go! Go!'
S: 'Are you without softness? Please, Devasena! Please!'
D: 'Go! Go away! Don't speak fond words!'
S: 'I am your beloved Lord of Tiruttani, dear Devasena!'
D: 'Let us be happy! Come, O Cenkalvaraya!'

On these words, the door is opened from the inside and peace is restored.

Apart from these devotional compositions portraying episodes from the god's life, entertainment was offered on specific occasions, such as when the god was seated in a pavilion and treated like a king, or when he was placed on a raft (*plava*) and floated on the temple tank. Such entertainment might consist of a full-scale dance concert,[11] the sounding of all musical instruments and the performance of several types of vocal compositions (*sarvavadyam*), or performance of group dance compositions to popular songs,[12] with or without sticks.

In addition to devotional songs and dances characterized by their topical and entertainment value, the devadasis also sang purely ritual songs such as 'eight-verse' praise poems (*astakam*), heralding songs (*curnikai; eccarikai*, Tamil), and songs determined by the hour of the day (*praharilu*).

The Repertoire for the Royal Court

In many temples, there was a direct link between attendance on the deity and attendance on the king. In Tiruttani, the palace of the king[13] borders on temple territory. In the days when Smt P. Ranganayaki was a devadasi, however, attendance on the king was limited to a few occasions each year: for example, during the Brahmotsava or great festival (see above); and during the festival for the goddess which lasts nine nights (Navaratri) and on the concluding tenth day on which the goddess reveals her victorious form (Vijayadasami). On both occasions, devadasis used to perform a full-scale dance concert (see n. 11). On the fifth day of the Brahmotsava, the concert was performed in the fourth circuit in front of the palace (locus 20). On Vijayadasami, a concert was performed in the palace of the king and accompanied by the purificatory 'waving of lamps' (*diparadhana*) on a grand scale. In other places such as Thanjavur where the court culture had received generous patronage and artistic attention, this creative side of the traditional devadasi repertoire was developed to a far greater degree of sophistication. After 1947, this concert suits was further chiselled into what has become known as Bharatanatyam, a term previously unknown.

The Repertoire for Rites of Passage

Even in 1986, when I was last in Tiruttani, people came to the house of Smt P. Ranganayaki to ask her to remove the evil eye from a family member who was either temporarily confused or suffering from headaches. When I returned from a long walk through the village, she thought it best to remove the evil eye from me as well. This demonstrates that not all trust and belief in, nor respect for, the power of the devadasi have vanished.

In the days of her grandmother, Smt Subburatnamma, devadasis were invited to small and grand social functions for reasons of both prestige and safety. The smaller functions are exemplified by the rites of passage (samskara), such as the name-giving ceremony or the ear- and nose-piercing ceremonies. On these occasions, devadasis sang auspicious songs and performed the ritual waving of lamps. An example of a grand social function is the wedding ceremony. In her day, Smt Subburatnamma used to prepare the wedding necklace for the bride, decorate her, and prepare the flower garlands and the wedding pavilion. Accompanied by other devadasis, she would sing auspicious and laudatory compositions as well as typical wedding songs, boat songs, and the swing songs. In addition to these more ritual songs, she composed many Tamil joke songs (contakavitvam) such as 'We have come from Bengal' (vankalam poyivarom), 'Tippu Sahib from Triplicane' (tiruvallikeni tippusayapu), and songs that mock the bridegroom such as 'The brother-in-law from Thanjavur taluk' (tancavur talukka attan):

You spoke about the artistic brother-in-law from Thanjavur taluk, but when one comes to see for-oneself in Thanjavur, he only beats a little drum, tra-la! You spoke about the brother-in-law who is a policeman in Pondicherrry, but once you set there, he is eating parched rice that he has picked up from the street, tra-la! You spoke about the brother-in-law in Mayuram who is a manager, but looking for oneself one discovers that he grazes cattle, tra-la!

In addition to such joke songs, marriages gave rise to rather obscene songs such as the request for a 'cooked' or 'ripe' woman (caminca ponnu, Tamil) in a rice-pounding song. Smt P. Ranganayaki beamed with delight as she recalled her grandmother's compositions. All this laughter and obscenity served not only to create a jovial mood but also to ensure the exclusion of the ever-lurking evil eye, jealous of any happiness. This corresponds with the text which one can find over the entrance of Tamil houses even today: 'Looking at me, laugh!' (ennai parkka ciri). To laugh means to break the tension of evil, jealous energy.

The ever-auspicious nature of the devadasi made her a welcome guest at marriages and at other important social functions which exposed the family members to an excess of public attention. Some very aristocratic and rich households even employed their own devadasi. Such a devadasi was called a *manikkam* (Tamil; usually translated 'ritual servant'); in this role, she took care both of the auspicious state of the puja-room (by singing songs and decorating the altar and its gods) and of the inauspicious evil eye that was believed to attach itself to family members returning home from outside. Nowadays, many of these functions have been taken over by secular family women (see sumangali, above); however, always with a slight feeling of danger.

THE CHARACTER OF THE REPERTOIRE

The repertoire of the devadasis as it was practised in the temples and during rites of passage has not been witnessed publicly since 1947, the year in which the Devadasi Act was passed. Even before the legal ban on devadasi ritual song, dance and action, the tradition had dwindled into a few, almost symbolic steps, gestures, and tunes. Among the remnants of the traditional temple and social repertoire of devadasis in general, the Tiruttani Sri Subrahmanyasvami Temple in particular, the heritage of Smt. Ranganayaki is unique.

However, in all the samples of ritual devotional repertoire once performed by devadasis in Tamilnadu it is clear that their art was marked by a minimal attempt to achieve aesthetic effect. The songs and dances are extremely straightforward and simple. It is clear that they were considered a ritual task, one which had to be performed for the sake of its occurrence and not for the sake of its artistic form. The ritual songs are set to a rhythm and tempo that sometimes resemble a military quick march. The dances make use of the idiom of the concert repertoire known today as Bharatanatyam (*catir*; see n. 11) but without either the rhythmical intricacies of its choreographic phrases or the sweep and flourish of the courtly tradition from which the modern dance form was derived.

The devadasis of Tiruttani performed these dances and songs without self-conscious pride. Their attitude towards the repertoire remains respectful but matter-of-fact. In the words of Smt P. Ranganayaki:

What is there? ... It is all gone; it will never come back ... Nowadays, anyone can do anything on the stage or in the film ... We were God-fearing. After we got our status as devadasis, we could decide for ourselves. If some of us were deserted by men, we still had our profession which afforded us a living ... We had our own discipline!

NOTES

1. The term devadasi means literally 'slave of god'. This translation led early Christian missionaries to compare her to the Christian nun (the 'bride of Christ'). Since the devadasi was allowed to choose a patron after her dedication and to bear children, this comparison proved to be misleading and even harmful to the Hindu tradition. For the devadasi was neither a vestal virgin or ascetic nun, nor their opposite a public woman or sacred harlot. Her function and identity was a third possibility away from the above-mentioned binary choice: she was primarily a ritual specialist whose professional qualification was rooted in her quality of auspiciousness; her powers were believed to bring good luck and to ward off evil. For further information on this and similar traditions in India, see Kersenboom 1987 and forthcoming (a); Marglin 1985. For the etymological derivation of tali, see Burrow and Emeneau 1961: 2594. In traditional Hindu homes, the puja-room contains the domestic altar.

2. This manuscript is written in the Telugu script. However, like the terminology of Indian dance in general, it incorporated a complex mixture of languages including Sanskrit, Tamil, Tamilized Sanskrit, Telugu, and Urdu. For the purposes of this volume, Indian-language terms are given in Sanskrit (or Tamilized Sanskrit) unless otherwise indicated. Non-Sanskrit terms are identified at their first occurrence.

3. I hope to publish this manuscript shortly (see Kersenboom, forthcoming (b)). All references to the songs and dances of the devadasi repertoire are taken from this text unless otherwise indicated. All translations (both from interviews and from this manuscript) are my own. For further information regarding concert practice, see note 11.

4. For further details of this rite of dedication (*muttirai*, literally 'branding', 'stamp' or 'mark'; Tamil), see below.

5. The full text of the Act may be found in the Government of Madras Archives (26 January 1948). See also Kersenboom-Story (1987: xxi, n. 15).

6. Saliva and blood are highly polluting substances in the ritual sphere. Birth, menstruation, and death should therefore be isolated from ritually clean places, objects, and persons.

7. Kumkum powder (kumkuma; *Crocus sativus*) is worn by women whose husbands are alive. Turmeric (*Curcuma longa*; *mancal*, Tamil) is used for protective, auspicious purposes.

8. For an elaborate discussion of the meaning and importance of this term, see Hart 1973; Zvelebil 1979.

9. This ritual of twilight (*sandhi*, literally, 'junction') worship was termed *cayaratcai* ('protection against the decrease of brightness'; Tamil) puja.

10. The god Sri Subrahmanyasvami, alias Murugan, is believed to have married two wives: Sri Devasena and Sri Valliyamma. In South India, Sri Valliyamma is the clear favourite: her festivals are celebrated with much more pomp and gusto

than those of her co-wife. However, the existence of two wives causes problems. In order to avoid confusion regarding whose turn it is to spend the night with the lord, the priests in Tiruttani have arrived at a practical solution. The bedroom images (*murti*) are kept in a little shrine in the inner or first circuit (*prakara*) behind the inner sanctum (or 'womb house', *garbhagrha*). The two ladies flanking the god are each given a wooden rod. The goddess who can look forward to the company of her lord is allowed to stand free while the other is barred by both rods. Each night this arrangement is adjusted by the priests.

11. The regular suite for a classical dance concert (*catir kacceri*, Urdu) consisted of: introductory tuning and prayer (*melaprapti*, Tamil and Sanskrit); a warming-up dance (*alarippu*, from the *alari* flower, Tamil; an abstract dance composition intended as a greeting); choreographic dance patterns based on musical notes (*jatisvaram*); a mythological anecdote in mime (*sabdam*, 'word'); a composition combing intricate abstract choreographies and mimetic interpretation of a text (*varnam*, 'colour'); a love-song rendered in mime (*padam*, akin to the courtly love-song or chanson d'amour of medieval France); an erotic song rendered in mime (*javali*, Telugu); and a grand finale in abstract dance choreography (*tillana*, 'ending').

12. Many of these dance compositions (*kolattam*, 'stick dance'; Tamil) are set to Western tunes which must have been popular at the turn of the century.

13. The raja of Karvetinagar in Chittoor district belonging to the Saluva dynasty.

REFERENCES

Burrow, Thomas and Murray B. Emeneau, 1961, *Dravidian Etymological Dictionary*, Oxford: Oxford University Press.

Hart, George L. III, 1973, 'Woman and the Sacred in Ancient Tamilnad', *Journal of the American Oriental Society*, 32 (2), pp. 233–50.

Kersenboom-Story, Saskia C., 1987, *Nityasumangali: Devadasi Tradition in South India*, Delhi: Motilal Banarsidass.

———, Forthcoming (a), 'Devadasi Murai', Sangeet Natak: *Journal of the Sangeet Natak Akademi*.

———, Forthcoming (b), *Devadasi Heritage: Ritual Songs and Dances of the Devadasis of Tiruttani*.

Marglin, Frederique Apffel, 1985, *Wives of the God-King: The Rituals of the Devadasis of Puri*, Delhi: Oxford University Press.

Zvelebil, Kamil V., 1977, 'Valli and Murugan: A Dravidian Myth', *Indo-Iranian Journal*, 22, pp. 227–46.

———, 1979, 'The Nature of Sacred Power in Old Tamil Texts', *Acta Orientalia*, 40, pp. 157–92.

———, 1980, 'The Valli and Murugan Myth: Its Development', *Indo-Iranian Journal*, 40, pp. 113–35.

Hari Krishnan

Inscribing Practice[1]

Reconfigurations and Textualizations of Devadasi Repertoire in Nineteenth and Early Twentieth-century South India

The cultural scripting of south Indian 'court dance' (variously known as *sadir kacheri, chaduru, kelikkai, melam* and *mejuvani*) was a process that drew from a variety of already established dance vocabularies and repertoires, yet was clearly renegotiated, manipulated, and extended by the culturally-hybrid artistic atmosphere of nineteenth and early twentieth-century south India. The cultural transformations of the dance of the Thanjavur court during the reign of King Serfoji II (1798–1832) and continuing through the reign of his son, Shivaji II (1832–55), involved the invention of new forms of cultural practice based on the linguistic pluralism of Thanjavur and the very tangible presence of Western artistic practices in this area (Subramanian 2004). Yet these new, hybrid cultural practices were short lived, as many dancers and musicians left Thanjavur after the death of Shivaji II in 1855 and the annexation of Thanjavur to the British in 1856. Most of these artists either moved back to their native areas (including parts of Andhra and Karnataka), or were hired by smaller feudal kingdoms such as Ramanathapuram and Pudukkottai in Tamil Nadu, or Pithapuram and Nuzvid in Andhra, or moved into the urban settings of Madras city.

It is widely known that at this highly precarious moment in colonial history, a systematization of court dance occurred at the hands of the 'Thanjavur Quartet' or *tanjai nalvar*, four brothers whose ancestors had been the court musicians of Thanjavur since the late-Nayaka period. However, the stimulus behind this systematization has never been clearly articulated. I would suggest that the potential loss of the dance in light of the emergent social reform movement directed towards female dancers in various parts of south India may have been a major impetus for the standardization of a formal repertoire and movement technique by

Thanjavur Quartet. Standardizing the practice at the court would (and indeed did) ensure the repertoire's survival into the next century.

In this article, I explore the central role played by texts in the formation and preservation of Thanjavur court dance, before, during, and after the time of the Quartet. I look at the ways in which systematization of the Thanjavur court dance predates the Quartet's activities, and I also look at the ways in which the compositions of the Quartet survive through twentieth century attempts to capture them using the written word. This essay is divided into two parts. In the first part, I explore an example of a pre-Quartet, eighteenth-century systematization of Thanjavur court dance in Tulaja Maharaja's Sanskrit text *Sangita Saramrita*. I then proceed to examine how the Quartet incorporated pre-existing form and structure into their compositions by looking at a *nritta* or pure dance section from a Marathi text called *Kumarasambhava Nirupana*. In the second part, I briefly examine two texts, Gangaimuttu Pillai's *Natanadi Vadya Ranjanam* (1898) and Devulapalli Viraraghavamurti Shastri's *Abhinaya Svayambodhini* (1915) that I posit as new attempts to document *devadasi* court repertoire. In this process, I hope to elucidate the complicated and entrenched relationships between text and practice, Sanskrit and vernacular in the devadasi dance traditions of nineteenth and twentieth-century south India.

PRE-QUARTET 'TEXTUALIZATION' OF THANJAVUR COURT DANCE

Certainly, twentieth-century 'revivalist' discourses centred around granting legitimacy to the reinvented forms by linking them to texts such as the *Natyashastra*. While recognizing the necessity to critique the primacy and elevated status given to Sanskrit dance texts in post-1930s dance history (Coorlawala 1994; Meduri 1996), I concede that the relationships between late Sanskrit and vernacular dance texts and devadasi dance are highly complex and varied. By the time of the Maratha rule in Thanjavur, and certainly throughout the late nineteenth century, there seems to have been a conscious attempt to notate, classify, and preserve songs of the dance repertoire in the form of written texts. While some of these types of texts are well known to most historians of south Indian dance—such as the Tamil *Kuravanjis*[2] danced in various temples that survive in manuscript form in various libraries and personal collections—other codifications of dance repertoire in textual form such as those I discuss here, are not.

Sangita Saramrita is a Sanskrit text attributed to King Tulaja I (r. 1729–35). Unfortunately, as V. Raghavan has noted in the production of a critical edition of the text in 1942, the dance section or *Nritta-prakaranam* is perhaps the most incomplete section in all of the available manuscript materials. However, the fragments are complete enough to provide us with a unique vision of the Maratha enterprise of re-working indigenous cultural practice. This text clearly reflects an attempt to reconcile the local traditions of dance with Sanskrit textual tradition. Its vocabulary is thus a unique amalgam of local (that is, Telugu/Tamil) for movements, which are called *adavu*s in the text, and representations of dance as found in medieval Sanskrit texts such as the *Sangita Ratnakara* of Sarangadeva, the *Sangita-muktavali* of Devenacharya, and the *Nrittaratnavali* of Jayappa, each of which Tulaja liberally cites. This is most clearly seen in the section called *Shrama-vidhi* (or 'directions for practice'). Below is an excerpt from the text that illustrates not only a new hybrid linguistic configuration for the dance, but also the detailed manner in which the text describes the practice of an adavu:

TEXT 1

Sangita Saramrita (shramavidhi)
Tulajaji [Tukkoji] Maharaja (r. 1729–35)

vilambadi prabhedena tadevavartate punah |
udaharanam: *theyyathai* iti |
nikhaya parshnimekaikam prithakpadena tadanam|
sa patakakaranvitam syat khanatpadakuttanam ||

This description of the *tattadavu* provides a Sanskrit equivalent (*khanatpada-kuttanam* or 'digging'-footstep). Moreover, it provides a description of the practice of the step in alternating speeds of *vilambita* ('slow') and the others, supplies the vocalized rhythm or *cholkattu* (which it transliterates as '*theyyathai*'), and gives a short description of the formation of the step, not unlike the well-known *karana* passages from the fourth chapter of the *Natyashastra*.

The *Sangita Saramrita* is, in a sense, a document of tremendous historic relevance, for it demonstrates that an indigenous form of what new critical scholarship refers to as a process of 'textualization' had in fact begun as early as the eighteenth century. While there is certainly a fundamental epistemological difference between the *Sangita Saramrita* and the products of later (Orientalist) 'textualization', it is important to note the significance of a pre-colonial text that clearly 'Sanskritizes' the local Thanjavur court dance traditions in terms of linking them ideologically to the Natyashastric tradition by reading them through the lens of Marathi observers and patrons.

THE THANJAVUR BROTHERS

The Thanjavur Brothers, Chinnaiya, Ponnaiya, Shivanandam, and Vadivel, descended from a clan of musicians who were patronized by the Nayaka and Maratha courts. Their earliest traceable ancestor is one Gopala Nattuvanar (b. 1638) who served in the Rajagopalasvami temple at Mannargudi, and was a chief musician of the court of King Vijayaraghava Nayaka in the seventeenth century. At the decline of the Nayaka rule in Thanjavur, this family moved to Madurai, and later to Tirunelveli. During the rule of King Tulaja II (r. 1763–87), three descendants of the family, the brothers Mahadevan (1734–91), Gangaimuttu (1737–98),[3] and Ramalingam (dates unknown) were invited back to the Thanjavur court. The present home of K.P. Kittappa Pillai on West Main Street in Thanjavur was gifted to the family at this time by Tulaja II. Gangaimuttu had two sons, Subbarayan (1758–1814)[4] and Chidambaram (dates unknown). Subbarayan's sons were the Thanjavur Brothers.

Chinnaiya (1802–56), the eldest of the four, was a great teacher of dance, and in addition was supposed to have been one of the few males who actually performed the dance. He later moved to the Mysore court of Krishnaraja Udaiyar III (r. 1811–68). We can thus surmise that of all the extant compositions attributed to the Thanjavur Brothers, the few dedicated to Krishnaraja Udaiyar III[5] are the creations of Chinnaiya. He also wrote a Telugu text called *Abhinaya Lakshanamu*, a re-worked version of the Sanskrit *Abhinayadarpana* of Nandikeshvara. The colophon of this text reads 'as dictated by Subbarayan', presumably Chinnaiya's father.[6] Ponnaiya (1804–64) was perhaps the most prolific composer among the brothers, and to him is credited the systematization of the sadir kacheri (concert dance repertoire). Most of the compositions by the brothers on Brihadishvara as well as several *nritta* compositions (*jatisvarams* and *tillanas*) are attributed to him. Ponnaiya also set the *mettu* (tunes) for the *Sarabhendra Bhupala Kuravanji*, a text that eulogized King Serfoji II by incorporating him into a Tamil literary genre performed in temples by devadasis. This Kuravanji continued to be performed at the Brihadishvara temple in Thanjavur well into the twentieth century on the ninth day of the annual 18-day long Chaitra Brahmotsavam in April-May.[7]

Before the innovations ushered in by the Quartet, court dance repertoire in the Kaveri Delta seems to have been very flexible. Numerous experiments were being conducted by court-poets, dance-masters, and female dancers themselves, in terms of the creation and manipulation of various genres. Like their contemporaries, the Thanjavur Brothers drew from a cultural pool of artistic materials related to solo female dance in the region. Their re-visioning of the court repertoire consisted of the development of seven primary genres for the solo female court dancer: *alarippu*, jatisvaram, *shabdam, varnam, padam, javali,* and tillana. These represented, in a well-balanced manner, both abstract dance technique (nritta) and textual interpretation (*abhinaya*). The aesthetic experiments of the brothers, Ponnaiya and Vadivel in particular, were 'tested' by three prominent female dancers: Kamalamuttu of Tiruvarur, Sarasammal of Thanjavur, and Minakshi of Mannargudi, who likely performed at the Maratha darbar. This systematization of various kinds of aesthetic material appears to have occurred sometime before 1834, when the Quartet were banished from Thanjavur because of a tryst with King Serfoji II, and moved temporarily to Travancore.[8]

In creating their sevenfold repertoire, the brothers were, in effect, weaving together various fragments of cultural practice. The compositions of the court-poets and dance-masters of other Maratha kings such as Shahaji and Pratapasimha, the Kuravanji temple dramas performed by devadasis, ritual dance in the Kaveri Delta temples, were among the sources they drew from. However, immediately before their establishment of the sevenfold repertoire, a set of Marathi texts for dance called *Nirupana*, also referred to by their Tamil name *Korvai* ('links' or 'chain'), were commissioned by Serfoji II. These Marathi texts are extremely important and provide one of the most important elements in the Quartet's vision of court dance. The court of King Serfoji II produced a cluster of these nirupanas that presented a series of new dance genres such as *sherva, tarana,* and *triputa* along with existing genres such as varnam, *abhinaya pada,* and shabda, couched in the context of a linear narrative presentation similar to the Telugu *yakshagana* court-dramas of the Nayaka and early Maratha periods. In these new genres, we see the roots for the structural aspects of the compositions of the Quartet.

For example, under the genre called sherva in the texts, for example, we find that it consists of three sections, called *tattakara, alaru,* and *aditya*:

TEXT 2

Kumarasambhava Nirupana
(attributed to Serfoji Maharaja II, r. 1798–1832)

Sherva

Raga Bilahari   Aditala

Tattakara—tathayyai thai dattatta

Alaru

tam tam thaikita taka || tam tam thaikita taka || (3x)
tam tam thaikita taka || tatdhi dhalangutaka tadhimginathom ||
takatdhidhalangutakatadhimginathomtatdhidhalangutakatdhidhalangu
dhalangutaka dhikitaka tadhimginathom || tadhimginathom ||
tam digi digi digi ||
dhiki taka taka dhiki taka taka dhiki taka dhalangutaka dhiki taka
tadhimginathom ||

Aditya

tam taka jhomtatta jhomta jhomtatta jhom jhamtari jagataku kumdata
kumdari tadhimginathom ||

The excerpt above is a sherva from a text called *Kumarasambhava Nirupana*, which re-tells Kalidasa's version of the birth of Skanda, through a series of songs meant for dance. The parts of the sherva (which is translated as 'Sabhai Vanakkam' or 'Song of Greeting to the Audience' by the Tamil editors of the text) are very similar in structure to elements of the repertoire developed by the Quartet, specifically, the genre called alarippu, the piece that begins the concert or court performance.

The first section of the sherva is called tattakara, a term used by the descendants of the Quartet even today. It consists of the recitation of a single line of vocalized rhythmic syllables or cholkattu. Here we see the sounds *ta-thay-yai thai dat-tatta*. The dancer would enter the performance arena with these sounds, while stamping her feet on the ground. The second section, alaru is more than likely the source of the genre that the Brothers call alarippu, from the Telugu word alaru ('flower' or 'blossom'). In this section, we see a configuration of syllables that looks almost exactly like the Quartet's alarippu. It ends with another form of tattakara, this time to the accompaniment of the sounds *digi digi digi*—a similar structure is also found at the end of the Quartet's alarippu. The composition ends with a section called aditya, which brings closure to the piece. This fragment of cholkattus bears a resemblance to a short *tirmanam* or flourish that concludes most rhythmic sequences.

DEVADASI DANCE TEXTS AFTER THE QUARTET

The effort to 'preserve' the devadasi dance also continued well after the time of the Quartet. Patrons and dance-masters appear to have been increasingly concerned about the potential loss of the art of dance, particularly in the first decade of the twentieth century, when there appears to have been a burgeoning interest in 'documenting' the devadasi music and dance repertoire in the form of Tamil and Telugu printed texts. The advent of print culture in south India played a major role in the sedimentation of new forms of cultural expression, and mediated the transmission of and accessibility to traditional forms of knowledge. As Stuart Blackburn has recently pointed out,

... even if it did not by itself standardize languages or fix canons or maintain colonial domination, the rise of print must be included in any attempt to explain cultural change in the nineteenth century (Blackburn 2003: 12).

In terms of our discussion of a new textualization of dance practice that occurs with the advent of print culture, on the one hand, it is important that printed texts serve, to some extent, to undermine traditional authority, or displace hereditary or other specialized knowledge. On the other hand, I propose that the set of printed texts we will be examining represent an anxiety about the loss of specialized knowledge. Brahmin men and *nattuvanars*, the 'brokers' of elite cultural forms in nineteenth-century south India, were eager to retain, remember, and reproduce the cultural practices that defined their identities in a changing public sphere.

One of the earliest examples of a printed work on dance is a Tamil work entitled *Abhinaya Sara Samputa* ('Vessel Containing the Essence of Abhinaya') by Chetlur Narayana Ayyangar, published in 1886. This work, and its companion, a text called *Abhinaya Navanita* ('Refined Essence of Abhinaya')[9] were edited by V. Raghavan and published in 1961 by the Madras Music Academy. The *Abhinaya Sara Samputa* is divided into six sections dealing with a range of topics related to the theory and practice of abhinaya, from discourses on *rasa* and *nayikas*, to the various typologies of head and neck movements and hand gestures, all based on the *Abhinayadarpana*. The final section, entitled *Bhava Prakasham* ('Illuminations on Bhava') is perhaps the most relevant for our discussion. It notates 'word-for-word' abhinaya for twenty padams in Tamil and Telugu, including Tamil compositions by Subbarama Ayyar and Telugu padams by Kshetrayya. These 'word-for-word' interpretations are suggestions for how to perform abhinaya for each word in the text of the song.[10] The author presents this as giving purport (*tatparyam*) to the representation of these songs (*Abhinaya Sara Samputa* 1961: 4).

We will now turn to an important Tamil work, *Natanadi Vadya Ranjanam* by Gangaimuttu Pillai (1837–1920), written in Tirunelveli in the year 1898. Gangaimuttu Pillai himself was a nattuvanar employed by the Minakshi temple in Madurai. Two other Tamil works, *Sabharanjita Chintamani* and *Sangita Bharata Sara Sangraham* are also attributed to him (Sundaram 1997: 41). Like the work of the Thanjavur Quartet, the *Natanadi Vadya Ranjanam* also seeks to 'document' older compositions that appear to be declining in current practice. The older compositions preserved herein are largely Telugu shabdams. Some of these appear to be compositions of Bharatam Kashinathayya, and thus date back to the time of Shahaji Maharaja (1684–1712), who is thought to have been Kashinathayya's patron.[11] Thus, we have the *Ramayana Shabdam, Tripurasamhara Shabdam,* a *Salam Shabdam* on King Pratapasimha, *Gopala Shabdam, Venkataramana Shabdam, Mukunda Shabdam, Kodandarama Shabdam* (likely a composition of the Quartet), and *Subrahmanya Shabdam,* all recorded in the first part (*purvabhagam*) of the *Natanadi Vadya Ranjanam.*

TEXT 3

Natanadi Vadya Ranjanam (1898)
by Gangaimuttu Pillai (1837–1920)

Venkataramana Shabdam
Talam Sarvalaghu

In Telugu transliteration:

chalamu valaduduru sukhayitu rara
jalam yala samiki mrokkera
valapu minchayika tamasam yala
prasanna venkataramana paraku

வேங்கிடாரமண சப்தம்
தாளம் சருவலகு.

தத்தி	இடதகஜெம்	நதிமித.	இடதகஜெம்
தக்கிடதகதிக்	இடதகதொம்கிட	தகணங்கிடதக	தகதரிஇடதக
தா	தெய்	தத்த	த்தா
சலமுவ	லதுதுரு.	சகபிஜ.	ஜார
ஜால	ம்யரலசச.	மிகிம்மொட.	க்கோ
வலபுஜி	ஞ்சபிக.	தாமச	ம்யரலஉ
ப்ரசன்ன	வேங்கட.	ரமணய.	ஜரகு
தளங்கு	தகதிதி	தகததி	ம்கிணதொஎம்

This composition is similar in structure and content to the Telugu salam-darus and shabdams that I have recovered from the repertoire of the devadasis of Viralimalai and Thanjavur. Though we have not yet been able to find this composition in practice among living devadasi families in south India, it is highly probable that this shabdam was part of Gangaimuttu Pillai's own sadir kacheri repertoire, likely a song that he would have taught to devadasis in Madurai.

In addition to courtly compositions such as the shabdams, the early part of the *Natanadi Vadya Ranjanam* also presents us with devadasi temple repertoire, in the form of ritual dances called *kavuttuvam*. The text contains the full cluster of the nine famous *navasandhi kavuttuvams*, and in addition, nine other *kavuttuvam* compositions. The navasandhi kavuttuvams are a set of nine compositions that invoke the deities of the eight cardinal directions (called *lokapalas* or *dikpalas*) plus the god Brahma in the centre (*brahmasthanam*) of the temple during a major festival (*mahotsava*). The ritual is accompanied by the worship of the structure called *balipitha* (seat of offering), and thus is thought of as part of a larger offering often called *balidana* or *baliharana*. Textual injunctions for the performance of such dances at the time of balidana is found in south Indian Sanskrit agamas such as the *Kumara Tantra* and in the Shaiva commentator Sadyojatashivacharya's manual for priests called *Kriyakramadyotika* (Kersenboom 1987: 115–28; Janaki 1988). In the form of the kavuttuvams that we find in the *Natanadi Vadya Ranjanam* however, these rituals were performed by devadasis at the Thanjavur Brihadishvara temple and the Madurai Minakshi temple until ca. 1946 in Thanjavur and 1955 in Madurai.[12]

The texts of the songs of the navasandhi kavuttuvam are descriptive in nature. They invoke both Sanskrit terms (such as the *krantaka* karana movement from the *Natyashastra*, and hand gestures *pataka* and *arala* mentioned as those used to depict Vayu in the *Abhinayadarpana*) and Tamil ones (including the names of the basic modes [*pans*] of ancient Tamil music):

TEXT 4

Natanadi Vadya Ranjanam
by Gangaimuttu Pillai (1837–1920)

Vayusandhi kavuttuvam
talam chaturashrajati rupakam

vayu disaiyil kodiyayudham shikhivahana madi anjana devi sahitamaga
In the direction of Lord Vayu [the North-West], who holds a flag as a weapon, riding a peacock, together with the Goddess Anjana Devi

sakala bhuvanapramana kartta simhasanadhiparku
[Resides] the Ruling Sovereign, who measures all the worlds.

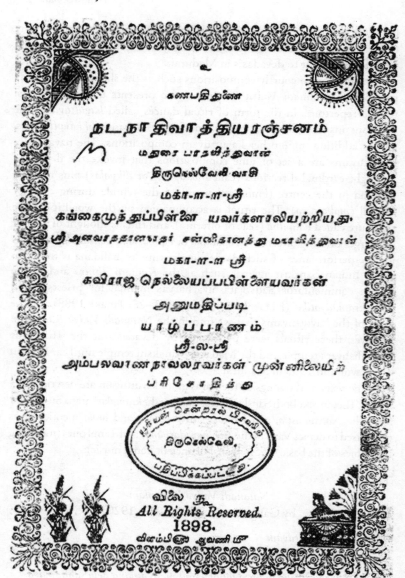

FIG. 12   Cover of the *Natanadi Vadya Ranjanam*
Published by Central Union Press, Tirunelveli in 1898

tanata jonuta dhimita kitata
pancha vadyam gitam makuta ramagiri
Using the instruments called *panchavadyam* and the song (*raga*) called
makutaramagiri,

sa ri ga ma pa dha ni sa
kanti nrittam ardhapatakaralamam
the dance movement called *kanti* [*krantaka*] and the hand-gestures pataka
and arala,
tam titaka tadhi mitakkitta tanata jonuta

pali talam takkesi raga pan meviya vayudisaik kavuttuvam
this is the *Vayu Sandhi Kautuvam,* in the *tala* [time-cycle] called *bali,* and
the pan [Tamil melody] called *takkesi.*

takanangi takatarikita
takataka tiki tadhingiōatom takku tikku takkitta
tonkiaa kitatakatan tangi kitataka tikki
tam tat ta tam tatta ||

The other kavuttuvams found in *Natanadi Vadya Ranjanam* are
the following: Ganapati kavuttuvam (on Ganesha); Subramaniyar
kavuttuvam (on Murugan); Sirkali Campantar kavuttuvam (on the
nayanar Tirujnanasambandar); Chidambara Natesar kavuttuvam
(on Shiva-Nataraja); Tiruvalankadu Kali kavuttuvam (on Kali);
Tiruchengodu Vishnu kavuttuvam (on Vishnu); Srivilliputtur Nachiyar
kavuttuvam (on the alvar Andal); Madurapuri Chokkar kavuttuvam
(on Shiva-Chokkanatha of Madurai); and Darukavanam Mahalinga
kavuttuvam (on Shiva-Mahalingasvami of Tiruvidaimarudur). Of these,
four (those on Ganesha, Murugan, Nataraja, and Tirujnanasambandar)
were among the five *panchamurti* kavuttuvams sung by the descendants of
the Thanjavur Quartet every year during the festival of Tiruvadirai (also
known as Arudra Darshana) at the Brihadishvara temple. These four
songs plus another kavuttuvam on the saint Chandikeshvara would be
sung by the dance-master as they played the cymbals (*talam*) while the
processional image of Shiva as Somaskanda would be taken around the
temple grounds.

Clearly then, the compositions in *Natanadi Vadya Ranjanam* were
specifically compiled in textual form by observing and recording the living
traditions of devadasi dance at a crucial point in history, and therefore
its significance as an early 'documentation' of the south Indian dance
repertoire cannot be understated.

Abhinaya Svayambodhini is a Telugu text written by Devulapalli
Viraraghavamurti Shastri (Fig. 13) in Kakinada in the year 1915. Like
the *Natanadi Vadya Ranjanam*, it too can be read as a text that documents
current practice. In the preface, its Brahmin author, Viraraghavamurti
Shastri explains why he has written this text. He claims that the repertoire
of the Andhra devadasis is fast disappearing before his very eyes, and
thus, this is perhaps the first conscious attempt to 'document' the living
traditions of the Godavari Delta for posterity. The text itself consists of
four sections (*adhyayas*). The first is an assemblage of concert music songs
(*kirtanas* and *svarajatis*); the second is purely devoted to *padavarnams*;
the third is dedicated to Kshetrayya padams; and the fourth, deals with
theory and dance technique such as *shirobhedas*, *drishtibhedas*, *grivabhedas*
(movements for the head, eyes and neck), and *hastas* (hand gestures) and
their applications. The fourth section clearly follows the codification in
the *Abhinayadarpana*, and here we should keep in mind that this was

FIG. 13   Devulapalli Viraraghavamurti Shastri, author of *Abhinaya Svayambodhini*
(From the frontispiece of the 1915 edition published by Sarasvati
Mudrakshara Shala, Kakinada)

published two years before Coomaraswamy and Duggirala's edition of the same text came to light.[13] The description of each composition includes the sahitya plus suggestions for how to interpret each word or phrase through abhinaya, much like the *Abhinaya Sara Samputa* discussed earlier. Shastri claims to have culled these abhinaya suggestions from the devadasis of the Godavari Delta region. Most importantly for us, the text also contains several compositions of the Thanjavur Quartet, indicative of their popularity in the Godavari region at the turn of the century. An examination of the content of the second section is telling—included in this list, for example, is Chinnaiya's padavarnam 'chalamu jesite' (the Telugu version of 'sakhiye inda velaiyil' in Anandabhairavi Raga) dedicated to King Krishnaraja Udaiyar III of Mysore (r. 1811–68):

TEXT 4

Abhinaya Svayambodhini (1915)
by Devulapalli Viraraghavamurti Shastri
Excerpt from *Table of Contents*

2 Adhyayamu (*padavarnamulu*)—pp. x–xi

*indicates compositions attributed to the Thanjavur Quartet
**also found in the *Sangita Sampradaya Pradarshini* (1904) of Subbarama Dikshitar (1839–1906)

The inclusion of Thanjavur Quartet compositions in the repertoire of the devadasis of the Godavari river delta in Telugu-speaking south India is remarkable. It is an index of the popularity of the compositions on the one hand, and also of the breadth of their dissemination on the other. Moreover, the fact that these compositions appear in the *Abhinaya Svayambodhini* with notes on how the coastal Andhra devadasis performed the abhinaya clearly marks it as a text that must be understood as a genuine attempt to preserve the songs and performance technique of these women.

Texts, and the literal 'scripting' of dance culture in Thanjavur, appear to have played a major role in the preservation and survival of devadasi dance in the midst of social reform of the nineteenth and twentieth centuries, and into the present. The compositions of the Thanjavur Brothers themselves, drawing from earlier attempts at systematization and codification, made their way as far north as coastal Andhra, while texts such as the *Natanadi Vadya Ranjanam* attempted to preserve them along with a host of other devadasi dance genres. As we have seen, the inclusion (or invocation) of Sanskritic dance culture, whether in the *Sangita Saramrita*'s classification of movement or the incorporation of names of hand gestures in the texts of the *navasandhi* kavuttuvam certainly *did* figure in the repertoire of devadasis, though clearly not in the ways in which contemporary histories of Bharatanatyam would like. The process of 'textualization' was indeed an indigenous one—the notebooks of the Quartet housed in their descendant's homes speak clearly of this—but ultimately the question of the *purpose* of such codifications must be raised. What use would Vadivel's notations of his own compositions be after his own death? In this article I have suggested that we take seriously the idea that there was a self-conscious attempt to preserve and sometimes even 'document' devadasi dance traditions that were undergoing major changes or were facing the threat of extinction. Such an understanding may help us move towards a critical reading of the performance practices of the devadasis of the late nineteenth and early twentieth centuries.

NOTES

1. Research for this project was supported by the Dance Department, Wesleyan University. I wish to acknowledge the help provided to me by Davesh Soneji at various points during this project. I am particularly indebted to B.M. Sundaram, whose pioneering work on dating and genealogies of nineteenth-century personalities has greatly impacted my own work. I also wish to thank my teachers, the late Kittappa Pillai of Thanjavur and R. Muttukkannammal (devadasi of the Murugan temple at Viralimalai), for their invaluable comments on dance history

in early twentieth-century south India. Finally, Indira Viswanathan Peterson and Lakshmi Subramanian have provided critical comments and suggestions through careful readings, and I am grateful to both of them.

2. The Kuravanji drama tradition formed a key component of the devadasi dance repertoire of many temples in the Tamil-speaking pats of south India. Kuravanji (lit. 'Drama of the Kura Woman') is a post-eighteenth-century literary and performance genre from Tamil Nadu. The second half of the typical plot of the Kuravanji texts revolves around the fortune-telling Kura woman from the hills (also called Kuratti or Singi) and her lover, a hunter or bird-catcher, known as Singan. See Muilwijk (1996) for a literary study of the *Kumaralingar Kuravanji*, and Peterson (1998) for an excellent critical study of the Kuravanji genre in transition.

3. This is *not* the same Gangaimuttu Nattuvanar who was the author of the text *Natanadi Vadya Ranjanam* discussed elsewhere in this paper. The author of this text came from Pasuvandanai, a village near Tirunelveli. The *Natanadi Vadya Ranjanam* was first published in Tirunelveli by the Union Central Press in 1898. According to B.M. Sundaram, the two were 'collateral relatives, and there has been great confusion about their identities' (Personal communication, January 1998). However, the *kavuttuvam* compositions found in the *Natanadi Vadya Ranjanam* may in fact be those of Gangaimuttu of the Thanjavur court.

4. According to T. Sankaran, Subbarayan was a musician who was highly respected by his peers including Melattur Venkatarama Shastri, Muttusvami Dikshitar, and Shyama Shastri. T. Sankaran cited in Higgins (1977), p. 26.

5. There is some discrepancy about the dates of Chinnaiya. Many of the compositions attributed to him are dedicated to Chamarajendra Udaiyar (r. 1868–94), son of Krishnaraja Udaiyar III. However, Chamarajendra only ascended the throne in 1868, and Chinnaiya passed away in 1856. K.P. Kittappa insists that all of the compositions on Chamarajendra are in fact by Chinnaiya and that he may have been alive well into the rule of Chamarajendra.

6. This text is currently being edited by B.M. Sundaram and should be available very soon.

7. The last time the Kuravanji was performed in the Brihadishvara temple was ca. 1947, when K.P. Kittappa Pillai provided vocal music for it. In 1994, he edited the musical notation of the entire text, and this was subsequently published by the Tamil University, Thanjavur. This text was erased from contemporary performances of Bharatanatyam dance, perhaps because it was deemed aesthetically inferior by revivalists such as Rukmini Arundale. See Peterson (1998) for details on the uses and interpretations of the *Sarabhendra Bhupala Kuravanji* by Arundale and others.

8. Sundaram's recent work (1997) indicates that the brothers were exiled from Thanjavur because of a confrontation with Serfoji II:

The service of the brothers continued for only a few years under this nominal ruler [Serfoji II]. During that time, they composed a few varnams honouring the new king. Ponnayya also composed music to *Sarabhenda Bhoopala Kuravanji* and *Manmatha Vilasam* and staged them in the Brihadishvara temple each year. But the situation gradually deteriorated. Serfoji II, a ward of Reverend Schwartz, had been educated in

English by him ... but Western music was more pleasing to his ears. He passed orders that all his court musicians must learn Western music and even went to the extent of fining his own minister, Varahappayya, 'because he was not ready to perform Western music'. On one occasion, Serfoji sent for the Quartet and declared that he planned to appoint a person for daily service in the Brihadeesvara temple in addition to them. The person was none other than the son of Serfoji's concubine and trained, to some extent, by the brothers themselves. The brothers submitted that the Raja should keep in mind the age and talents of the appointee before taking a decision. But Serfoji promulgated a *firman* [official order] by which the new incumbent would not only be appointed in the temple, but would also have exclusive right to temple honours such as *parivattam* [the ritual honour of wearing the cloth of the deity around one's head]. This was an insult to the brothers so they left Thanjavur. (Sundaram 1997: 34)

9.   The *Abhinaya Navanita* (lit. 'Clarified Butter of Abhinaya') was written by Ayyangar in collaboration with Panchapakesa Nattuvanar (1842–1902) from Thanjavur, father of the famous Tiruvidaimarudur Kuppaiya Nattuvanar (1887–1981) who founded the Sri Rajarajeswari Bharatanatya Kala Mandir in Bombay in 1945.

10.   Such 'word-for-word' abhinaya texts are not new in themselves. This appears to have been a standard way of notating abhinaya in south India. Manuscript sources from the eighteenth and nineteenth centuries confirm this. For example, in 1950, K. Vasudeva Sastri, pandit at the Sarasvati Mahal library in Thanjavur edited and published an edition of Jayadeva's *Gitagovinda* that provides word-for-word suggestions for performing abhinaya to each of the *ashtapadis*. His sources were two paper manuscripts found in the library. The performance of ashtapadis by devadasis since at least the nineteenth century has been documented in both Thanjavur and the Godavari River Delta (Soneji 2004). But instead of positing that these relatively recent paper manuscripts may have belonged to a nattuvanar in the Thanjavur area, Vasudeva Sastri, who feels that 'the traditional practice has suffered by the general break of tradition due to the foreign invasion and foreign influence,' (Sastri 1950: ix) wishes to posit a north Indian origin for the manuscripts:

It is ... clear that this work must have been composed before the mixing up of the Indian and Persion [sic] styles of Dance, under the Afghan and Mughal rule of the 14th to 17th century in Northern India. It is extremely probable that this work was composed by the direct disciples of Sri Jayadeva himself or those just after him. (Sastri 1950: x)

The content of these manuscripts employs the abhinaya and gestural language described in the *Abhinayadarpana*, whose techniques are used so widely by nattuvanars in the region. It is clear that the manuscripts must have a southern origin, and that this text is an early precursor of other 'word-for-word' abhinaya manuals that follow after the advent of the printing press in south India.

11.   Bharatam Kashinathakavi is accredited with the composition of *salamdarus*, also called tala-cholkattu or shabdam. Usually addressed to a king of a local deity, they involve the recitation of rhythmic utterances (cholkattu) and epithets of the hero. They usually end with Urdu words like salam (hence the name of the genre,

salam-daru) or *shabash* ('well done!' or 'bravo!'), reflective of the multilingual nature of the Thanjavur court. For details, see N. Visvanathan's Tamil work (1985), *Sabdam alias Tala Solkattu of Bharatam Kasinathakavi, King Sahaji and Bharatam Narana Kavi*.

12. As Davesh Soneji notes, the baliharana rites were also found among Telugu-speaking devadasis in what is now coastal Andhra Pradesh, and were common to both Vaikhanasa-Vaishnava and Shaiva temples in this region. (Soneji 2004: 98).

13. In 1917, Ananda Coomaraswamy and Gopala Krishnayya Duggirala, a Telugu scholar, edited and translated the *Abhinayadarpana* for the first time. The majority of manuscripts available were in Telugu script, and were likely found, like many manuscripts of *Bhamakalapam* and *Gitagovinda*, in the homes of Telugu poets who interacted with Telugu-speaking devadasis (Soneji 2004: 106–9, 145–7).

REFERENCES

(Primary Telugu and Tamil Texts)

Ayyar, B. Rajam and S. Ramanathan (eds), under the supervision of L. Venkatarama Iyer, C. Venkatarama Iyer, and V. Raghavan, 1961–83, *Sangita Sampradaya Pradarshini*, Subbarama Dikshitar (5 vols), Madras: The Music Academy.

Kittappa, K.P. and Gnana Kulendran (eds), 1994, *Natya Pattisai: Tanjai Sarabhendra Bhupala Kuravanji*, Thanjavur: Tamil Palakalaikkalagam.

Kittappa, K.P. and K.P. Sivanandam (eds), 1961, *The Dance Compositions of the Tanjore Quartet*, Ahmedabad: Darpana Publications.

———, 1964, *Adi Bharata Kala Manjari*, Madras: Natyalaya.

Pillai, Gangaimuttu, 1898, *Natanadi Vadya Ranjanam*, Tirunelveli: Union Central Press.

Pillai, K. Ponnaiya (ed.), 1940, *Tanjai Peruvudayan Perisai*, Madras.

Pillai, K.P. Kittappa (ed.), 1999, *Tanjai Nalvarin Natya Isai*, Chennai: The Music Academy.

Raghavan, V. (ed.), 1961, *Abhinaya Sara Samputa*. Chetlur Narayana Ayyangar and *Abhinaya Navanita*, Chetlur Narayana Ayyangar and Tanjore Panchapagesa Nattuvanar, Madras: The Music Academy.

Shastri, Devulapalli Viraraghavamurti, 1915, *Abhinaya Svayambodhini*, Kakinada: Sarasvati Mudrakshara Shala.

Srinivasan, A. (ed.), 1988, *Sarabhendra Bhupala Kuravanji*, Madras: Aintinai.

Sanskrit Texts and Translations

Sastri, K. Vasudeva (ed.), 1989, *Bharatarnavam*, Thanjavur: Saraswathi Mahal Library Society.

Sastri, K. Vasudeva, 1950, *Gita Govinda with Abhinaya*, Thanjavur: Thanjavur Maharaja Serfoji's Sarasvati Mahal Library Society.

Sastri, S. Subrahmanya (ed.), 1942, *Sangita Saramrita*, Madras: The Music Academy.

Secondary Sources

Blackburn, Stuart, 2003, *Print, Folklore, and Nationalism in Colonial South India*, New Delhi: Permanent Black.

Coorlawala, Uttara Asha, 1994, 'Classical and Contemporary Indian Dance: Overview, Criteria and a Choreographic Analysis', PhD dissertation, New York University.

Higgins, Jon, 1993, *The Music of Bharata Natyam*, New Delhi: ARCE-AIIS/ Oxford and IBH.

Janaki, S.S., 1988, 'Dhvaja-Stambha: Critical Account of its Structural and Ritualistic Details', in S.S. Janaki (ed.), *Siva Temple and Temple Rituals*, Madras: Kuppuswami Research Institute.

Kersenboom, Saskia, 1987, *Nityasumangali: Devadasi Tradition in South India*, New Delhi: Motilal Banarsidass.

Meduri, Avanthi, 1996, 'Nation, Woman, Representation: The Sutured History of the Devadasi and Her Dance', PhD Dissertation, Department of Performance Studies, Tisch School of the Arts, New York University.

Muilwijk, Marina, 1996, *The Divine Kura Tribe: Kuravanci and other Prabandhams*, Groningen: Egbert Forsten.

Peterson, Indira Viswanathan, 1998, 'The Evolution of the Kuravanci Dance Drama in Tamil Nadu: Negotiating the "Folk" and the "Classical" in the Bharata Natyam Canon', *South Asia Research*, 18, pp. 39–72.

Soneji, Davesh, 2004, *Performing Satyabhama: Text, Context, Memory and Mimesis in Telugu-Speaking South India*, PhD dissertation, McGill University.

Sundaram, B.M., 1997, 'Towards a Genealogy of Some Tanjavur Natyacharyas and their Kinsfolk', *Sangeet Natak*, 124, pp. 30–41.

Davesh Soneji

Salon to Cinema

The Distinctly Modern Life of the Telugu Javali*

In 1960, eminent Sanskritist V. Raghavan was asked to write the preface to a volume of Telugu *javali* songs. Dr Raghavan appears frustrated in the preface, unable to crack the historical puzzle of the javali. He writes: 'curiously for a type which has come up in times so near to us, the Javali is really obscure in its origins.'[1] But Raghavan is not alone. Over the past century, the javali has been contentious both in terms of its origins and its status. Excepting Raghavan and a few others, most contemporary writers and performers dismiss javalis as degenerate expressions of poetry that are meant to arouse the senses, and nothing more.[2] Unlike the songs of the older Telugu *padam* genre from which they derive their structure and narrative contexts, javalis are rarely thought of as 'highbrow' or 'classical' songs. Traditionally associated with *devadasis* in colonial Madras and their upper-caste male patrons, javalis bear the sign of private salon performances by courtesans in South India. They unsettle nationalist re-inventions of dance as temple-based and purely religious, and perhaps because of this, they are rarely heard in contemporary performances of Bharatanatyam dance and Karnatak music.

In form and structure the javali is basically indistinguishable from the padam, except perhaps for its lighter, more playful style. What makes the javali unique, and what has perhaps contributed to its opacity as a form, is the very context of its performance, the relations that it proposes between dancer and audience. The field of its production is also radically

* Funding for this research was provided by the Social Science and Humanities Research Council of Canada (SSHRC). I would like to express my gratitude to B.M. Sundaram, Hari Krishnan, and Voleti Rangamani for helping me navigate through a number of complex sources that form the basis of this work. I am also grateful to Kathryn Hansen, Indira Viswanathan Peterson, and Simon Reader for their insightful comments on earlier versions of this essay.

different from that of the padams composed by apotheosized Telugu poets such as Annamayya and Kshetrayya. While these composers lived and worked at medieval centres of religious pilgrimage and devotion like Tirupati, javali composers (*javalikartas*) worked in the civic heart of the colonial city, employed as Taluk clerks or post office workers.

Located between the demise of courtly forms of the late medieval period on the one hand, and the emergent modern forms of the mid-twentieth century on the other, nineteenth-century Indian literary and performance genres elude obvious categories. In this paper I argue that it is precisely this 'transitional' status of the javali that has made it an unsolvable riddle for scholars and historians like Raghavan. Javalis lie at the furthest edges of courtly dance practices, and at the cusp of India's emergent entertainment industry in the early twentieth century. As texts, they are sites for multiple experiments in syncretism with regard to language and music. They are incorporated into Parsi-theatre inspired Tamil plays, sometimes written in a combination of South Indian languages and English, are subject to Orientalist analyses, and even enter films. This paper charts the flows of this highly malleable and ever-shifting genre, as it dramatizes these multiple transformations.

For over a century, scholars have grappled with the definition and etymology of the javali. In 1894, Reverend F. Kittel in his *Kannada-English Dictionary* defined javali as 'a kind of lewd poetry,' evidently derived from the Kannada word *javala* which he translates as 'common, vulgar, or insignificant.' Kittel's definition appears to have been the point of reference for nearly all subsequent attempts to pin down an etymology for the word. Similarly, when it comes to the content of the javali—namely exactly how it is different from the padam—there is an absolute lack of consensus. The javali shares the tripartite structure of the padam: it contains *pallavi*, *anupallavi*, and *caranam*. This three-fold unravelling of the poem, literally from the 'sprout' of the poem (pallavi) to the elaborate caranam stanzas, enables narrative and aesthetic movement through the text. Like songs in the Telugu padam genre, javalis are usually dedicated to a localized form of Krishna. Often the *mudra* or 'signature' of the composer of the javali is the name of the God. So, for example, the javalis of Patnam Subrahmanya Ayyar are identifiable through their inclusion of the names 'Venkatesha' or 'Varada-Venkatesha.' These similarities, combined with the emphasis on eroticism or *shringara* in both the padam and javali, make them nearly indistinguishable. So much so, that one Telugu scholar, hands thrown up in aggravation, insists on referring to javalis as 'nothing more than mini padams'.

Two major historical trajectories prevail when it comes to the invention of the javali as a musical form. The first, and perhaps more historically accurate narrative, situates the genesis of the genre at the Mysore court under the patronage of the kings Mummadi Krishnaraja Udaiyar III (1799–1868) and Chamaraja Udaiyar IX (1881–94). Two Kannada paper manuscripts from the time of Krishnaraja Udaiyar that are preserved in the library of the Institute of Kannada Studies at the University of Mysore attest to the fact that the genre was in existence during his reign.[3] Later, under the patronage of both of these kings, the dance master Cinnaiya (1802–1856, one among the famous 'Thanjavur Quartet') who was employed by the king, and others are known to have composed songs that were known as *javadis* or javalis. The other narrative revolves around events at the court of the last king of Travancore, Maharaja Svati Tirunal (1813–1846). Here, the first javali is said to have been crafted in the hands of the dance-master Vativelu of Thanjavur (1810–1847, younger brother of Cinnaiya). On the whole, there appears to be less evidence to support such a claim.[4]

Sources for studying javalis as literature or as scripts for performance are few and far between. With the exception of the two Kannada paper manuscripts mentioned above, manuscripts of javalis do not exist in library collections. Notations of javalis can be found in the personal notebooks of some *nattuvanars* or dance-masters, such the one belonging to Chennai Nellaiyappa Nattuvanar (1859–1905), a descendant of the 'Thanjavur Quartet' who lived and worked in Madras city. This book, currently in the possession of one of his descendants in Chennai, contains over 150 compositions meant for devadasi performance, including javalis. Other sources include nineteenth- and twentieth-century print materials in Tamil and Telugu, such the chapbook entitled *Telunku Cinkara Javali* (Telugu Srngara Javalis) published in 1924 (Fig. 14) and more elaborate books on South Indian concert music, such as the treatises of Taccur Singaracharyulu[5] and the *Gandharvakalpavalli* (Fig. 15).[6] This last work by P.S. Ramulu Chetti was published in both Telugu and Tamil versions in Madras from 1911–12. Not much is known about Ramulu Chetti other than the fact that he was a non-Brahmin master of the harmonium, an instrument that was banned by All India Radio in 1930, and much despised by many traditional Brahmin musicians in South India. The large number of compositions in this work that are traditionally associated with devadasi performance point to the fact that he may have been in

FIG. 14   The cover of *Telunku Cinkara Javali* (1924)

contact with devadasis, perhaps even in the capacity of an accompanist. We shall return to this text later.

The last and perhaps most abundant source of javalis comes from within the traditional community of javali performers, the devadasi-courtesans of South India themselves. In both the Tamil and

FIG. 15   The cover and frontispiece of the Tamil edition of Ramulu Chetti's *Gandharvakalpavalli* (1912)

Telugu-speaking regions—from the northern tip of the Godavari delta to the Kanyakumari district in the deep South—these women have continued to preserve the texts and performance techniques of javalis. In the latter half of this paper, we will observe the ways in which memory allows us to access the texts and performance practices traditionally associated with javalis.

Though the javali is traditionally understood as a Telugu or Kannada genre, between roughly 1880 and 1910, javalis become extremely popular as Tamil *devotional* songs meant for theatrical performance. These circulate in the form of small inexpensive chapbooks, usually 8–10 pages in length, each of which consists of a set of songs dedicated to localized Tamil deities. Thus, we have collections of Tamil 'javalis' called *Citamparam Nataraja Civakamiyin Peril Parsi Ati Arputa Javali* (1906) dedicated to Nataraja and his consort at Chidambaram, and *Maturai Cuntaresvarar Javali* (1888) dedicated to Siva as Sundaresvara at Madurai. Here the javali as a 'popular' genre of literature and music easily fits into the emergent contexts of Tamil theatre that consciously presented itself as *innovative* (note the word *ati arputa* 'astonishing,' in the title above), and linked itself to the Parsi theatre.

Most of these songs were composed by non-Brahmin Velalars who were involved in the emergent world of Tamil popular drama known as *isai natakam* or 'special' *natakam* that was shaped by Sankaradas Swamigal (1867–1922) between 1887 and 1922. Indeed, many of the chapbooks are written and/or published by members of popular early drama companies in Madras with names such as 'Chennai Manoranjita Nataka Sabha.' These songs are also part of a new set of performance practices deeply affected by Parsi theatre companies that toured the Madras Presidency in this period. As Susan Seizer (2005: 52–4) has convincingly demonstrated, the aesthetics of popular theatre in Tamilnadu emerge out of a peculiar kind of nineteenth-century cultural modernity in which Velalars and Tevars are literally the nouveaux *dramatis personae*, deploying consciously innovative staging, music, and acting technique.

More generally, early South Indian print materials on music also contain large sections on 'Parsi Pattukal,' and often javalis are subsumed under this category, which usually contains Hindi and Urdu love songs from Parsi plays such as *Aao ji aao* from the play *King Lear*.[7] These songs, which employed North Indian melodies adapted from Hindustani ragas, gave rise to a catch-all genre in South Indian music, called '*parsi mettu*' or Parsi tunes. Thus, many javalis are not in known South Indian ragas, but in their printed forms are listed as set to the 'parsi mettu.' By the 1920s,

FIG. 16   'God Save the King' in Sanskrit (*sarasa sarvabhauma jarjinama bhupa*)
from Ramulu Chetti's *Gandharvakalpavalli* (1912)

the terms 'parsi mettu' or 'Hindustan mettu' referred to any 'odd' tune or
song that could not be classified as part of the indigenous South Indian
music or dance repertoire. These included javalis, 'gramophone songs,'
and even popular everyday Tamil song-genres such as *nalanku* (wedding
songs) and *otam* (boat songs). In the *Gandharvakalpavalli*, the final tune
listed under 'Parsi Pattukal' is a Sanskrit version of 'God Save the King'
entitled 'sarasa sarvabhauma jarjinama bhupa' in honour of King George
V and his wife Queen Mary, who visited India in 1911 and staged the
Coronation Darbar in Delhi that same year (Fig. 16).

The forms of cultural hybridity that surround genres like the javali
also include radical experiments with language. For example, in the
Gandharvakalpavalli, we also find a javali in a mixed-language genre,
consisting of four languages—Tamil, Telugu, Kannada, and English.
Composed by a Tamil poet Sivaramayya from the village of Karur near
Trichy, nearly each word in this song alternates between the languages, and
clearly, the song is meant for consumption by a cosmopolitan audience.[8]

Javali in Four Langauges (*caturbhasa* javali)
Raga: Kambodhi; Tala: Adi; Composer: Karur Sivaramayya (*c.* 1798–
1820)

Pallavi (refrain)

| my dear come | varuvai | i vela |
| [English] | [Tamil] | [Telugu] |

Caranam (stanza)

ninnujuci cala	*divasa ayite manna*	*ni na manasu impaina*
[Telugu]	[Kannada]	[Telugu]

kalaharanaminca	*for me now*	*belatingalu bisallavayite*
[Telugu]	[English]	[Kannada]

kuluku talakugala	*come*	*birana*	*well I shall sing*	*Sivaramuni*	*songs*
[Telugu]	[English]	[Telugu]	[English]	[Telugu]	[English]

A translation would read something like this:

My dear come, come here now! Many days have passed since I have seen you. O King! Fill my heart with your sweetness. Why do you delay for me now? Months have passed—it all seems a waste! With all your charms, come quickly, well I shall sing Sivarama's songs.

Despite what received nationalist histories of dance in South India tell us, the majority of performances by devadasis in the nineteenth and early twentieth century did *not* take place in temples. Rather private gatherings, largely consisting of elite men, were the primary sites of devadasi performance. In one sense, this 'salon culture' as I call it, can be seen as an extension of cultural performances at courts like that of Thanjavur in the eighteenth and nineteenth centuries. Elite social gatherings for 'men of affairs' in colonial Madras provide us with some of the earliest documented scenes of salons in South India. Literary works such as the Sanskrit *Sarvadevavilasa* ('Sport of All the Gods', likely composed around 1820) and the Telugu *Cennapurivilasamu* ('Sport in the City of Chennai,' composed by Narasimha Sastri in 1863) describe private gatherings in homes that cemented social relations among high-ranking men.[9] In the *Sarvadevavilasa*, the *dubash*es of Kovur and Manali, merchants, and non-Brahmin temple administrators (*dharmakartas*), are imaged as regal patrons of learning and the arts, creating the illusion that they were free from any superior authority.[10] They hosted lavish assemblies known as *sadas*, both inside and outside temple contexts, and on festivals such as Navaratri, these soirees revolved around the presentation of concerts of music and dance. In the *Sarvadevavilasa*, many of these men are depicted with their courtesan-mistresses who are described as famous singers and dancers of the time, and are referred to as *ganikas* and *dasis*. Thus we have the names of Narayani of Kumbhakonam, Mangai of Thanjavur, and Minaksi of Salem.[11] The last of these figures was a very prominent courtesan of Madras who paid for the Brahmin vocalist, Patnam

Subrahmanya Ayyar (1845–1902) to move to the city from Tiruvaiyaru in Thanjavur district, so that he could teach her daughters vocal music. He stayed in the city for 12 years in the outhouse of Salem Minakshi, who paid him Rs 100 a month. It is here that he composed a large number of javalis that he taught to his devadasi students.

Representations of salon performances in Madras city are also found in other literary sources. The popularization of print culture in the Presidency in the middle of the nineteenth century enables the circulation of Tamil, Telugu, and English poetic literature on dancing women between c. 1850 and 1950.[12] All of the works are written by men, and all describe private performances as the primary sites for performances of dance. The texts inevitably vilify the devadasis, presenting them as money-hungry gold-diggers and diseased prostitutes. Texts such as the Telugu *Ganikagunapravartana Taravali* ('Poem on the Transformation of the Courtesan's Nature'), written by Racavetikavi, a resident of Tiruttani, in 1864, talks about the cunning nature of the dasis who ensnare 'innocent' men into their traps of sexual pleasure, greed, and disease. It juxtaposes graphic descriptions of sexual intercourse with depictions of the pain of venereal disease that has affected the male character. No doubt, there is a titillating dimension to this literature meant for its elite male consumers. Another text is *Varakanta*, subtitled in English as 'The Nautch Girl', (Fig. 17) a Telugu novel by Raja M. Bhujanga Rau Bahadur, Zamindar of Eluru, published in the year 1904. Bhujanga Rau was a scholar of Telugu literature, and in 1928 co-authored an English work called *A History of Telugu Literature* with P. Chenchiah. *Varakanta* is a complex narrative that focuses on a professional dancing woman named Kanakangi and her relationship with a married man named Kesava Rao. Kanakangi and her mother Papa con Kesava Rao into giving up all his money, and eventually take him to court, arguing that even his house should rightfully belong to them. They win the case, since *vesyas* are dharmically entitled to support from their patrons. A broken man, Kesava Rao seeks solace in his virtuous wife and friends, and ultimately is consoled by them. The text contains a lengthy section entitled 'The Commencement of the Mejuvani (dance performance)' that runs for two pages. In it we see that the author is clearly conversant with many of the technical dimensions of courtesan performance, but he ultimately foreshadows the tragic end of the narrative with a recurrent moralizing discourse on the dangers of associating with *sanis* or courtesans.

Much later, we see a Tamil text written in the same attitude, *Dasikal Tankappattu*, or 'Songs about the Dasis who Left Madras and Ran Away

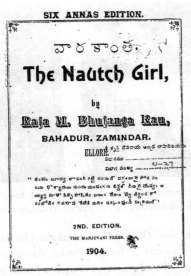

FIG. 17 The cover of *Varakanta: The Nautch Girl* by M. Bhujanga Rau (1904).
This Telugu novel contains long and detailed descriptions of mejuvani
performed by Telugu-speaking courtesans

to the Villages' by K. Kurucamitas. Published in Kumbhakonam in 1943, the work is meant to be sung 'in the Hindustani tune' (*intustan mettu*), and also speaks of the 'vesya whores' (*veci-muntaikal*) who 'pollute' Madras city, and out of fear of being persecuted under the new Devadasi Abolition Bill of 1929 are 'running back' to their villages in the Kaveri delta. The writing style and content is continuous with the *Ganikagunapravartana Taravali*. The focus is on the intensity of the sexual experiences shared by the dasis and their lovers, but the 'innocent young men' are fleeced by the dasis, wander about Madras like emasculated beggars, and ultimately contract venereal disease. A lot can be said about these kinds of literary works, particularly about their relationship to the emergence of nationalist masculinity, but for now, it is important for us to note that these texts are *not* about the idealized 'devadasi temple-woman' retrieved by historians, but rather about the courtesans—non-dedicated professional dancing women. It is also important that the stereotypes embedded in this kind of literature fuel the conscious exclusion of the history of salon performances from the writings of nationalist historians of dance. And it is precisely *this* omission that has disabled the historical contextualization of javalis.

Many prominent devadasis and nattuvanars from Thanjavur moved to Madras after the annexation of Thanjavur to the British in

FIG. 18   Vina Dhanammal with her daughter Lakshmiratnam, 1918, and Dharmapuri Subbbaraya Ayyar. Photos courtesy the late T. Sankaran

1856. Among them was Thanjavur Kamakshi (1810–90), great-great grandmother of the famous T. Balasaraswati. Around 1857, Kamakshi moved to Madras from Thanjavur, and bought a house on Nattu Pillaiyar Koyil Street in Georgetown. She supplemented her income as a dancer by giving private recitals of *Tiruppukal* hymns at the family shrine in the home of a prominent merchant named Rangoon Krishnaswami Mudaliar every week (B.M. Sundaram, personal communication; Menon 1999: 56). Vina Dhanammal (1867–1939), Kamakshi's granddaughter, met Dharmapuri Subbaraya Ayyar (Fig. 18), a clerk in the Taluk office at Hosur while she was singing at a festival in Tiruvottriyur just outside Madras (Sankaran 1982: 24). The two shared an intimate relationship, and it was for her and her family that Subbaraya Ayyar, who was also an accomplished musician, composed over 30 javalis. In a couple of these javalis, we even find anecdotal references to their relationship.[13] In some senses, this exemplifies the social dynamics that characterize the creation of most javalis—composed by upper-caste men, performed by courtesans, and usually symptomatic of an intimate relationship between the two.

This tradition of salon-based performance was also very common in the Telugu-speaking parts of the Madras Presidency from the late eighteenth century onward. Troupes of courtesan performers who were known as *bhogamvallu* were contracted to perform in the homes of Brahmin and non-Brahmin elites, and would receive obligatory fees and gifts called *osagulu* for their performances. In Telugu these salon performances were called *mejuvani* or *mezuvani*, from the Urdu word *mezban* or *mezman*, meaning 'landlord, master of the house, host of a feast, a man who entertains guests.' But in fact the repertoire they performed was continuous with the repertoire of their Tamil-speaking counterparts. For example, they performed compositions dedicated to the Thanjavur kings, Serfoji and Sivaji, and also javalis composed by Patnam Subrahmanya Ayyar of Madras, whom we have already discussed.[14]

Socially speaking, courtesans in South India were incorporated into a complex dynamic of simultaneous privilege and constraint. As Regula Qureshi notes in her work on tawa'ifs in Lucknow, 'it is the dancer's unencumbered identity as a woman [in the salon context] that enabled the courtesan to produce a sensual gendered cultural experience for her male patrons in return for the rewards they offer.' (Qureshi 2006: 322). In both the Tamil and Telugu-speaking parts of South India, devadasi-courtesans were usually the mistresses upper-caste patrons. On the one hand, they possessed a degree of agency, in that they were not bound by the norms of patrifocal kinship. They often lived in matrifocal and quasi-matrilineal communities and had access to literacy at moments in history when most South Indian women did not. But like 'respectable' family women, as the 'second wives' of South Indian elites, they too were implicated in a larger world of servitude that usually focused on the fulfillment of male desires.

Literally embodying the aestheticized ideal of the nayika or heroine of the padams and javalis, the South Indian dancing woman relied on artful self-representation in the salon context. The bulk of Telugu javali texts are written from the perspective of the nayika, and it is not surprising that there is a certain self-consciousness among courtesans today when they talk about these texts. Kotipalli Hymavathi, a 59 year-old woman from a bhogam community in the village of Muramanda in coastal Andhra told me 'Javalis are my favourite songs. I like how the woman talks to the nayaka in these songs. She can tell him what she really thinks, and there's nothing wrong with that (emi tappu ledu)!'

Indeed, the themes of javalis are sometimes bolder than those of the Telugu padam. In one very popular javali from coastal Andhra composed by Neti Subbarayudu Sastri (c. 1880–1950), the heroine admonishes Krsna for approaching her on the days of her menstrual period. She says 'you made the rules of purity and pollution, and now you want to break them? No way! You'll just have to wait.'[15] Javalis also commonly deploy rhetorical strategies familiar from other bhakti contexts, such as those of ninda-stuti (or 'complaint-praise'), and of course the use of sexual metaphors. But when we watch a performance of javalis by courtesans, these ideas clearly recede

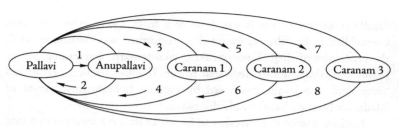

FIG. 19   Movement through the text of a javali,
after Matthew Allen (1992: 288)

to the background. The javali is, like the *thumri* of the North Indian *baiji*, or the *lavani* of Maharashtrian *kalavant*, a dance genre whose primary function is to entertain. The aesthetics of the genre—as an erotic composition meant specifically to entertain urban audiences—drew from the standard tropes that already existed in the texts for courtesan performance. As with Telugu and Tamil padams, the primary actors in javali poetry are the heroine (nayika), the hero (*nayaka*), and the heroine's confidante (*sakhi*). As Matthew Allen notes in his discussion of Tamil padams, courtesan poetry employs both direct and indirect rhetorical stances, with the nayika or heroine either directly addressing the hero, or speaking to him through her confidante (Allen 1992: 337–9).

The movement through the poetry of a javali, like that of a padam, is cyclical. The performance of padams and javalis as music for dance is itself a lyrical act. The artist renders the text through a movement that returns to a central theme encapsulated in the refrain or *pallavi*. The anupallavi and multiple caranams have the pallavi as their point of reference. Poems meant for performance by devadasi-courtesans are rarely linear 'storytelling,' but rather cyclical, lyrical texts that suggest emotive landscapes and invoke fleeting visions of erotic and social situations. The cyclical nature of this rendition also allows javalis to invoke memory and oscillate between past and present (Fig. 19).

The javali that follows was composed for the family of Vina Dhanammal in Madras by Dharmapuri Subbaraya Ayyar in the raga Khamas. The heroine's confidante speaks to the hero, asking him to reunite with the heroine who longs to make love to him:

Pallavi
narimani nikainadira jaracora ma   Crafty lover!
                                          This matchless woman is the one
                                          for you.

Anupallavi
dhira vinara sri dharmapuradhipa
ma cakkani

Listen,
Sweet Hero of Dharmapuri
She's the one

Caranam 1
boti nercina ratipatalu saiyatale
vadhutiyu sarisatila patiyana
kadata ma

She has learnt her erotic lessons.
No woman can outplay her!
She's the one

Caranam 2
marubalkerugani manini gadara
kamini
taradhipa ni bhavakadanare
sarasaku

She'll never say no to you,
moon-faced one,
she knows all your lovemaking
moods
She's the one

Caranam 3
maraviruni virisaramula korvadika
rara saragunanu cekora marukeliki
ma

She can't suffer Kama's arrows
anymore—
come play his games with her
She's the one

In her attempts to entice the hero, the confidante extols the heroine's skills in lovemaking, and these kinds of poetic passages traditionally provide courtesans ample scope for depicting various kinds of sexual union through elaborate metaphors and complex gestural vocabulary. The Telugu-speaking courtesans of the Godavari river delta deployed *rati*—*mudras*—a set of over fifty different hand gestures that depicted the positions (*bandhalu*) of lovemaking—in their performances of javalis (Fig. 20). They also performed another technique known as *nakha-sikha varnanam*, 'praise [of a woman's body] from the toenails to the crown of the head.' Here, the various parts of a woman's body are compared to images found in the natural world, largely in keeping with lyrical conventions used by Telugu and Sanskrit poets. Variation and improvisation are at the heart of courtesan interpretations of songs like padams and javalis; therefore the texts themselves are often open-ended to allow for flexibility in their interpretation through abhinaya. In addition to the complex improvisations in abhinaya, javalis also provided an occasion for the display of improvised patterns of abstract movement for the body (*adavu* or *adugulu*) among Telugu-speaking courtesans. At the conclusion of the last line of the javali, the musicians improvise on the raga and abstract

FIG. 20 Maddula Janakamma (b. 1932) demonstrates the use of *rati-mudra*s in the rendering of compositions like padams and javalis. Manepalli village, East Godavari district, Andhra Pradesh, 2002. Photograph by author

dance movements are performed to this musical sequence. The clusters of movement end with a tripartite cadence called *muktayi*. This technique, which almost always follows the rendition of javalis by Telugu-speaking courtesans, is called *gaptu-varusa*, a 'string of dance movements,' and was an indispensable technique in the performance of javalis in the Godavari delta region.

Another new performance opportunity is presented to professional dancing women in the first decades of the twentieth century, namely that of gramophone recordings. As Stephen Hughes (2002: 450–1) has noted, recording companies promoted these recordings by emphasizing the 'respectability' of the listening experience—that is, enjoying devadasi music without any personal contact with performer herself. Printed indexes to gramophone recordings with titles like 'Gramophone Kirtanamrtam,' contain the texts of several javalis sung by devadasis such as Tiruchendur Shanmukha Vadivu, Tiruvidaimarudur Bhavani, Coimbatore Thayi, and Salem Godavari, all of whom produced top-selling records for company labels such as HMV in the first two decades of the twentieth century (Hughes 2002, 2007; Weidman 2006).[16]

The first women to appear on gramophone recordings made in India were courtesans from Calcutta—Soshi Mukhi, Fani Bala, Saila Bai, and Gauhar Jan (Kinnear 1994). Gauhar Jan, born to Jewish-Armenian parents as Angelina Yeoward, produced some of the most famous recordings of all.[17] In 1910, Gauhar Jan came to Madras for a performance at the Victoria Public Hall, organized by C. Gopala Chetty, a wealthy textile merchant and music connoisseur.[18] By this time, Gauhar Jan was a celebrity, with hundreds of her songs circulating across India from 1903 onward. In Madras, Gauhar Jan was hosted by a devadasi named Salem Godavari. Vina Dhanammal organized a catered dinner in honour of Gauhar Jan, and taught her a Telugu *kirtana* by Tyagaraja which Gauhar Jan recorded a year later. By 1912, the texts of Gauhan Jan's recordings of Hindi songs were already circulating in Tamil print, for example in our *Gandharvakalpavalli*, where they are found under the heading 'Songs by Gauhar Jan of Calcutta' (*kalkatta kohar jan pattukal*), but still under the meta-genre of Parsi theatre songs.[19]

Just as devadasis were employed by gramophone companies, they were also in high demand in early Indian cinema. Prominent early film producers and directors such as Lakshmana Chettiyar and K. Subrahmanyam recruited devadasis to act in their films, some of whom, like M.S. Subbulakshmi, gained iconic status largely because they *left* cinema to pursue more respectable professions early in their career. Others, such as S.P.L Dhanalakshmi, daughter of a devadasi named Kuchalambal of Thanjavur, remained stigmatized as women suitable only for cinema, and failed when they attempted to become gramophone artists or concert musicians.

In the context of cinema, we see how the javali indexes a major cultural transition—from the intimate salons of Madras elites to the artefacts of mass culture. The journey of one javali as it travels from the traditional community of performers through the fieldnotes of an Orientalist musicologist into a Telugu film, foregrounds the javali genre's distinctively modern life. The javali 'amtalone tellavare' has been attributed to Dharmapuri Subbaraya Ayyar, but this is open to debate. It describes a married woman after a night of illicit lovemaking. She wakes in the bed of Krishna who is 'full of desire,' (*makkuvato gopaludu*) and sings: 'In the meanwhile, dawn has come. Ayyo! What can I do?' This composition makes an early appearance in a text by Captain C.P. Day, who wrote his famous work the *Music and Musical Instruments of Southern India and the Deccan* in 1891. This work provides the javali in Western staff notation and indicates that it is in the Sankarabharanam raga, and *rupaka tala*.

FIG. 21   The javali 'amtalone tellavare' from C.P. Day's *Music and Musical Instruments of Southern India and the Deccan* (1891)

Captain Day also notes that this 'perhaps the most popular' of 'javadi airs' danced by the nautch girls of the Madras Presidency (Fig. 21).

Oddly, the same song also appears as one of the javalis composed by Dharmapuri Subbaraya Ayyar in a text called *Tarumapuri Cupparayar Javali* (1896) which was published during the composer's own lifetime. Here we see it in the raga Behag (Fig. 22). It is highly improbable that Dharmapuri Subbaraya Ayyar composed this song, since it does not contain the characteristic 'signature words' (*mukuta* or mudra) used by Subbaraya Ayyar, but instead contains the obscure signature 'simhabhupala'.

FIG. 22   The cover of *Tarumapuri Cupparayar Javali* (1896), an anthology of javalis attributed to Dharmapuri Subbaraya Ayyar published during his own lifetime

The next appearance of this javali is in the Telugu film *Muddu Bidda* ('Darling Child') directed by K.B. Tilak in the year 1956 (Fig. 23).[20] In this film, one of the young male protagonists is chastised for watching a performance of dance by the courtesans or bhogamvallu. But the scene that depicts the performance by the *bhogamelam* seems to celebrate the culture of courtesan dance, leaving the viewer confounded by a spectacle that animates the simultaneous desirability and vilification of the courtesan and her art, an anxiety that is so much a part of reform discourse in this period, which is largely engineered by *smarta* Brahmins, Chettiyars, Mudaliyars, and other elite men. The release of this film also happens to coincide with another intervention—the passing of the Andhra Pradesh State Government's amendment to the Madras Anti-Devadasi Act, on August 14th, 1956. The original Madras Devadasi (Prevention of Dedication) Act of 1947 only banned the temple dedication rituals and temple-oriented performances by devadasis, and so in most parts of South India, especially coastal Andhra, salon performances by courtesan troupes continued well into the 1950s. This 1956 amendment criminalized performances by women from hereditary courtesan communities at marriages and other private social events. This film, in many ways, represents the last official nod to the culture of the salon in Telugu-speaking South India. The poignancy of the film sequence is remarkable—the women performing in the troupe are likely bhogamvallu from the region around the town of Manepalli in East Godavari district, whose names do not appear in the credits. The distinctive feature of javali rendition in that region—the *gaptu-varusa* or improvised dance sequence at the end—undeniably marks the technical and aesthetic continuity of javali rendition in the courtesan community. It is a reminder of the precarious fate of traditional javali performance. The social reform movement directed toward devadasis

FIG. 23   Stills from the Telugu film *Muddu Bidda* (1956) depicting a performance of the javali 'amtalone tellavare'. Performers unknown

in this period, as I have argued elsewhere, was not so much directed at dancing in temples, but toward dance performed at private events, or in colonial parlance, the South Indian *nautch*. For the women who were the traditional keepers of these cultural practices, the javali oddly presented opportunity in the new world of colonial modernity, but also would come to be seen as morally questionable and would eventually play a role in the criminalization of their lifestyles.

As indices of the transformations of culture—traversing zamindari courts, print materials, salons, gramophone recordings, and films—javalis live complex and multivalent lives. As we have seen in our examples, javalis also carry with them traces of bhakti poetics, both in style and content. But our discussions of the javalis' complex colonial history have demonstrated that they can neither be construed as 'degenerate' excesses of poetry, nor can we apologize for them by attempting link them to an unbroken bhakti past—indeed the story of the javali foregrounds the historical fissures and uneven movements that underwrite the project of modernity in South India. The various historical, aesthetic, and even affective registers of javalis can only be understood in the context of a hybrid, cosmopolitan Madras Presidency, in which the new flows of culture involved Telugu poetics, European languages and performance idioms, and an unstable political and sexual economy. I would argue that it is the fundamental linguistic, social, and performative hybridity of devadasi dance in the nineteenth and early twentieth centuries that enables the development of the javali, and allows it to move so quickly and effortlessly though the sites of urban cultural practice and innovation we have discussed. Lodged as they were in the *in-between* spaces of colonial modernity and the emergent nationalist reinvention of South India's arts in the 1930s, it is easy to imagine how javalis, like devadasis themselves, have slipped through the cracks of historicization and historiography.

NOTES

1. This was for a volume of javalis edited by T. Brinda (1912–96), granddaughter of Vina Dhanammal (1867–1939), one of the most prominent courtesans in colonial Madras. The volume, dedicated to the memory of Dhanammal, consists of 30 javalis with *svara* notation, many of which were composed during Dhanammal's lifetime. See Brinda (1960).

2. Studies on the javali as a genre are few and far between. Excepting the studies by Arudra (1986a; 1986b), Chennakeshaviah (1974), Sastri (1974), Suryanarayana Rao (1964) and a few others, most writing on javalis consists of short introductions to compilations of javalis meant for performers (see for example Brinda 1960; Kittappa 1979; Kuppuswamy and Hariharan 1996; and Parthasarathi and Parthasarathi 1980). The essays by Arudra (1986a; 1986b)

and also T. Sankaran (1982a; 1982b) contain some invaluable biographical information about javali composers.

3. Mss. KB 240/2, Kannada Adhyayana Samsthe (Institute of Kannada Studies), Mysore. For more on Kannada javalis and the Mysore court, see Sastri (1974) and Pranesh (2003). Javalis continue to be popular in the Kannada-speaking regions until the middle of the twentieth century. Poets such as Ullahalli Ramanna (1854–1918) were among the most famous javalikartas from this region (Chennakeshavaiah 1974; Sastri 1974). To be sure, hundreds of javalis exist in Kannada, and these were performed by courtesans at the Mysore court and at privately sponsored performances inside homes. In the recent past, late nineteenth and early twentieth-century courtesans such as Mugur Jejamma, K. Venkatalakshamma, Mysore Sundaramma, and Nanjangud Nagaratnamma performed javalis on a regular basis in and around Mysore and Bengaluru.

4. This is an oral tradition that has been maintained by the descendants of the Thanjavur Quartet. They claim that a single javali, 'itu sahasamulu elara' in Saindhavi raga is the earliest song in this genre, and was composed at the Travancore court. There are no records to substantiate this claim, although we do know that Vativelu did indeed teach dance at the Travancore court, and in the year 1834, Maharaja Svati Tirunal gifted him with an ivory violin and an ivory box full of jewels. Both of these artifacts are in the possession of the descendants of the Quartet who live in Thanjavur and Chennai.

5. Tacchur Singaracharyulu (1834–1892) and his brother Chinna Singaracharyulu, wrote seven treatises on music that were commissioned by Nalvadi Krishnaraja Utaiyar. These included *Gayakaparijatam* (1882); *Gayakalocana* (1884); *Sangita Kalanidhi* (1889); *Gayaka Siddhanjanam* (Part I, 1890; Part II, 1905); *Ganendu Sekharam* (1912), and *Svaramanjari* (1914). All were published in Madras. Singaracaryulu also organized annual 'salon style' concerts on the festival of Ramanavami near his house in Georgetown.

6. The *Gandharvakalpavalli* is subtitled in English as 'A Self-Instructor in Music'. Many such 'teach yourself' books on music and dance were composed in the early twentieth century. Another important example related to dance is *Abhinaya Svayambodhini* ('Teach Yourself Abhinaya', 1915) by Devulapalli Viraraghavamurti Sastri. In the preface to this work, the author talks about the instrumentality of the book:'To make it easy for *vesya stris* and other women who wish to learn this art, I have written this text in Telugu, so they need not look elsewhere. One can [now] learn the art with the help of this book.' This text has also been discussed in Krishnan (2008).

7. Agha Mohammad Shah (1879–1935), later known as Agha Hashr Kashmiri, wrote an Urdu adaptation of *King Lear* for Parsi theatre entitled *Safed Khun* ('White Blood', 1906). This combined Urdu prose and poetry with Hindustani music. For details see Kapur (2006). Also see Somnath Gupt, 2005, *The Parsi Theatre: Its Origins and Development*, translated and edited by Kathryn Hansen.

8. Karur Sivaramayya (c. 1798–1820) also composed the javali 'O My Lovely Lalana' (Kharaharapriya raga) in a mix of English and Telugu which also appears in the *Gandharvakalpavalli*. Sivaramayya lived most of his life in Karur, near

Trichy. One of his descendants was the famous violinist Papa Venkataramayya (1901–72).

9. Here, for example, is an excerpt from the 'Vesya Prakaranam' chapter of the *Cennapurivilasamu* that describes the courtesans' quarters in Madras:

There are many girls with pleasant eyes and full breasts who have been taught rhythms like *jhampa-tala* [a 10-beat rhythm cycle] by dance-masters (*natya bharatacaryas*). In Suryam Pasyalpuri there are plenty of vesyas on the *nodakal vidhi*. They have beautiful teeth, a *kumkuma* mark on their foreheads, and their faces shine bright as blue lilies. As they perform the beautiful *lasya* dance, their graceful gait appears like that of swans. Like lotuses swaying from side to side, they enact a play (*lila*) of *abhinaya*.

They are born of the secret desire of Rati and Kama. In that *nodakal vidhi*, live the women who are victorious over Kama himself (*smara jaya strilu*). They exhibit beautiful bodily movements and alluring qualities. They do not appear to be worried about anything. Their attractive features hunt down young men, and they wait, keeping their doors open. Such vesyas are on that street. The sweet ambrosia of their music (*ganamrta*) showers down, like flowers falling from the branches of a beautiful tree. Those who witness their performances are knowledgeable in the art of lasya. This assembly of connoisseurs adds lustre to the art of the vesyas. On this street, live vesyas who are like the mantric powers of illusion wielded by Kama.

10. The Mutaliyar dubash family of Manali, just outside Madras, maintained connections with the Thanjavur court. For more on these connections see Neild (1977); for details on company dubashes and culture in colonial Madras, see Mukund (2005), Neild-Basu (1984), and Waghorne (2004).

11. *Sarvadevavilasa*, 5.21–3.

12. In a forthcoming work, I discuss these texts in greater detail. Over and above the few works I have mentioned in this essay, a number of others in Tamil also exist. A very early example, in the form of a Tamil drama titled *Tevataci* ('Devadasi') was composed in the early nineteenth century by a poet named Paracurama Kavirayar, and then translated in 1868 into French by Louis Jacolliot under the title *La Devadassi, Bayadere* (Zvelebil 1998). Other literary works about devadasi-courtesans in Madras include *Mattappucuntaram allatu Tacikalin Ceykai* ('The Beauty of Fireworks, or the Deeds of the Dasis', 1916) by Kirusnacami Ayyar, *Tanapalan allatu Tacikalin Mayavancaka Culccikal.* ('Dhanapalan, or the Devious Crimes of the Dasis', 1931) by Kovintacami Pillai, and the play *Tacikalum Tacikantarkalum* ('Dasis and the Dasis' Lovers', 1947) by E. Cokkalinkam Pillai. This type of writing also includes works in English, such as *The Days of a Dancing Girl, or, The Inner Life of India Unveiled: A Book of Revelations in the Life of the Rich and Religious in India as seen through the Private Life of an Indian Prostitute* by R. Balasundara Mudali (1913) and the essay *Pen-Pictures of the Dancing Girl*, by M.S. Mani in 1926. Many of these works also resonated deeply with Victorian writing in English on concubines and professional performing artists in colonial India. For an example of such writing see Penny (1898); for an analysis see Paxton (1999).

13. For example, in the javali in Paras raga, 'smara sundaranguni sari evvare', the heroine notes that as she plays her vina, her lover encourages her by exclaiming

'*sabash* (bravo)!' T. Sankaran, a descendant of Dhanammal, in a biographical essay on Subbaraya Ayyar notes that another javali in Jhanjhuti raga, 'prana sakhuditu' also refers to the relationship between Ayyar and Dhanammal. He writes: 'Some time before his death, he had left Madras, promising Dhanammal that he would return soon. But circumstances beyond his control detained him at Dharmapuri… When he came back, on learning that Dhanammal was going through hard times, instead of the usual paltry monetary help, he gifted to her this priceless javali.' (Sankaran 1982: 25)

14. Having noted the continuities between dance and aesthetics throughout the colonial Madras Presidency, it is significant that a number of javalis were composed in the late nineteenth and early twentieth centuries exclusively for professional dancing women in the coastal Andhra region. These include the javalis of Neti Subbarayudu Sastri. Another example of a localized javali tradition comes from the village of Ballipadu in the West Godavari district, where courtesans who had connections with the festival worship of Krsna at the Madanagopalasvami temple sang a number of javalis composed for this purpose. During my fieldwork with Saride Anusuya (1910–2005) who was dedicated to this temple, I recorded one such javali, 'idi nyayama sami' in Jhanjhuti (Cencurutti) raga, which made specific reference to the temple at Ballipadu, and it was clearly used in this highly localized context.

15. This is the javali in Kalyani raga 'ceragu mase emi setura' by Neti Subbraya Sastri. I have commented on this javali in detail elsewhere (Soneji 2008).

16. The story of Coimbatore Thayi is particularly interesting. Her lineage can be traced to a devadasi named Visalakshi in the village of Avinasi in the Kongu region. Visalakshi had two daughters, Shanmukattammal and Venkammal, both of whom settled in Coimbatore city. In 1872, Venkatammal gave birth to a daughter whom she named Palanikunjaram, nicknamed 'Thayi'. She had her formal debut in dance (*arankerram*) at the age of eleven, and continued to perform dance till she was nineteen, when she shifted her focus to vocal music performances. She purchased a house on Nattu Pillaiyar Koyil Street in Georgetown, Madras, and moved there around 1892. In Madras, she received further training in music from Tiruvottriyur Tyagayyar (1845–1917) and Dharmapuri Subbaraya Ayyar. Coimbatore Thayi was also the inspiration for a somewhat unique European experiment in music. Maurice Delage (1879–1961), an amateur French composer, came to India in 1912. Delage wanted to access music from all over the country, and so began to purchase gramophone records, including those produced in Madras (Pasler 2000: 102). As Jann Pasler has observed, Delage's interest in India was rooted in his 'own essentially Western preoccupations,' namely his obsession with modernist aesthetics. Delage was attracted to the techniques of Indian music largely with an eye to mine them for a 'future-oriented' modernism in European music (ibid.: 102). His stay in India resulted in two major musical works, *Quatre poèmes hindous* ('Four Hindu Poems', 1912–13), inspired largely by North Indian music, and *Ragamalika* ('Garland of Ragas', 1912–22), a virtual re-creation of a single recording by Coimbatore Thayi. *Ragamalika* is based on Thayi's recording of Tamil devotional hymns called *Arutpa* or *Tiruvarutpa* by the saint Iramalinka Atikalar (1823–1874). Thayi died on 17 August 1917.

17. The first women to appear on gramophone recordings made in India were courtesans from Calcutta—Soshi Mukhi, Fani Bala, Saila Bai and Gauhar Jan (1873–1930). Born to Jewish-Armenian parents as Angelina Yeoward, Gauhar Jan and her mother converted to Islam in 1881, and changed their names to Gauhar Jan and Badi Malka Jan respectively. Both mother and daughter were trained in music and dance, and eventually became renowned courtesan-artists. Badi Malka Jan received the patronage of Wajid Ali Shah (1822–1887) who was exiled from Awadh to Matiaburj outside Calcutta following the annexation of Awadh to the British in 1856. At Wajid Ali's relocated court, Gauhar Jan learnt Kathak dance under Bindadin Maharaj (1830–1918), and studied music with respected teachers such as Kale Khan of Patiala.

18. This was not Gauhar Jan's only visit to South India. Toward the end of her life, in the year 1928, Gauhar Jan was invited to the Mysore court of Nalvadi Krishnaraja Utaiyar (r. 1902–40). She was appointed as a palace musician, and died of pneumonia at the Krishnarajendra Hospital in 1930 at the age of fifty-seven.

19. Three of Gauhar Jan's songs are listed with South Indian svara (solfa) notation in both the Tamil and Telugu editions of P.S. Ramulu Chetti's *Gandharvakalpavalli* (1912).

20. The music for this film was by Pendyala Nageshwara Rao (1924–1984), and the lyrics were by the poet and historian Arudra (1925–1998), who also likely wrote two of the caranams in this version of 'amtalone tellavare.' In the film, the javali was sung by playback singer P. Susheela (b. 1935).

REFERENCES

Arudra, 1986a, 'Javalis: Jewels of the Dance Repertoire', *Sruti* 23–23S, pp. 43–6.
———, 1986b, 'Javalis: Jewels of the Dance Repertoire II: Salvaging After the Decline and Fall', *Sruti*, 25, pp. 33–6.
Bhujanga Rau, Raja M., 1904, *Varakanta: The Nautch Girl* (2nd edition), Ellore: The Manjuvani Press.
Balasundara Mudali, R., 1913, *The Days of a Dancing Girl, or, The Inner Life of India Unveiled: A Book of Revelations in the Life of the Rich and Religious in India as seen through the Private Life of an Indian Prostitute*, Sowcarpet, Madras: Coronation Book Depot.
Brinda, T., 1960, *Javalis of Patnam Subrahmanya Iyer, Tiruppanandal Pattabhiramayya, Dharmapuri Subbarayar, Tirupathi Narayanaswami and Others*, Madras: The Music Academy.
Canmuka Mutaliyar, 1896, *Tarumapuri Cupparayar Javali*, Madras: Viveka Vilakka Accukkutam.
Chennakeshavaiah, N., 1974, 'Javalis in Kannada: Ramanna, A Kannada Javali Composer', *Journal of the Madras Music Academy* XLV, pp. 155–8.
Chetti, P.S. Ramulu, 1912, *Gandharvakalpavalli, being a Self-Instructor in Music*, Madras: The India Printing Works.
Day, Charles P., 1891, *Music and Musical Instruments of Southern India and the Deccan*, London and New York: Novello, Ewer.

Farrell, Gerry, 1998, 'The Early Days of the Gramophone Industry in India: Historical, Social, and Musical Perspectives', in Andrew Leyshon et al. (eds), *The Place of Music*, New York: Guilford Press.

Gupt, Somnath, 2005, *The Parsi Theatre: Its Origins and Development*, translated and edited by Kathryn Hansen, Calcutta: Seagull Books.

Hughes, Stephen P., 2007, 'Music in the Age of Mechanical Reproduction: Drama, Gramophone, and the Beginnings of Tamil Cinema', *Journal of Asian Studies*, 66 (1), pp. 3–34.

———, 2002, 'The "Music Boom" in Tamil South India: Gramophone, Radio and the Making of Mass Culture', *Historical Journal of Film, Radio and Television*, 22 (4), pp. 445–73.

Kapur, Anuradha, 2006, 'Love in the Time of Parsi Theatre', in Francesca Orsini (ed.), *Love in South Asia: A Cultural History*, Cambridge: Cambridge University Press.

Kinnear, Michael S., 1994, *The Gramophone Company's First Indian Recordings, 1899–1908*, Bombay: Popular Prakashan.

Kirusnacami Ayyar, Ma., 1916, *Mattappucuntaram allatu Tacikalin Ceykai*, Kumpakonam: Amirtavarsani Accukkutam.

Kittappa, K.P., 1979, *Javalis of Sri Chinniah*, Bangalore: Ponniah Natya Shala.

Kittel, Ferdinand, 1894, *A Kannada-English Dictionary*, Mangalore: Basel Mission Book and Tract Depository.

Kovintacami Pillai, Cu. Ku, 1931, *Tanapalan allatu Tacikalin Mayavancaka Culccikal*, Mataras: Kaurivilaca Puttakacalai.

Krishnan, Hari, 2008, 'Inscribing Practice: Reconfigurations and Textualizations of Devadasi Repertoire in Nineteenth and Early Twentieth Century South India', in Indira Viswanathan Peterson and Davesh Soneji (eds), *Performing Pasts: Reinventing the Arts in Modern South India*, Delhi: Oxford University Press.

Kuppuswamy, Gowri and M. Hariharan, 1996, *Javali*, Trivandrum: CBH Publications.

Kurucamitas, K., 1943, *Metracai Vittu Nattipurattukku Ottam Pititta Tacikal Tankappattu*, Kumpakonam: K. Kurucamitas.

Mani, M.S., 1926, *The Pen Pictures of the Dancing Girl (With a side-light on the Legal Profession)*, Salem: Srinivasa Printing Works.

Menon, Indira, 1999, *The Madras Quartet: Women in Karnatak Music*, Delhi: Roli Books.

Mukund, Kanakalatha, 2005, *The View from Below: Indigenous Society, Temples and the Early Colonial State in Tamilnadu, 1700–1835*, New Delhi: Orient Longman.

Narayana Rao, Velcheru and David Shulman, 2005, *God on the Hill: Temple Poems from Tirupati*, New York: Oxford University Press.

Neild, Susan Margaret, 1977, 'Madras: The Growth of a Colonial City, 1780–1840', PhD Dissertation, Department of History, University of Chicago.

Neild-Basu, Susan, 1984, 'The Dubashes of Madras', *Modern Asian Studies*, 18 (1), pp. 1–31.

Nrsimhasastri, Matukumalli Kanakadrisastri, 1864, *Cennapurivilasamu*, Cennapuri: Ma. Sundaresvara Nayani.

Pasler, Jann, 2000, 'Race, Orientalism, and Distinction in the Wake of the "Yellow Peril"' in Georgina Born and David Hesmondhalgh(eds), *Western Music and its Others: Difference, Representation, and Appropriation in Music*, Berkeley: University of California Press.

Parthasarathi, N.C. and Dvaraka Parthasarathi, 1980, *Javalilu: Svarasahitamu*, Hyderabad: Andhra Pradesh Sangeeta Nataka Akademi.

Paxton, Nancy L., 1999, *Writing under the Raj: Gender, Race, and Rape in the British Colonial Imagination, 1830–1947*, New Brunswick, NJ: Rutgers University Press.

Penny, Mrs Frank, 1898, *The Romance of a Nautch Girl: A Novel*, London: Swan Sonnenschein & Co. Ltd.

Pranesh, Meera Rajaram, 2003, *Musical Composers during Wodeyar Dynasty*, Bangalore: Vee Emm Publications.

Qureshi, Regula Burckhardt, 2006, 'Female Agency and Patrilineal Constraints: Situating Courtesans in the Twentieth-Century India', in Martha Feldman and Bonnie Gordon (eds), *The Courtesan's Arts: Cross-Cultural Perspectives*, New York: Oxford University Press.

Racavetikavi, 1864, *Ganikagunapravartana Taravali*, Cennapuri: Ma. Sundaresvara Nayani.

Raghavan, V., 1959, *Sarvadevavilasa* with Critical Introduction and Notes, Madras: The Adyar Library and Research Centre; first published in the *Adyar Library Bulletin* 21, No. 3 and 4 (December 1957).

Ramanujan, A.K., Velcheru Narayana Rao, and David Shulman, 1994, *When God is a Customer: Telugu Courtesan Songs by Ksetrayya and Others*, Berkeley: University of California Press.

Sankaran, T., 1970, 'A Javali and Swarajati of Sri Tirupati Narayanaswamy Naidu', *Journal of the Madras Music Academy*, XLI, pp. 238–41.

———, 1982a, 'Dharmapuri Subbarayar', in Gowry Kuppuswamy and M. Hariharan (eds), *Glimpses of Indian Music*, Delhi: Sundeep Prakashan.

———, 1982b, 'Pattabhiramayya', in Gowry Kuppuswamy and M. Hariharan (eds), *Glimpses of Indian Music*, Delhi: Sundeep Prakashan.

———, 1984, 'Kanchipuram Dhanakoti Ammal', *Sruti* 11 (September 1984), pp. 31–2.

———, 1986, 'Women Singers', *Kalakshetra Quarterly* VIII (1–2), pp. 58–65.

Sastri, Devulapalli Viraraghava, 1915, *Abhinaya Svayambodhini*, Kakinada: Sarasvati Mudraksara Sala.

Sastri, B.V.K., 1974, 'Kannada Javalis', *Journal of the Madras Music Academy* XLV, pp. 159–66.

Soneji, Davesh, 2008, 'Memory and the Recovery of Identity: Living Histories and the Kalavantulu of Coastal Andhra Pradesh', in Indira Viswanathan Peterson and Davesh Soneji (eds), *Performing Pasts: Reinventing the Arts in Modern South India*, Delhi: Oxford University Press.

Subramanian, Lakshmi, 2006, *From the Tanjore Court to the Madras Music Academy: A Social History of Music in South India*, Delhi: Oxford University Press.

Suryanarayana Rao, Y., 1964, 'Jhavali', *Journal of the Madras Music Academy* XXXV, pp. 224–7.

Waghorne, Joanne Punzo, 2004, *Diaspora of the Gods: Modern Hindu Temples in an Urban Middle Class*, New York: Oxford University Press.

Weidman, Amanda, 2006, *Singing the Classical, Voicing the Modern: The Postcolonial Politics of Music in South India*, Durham: Duke University Press.

Zvelebil, Kamil V., 1998, 'Paracurama Kavirayar's *Tevataci*', *Journal of the Institute of Asian Studies* (Madras), XV (2), pp. 1–14.

Anti-Nautch Revisited

S. Muthulakshmi Reddi

Why should the Devadasi Institution in the Hindu Temples be Abolished?

This council recommends to the Government to undertake legislation or if that for any reason be impracticable, to recommend to the central Government to under take legislation at a very early date to put a stop to the practice of dedicating young girls or young women to Hindu temples which has generally resulted in exposing them to an immoral life.

I beg to move this resolution which stands in my name in response to the wishes of all the women's associations in this Presidency who feel this practice of dedicating young girls or young women to temples for immoral purposes as a slur on Indian womanhood and a great wrong and injustice done to the innocent young of the country, and in response to the incessant demands of the enlightened section of the aggrieved communities themselves, whose rightly developed moral sense naturally revolts at the practice of such a notorious custom prevalent among the unenlightened of their community and who with their persuasive methods and educative propaganda work among those illiterate, are unable to suppress this vice without further legislation and above all in deference to my own personal conviction that in the cause of humanity and justice, we can no longer delay this piece of beneficial legislation, a reform by which we can rescue thousands of young innocent children from a life of immorality and vice, from life-long invalidism, suffering, disease and death resulting from infection with venereal disease.

THEIR ORIGIN

It is a well known fact that the Devadasis are recruited from various castes among the Hindus having different names in different districts and their strength is kept up by adoption from other Hindu communities, because when the old Devadasis become sterile, which they very often are by the nature of their profession, buy girls from other poor caste-Hindus and so every Hindu community at one time or other shares in the degradation and misery of such a life. I want the Hon. Members of this House to understand that these people are neither descended from heaven nor imported from foreign countries, but they belong to us, they are our own kith and kin. I am forced to make this statement because as you are all aware, of late there has been a quarrel in the press about their origin.

One more point I like to impress upon the attention of the Hindu public is that this practice, though prevalent only among certain sections of the Hindus in Southern India, but as it affects the morality, health and well being of the Hindu Society at large, loses its communal nature and becomes a question of national importance and interest.

THEIR HABITS AND CUSTOMS

Now the appellation 'dasi' as every one of us here knows, whatever the original meaning might have been, stands for a prostitute. None of us in the south who are too familiar with their customs can dispute that fact.

The most pathetic, the most regrettable and the most revolting nature of this custom is that the training for the immoral trade begins for these girls even from their childhood, that is at an age when they cannot think and act for themselves. As a certain good lady has so feelingly remarked 'it was a wax, a little tender, innocent child in the hands of a wicked power when the fashioning process began,' these innocent girls, both the adopted and the legitimate children of the dasis are taught music, dancing and all other fine accomplishments to make them attractive to vice and these accomplished girls well tutored in that art of evil trade are taken to the temples and made to undergo a form of nominal marriage with a dagger, with an idol etc., which ceremony prohibits them from lawful marriage afterwards and then gives them a license to promiscuity, but nowadays as the penal code prohibits girls of tender age below 18 years to be so dedicated, the parents or the guardians successfully evade the law by having the ceremony performed after their 18th year. You may rightly ask this question, that after the 18th year they are majors and as such are at liberty to choose the life before them, but I may impress upon the Hon. Members of this House they are not in a position to do so, because these victims are taught from their tender age to look upon this practice as their caste-duty or dharma and in their ignorance and superstition, imagine also that the Gods will be displeased or out of jealousy will visit them with some punishment if they do at all marry.

Such unhealthy and superstitious notions are constantly dinned into the minds of these girls during their very impressionable age, and no wonder then, even after these girls attain their maturity then of their own free will, choose a life of shame. What else do you expect from those young women, when even from their childhood are thus tutored and advised by word and deed both by their superstitious and orthodox relations.

THE INIQUITY OF THE PRACTICE

The most good-looking and the most intelligent children of a family in those communities are set a part for this purpose and are thus sacrificed to a most blind and degrading custom. Certainly we cannot boast of any culture or civilization if some of us in our ignorance of actual facts should try to minimize the evil by consoling ourselves that this obtains only in a small section of the Hindu community with whom no respectable member associates. I wish it were true. I wish that no member of our society associates with these women. Then there would never have been any necessity for me to move this resolution before this House, but alas it is otherwise. We know too well they are not allowed to remain as virgins for long. We recognize the evil and it has been also pointed out to us both by our friends and foes in time and out of time.

Still some of us who have both education and enlightenment, knowingly or unknowingly, tolerate a system by which the young and innocent children of those communities, who if left alone or removed to better environments, would become virtuous and loyal wives, affectionate mothers and useful citizens, are slowly introduced into an evil life which subjects them to very painful, very debilitating, disfiguring and contagious diseases in addition to all the horrors of a prostitute's life. At an age when they are helpless and innocent, these children are allowed to be exploited and initiated into all these unhealthy ideas which having a demoralizing tendency converts them into mental, moral and physical wrecks.

DEDICATION OF GIRLS TO TEMPLES AS COMPARED WITH THE STATE REGULATION OF VICE

This system of dedication that obtains in Southern India resemble in certain respects the 'State regulation of vice' that is tolerated in a few of the European countries, which system in my opinion is a much more humane method of tolerating vices. Even against that system, the noble British woman Josephine Butler, who is a pride to her country and an honour to her sex, had fought ceaselessly till that abominable practice had become eradicated in the year 1886 not only in Britain but in all the forward countries of the West. This custom of dedication that at present obtains in our temples and even outside, under the cloak of religion and under the guise of custom is a much more barbarous and a more iniquitous one, because by state regulation only adult women, who willingly and with the full knowledge of the life before them take to an immoral life, are made to register their names in the police register. Then they are segregated and subjected to medical inspection and treatment and then certified as to their fitness to carry on that evil trade. Mrs Josephine Butler, the first woman who had the moral courage to break open the conspiracy of silence on this subject and exposed the iniquity of that system, used these arguments that the state which ought to guard the morals of the individual and the society, by recognizing such evils gives a sanction to the practice of vice and thus encourages the immoral traffic in women.

As the result of her noble and valiant fight and agitation, state regulation, a system of tolerated brothels, was abolished in 1885 not only in Britain but also in her colonies. This humane legislation could not touch our temples. Most probably even in those days a few pillars of orthodoxy might have defended this heinous practice on the plea of custom, religion or tradition as some had come forward to defend even in 1922 when a similar measure was taken up by the Legislative Assembly stating that the abolition of such a practice is likely to wound the pious feelings of the people. The Government being foreign and on account of their avowed principle of religious neutrality could not take a forward step, nor were they interested in such a piece of legislation affecting the morals of different race.

That noble woman Josephine Butler, when pleading for the abolition of state regulation of vice, characterizes that practice as follows—

This system necessitates the greatest crime of which earth can witness the crime of blotting out the soul by depriving God's creatures of free will, choice and of responsibility and by reducing the human being to the condition of a passive, suffering minister to the basest passions.

When she thought it fit to decry in that soul-stirring appeal a system which subjected only adult prostitutes to the indignity and necessity of registration, medical inspection and segregation, how much more inhuman and barbarous is our practice, by which the young, innocent and helpless children are turned into sinners and criminals and then stigmatized and treated as outcastes.

Here are the impressions of a pure-hearted woman on the Devadasis and the treatment given to them:

So let us deal gently with those who least deserve our blame and reserve our condemnation for those responsible for the creation of the temple woman. Is it fair that the helpless child, who has never once been given the choice of any other life, should be held responsible afterwards for living the life to which alone she has been trained? Is it fair to call her by a name which belongs by right to one who is different, in that her life is self-chosen? No word can cut too keenly at the root of this iniquity; but let us deal gently with the mishandled flower. Let it be remembered that she is not responsible for what she is.

However that was not the original idea of the inventors of the Devadasi institution as the name 'dasi' itself signifies. The following from a speech of Dr Besant regarding the origin of the dancing class woman attached to the temples which exonerates our ancestors from any such evil motives is worthy of our earnest attention.

There was a band of pure virgin devotees attached to the ancient Hindu temples. They used to preach religion like any other religious teacher to the common people that resort to the temple for their daily worship. In those days they were held in high esteem and respect and were very well looked after. They would spend their time in doing religious service to the Gods and the devotees of the temple as the word 'dasi' itself signifies. They would follow the procession of Gods dressed in the simplest sanyasi garbs and singing pious hymns suitable to the occasion. This is the history and origin of the Devadasi class.

So there are authentic records to prove these dasi girls were pure virgins spending their time in religious study, meditation and devotional service in the temples akin to the Roman catholic nuns of the present day. Now-a-days we find to our great sorrow that all their accomplishments such as music and dance are being utilized in the majority of cases to promote their evil and immoral trade and to drag the imprudent and the unwary youth of the country into immorality and vice and hence the word 'dasi' has become one of reproach.

THE REMEDY

The agitation for the enaction of these good measures has been started even as early as 1868. (In this connection it is significant to note that about the same time the campaign against the state regulation of vice was started by that eminent English woman Josephine Butler in England and was carried to a successful termination in 1886). What was easy there has been rendered very difficult here because of its association with religion and the existence of caste in this country.

In 1906–07, we find the central government referring the matter to the local government when they had to sign the international convention for the suppression of immoral traffic in women and children. Even then our friend and benefactor Dr Gour did not keep quiet, and pressed this matter upon the attention of the central government.

In 1912 three bills to suppress this evil were brought by Manekji Dadabhoy, Mudholkar and Madge. Even though there were many supporters for the bill it was quietly dropped on the plea that there were no Hindu Homes to lodge these girls that are rescued, but the truth is, we find on a closer study, that the local government did not send a satisfactory reply. Even at that time in 1912 Pandit Mohan Malaviya, the so-called Pillar of Orthodoxy, to his credit it must be said, has strongly supported this measure in the following terms.

I hope that not a man in the country will be able to put forward one single text which will justify a thing which is so irreligious and sinful as the dedication of minor girls in a position where they must be compelled to lead a life of sin and shame. My Lord, I hope that all sound men will be united in the desire to support the Government in any legislation which shall secure that no girl shall be led, induced or compelled to take to a life of shame or placed in a position where they may be helplessly led to adopt it until she has attain to discretion; and so far as that is concerned, I hope and trust, that the measure will receive the support of all right-thinking men throughout the country.

Then in 1922 Dr Hari Singh Gour, the brave champion of woman's cause in this country, moved a resolution similar to mine in the Assembly. The speech he then made supplemented with facts and figures, accurately and vividly described the evil custom prevailing in the south in its true colours, his strong plea on behalf of those poor girls will do him credit for ever. Which speech I read to-day with a feeling of gratitude and intense admiration. Every word of Dr Gour's speech I am in a position to endorse. Still the Madras and Bombay representatives to the Assembly (I really felt sorry when I read their speech) had accused Dr Gour, the patriot and saint, of ignorance and even called him a non-Hindu missionary. This unholy attack on Dr Gour surely has showed us to a much greater disadvantage than even Miss Mayo's attack on India (vide page 2605 of the Assembly Proceedings, Vol. II, 1922).

During that discussion it was stated that the Penal Code enactment prohibits the dedication of girls below the age of 18 years and the religious tenets prohibit that practice about that age and so they who defended this infamous institution tried to impress upon the audience that there was not much need for any more legislation. I may inform the Hon. Members of this House that the above statement was not founded on facts because to my personal knowledge the law has been rendered ineffective by the parents or the guardians of the girls waiting till the completion of the 18th year and then dedicating them to the temples. Many girl has been brought to me for a certificate to say that the girl has attained 18. So the religious tenets which had enjoined dedication before the girl attains puberty had failed to arrest the practice. Therefore I like to impress upon the Government with all the emphasis that I could command that any amount of age limit will not do these people any good so long as the temple sanctions such a vicious practice, so long these communities, the Dharmagarthas and the general illiterate public imagine that Gods in the temples want these dasis for service. I will repeat once more that any amount of outside legislation or the penal code amendment will not take us one step further unless the temple is reformed.

Then again who is to enforce the law and bring the offenders to the Magistrate? I am afraid that further amending the penal code will give only more power to the police resulting in useless litigation and in the oppression of the weak without any proportionate good resulting from it. I may point out in this connection that in England even before 1885 a mother who was living a life of immorality would not be entitled to the guardianship of her child. The Court of Chancery had laid it down repeatedly. We want a similar provision in the law here also to prevent dedication of girls that may take place outside the temples.

The Hon. Law Member Mr S.R. Doss in his reply to the Hon. Mr Ramadas has asked him 'to move the people of Madras to institute vigilance associations, to see that prosecution is launched in every case against the person who dedicates as well as the person who obtains possession of girls etc.,' for which we require an enlightened public opinion, any number of devoted social workers, the co-operation of the communities and the temple authorities. Unless all these co-operate such moves on our part will never solve this problem of dedication as has been proved by experience.

SO THE REMEDY I SUGGEST IS THIS

The temples have allotted lands to these families which they have been enjoying from time immemorial as hereditary in lieu of their services in the temples. So when these women become sterile they go to the extent of buying girls from other communities in dedicating them to enjoy the benefit of those lands and also there is a superstitious notion prevalent among them that the Gods will visit them with some punishment if they don't continue such a practice. In most cases it is ignorance combined with poverty that seems to be responsible for such a thing. I think that if these lands could be permanently settled upon them without any expectation of service from them in return, automatically they will be forced to give up this abominable custom. This is what they have done is some of the native states such as Mysore.

MYSORE ORDER

The Government now observes that whatever might have been the original object of the Devadasi institution in temples, the state of immorality in which these temple servants are now found, fully justifies the action taken by them in excluding the Devadasis from every kind of service in sacred institutions like temples.

When land or other Inams, have been specially granted to any individuals, the Government directs that such Inams be confirmed under Rule VIII, Clause F, of the Inam rules to the holders thereof as permanent and alienable property, subject to the payment of quit-rent as laid down therein. The quit-rent thus imposed will be credited to the Government and an equivalent amount will be granted as cash Inam to the temple concerned.

DEVADASIS AND BROTHEL WOMEN

I may point out for the benefit of the non-Hindu members of this House that these women do not belong to the brothel class and they are only the victims of tradition, custom or a mistaken religious fervour and there is no innate tendency in them for vice. There have been a few good and pure women in these communities, who dedicated as they may be, in spite of their caste laws and their early training retain their virginity and when they have the singular fortune of coming across suitable mates, turn virtuous women, make faithful wives and model mothers even in the absence of the marriage bond which is a proof what healthy associations and change of surroundings can do even for these adult women and how the divine element in the human soul asserts itself sometimes in spite of training and environments, but alas these virtuous women form only a small percentage of the total number.

HOW RELIGION AND CUSTOM ARE RESPONSIBLE FOR THIS PRACTICE

I have already compared and contrasted the state regulation of vice in a few of the European countries with our temple dedication. By the former the existing brothels in those countries are licensed, while the latter converts the innocent girls of a particular caste (in the absence of whom the old Devadasis purchase children from other communities) into wretched human beings. The unholy feature of this institution is that the Hindu temples holding out Inams or salaries for such dedication creates an impression in the minds of the ignorant people that impurity and immorality in a particular caste is no sin, no crime, so long they undergo the ceremony of dedication. In temple dedication two factors stand out pre-eminently which differentiate it from prostitution tolerated in other countries.

First of all here these innocent children are made victims and are prepared for an immoral life by a course of training from their early days.

Secondly the temple and the illiterate Hindu public are responsible for developing a kind of mentality in those children which makes them when they grow to be a woman, view a criminal an unholy and anti-social act, an act productive of the most virulent diseases to the individual and the community, the practice of which demoralizes the individual in every way, such an act as a hereditary right and caste dharma.

In this connection, I may bring to your notice the Geneva convention on children, the principles of which were agreed to by all civilized nations—

Men and women of all nations recognising that mankind owes to the child the best that it has to give, declare and accept it their duty that beyond and above all considerations of race, nationality or creed, the child must be given the means requisite for its normal development both materially and spiritually.

So, are we justified in keeping indifferent over a matter which concerns the health and happiness of so many of our young girls? This evil custom as tolerated by our society, as having the holy sanction of our temple, is it not a worse from of 'Sati'? More than that is it not a 'hygienic mistake', 'a social injustice,' 'a moral monstrosity,' and a 'religious crime' and as such does it not deserve condemnation from every right-minded person, from every parent and above all from the state, because it is the duty of the state as the guardian of the people to suppress evil wherever found under any circumstances. So, I expect all patriots and great and good people of this land to bring about speedy legislation to suppress this notorious and barbarous practice which is revolting to our sense of justice and morality and to our feelings of humanity.

VIRTUE OF CONTINENCE

Again we all knew how sexual promiscuity either in men or women, is condemned by all religions and by all good people of any country, and in our country chastity in women has been looked upon as the supreme virtue of womanhood and even supernatural powers have been ascribed to such virtuous women by our poets and philosophers. Under such conditions it surpasses my understanding how sexual promiscuity in a certain class of women has been regarded by the majority of our people as a caste duty and a thing sanctioned by our religion and as such tolerated even within the precincts of our holy temples and again it is beyond my comprehension how in a country which can boast of innumerable saints, sages and rishis, who in their lives have demonstrated to us how much continence in sexual matters contributes to one's physical and mental health and vigour, how irresponsibility in vice has been ignored and even encouraged in men to the detriment of the individual and the future race.

I may say that the safety valve theory has long ago been exploded in other countries. The principles that are advocated by good men and women of the west to suppress the vice of prostitution are based upon justice, the same right for all, for men and women. 'The first condition for any measure for abolishing evil is this: it must itself conform to the highest ideals of morality and justice. Only when the measures taken are themselves moral, can measures against prostitution and venereal disease prove a power of educating and elevating human beings.' We cannot prove this but experiences of other countries demonstrate this truth beyond any doubt; measures directed against women alone are as unsuccessful as they are unreasonable. They declare that when the women alone are burdened with the consequences of a mutual act, the state or the society propagates the disastrous idea that there is a different morality for the two sexes. By providing for men security and irresponsibility in vice, the society breaks down the whole idea of responsibility, the basis of all morality.

Prostitution has been recognized as an evil trade, a crime and an anti-social act. A trade necessarily involves buyers as well as sellers. If it is to be made unlawful, it must be unlawful for both; to punish one only is unjust and ineffective; the receiver of stolen goods is a criminal as the thief and is rightly treated by law.

We know public opinion demands that the woman shall be chaste, but admits that the same is not to be expected of man. Can we protect a youth from the insidious poison of such a false public opinion that the sowing of wild cats on the part of young men is practically inevitable and the existence of a prostitute class appears therefore to be an obvious necessity, that the presence of these does not check the simultaneous activity of such a large army of 'unlawful traders', the so-called clandestine prostitutes who prefer to ply their business without the sanction of the society is a universal experience.

Again modern science has proved that continence is conducive to the health and well-being of the individual, the family and the future race and that sexual immorality, just like any other anti-social habit like theft, drink, and murder is productive of much harm to the individual and to the country.

Statistics in other civilized countries reveal that venereal disease, the produce of sexual promiscuity, is responsible for more than 50 per cent of child blindness and deafness and for a large percentage of insanes and imbeciles in the country and for many of the disabling diseases such as paralysis, liver, kidney and heart diseases in the old as well as in the young.

In women it accounts for 50 to 75 per cent of abortions, miscarriage, and sterility and is the chief cause of most of the gynic disorders in our women. Above all it is a racial poison capable of being transmitted to one's children, the second or even the third generation. Knowing as we do the serious and far-reaching nature of venereal diseases which affect the guilty as well as the innocent married women and children and which are the invariable accompaniments of a prostitute's life, how could we have the heart to remain indifferent to the fate of thousands of our young innocent children who are wantonly introduced into such an evil life through the apathy of our society and the ignorance and superstition or our people. Mrs Rolfe, the delegate sent to this country by the British Social Hygiene Council to study the prevalence of venereal disease in this country, when addressing the members of the Rotatary Club in Calcutta has remarked that it is four times more prevalent here than in England and Wales. When it is so, you can very well imagine the heavy toll by means of disease and death that our people have to pay every year to the unchecked prevalence of these baneful diseases. The prohibition of drink is in your hands while this reform lies in our hands, which is as necessary if not more, to the well being of the individual and the community, and by granting the one which is in your hands make yourself worthy of the other.

WHY THE DELAY

Dr Sapru in 1922 speaking on behalf of the Government during the introduction of Dr Gour's bill (which bill by the bye was passed unanimously by the Assembly) had stated that the initial difficulty in giving effect to such a resolution was to find a Home for those women who are thus rescued. Perhaps he was under the impression that these women lived in the temple premises, but we know that they have their own Homes and we have no right to dislodge them from their places, but only we have to provide them with some means of livelihood by settling those lands upon their names as Mysore has done.

As for providing a safe place for these minor girls, there need not be any difficulty in these days as we have already a number of Homes in Madras, which are taking girl orphans, the destitute, the delinquent and even girls rescued from brothels. As it is we are treating the end of the disease and not the beginning, not the root cause of the disease which is not a wise plan. Even supposing that a special Home is necessary for these type of girls I feel most strongly from the health, moral and humanitarian point of view that some of the money proposed to be spent upon the blind, the deaf, the lunatics and upon the venereal campaign could be profitably and easily diverted into this direction because preventing healthy children, healthy in mind and body from becoming the victims of the above disabilities is a much wiser, much saner and a more farsighted policy than allowing them to get diseases and then seeking the remedies, which remedy in most cases comes too late and does not consequently cure their deep-rooted ailments.

What will be the result of such a reform?

The result will be that the moral tone of the society will be strengthened.

In the words of that famous French woman Madame-de-witt-Schlumberger who was engaged in a similar kind of rescue work in France and who had rightly said 'the moral rescuing of each young girl, of whom they have made a good woman, is a small but useful stone for constructing the magnificent moral edifice which must be rebuilt.' In this connection I may bring to the notice of the Hon. Members of this House that in social legislation the European countries have taken a very forward step.

Then are we whose ancestors had practiced the highest ideals of sexual purity which human nature is capable of and had attained the utmost height of spirituality to be left behind and pointed out as a morally backward race?

I feel sure that every Hindu remembers the story of the rishi Vishwamitra, how the great rishi had to forego so much of his spiritual power and thus fell in the estimation of the Devas because he yielded to the amorous solicitation of the most beautiful woman Menakai and again we have not forgotten the story of Indra, the king of Devas whose body was disfigured with very ugly spots as a mark of punishment for his unholy act of outraging the modesty of Ahalya.

To be worthy of our past records and to deserve well of the present, let us blot out this evil once for all from our midst and put an end to this legitimate agitation that was started even as for back as 1863 by our high-minded Hindus, by our patriots and benefactors of society, again and again to be taken up, only to be discussed and then shelved aside on some excuse or other owing to the apathy of the local government and the timidity of the central government to interfere with our social matters. More than that I feel the real cause was that the magnitude of the evil had not been sufficiently realized till now and presented before the ignorant public.

Now I appeal to you in the name of humanity, in the name of justice and on behalf of the thousands of our young innocent girls who are sacrificed on the altar of immorality and vice, that Madras may take the lead in enacting a permanent measure to put a stop to this evil as even it has taken its first place in the granting of political rights to its women, a status unequalled in the history of any other nation in the world.

Let your righteous indignation result in determined efforts to blot out on the face of this earth the most heinous sin that was committed in the name of the Holy and in the name of religion, a religion advocating such virtues as Bramacharya, self-control, continence as conducive for the attainment of the worldly fame and heavenly bliss, which grand truths came to light in the west only a few years before.

Again to those Hon. Members who love and serve Jesus Christ I will remind them of His love which it would seem, went forth in preference to the tax-gatherers, to the sinners, but whose words severely and mercilessly rebuked all accused of injustice and also I will appeal to our Mussalman friends to be true to their Prophet's injunctions that do not advocate any tolerated institution of vice and hence I will in all humility ask them to follow the lead given by the worthy Mussalman representatives in the Council of State who have unanimously supported Hon. Mr V Ramadas's resolution.

So let that honour of being the first council to dictate to the central government a practical policy to save the girl children of this land from an evil life and lead them to good, let that unique honour and that sacred responsibility be yours.

(The resolution was carried unanimously in the Madras Legislative Council).

Madras Devadasis Association

The Humble Memorial of
Devadasis of the Madras Presidency

The Humble Memorial of the Devadasis of the Presidency of Madras Most Respectfully Showeth—

1. Dr Muthulakshmi Reddi's Resolution—Dr S. Muthulakshmi Reddi of the Madras Legislative Council brought a resolution in our legislative council which reads thus as amended—

This Council recommends to the Government to undertake legislation at a very early date to put a stop to the practice of dedicating young Girls and women to Hindu temples which has generally resulted in exposing them to an immoral life.

This recommendation was moved on 5-11-27 and accepted by the local Legislative Council.

2. Our protest against it—We most emphatically raise our voice of protest against the resolution and against any attempt at legislation which has for its object the stopping or prevention in any measure whatsoever of the dedication of young girls and young women to Hindu temples. We shall firstly deal with the ostensible objects of this resolution and of any legislation which may be brought to fulfil the spirit of this resolution and show how the objects of the legislators cannot be fulfilled by the proposed legislation and how the proposed legislation would bring results just the reverse of what is intended and we shall then specify our specific reasons for not allowing any such contemplated legislation to be taken up.

3. Devadasis are not prostitutes—The first and foremost and the only object of the proposed legislation is that such a dedication of Hindu girls and women generally resulted in exposing them to an immoral life. This sympathizes with the future of our womanhood and is generally against an immoral life. Let us calmly analyse the implications of this idea of legislation. The community which dedicates their women to temple service is known as *Devadasis*. It is a compound of two words God and Devotee and means the devotees of God. *Dasi* is the feminine of the word *Dasa* occurring in such words as Ramadasa. Popularly our caste is styled by the name of dancing girls probably due to the reason that most of our caste women are experts in dancing and music. Such a hoary name is unfortunately mingled up and associated with an immoral life. It would, we submit, be easily conceded by every one that the institution of dedicating one's life to a temple has nothing to do with prostitution. This is not merely our own self-glorified opinion but the considered judgment of some of the most eminent judges of our High Court. No less a person than Mr Justice Muthuswamy Iyer with his keen observation of South Indian customs laid down in a case (I.L.R. 11 Madras 393 at page 402) that 'it should not therefore in the case of dancing girl be confounded with prostitution which is neither its essential condition nor *necessary consequence*.' The italics is that of the learned judge. This observation is accepted and reiterated by another learned judge of the same High Court, Parker J. in I.L.R. 12 Madras and again the same learned judge stated 'It has been held in two cases that prostitution is not the essential condition or necessary consequence of becoming a dancing girl and a fortiori it is not the necessary consequence of education to become one'. Another learned judge Mr Justice Subramania Iyer has said in I.L.R. 19 Madras 127 at page 130 that 'it is scarcely necessary to say that neither in theory nor in practice, is the dedication to the temple looked upon as essential to a woman of the dancing girls caste becoming a prostitute. But on the other hand there is an immediate and clear connexion between the ceremony (tying the Pottu) and the Mirasi office (of dancer claimed in the case) in as much as the former is a necessary preliminary to his entering upon the duties of that office and to her enjoying the emoluments attached thereto'. The learned Judge finally established the proposition that 'no true relation exists between the ceremony (of tying Pottu or Tali) and prostitution.' We must humbly state that we cannot add anything to the above remarks of the illustrious judges. In spite of this a sad confusion of thought arises and we submit that this confusion of thought underlies the object of this resolution. Hence we make bold to question the implied identification of Devadasis with prostitutes.

4. **Prostitution as such may be suppressed**—If the object of the measure is to suppress prostitution, why not check prostitution wherever it is found and by whomsoever it is committed? Why should anyone deal with Devadasis for that? We have to state that prostitutes come from all classes of Society and prostitution is an incident of Social influences. We need

130   Bharatanatyam

not here analyse the underlying motives for prostitution. Prostitutes are a low class of people who degrade themselves by their immoral conduct and are consequently unfit to mix in decent society. They are to be found among all castes and creeds. We are given to understand that prostitution as such is not an offence in India and we can have no objection to any measure, however severe it may be, to check prostitution. We welcome such a measure because if an act is passed preventing prostitution, the few of our members who have erred would become rectified. If some of our members have gone astray from the path of virtue and rectitude, is the whole community to suffer? Similarly as prostitutes are found amongst all castes and creeds, it would follow that all castes and creeds should be condemned for the sins of a few. This, we would submit and you would certainly agree with us, is neither logic nor justice.

5. Real purpose of our caste is Religion & Service—We would most respectfully appeal to you that the real purpose or object of our caste is to dedicate oneself to a life of religion and service. Who will object to this? We were associated with the various temples and Mutts throughout the length and breadth of our Presidency. Our institution is similar to the institution of Mutts presided by Sanyasis for the propagation of religion and is an embodiment of a life of service which has taken a deep root in the national life of our country. We may again compare our institution with that of the Buddistic Nuns and the several Roman Catholic Nunnaries of the west. We can be compared to female Sanyasis who are more at home and are attached to the respective temples and Mutts. We submit that this is our object and the main purpose of our ancient institution.

6. Fundamental Principle—Service to God—We beg to remind in this connection that one of the main and most fundamental of our principles is the Service of God in all its aspects. We therefore say that we marry none but God and that God alone is our Lord and Master. As a man ties a tali round the neck of his wife as a symbol of wedlock, we go to the temple and symbolically associate the tali or Pottu being tied to our necks by the Lord Almighty himself. This religious symbol denotes that we have from that day forward become devotees of God. This idea of marrying is not new to our religion and religious ideals. One has to read the devotional Songs of Tamil Literature and the most inspiring of them the Thevaram of the Saivite Acharyas and the Nalayira Prabandam of the Vaishnavite Alwars; and then one feels how this idea of a devotee marrying God has been sung in some of the most devotional songs of Tamil Literature and it was practiced in the lives of many of these religious teachers as in the case of Andal. These ideals did not merely live in books and songs but so affected the life of some of the religious amongst us that many began to imitate the ideal sung in the hymns and follow the life led by the composers of the hymns. This is the vivifying force which has shaped us in course of time into a separate body. Can any one condemn with any sense of fairness such a holy ideal or the persons who tried to live in their practical lives such an ideal?

7. **Life of Devadasis**—Such an ideal cultivated in practice brought into the Hindu world the Devadasis. Dr Annie Besant says in her speeches about our life 'There was a band of pure virgin devotees attached to the ancient Hindu Temples. They used to preach religion like other religious teachers to the common people that resort to the temples for their daily worship. In those days they were held in high esteem and were very well looked after. They would spend their time in doing religious service to the Gods and devotees of the temples as the word dasi itself signifies. They would follow the procession of Gods dressed in the simplest Sanyasi garbs and singing pious hymns suitable to the occasion. This is the *History* and origin of the Devadasi class'. Thus these pure virgins were spending their time is religious service and travelling abroad to understand and unravel philosophical disquisition. Let any one read the work entitled 'MANIMEKALAI' written in the Sangam age of Tamil Literature and he will surely appreciate the truth of the above observations.

8. **Religion is in danger**—Hence we submit that any legislation which prevents us from pursuing our ancient ideal in as humble a manner as is possible for us in these troublous times is really affecting our freedom to hold and practice our religious beliefs. Our opponents know this principle very well; but still they contend that the principle of religious neutrality should be easily brushed aside with a light hand. This principle has been granted to our land in the Proclamation of the great Queen Victoria whose words are considered even today as the Magna Charta of India, whose message is so noble and liberal in its spirit and so magnificently just in its policy that it has won the eternal gratitude and unflinching loyalty of her Indian subjects. This fundamental principle of religious neutrality is sought to be treated as a mere scrap of paper by the introducers of the bill.

9. **Whole community cannot be condemned for sins of a few**—Let us be permitted also to point out that any legislation abolishing dedication to God affects our freedom of conscience and freedom to follow our own religious ideals. In proposing this legislation they attempt to do away for ever with our sect. Assuming, without conceding, that a few of our

community have gone astray why should a whole class be condemned to a practical annihilation of itself. We like to expect cold logic in all its barest aspects. If a single member of a family goes astray, should the whole family be ordered to be extinguished or be given an injunction not to procreate itself lest another erring member be born. If a member, say of one class, misbehaves, should the whole class be condemned for ever. Such a legislation is unheard of in any civilized world. Not even the fines imposed on the Anglo Saxon family for the thefts committed by one of its members is any near parallel to this proposed legislation. An attempt to annihilate a whole class recalls to our minds the mad frenzy of the French Revolution and the barbarous outbursts of the Modern Russian innovator—not legislator. Even to-day, France has not recovered from the results of its revolution and it will take a long time before Russia can realize the effect of her experiments. We most humbly beg in the interests of the future of this great and ancient land that our class as a whole should not be doomed to destruction.

10. **Our right to live**—We base our claim to live as a class upon our hoary past, upon our utility to other classes in the life of the nation to-day and in the immense possibilities of our usefulness to the common wealth in the near and distant future. The accounts given of our lives in histories and in the extract quoted above from the writing of Dr Annie Besant, would be sufficient to bring home to the minds of every one what we had stood and lived for in the past. We had been a necessary adjunct to the temples and Mutts of our land, preaching religion and leading a life of renunciation and service. Our class is mentioned in all the works of literature and religion of our country throughout its various epochs. A class which had such a magnificent past deserves per se to exist. In the life of to-day every one will readily admit that we have been the guardian angels of two of the most useful of arts to modern civilization viz. music and dancing and without any support from the Government, we have known to attach ourselves to these arts with a devotion that bears comparison with the ardour of the pundit reading his Vedas in preference to more lucrative modern pursuits. Some of our community have actually come out to preach religion as Bhaghavathars and today we can proudly boast that the orthodox pundit as well as the modern English educated young men listen to their teachings with the enthusiasm which they deserve. The loss to the nation at large can very well be conceived if all of us ceased to exist on a single day and this is exactly what the bill attempts to do. We are doing our costomary services in the temples and mutts and thus form an integral part of the religious life of the nation. In the future, we believe

that we shall strive our best with the advantages of a free and compulsory education which we pray that the legislature may bestow, to achieve the ideals of our past and lead the sacred life described in the preceding part of our memorial.

11. **Support of Shastras**—Not only are we entitled to exist because of our brilliant past, present usefulness to Society and our immense future possibilities, but our community has specific Shastraic sanction and support for our existence. The various Agamas of our community both Saivite and Vaishnavite refer to our community and the absolute imperative necessity of our being associated in the temples during the times of religious worship. Hear the words of the Lord Siva in the Kamikagama one of the most authoritative and widely read Agamas. He describes the origin of Devadasis and says, 'Therefore to please me during my puja, arrangements must be made daily for Shudda Nritta (dance). This should be danced by females born of such families and the five Acharyas should form the accompaniments.' Shudda Nritya is the dance called Bharata Natyam.

Again Lord Siva says, 'Therefore let (every day) the dance be arranged only by those born of the dancing girl caste.' There are other religious texts which but for want of space may be quoted here.

These injunctions of God clearly sanction not merely the existence of the dancing girl caste but their continuance. Let every legislator carefully read these and ponder over the sanction of religion which created our caste and which holds us to these temples and mutts. These Agamas are held in the most reverential admiration by every Hindu however modern and educated he may be and they form a part of the religious and sacred Literature of our ancient land. What reason can there be, we ask, for our community not to thrive and exist as necessary adjuncts of temple service.

12. **Our right of property affected**—We also beg to bring to your notice that we have large grants of land in our favour scattered throughout the presidency as remuneration to our services in the temples and Mutts. These we enjoy from generation to generation. The lands are burdened with our obligation to perform these services. What is to become of these lands? We believe that these lands would be taken away from us. Any attempt in this direction is inconceivable of any stable government and is fraught with the most dangerous results to the community. No one would think of annexing the lands of a family because some one of its members offended the ethical conscience of the public, and we are not in

the hands of the Bolschevic legislators. Some many argue that the lands may be granted to us free but we venture to ask as to why our children and their children should be deprived of their means of honest living and reciprocal religious service. The vested rights in land of any community has not been lightly interfered with in any age or clime.

13. **Legislation increases tendency to prostitution**—Such an interference with our Inams would deprive us of the honourable source of living and if we are turned as paupers, prostitution is certain to invite some of us and they may fall an easy prey to it. One of the main reasons of prostitution is poverty and why should we be turned out as destitutes. Even those of us who do not own lands at present are deprived of all chances of acquiring grants of land in the future and of leading decent lives. The legislation which has the sole object of putting an end to prostitution will surely dismantle many a peaceful and joyous home and throw many of us into the very jaws of hunger, despair and prostitution.

14. **Lines of Gradual Evolution**—Instead of trying to cut us entirely adrift in this wide world, let any one notice the path of gradual evolution which one can notice in the life of our community. Some of us surely aspire to the pristine purity of life as Saints and Devotees of Gods; and we have no hesitation in stating that many of us are living peaceful lives after marrying a husband like many other people. One may call it a permanent concubinage instead of marriage. Even then under the law as it is at present administered to us we are informed that authoritative decisions of Full Benches of the several High Courts in India and the Privy Council have laid down that the offspring of such permanent connections are entitled to rights of inheritance and maintenance in the father's estate. If we may respectfully suggest, if such permanent connections are held in law to have all the legal effects of a regular marriage, then we can surely assert that there can be no difference between such a life and that of a legally married couple. This is the right direction in which one should attempt at legislation. If some of us go astray and lead a life of shame they will be outcasted and they alone will be rightly classed along with prostitutes who come from all the classes of the community.

15. **Attempted Legislation Revolutionary**—When our community will thus along with the other sects of this land work out its salvation in a slow but emphatic manner, any legislation to wipe us out of existence is revolutionary. Such a legislation is fraught with the same dangers as every revolution will inevitably bring in its wake. In trying to remedy an evil existing in a caste, the caste itself is condemned to death and hence

it is argued that the evil cannot therefore exist. Which Doctor decreed that his patient should die and therefore reasoned that he had cured him of all his ills? This we submit is a just comparison of this attempt at legislation. Again they compare the ideal life of our past and the miserable present life of a few of our community and arrive at the conclusion that the community does not deserve to exist. If one were in a similar manner compare the rights and duties of the various castes in the Manu Smrithi for instance and look at the lives led by some of them to-day one should logically hold that all the castes deserve to be extinguished by one stroke of the pen or a single act of the legislature and we will cease to exist as a nation. We fully trust and believe that these revolutionary principles of legislation would not commend themselves to any member of the Government and the public.

16. **Alleged public Support to Legislation**—When so revolutionary are the underlying principles of this attempted legislation we are told by Dr Muthulakshmi Reddi that her resolution is in response to the wishes of the women's associations in this Presidency. We wish to point out that public opinion has to consider all the foregoing considerations earnestly submitted by us, test them without prejudice and prepossession, unmoved by personalities and arrive at a calm and correct conclusion. We venture to assert that such public opinion does not exist to-day and when it does so exist we fully believe that it will vote in favour of the retention of our community. Only the other day on the 12th of September 1927, the Honourable Mr S.R. Das the Law Member of the Government of India spoke in the Council of State on the resolution of the Hon'ble V. Ramadoss Pantulu to introduce legislation for abolishing Devadasis and he emphatically stated that public opinion should be educated in this matter. On this the Hon'ble V. Ramadoss Pantulu withdrew his resolution. It would in all fairness, we submit, be conceded that public opinion has not yet asserted itself to-day in any manner what-so-ever and it is wrong to suppose that what did not exist as public opinion on 12-9-27 in the eyes of the Government of India has since come into existence within the space of hardly two months. Secondly, we beg to submit that any strong condemnation of prostitution does not amount to condemning Devadasis as a community. We are behind no one in trying to put down prostitution but that does not imply that we vote for our extinction as a class. The violent and untrue description given by a wandering globe-trotter ought not to dim our eyes with respect to real facts of the situation. Under these circumstances, we venture to assert that public opinion has not yet considered this attempt at legislation in

all its bearings and we do hope that when public opinion asserts itself, it world certainly favour the preservation of our community.

17. **Our proposed means of testing the opinion of our caste**—Before getting the opinion of other members of the community, it would certainly be admitted that the views of our community should primarily be taken into consideration. We propose to submit memorials to the authorities with the signatures of all the adult members of our community scattered over this Presidency. This is a huge and gigantic undertaking, but in the interests of the future of our community and the country at large, we have voluntarily shouldered this labour of love. We propose organizing ourselves into several associations in the principal towns and cities of this province with a Head Association in the city of Madras. In this way we will be able to show to you what we feel in this matter and we trust you will understand the strength of our cause, the legality of our claims and the justice of our demands to you. Our proposal resembles in a large measure the ascertainment of public opinion by the well known principle of *Referendum* known to many of the civilized countries of the west. In so ascertaining our opinion we believe that our opinion will have the greatest weight with you.

18. **A few of our detractors and their interest**—We have to admit that a very few sprinkling of us are now on the opposition and we hope to win them on our side also. You are well aware that under the law of inheritance and succession as administered to us at the present day, a female succeeds in preference to a male, and hence a few male members of our community actuated by self interest are trying to sow dissensions amongst us; and self interest creates at least a bias in one's mind if it does not actually corrupt the heart. Hence any opposition from that quarter ought not to be considered against us.

19. **Appeal to the Press and Public**—As we have prejudice and pre-possession to fight against in establishing our claims to existence, we crave the press to give us support in publishing our proceedings, resolutions in the respective newspapers of our Presidency, English and vernacular. It should be admitted that an ostracism or a one sided view by the press makes the apparent appear real and vice versa; we hope that the press will cordially extend its hand of support to ventilate our side of the case. The public should also judge of us by the principles which we stand and fight for, the underlying motive for the attempted legislation and how far it will bring the desired end—in a calm and cool manner regardless of

personalities who move or support the attempted legislation but regardful only of the basic principles underlying the legislation.

20. **Our great need is education**—Having considered our case with the care characteristic of a scientific investigator regardful only of truth without any passion or prejudice, we believe you will realise that the one and great pressing need of our community is education. You will admit that many of us are devotees to the arts of music and dancing. A few of us are able to perform Kalakshepams to the public. Give us education, religious, literary and artistic. Education will dispel ignorance and we will occupy once again the same rank which we held in the national life of the past. It seems to us a paradox at once touched with humour and tragedy that in this advanced stage of civilization in the 20th century, it should still be necessary for us to appeal to you to vote for the retention of our class which in the onward march of history and Indian civilization, had contributed to the world's progress, radiant examples of women of the highest genius, widest culture and deepest devotion. But as by some irony of evolution the paradox stands to the shame of our countrymen to-day that instead of giving us education and achieving something at once fruitful to the future of our country, they are trying to kill us root and branch. Does one man dare to deprive another of his birthright to God's pure air which nourishes his body. How then shall a man dare to deprive a human soul of its immemorial inheritance of liberty and life. Teach us the Tevaram of the Saivaite Saints and the Nalayiram of the Vaishnavite Acharyas. Instil us into the religion of the Gita and the beauty of the Ramayana. Give us education in the vernacular and in the Sanskrit Literature. Explain to us the Agamas and the rites of worship. When anyone shows capacity for deeper thought, let her pursue higher philosophical studies. Do all this so that opportunity may be afforded for the reappearance of the type of women of which Maitreyi and Gargi, Manimekalai and the women singers of the Vedas were shining examples, that we might once again become the preachers of morality and religion, that we may be embodiments of that practical spirit of self-sacrifice which appears as public spirit when it is carried out into public life and which looks on the interests of the country as greater than the interests of the individual.

21. **Appeal for justice**—Finally we beg to close this appeal to you not to pass any legislation suppressing or interfering in any manner whatsoever with our dedicating ourselves to a life of religion and service. Kindly

consider our great past and the ever brightful future. Do not be blinded away by prejudice and personalities or be guided by impulses. In trying to mend an evil do not end the institution. Remember that every nation is a body politic, that every nation has one life, that neglect of one part injures all. Give us our birthright to live and work for the cause of our country. Encourage and foster our ideals of love and religion and service and our arts of music and dancing. We are the modern descendants of those who in the past held aloft the torch of civilization. Do not mistake the opinions of the few interested champions for public opinion. You who stood for religion, toleration and freedom of religious and philosophical opinions in the past, you who boast of your tender love for small communities we pray that you may allow us to live and work out our salvation and manifest ourselves in the dual aspect of wisdom and devotion, Gnana and Bhakti and show to the world both the aspects of spirituality and the noblest religion enshrined in the sublimest philosophy and that we keep alight the torch of India's religion amidst the fogs and storms of increasing materialism and interpret the message of India to the nations of the world.

We beg to remain,
Your most obedient Servants,
The members of the Deputation of
The Devadasis of the Presidency of Madras

Amrit Srinivasan

Reform or Conformity?

Temple 'Prostitution' and the Community in the Madras Presidency[1]

This paper describes the changes that affected an artist community of Tamil Nadu in the wake of reform agitation begun in the late nineteenth century, concerning the idiosyncratic lifestyle of a section of its women—the *devadasis*. The term devadasi, a shortened form of the Tamil *tevaradiyal*,[2] was applied to that class of women who, through various ceremonies of 'marriage' dedicated themselves to the deities of temples and other ritual objects. The use of the term 'caste', *jati*, in relation to the devadasis is misconceived; according to the devadasis themselves there existed a devadasi way of life or professional ethic (*vrtti, murai*), but not a devadasi jati. The profession of devadasi was hereditary but it did not confer the right to work *without adequate qualification*. There were certain local communities associated with the devadasis such as the Melakkarar, the Nayanakkarar and the Dasi in Tanjore district, who either recruited (through birth and/or adoption) and trained them or were functionally connected with them in the tasks of temple service. But it was only *after* the reforms that these individual and distinctive service categories merged under the prestigious 'caste' title, Isai Vellala,[3] in a bid to overcome the disrepute attaching to their past association with the devadasis. In a very real sense this marked the transition from a loosely-integrated occupational, temple social system to a highly politicised, communal caste association which utilised the cultural propaganda of the regional non-Brahmin party organisations, the Dravida Kazhagam and the Dravida Munnetra Kazhagam, to achieve corporate identity and prestige.

The first half of the paper reconstructs the devadasi system as it prevailed prior to the legislation of 1947, which banned all ceremonies and procedures by which young girls were dedicated to Hindu shrines.[4]

The second half describes the 'reforms' instituted in the social, religious and domestic status of the devadasis in the wake of the legislation, and questions to what extent these changes constituted an 'improvement' over their past position. The colonial context of the devadasi debate which kept the whole issue of reform very much at the forefront of conservative, native political activity is borne in mind throughout the discussion.

In Tamil Nadu, or the Province of Madras as it was earlier known, it was the devadasi, or D.G. (short for dancing-girl in Anglo-Indian coinage) who was the *nautch* girl of elsewhere. With appropriate variations, she danced this style before the deity in the temple and also at royal courts, the domestic celebrations of the local elite, public ceremonies of honour, and temple festivals. The performance of the nautch, the *cinnamelam*[5] or *sadir kacheri*[6] as it was variously called in Madras, was obligatory and a matter of etiquette at society occasions. Besides, of course, it proclaimed the wealth and prestige of patrons who maintained the dancing-girls (as concubines) and their bands of musicians, all at great cost.

The campaign against the dedication of women to temple service began in earnest in 1892. Articulated primarily by educated Hindus, Brahmin and non-Brahmin alike, the campaign formed part of the whole complex of reforms relating to women, such as the ban on sati, female infanticide, the encouragement of widow-remarriage and the raising of the age of consent, which had earlier been pressed forward by the English missionaries and officials themselves. The overall moral, political and scientific 'experiment' tried out in India by the Utilitarians and enlightened Protestants, had however proved to be a dangerous failure. The 'mutiny' of 1857 and growing local protests had brought home to the British Parliament the impracticality of interfering with their subjects' private lives. In 1858, the governing of India was transferred from the East India Company to the Crown, and Her Majesty, Queen Victoria, promised the Indian people tolerance and non-interference in all matters relating to religious faith and observance. The equal and impartial protection of a rational system of civil law was, in the same breath, offered as a privilege available to all.

The move for greater neutrality in the religious affairs of the Indians had been initiated by the missionaries, who saw in the government's 'protective' attitudes towards the Hindu temples, for instance, a patronage of precepts and practices at variance with Christianity. As early as 1833, the Directors of the East India Company sought to withdraw all control and sever connections with the management of religious institutions. Despite the enormous complications of such a move (given the government's deep involvement in temple affairs) they set about it, while yet continuing to draw what benefits they could from the temples, as for instance, the utilisation of surplus endowments on matters requiring public spending. Her Majesty's assurance consequently was increasingly viewed by the Indian public as a desire on the part of the government to withdraw from the responsibilities of rule. If earlier the people had made their anger felt at the comprehensive programmes of religious (Christian) attack on idolatry, caste practices and other social customs, they now went about letting the government know that its duty lay not in indifference but in the ratification of the people's wishes and expectations even in private and/or religious matters.

The government's proclaimed policy of neutrality combined with its potential power to legislate was destined to greatly politicise the Indian people who competed with one another to somehow gain official attention. Beginning in the second half of the nineteenth century, the tremendous spurt in both constitutional and unconstitutional agitations for secular and religious reform has been well documented by political historians. Lobbies, associations and other pressure groups were formed to let the 'consensus' be known, on which government action could be based and were, in a sense, encouraged by the British. It is in the context of this greatly accelerated political activity that many of the older questions relating to women's issues were regenerated, this time largely through indigenous initiative. There was nothing particularly new in this for Indians; the tradition of liberation and reform was as much a part of shared history as conservatism and conformity and went back to a period much earlier than the advent of the British. What *was* new was that given the alien impersonal bias of British law, these movements were more likely than ever before to be couched in terms of a universalistic jargon essentially insensitive to socio-historical complexity.

If sacrificial infanticide and sati had been banned earlier as 'murder', then by the late nineteenth century temple-dancers were being presented as 'prostitutes', and early marriage for women as 'rape' and 'child-molestation'. Given the dual role of the British, both as administrators and legislators, there was a premium on social issues being presented in a 'language' understood by them, on which their actions could be based. This imposition on all manner of public activity, of an alien framework of understanding, played up the apparent contradictions within Indian social reality permitting the politicisation of many civil issues. In the case of the devadasi controversy, if some viewed it as a pernicious social evil, there were others who viewed it as a perfectly valid religious profession with the devadasi having her own distinctive code of conduct. This sympathy extended even to a defence of her legal rights:

'Raising the consent age above 14 in extramarital cases would be unfair to devadasis as that would prevent them earning their livelihood.' (Testimony of Mr Pandit, Asst. Commissioner of Belgaum, Age of Consent Committee, Poona hearing. Appearing in Associated Press despatch, Bombay *Daily Mail*, 1928, November 5.)

As history informs us, however, the vigour of the reform movement was such that the devadasi had stopped dancing much *before* formal legislation was enacted against temple dedication in 1947. A reconstruction of the devadasi system as it actually worked in the Tamil region may reveal the nature of the incomprehension that underlay the huge success of the reform campaign.

Traditionally the young devadasi underwent a ceremony of dedication to the deity of the local temple which resembled, in its ritual structure, the upper-caste Tamil marriage ceremony. Following this ceremony she was set apart from her non-dedicated sisters in that she was not *permitted* to marry and her celibate or unmarried status was legal in customary terms. Significantly, however, she was not prevented from leading a 'normal' life involving economic activity, sexual activity and child-bearing.[7] The very rituals which marked and confirmed her incorporation into temple service also committed her to the rigorous emotional and physical training in the classical dance, her hereditary profession. In addition, they served to advertise, in a perfectly open and public manner, her availability for sexual liaisons with a 'proper' patron and protector. Very often, in fact, the costs of temple dedication were met by a man who wished thus to anticipate a particular devadasi's favours after she had attained puberty.

It was, crucially, a woman's dedicated status which made it a symbol of social prestige and privilege to maintain her. The devadasi's sexual partner was always chosen by 'arrangement' with her mother and grandmother. Alliance with a Muslim, a Christian or a lower caste man was forbidden, while a Brahmin or member of the landed and commercial elite was preferred for the good breeding and/or wealth he would bring into the family. The non-domestic nature of the contract was an understood part of the agreement, with the devadasi owing the man neither any householding services nor her offspring. The children in turn could not hope to make any legal claims on the ancestral property of their father whom they met largely in their mother's home when he came to visit.

The temple institution's sanction to the pursuit of feminine skills and the exercise of sex and child-bearing functions outside the conventional domestic (*grihasta*)[8] context was evident in many ways. Till 1910 the rituals of dedication were public and elaborately advertised ceremonies which required the permission and full cooperation of the religious authorities for their proper performance. The *pottukattu* or *tali*-tying ceremony which initiated the young *dasi* into her profession was performed in the temple through the mediation of the priest. The insistence on the pre-pubertal state of the girl was in imitation of Brahminical custom which saw marriage as the only religious initiation (*diksha*) permissible to women. Similarly, the *sadanku* or puberty ceremonies of the devadasi which confirmed her 'married' status as wife-of-the-god, were performed with an emblem of god borrowed from the temple as stand-in 'bridegroom'. On this occasion the procreative and nuptial rites performed at the time of actual consummation of a Brahmin marriage (shortly after the girl attains maturity) were also carried out and auspicious wedding songs celebrating sexual union sung before the 'couple'. From now onwards the devadasi was considered *nitya sumangali*, a woman eternally free from the adversity of widowhood, and in that auspicious capacity, she performed for the first time her ritual and artistic duties in the temple. The puberty ceremonies were an occasion not only for temple honour but for community feasting and celebration in which the local elite also participated. The music and dance and public display of the girl was meant to attract patrons just as amongst upper-caste non-Brahmin groups they served to invite marriage proposals from the family network.

A variety of competitive social pressures and traditional community obligations worked towards the setting up of particular arrangements between dancing girls and rich landed or business households. The men of the patron class were expected to accept a young devadasi as a concubine despite the enormous expense it eventually entailed. The fact that it was the eldest son alone (and that too one who was already married) who had the right to take on such a partnership showed the normative co-existence of a private 'decent' way of life with one that was more wayward and idiosyncratic. For the devadasis their temple attachment granted sectarian purity and the promotional avenues to pursue a prosperous career. The economic and professional benefits were considerable and most importantly, not lacking in social honour.

'Touching the dancing women, speaking to them or looking at them,' was mentioned as a ritual offence in the sectarian texts laying out the etiquette to be followed by worshippers when visiting temples. This misconduct was considered equivalent in blame to other varieties of desecration such as spitting in the temple, turning one's back to the shrine, looking covetously at consecrated property, etc. Life honours were granted to the devadasi at the time of her death. Flowers, sandal paste and a garland from the god of the temple were sent on the occasion of her last rites. In some temples the fire of the kitchen in the temple was used to light her pyre and the deity observed 'pollution' for a token period of one day when no puja was performed at the shrine. Usually, a funeral procession is not meant to stop anywhere, but in the case of the devadasi the bier was placed for a moment on the floor near the entrance to the temple when the gifts mentioned above were made.

As nitya sumangali, a woman with the protection of a living husband—the deity and lord of the temple corporation—the devadasi was provided with the excuse to enter secular society and improve her artistic skills amongst the connoisseurs and their families who were obliged to respect her and treat her with chivalry. What in ordinary homes was performed by the sumangalis of the family—ceremonies welcoming the bridegroom and guests, singing songs of festivity at marriage and puberty ceremonies, tying the red beads on a woman's marriage necklace, etc.—were in the big houses of the locality performed by the devadasi. As a symbol of good luck, beauty and fame the devadasi was welcome in all rich men's homes on happy occasions of celebration and honour. Her strict professionalism made her an adjunct to conservative domestic society, not its ravager. It is this which lay behind the customary acceptance of married and financially secure family men as patrons. As the wives of men who had maintained dancing women often said, they far preferred a devadasi to a second wife as a rival, as the latter would make domestic life intolerable. Even amongst some non-Brahmin groups where the devadasi could assume the status of a common-law wife of her patron, she never resided with him.

By cooperating in the ceremonies which conferred prestigious sumangali status on a section of its female personnel, the temple permitted the most intimate connections to develop between sectarian specialists and the laity. Crucially, however, its mediation helped to simultaneously institutionalise and depersonalise these dyadic, erotic relationships. The triple-cornered communication between the temple, the devadasi and her patron permitted the legitimate pursuit of interests even in the absence of 'market' conditions. For the civil elite a sexual relationship with temple women did not reflect secret needs of a ritual or orgiastic nature. As far as my field information goes, the man did not go to her to get special powers (sakti) or other such magical returns. The very publicity and singularity of the connections between a devadasi and her patron ruled out the cultic context more typical of Tantrik rites which involve high-caste men with female partners who are 'low' with a vengeance—usually untouchable. The competitiveness of the enterprise was evident from the fact that it was the devadasi's original sacramental husband, the Lord of the temple, who provided the momentum for her subsequent attraction for men who wished to approximate and imitate it in human terms. The fascination of a 'wife-of the-god' may be mythic just as the fascination for a bed in which Napoleon slept or for a saint's relic. But what is crucial for us is that it converts itself into exchange value when the socialite-client, collector or believer wishes to own the commodity in question or touch it for himself. Intimacy with a devadasi consequently demonstrated public success which visibly marked a man apart from his peers.

Seen in this light, the devadasi represented a badge of fortune, a form of honour managed for civil society by the temple. Land grants were given to individuals by rulers and patrons expressly for meeting their 'entertainment' expenses—the upkeep of a devadasi and her band of musicians. The whole idiom of temple 'honours' (mariyadai) in which the devadasi participated permitted a privileged contact with the deity and/or his possessions to have a more clearly secular significance and value. The temple for its own part was no disinterested participant, for the patronage extended to the devadasi was by no means passive. It recognised that her art and physical charms attracted connoisseurs (in the garb of devotees) to the temple eager to promote her as their protegee in the world at large. The devadasi acted as a conduit for honour, divine acceptance and competitive reward at the same time that she invited 'investment', economic, political and emotional, in the deity. In this way the competitive vanities of local patrons, their weakness for one-upmanship with their equals and rivals become inextricably linked with the temple institution. The efficacy of the devadasi as a woman and dancer began to converge with the efficacy of the temple as a living centre of religious and social life, in all its political, commercial and cultural aspects.

The temple's sanction to the system of extra-marital alliance described above was particularly evident from the fact that it was the offspring of these 'mixed-unions' who were given prime monopoly over temple service. The temple also ensured in this way a permanent task-force committed to temple duties over all others. In an inter-caste context, the religious sanction given to female celibacy institutionalised sexual intimacy between devadasis and patrons. In an intra-caste context, it enforced sexual separation in excess of incest prohibitions normally operating within the kin group. The devadasi was permanently denied to any and every man of her community as a marriage or sexual partner. The artificial dichotomy within the community between the householding and the celibate female population gave rise to the 'pure' or 'closed' and the 'mixed' or 'open' sections of the community. The former perpetuated itself through marriage, the latter through both marriage and 'mixed' sex. (The sons and brothers of the devadasi were permitted to marry as also the non-dedicated girls of the group.) These internal divisions were closely linked to aesthetic specialisation within the community.

The allied arts of Tamil bhakti worship—sadir (dance), nagaswaram (instrumental music) and nattuvangam (dance-conducting)—were traditionally organised into two orchestras: the periamelam (in Tamil, literally, 'big drum') and the cinnamelam ('small drum').[9] The periamelam was focussed around the male nagaswaram virtuoso and was the hereditary specialisation of the 'pure' section of the community. The cinnamelam, on the other hand, was focussed around the devadasi or female dancer and her male guru or nattuvanar, and was the hereditary specialisation of the 'mixed' section of the community. The requirement for both heredity and skill in temple positions was evident in that it was not enough to be born into the community, one had to be competent in order to gain rights to temple service, just as it was difficult to be competent in the particular service unless born or adopted and resident in the community with its internal training facilities. Professional divisions such as peria and cinnamelam reflected an involution and greater sophistication of the artistic services rendered by the community under the influence of the Bhakti temple institution. Both the technical instrumental organisation as also the aesthetic and functional speciality of the music provided by the two orchestras reflected this fact. The statutory requirement to live proximate to the deity intensified local community relations which (as they saw it) had helped 'concentrate' and develop their skills. Art as a corporate function and mode of livelihood ensured competence and continuity of practice. An extremely telling metaphor used to justify their artistic capacities was that of the plantain (vazai) which kept perpetuating itself over the year from the original parent stock (vazai-adi-vazai).

What is significant for our purpose, however, is that in the context of an otherwise shared community culture where the sadir 'people' (also referred to as the cinnamelam) and the nagaswaram 'people' (also referred to as the periamelam) lived, married and worked together, it was the female profession which instituted competitiveness. Most of the nagaswaram players remarked on the greater wealth, fame and glamour that had been possible for the dancing girls as compared to themselves. Significantly, they claimed this to be the effect of an unfair advantage arising out of the natural attraction of women. According to them the temple authorities gave the dance pre-eminence at festivals knowing that the people would flock to see the devadasis. The devadasis were certainly permitted privileges and honours and a physical closeness to the deity denied to the men of their community. The artistic and monetary dominance of the female art form was also linked to its earnings as a concert item—before the 1940s nagaswaram played only at outdoor occasions. Even their sense of comparative social superiority ('we take our father's initials ...') offered the nagaswaram artists little recompense since they were forced to acknowledge that it was the devadasi's distinctive lifestyle which permitted her greater artistic and worldly success. In addition, one cannot help feeling the privileged access of women artistes to rich patrons and their wealth underscored more sharply their absolute non-availability to their own men. The antagonism felt for the cinnamelam was in recognition consequently of the power and influence the devadasis had *as women* and as artists. The leading role played by the men of the community in the subsequent reform campaign to abolish the female profession of temple-dancing cannot be understood without reference to this potent fact.

It was the radical factor of female celibacy which permitted the group to go beyond a purely domestic organisation of internal social relations. The professional division within the community between the male and female art forms was not restricted to household specialisation. In the nagaswaram tradition the women of the group were scrupulously kept out of public, professional life. In the dance tradition, too, despite the involvement of both men and women in the occupational tasks of the group, various mechanisms operated which kept the relationship free of any domestic obligations. As we have seen, married girls were not permitted to specialise in the classical temple dance and its allied music. Conversely, those girls who were dedicated to the deity were not permitted to cook or perform mundane domestic tasks either for the men of their own household or for their gurus. The latter in fact were necessarily men from a separate household tradition to that of their students even though they might reside together for the period of training.

The peria and cinna social divisions clearly did not reflect the mechanical repetitiveness of a uniform domestic structure. The 'rationalisation' of diffuse kinship ties and the 'pre-industrial' economy seen as characteristic of caste society was most evident in the structure and organisation of the devadasi household. The methods and means employed here to encourage artistic excellence, monetary profit and a greater systematisation in the achievement of life's goals reflected an unusual household and cultural tradition which saw itself as perpetuated in a natural *and* moral/social sense, by its women. The direct link that obtained between women as the bread-winners, the kind of income they fetched and their household supremacy, not only in spending and managerial matters but in a political sense as well, will now be briefly described.

It was conscious economic motivation which lay behind the temple dedications, whatever the voiced religious reasons for their performance. Although the temple cooperated in the rituals, pressures to perform the ceremony remained internal to the household and reflected not only the self-interest of the family against 'outsiders' but also internal mechanisms of competition and rivalry which often raised disputes over claims.[10] The insistence on the minor status of the girl to be dedicated reflected this fact since it ensured the retention of hereditary rights by her to service and land benefits in a given temple. The temple tenurial system of pre-colonial India granted a service allotment or *maniam* which was meant for the enjoyment, 'over the generations' (*vamshaparambirayam*), of a set of dasis attached to a given shrine. They had no right to alienate it since it was not in their name but the temple's, more specifically in the name of the deity or the head of the controlling *matha*. The organisation of shares (*panku*) in this land, just as the organisation of training and arrangement of daily duties, was a matter of internal management by the community. The property transmission within the household recognised the joint and inalienable nature of privileged land-use which could only remain with the family so long as there was a member actively employed in the temple.

The clear desire to keep the economic backbone of the household a female one was consequently linked to the fact that it was the women who were the primary source of both earned and ancestral property. But it was also in recognition of the fact, with no recriminations involved, that the moment a boy made good in an independent career, be it in music or dance or trade, he would move out and maintain a separate household with his own wife and children. Men stayed on as appendages of their sister's or mother's household only on sufferance. A man who had made his own name in his particular field of musical specialisation could not allow professional pride to be compromised by continuing to depend on his women. In any case in purely economic terms, he would be able to move out only once he had established his own reputation and consolidated his earnings. Under ordinary circumstances, it was the women who provided the men with a livelihood, arranged their marriages and gave them a home. The men, it was further felt, always had the choice and the opportunity to make their livelihood elsewhere, not necessarily in the art field, but the women were restricted and had no freedom in the matter. For these various reasons women were favoured over men in property matters. Devadasis were the only women allowed to adopt a child under customary Hindu law and often an adopted daughter was favoured over an only son in the matter of inheritance.

The dominance of women even at the level of formal authority within the home was in a large measure due to the very nature of its economic base. Household property was largely earned income acquired in the form of cash, jewellery and goods, and it was through its women that the household made profits in this sphere. The land endowments, by the very terms of their enjoyment, could not be alienated or capitalised on. Neither did the community have the agricultural skills necessary to profit from the land they owned—they saw themselves primarily as artists and professionals.

The person 'in charge' in the dasi establishment, the *taikkizhavi* or 'old mother', was the seniormost female member who was normally one of the more renowned dancers of her time who, after retirement, exercised control over the younger members. The strict discipline of this old lady over both the private and professional lives of her relatives, her control over joint income, its pooling and expenditure, provided the fundamental source of unity for the dasi household. The critical role she thereby played in the status and prestige of an establishment was appreciable. Considering that much of the income brought into the house was made on an individual basis it was the intervention and managerial control of the old woman which prevented household fission. All community members agreed in this and referred to their mother's or grandmother's special gifts with honour and reverence. Most homes had photographs on the walls of previous such leading lights of the family before whom daily worship was offered.

Quite clearly, it was the women who were considered precious in any given household for its social and professional reputation and continuity. The men acquiesced in the priorities of the household for they too saw their future prosperity as inextricably linked with the emergence of a beautiful and talented sister or niece who would consolidate resources. The alliances made by one's female relatives were significant both for the material and symbolic wealth of the household, and the caste status of the 'father' provided a kind of axis along which different members of the group were graded. Given the peculiarities of the domestic economy in the charge of women, it would not be far wrong to say that it suited men to stay in the background. For not only was household wealth linked to the rather shaming (for men) category of 'women's earnings' but it reflected an area of insecurity and periodic want.

The money flow into a devadasi household remained rather uneven and individual prosperity varied greatly. The excessive lifestyle and lavish spending on hospitality, food and clothing rarely left anything over to be invested in more profitable ways. The taikkizhavi, though head of the household, did not gain public recognition or any specific material advantage for her troubles. Given all this, the brothers and uncles of the devadasis acquiesced in their subordinate position because it relieved them of economic cares and responsibilities.

Significantly, these various matri-centred features of the devadasi household encouraged a greater functional specificity and technical excellence of the dance tradition. As mentioned earlier the sexual division of labour underlying the dance was of a non-domestic nature. Despite female household authority, in the professional sphere it was the male guru who exercised control over the dancer. Even when a nattuvanar resided with his mother or sister, his superior authority vis-à-vis the female student was ensured by the fact that she came from a separate household. With the achievement of a special renown, however, his subordinate position in his own household clearly led to an ambiguous situation. Given the strong force of the taikkizhavi and her complete authority in the household, any man with self-esteem would, it was considered, move out whenever possible and rule supreme in his own domain. Financially as well, the nattuvanar who set up on his own had much to gain since he was under no further obligation to pool his earnings with his mother and sisters. Residential separation consequently for the dance guru who continued to be associated with women professionally, conclusively asserted his position of dominance over them.

The self-conscious and competitive functional division within the dance tradition between 'male' (teaching) and 'female' (performing) skills was reflected most dramatically in the emergence of two distinct structures of household organisation. The socio-spatial forces underlying this process related specifically to men and their need to develop an independent tradition for themselves, matching that of their illustrious womenfolk in wealth and prestige.[11] The dasi or matrifocal household was characterised by the following features: (i) large size (an average of thirty residents) and excess of female residents (women married into the house but few married out; besides girls were adopted for professional purposes); (*ii*) dichotomous power structure (female members exercised household control, male members exercised professional control); and (*iii*) dichotomous ethical structure (conjugal and celibate codes both coexisted within it). The guru or patrifocal household on the other hand, displayed a consistency of political and moral structure and had a smaller size, made up on an average of an equal number of males and females.

The flexibility and heterogeneity of the dance's social organisation described above paid considerable artistic and economic dividends. Members of the community often related the sophistication of their art as a concert item to the teaching of the dance. It was the access of the women of the community to closely related gurus, specialists in the female classical dance, which made the sadir tradition aesthetically perfect. Dance teaching was more closely modelled on the Tamil sectarian traditions of spiritual teaching and secular education which required a close and intimate life-long relationship between the adept and the student. The devadasi, we must not forget, was permitted to learn to read and write and pursue vocational skills traditionally denied to all other women in India. The dasis feared and respected their gurus *as teachers* and artists and informal religious leaders of the community whose curse could ruin a girl's career and prospects. At the same time the community context prevented the inherent asymmetry of the guru-shishya relationship from becoming exploitative. Households very often stood in a 'student' relationship to some and a 'teaching' relationship to others. The chances of permanent structural asymmetry within the dance organisation were in this way obviated. The continuity of marriage exchange, furthermore, between gurus and undedicated women of student households balanced the tensions inherent to the *gurukulam*.

It was the more wealthy and prestigious patrifocal nattuvanar households which showed a marked tendency not only to prohibit their women a professional career but also to restrict the circle of marriage exchange. Quite understandably this aggravated specialisation and claim to 'purity' was seen by community members as being detrimental to art. According to them such extreme professionalism on the part of gurus made it unprofitable for the girls to dance. The accumulation of wealth and power through the exploitation of students and their earnings destroyed community and its 'give and take'. It was only through the continuity of the gurukulam—the transgenerational exchange between the teaching and practicing adepts and their respective households— that the excellence of a particular 'school' of dance could be maintained.

Real motivations of economic self-interest lay behind this professional and community code of conduct. The skill of a particular nattuvanar belonging to a famous tradition could directly affect a student's 'market' both in the dance and entertainment world for the better and enhance her household's prosperity. Equally, for the nattuvanar, she was the proverbial goose that laid the golden egg whose talents, if handled properly, yielded steady financial dividends over the year in the shape of fees and gifts.

The unusual social gradation described above sanctioned: (i) a particular model of women which constituted a unique religious office— the conscious theological rejection of the harsh, puritanical ascetic ideal for women in the bhakti sects, softened for the devadasi the rigours of domestic asceticism in the shape of the widow, and the religious asceticism in the shape of the Jain and Buddhist nun; (ii) a particular community or 'caste' which was a necessary corollary to the institutionalisation both of celibacy with sexuality in the devadasi's person. The devadasi stood at the root of a rather unique and specialised temple artisan community, which displayed in its internal organisation the operation of pragmatic, competitive and economic considerations encouraging sophisticated, professional and artistic activity. The innovations introduced into the community through the fact of independent female professional skills contrasted well with the more conservative male profession which was also poorer, economically. The abstract sectarian truths of Hinduism which see the male element as 'passive' and the female as 'active' in their cosmologies appear here to receive confirmation on the sociological plane.

For the reform lobbyists—missionaries, doctors, journalists, administrators and social workers—strongly influenced by Christian morality and religion, it was precisely these features of the devadasi institution which were reprehensible in the utmost. The publicisation of the devadasi system as prostitution sought to advertise the moral grotesqueness of the subject population for political ends. For those who supported imperialism on the grounds of its 'civilising' function, programmes of reform, it must be remembered, were not without their ideological rewards. The movement urging the abolition of all ceremonies and procedures by which young girls dedicated themselves as devadasis to Hindu temples, was articulated in the first instance as an anti-nautch campaign. The very use of the term nautch (a corruption of the Hindi term nach, a dance performed by a more common class of northern dancing girl) suggested the smear campaign that was to follow.

The anti-nautch supporters, largely educated professionals and Hindus, began their attack on the devadasis' dance, using the declamatory and journalistic skills at their disposal to full effect. Collective public action took the form of signature protests and marches to the homes of the elite who refused to heed the call for boycotting the dance at private celebrations. At the official level memoranda urging legislative action and a ban on the dance were presented to the Viceroy of India and the Governor of Madras who were assured that these performances were '... of women who, as everybody knows, are prostitutes, and Their Excellencies hereafter at least must know to be such ...' After much pressure and recrimination both from the missionaries and the lobbyists, the government agreed to take sides, and by 1911 a despatch was issued desiring nationwide action to be taken against these performances.

The emergence of a vigorous reform movement focusing on the devadasis' dance was a consequence of its politicisation. The so-called 'reformist' approach which characterised Indian political activity in the latter half of colonial rule was reflected in its organisation. By the 1920s the anti-nautch agitation had become inextricably linked up with the communal politics of the Dravidian movement. The abolition of the practice of female dedication became a powerful political and legislative cause espoused by the backward non-Brahmins as part of the over-all self-respect campaign initiated by Ramaswami Naicker in 1925. The extraordinary success of the reforms was not unconnected with the fact that the community menfolk stood to gain by the legislation. Given the shastraic sanction to the devadasis' celibate, professional ethic and duty, their marriages could not become valid till the passing of the Act in 1947. In the interim period, the tremendous social disabilities they faced worked to the advantage of the men of the community. For most devadasis there was opposition to their getting married particularly if they had been through the dedication ceremony already. To flout the prohibition placed on profane marriage by the sacrament of dedication was viewed as equivalent in moral blame to remarriage for an upper-caste widow. Community members took advantage of this 'blot' on the girls' character and would either demand sums of money as dowry before agreeing to marry the girl or offer opposition in other forms: the astrologer would tell the boy's family that, if married, such a girl would surely die, and so on. At the time of the reform campaign some eminent men did take devadasis as wives, but these exceptions (as in the case of the few reported widow re-marriages of the time) only served to prove the rule. It was the very beautiful or gifted dasis alone who managed to make good matches—M.S. Subbulakshmi, today's renowned singer, married a Brahmin despite her dasi parentage; Jayalakshmi, the famous dancing girl of Pandanallur became the Rani of Ramnad, to mention only two. For the majority however, marriage remained an expensive and difficult proposition.

The reform campaign forced the devadasis to acknowledge the moral supremacy of domestic values; even more importantly, it obliged them to relinquish all rights to temple service and its privileges. The men on the other hand continued to perform both in the temples and in people's homes. The immense patronage they received from the DK/DMK regional party organisations favoured them financially. The nagaswaram even today is performed as a concert art. With respect to land rights as well, as explained below, the abolition of the devadasi system benefitted the men of the community over the women in direct contrast to the historical situation.

In the 1920s the non-Brahmin Justice Party (the more elitist precursor of the DK) had taken great care to protect service benefits in terms of lands and buildings attached to the devadasi's office before finally pushing through the Legislature Bill in 1930. The Madras Act of 1929 enfranchising *inam*s and *maniam*s, as the tax-free land privileges were called, was justified on the grounds of social justice: the devadasi 'bond-slave' to the temple authorities could now own the house and land without the extortion of service. The process of converting traditional usufructary rights to public land (attached to office) into private taxable 'property', however, favoured the men over the women in that they, too, could now inherit the shares earlier kept aside for their dedicated sisters. With land coming into the market through the introduction of the *patta* (land deed) system under the British, the economic and moral infrastructure of matri-centred householding suffered. Internal strife over property division increased and the wealthier sections of the community benefitted over the less fortunate. Most interestingly, however, the processes of rational, western, social change initiated by the reform campaign, far from reducing casteism actually increased communal tendencies within the community. The imperial census data of the 1901–21 period reveal this process of transition of the devadasi community from a professional class with a *higher* percentage of women (quite unusual for India) to a 'caste with a more typical sex distribution.'[12]

The resentment freely expressed by the devadasis at the loss of power and privilege through the legislation provided ample, verbal testimony that the 'reforms' had been pushed through largely by a politically aware minority of the community, pre-dominantly men. By contrast, the far greater resistance at the time to reforms seeking to change Brahmin female institutions such as dowry, virgin-widowhood and child-marriage was a consequence of the threat they posed to the interests of elite men. The aggressive anti-Brahminism and anti-ritualism of the Backward Classes Movement of the south provided the men of the devadasi group with a powerful ideology to overcome the humiliation of the anti-nautch campaign and fight for dominance both within the household and in the wider political society.

British officialdom's stake in encouraging regionalism and cultural divisiveness directly linked them with those who pressed for its ban. The colonial framework of formal confrontation not only greatly politicised the Indian people but also provided the very rhetoric and 'facts' on which reform action was based. It was essentially alien currents of thought that were utilised by the reform lobby to advertise its public campaign. Even in sensitive areas such as women's reforms it was the power of 'facts' and arguments based on western rationality and reason, and not the authority of the Sanskrit shastras, that was increasingly invoked by Indians to bring about socio-cultural change. The reform movement associated with the Hindu temple-dancer continued on the scientific plane, 'civilising' arguments pushed forward earlier (with far less success) on the religious plane by the missionaries and the British government. The atheist programme of the Backward Classes Movement clearly stressed the benefits of western education and 'rationalism' to bring about desired social change.

Science, religion and the politics of reform became absolutely intertwined in the person of the female missionary/doctor towards the close of the nineteenth century. Through the sensational and selective publicisation of the medical 'facts' of immature sex, missionaries sought to discredit upper-caste customs and habits on humanistic grounds. The patronage of temple dancers and the practice of pre-pubertal marriage were declared equally abominable, and despite official policies of neutrality in civil affairs, the prestige of science gave missionary interference a renewed legitimacy. It is significant that even with direct community involvement, it was a professional doctor, Dr (Mrs) S. Muthulakshmi Reddi, who headed the legislative battle for the abolition of temple dedication.

Paradoxically, however, almost simultaneous with the reform movement there emerged a movement urging the 'revival' of the devadasi's dance. Those seeking to abolish the devadasi system had utilised the British machinery of regional party politics and the rhetoric of empiricism to achieve their local ends. Those urging the resurrection of the devadasi's art, separated from her way of life, on the other hand, consciously stepped outside the requirements of state electoral politics and western scientific traditions to achieve their particular ends. The Theosophical Society's[13] notoriously anti-official stance and interest in an Indian cultural and political renaissance bound them with the revival of the dance. At the same time, the nationalisation of Indian art and life and its almost 'religious' idealisation by the Theosophists and thinkers such as Coomaraswamy, Havell and Tagore was in no small measure itself an effect of westernisation. The re-classification of regional, artistic traditions within a unique territorially-defined framework of unity was now proposed in terms of the spiritual and civilisational advantages of Indian and eastern philosophies and techniques.

The British government officials and missionaries were not slow to play up non-Brahmin suspicion of Indian nationalism, coming as it did from the largely Brahmin-dominated Theosophical circles and Congress alike. With political lines drawn in twentieth century Madras between the British (official)-Christian missionary-'Backward' non-Brahmin complex, on the one hand, and the British (unofficial)-Theosophist-Brahmin[14] complex on the other, it should not be difficult to understand why, by the time the former had done their best to kill the dance and its 'caste' of performers, it should be the latter who would promote it as a 'national' art. When Dr Reddi's Bill of 1930 asking for the abolition of temple dedications finally came to be passed into law (1947), it seemed to have been pushed through not so much to deal the death of the Tamil caste of professional temple dancers as to approve and permit the birth of a new elite class of amateur performers.[15]

The legislation came at a time when the practice of dedication was already quite dead and it was the official sponsorship and patronage of traditional arts which was at a premium. With newly-won independence to spur on the Congress Party ministry of that time, the Bill was passed into law with the qualification that ... 'This legislation should not cut at the root of art and culture ... This culture has come to us from generations past .... These things should not be killed in our jealousy for social reform.' (The Hon. Dr P. Subbarayan in the Legislative Assembly Debates on the Bill, October 9, 1947.) By 1947, the programme for the revival of sadir as Bharatanatyam, India's ancient classical dance, was already well underway with the patronage and support of Brahmin dominated Congress lobbies of elite Indians drawn from all parts of the country.

All revivals, however, present a utopian view of the past which is usually an interpretation fitting in with a changed *contemporary* situation. Given the upper-class Christian religious biases of the Theosophists and the deep influence of evolutionary theories on their 'science', it was the model of the ancient temple-dancer as a pure and holy, sexually chaste woman which was stressed in their performance. By thus marking her off from the 'living' devadasi, they hoped to attract the right sort of clientele for the dance. The argument that without the attendant immorality the dance was a form of yoga—an individual spiritual exercise—abstracted it from its specific community context, permitting its rebirth amongst the urban, educated and westernised elite. The pre-eminence of the women of this class in the field of Bharatanatyam today conclusively indicates that the art has come to be preserved in that very section of Indian society that had been drawn to theosophy in the first place. The modifications introduced into the content of the dance-style were a consequence not so much of its 'purification' (as the revivalists liked to see it) as its rebirth in a more 'proper' class.

In Tamil Nadu today, the art of sadir/Bharatanatyam is monopolised by Brahmins who clearly see themselves as having 'rescued' it from the fallen 'prostitute', the devadasi. Yet in a very real and practical sense it is only the devadasi dance they are perpetuating. In essence the dance technique remains unchanged and was learnt from the very community nattuvanars and performers who had become redundant after the reform agitation. In the absence of any textual choreography, the widespread renaissance of the dance was really only possible with their help. Many of the best known artists in the field proudly acknowledge training in the secrets of the art from old, defunct devadasis. In the midst of new forms of vulgarity surrounding the dance profession today, such as the commercial cinema, it is the devadasi tradition alone which is propagated by the elite schools as representative of the ancient and pure Bharatanatyam. But we may ask, if the devadasi's dance was a sacred tradition worth preserving and the legislation (justified though it was on the grounds of anti-prostitution) came down with a punitive hand not on prostitutes in general but on the devadasi alone—why did the devadasi need to go?

NOTES

1. The paper draws upon my research work for a doctoral degree at the Department of Social Anthropology, University of Cambridge, England. Data on the devadasis were collected through both field and library research. The documentary material focussed on (i) the specifically British, official and non-official tradition of scholarship on India in the colonial period, and (ii) on the orthogenetic textual tradition. In the field, research was carried out in two stretches covering a total of one and a half years from 1979–81 and focussed primarily on the Tanjore district of Tamil Nadu. The main aim of field research was to contact and interview the devadasis—the living representatives of a changed

cultural position, in order to grasp their evaluation and interpretation of the past. All those who could provide eye-witness accounts of the institution of temple-dancing as a working system, such as dance teachers, temple priests, musicians and local landlords, were interviewed as well. Supplementing these interviews was the collection of biographies, extended case-studies and genealogies, archival accounts, temple and social histories, court and temple records and scripts of dance lyrics and ritual songs.

2. The term translates (not very well) as 'slave of the gods'; literally it means 'at the feet of the lord' which clearly distinguishes it from the cruder term, *tevadiya* or 'available for men', which is used to refer to a common class of prostitute.

3. The term *isai* appears in classical Tamil literature and refers to a special music played in the courts of kings. In association with Vellala, a respected caste name for dominant Tamil non-Brahmins, it represents a modern version of the term *icai-karar* or *icai-panar* which referred to the prestigious bards and court minstrels who performed this music in ancient times (Tamil Lexicon, Vol. I, pp. 272–3). This title was adopted by the caste association, the Isai Vellala Sangam, at a conference in Kumbakonam in 1948.

4. The full text of the Act is found in the archives of the Government of Madras, Law (Legislative) Department G.O. No. 23, January 26, 1948: Acts— The Madras Devadasis (Prevention of Dedication) Act, 1947, Publ. Madras Act XXXI of 1947.

5. The band which accompanied the dancing-girl, as against the *periamelam* which accompanied the male temple-pipers.

6. The term sadir is not a Tamil one; some derive it from the Urdu or Hindustani word, *sadar* meaning public court. In usage it referred to the public, solo concert (kacheri) dancing at rich mens' homes on ceremonial occasions.

7. In Christian traditions of celibacy for the priesthood and consecrated life, sexual chastity is a normative aspect of the vows taken. Before the Reformation, however, the prevalence of priestly concubinage provides sufficient evidence to indicate that in an earlier period the institutionalised stipulation against marriage was more crucial than rigorous sexual chastity. There is no denying, however, that the ordinary understanding of celibacy today implies sexual abstinence. Particularly in the case of nuns the passionless ideal is more strictly enforced and adhered to. For the reform, strongly influenced by Christian monastic ideals in the colonial period, it made more sense consequently to publicise the devadasi system as a degenerate one. Ancient ideals of sexual purity it propogandised had been corrupted by the strength of commercialism and modern-day immorality. But if one is to understand the devadasi system, it is crucial to accept that though the ceremony of dedication prevented her from contracting a legal marriage, it never demanded sexual abstinence. If anything Tamil bhakti traditions, of which the devadasi was an integral part, rejected puritanism as a valid religious ethic for its female votaries.

8. In the indigenous tradition, grihasta refers specifically to householding life based on the marriage of a man and woman, and the duties and rights that flow from it. The devadasis always lived as members of a household but it was not a 'domestic' (grihasta) structure.

9. The periamelam was constituted of the nagaswaram (a kind of oboe) the *tavil* or 'big' outdoor drum, the *ottu* (drone) and cymbals. The cinnamelam was constituted by the *mukha-vina* (a diminutive nagaswaram), the *mridangam* or 'small' concert drum, the *tutti* (a bagpipe shaped drone) and cymbals.

10. In the section on devadasis in his prodigious work on the ethnography of South India, E. Thurston, Superintendent of the Madras Government Museum, gives evidence of the increasing involvement of secular law with the devadasis and their disputes in the late nineteenth century. (*Castes and Tribes of Southern India* in seven volumes, 1909, Madras.)

11. The discussion, rather than view the process of household formation as wholly influenced and controlled by customary, kinship factors, seeks to emphasise the play of rational choices and competitive pressures in areas of internal caste organisation.

12. The census returns showed the following statistical variations for the dasi group:

Census Year	Dasi	
	Males	Females
1901	1568	5294
1911	1691	3290
1921	5050	5970

Sources: Francis, W., 1902, *Census of India 1901*, Vol. XV-A Pt. 2, Madras, p. 158.

Molony, J.C., 1912, *Census of India 1911*, Vol. XII, Pt.2, Madras, pp. 112–13.

Boag, G.T., 1922, *Census of India 1921*, Vol. XIII, Pt. 2, Madras, p. 114.

13. At the time of its inception, the leading lights of the Theosophical Movement, Madame H.P. Blavatsky and Colonel H.S. Olcott, had toured the southern parts of India and gained support from all sections of the native elite by their public denouncement and denigration of western Christian morality and materialism. In 1882, the Society had set up its headquarters in Adyar, Madras, with the set goal of working towards the restoration of India's ancient glory, her art, science and philosophy. The support later given to the revival of sadir as Bharatanatyam by the Theosophical Society was largely due to the efforts of Rukmini Arundale, an eminent Theosophist herself. The direction the dance took under her protective wing cannot be severed from the all-embracing influence of theosophy on her life and career.

14. In the existing literature on the Theosophical Society's activities in India, it is their anti-Christian image which is constantly portrayed to justify its appeal to the Hindus. Theosophy was rebelling, however, not against Christianity *per se* but against a particular version of it—non-conformist Protestantism, espoused by the missionaries in India.

15. For background information on the implications of the Brahmin-non-Brahmin conflict of South India for the nationalist movement as a whole, readers are referred to: M.R. Barnell, 1976, *The Politics of Cultural Nationalism in South India*, Princeton; R. Suntheralingam, 1974, *Politics and Nationalist Awakening in South India 1852–1891*, Arizona.

Teresa Hubel

The High Cost of Dancing

When the Indian Women's Movement Went after the Devadasis

On the other side of patriarchal histories are women who are irrecoverably elusive, whose convictions and the examples their lives might have left to us—their everyday resistances as well as their capitulations to authority—are at some fundamental level lost. These are the vast majority of women who never wrote the history books that shape the manner in which we, at any particular historical juncture, are trained to remember; they did not give speeches that were recorded and carefully collected for posterity; their ideals, sayings, beliefs, and approaches to issues were not painstakingly preserved and then quoted century after century. And precisely because they so obviously lived and believed on the underside of various structures of power, probably consistently at odds with those structures, we are eager to hear their voices and their views. The problem is that their individual lives and collective ways of living them are impossible to recover in any form that has not already been altered by our own concerns. In making them speak, by whatever means we might use (archives, testimonials, court records, personal letters, government policy), we are invariably fictionalizing them because we are integrating them into narratives that belong to us, that are about us.[1] Given the inevitability of our using them for our own purposes, we cannot justify taking that all-too-easy (and, as this essay will suggest), middle-class stance that posits us as their champions, their rescuers from history. It falls to us to find other motives for doing work that seeks them.

In the case of this essay, the *them* are the *devadasis* or temple dancers of what is now Tamilnadu in southern India (the term devadasi literally translates as 'female servant of God'), especially those dancers who were alive during the six decades of the nationalist movement. This movement was meant to grant Indians freedom from colonial oppression and give them a nationalist identity, but if it succeeded, at least to some extent, in accomplishing these things, it did so at the cost of the devadasis and their dance traditions. Janet O'Shea (1998) explains the logic through which the newer institution, nationalism, drove out the older one, the profession and culture of the devadasis: 'Indian nationalism has often required a shift away from cultural diversity in order to construct a unified image of nationhood ... The devadasis were threatening ... because they represented, for the new nation, an uncomfortable diversity of cultural practices and cultural origins' (p. 55). Most scholars who have written about the modern history of the devadasis would agree with this explanation.[2] To the elite men and women who had the greatest say in what would constitute the new Indian nation, the devadasis were an embarrassing remnant of the pre-colonial and pre-nationalist feudal age and, as such, could not be permitted to cross over into the homogeneity that the nationalists hoped would be postcolonial India. The campaign to suppress the devadasis and to eliminate their livelihoods culminated in the Madras Devadasis Prevention of Dedication Act of 1947, an act brought about largely through the efforts of middle-class Indian nationalists who were also social reformers and, often, feminists—that is, advocates not only of nationalism but of the burgeoning women's movement that was to ensure so many of the legal rights Indian women enjoy today. That feminists who were determined to extend the rights of some women should also work to deny rights to other women is the conundrum that this essay examines.

Its subject generally, then, is the colonial confrontation between the Indian women's movement and the devadasis of South India. Initially analysing the representation of these dancing women in selected historical and literary texts, it next charts the involvement of early twentieth-century feminism in the decades-long persecution of this female profession. I subsequently explore the reasons behind the participation of one female group in the suppression of another, ending finally with an inquiry into the implications, particularly for middle-class feminists, of choosing a course of action that requires the conquest of female collectives outside the mainstream norm. As I indicated above, what I cannot hope to achieve in the course of this essay is the recovery of some kind of authentic devadasi voice; it simply isn't possible. But I do plan to use the modern history of these female dancers, matriarchs, and religious devotees to suggest the dangers for feminists and dancers of colluding with forces of homogeneity, even anti-imperialist and liberal ones such as Indian nationalism.

THE HISTORICAL REPRESENTATION OF THE DEVADASI

The entrance of the devadasis into Western discourse coincides with the advent of European imperialism. Travel memoirs, dating from the earliest period of European trade expansion into India, often include descriptions of these women. Not surprisingly, they symbolize the wealth, the wonder, and the sexual license that Europeans equated with the East. For writers like Domingos Paes, who accompanied the Portuguese envoy to the court of Krishna Raya at Vijayanagar early in the sixteenth century, the dancers are curiosities, notable for their baffling practices and their tantalizing sexual reputations. Paes (cited in Kersenboom-Story, 1987) composed his narrative for European readers, who were at this time largely unfamiliar with the everyday details of Indian life. Consequently, his images of India, especially of the dancers he saw in the court, are predictably exoticized:

They feed the idol every day, for they say he eats; and when he eats women dance before him who belong to that pagoda, and they give him food and all that is necessary, and all the girls born of these women belong to the temple. These women are of loose character, and live in the best streets that there are in the city; it is the same in all their cities, their streets have the best row of houses. They are very much esteemed, and are classed amongst those honoured ones who are the mistresses of the captains; any respectable man may go to their houses without any blame attaching thereto. (p. 36)

That he bothers to mention that such 'women ... of loose character' live in the 'best streets' and the 'best ... houses' and that 'respectable' men may visit them without suffering public censure suggests just how bewildering Paes finds the devadasis and their position in the elite Hindu society of Vijayanagar. Paes was one of the very first European writers to associate the devadasis with the profession of prostitution, but many others followed his example, including the Indian social reformers of the late nineteenth century. What is behind this labelling is the questionable assumption that the devadasis' unconventional sexuality—their tendency to participate in sexual relationships outside of the traditional Hindu marriage—was analogous to that of the prostitutes of Europe. However, in his desire to make the unfamiliar knowable by constructing a seamless comparison between it and that with which he was familiar, between the devadasis and European prostitutes, Paes and the writers who came after him demonstrate a telling inability to confront the profound difference that these often affluent, and always literate and religiously devout dancing women represented for European conceptions of female sexuality.

Devadasis also appear as figures or characters in imaginative constructions of India: fiction and poetry written by Indians and Europeans alike.

Frequently, they are marginal figures whose function in the text is to lend it an exotic and erotic flavour. It might be argued that the second-century Tamil classic *Silappadikaram*, in which a dancing girl, Madhavi, wins the heart of someone else's husband, only to lose it again because of the irrepressible devotion of his wife, constitutes an early exception to this typical rendition. Still, although rich in its depiction of early dance culture in southern India, *Silappadikaram* is ultimately a story about conventional domestic relationships. Madhavi is a secondary character, a kind of foil for the persistent wife Kanagi. It is Kanagi whom the story celebrates and privileges.

A similar sort of argument could be made about the devadasi character in R.K. Narayan's delightful novel *The Man-Eater of Malgudi*. Like so many of the female characters that Narayan has created, Rangi is an adjunct; the main narrative concerns a gentle male protagonist, Nataraj, and his ferociously male adversary, Vasu. Rangi, who is Vasu's girlfriend, plays out her role on the fringes of the masculine tale that the novel seems most determined to tell. However, as I've argued in another place (Hubel, 1994), interpreting the text through the character of Rangi, though she is undoubtedly secondary, allows a reading that disturbs the main narrative. Her defiance of the role that the Hindu patriarchy insists she fulfil, that of the middle-class wife, threatens Nataraj's world even more so than do the antics of Vasu. So even in a relatively recent piece of writing—Narayan's novel was published in 1961—the devadasi's sexuality stands in counterpoint to some female standard erected by an overriding patriarchy.

The nationalist and social reform movements in India tended to focus on their sexual lives as well. The only occasional mention of devadasis in books, speeches, and newspaper articles from the nationalist period in Indian history belies their formidable significance to the predominantly middle-class and upper-caste values that formed the bedrock of assumptions that fuelled nationalism. Seeming sympathetic to what they saw as the deplorable plight of the helpless devadasis, the nationalists generally portrayed them as women caught in an evil practice, a practice that desperately needed to be abolished. This is how Gandhi (1946) described them in a 1925 article for *Young India*, 'Of all the addresses I received in the South, the most touching was one on behalf of the devadasis—a euphemism for prostitutes. It was prepared and brought by people who belong to the clan from which these unfortunate sisters are drawn' (p. 166).

Gandhi closes the article with a rousing call to the men of India to root out corruption everywhere, 'And let every pure man, wherever he is, do what he can to purify his neighbourhood' (pp. 166–7). The premise underlying his injunction is that the men of the devadasi clan are doing just that—purifying their neighbourhood by working with Gandhi to put an end to the profession of their 'unfortunate sisters.' In these nationalist texts, the devadasis are merely somewhat contemptible victims because, by this time in Indian history, their status as prostitutes has been taken for granted. That they might be something else—dancers, wives of gods, professional women—is not even considered.

Depictions of the devadasis are also common in the history sections of numerous books about the classical dances of India. However, these glimpses of the temple dancers and their dance are extraordinarily insubstantial and usually filtered through the eyes of some long-dead European—a priest, an amateur anthropologist, or a merchant traveller like Domingo Paes writing his memoirs. Such portraits are invariably shaped by the writers' specific agendas, many of which were imperialist or nationalist as well as powerfully elite-class and androcentric in their allegiances. For instance, Beryl De Zoete, while providing no evidence whatsoever for her assertion, confidently writes in her 1953 book *The Other Mind: A Study of Dance in South India*, 'There is no doubt that the Philistinism of their English rulers, like the Puritanism of the Muslims they succeeded, helped to debase the art of the devadasi. The professional, secular Nautch girls were too often ignorant of their art, vulgar and degraded' (p. 162). We can trace her confidence in this particular opinion to her unquestioning acceptance of Indian nationalist and middle-class views of the subject. Significantly, this class was one of the groups that benefited from the official suppression of the devadasi culture.

All of these constructions of devadasis have at least one thing in common: They constitute the devadasi as an object of knowledge. In other words, we are permitted to see the devadasi only as she is seen by another—a European visitor to India, an Indian nationalist, or an English dance scholar. What little we know about these women is usually mediated through the perspectives of people who are not devadasis. In most Indian history, devadasis usually do not speak but are only spoken about. The scarcity of published material recording the subjectivity of the devadasis themselves represents a considerable gap in our knowledge of this history and these women, a gap we are wise to keep in mind when we write about them. As sympathetic as I am to the historical devadasis, I cannot, because of this present gap, recover them as anything more than victims of history, a depiction that is surely too simple to do real justice to these women's lives over the centuries. A community that speaks divergently for itself (that is, through the mouths of more than a tiny minority of its people), though it inevitably speaks through ideological filters over which it may have little control, nevertheless emerges into history in much more complex ways than one that is mostly spoken about. Thus it is crucial to remember that the case I make here—this exploration of the missing connection between the devadasis and the Indian women's movement of the first half of the twentieth century—is imbalanced. Because there exists much information about the women's movement from the perspective of the women who helped to create it and few records of the devadasis' undoubtedly diverse perceptions about their profession and its suppression, the only point of view this essay can examine in any depth at all is that of some of the upper- and middle-class women who constituted the movement's leadership. How the devadasis might have returned their gaze or how their experiences as temple dancers might have undermined or bolstered the anti-Nautch campaign that sought to rid India of their traces is a more formidable subject, best left for another essay.

THE NEW PATRIARCHY AND THE SUPPRESSION OF THE DEVADASIS

In her detailed and carefully argued article, 'Reform and Revival,' Amrit Srinivasan (1985) explores the alternate efforts of various social reform parties and of the Theosophical Society to ensure the repression and eventual extinction of the devadasi culture. This event, which began in 1892 with the anti-Nautch campaign and was crowned by the 1947 Act, was successful, according to Srinivasan, in part because a politically astute faction—most of whom were men—of the caste community to which the devadasis belonged was determined to stamp out the woman-centered tradition that the devadasis had managed to sustain. Srinivasan leaves no doubt that these men were motivated by a desire to usurp the power and authority that their women had built up for themselves over the years. She writes, 'The aggressive anti-Brahmanism and anti-ritualism of the Backward Classes Movement of the South provided the men of the devadasi group with a powerful ideology with which to overcome the humiliation of the Anti-Nautch campaign and fight for dominance both within the household and wider political society' (p. 1874). Under the guise of rescuing their women from the clutch of Brahminism, the devadasis' men managed to secure for themselves the property and inheritance rights that devadasi custom had guaranteed mostly to the women in their matrilineal lines. They were also not, as already suggested, alone in their crusade. They had joined forces with social reformers and members of the Dravidian movement—again, most of whom were men—to almost obliterate the female profession of dance and temple service. It is perhaps not so surprising that the men of the devadasi community should collaborate with the new Indian patriarchy, which had, in part, been created by the imperatives of a nineteenth-century middle-class social reform movement. After all, both the devadasis' menfolk—their sons, uncles, brothers, as well as other men from their castes—and the social reformers were committed to the belief that Indian women *should* be defined only by their domestic relationships with men. As Kumari Jayawardena (1986) has pointed out in *Feminism and Nationalism in the Third World*, the 'issues tackled by the reform movement ... were raised by bourgeois, male social reformers from urban areas who tended to idealize women's role as wife and mother in the context of patriarchy' (p. 79). Being the wives of gods and dancers by profession, the devadasis hardly fit into this androcentric and uniform conception of Indian womanhood, which the new patriarchy was intent on establishing in India.

THE SUPPORT OF THE WOMEN'S MOVEMENT

What is surprising, however, is how much support the men of the devadasi community and the social reformers received from the Indian women's movement. The Irish feminist Annie Besant, who went to India in 1893 to contribute to the nationalist struggle for independence and who helped found the Women's Indian Association in 1917, joined the anti-Nautch campaigners in condemning the devadasis. She was quoted in the July 14, 1894, issue of the *Madura Mail* as an opponent of a group of Hindu revivalists who were dedicated to the task of preserving the devadasi tradition. Besant's attack on the temple dancers was grounded in the premise that, because they were sexually active, they were no longer authentic practitioners of their dance, 'It is absurd to speak of dancing-girls as "accredited ministers". The ancient religion trained them as chaste virgins, and their ancient religious functions were dependent on their virginity. Losing that, they have lost their ministry' (quoted in Marglin, 1985, p. 10). I have yet to find any evidence to support this representation of the nineteenth-century devadasis as degenerate artists-cum-devotees, a representation that has become a truism in certain dance academies and schools in India. Various song lyrics as well as the historical records of the devadasis that exist would seem to suggest that sexual abstinence was never a requirement of the profession. Srinivasan's (1985) research has led her to the same conclusion. She writes, 'If anything the Tamil Bhakti tradition of which the devadasi was an integral part, rejected Puritanism as a valid religious ethic for its female votaries' (p. 1876).

Dr S. Muthulakshmi Reddi, a powerful leader of the women's movement who has been described by two contemporary feminists as 'India's greatest woman social reformer' (Basu & Ray, 1990, p. 184), was one of the most outspoken critics of the temple dancing tradition and was at the forefront of the legislative battle to abolish temple dedication, the ritual through which a woman became a devadasi. Her name was also associated with another famous social reform crusade of the 1920s, 1930s, and 1940s, the struggle to put an end to the Brahmin institution of child marriage. Reddi was fierce in her denunciation of both of these Hindu practices. Indeed, she saw herself as a rescuer of Indian women and girls less fortunate than herself, like child brides and temple dancers. This attitude is evident in much of her writing on these issues. For example, among her papers in the archives of the Nehru Museum and Memorial Library is an undated article, entitled 'An appeal to the public' and clearly meant for publication in a newspaper, that castigates those men from the Brahmin community who continue to support and participate in arranged marriages to pre-pubertal girls. The article probably dates from the 1920s, when Reddi was lobbying the Indian government to pass the Sarda Act. This was a bill that had been introduced into the Legislative Assembly in 1927 with the object of preventing child marriages by prescribing a minimum age for marriage and a punishment for those who failed to conform to the new law. In her article Reddi asserts that while the 'enlightened womanhood of the land ... have been pleading so eloquently for the innocent suffering womanhood of the country,' various orthodox men of the Brahmin community, particularly the young university students, continue to 'come forward with out-of-date and antiquated shastraic quotations [about the religious sanction accorded the practice of marrying girls before they have reached puberty] without any regard to the very deplorable conditions prevailing in ... society.' She ends the article with a threat. If the orthodox persist in quoting 'their out-of-date and antiquated authorities,' she will publish the names of Brahmin men who have recently married little girls; 'many of such are even to-day to be found at Madras in the well-to-do and educated families,' she adds.

What this example of Reddi's courageous and forthright politics shows us is the paternalism implicit in her approach to certain Indian females—those whom she feels are unable to defend themselves. This was exactly the stance she along with many other feminists of the All India

Women's Conference (AIWC) chose to take in regard to the devadasis. As the first woman elected to the Madras legislature, she introduced a bill in 1927 that would prohibit the devadasi system. In 1929 she put forth another bill, this one designed to force the Madras government to release all the devadasis of the province from their temple obligations. By this time, the anti-Nautch campaign had begun to seriously undermine the devadasi heritage, making it an increasingly socially unacceptable profession among the middle- and upper-class Hindu communities of the south. However, Reddi's contention that what was needed to alleviate the situation of the devadasis was not laws so much as 'strong public opinion to back these laws' (Basu & Ray 1990: 63) suggests that even as late as 1929 South Indian communities were not entirely in support of this feminist movement to end the devadasi involvement in the religious service of the temples. But Reddi and various other women of the AIWC justified their intervention in the lives and choices of the devadasis by constructing them as mostly guileless 'girls' rather than women, girls who could be defined solely by their sexual practices, which, in turn, could be understood only as prostitution. From the time she first introduced a bill to outlaw the devadasi system until 1947, when a law was enacted, effectively ending the devadasi profession, Reddi and her middle-class, upper-caste feminist supporters worked to sway public opinion against the temple dancers, though they were usually careful to depict them as pawns in a system run by men, thereby suggesting that it was not other women or a woman's livelihood they were undermining so much as the immoral men who were living off these women and directing this livelihood. In a 1937 letter to Gandhi, in which she thanked him for his support for her bill, Reddi made it clear just how important this issue was for her: 'I place the honour of an innocent girl, and saving her from a life of shame and immorality, even above Swaraj [Gandhi's word for Indian self-government] .... I will value Swaraj in as much as it gives protection to these women by the speedy abolition of unhealthy and pernicious customs' (quoted in Asaf Ali 1991: 220). Clearly, Reddi saw herself as the champion who would save these powerless women and their daughters from the 'unhealthy and pernicious customs' that were enslaving them.

Whether or not the devadasis saw themselves as enslaved seemed beside the point for Reddi and the other participants in the women's movement. In fact, Reddi made it clear that she was abundantly uninterested in any opinions on the subject from the devadasis. When a number of devadasi associations protested against the 1927 bill to the then

Law Minister C.P. Ramaswamy Iyer, insisting on their right to continue their profession, Reddi (quoted in Anandhi 1991) responded, 'As far as the local devadasis' protest, they are all set [sic] of prostitutes, who have been set up by their keepers. How can the government take cognisance of such a protest? ... So I would request you not to pay any heed to such protests from a most objectionable class of people in the society' (p. 741). Obviously, for Reddi, devadasis were alternately innocent and helpless girls or degraded and hence untrustworthy women, their condition at any given moment being dependent on what she needed them to be. Rather than existing for her as people as 'real' as she was, with personal as well as collective agency and views, they were, as Anandhi maintains in her essay on the subject, a metaphor to be deployed variously in Reddi's self-interested narrative of enlightened womanhood.

Let me emphasize again that the opinion of the devadasis on the eradication of their profession is neither easy to establish nor simple to assess. But there is evidence, similar to the devadasi protest mentioned above, that points to a considerable amount of resistance on the part of these temple dancers to the anti-Nautch campaign. In her doctoral dissertation entitled 'Another Stage in the Life of the Nation: *Sadir, Bharatanatyam*, Feminist Theory,' Srividya Natarajan (1997) quotes a series of memorials and testimonials that various groups of devadasis submitted to the government of Madras in an attempt to retain control of their profession and the meanings that could be ascribed to it. The following 1927 self-description from the South India Devadasi Association is one such example:

The community which dedicates their women to temple service are known as *DEVADASIS*. It is a compound of two words God and Devotee and means the devotee of God. Dasi is the feminine of the word Dasa occurring in such words as Ramadasa. Popularly our caste is styled by the name of dancing girls probably due to the reason that most of our caste women are experts in dancing and music. Such a hoary name is now unfortunately mingled up and associated with an immoral life. It would, we submit, be easily conceded by everyone that the institution of dedicating one's life to a temple has nothing to do with prostitution. (p. 124)

The translating of their title, devadasi, from the Sanskrit is meant to remind elite Indians not only of their profession's ancient roots but of the religious component in their temple service. These devadasis were obviously aware that they and their culture were being unfairly judged by an alien moral order that was antagonistic to them and to the set of values that had sustained their customs. They were forced, however, to make their case within the terms of the very moral framework that had already condemned them as degraded and to call on that system for a fair hearing: 'We want that we should be heard. The fundamental maxim of law and justice is that one should be heard before anything affecting him is passed and we therefore pray that we should be heard and full justice rendered to us' (quoted in Natarajan 1997: 127). Far from being heard, the voices of the devadasis who objected to the actions of the anti-Nautch campaigners were drowned out in the chorus of nationalist, social reformist, and feminist calls for the extermination of their way of living.[3]

In their encounter with the devadasi system, Reddi and her feminist colleagues adopted the same paternalism that they simultaneously used in their political movement to end the Hindu custom of arranging the marriage of high-caste girls. But while such paternalism might have been considered appropriate when it was wielded on behalf of helpless children from their own caste and class group, girls whose youth prevented them from being able to resist such patriarchal subjugation as child marriage and whose oppression these women could be expected to comprehend either because of their personal experience of it or because they themselves had been able to witness it close up, it could only be seen as presumptuous when it was used in regards to the devadasis, most of whom were adults earning independent livings and managing extended family households. Furthermore, with the exception of Reddi herself, who was, interestingly enough, the daughter of a devadasi, the elite-class and upper-caste women of the Indian women's movement had little knowledge, personal or otherwise, of the devadasis and their everyday lives.

The culture of the elite Hindu castes and classes and the devadasi tradition of South India, though they frequently intersected, particularly on special public occasions such as temple festivals and Hindu weddings, were radically dissimilar in their respective value systems and in the practices associated with them. Nowhere is this more apparent than in their disparate marriage customs. Although devadasi custom also allowed for the marrying of daughters before puberty, significant differences existed between more conventional upper-caste marriages and those in which the devadasis participated, the most obvious one being that these girls were married to gods, not men, an act that conferred on them the status of *nitya sumanguli*. Saskia Kersenboom-Story (1987) explicates the term:

The traditional view holds that all women share, by their very nature, the power of the goddess. A regular progress is imagined in the degrees of auspiciousness of varying status of women: at the top of the scale is the married woman whose husband is alive and who has borne several children; she is called *su-mangali* 'auspicious female'. At the lowest rung of the ladder is the widow who is considered highly inauspicious. As a ritual person, the devadasi exceeds even the su-mangali in auspiciousness. Firstly, because her individual female powers are ritually merged with those of the goddess, and secondly, because she is dedicated to a divine husband, i.e., a husband who can *never die*. In consequence, she can never lose her (double) auspiciousness and is therefore called *nitya-su-mangali*, the 'ever-auspicious-female.' (p. 204)

Protected throughout their lives from the possibility of becoming widows, devadasis were considered lucky by the Hindu community of the pre-colonial and colonial periods, up until the various campaigns against them of the mid- to late nineteenth century and were therefore accorded a certain respect and admiration denied to most other Hindu women of the time. Furthermore, while the devadasi's marriage was generally consummated by a man who would later serve as her patron, often a wealthy Brahmin or member of the landed and commercial elite, and while this man usually became her sexual partner, unlike a conventional wife, she was not required to maintain his household or any other man's household or to surrender her rights to their offspring. The children of the devadasis belonged only to the devadasis and not to any men at all. The consequence of this practice was that the devadasi culture was one of the only matrilineal *and* matrifocal cultures in India. Moreover, because the female line was given precedence and because the females were the main source of income for the extended families in which they lived (outside the temple they were paid for their dancing, while temple tradition guaranteed them income from inherited temple lands), female children of devadasis were favoured over male children when it came to inheritance. Obviously, the power and authority available to the devadasis far surpassed that of the average Hindu wife and mother. At a time in India when most high-caste women did not work outside their homes and were therefore made dependent on male providers, the devadasis were able not only to support themselves through the practice of their artistic profession but to maintain entire households.[4] Given the devadasi's, at one time, unique but still honourable place within the larger Hindu community, Reddi's determination to rescue her from her apparently debased conditions seems at best misguided philanthropy and at worst middle-class arrogance.

THE COMMON GROUND BETWEEN THEM

No solidarity was ever achieved between the women of the women's movement and the female temple dancers. I find this surprising because, putting aside their contentious sexuality, the devadasis had something that the feminists of the 1920s, 1930s, and 1940s seemed determined to achieve for themselves: economic independence in a profession that at least at one time was considered respectable and was frequently profitable. This desire on the part of middle-class Hindu women for financial autonomy from the men in their households—the fathers, husbands, brothers, and sons whose welfare was deemed by Hindu scripture the primary concern of women—had not always been an issue in the history of the Indian women's movement. In the nineteenth century, for instance, the middle- and upper-class women promoting female emancipation seemed more interested in redefining their roles as wives and mothers in order to accommodate their new literacy and politicization. But by the third decade of the twentieth century, a note of dissension had crept into the rhetoric of the women who took over the movement from the elder generation (Hubel 1993). These second wave feminists began to talk of their right to an education similar to that permitted to men and to an occupation outside the home should they wish to pursue one. In her 1945 presidential address to the AIWC, Hansa Mehta (1981) was straightforward in staking women's claims to these prerogatives: 'It is in the economic sphere that women will have to fight hard to establish their position. We must demand the right for every woman to work. Let no disability be attached to her on the ground of her sex in regard to public employment, office of power or in the exercises of trade or calling and women must receive the same payment as men for the same amount of work' (pp. 8–9). Yet in their attempt to find new categories for womanhood, ones that would accommodate their public lives and professionalism, which they had developed as a result of their participation in the nationalist political arena, the women of the women's movement overlooked one indigenous women's profession that might have served as an ally, maybe even as an example.

THE DEVADASIS' SEXUALITY AND MIDDLE-CLASS WOMANHOOD

Why did they do this? In part, it was the sexual lives of the devadasis that prevented the women activists from appreciating this female-dominated culture. Nationalism in India, in both its early and later phases, encouraged an asexuality in women because it placed enormous emphasis on their potential or actual motherhood. Even the role of wife was subordinated to this celebration of Indian motherhood, which reached its apotheosis in the construction of India as the motherland. Within the terms of this representation, the role of woman as the lover of man was elided. Female erotic sexuality is therefore a subject notably absent in nationalist writings and speeches, and, because of the close connections between nationalism and feminism during this period, in feminist works as well. The consequence of this deliberate erasure, then, was that the sexuality of the devadasis inevitably seemed excessive and aberrant. Thus it was because of this fundamental inability to come to terms with a female sexuality that was exercised outside the acceptable borders of middle-class and upper-caste womanhood that the women of the women's movement allowed the devadasi culture to be destroyed or, as in the cases of Besant, Reddi, and numerous others, actually assisted in delivering the final blows.

And yet for centuries in India the world of the Hindu temple dancers existed, if not in conjunction, at least alongside that of the upper-caste Hindu woman. Occasionally, these two groups of women even shared the same men, the Hindu husbands who visited the homes of the devadasis and sometimes served as their patrons and lovers. Although often depicted in a dichotomous relationship with one another, the wife versus the dancer, these two kinds of women were nevertheless both conspicuous figures within the various historical Hindu patriarchies of South India that preceded the nationalist era. It was only the late nineteenth and early twentieth centuries that saw the one female group consume the other. The historical shift that enabled this massive alteration to a status quo that had, in various forms, lasted for so very long is the consequence not only of the nationalist ideology that redefined the Indian woman but also of the growing dominance of the middle class in India, a class that understood itself in liberal humanist terms as universally significant, that identified its own values and way of living as the only legitimate moral choices. Hence, while earlier forms of Hindu upper-caste patriarchy tolerated and even encouraged a certain diversity among the subordinate female groups within its reach (a diversity, it is important to remember, that still worked to the primary advantage of the upper-caste men in whose interest these patriarchal structures functioned), the new liberal humanist patriarchy, with its increasingly ascendant middle class, set itself up as the yardstick by which all other caste and gender groups would be measured and in so doing stifled the diversity of those whom it also marginalized.

Owing to the tendency toward universalization at the heart of this class's humanist perspective, Indian feminists from the middle class were fundamentally unable to conceive of a world not made in their own image. With the gradual adoption of a secularist philosophy among the liberal men who were the nationalists and social reformers as well as among the women in these families, middle-classness also came to be seen as the *definitive* characteristic of these elites, a move that, in its substitution of class for caste, made their upper-caste positioning or (in the case of Reddi) identification invisible. Congruently, caste began to be constructed as something possessed only by people lower down on the social and political ladder, people like, for instance, the devadasis, who, although they did not constitute a caste on their own but became devadasi through initiation rituals (see Kersenboom-Story 1987), nonetheless were predominantly associated with the non-elite artisan castes. This public erasure of upper-caste status in its relation to lower-caste identities allowed for the emergence of middle-classness as a norm and an ideal rather than as a distinct and dominant site in a social and political hierarchy, which is what it was and is. The middle-class women of the early women's movement (including Reddi who, although not upper caste by birth was still middle class by marriage, education, and identification) could therefore define themselves and their views as normal, natural, moral, and obviously right and correspondingly paint the devadasis as purveyors of an antiquated and morally repugnant caste tradition that was best left in the Indian past. The erasure (but not the extinction) of their own upper-casteness prevented these women from being able to see their involvement in the suppression of this female profession as an exercise of power, through which a high-caste and middle-class community forced its will on a lower-caste group. That this group was also female in its composition made it even more vulnerable to that community's insistences, since the men who held the ultimate authority under this new liberal patriarchy, on behalf of which the middle-class feminists were unwittingly working, could legally and culturally control and define the meaning of femaleness. And they did. To their own women, they assigned the quality of purity, while the devadasi was made to play the oppositional role. Forced to inhabit an identity associated with impurity, her reputation as 'ever-auspicious' became moot.[5]

THE REVIVAL OF THE DEVADASIS' DANCE

But the devadasi tradition did not entirely die out. Some of the attributes and accoutrements of their dance were preserved through the vehicle of what has been called a revival movement, orchestrated principally by another group of women from the upper castes and middle classes: not the freedom fighters and social reformers who worked to outlaw the devadasi tradition, but artists and theosophists, whose justification for appropriating the dance of the devadasis involved the construction of the dance as a national trophy belonging to all Indians. The devadasis' sadir, a regionally specific art form performed by a clearly demarcated group of female professionals, became *bharatanatyam*, an emblem of Indianness designed to display modern India's ties to its gloriously ancient past as well as a dance that middle-class, upper-caste girls and women could do without losing their decency. In the process of this transformation, the problematic sexuality of the temple dancers was expunged. As one of the recipients of the reconstructed dance tradition, I have firsthand experience of how this metamorphosis was accomplished.

In 1983 I started studying *bharatanatyam* in Kingston, Ontario, Canada. My first teacher was a Brahmin woman from South India who had the good fortune to learn dance for a time with the most famous of devadasi dancers to survive the social reform campaign, Balasaraswati. Drawing an artistic genealogical line between me and that great dancer, my first teacher told me a few small, though somewhat unconnected details about the temple dancers and their difficult history. With her encouragement I went to India to study dance for a year in 1985–6. I was accepted into the famous performing arts college in Madras, now Chennai, called Kalákshetra. Kalakshetra was founded in the 1930s by a South Indian Brahmin woman named Rukmini Devi, and it is renowned for its teaching of bharatanatyam. Rukmini Devi was one of those middle-class, upper-caste dancers credited with the revival of the dance, which, we were told at the school, would have been lost had it not been for her. By being among the first Brahmin women to do the dance in public, she lent it a respectability it did not have when the devadasis alone did it.

There was a great deal of talk at Kalakshetra about *bhakti*, an attitude of pure spiritual devotion thought appropriate for a dancer of bharatanatyam, and little mention made of *sringara*, which my first teacher had taught me to understand as the expression of erotic and sexual love, also intimately connected to spiritual devotion. Kalakshetra, though it was many wonderful things, was one of the least erotic places I have ever been. The rules there were strict, especially concerning the behaviour of its young female students. I was a 25-year-old woman at the time, whose Canadian parents had long since ceased to be concerned about the quotidian details of my relationships with young men, and so I found the life at Kalakshetra to be a little bewildering and confining. I was told, for instance, by one of my fellow students, a young Tamil man from Malaysia whose homosexuality was well known even among the teachers, that I should refrain from touching him on the arm, as I tended to do as a gesture of affection, because the teachers wouldn't like it. Off the school grounds was a different story. Here we could demonstrate physical affection toward each other all we wanted. My point is that any gesture between a young man and woman that might be construed as erotic or sexual was not permitted. Similarly, in the realm of dance, sringara was not permitted, and young dancers who demonstrated this expression were thought to be vulgar, both by the students and the teachers. I of course, amended my conduct in this and in other ways because I felt it was a small price to pay for the privilege of attending such an extraordinary school.

I had gone to Kalakshetra expecting that in the course of my education I would find out more about the devadasis. I didn't, and it wasn't until years later that I began to recognize that the existence of Kalakshetra—with its bhakti-minus-sringara-oriented dance—was predicated on the absence of the devadasis. Although Rukmini Devi's bharatanatyam was an offshoot of the devadasis' *sadir*—indeed she developed the Kalakshetra style after learning sadir from one of the best-known of the devadasi gurus in the 1920s and 1930s, Pandanallur Meenakshisundaram Pillai, and one of its most prominent practitioners, Mylapore Gowri Ammal—these dance forms could not occupy the same space. In fact, the one was working assiduously to annihilate the other by insisting that its own version was more authentic, more true to ancient Indian tradition than the other. What the crafters of bharatanatyam did to erase the dance's associations with the devadasis' sringara-inflected sadir was to claim to have gotten their inspiration for the dance *solely* from certain ancient Sanskrit texts on performance, for instance, the *Natyasastra* and the *Abhinaya Darpana*. Such erasure could not, however, entirely disguise bharatanatyam's indebtedness to sadir, for, as Natarajan points out, despite the declaration by Rukmini Devi and other Brahmin dancers that they were resurrecting the dance from ancient Sanskrit texts, there was really only sadir from which to mount such a resurrection.[6] She describes this so-called resurrection in comparison to the historical borrowings between various geographically based styles of sadir (the Pandanallur style, the Vazhuvoor style, etc.) that had characterized earlier interactions among devadasi dance traditions: 'The slow rhythms of cross-fertilization and exchange between ... styles gave way, in the period of the Brahmin takeover, to the abrupt disturbance and acceleration that marked the advent of the universal modern: grossly undiscriminating hands rummaged through finely nuanced regional forms, selecting a theme here and a movement there, to produce the hegemonic version of bharatanatyam' (p. 209).

It is the hegemony of bharatanatyam with its attendant all-India ideology that should be troubling for dancers today, whether they claim descent from the devadasis' sadir or from the more recently invented form. For such hegemony freezes the meanings that the dance might generate, in India as well as abroad, limiting those meanings to the narrow confines of a Brahmin-sponsored Sanskritic tradition and to an expression of a distinctly unempowering middle-class femininity. In fact, Natarajan herself, a dancer as well as a scholar, goes so far as to make this assertion about bharatanatyam in contemporary India: 'The dance in India is so congealed in this alliance with the "tradition" and the disabling aesthetic (re)invented by Brahmin activists that it is hopelessly incapable of adapting itself to address the ethos of the modern' (p. 236). Innovation, the force that makes art forms relevant and inspiring to successive generations of artists and audiences, is difficult to produce when a dance has been made to reiterate again and again an unchanging and eternal Indian heritage.

Kalakshetra taught me a lot of things, but it could not, in good faith, teach me about the devadasis because to do so would be to call into question the fundamental assumption on which the school operated— the assumption that people who had not been initiated into the devadasi system could, nevertheless, in the new independent India, teach and learn the devadasis' dance. I might add that it was precisely this assumption that created the reality that enabled *me* to learn this South Indian dance though I was neither a dancer by inheritance nor even an Indian.

I no longer study or practice bharatanatyam, but the position I fill now as a professor of English in a small Canadian university college, a professor whose area of specialization is Indian literature in English and British literature about India is entirely the result of those eight years studying bharatanatyam, including that one incomparable year at Kalakshetra. I am, consequently, in a precarious position: indebted to a disjunction in Indian history that shifted the dance from out of the hands of the temple dancers and into those of the more politically powerful revivalists, I still cannot help but lament the displacement of the devadasi from the public arena of dance, and not for nostalgic or romantic reasons. I regret the defeat of the devadasi heritage, profession, and tradition by the forces of feminism because, if feminism is indeed, as we all believe and hope, a project of emancipation, the liberation of one female group at the expense of another undercuts the ideals that propel this worldwide project. The field of emancipation isn't expanded to include more women; instead, various freedoms and advantages are simply transferred from one female place to another. And in the 'modern' societies of the new millennial globe, it's almost always the working-class or otherwise subaltern women whose concerns are sidestepped and whose authority is subverted by a feminist programme that is, inadvertently, or not, pursuing middle-class interests. That this situation is pertinent to Indian feminism today is borne out by an article in one of the more recent Subaltern Studies collections. In 'Problems for a Contemporary Theory of Gender,' Susie Tharu and Tejaswini Niranjana (1997) argue that 'A wide range of issues rendered critical by feminism are now being invested in and annexed by projects that contain and deflect that initiative. Possibilities of alliance with other subaltern forces (dalits, for example) that are opening up in civil society are often blocked, and feminists find themselves drawn into disturbing configurations within the dominant culture' (p. 233). Avoiding such disturbing configurations must surely be one of the paramount aims of global feminism as it recreates itself in the twenty-first century. Let the history of the devadasis be a cautionary tale, then.

NOTES

1. There have been many feminist scholars who have made this point or something like it over the last 20 years or so, among them Rosalind O'Hanlon (1988) in her essay 'Recovering the Subject', Gayatri Spivak (1988) in 'Can the Subaltern Speak?', and, more recently, Anne Hardgrove (1995) in 'South Asian Women's Communal Identities.'

2. There are a number of scholarly texts that should be standard reading for anyone interested in the nationalist history of the devadasis: Amrit Srinivasan's 1985 essay 'Reform and Revival', Frédérique Apfel Marglin's (1985) book *Wives of the God-King*, Anandhi's (1991) essay 'Representing Devadasis', Janaki Nair's (1994), 'The Devadasi, Dharma, and the State', and an excellent doctoral dissertation by Srividya Natarajan (1997) entitled 'Another Stage in the Life of the Nation: Sadir, Bharatanatyam, Feminist Theory.' For a reading that focuses on the response of the British courts in late colonial India to the changing status of the devadasis, see Kunal M. Parker's (1998), *A Corporation of Superior Prostitutes*.

3. To maintain a sense of the diversity of this community, I should note that not all devadasis sought to preserve their traditions of temple service, music, and dance. Social activist and novelist Moovalur Ramamirtham Ammaiyar, for instance, who was herself once a devadasi as well as being born to one of the castes from which devadasis were drawn, saw the profession as the product of the patriarchal and upper-caste insistence on having sexual access to low-caste women. Initially aligning her politics with that of the Indian National Congress and Muthulakshmi Reddi, and subsequently rejecting them both as Brahmin-dominated, Ramamirtham Ammaiyar joined the anti-Brahmin Self Respect Movement and worked to bring an end to the practice of temple dedication. Her novel is analysed in relation to the anti-Nautch campaign in a very interesting essay by Anandhi (1991) called 'Representing Devadasis: "Dasigal Mosavalai" as a Radical Text.'

4. Scholars who write about devadasis often address what they see as a tendency among contemporary feminists to romanticize the lives and practices of the devadasis of South India. For example, Nair (1994) insists, 'We must not

exaggerate the power enjoyed by devadasis, who despite their relative autonomy nevertheless remained dependent on that triad of men within the political economy of the temple, the priest, the guru and patron' (p. 3161). Similarly, Anandhi (1991) declares, 'it was not a free flow of devadasis' desire which marked out the system, but its almost exclusive control by the landed patrons' (p.739). These are important reminders of the patriarchal orbit that circled the profession of the devadasis, in many ways placing them on something of the same footing as their counterparts, the Hindu wives. Still, it also needs to be conceded that the celebration implicit in much recent scholarship on these temple dancers, including in this essay, can be traced to their significance as markers of female diversity in the larger picture of pre-independent India. That there should be more disparate roles and accepted behavioural patterns for women in the world, rather than fewer, is one of the most fundamental of feminist ideals. The devadasis, at one time, represented an alternative to the principal life script allotted to Indian women, that which led only to wifehood and motherhood. Though their economic decisions and sexual choices were also circumscribed by patriarchal dictates, the devadasis and their history continue to point the way towards inspiring possibilities for women. At this moment in India, when Hindu fundamentalism works to essentialize women once again, it seems especially crucial to celebrate those who don't or didn't fit comfortably into Hindu patriarchy's coercive narrative.

5. Much recent scholarship on devadasis concerns not the historical temple dancers of colonial India but devadasis in India today, many of whom are drawn from lower-caste and dalit populations and whose profession does not include dancing. Like the middle-class crusade to end the historical practice of temple dedication and temple dance, current writing on these contemporary devadasis, although clearly driven by such admirable intentions as the desire to draw attention to and hence bring about the end of the sexual exploitation of working-class women by middle-class and upper-caste men, also often contains middle-class, universalist assumptions about appropriate sexual conduct for women and the inherent inferiority of non-middle-class cultures and peoples. See, for instance, Kay K. Jordan's (2002) essay 'Devadasi Reform', in which the following statement occurs: 'The poverty and ignorance prevalent in these [scheduled] castes cause parents to dedicate daughters to serve deities' (p. 47). Although Jordan earlier acknowledges the complicated reasons why impoverished parents might want their daughters to be devadasis, including the fact that such status sometimes confers social auspiciousness and esteem, she seems finally to shrug off these complications to paint the devadasis and their parents as simply desperate dupes of an ideology that only benefits the upper castes. The devadasis and their families emerge in such depictions as incapable of making their own decisions regarding their own lives, implicitly leaving the field clear for non-impoverished and non-ignorant (meaning educated in acceptably middle-class ways) crusaders to save these people and their daughters. As I've tried to demonstrate in this essay, analysis like this purveys middle-class values in the guise of objective scholarship and runs the risk of becoming complicit with elite-class and upper-caste exercises of power against working-class and dalit persons and communities.

6. A visual example of the Brahmin revivalists' success in erasing the devadasis' sadir is available in *Dance Magazine* by dance scholar Kimerer L. LaMothe (2001) entitled 'Sacred Dance, A Glimpse Around the World.' In it, LaMothe outlines the significance of a mid-day dance performed by devadasis at the Jagannatha temple in Puri as a ritual that transforms a meal into nourishment for both gods and pilgrims. The photograph that accompanies the short piece, however, is not of a devadasi but of a bharatanatyam dancer, and in the text below the photograph, bharatanatyam is described as 'a classical Indian style danced by the devadasis' (p. 64).

REFERENCES

Anandhi, S., 1991, 'Representing Devadasis: "Dasigal Mosavalai" as a Radical Text', *Economic and Political Weekly*, 11 and 12(26), pp. 739–46.

Asaf Ali, A., 1991, *The Resurgence of Indian Women*, New Delhi: Radiant.

Basu, A. and B. Ray, 1990, *Women's Struggle: A History of the All India Women's Conference, 1927–1990*, New Delhi: Manohar.

De Zoete, B., 1953, *The Other Mind: A Study of Dance in South India*, London: Victor Gollancz.

Gandhi, M.K., 1946, *To the Women: Gandhi Series*, A.T. Hingorani (ed.), 3rd edn, Vol. 2, Karachi: Hingorani.

Hardgrove, A., 1995, 'South Asian Women's Communal Identities', *Economic and Political Weekly*, 39(30), pp. 2427–30.

Hubel, T., 1993, 'Charting the anger of Indian Women through Narayan's Savitri', *Modern Fiction Studies*, 39(1), pp. 113–30.

Hubel, T., 1994, 'Devadasi Defiance and *The Man-Eater of Malgudi*', *The Journal of Commonwealth Literature*, 29(1), pp. 15–28.

Jayawardena, K., 1986, *Feminism and Nationalism in the Third World*, London: Zed.

Jordan, K.K., 2002, 'Devadasi Reform: Driving the Priestesses or the Prostitutes Out of Hindu Temples?', in L.J. Peach (ed.), *Women and World Religions*, Upper Saddle River, New Jersey: Prentice-Hall, pp. 39–49.

Kersenboom-Story, S.C., 1987, *Nityasumangali: Devadasi Tradition in South India*, Delhi: Motilal Banarsidass.

LaMothe, K.L., 2001, 'Sacred Dance, A Glimpse around the World', *Dance Magazine*, 75(12), pp. 64–5.

Marglin, F.A., 1985, *Wives of the God-King: The Rituals of the Devadasis of Puri*, Delhi: Oxford University Press.

Mehta, H., 1981, *Indian Woman*, Delhi: Butala.

Nair, J., 1994, 'The Devadasi, Dharma and the State', *Economic and Political Weekly*, 50(29), pp. 3157–67.

Natarajan, S., 1997, 'Another Stage in the Life of the Nation: Sadir, Bharatanatyam, Feminist Theory', Unpublished doctoral dissertation, University of Hyderabad, India.

O'Hanlon, R., 1988, 'Recovering the Subject: Subaltern Studies and Histories of Resistance in Colonial South Asia', *Modern Asian Studies*, 22(1), pp. 189–224.

O'Shea, J., 1998, "'Traditional" Indian Dance and the Making of Interpretive Communities', *Asian Theater Journal*, 15(1), pp. 45–63.

Parker, K.M., 1998, "'A Corporation of Superior Prostitutes": Anglo-Indian Legal Conceptions of Temple Dancing Girls, 1800–1914', *Modern Asian Studies*, 32(3), pp. 559–663.

Reddi, M., Papers in Nehru Museum and Memorial Library, New Delhi, India.

Spivak, G.C., 1988, 'Can the Subaltern Speak?', in C. Nelson and L. Grossberg (eds), *Marxism and the Interpretation of Culture*, Champaign-Urbana: University of Illinois Press, pp. 271–313.

Srinivasan, A., 1985,. 'Reform and Revival: The Devadasi and her Dance', *Economic and Political Weekly*, 44(20), pp. 1869–76.

Tharu, S. and T. Niranjana, 1997, 'Problems for a Contemporary Theory of Gender', in S. Amin and D. Chakrabarty (eds), *Subaltern Studies IX: Writings on South Asian History and Society*, Delhi, India: Oxford University Press, pp. 232–60.

PART II

Reinventing Dance in South India

New Beginnings?
Voices from Twentieth Century Madras

Part II

V. Raghavan (Bhava Raga Tala)

Bharata Natya—Classic Indian Dance

The South Indian Sadir-Nautch

The Recent Controversy Over the Art

The controversy over Nautch carried on in the columns of the Madras Dailies may be fresh in the memory of the pubic, at least of the art-loving section of it. We are thankful to the Anglo-Indian Daily of Madras, *The Madras Mail* and its Editor for having taken so much interest in it. Though the controversy has subsided for the present, the lover of indigenous art cannot forget it and must be anxiously bestirring himself over the means to protect the art and secure the pure and perfect spreading of it. It is meet that the Madras Music Academy condemned the Anti-Nautch activities and in the recent conference in December, 1932, affirmed its patronage and propagation of the art as forming part of the Academy's aims.

The Anti-Nautch movement is an old one in Madras. One of its leaders said that fifty years of its activities have completely killed the art in Andhradesa where the art had attained perfection. Even before the Willingdon entertainment shocked the moral sensitiveness of the social reformers and brought forth their condemnation of civilized citizens patronizing the art of dance, there had appeared in the *Hindu* reports of a conference of women social reformers having passed resolutions for the suppression of Devadasi music and Devadasi dance. It is well that the question attained some importance and many protests against the reformers appeared in the papers. It was most satisfying to see that the quiet community of Devadasis itself expressed forcibly its protest against the attack upon it by the vociferous world of social reformers, exposing the arguments of Nautch-iconoclasts.

First and foremost must be considered the moral objection to the dance performed by the community of Devadasis. Music and dance are not the causes of promiscuous sexual life nor is such life found only in that community. The charge of promiscuous sexual life itself is not proved by the actual facts obtaining in the community which is not lacking in examples of single-hearted devotion to single lovers, as can be seen by the evidence of life and literature. The community has its own code and mixes only with those cultured in the arts. It knows that promiscuous sexual life is ruinous to the great arts of music and dance of which they are the repositories, and it is wrong to condemn a whole community, much more so, the art they are exhibiting, for a fraction of its members who have fallen from art and thus being devoid of *kala* become *Bhoga-Murtis*, seeking life by other ways. Heredity counts much and as authorities on Eugenics say, Nurture as compared to Nature is only one-fifth. It is good to preserve the community in which women enjoy so much means to devote themselves wholesale to fine arts. If some of them lead also bad lives they may be driven to it and the greatest cause thereof is ourselves, the society, which, not being sufficiently interested in the great art they exhibit on account of our denationalized tastes and on account of our ignorance of and apathy towards indigenous art, interest ourselves rather in the exponent. If that great art gets the great patronage it once enjoyed and which it does deserve, there is no reason why its exponents should have supplementary careers, which none knows more than they do, will be ruinous to their art. But the question fundamentally resolves itself into one of art versus morals, and twenty centuries of Christian Era and many more of this old world have not solved the problem. We must not demolish one community and in its place, sow seeds for the gradual growth of a similar community of persons who, to adopt the Sanskrit saying, are lost both ways—'Ito Brashtas Tato Brashtah'; for, as is well-known and human nature being what it is, it is impractical and extremely unreal to talk of family women developing into the future repositories of Bharata Natya. The part of the family women in the realm of the art of dance shall be separately considered. Here this must be pointed out; knowing human nature to be what it is, how are we going to solve the problem of the extra-artistic or 'aftermath' influence of art on morals? Leaving aside Dance, even as regards music, the Vedas with their unerring psychological insight say, 'Tasmat Gayantam Kamayante Striyah'—'Women fall in love with those who sing'; and consequently a community of ancient ultra-purists had declared that musicians are *Apankteyas*, unfit to be had as guests in our houses. Some had excelled the modern social reformers by declaring that even talks of poetry should be avoided—'Kavyalapamscha Varjayet.' Therefore there is no use crying down the community and killing the art along with it. The disease must be diagnosed, located and remedied. The audience it is that imposes standards and conduct on the artists. If we are but genuine in the admiration for that art, if we but pay greater attention to this great indigenous art than to the cinema halls where we are not surely under the influence of more moral and spiritual circumstances, the art is bound to flourish under healthy circumstances.

It is suggested that the community must first be done away with and that 'respectable' women must then take to the art. This wisdom reminds one of the wiseacre who cut at the root himself sitting upon the branch. The question does not seem to be a purely moral question, for other conditions in social life contributing to lax moral life of girls and ladies are not attacked and the Devadasi community is picked out as if for killing its arts. A social reform Tamil novelist has deprecated the custom of richmen arranging dance by courtesans during marriages which ought to be times too sacred for such immoral performances. But how is it better when a modernly married metropolitan couple repair to the cinema or talkie house and celebrate their marriage by seeing American nature-clad stars, in shows punctuated with osculations, acting scandalous stories. It seems as if this side of modern life and its modern entertainment will persistently be refused to be seen and only Devadasi music and dance will be attacked by social reformers so sensitive to the health of the race. Let it be granted that family women take to dance and attain great perfection in it. Will they waste their talents in the courtyard of their houses or will they come in public and exhibit their art to the city? How are the delicate questions regarding the consequences of such ideals to be solved before we glibly talk of family women taking to the art?

Above all, I am of opinion, that pure art for art's sake and persued to perfection, is not the realm of family women for this reason, if not anything else, that they have not the time and other facilities for it. Even as regards music, few are the family women who are *Pallavi-Vidwan*s or Vidwan enough to give a sustained performance. Even admitting that there are some among them reaching that height, has the field of Music been cleared of professionals of other descriptions by the inrush of family women. It will be laughed at now if one repeats the maxims of the great thinkers that woman is for the home and that all her accomplishments are for beautifying the home and home-life. Her arts are of that level and are such as are enough for that purpose. A good deal can be done by the girls and ladies of the families to keep alive the various folk-arts in the realm of drawing, singing and dancing which are the rich heritage of the Indian homes. Some modern Renaissance art and dance movements are cited by the reformers as proof of the possibility of the new condition of things they are dreaming of. As for instance, mention was made in the controversy of Tagore-dance. Whatever be the merit of the said dance, it must be remembered that we are trying to solve the problem of the pure preservation of Bharata Natya and not to displace one art by another. Bharata Natya must be protected and Tagore-dance or any other dance which we often hear advertised by Renaissance movements are no substitute for it. Conditions are such now that one really fears the word 'Renaissance' and the more obscure, fantastic and bizarre the thing goes on, the more is it believed to be Indian Art. It seems to be very easy to impose abroad and carry on as an exponent of Indian dance. Not only do Indians play the game but foreigners like American women and others compete. Such a state of affairs should not be encouraged. Rank amateurishness, lowering of the standard of perfection, lack of fidelity and system, flimsiness, self-complacent contentment with trifling achievement—these must not be mistaken for Renaissance.

The family women are not capable of devoting the time and attention needed to develop to perfection this art of Bharata Natya. Domestic circumstances of work and care are not promotive of the spirit for it. The arts must come by themselves and practice especially of gestures and *Tirmanas* must begin from an early age. The body has to be specially nourished into perfect grace and beauty and without the artist's personality—*Patra Guna*—the art does not shine. For these a separate community exists. But what can the family woman do? They can do infinite work in the realm of folk-art, folk-music and folk-dance in which no modern English educated girl can be called to be rich. She does not know *kolam* but knows of compass, set square and the instrument box. She knows little of the huge mass of songs that our grandmothers sang on every festive occasion; she has not heard of *Pasavan, Kol-Attam, Kummi* and other girl festivals but can give out to you song-hits from this and that Hollywood talkie. There is the department of the folk-art of dance in its numerous varieties in which are combined graceful types of physical exercises also, in the resuscitation of which family women have got to play a great part. Leaders of women movements can do research in this direction and devote some of their time to the reviving of the dying household arts in painting, music and dance. Of course, genius cannot be stifled and exceptional cases of such women attaining great mastery over the pure-arts of music and dance are not ruled out. The law of life, nature and self-expression rules everywhere.

Third, the Anti-Nautchers say that they have the greatest admiration for the art of Bharata Natya. How have they proved their bonafides? What have they done for the art and its propagation according to their own methods and ideals all this time? This aspect of the question resolves into one of a basic and serious nature of the general apathy of the society towards indigenous art. Society now prefers Hollywood pictures—all singing, all dancing talkies to Bharata Natya. The evil presents itself everywhere. There are college students who whistle tunes from 'Sunny Side Up' or this Chevalier number or that but who know next to nothing of Tyagayya or Carnatic music. Kicking of limbs passing for dance is paid for and seen, and there are not youngsters lacking who denounce the graceful art of Bharata. In literature, drama etc., too, denationalization of our tastes has not yet been extirpated. Renaissance Theatres must mean the Renaissance of Indian drama and dance, of Bharata's art, of the plays of Kalidasa, Sudraka and Bhavabhuti or of modern vernacular dramatic movements but not of Shakespeare's *Hamlet*, *Othello*, *Julius Cæsar*, etc. The *Bommalattam* shows with their dexterous puppet-artists, the old *Natakams* based on Bharata's system, the *Nattuvans* and the *Natyacharyas* are all dying, if they are not already dead.

Let us leave aside the Nautch. It is one variety in the vast theatre of Bharata. The world knows the famous Chinese male artists who astound the public by their extremely perfect playing of feminine emotions. Does the social reform world know of the great art of Bharata and of those of its varieties which are not deposited in women, in Devadasis, but which are handed down through males, through a pious race of Brahmin *Bhagavatars*, perhaps greater artists than the said Chinese. Do the art-critics know that greater in importance and systematic fidelity to Bharata's art than even the Malabar *Kathakali*, there are, even to this day, enacted in such villages of Tanjore District as Sulamangalam and Uttukadu, traditional Natakams by select families of Brahmin male artists called Bhagavatars? What has been done by the reformers in Andhra for the preservation and greater spread of the art of Bharata Natya which is not in the bands of Devadasis but in the hands of males, the pious Brahmins called *Kuchipuri Bhagavatars*? Again how much has the modern art-critic and art-lover interested himself in the same art of Bharata with which the *Arayars* (males) expound in *Abhinaya*—gestures—the *Vaishnavite* lyrics in the month of Marga Sirsha? The slogan of 'Buy Indian' and 'Buy *Swadesi*' in the field of economic revival of India is heard everywhere at present; but not even faint sounds are heard of the most needed slogans of *Swadharma*, Swadesi and *Swarajya* in the field of art.

It is happy however to note that Dr Muthulakshmi Reddi has expressed the reformers' appreciation of the greatness of the art of *Natya*. But curiously enough, she is excelled by the Rt. Hon. V.S. Sastry who is the only person to express himself in an interview to the correspondent of the *Madras Mail* that the art of Bharata Natya is of 'doubtful merit.' It is all the more pitiable that one of such public eminence should mislead the world with such *obiter dicta*; still more pitiable it is that it should fall from the lips of one who is not only a political ambassador of India but is considered as an ambassador of Indian culture too. The Rt. Hon. Sastry however accepted that his grievance against the art might be due to his ignorance of it, which seems to be the fact. He has explained himself by saying that the signs or gestures shown by the dancers do not seem to have any relation with the idea or thing intended to be expressed. That is what a layman thinks of it and that is the sort of intelligent interest the most cultured among us take in the art and trouble to understand it. Those who have devoted some attention to it know that every gesture—Abhinaya—is not meaninglessly shown so that any impostor may show his or her finger this side and that and pass off as a great exponent of Bharata Natya. The symbols have their basis on Nature and are derived from Nature. After giving the gesture-symbols for certain number of ideas and objects, Bharata says that when a new idea or thing confronts the artist he has to create the Abhinaya or gesture for it himself by 'shape or form, by the dominant action, by some other persistent sign, by the class of the object as seen in the world.' (Bharata's *Natya Sastra*, IX Slokas 151–2), that is, that characteristic by which we at once recognize a thing in the world is made into the gesture-symbol which *suggests* the thing. When people devote some attention they can clearly see the simple symbolic gestures which suggest Lord Krishna by the action of the two hands playing on the flute. It is not known how one is not able to see the relation of the gesture to the idea gestured when the artist says 'tiger' and renders it by gesturing the two palms with its fingers bent in the shape of the claws of a wild beast. Anybody can see that a horned animal like a cow is suggested by the symbol of the hand with the last small finger and the finger next to the thumb lifted up like horns and the three other fingers joined at their tips to resemble exactly a cow's or a deer's face. There is perfect realism in the symbology of Bharata Natya. Further the understanding of the gestures is facilitated to a large extent by the verbal text of the song or musical theme which is first sung by the dansuese and after which the gestures of the words in the song follow.

The same critic wishes that the art should be more simple. I do not know which art is so simple as to enable people to understand it even without the slightest effort or desire on their part to do so. How many understand even music and its subtilities? But let it be granted that Bharata Natya is a complex thing. It must be known by these critics that Bharata's dance is of two kinds—*Nritya* and *Nritta*. The former it is that involves symbolic interpretation of an emotional theme through gestures or Abhinayas and can thus be open to the objection of indifferent men calling it as not being simple. The latter—*Nrittam* or *Attam* is mere rhythm and absolutely simple to be understood; for there is in it the mere beauty of motion, of *Laya*, which directly appeals. This forms part of Natya and comes in at the end of the Abhinaya of each part of the song and is sometimes done as separate items. These Tirmanas or *Adavuvarisai*s are set to various *gatis* in various *Talas* and lift the art above the European dance. This simpler dance of Nritta can be enjoyed by everybody and a study of the Bharata *Natya Sastra* reveals the existence of many a graceful variety of such dance by a single artist, by two and by a group of ballet-dancers. These involve no mysterious gesture symbology for they are not interpretative Nritya. Bharata says that this Nritta depicts no emotional idea except pure joy and beauty of motion. It is devised for this reason. Such forms can be studied and revived and here can be had for women the art of dance along with physical culture.

To conclude, the Nautch by women, by Devadasis, is not the only variety of Bharata's great art of Natya. Simple forms of it, varieties of it that males expound are available. Any new development based upon Bharata's art can be had. But what is urgent is the need of the pubic to cast off its apathy towards great indigenous arts and to take an overgrowing interest in them. We must have, to repeat again, Swadharma, Swadesi and Swarajya in the kingdom of art. That is true Renaissance.

Rukmini Devi Arundale

The Spiritual Background of Indian Dance

One of the greatest and most ancient arts of India is the dance and as far as I know India alone has given it so high a place in both national and spiritual life. No one was too low born for this sacred art, nor anyone too great or spiritual for it. From the Sublime Being comes the inspiration and example. Therefore, everyone who is but part of Him, every living creature, is animated by that spirit of creation which is the dance. It is because the whole conception of art is cosmic and all-embracing that in reality it is undying and eternal. Its expression is many, for it is like the light of the sun which sparkles on the ocean. From the oneness of that life comes the creative genius in man. Man intuits the spirit and absorbs his environment. From the harmony of the environment, the life, the thought, the philosophy and nature all around, with the creative spirit within, inspiration is born, and art is the expression. Environment is of tremendous importance to the actual form of art. The environment is what we call national life. If in India, the dance, as any other art, is essentially spiritual and philosophical, it is merely because the sages have given a spiritual meaning to it. It is also because the very same sages have, at the same time, helped to build the nation so that there is no fundamental difference between the spiritual and the physical, nor is there a difference between the manifest and the unmanifest. This has been the uniqueness in the civilization of India. If we understand the highest, we understand the least also—for both are one.

IMPORTANCE OF MUSIC

From this point of view comes the dance tradition of our country. Dance is not an art by itself. It is a unique expression, through the body, synthesizing all arts. In reality, though it is the nature of the body to respond to rhythm, yet it is *thamasic* in nature and its inertia expression, which we call dance. Therefore, the perfect harmony of the physical and emotional produces the dance. How is emotion stirred? It is flexible and quickly affected and that which stirs it most is sound. Sound as movement expresses itself in music. Music is the speech of the Highest. The first manifestation is in terms of sound, which is speech or music. All this is so magnificently conceived and presented to humanity through the form of Nataraja, the great Yogis of Yogi. In Him is synthesized all the planes of consciousness and all the arts.

We find that the instinct of dance is in the savage as in the cultured. When the dance becomes an art that transcends the physical, it becomes art, giving pleasure to all, to the devas as well as human beings. It is equally an art that pleases all tastes. In dance there is music for the musician, for dance is but the music of the body. It is said that when music, in terms of poetry, song and rhythm, blends with the instruments, it becomes complete music. There is music in the dance as there is dance in music. Without the spirit of music within, it is impossible to dance; for music is the expression of the highest emotion, through gesture, movement or mime. When it is perfectly expressed through gesture of *hasta-abhinaya*, movement or *angika-abhinaya* and *satvika-abhinaya* or facial expression, the dancer becomes something beyond and unfolds another great art into herself—the art of *natya* or drama. Then she becomes the story-teller or the actress. To do perfect justice to the story telling or in delineating a particular character in drama, *aharya-abhinaya* (expression through costume) becomes part of the four-fold aspects of the dance.

In Bharata Natya as danced in solo performances, the dancer is the story-teller and aharya abhinaya or the expression of a character through beautiful costumes and jewels is elaborate but simple in one sense. The dancer has merely to prepare herself to be beautiful and pleasant and to create a personality that can make her story attractive. Her art is music in the form of dance and every emotion of every song and every character is in her. In the dance-drama where the dancer is a particular character, the art of costume is itself expressive of a *rasa* or an aspect of the fundamental state and no movement is expressive by itself. The truest expression is in the experience within, which is dependent on so many things—especially on the spiritual development and perception of the artist.

DANCE AND OUR HERITAGE

Thus dance becomes an art that unifies art. The painter sees beauty of line and colour, the sculptor sees the grace and the form, the actor sees the portrayal of life, and the musician and poet alike see the very embodiment of poetry in motion. With all these blended in one who is dedicated body and soul, the dancer becomes the very expression of Nataraja Himself, of whom it is described that His *Angika* or the movement of His limbs is the world around the *Vachika*, the poetry of His dance, is the language within all speech, the *Aharya*, His costume and jewellery, are the moon and the stars, while the *Satvika*, the true expression, is the essence of Being, Siva Himself. In Him is all united and in Him is all transcended by the divine spirit. This is the dance and this is our heritage.

In this spirit we can still see true dance in India. Bharata Natya is the root and origin of all dance in India. Essentially, all real Indian dancing is Bharata Natya, though now only one particular school of art is known by the name. The most ancient authority on dance is the *Natya Sastra* of Bharata. In the South, there is what is known as the Tanjore School of Bharata Natya, but Kancheepuram and other cities are equally famous for the practice of the art. In every temple and on all auspicious occasions, there were dance performances. The art very nearly died as it had become a means for remembering the body rather than of forgetting it. Yet, those whom the world denounced as having become corrupt, gave themselves up with devotion and sincerity to the art they loved. The art was their very life and they worked and sacrificed their bodies for perfecting the art.

DIVINITY IN INDIAN DANCE

According to the Indian conception, character and dance go together. In reality they are one and the same, for what is without is but what is within. Through the portrayal of Gods and Goddesses one becomes divine. Indian dance being spiritual, it is suited only for spiritual expression. Through *bhava* one portrays in story-form the lives of Gods and Goddesses. The Indian genius has shown that humanity is divine and divinity is human; hence the stories of Gods and Goddesses who live and speak like humans. This was so in every part of India. There were the dance-dramas of the *Bhagavatar*s (men-dancers) in the Tanjore district, of Kuchipudi in the Telugu districts and Chakiar Koothu in Malabar where it still survives. Through these and through the still-living dance drama of Kathakali in Malabar, religion lived, philosophy lived and art lived. As you travel all over India we find no part of the country where dance did not flourish, although, except in Assam, Orissa and one or two places in the later years, dance was considered as an art of the vulgar. Yet one hears of the great Kathak dancers of United Provinces as flourishing under the patronage of rulers and noblemen. One never hears of Kathak being performed in temples but only in courts as temples had been destroyed, and the temple lost its place as a centre of art and culture. In Assam it is a respected art and it lives as a sacred expression enjoyed by all. Though the style is different from orthodox Bharata Natya, yet in essence it is the same, giving the same age-old atmosphere, and telling the stories of Krishna, Rama and the dance as an art-form lives everywhere, in the temples, in the courts, in the fields, among the peasants and even ordinary people all over India.

Because we forgot our heritage, the art almost disappeared. Today there is a sudden awakening to the glory of the art, and people everywhere are thinking and speaking of the dance. Entertainments are given everywhere and new names of famous exemplars of the art are heard.

REVIVAL OF THE ART

But if the art is to live, we have first to remember that it is an essential part of our lives. India's real achievement depends upon her understanding of the place of art in life. To know this, one must understand India, the very heart of India herself. We cannot revive the art by forgetting India. Indians today are forgetting India. They try to express in dance, a spiritual medium, ideas totally foreign to our genius. People try to portray Rama but disbelieve in Rama! That is why in modern India, art fails for want of sincerity. We tried apparently to rescure the art from the corrupt, but because we lack devotion, dedication and sincerity, we are gradually corrupting art itself. There is a general lowering of standards and the decline has been so fast that one dreads what is in store for the future. Will the dance have to go through another death before it regains its own glory? As dance is part of life itself, the nation and its consciousness will have to go through a revolutionary change in character. Indian arts have been slowly deteriorating because crudities have crept in. The sense of colour has almost vanished, equally the sense of form and line. The ordinary dramas portraying religious stories like the Ramayana and Mahabharata were crude and childish in presentation, though sincere is spirit. Today sophisticated vulgarity has taken the place of simple crudeness. Which is preferable, the crudeness of the ignorant or the vulgarity of the sophisticated? The latter has no compensations and is subtle and dangerous while the former had at least its merits. Hard work was its feature, inspiration its source, and devotion its aim. Today, there is dance without hard work. People want either diplomas or headlines. It is easy to have both because we do not have today, trained audiences, including art critics and the public will take one at one's own valuation. If that valuation is high as it is bound to be in the mind of the ignorant, the 'fame' achieved is indeed great. It was said by Kathakali teachers of the old type that it took 12 years of hard training before a dancer could even take a minor part on the stage. In Bharata Natya it took no less than seven or eight years of hard work. Today, even twelve months is too long. Owing to the lack of devotion, there is lack of discipline and, as a consequence, there is a deficiency in technique. The result is that there is no inspiration. To make up for this, false stimulation from outside is resorted to, instead of true stimulation from within. This naturally kills the creative spirit and, therefore, there has to be copying from others, and perhaps also borrowing from foreign countries. True art never copies. It is like a well of deep cool waters from which flows fresh ideas and life. India understood the dance as joy which is why Nataraja's dance is called *Ananda-Tandava*. This joy is that of a Yogi. What sort of a Yogi? One who has forgotten his body. The forgetfulness is not due to negligence but due to control. After training the body, one forgets it. This is the technique of 'art which conceals art'. This is why the dance is called a Yoga. People think that technique is the antithesis of creative expression. This is a wrong notion, since the creative spirit is but the achievement of a technique by which the technique itself vanishes, and uniqueness is the result. This final outcome is the supreme joy of creation. Even in folk art there is the expression of joy. Every part of India has its folk art, solo or group dramas, and dance-dramas. Each type expressed the uniqueness of the life and thought around, all different from each other like the Garba and the Rasa Lila of Gujarat, the Kaikottikali and Kolkali of Malabar, Kummi and Kolattam of the Tamil country, the village dances of Assam, Orissa and other places. For groups of every level of thought there is the dance from the lowest to the highest, from the child to the adult, filling the country with music and movement. When Indians realize what is Indian in essence, art will regain its original height and the dance will return to the people in all its pristine purity.

Dance is being revived but if this revival is to continue, we must know the spiritual message of art and make art a part of our lives. Then our very lives will become works of art and India will become a Land of Beauty; a fit vehicle for the message of the Sages and Saviour of humanity.

T. Balasaraswati

Bharata Natyam[*]

I am sincerely grateful to the Tamil Isai Sangam for giving me the honour of presiding over the Conference this year. I consider it a great privilege to have this honour conferred on me in the year of the 600th anniversary of *Arunagirinathar*[1] who sang the praise of *Arumugan*, the darling deity of Tamil Nadu.

There is a special relationship between Tamil music and Bharata Natyam. The Tamil lyrics of Muthuthandavar, Ganam Krishna Iyer and Subbarama Iyer lend themselves wonderfully well for dancing with intense participation. It is the distinguishing feature of Tamil music that compositions, coming in an unbroken line from the Vaishnava and Shaiva Saints through Gopalakrishna Bharathi down to the composers of our own time, are replete with moods and feelings suitable for *abhinaya*.

As far as I know, Bharata Natyam is *bhakti*; Tamil is also nothing but bhakti. I believe, therefore, that Tamil and bhakti are part of the same tradition.

In *Silappadikaram*[2], eleven dances[3] are referred to which were danced by divinities like Shiva, Tirumal (Vishnu), Murugan, Kama, Kali, Tirumagal (Lakshmi) and Indrani. They depict the destruction of various demons and symbolise the triumph of good over evil. This is evidence enough that the dance was a divine art whose theme was the destruction of evil and the purification of the spirit.

In these early dance forms, valour and wrath are the predominant emotions. Yet, *shringara* which was later to become the ruling mood of *abhinaya* was pre-eminent in the Tamil dance tradition right from the beginning. In the two important dance forms, the Court dance and the Common dance, which relate respectively to the inner and the outer life of man, shringara belongs to the Court and to the inner life. This explains

---

[*] Presidential Address of Dr T. Balasaraswati at the 33rd Annual Concerence of the Tamil Isai Sangam, Madras, 21st December 1975.

the eminence of shringara as a mood. In dances such as the Group Dance of the Cowherd Girls, this same *shringara* becomes the love of God. This *bhakti* is beautifully expressed in the following verses of *Silappadikaram*:

A girl to her companion:

The Magical One,
Who shook the young tree like a stick,
And brought the fruits down—
Should he come amidst our cattle,
Shall we not hear again,
The music of the sweet konrai flute
On His lips!

and

Oh, the look on her face!
Her garment and bangles slipped away
With her hands, she covered herself.
Seeing her,
Who hid herself with her hands,
His shame and pity became wild passion.
Oh, the look on His face!

It is this stream of shringara that swells into the mighty river of the lover-beloved songs of the Vaishnava and Shaiva Saints, the *ashtapadi*-s of Jayadeva and the compositions of Kshetragna. In Bharata Natayam, too, when it comes to abhinaya, shringara has been the dominant mood.

I emphasise all this because of some who seek to 'purify' Bharata Natyam by replacing the traditional lyrics which express shringara with devotional songs. I respectfully submit to such protagonists that there is nothing in Bharata Natyam which can be purified afresh; it is divine as it is and innately so. The shringara we experience in Bharata Natyam is never carnal; never, never. For those who have yielded themselves to its discipline with total dedication, dance like music is the practice of the Presence; it cannot be merely the body's rapture.

Bharata Natyam is an art which consecrates the body which is considered to be in itself of no value. The yogi by controlling his breath and by modifying his body acquires the halo of sanctity. Even so, the dancer, who dissolves her identity in rhythm and music, makes her body an instrument, at least for the duration of the dance, for the experience and expression of the spirit.

I believe that the traditional order of the Bharata Natyam recital viz., *alarippu, jatiswaram, shabdam, varnam, padam*-s, *tillana* and the *shloka* is the correct sequence in the practice of this art, which is an artistic yoga, for revealing the spiritual through the corporeal.

The greatness of this traditional concert-pattern will be apparent even from a purely aesthetic point of view. In the beginning, alarippu, which is based of rhythm alone, brings out the special charm of pure dance. The movements of alarippu relax the dancer's body and thereby her mind, loosen and coordinate her limbs and prepare her for the dance. Rhythm has a rare capacity to concentrate. Alarippu is most valuable in freeing the dancer from distraction and making her single-minded.

The joy of pure rhythm in alarippu is followed by jatiswaram where there is the added joy of melody. Melody, without word or syllable, has a special power to unite us with our being. In jatiswaram, melody and movement come together. Then comes the shabdam. It is here that compositions, with words and meanings, which enable the expression of the myriad moods of Bharata Natyam are introduced.

The Bharata Natyam recital is structured like a Great Temple: we enter through the *gopuram* (outer hall) of alarippu, cross the *ardhamandapam* (half-way hall) of jatiswaram, then the *mandapa* (great hall) of shabdam, and enter the holy precinct of the deity in the varnam. This is the place, the space, which gives the dancer expansive scope to revel in the rhythm, moods and music of the dance. The varnam is the continuum which gives ever-expanding room to the dancer to delight in her self-fulfilment, by providing the fullest scope to her own creativity as well as to the tradition of the art.

The padam-s now follow. In dancing to the padam-s, one experiences the containment, cool and quiet, of entering the sanctum from its external precinct. The expanse and brilliance of the outer corridors disappear in the dark inner sanctum; and the rhythmic virtuosities of the varnam yield to the soul-stirring music and abhinaya of the padam. Dancing to the padam is akin to the juncture when the cascading lights of worship are withdrawn and the drum beats die down to the simple and solemn chanting of sacred verses in the closeness of God. Then, the tillana breaks into movement like the final burning of camphor accompanied by a measure of din and bustle. In conclusion, the devotee takes to his heart the god he has so far glorified outside; and the dancer completes the traditional order by dancing to a simple devotional verse.

At first, mere metre; then, melody and metre; continuing with music, meaning and metre; its expansion in the centerpiece of the varnam;

thereafter, music and meaning without metre; in variation of this, melody and metre; in contrast to the pure rhythmical beginning a non-metrical song at the end. We see a most wonderful completeness and symmetry in this art. Surely the traditional votaries of our music and dance would not wish us to take any liberties with this sequence.

The aesthetics and the artistry of Bharata Natyam alike make us realise that shringara has pride of place here. In a sense, Bharata Natyam is a combination of the yoga and *mantra shastra*-s. The *mudra*-s of the mantra shastra are the same as the hand gestures of Bharata Natyam. When dancing to the beat of the rhythm, as in a yoga exercise, the dancer's body is rid of its human weaknesses and is purified into a conduit of the spiritual and the beautiful. However, the experience of the art can be total only if a variety of moods and feelings are portrayed; and variety is the soul of art. But these feelings should be universalised into aspects of divinity and not remain the limited experience of an insignificant human being. The mood of a song may tend to get portrayed as the subjective feeling of one individual; but true art lies in universalising this experience. To train the dancer in this art, melody and metre join together in jatiswaram. The dancer takes leave of her subjective consciousness in the alarippu and identifies herself with the universal consciousness in the jatiswaram. Hereafter, she is ready to explore and express the infinitely varied nuances of the entire gamut of emotions and feelings not in terms of her subjective self but in terms which bring out their universal essence.

Shringara stands supreme in the range of emotions. No other emotion is capable of better reflecting the mystic union of the human with the divine. I say this with deep personal experience of dancing to many great devotional songs which have had no element of shringara in them. Devotional songs are, of course, necessary. However, shringara is the cardinal emotion which gives the fullest scope for artistic improvisation, branching off continually, as it does, into the portrayal of innumerable moods full or newness and nuance.

If we approach Bharata Natyam with humility, learn it with dedication, and practise it with devotion to God, shringara which brings out the great beauties of this dance can be portrayed with all the purity of the spirit. The flesh, which is considered to be an enemy of the spirit, having been made a vehicle of the divine in the discipline of the dance, shringara, which is considered to be the greatest obstacle to spiritual realisation, has itself, we shall realise, become an instrument for uniting the dancer with Divinity.

Since the dancer has universalised her experience, all that she goes through is also felt and experienced by the spectator.

Refined in the crucible of alarippu and jatiswaram, the dancer portrays the emotions of the musical text in the shabdam in their pristine purity. In the shabdam, emotions are withheld at the beginning; thereafter, when the dancer has clarified herself, they are released in a measured and disciplined manner. It is after mastering this discipline that she dances the varnam which is a living river that holds together movement and interpretation.

The composer of shabdam or a varnam might have dedicated it to a prince or a nobleman. But as far as the dancer is concerned, the hero can only be the king of kings, the Lord of the wide world. It is impossible for her to dedicate her art, which has sanctified her body and has made her heart sacred, to a mere mortal. She can experience and communicate the sacred in what appears to be secular. After all, our composers have been steeped in the tradition of bhakti. While singing the praise of secular heroes, they begin to dwell on his devotion to Brihadishwara of Thanjavur or to Tyagesha of Tiruvarur or to Padmanabha of Tiruvanandapuram. The dancer taking the cue enters the realm of bhakti, enjoys the play and pranks of the deity concerned and displays them in her abhinaya. The divine, so far mixed with the secular, now becomes explicit in the dance and impresses itself deep in the heart. Various rhythmic movements are inter-twined with her abhinaya; this saves her from degenerating into the human, and keeps her fresh and pure in the yoga of the dance.

It is after passing through this ordeal of fire that the dancer fully qualifies herself to do abhinaya for the padam-s. If she has dedicated herself to the art, there will be no carnal distortions in her interpretations of the padam. Steeped in art and beauty, which are pure spiritual states, she expresses the joy which is at the basis of different moods and emotions. Such a dancer will feel no need to 'purify' any item in the traditional order of Bharata Natyam.

Indeed, the effort to purify Bharata Natyam through the introduction of novel ideas is like putting a gloss on burnished gold or painting the lotus.

The inadequacies that are felt in this art arise from the inadequacies of the dancer herself. If Bharata Natyam is studied with devotion, dedication, patience and thoroughness, its completeness in its traditional form will be crystal clear. The traditional sequence and structure of the recital secures and safeguards this completeness. There is, therefore, no need to purify perfection by amending, adding or subtracting any of the elements in the traditional order of the recital.

The traditional recital is a rich combination of diverse aesthetic and psychological elements which produces complete enjoyment. To alter this arrangement because it is considered 'boring' is to destroy the integrity of aesthetic enjoyment.

Let those who create novel dance forms present them as separate performances; they need not make a hash of the Bharata Natyam recital by interpolations of novelties. Of Madhavi's dancing master, the *Silappadikaram* says that 'he knew when only one hand had to be used (*pindi*) and when both the hands had to be used (*pinaiyal*). He also knew when the hands had to be used for exhibiting action (*tolirkai*) and for graceful effect (*elirkai*). Knowing as he did the conventions of dancing, he did not mix up the single-handed demonstration (*kutai*) with the double-handed (*varam*) and vice versa, as also pure gesture with gesticulatory movement and vice versa. In the movements of the feet also he did not mix up the *kuravai* with the *vari*. He was such an expert.'

The dancer can integrate herself with her discipline if she goes through the traditional sequence in one continuous flow without too much of an interval between one item and another; and the completeness of the recital in its entirety will assert itself. My personal opinion is that this concerted effect of the experience of dancing, which needs mental concentration, is spoilt by frequent changes of costume.

Silappadikaram and *Manimekalai* list dance, music and the personal beauty of the dancer in that order. Yet unfortunately the last and least of them has come to the forefront at the present time. When so much importance is attached to the looks of the dancer, it is but natural that dancing is considered carnal and shringara vulgar. The truth is exactly the opposite; it is her dance and music alone that make a dancer beautiful.

Kalidasa describes Malavika standing tired and perspiring after her dance as the best of all her abhinaya. This is not just poetic conceit. Even when the collyrium gets smudged and the make-up is disturbed in the course of the dance, that itself is a tribute to the dancer's dedication.

When the continuity of the dance is interrupted by costume changes, announcements and explanations, the congealing of inner feeling becomes impossible and concentration is shattered.

The greatest blessing of Bharata Natyam is its ability to control the mind. Most of us are incapable of single-minded contemplation even when actions are abandoned. On the other hand, in Bharata Natyam actions are not avoided; there is much to do but it is the harmony of various actions that results in the concentration we seek. The burden of action is forgotten in the pleasant charm of the art. The feet keeping to time, hands expressing gesture, the eye following the hand with expression, the ear listening to the dance master's music and the dancer's own singing—by harmonising these five elements the mind achieves concentration and attains clarity in the very richness of participation. The inner feeling of the dancer is the sixth sense which harnesses these five mental and mechanical elements to create the experience and enjoyment of beauty. It is the spark which gives the dancer her sense of spiritual freedom in the midst of the constraints and discipline of the dance. The yogi achieves serenity through concentration that comes from discipline. The dancer brings together her feet, hands, eyes, ears and singing into a fusion which transforms the serenity of the yogi into a torrent of beauty. The spectator, who is absorbed in intently watching this, has his mind freed of distractions and feels a great sense of clarity. In their shared involvement, the dancer and the spectator are both released from the weight of worldly life, and experience the divine joy of the art with a sense of total freedom.

To experience this rare rapture, a dancer has only to submit herself willingly to discipline. It will be difficult in the beginning to conform to the demands and discipline of rhythm and melody and to the norms and codes of the tradition. But if she humbly submits to the greatness of this art, soon enough she will find joy in that discipline; and she will realise that discipline makes her free in the joyful realm of the art.

The greatest authorities on the dance have definitively recognised that it is the orthodoxy of traditional discipline which gives the fullest freedom to the individual creativity of the dancer.

Young dancers who go in for novelties will find that their razzle-dazzle does not last long. On the other hand, if they hold firm to the tradition, which like the Great Banyan strikes deep roots and spreads wide branches, they will gain for themselves and those who watch them the dignity and joy of Bharata Natyam. I come out with these submissions only because of my anxiety that they should realise this. The young will recognise the greatness of this art if they study it with intense participation, calmly and without haste.

One has to begin early and learn it for many years to reach a devout understanding of the immanent greatness of this art. Then comes the recognition of one's great good fortune in being chosen to practice this art; this recognition leads the dancer to surrender herself to her art. Such surrender makes her aware of the divinity and wholeness of Bharata Natyam. And the art will continue to flourish without the aid of new techniques which aim at 'purifying' it or changes in dress, ornament, make-up and the interpolation of new items which seek to make it more 'complete'. This is my prayer.

It is the Tamil tradition to honour a dancer by presenting her with a *talaicol*.[4] I look upon the Presidentship of the Conference which the Tamil Isai Sangam has conferred upon me as a talaicol which I have received through the grace of Nataraja who keeps the myriad worlds in movement.

NOTES

1. Saint-poet of Tamil Nadu, author of *Tirupugazh* or the 'Holy Praise' of Arumugan or Subrahmanya, son of Shiva.

2. *Silappadikaram*—Tamil classic of the second century AD.

3. The eleven dances referred to in the *Silappadikaram* are: (*i*) *kodukotti* danced by Shiva on the burial ground; (*ii*) *pandaranga* dance which Shiva displayed before Brahma standing in His chariot; (*iii*) *alliyam* performed by Vishnu after disposing of the treacherous devices of Kamsa; (*iv*) *mallu* performed by Vishnu after the destruction of the demon Bana; (*v*) *tudi* (drum-dance) of Subrahmanya which was the war-dance of triumph, on destroying the demon Surapadma, on the heaving wave-platform of the ocean to the accompaniment of the rattle of his drum; (*vi*) *kudai* (umbrella-dance) danced by Subrahmanya lowering the umbrella before the demons who gave up their arms; (*vii*) *kudam* (pot-dance) danced by Vishnu after walking through the streets of Banasura's city; (*viii*) *pedi* danced by Kama (Cupid); (*ix*) *marakkal* dance of Durga; (*x*) *pavai* dance of Lakshmi; (*xi*) *kadayam* dance of Indrani at the northern gate of Bana's city.

4. *Talaicol*—Staff of honour given to musicians, poets and dancers. It was the central shaft of a splendid white umbrella captured in battle from the enemy-king.

(*Translated from the original Tamil into English by S. Guhan*)

Matthew Harp Allen

Rewriting the Script for South Indian Dance

For the past several years I have been investigating the local circumstances of what is commonly referred to as a 'revival' of dance is South India in the 1930s, working outward form a study of the *padam* genre of dance music.[1] Reading the work of Jennifer Post (1989), Regula Qureshi (1991), and Tapati Guha-Thakurta (1992), which describes and theorises 'revivals' in the performing and visual arts in the northern part of the subcontinent, has convinced me that the events in South India bear study as part of a larger pattern. Accordingly, I have been led to an investigation of pan-South Asian patterns of revival and of intellectual influences from outside South Asia upon these (self-consciously nationalistic) complexes of events.

This study centers on Rukmini Devi (1904–1986), a central local figure in the South Indian revival of dance, and on Nataraja (literally, *raja*, king, of *natanam*, of dance), a primarily South Indian manifestation of the Hindu god Siva, who became the central icon and master metaphor for the revival of dance and, arguably, for the Indian nationalist movement as a whole. In an attempt to understand these local actors—one human, one divine—my gaze has been drawn outward from South India toward Bengal, which as the capital of British India served as a major conduit for intellectual currents between India and Europe; to the Theosophical Society (founded in 1875), a transnational creature bred by the United States, Europe, and India;[2] to Ananda Kentish Coomaraswamy (1877–1947), initially a geologist, later a disciple of the British Arts and Crafts Movement, and finally a world-renowned aesthetician and historian of South Asian art; and to three American and European dancers who choreographed along Indian themes and performed these creations in the Americas, Europe, and Asia during the decades leading up to the revival.

The term 'revival' is a drastically reductive linguistic summary of a complex process—a deliberate selection from among many possibilities—which cries out to be examined from more than one point of view. While the 'revival' of South Indian dance certainly *involved* a re-vivification or bringing back to life, it was equally a re-population (one social community appropriating a practice from another), a re-construction (altering and replacing elements of repertoire and choreography), a re-naming (from *nautch* and other terms to *bharata natyam*³), a re-situation (from temple, court, and salon to the public stage), and a re-storation (as used in Schechner 1985: 69, a splicing together of selected 'strips' of performative behaviour in a manner that simultaneously creates a new practice and invents an historical one). The discourse on South Indian dance to date has privileged the term 'revival' over other equally descriptive ones, obscuring the complexity of the process, focusing attention onto a simple, celebrative vision of the giving of new life.

Rukmini Devi was not the only dancer central to the revival, and she was not the most popular dancer to emerge from it. It is the role which she ascribed to herself and which posterity has granted her—in the words of N. Pattabhiraman, 'her unique contribution was to destroy what was crude and vulgar in the inherited traditions of dance and to replace them with sophistication and refined taste' (1988: 24)—which placed her at the center of this essay along with Siva-Nataraja, the deity who became her model for action. Detailed consideration of T. Balasaraswati, the world-renowned bharata natyam artist from the hereditary dance tradition who, virtually alone from her community, continued to dance after 1940, and of 'Baby' Kamala, who as a young girl became the first Brahmin 'star' of the dance in the early 1940s, is not possible here.

Nataraja, an ancient form of the god Siva indigenous to South India, would serve as the perfect *nayaka* (lord) of the revived dance. The astonishingly beautiful bronze sculpture of Nataraja from the Cola era (ca. 9–11th century CE) is today the focus of his renown in the international art world, but even earlier (ca. 530 CE) Nataraja was depicted in stone in the Chalukya center of Badami, dancing with the wives of the *rishi*s (sages) in the forest. As we will see, however, despite his deep roots in South Indian religious tradition, Nataraja had never before been asked to play a role quite like the one reserved for him in the 20th-century revival.

The groundwork for this complex process of 'revival' and other 're's' was laid by intertwined cultural and political forces within the Indian nationalist movement, itself grounded substantially in Orientalist thought and Victorian morality. Key figures in the movement to revive Indian high culture, such as <u>Rukmini Devi and Ananda Coomaraswamy</u>, far from being isolated mono-cultural social actors, embody in their persons and their intimate associations this intellectually and culturally hybrid world.

I'm happy [...] I was able to prove we could do without them.

—Rukmini Devi (in Sarada [1943] 1985: 50)

I begin with a 1943 quotation by Rukmini Devi, the first Brahmin woman to perform dance in modern South Indian history[4] and the founder and long-time director of the pre-eminent dance training institution in South India, Kalakshetra:

One great new thing that has come as a result of these difficulties is the complete separation of our work form the traditional dance teachers. It is a well-known fact that they are a small clan of people who have never believed it possible for anybody else to conduct a dance performance. I have always had a determination that this must go. They used to think that, except the usual class of people, no one else would be able to dance. Now there are so many girls from good families who are excellent dancers. The second aspect is to train Nattuvanars [dance teachers] from good families. I am happy that on Vijayadasami day I was able to prove that we could do without them. (in Sarada 1985: 50)

What *great new thing* has been accomplished? What were the *difficulties?* Who are they, this *usual class?* And who are we, the *good families?* How can an intelligent, idealistic human being like Rukmini Devi exult that on an auspicious day she is able to dispense with the artistic collaboration of an entire class of fellow human beings?[5] Why did she think that appropriation—though she probably never used this term, it is implicit in her use of *separation* above—of the dance art was legitimate, indeed imperative? Given the centrality of Rukmini Devi to the 1930s revival, and given the tremendous prestige that bharata natyam has come to enjoy as an all-India and an international 'classical' dance art, it behooves us both to search for answers to particular local questions and to study the webs—the social, political, intellectual, and artistic currents of the late 19th and early 20th centuries in and outside India—in which her statement hangs suspended.

Let us consider the specific local questions posed above: The 'great thing,' the 'separation of our work from the traditional dance teachers,' was to Rukmini Devi the second and final *aspect* or stage of the appropriation of a dance art from a hereditary community of artists. In the first stage, the we, young women from 'good families,' had begun studying and performing dance in the mid-1930s, Rukmini Devi being one of the first Brahmin women to do this. For instruction, however, *we* were compelled to go to *them*, the *nattuvanars*, dancemaster–teachers and kinsmen of the community of women dancers known as *devadasis*. Devadasis (*dasi*, servant, of *deva*, god) were female Hindu ritual practitioners, women who underwent training and initiation in religious-artistic service, including dance and vocal music. After her period of training, a devadasi was ritually married to the god of a Hindu temple and therefore became *nityasumangali*, always-auspicious, by virtue of the fact that, married to the god, she could never become a widow.[6]

In the first aspect, or stage, of appropriation, the hereditary community of devadasi dancers was replaced by a new community of upper-caste dancers. This was a gradual process and not an uncontested one; arguments abounded in the early 1930s between those who thought the existing human 'vessel' needed to be replaced by a new (pure) one, and those who claimed that the vessel had integrity and only needed a better coating and a proper venue for display. Through the decade of the 1930s, a stream of non-Brahmin dancers from the traditional community were presented at the Music Academy, the most prestigious public performance venue in Madras (founded in 1928), by the lawyer E. Krishna Ayyar (1897–1968) and other Brahmin arts connoisseurs (Arudra 1987: 23–8). These performances proved instrumental in encouraging 'middle-class' women (an Indian-English euphemism referring substantially to the Brahmin community) such as Rukmini Devi to see and then to study dance. By 1940, most of the dancers from the traditional community who had danced at the Music Academy during the 1930s had stopped performing publicly, with the notable exception of T. Balasaraswati (1918–84). She established a dance school on the Music Academy premises, performed from the 1930s to 1970s in the Academy's December 'music season' concert series, made repeated international tours and trained many foreign students beginning in the 1960s, and was elected to the Academy's highest honour, the *Sangita Kalanidhi*, in 1973.[7]

What were the recent *difficulties*? The new students depended on teachers from the traditional community who possessed the techniques of the dance art. In 1943 Pandanallur Chokkalingam Pillai (see Singer 1972: 176–80), a nattuvanar teaching at Rukmini Devi's school, left her employ for a more lucrative offer elsewhere, on the eve of several important concerts and after a variety of interchanges which he likely viewed as demeaning and she likely viewed as impudent. A series of tensions between Rukmini Devi and nattuvanars preceded Chokkalingam Pillai's departure, beginning back in 1935 with her decision to perform for the Diamond Jubilee Celebrations of the Theosophical Society before her earlier *guru*, Chokkalingam Pillai's venerable father-in-law Pandanallur Minakshisundaram Pillai (1869–1954), thought her ready (Meduri 1996: 277, 299). This would have been unthinkable in the traditional teacher-student relationship, in which the teacher determines the date of the student's *arangerram* (premiere performance). It was also a traditional practice for a nattuvanar to receive handsome gifts on the occasion of a dancer's arangerram in addition to gifts (or cash salary, in the case of new institutions such as Kalakshetra) given during the course of instruction—a custom which Rukmini Devi did not follow. Such conflicts are illustrative of the inherent clash of cultures that occurred when a student came to the practice from outside the hereditary community, bringing an explicit agenda involving appropriation based on a worldview which considered the hereditary keepers of the tradition as unworthy.

In the second stage of revival, according to Rukmini Devi's thinking, the services of the troublesome dance teachers were thus to be dispensed with, completing the removal of the entire traditional community, dancers and teachers, from the profession. As the traditional nattuvanars did not simply teach their students but also actively directed their performances onstage—reciting rhythmic compositions which the dancers performed through their non-representational *nritta* ('pure dance' in bharata natyam parlance) and serving other functions as well—the lack of a nattuvanar onstage to direct the dance presented a serious problem. Rukmini Devi clearly felt that the solution was to train nattuvanars from within her own social community. As she stated in 1943, at that time she had trained new nattuvanars from *good families* who could take over the work (to her satisfaction, at least), and several Kalakshetra performances that year were conducted by student-nattuvanars. By dispensing with traditional teachers and using her own students as nattuvanars, Rukmini Devi dramatically altered the modalities of communication in performance. In the new situation, the student-nattuvanar was in no way able to direct the dance in the manner of the traditional teacher but simply was to try to follow it; hence the slighting term *tattuvanar* used by critics to describe such new, non-traditional nattuvanars (*tattu* simply means to beat a stick; i.e., the student-nattuvanars needed neither talent nor depth of experience to do their job—only the ability to keep time).

Unlike the first stage, this second stage appropriation, replacement of the traditional nattuvanars, was never completed. Although Rukmini Devi ended her institution's employment of nattuvanars from the hereditary community in 1943, a number of traditional nattuvanars thrived, or at least survived, outside Kalakshetra, and some nattuvanars descended from the early 19th-century Tanjavur Quartette (four eminent nattuvanar-composer brothers) remain a major force in bharata natyam training to the present day.[8] Still, the lines of power and authority between student and teacher have shifted considerably, a process which Rukmini Devi was instrumental in initiating. Formerly, the teacher wielded near-complete authority over his charge from youth through her maturity, invariably directing the dancer's performances and retaining considerable control over her career. Today, students engage teachers and pay cash tuition for training. (This has resonances of the modern consumer, shopping for instruction.) Once mature, dancers rarely use their guru as the nattuvanar onstage for their performances, relying instead on a cadre of more-or-less freelance nattuvanars and accompanying musicians, or even on taped music.[9]

Finally, a basic question: Why did Rukmini Devi and others deem a separation of *our* work from *theirs* necessary? The question is answered in a narrative given to Avanthi Meduri by her own Brahmin dance teachers in Madras (themselves products of Kalakshetra), a narrative that thousands of young middle-class Indian dance students have absorbed in essentially the same form since the 1930s—one which surfaces in countless books on and reviews of dance:

My dance teachers told me a story, a story they were never tired of repeating [...], that this dance was once called *sadir* and that it was performed in the sacred precincts of the temple. They said that the *devadasi* (temple dancers) who practiced this art form lived and danced happily in the temple environments [...] But then the *devadasi* turned 'corrupt' and profaned the art form, they said suddenly, and rather angrily. Frightened by their anger, I asked rather hesitantly about how they had profaned the art. They looked around them to see if anybody was eavesdropping, and whispered into my ear: they said that dancing became associated with *nautch* girls because of the corrupt ways of the *devadasi*. [...] A highly complex system rooted in religion had become 'corrupted' until the 'respectable' people of the south initiated a campaign in the late 1920s to abolish the ill-reputed *devadasi* system. (Meduri 1988: 1)

NATIONALISM, COLONIALISM, AND 'REVIVAL' IN SOUTH ASIA

There is strong evidence that events taking place in South India were part of a larger pattern. In the world of musicology there were significant currents of influence flowing between scholars of Hindustani (North Indian) and Karnataka (South Indian) music in the early 20th century, a fact that has remained a subtext in the scholarly discourse, proceeding as it has tended to along two parallel tracks (very few performers or scholars are intimately involved with both traditions). First, the North Indian (Marathi) lawyer-scholar V.N. Bhatkhande (1860–1936) travelled south in 1904 and met Subbarama Dikshitar (1839–1936), author of the treatise *Sangita Sampradaya Pradarsini* (1904) and adopted grandson of the composer Muttusvami Dikshitar.[10] Bhatkande familiarised himself with the Karnataka *melakarta*, the scale-based system for classification of *ragas* (melodic modes), which then became a formative influence in his own systematisation of Hindustani musical practice. Dikshitar provided Bhatkande with manuscripts from the 15th–18th centuries which demonstrated to Bhatkande's delight that—unlike in the North where (he felt) the tradition was in the hands of unlettered practitioners—'the music that is practiced there [in the South] has the authority of the texts' (in Ratanjankar 1967: 17). While Karnataka music theory thus proved a direct inspiration for the development of the *that* system of raga classification in the North, the idea of the music conference was first established in the North, and was later taken up in the South. At the first All-India Music Conference in 1916, organized by Bhatkhande under the sponsorship of the Maharajah of Baroda, the South Indian musicologist Abraham Panditar of Tanjavur was in attendance and presented a paper. Eleven years later in 1927, the first music conference in South India took place as an appendage of the annual Congress Party meeting in Madras— an event which led to the founding of the Music Academy of Madras the following year. (The doyen among Madras *sabhas*, music-sponsoring organisations, the Music Academy hosts a yearly music conference with scholarly paper sessions as well as performances of music and dance, maintains a research library, and has published a scholarly journal since the early 1930s.)

Regula Qureshi has documented a process of revival/appropriation in the northern part of the subcontinent which appears strikingly similar to the process in the South. Qureshi notes the goals and methods of the revivalists in the North—a primary goal being reclamation of the spiritual status of music, and a primary method to achieve that goal being a shift of personnel—and argues that European Orientalist thought played a major role in this nationalist endeavour:

> Somewhat ironically, it was British Indology which showed the way to reclaiming the spiritual status of music, through its paradigm originating in European alienation and today debunked by Marxist historians (Thapar 1977): The Hindu Golden Age of Spirituality, whose ideation and historical reality is enshrined in Sanskrit texts. [...]

The visionary who set out to achieve the new goal in a comprehensive way is V.N. Bhatkande. He directly embodies this 'engaged' pursuit of historical scholarship as a pivotal figure in the entire enterprise of musical revival and of redefining Hindustani music. Pandit Bhatkande was the 'father of music conferences'; as the life and soul of the first five such events, he engaged nationalists and their noble patrons to support socially acceptable teaching and performing venues. [...]

But there was a major shift required to realize this musical transformation: that of personnel. Initiated and articulated very clearly by Bhatkande, it became the agenda for middle-class Hindu music lovers for a generation: to take music out of the hands of the Muslim hereditary professionals and win it for the Hindu elite through discipleship and devotion. (1991: 160–61)

While, in the course of the revival, communities of Muslim musicians and dancers in the north of the subcontinent were disenfranchised, the hereditary community of non-Brahmin Hindu dancers was replaced in the South. In both cases, the replacement performers came form high-caste, almost exclusively Brahmin, Hindu communities.[11] Leaving behind the practice of dance in the face of overwhelming social pressures, a significant number of women from the traditional dancing community nevertheless continued in the profession of musical (most often vocal) performance, where they have achieved great recognition; however, in the 1990s, very few of the women descendants of this community are going into musical performance.

Neither the mother nor grandmother of T. Balasaraswati performed dance, though their female ancestors had been court dancers at Tanjavur. Leaving dance behind, like many members of their community, the women in this family began to concentrate in the late 19th century on vocal or instrumental musical performance. (When Balasaraswati wanted to begin dance training as a young girl in the 1920s, it was the subject of a heated debate among family members and close friends.) The women of this family are atypical in that they continue as professional musicians today, while most women of the community have stopped singing as well as dancing. The decline in the number of hereditary South Indian women performers closely parallels the two-stage withdrawal of women from artistic performance in western India. According to an account by Jennifer Post, the women of western India first left dance to concentrate on vocal music and then, one or two generations later, ceased performing music as well (1989).

Qureshi notes that the replacement of Muslim musicians by upper-caste Hindus in North India had the extraordinary effect of closing the social gulf between performer and audience, a chasm in the patron-artist relationship that had existed for centuries. The revival of dance in the South led to the same change there, as thereafter the connoisseurs were from the same community as the performers. V.N. Bhatkhande and Rukmini Devi played analogous roles in a drama of appropriation and legitimation within a pan-South Asian framework of nationalist aspiration and cultural regeneration. The arts were 'revived'—renamed, appropriated and repopulated, reconstructed, represented—as one wing of the nationalist enterprise. In South India, as we have seen, it was a national meeting of the Congress Party in Madras in 1927 that led to the founding of the Music Academy. Furthermore, important figures associated with the early days of the Music Academy, such as E. Krishna Ayyar (whose presentation of devadasi dancers at the Music Academy first gave Rukmini Devi the opportunity to see dance in a 'respectable' setting), were intimately involved with the nationalist movement. Krishna Ayyar, a member of the socialist section of the Indian National Congress who shocked his contemporaries by performing devadasi-style dance in drag as early as 1926 (Meduri 1996: 158–60), was in and out of jail for nationalist activities in the 1930s (Arudra 1987: 35–36).

In her study of the creation of a new 'Indian' art in Bengal (her quotation marks signifying an attention to not only the constructed, restored nature of artistic practice but of the nation itself), Tapati Guha-Thakurta argues that Indian nationalist thought was inextricably intertwined with international intellectual and political networks, oriented to the seat of colonial power in England:

The new nationalist ideology of Indian art, its aesthetic self-definitions and its search for a 'tradition' had strong roots in Orientalist writing and debates. British Orientalism produced and structured much of its notion of an Indian art tradition. While it had provided the core of historical knowledge and archaeological expertise on the subject, it would also stand at the helm of the aesthetic reinterpretation of Indian art during the turn of the century. (1992: 146)

The motivation for such an interest on the part of the British was complex and notably political. To study in order to consolidate influence was an implicit agenda of British colonialists since at least the time of the founding of the Asiatic Society of Bengal by Warren Hastings in 1784— an agenda which by the turn of the 20th century had become quite explicit. Guha-Thakurta quotes Lord Curzon, chief English administrator of India from 1898 to 1905:

The development of Orientalist studies in India was, for rulers like Curzon, a great imperial obligation: 'Our capacity to understand what may be called the genius of the East is the sole basis upon which we are likely to be able to maintain in future the position we have won.' (1992: 147)

The major British figure involved in the creation of this new 'Indian' art was the art educator Ernest Binfield Havell (1861–1934), who first came to India in 1884 to take up the position of Superintendent at the Madras School of Arts. After spending a decade in South India, he was Superintendent of the Government School of Art, Calcutta, from 1896 to 1906. During his tenure in Calcutta his interest gradually turned from encouragement of what he viewed as Indian 'crafts' towards the 'fine arts' (a shift of focus we will see occurring as well in the early career of a young scholar inspired by Havell, Ananda Coomaraswamy). In Calcutta, Havell became intimately involved in promoting a young Bengali painter, Abanindranath Tagore (1871–1951), as the front for a school of truly Indian art: 'His protégé Abanindranath and his pupils engaged with utmost seriousness in reviving what they considered "the lost language of Indian art," as part of their concerted campaign against the Westernization of art in India' (Mitter 1984: 80). Havell sold off pieces from the mediocre European collections of the Calcutta Art Gallery in order to buy Mughal paintings and other examples of Indian art, a move that earned him criticism not only from some British quarters, but also from the Bengal nationalist press. In 1906 Havell was recalled to Britain, declared 'unfit for further service in India' by a government irritated at his 'meddling in the arts revival' (Meduri 1996: 96). Havell thus became a somewhat oppositional 'internationalist' figure (Meduri 1996: xxiii) within British Orientalism, as did Coomaraswamy and the woman who would have the most profound effect on Rukmini Devi, Annie Besant (1847–1933).

RUKMINI DEVI AND THE THEOSOPHICAL SOCIETY

Although born into a South Indian Brahmin family, Rukmini Devi would not grow into the stereotypical life of an early 20th-century Brahmin woman, illiterate and cloistered in a circle of domestic duties. Due to her family's intellectual temperament, notably her father's involvement with the international Theosophical movement, she was highly educated—her studies included Sanskrit, at that time the almost exclusive preserve of Brahmin males—and was raised in close contact with American and European intellectuals and artists, male and female. Rukmini Devi's father, Nilakantha Sastri, who came from a family of Sanskrit scholars, was a civil engineer for the government, a position which necessitated frequent moves for the family around South India. Intellectually curious and impressed with the Theosophical literature he had read, he was initiated into the Society by co-founder Colonel Henry Olcott (Ramnarayan

1984a: 20). When he retired from government service, Sastri moved the family to a house just outside the Theosophical compound in Adyar in the southern suburbs of Madras and placed young Rukmini and her siblings at the epicentre of the society's activities in India.

The question of agency is central to a consideration of Rukmini Devi. The discourse on South Indian dance to date has stressed and celebrated her independence as an actor, her courage and vision in achieving the unbelievable in the face of all kinds of odds. What has gone almost completely unremarked or at least unwritten by dance scholars, social historians, and biographers (excluding a major study by Avanthi Meduri [1996] and the attention given to her in Arthur Nethercot's 1963 biography of Annie Besant) is the extent to which her young person was the site of absolutely feverish Orientalist-internationalist Theosophical activity, culminating in the proclamation of Rukmini Devi as World Mother (twice, in 1925 and again in 1928), and further, the extent to which this activity may have coloured and shaped Rukmini Devi's subsequent involvement with the so-called revival of dance in South India.

The Theosophical Society was founded by Olcott and H.P. Blavatsky in 1875 in New York. By the time Annie Besant first set foot in India in 1893, an Eastern 'Esoteric' section of the Society had been started by Olcott, who called Besant its 'sweet spirit and guiding star' (Nethercot 1963: 18[12]). An idyllic site for the future headquarters' grounds and buildings had been obtained on the south bank of the Adyar River in Madras, and spurred by Theosophical interest in 'Eastern' religions, many wealthy Americans and Europeans (some titled aristocracy) liberally supported this expansion. Besant, who to the astonishment of both supporters and adversaries back in England had been 'converted to Theosophy at the height of her career as a materialist, an atheist, an anathematised advocate of birth-control, and a feminist crusader in all the new advanced movements' (Nethercot 1963: 11), dived into her work in India with total dedication. By all accounts she was determined to position and maintain the Theosophical Society not simply as a mystical or occult organization, but as a major force in Indian society. She made the Society a potent player in the Indian nationalist movement, even serving as President of the India National Congress Party in 1917/18, though her self-insertion into nationalist politics came to be resented by many Indian leaders who 'had not been informed that she was acting in accordance with the wishes of the Rishi Agastya' (Nethercot 1963: 273).[13] She founded several universities and the Young Men's Indian Association (a counterpart to the YMCA), helped start the Boy Scout movement in India, and carried on a plethora of other community activities. The simultaneous involvement of the Theosophical Society in matters spiritual and political is telling, as we will see; the mentoring of Rukmini Devi by Theosophical leaders argues a strong role for the Society, with all its international implications, in the revival of dance in South India.

As a young man, George Arundale (1878–1945), the nephew and adopted son of the wealthy, unmarried Theosophist, Francesca Arundale, became a protégé of Theosophical leader Charles Leadbeater (1847–1934). Arundale came to India in 1903 as Principal of the Central Hindu College in Banaras, one of the institutions founded by Annie Besant. In 1913, he met Rukmini Devi at a party given by his aunt (Ramnarayan 1984: 26). She was about nine years old. Seven years later, one year after the death of her father in 1919, Arundale, aged 40, shocked orthodox Brahmin Madras society by proposing marriage to the 16-year-old girl. Upon her acceptance, the marriage took place in Bombay, away from the furore in Madras, on 29 April 1920. After she was named President of the All India Federation of Young Theosophists in 1923, and of the World Federation of Young Theosophists in 1925 (Ramnarayan 1984a: 27–28), the new and exalted role of World Mother was conceived for Rukmini Devi by the leaders of the Theosophical Society. The flavour of Theosophical esoteric transactions is captured somewhat tongue-in-cheek by Arthur Nethercot, here discussing events at the 1925 Theosophical Star Camp in Ommen, Holland, leading up to the selection by the Society's astral advisors of Rukmini Devi as the head of the new World Mother organization:

That night George [Arundale] was consecrated Bishop—so they were told the next morning—in a beautiful ceremony by no less than the Lord Maitreya himself, with all the Masters present. The Masters now began to hand down many instructions through the newly made Bishop. [...] Rukmini astonished them all with the nightly experiences, and her husband reported that it was said of her in the other world that she had no fault. [...] On the morning of 10th August [1925], Bishop Arundale disclosed that during the night he had been entrusted with a message of incredible importance by the Masters. [...]

These announcements came just in time, because the Star Camp at Ommen opened later the same day. Annie Besant hastily summoned a meeting of the special pupils and electrified them with a general disclosure of what had occurred. The next day she divulged that Rukmini, Lady Emily [Lutyens, daughter of the Earl of Lytton, at one time Viceroy of India], and [B.] Shiva Rao [a young protégé of Besant] had passed further Initiations the preceding night, though all that Lady Emily could remember was that she had spent a very disturbed time fighting with a bat in her room.

But that night at the Camp Fire, Annie in a long address broke the thrilling news to everyone. [...] Her 'daughter,' Rukmini Arundale, she predicted, would pass [initiation as one of the twelve apostles for J. Krishnamurti, the coming messiah] in a few days, and, 'hearing the call of her Master very, very early in life, will be the Rishi Agastya's messenger to the women and young ones in India, taking up a large part of the work there I have been carrying on for years.' (1963: 364–65)

The creation of a World Mother organization placed Rukmini Devi in a position parallel to that of the young J. Krishnamurti (1895–1986), at that time being groomed to be the vehicle for the second coming of the messiah. The childhoods of these two Theosophical chosen-ones had striking parallels as well. Like Rukmini Devi's father, Krishnamurti's father Narayaniah was a frequently transferred government employee (revenue collector) and Theosophist. As upon his retirement Rukmini Devi's father had moved the family close to the headquarters in Adyar, so had Krishnamurti's father moved his children there upon his retirement in 1907 (his wife had died in 1905). One day, Krishnamurti, standing on the banks of the Adyar River with his brother Nityananda 'shyly watch[ing] a group of young Theosophists cavorting in the waves,' was noticed by Charles Leadbeater. Struck by the young boy's aura, Leadbeater 'concluded form this initial impression, that Krishna[murti] might prove to be the vehicle that he believed the Masters were directing him to find. Before long he stated he had been instructed by the Master Kuthumi to train this boy' (Sloss 1991: 25). Leadbeater initiated the process of taking control of the two boys from their father, raising them, and educating them within the compound. 'At the age of 14, only eight months after being discovered by Leadbeater (when he had known no English at all) with Leadbeater's probable assistance, Krishna wrote affectionate and grammatical letters to Mrs Besant. He saw her as a new mother and begged her to let him address her as such' (Sloss 1991: 29). In 1911, Krishnamurti underwent his first initiation and was formally announced as the vehicle for the message of the coming world teacher. A major organization whose membership quickly swelled into the thousands, the Order of the Star in the East (first called the Order of the Rising Sun) was created by Besant and Leadbeater in 1911 as the organizational vehicle for the new messiah.

Though a dedicated Theosophisst, Narayaniah was, naturally enough, alarmed at what amounted to the kidnapping of his sons Krishnamurti and Nityananda. He initiated a custody suit in 1912 (while they were in Sicily, far from his grasp), which succeeded in the Indian courts but was overturned on appeal by the Privy Council in London (Sloss 1991:

32). Upon attaining legal maturity in 1913, Krishnamurti elected to stay with his Theosophical sponsors. Over the next decade and a half he led a peripatetic life, moving between Europe, the United States, and India at the behest of his Theosophical sponsors. Krishnamurti grew increasingly disenchanted with the role created for him and with certain tendencies within the Theosophical bureaucracy. He showed pointed irritation with Arundale as he spun out more and more layers of mystical hierarchy (as in the set of 'apostles' created at Ommen) and with the whole idea of a World Mother movement. Finally, declaring that 'truth is a pathless land,' Krishnamurti dissolved the Order of the Star in the East in 1929, sending shock waves throughout the international Theosophical community and causing the World Mother movement to wither on the vine (Nethercot 1963: 423). In 1933, soon after the demise of the World Mother movement, Annie Besant passed away. George Arundale assumed the presidency of the Society and, I believe, a central role in the formulation of what would be his wife's next and most celebrated activity, the 'revival' of dance.

The narrative of Rukmini Devi's seeking out and then taking up Indian dance has acquired several iterations. Meduri reports that Rukmini Devi went to see the 'Kalyani Daughters,' Jeevaratnam and Rajalakshmi (student of Pandanallur Minakshisundaram Pillai and daughters of the eminent dancer Tiruvalaputtur Kalyani), at the Music Academy in 1933 (1996: 231). Gowri Ramnarayan agrees that this dance performance was the catalytic event but states that E. Krishna Ayyar invited her to attend this performance not in 1933 but two years later, in 1935 (1984b: 18). For his part, Arudra concurs that Rukmini Devi first went to the Music Academy at E. Krishna Ayyar's invitation on New Year's Day 1935, but notes that the performance that day involved not the Kalyani Daughters but instead the sisters Sabharanjitham and Nagaratnam, daughters of a Smt. (Ms) Nagamma and also disciples of Minakshisundaram Pillai (1987: 30).

Music Academy festival souvenirs I have seen indicate that the Kalyani Daughters danced at the Music Academy in 1931 and 1933, while Sabharanjitham and Nagaratnam danced in 1935 (this would imply an anomaly in Ramnarayan's account). We may summarise that, at the invitation of E. Krishna Ayyar, Rukmini Devi either first went to the Music Academy to see the dance performance of the Kalyani Daughters on 1 January 1933 or that of Sabharanjitham and Nagaratnam on 1 January 1935. After seeing Minakshisundaram Pillai conducting the recital of his students, she decided he was the teacher she wanted to study with and approached him (sometime, then between 1933 and 1935). Interviewed by Ramnarayan (1984b: 18), Rukmini Devi introduces another teacher into the narrative, saying that in advance of studying with Minakshisundaram, she had already taken lessons from the devadasi dancer Mylapore Gowri Ammal, a renowned expert in *abhinaya* (mimetic gestural language). Then, either in December 1935 (Ramnarayan 1984b: 20) or March 1936 (Arudra 1987: 30), Rukmini Devi decided to have her dance debut on the occasion of the Theosophical Society's Diamond Jubilee celebrations. As noted earlier, in making this decision herself she usurped the guru's traditional prerogative, angering Minakshisundaram Pillai, who left to return to his home in Tanjavur District.[14]

The role played by George Arundale in his wife's career has been characterized in various ways. Sources disagree, for example, on whether Devi or Arundale was the prime force behind the founding of the International Institute of the Arts in 1936, renamed Kalakshetra (*kshetra*, womb or place, of *kala*, arts) in 1938. S. Sarada, for one, foregrounds Rukmini Devi while acknowledging Arundale: 'Inspired by the noble ideals and magnificent educational mission of Dr G.S. Arundale, *she* established [...]' (1985: frontispiece; emphasis added). Who actually had the idea for the institute is probably impossible to answer and is, in any case, less interesting than the question of why an active, direct role for Arundale has been discounted in much of dance scholarship. At several points in the account by Ramnarayan (whose mother Anandhi Ramachandran was one of the early students of Kalakshetra), Arundale is assigned an essentially passive role, that of a husband supporting a wife's recreational pastime. For example: 'Dr Arundale for one encouraged his wife in her new interest, for he considered dancing to be an excellent form of enjoyment and relaxation' (Ramnarayan 1984b: 20). But anecdotes sprinkled throughout the literature point to, I believe, a greater involvement. Ramnarayan quotes the Theosophist James Cousins, writing about Rukmini Devi's premiere performance for the Diamond Jubilee:

A large international audience was stirred to enthusiasm by a new beauty of rhythmical expression; a group of indigenous art critics saw the beginning of a cultural era that broke bounds and opened up incalculable possibilities; *the dancer's English husband, an incorrigible idealist, saw his wife as the ordained instrument of a new and extraordinarily potent revelation of spiritual reality through art.* (in Ramnarayan 1984b: 21; emphasis added)

Tours of the Kalakshetra dance troupe were sometimes combined with Arundale's Theosophical lecture tours (Sarada 1985: 13–14), a fact which supports a more activist interpretation of Arundale's role in his wife's activities, as do apocryphal comments such as, 'Dr Arundale himself, it seems, would be meditating in the wings during his wife's performances' (Ramnarayan 1984b: 27), and Sarada's account of Arundale serving as the arbiter on whether a particular padam should be a part of his wife's repertoire. Asked whether the 'sringara [love sentiment] it expressed was too physical' or not, 'he finally decided that she could dance for this padam' (1985: 46). Finally, according to Sarada, after Rukmini Devi went to Cidambaram in 1937 (or 1938) to perform a dance offering for the god Siva enshrined there in the form of Nataraja,

Dr Arundale called for a special meeting which my grandfather attended. He told me that Dr Arundale had said that this art work of Rukmini Devi was for the welfare of India. The work would advance the emancipation of our Nation. It could be used as a channel for the spiritual power of Lord Nataraja. (Sarada 1985: 5)

Several powerful themes are tied together by Arundale, suggesting that he had a quite specific vision for the use of dance towards, simultaneously, national and spiritual ends. His invocation of Nataraja was no coincidence: this one particular manifestation of Hindu deity was to take on the character of a master metaphor for the dance 'revival' and, perhaps, the Indian nationalist movement as a whole.

Murugan and Krishna are the Love Rajas.

—Kalanidhi Narayanan (1990)

In the course of research on the performance history of the padam genre in South India (Allen 1992), all sources I have been able to consult suggest that in the performances of the hereditary community of devadasi dancers before 1930, the god Siva in his form of the 'cosmic dancer' Nataraja was neither a primary subject of, nor a patron deity for, dance. Interviews with consultants, catalogues of 78 RPM recordings produced in the first part of the century (beginning ca. 1904), and early printed concert programmes (beginning ca. 1931), indicate that the devadasi performing repertoire was made up of primarily *sringara prabandhas*—songs involving one or more aspect of romantic love—such as the *ashtapadis* of Jayadeva's 12th century CE Sanskrit poem *Gita Govinda* and compositions in the padam and *javali*[15] genres. The padams, written between the 17th and 19th centuries by Telugu and Tamil composers, were and still are considered by most *rasikas* (connoisseurs) to be the major expressive element of the dance repertoire:

The padam is justifiably the best known of dance music compositions; from the point of view of musical and poetic content, no other compositional form effects a comparable integration of sound and meaning. The true connoisseur awaits this portion of the dance recital before passing final judgment upon the dancer, for it is the padam which tests to the limit a dancer's interpretive range and artistic resources. (Higgins 1993: 111)

In a padam, the relationship between the *nayaki*, a female devotee, and the *nayaka*, a male deity (or human patron), is cast primarily in the mold of lover/beloved, using a tripartite rhetorical scheme in which direct communication (often confrontation) is usually mediated through a female *sakhi*, friend (in some Vaishnava theological interpretations, the guru), who carries messages between the two lovers, sometimes straying into the nayaka's arms along the way. This rhetorical scheme involving an indirect communication between lover and beloved dates back to the first centuries after Christ in the Tamil region of South India (see Ramanujan 1985). The overwhelming majority of songs in the padam genre focus on either Krishna as the nayaka (if in the Telugu language) or Murugan (if in Tamil), gods whose mythologies are saturated with youthful, playful, and virile resonances and stories. Though Murugan has been integrated into the Hindu pantheon as a son of Siva, the son is not a carbon copy of the father; in the Tamil-speaking region, Murugan has an independent set of associations strikingly similar to those of Krishna, the divine 'romantic lead' par excellence of the song literature in Telugu and most of northern South Asia.[16]

An extremely popular and textually typical Tamil padam on Murugan is 'Padari varuhudu' (My Heart Is Trembling) by the 19th-century Tamil composer Ghanam Krishna Ayyar.[17] Never directly addressing the object of her affection (Lord Murugan, addressed by his epithet *Velavar*, holder of the lance), the heroine asks her friend to take a message to him. In the opening *pallavi* section, she manifests some disorientation at her friend's apparent indifference to her heartsickness, and by the second *caranam* section (found in a catalogue of 78 RPM recordings but not sung in any versions I have heard) she has formulated a possible reason for this in her tortured mind (the bracketed phrase at the end of the *anupallavi* and caranam sections indicates that a brief reprise of the pallavi is taken at the conclusion of these other sections):

Pallavi
My heart is trembling, my soul is melting!
Go and tell him, woman! But, wait—stop a moment, friend
Is your heart of stone?
How can you gaily, pompously strut around like that
When I am in such a state? Now go!

Anupallavi
The holder of the lance [Velavar] who dwells in Parani, the place without
    equal
I have kept him within my heart
Ayyo! What is happening to me?
Kama's arrows in my breast make me swoon
Go and bring my lord to me! [My heart is trembling...]

Caranam 1
Come woman, and bring my Murugan to me
To play with me, to embrace and love
He will sing Kambhoji raga*, and he'll sprinkle magic powder all over
    me—Go!
Is there any equal to him, my friend?
He took my hand, he gave me the most precious of jewels
Go and find him—sing his favourite beautifully worded padam for him
Don't quarrel with me! Go running, and bring him to me! [My heart is
    trembling ...]

Caranam 2
When he gently put his hand around your waist, woman, and spoke
    assurances to you
Your mind became intoxicated, and you stood there confused
When you saw Lord Murugan who holds the lance, you fell in love with
    him
Right in and among your full young breasts, his twelve hands** started
    playing
I saw this with my own eyes!
Bring him to me now, and the truth will all come out, oh soft-flower
    woman!
Go, pay obeisances to him and bring him here! [My heart is trembling...]
(Ghanam Krishna Ayyar, translated in Allen 1992, vol. 2: A12)

* Kambhoji is the melodic mode in which this composition is set.
** A playful reference to one of Murugan's names, Shanmukham, 'six-faced.' A
six-headed deity would possess the requisite number of arms for this passage to
make sense.

In this piece we are 'left in doubt' (to use the Indian-English phrase)
as to the sakhi's loyalties because she seems less than bereft at the heroine's
plight; indeed, following one time-honoured padam scenario, the friend
has been to the hero with a message and herself ended up in his arms.

Murugan and Krishna are admirably fit for the padam genre, perfectly cast as its nayaka, or hero.

Nataraja on the other hand is a deity with a quite different set of resonances. As the respected senior exponent of abhinaya, Kalanidhi Narayanan (b. 1928), quoted above, told me, Nataraja's (and Rama's) resonances are generally more severe than those of Murugan and Krishna—whom she dubbed 'Love Rajas,' not having what Indian performers like to call 'scope' for development in the sringara erotic-devotional mode so central to the devadasi tradition of dance (1990). Saskia Kersenboom writes of Nataraja, 'This form of Siva indicates his Rudra aspect of the cosmic destruction of all impure, gross forces by means of his cosmic dance that burns all impurities to retain only the purest substance, namely gold' (1987: 146). A dance that incinerates impurity is quite outside the modality of the devadasi dance, a dance preoccupied with cataloguing the infinite shadings of feeling in love.

I have found two exceptions, of different types, to the exclusion of Nataraja from the devadasi performing repertoire. First is a group of padams written and performed in or nearby the town of Cidambaram, seat of the Nataraja cult in South India. Some of the compositions on Nataraja by the earliest known composer of Tamil padams, Muttuttandavar (17th century), such as the famous 'Teruvil varano' (Won't He Come Down My Street?), treat him as a lover-lord (Allen 1992, vol. 2: A13). This is perhaps due to the fact that Muttuttandavar lived and wrote his songs in the Cidambaram area; one might argue that they were therefore written (and danced) not on Nataraja as a transcendent cosmic deity or abstract principle so much as on Nataraja the local, literally neighbourhood, lord. Two gracious and generous consultants with deep knowledge of the Cidambaram temple, Vanaja Jeyaraman of Cidambaram and T.A. Sundarambal of Mayavaram, sang a series of padams for me (of unknown authorship) composed on Nataraja as a lover and told me that these were typical of the local Cidambaram town repertoire (1990; see also Allen 1992, vol. 2: A5).

The second type of exception is a group of Tamil compositions that give an original interpretive twist to a particular part of Nataraja's anatomy. The dancing Nataraja's raised left leg is often interpreted as an auspicious gesture of blessing:

Unmai vilakkam, verse 36, tells us: 'Creation arises from the drum: protection proceeds from the hand of hope: from fire proceeds destruction: the foot held aloft gives release.' It will be observed that the fourth hand points to this lifted foot, the refuge of the soul.

We have also the following from *Chidambara mummani kovai*: 'O my lord
[...] it is Thy lifted foot that grants eternal bliss to those that approach Thee.'
(Coomaraswamy [1918] 1957: 71)

In this second category of exception, songs on Nataraja in the devadasi
repertoire before 1940 that I've documented cast him neither in the role of
lover nor in that of destroyer-rectreator of the universe. These compositions
are almost exclusively in the genre known as *ecal* (in Tamil) or *ninda stuti*
(Sanskrit), where the god is not treated as lover, not worshipped in awe,
but *teased* by the devotee. Contrast, for example, the mood of the verses
quoted above by Coomaraswamy with 'Enneramum' (Always), an ecal
composition by the 18th-century Tamil composer Marimutta Pillai. The
devotee-singer immediately and directly accosts Nataraja (no indirect or
subtle approach here) in the pallavi section—'You always have one leg
raised: Why such lameness, Lord?' Then in the three caranams (two of
which are translated below), successive possible reasons for his disability
are put forth in question form. I found documentation of only one dance
performance of this composition, by Smt. Swarnasaraswati (a performer
from the traditional hereditary community) in 1936:

Pallavi
You always have one leg raised
Why such lameness, Lord?

Anupallavi
Great kings and good people praise you, O dweller of the golden hall at
    Cidambaram
Still, but even now you are not resting that leg! [You always have one leg
    raised...]

Caranam 1
You walked all the way to Daksha's house and put out his sacrificial fire,
    didn't you?
And that time you kicked Yama, the god of death, did you sprain your leg
    and have to raise it, limping?
When you firmly caught the moon and rubbed it into the ground, did
    that give you rheumatism?
Were you tired out by your dance contest with the fierce goddess Kali?
When you held the poison in your throat to save the world, did it spread
    down through your body to that leg?
Did your dance display for Vyaghrapada the tiger and Patanjali the snake
    leave you exhausted?

Does your golden foot have an ache, after all these experiences? Is that it, Lord?

[You always have one leg raised...]

Caranam 3

When bracing yourself to bend the mountain bow, did your foot become dislocated?

When the devas were worshipping you, did it somehow affect your matted locks?

When you left famed Kailasa in the far north and came walking all the way down south to Cidambaram, did your leg experience some pain?

That golden anklet that jingles 'kalakala' when you dance—did it rub and irritate your leg?

Did the demon's coarse, unruly hair irritate your leg as you stood atop him?

Among so many possible causes, which could be the one?

I just do not know, O dweller of the Golden Hall, O Lord Natesa (Nataraja) of Cidambaram

[You always have one leg raised...]

(Marimutta Pillai, translated in Allen 1992, vol. 2: D1)

Another popular Tamil ecal padam is 'Nadamadi tirinda' (Wandering About) by the 18th-century composer Papvinasa Mudaliar. After positing a similar set of causes for the poor god's disability the devotee-singer comes to the ingenious conclusion that maybe, after all, it's his own fault: 'Was it because of one of these things, or *was it due to my sins*? O my Siva! Didn't you used to say you were first among the three great gods?' (in Allen 1992, vol. 2: D4).

NATARAJA AS NEW NAYAKA
Re-Sanctifying a Recently Secularized Dance

During the 1930s, several linked changes took place in dance practice in South India, foremost among them the replacement of the traditional community of dancers. Affiliated changes were the renaming of the dance as bharata natyam, evoking a connection with a presumed glorious Hindu golden age; the excising from the repertoire of songs (or parts of songs) that contained textual references judged to be erotically suggestive; a general increase in tempo and in nritta, the rhythmic component of the dance[18] (at the expense of the graceful mimetic technique of abhinaya, which flourishes best in a leisurely tempo); the movement of dance from the premises of temple and salon to the public stage; and the advent of Nataraja as both a patron deity *for* dance and a subject for portrayal *in* dance.

While cultural workers like E. Krishna Ayyar and Rukmini Devi moved dance practice quite deliberately out of the temple to what they felt would be a more respectable home on the secular stage, dancers and programme presenters quickly came to feel that the new stage needed some type of spiritual resonance. The severing of dance's temple roots cut off perhaps the most vital source of nourishment for animating and guiding dancers' limbs in the new setting. As a result, it became the custom during the 1930s to place a religious icon on the secular stage, providing/restoring a semblance of a devotional setting. Looking back, Rukmini Devi states: 'My intention was that dance, now abolished in the temple, should create the temple atmosphere on the stage' (Ramnarayan 1984b: 29). Though there is no consensus on who started the practice of placing an idol of Nataraja onstage, it is certain that Rukmini Devi was one of the first dancers to do this, just as it is certain that Balasaraswati disliked and criticized the practice. Arudra writes that while other dancers placed Nataraja onstage, 'Balasaraswati flatly refused to follow suit. She used to say, quite vehemently, that the would not show any disrespect to Nataraja's idol with her lifted food pointing towards him in dance movements' (1986: 12). While Nataraja soon became the standard patron deity for dance, a niche he occupies on dance stages around the world to this day, it appears that he was neither the first nor the only deity to be so invoked:

Even people who have been regularly witnessing Bharatanatyam recitals for the last four and a half decades cannot be definite who started this practice of placing a divine figure on the stage. [...]

Some people think it was Kalki Krishnamurthi that initiated that custom when his daughter Anandhi [Ramachandran] and her partner Radha [Viswanathan] used to dance in the early days. Anandhi says she was too young to remember whether there was any icon on the stage but she vividly remembers her father's innovation of an additional curtain just behind the usual front curtain. When the curtain supplied by the theatre people was raised or drawn across, the second curtain with a painting of a large Nandi on it was there to be seen and admired by the audience for four or five minutes. [...]

Anandhi Ramachandran believes that Rukmini Devi, the founder of Kalakshetra, was the first person to place the icon [of Nataraja] on the state to bring the temple spirit to the temporal dance stage. (Arudra 1986: 12)

Planted in a corner of the dance stage, Nataraja thus became a symbolic *patron for* dance, with bharata natyam dancers performing a brief puja (worship) to his icon before beginning their recital—a custom retained to this day by the vast majority of dancers. Nataraja also became a *subject of* dance, his *ananda tandava,* 'blissful vigorous dance', described and sometimes even mimed by the new generation of dancers in a manner totally foreign to the *lasya,* graceful and feminine, devadasi dance practice. Indeed, Ramnarayan specifically cites the 'creation of dances to music previously not even thought of as possible dance material (such as the dance of Nataraja)' as one of Rukmini Devi's personal innovations (1984c: 29). The number of compositions in the dance repertoire on Nataraja *as* a cosmic dancer increased dramatically during the 'revival'. By far the most popular song on this theme from the late 1930s through the 1960s was 'Natanam adinar' (He Danced), a composition of the Tamil composer Gopalakrishna Bharati (1810–1896). Though new to the dance proscenium, it should be pointed out that this and other compositions of Gopalakrishna Bharati were not new songs, but songs already popular in vocal concerts; the songs were imported into dance in the 1930s and '40s as an explicitly articulated strategy of revival. Rukmini Devi and others choreographed a range of existing compositions that had never been danced before, including the *kritis* (the primary genre of concert music) of the 19th-century 'Trinity' of venerated Karnataka composers: Syama Sastri (1762–1827), Tyagaraja (1767–1847), and Muttusvami Dikshitar (1775–1835).

The earliest mention I found of a dance performance of 'Natanam adinar' was in 1939 by 'Miss Lakshmi Sastri' (Lakshmi Shankar, an eminent Hindustani vocalist today); I documented 25 additional performances between 1940 and 1970, by far the greatest frequency of dance performance of any song. According to Sarada, 'Natanam adinar' became one of two 'masterpieces' of Rukmini Devi: 'In "Natanam adinar," she pictures Lord Nataraja's dance in all its glory and sacredness. The different poses of the god of dance she used were perfect. She usually ended her dance recitals with "Natanam adinar"' (1985: 47).

'Natanam adinar' also became a standard item in the performances of Kamala (b. 1934); I documented nine performances of it between the years 1948 and 1961. A child prodigy who retained the stage name 'Baby Kamala' well into her teens, Kamala had her *arangerram* in 1941. In 1948 at age 14 she danced for the first time as part of the Music Academy's season and became a fixture at its yearly festival thereafter. While Rukmini Devi and Kamala began studying Indian dance within a few years of each other (ca. 1935 and 1937 respectively), Rukmini Devi was about age 30 at the time she began, while Kamala was only three. Partly due to her youth and innocence, Kamala and not Rukmini Devi was the first Brahmin woman dancer to become a major star, on the screen as well as onstage:

When Rukmini Devi gave a jolt to middle-class morality by learning an art practised until then, with very few exceptions, by devadasis alone, the response was not wholly positive. Her efforts did not at once break the dark spell cast on the art. She was dubbed a maverick and the opposition she had to face even from the elite and enlightened is already history.

It was Kamala who transformed, almost overnight, the loathsome into the laudable. The timing was perfect. The conditions ideal. And her age was just right. She was still a child, a 'baby' and her innocence and charm endeared her to one and all. In addition she possessed the required blend of glamour and appeal that rendered Bharatanatyam a vitally alive artform of contemporary relevance. (Vijayaraghavan 1988: 24–25)

'Natanam adinar' narrates the story of how Siva came down form the Himalayas and danced in the form of Nataraja for the benefit of his devotees in the Golden Hall at Cidambaram. A notable feature of this song is a *jati*, a passage of rhythmic solfège syllables (partially transcribed below) coming after the anupallavi, which imitates and was invoked by the new generation of dancers to mime Nataraja's dance:

Pallavi
He [Nataraja] danced so beautifully, so artfully,
A blissful dance in the golden hall of Cidambaram

Anupallavi
Long ago on Mount Kailasa in the North
Keeping his promise to the great sages
Without fail, he came to the city of Cidambaram
In the month of Tai, on the full moon anniversary of the guru

Jati
And he danced: 'tam, takita takajam takanam tari kundari...' [He danced
   so beautifully...]

Caranam
He danced, and all the eight directions shook—'gidu gidunga'
The head of the cosmic snake Sedan trembled, the whole earth shivered
Water drops from the Ganges splashed over the land and the gods
   celebrated
Krishna sang lovingly for his [Nataraja's] dance
Siva's matted locks swayed in the air while the cobra danced with its hood
   spread
He danced about, giving all assembled his blessings with the sound of
   'tontom tantom'

And he danced: 'tam, takita takajam takanam tari kundari...' [He danced
so beautifully...]
(Gopalakrishna Bharati, translated in Allen 1992, vol. 2: G1)

Based on my documentation of repertoire change, I feel that the new
class of women entering the profession of dance must have embraced
'Natanam adinar' as an anthem, just as they embraced Nataraja himself
as a new kind of nayaka, hero, for dance. Siva as the cosmic dancer
Nataraja was free from the kind of criticism that an earthy, sensual,
often philandering Murugan or Krishna could come under from social
reformers and was full of resonances suggesting spiritual detachment and
masculine power, images invoked by both revivers of dance and Indian
nationalist politicians.

Iconographically, we can see the rise of Nataraja and the domestication
of the dance in two images that frame the critical years of the revival.
The first is from August 1933 (Fig. 24), coming not long after devadasi
dance was first presented at the Music Academy (in 1931), a year or so
before Rukmini Devi started her study of Indian dance, and just after a

FIG. 24   A racy 1933 advertisement for 'Devi the Dancer,' a serial story about a
devadasi dancer written by Deisvi, whose previous story 'set all South
India thinking and talking.' This ad was placed in *The Hindu*, the primary
English-language daily newspaper based in Madras, Tamil Nadu, South
India. (Photo courtesy of Matthew Harp Allen)

flashpoint in the public debate on the devadasi and her dance (a long-simmering debate that dated back to at least the early 1890s: see Meduri 1996: 56). In early December 1932, after the Raja of Bobilli invited the devadasi dancer Sitaramudu to perform at a function commemorating his election as the leader of the Legislative Council and Premier of the Madras Presidency, the social reformer Dr Muthulakshmi Reddi (1886–1968), a medical doctor herself coming from a devadasi family background, wrote in protest to the English-language Madras newspapers the *Hindu* and *Madras Mail*. Outraged, she felt betrayed that prominent citizens who had vowed not to attend devadasi dance performances had attended the Raja's function (Meduri 1996: 222). Her criticism met with a rejoinder from E. Krishna Ayyar, touching off a prolonged exchange of letters between the two; upon the conclusion of both Krishna Ayyar's letter to the *Hindu* of 14 December 1932 and Dr Reddi's response of 19 December, an increasingly fatigued editor writes in brackets, 'Correspondence on this subject will now cease—Ed. H.'! While Krishna Ayyar argued for giving the hereditary dancers a 'respectable' venue in which to perform (a belief he was putting into practice at the Music Academy at this very time), Reddi was for stopping devadasi dance performance as well as banning the religious initiation and dedication of devadasis, which she saw as the root cause of the degradation of her community. It was into such a conceptual space that Rukmini Devi stepped with the idea that dance should be preserved in a (supposedly) more worthy social community.

The 1933 image is an advertisement for a serialized popular story, and the textual references are quite racy, averring that the author's previous story *Bala the Bad Woman* 'set all South India thinking and talking.' (I have not yet been successful in finding any stories by 'Deisvi.') In it, a dancer performs in a temple setting while her musical accompanists, some clad in turbans, stand and move with her. That this is an accurate portrayal of performance practice up until the 1930s is attested to by V.K. Narayana Menon:

Reform was certainly necessary not only in the social attitude to the Dance, but in the practice and presentation of the art itself. Public performances of *Bharatanatyam* in the early years of this century were somewhat crude. Recitals often lasted the whole night. The music was hardly ever of good quality. Bagpipes (!) were the order of the day for drones. Three of four male singers dressed in green and red turbans stood on one corner of the platform, the drummer often standing behind the dancer and walking up and down the stage. The *Nattuvanar* and the musicians began to sit on the platform and they dressed soberly. The bagpipe gave place to the tambura. The dress and the make-up of the dancer (who used to be overdressed, over-made up and over-ornamented) were improved. The dignity of the platform was sternly maintained and overtures from the audience severely snubbed. (1963: 18; emphasis [!] in original)

The placement of Nataraja in this advertisement is I think quite suggestive: outside the main frame of action, he hovers in an inset at the upper right corner. He seems to be waiting in the wings, as it were, for his grand entry into the 'revived' dance.

By the mid-1940s, the appropriation and domestication of bharata natyam by 'middle-class' dancers was virtually complete. Rukmini Devi had moved away from solo dance performance and was producing dance dramas at Kalakshetra (see Meduri 1996: 376–82), and a barely pre-teen 'Baby' Kamala was making her mark in the dance world. In an advertisement from a 1946 dance souvenir (Fig. 25), a bright-faced young boy and girl illustrate the fact that social permission had by this time been given for children of 'good' families to dance. Indeed, this course of action is here not merely given tacit approval but is actively marketed to the English-speaking Madras audience. Nataraja in this image is the radiant glow to which the children direct the eye as they dance to his cosmic rhythm (and by implication the rhythms of Ram Gopal, whose recordings are herein advertised).

HOW NATARAJA BECAME A NEW NAYAKA

Ananda Coomaraswamy and 'The Dance of Shiva'

The central figure in promoting Nataraja as the symbol of the synthetic grandeur of ancient (specifically Hindu) Indian art, science, and religion was Ananda Kentish Coomaraswamy. As iconic as the composition 'Natanam adinar' has been to the revived bharata natyam tradition, and as Nataraja himself has been as a patron deity and new subject for the revived dance, Coomaraswamy's essay 'The Dance of Shiva' (first published in the book of the same name in 1918) has been the most influential publication in the phenomenal 20th-century popularisation of the Nataraja image.[19] Today, the icon of Nataraja is found in many places. A 1993 PBS television special on dance visually references Nataraja at the beginning of its segment on India, the camera panning slowly around a huge bronze while the narrator intones, 'In India, the gods dance!' (Dunlop and Alexander 1993); affluent Indians and Indophiles place reproductions of Nataraja bronzes in their homes and corporate boardrooms; the icon of Nataraja is present at many Indian cultural functions; and non-Indians who come into contact with Indian art, philosophy, religion, or aesthetics cannot fail to encounter this most potent symbol:

FIG. 25   With the 'revival' of South Indian dance, children from 'good,' middle-caste families began to practice the genre. Here, 'Let Your Children Dance to the Rhythm' advertises dance records in a souvenir brochure from the Natana Niketan (The Indian School of Kathakali Dancing), where Guru Gopinath was its chief teacher in 1946. (Photo courtesy of Matthew Harp Allen)

Five years ago, I had a beautiful experience which set me on a road which had led to the writing of this book. I was sitting by the ocean one late summer afternoon, watching the waves rolling in and feeling the rhythm of my breathing, when I suddenly became aware of my whole environment as being engaged in a gigantic cosmic dance. [...] I felt its rhythm and 'heard' its sound, and at that moment, I *knew* that this was the dance of Shiva, the Lord of Dancers worshiped by the Hindus. (Capra 1977: xv)

Where did the author of *The Tao of Physics* come across such an idea? As his book unfolds it is clear that it came to Fritjof Capra from the same source that reached the dancer Ted Shawn (to be discussed below), the same source to which my Karnataka teacher, T. Viswanathan, first referred me when I asked him early on in my training for readings on the arts in India: the essay by Coomaraswamy.

Nataraja's status today as an ubiquitous symbol for everything majestic and noble in Indian culture (in conjunction with his presence throughout antiquity in sculpture and literature) might tend to obscure the fact that he was not so well-known just a few decades ago. V. Subramaniam argues that there has been a major growth in awareness and appreciation of Nataraja (unfortunately matched by a corresponding increase in 'vulgarization') in this century:

The Nataraja image itself, *almost unknown outside South India round the turn of this century*, is now found in all the posh lounges of Indo-Philic Western homes, offices and universities all over the world and practically in every Western museum either as an original or in a good replica. The dramatic story of the recent theft of the Sivapuram Nataraja, its detection by a British art critic, its valuation at over 4 million dollars, the well publicized legal action and its impending restoration to India have all highlighted the glory of the Nataraja image beyond all doubt. We may also add that through a study of this icon and that of Sivakama Sundari, the consort of Nataraja, Western artists and art critics have come to appreciate the basic principles and standards of Indian sculpture more than through any other means. On the other hand, we cannot also forget the story of vulgarisation. The icon has become a prestige symbol, regardless of the quality of the casting and as a result, these icons are made in every State of India and with all sorts of alloys and even the Tibetan refugees in Janpath, Delhi, do a roaring trade with ugly icons of the dancing lord. (1980: xviii; emphasis added)

Like Rukmini Devi, Ananda Coomaraswamy was a person deeply steeped in European as well as South Asian culture and thought; as the child of a Ceylonese father of Tamil background and a British mother, he quite literally embodied the two cultures. His father, Sir Mutu Coomaraswamy, born in 1833, became the first Asian accredited for the practice of law in English (and the hero of an unfinished novel by Disraeli!). In 1876 he and Elizabeth Beeby were married by the Archbishop of Canterbury, and Ananda was born the next year in Ceylon (today Sri Lanka). The elder Coomaraswamy died in 1879, as he was about to board a ship for England to enter Parliament. Ananda grew up in England, training in geology and receiving a doctorate from London University in 1906 (Lipsey 1977: 9–11). While conducting geological research in Ceylon he was struck by the desuetude of native crafts. He longed for the 'possibility of a true regeneration [...] of the national life of the Sinhalese people' (Guha-Thakurta 1992: 160). This led to his first work in the realm of aesthetics, *Medieval Sinhalese Art* (1908):

The basic intent of the book was polemical. [...] Tradition was located in the medieval Ceylon that existed prior to British occupation, especially in her arts and crafts that flourished until the invasion of Western commerce and machine-industry. [...] The book thus came to stand as a manifesto of the Arts and Crafts idealists in England. C.R. Ashbee's vision of 'a nobler, finer and saner order of things' and 'the protection of standard in life' was given the reality of a preindustrial, traditional world of craftsmanship in the medieval kingdom of Ceylon. The nostalgia for a medieval past found, here, a model world, more accessible in time than the European middle ages for it had preserved itself right into the nineteenth century, and traces of it still lingered on. (Guha-Thakurta 1992: 160–61)

Coomaraswamy was clearly influenced by the British Arts and Crafts Movement, in particular the work of William Morris; *Medieval Sinhalese Art* was printed on Morris's Kelmscot Press, which Coomaraswamy had moved to his house and resuscitated in 1907 (Lipsey 1977: 44–45). Guha-Thakurta stresses that at the same time, however, *Medieval Sinhalese Art* 'marked a subtle transition in Coomaraswamy from his Arts and Crafts preoccupations to a new concern with the propagation of Oriental art and aesthetics, from a purely "Eastern standpoint"' (1992: 160). As with Havell before him, Coomaraswamy's attention evolved in the first decade of the 20th century from an emphasis on crafts towards an overriding concern with Hindu India's 'classical' heritage in the arts—a concern both to demonstrate the existence of an ancient, sophisticated heritage based on ideals of Vedanta and yoga and to revive that heritage in the present day:

This neo-Platonic aesthetic in vogue in 19th century Europe, which enjoyed a great preponderance with all nineteenth-century critics of Academic and Neo-Classical art, also lodged itself at the center of the new Orientalist view of Indian art. To explain and justify their admiration for it, 'fine arts' in India was associated with a profoundly transcendental view of art in Indian philosophy. Havell's and Coomaraswamy's natural choice here was the Vedanta school of Indian philosophy, which considered the material world to be an illusion (*maya*), the veil of which had to be removed in order to perceive the ideal. [...]

While Greek artists took as their model an ideal physical type of an athlete or a warrior, the Hindu artists sought their ideal in forms that 'transcended' nature into something supernatural and divine. Their ideal type was said to be embodied in the figure of the *Yogi*. [...] Coomaraswamy joined Havell in an elaborate exposition on the links between art, asceticism and *Yoga* in the Indian tradition, showing how the worshipper and artist became one in the construction of divine images. (Guha-Thakurta 1992: 178)

An emphasis on a high art grounded in a specifically Hindu spirituality was reflected in Coomaraswamy's next major work, *Rajput Art*, published in 1916, and then in *The Dance of Shiva*, published 1918. After unsuccessfully trying during World War I to interest the Banaras Hindu University in the establishment of a museum of Indian arts (to be based substantially on his growing personal collection), by 1920 Coomaraswamy had accepted a position at the Boston Museum of Fine Arts and moved his entire collection to the United States (Lipsey 1977: 124–26).

RUTH ST DENIS AND TED SHAWN

As a young girl in Somerville, New Jersey, Ruth Dennis (1879–1968) listened at her parents' farmhouse as summer boarders from New York City with intellectual pretensions debated the relative merits of the newly formed Theosophical Society and Christian Science sect (both were founded in 1875). Her mother, the first woman M.D. graduate of the University of Michigan, took her periodically into New York and encouraged her growing interest in Asian religions. Mother and daughter both soaked themselves in Orientalia such as the actor Edward Russell's popular society readings from Sir Edwin Arnold's *Light of Asia* (Shelton 1981: 49)—a play Rukmini Devi would produce at the Theosophical Society in Madras several decades later, circa 1935 (Sarada 1985: 2).

The impressionable Dennis (who would take the professional name St Denis in 1906) soon imbibed the Orient from a rather different type of source. In May 1903, the extravagant Luna Park amusement center at Coney Island opened. Its entrepreneurs, taking their cue from the Midway Plaisance at the Columbian Exposition in Chicago (1893, itself inspired by earlier international expositions in Paris) introduced for the 1904 season an exhibit called 'The Streets of Delhi' (Kasson 1978: 63, 69). St Denis later wrote in her autobiography, *An Unfinished Life*:

During these days someone took me down to Coney Island. I was mildly intrigued by the sights and sounds, but my whole attention was not captured until I came to an East Indian village which had been brought over in its entirely by the owners of the Hippodrome. Here, for the first time, I saw snake charmers and holy men and Nautch dancers, and something of the remarkable fascination of India caught hold of me.

When I reached home that evening I determined to create one or two Nautch dances. [...] With these I was sure I would find some vaudeville bookings and, with the money earned, produce *Egypta* [a dance project preoccupying her at the time]. I was very happy over my decision, and went the next day to the Astor Library to do a little research in Nautch costumes.

Everything went according to plan for a few days. But when pictures of Nautch dancing girls led me to the Devidassi, who were temple dancers, and they in turn brought me to the temples themselves and the name of Radha, the shifting center of interest began, ever so slightly, to move away from Egypt and towards these strange new mysteries of Hindu religion. [...] I read everything I could lay my hands on; in the library I called for pictures of Nautch dancers, of temples, of the Himalayas, of the jungles, and saturated myself in this atmosphere. (1939: 55)

St Denis created the dance *Radha* in 1905/06, hiring a ragtag troupe of 'supernumeraries' (including, sometimes, family members) to assist her in her planned vaudeville act (Shelton 1981: 197). What strikes me in hearing her discuss the development of this dance is her disarming candour—she lays no claim to authenticity either in choreography or in representation of mythology:

My first Indian dance was a jumble of everything I was aware of in Indian art, but with little sense of balance and continuity. Ideas came in a stream and from quite unrelated sources. One morning at breakfast Mother and I planned the scene for the *Cobra* dance with bits of toast and a saltcellar. I thought in terms of scenes and not of technical virtuosity. Mother and I moved our bits of toast about to indicate where the Indian water carrier came in and spoke to the fruit seller, where the merchant's stall was, and where the brass seller squatted to watch the snake charmer's exhibition.

By now, as you will see, I had expanded my plans to include supernumeraries. My intense interest in India had sent me into the byways of New York and I collected a little company, which used to meet in our flat to rehearse two or three times a week. They were of all varieties—Hindus, Moslems, Buddhists. Some were clerks from shops, some were students at Columbia, and one or two were unmistakable ne'er-do-wells. They would sit on the floor and answer in a chorus the questions that I flung at them. One night Father had to separate two combatants in a religious war. I had unwittingly asked a Moslem instead of a Hindu the rituals of a Hindu temple. [...]

Out of my jumbled and confused ideas two dances began to emerge, the *Nautch* and the *Incense*. [...] But *Radha* was, I sensed, to be the blossom of all these little plantings. I conceived of her as an idol in her temple, who for a brief time was infused with life and danced a message for her devotees. Theologically speaking, this was inaccurate, for Radha, although the beloved of Krishna, the god of love, was seldom worshiped on her own account; but at no time, then or in the future, have I been sufficiently the scholar or sufficiently interested to imitate or try to reproduce any Oriental ritual or actual dance—the mood to me is all, and inevitably manifests its own pattern. (1939: 56–57)

The heart of *Radha* is a five-part 'dance of the senses' culminating in a 'delirium of the senses'; these six segments are framed within beginning and ending tableaux where the goddess sits in Lotus position on a pedestal. A group of 'priests' enters at the beginning and sits in a semicircle to watch her dance a progression 'from the senses of far distance to the more intimate ones,' ending in the 'delirium' which leaves her supine on the floor. The description refers to a 1941 film of St Denis performing *Radha*:

The lights come up on a chastened Radha, lifting her arms in supplication. After tracing the petals of a lotus blossom on the floor, she withdraws to her shrine. The final image shows her sitting on her pedestal, transformed by *samadhi*, self-realization. (Desmond 1991: 32–33)

St Denis identified so much with this dance that for a time she adopted Radha as her professional name (Sherman 1979: 3).

As her career evolved St Denis picked up a like-minded partner, and together they assiduously cultivated the personae of 'divine dancers' in an extremely heterodox performing environment, moving between vaudeville and more 'legitimate' venues, crisscrossing the United States, Europe, and Asia. Their voracious interest in world dance traditions would lead to choreography of cross-cultural impressions ranging from *Egyptian Ballet* (1922) to *Cuadro Flamenco* (1923) to *Ishtar of the Seven Gates* (1923) to *A Legend of Pelee* (1925) to *General Wu Says Farewell to His Wife Gates* (1926). It was while she was on tour in Denver in 1911 that Ted Shawn (1891–1972) had his first glimpse of Ruth St Denis:

In her audience was an impressionable, idealistic youth, a divinity student-turned-dancer, only nineteen years old. Ted Shawn saw before him a glamorous goddess who blended the two ideals most dear to his heart, divinity and dance. Watching St Denis, he vowed that he too would become a 'divine dancer,' though he did not suspect that he would marry the high priestess herself. (Shelton 1981: 102)

Three years intervened before, in 1914, Ted Shawn requested an interview with St Denis through her brother. He auditioned for her, costumed as an Aztec warrior; St Denis found him adorable and talented. That spring, she invited Shawn to tour with her company and, a week into the tour, he proposed to her: 'Ruth was amused. Her road romances dated back to the days of Jack Hoey and *The Man in the Moon*. She had always attracted ardent suitors, but marriage was out of the question' (Shelton 1981: 121–22). He was persistent, she grew increasingly fond of and reliant on him, and they were married in August 1914, leading to the birth of their Denishawn company. Taken with the idea of 'divine' dance, which he had seen in St Denis's performance, Shawn researched and developed dances based on mythology and movement in many cultures, always valorizing what he considered healthy masculine elements:

Some eight or ten years ago, Gertrude Hoffman had two Sinhalese dancers with her in vaudeville who performed a stick dance without masks. Both of these dancers seemed pathetically effeminate. It was with real surprise then that I saw one group of dancers after another in Kandy, the ancient capital of Ceylon, dancing robustly, energetically and with one hundred per cent masculinity. (Shawn 1929: 139)

For a time the Denishawn style 'was a happy hybrid, a blending of St Denis's romanticism with Shawn's sentimentality, her exoticism and his eye for the vernacular' (Shelton 1981: 165). Choreographic ideas from *Radha*, the 'motherlode' of St Denis's expanding repertoire (Shelton 1981: 62), eventually crystallized into her *Nautch* (1919) and *Dance of the Black and Gold Sari* (1923), which were by far the most popular dances in the India portion of the Denishawn Dancers tour of Asia in 1925/26. Sherman (1979: 35–38) reports that St Denis initially did not intend to perform the *Nautch* for Indian audience, but after an enthusiastic reception—by a largely Indian audience—in Rangoon, she overcame her reluctance. Though contemporary observers agreed that St Denis's *Nautch* was a tremendous success in India, they disagreed on the possible reasons for its popularity:

During that first Calcutta engagement Ruth had the courage to perform two of her Indian dances, the *Dance of the Black and Gold Sari* and the *Nautch*, which she had tested on a Rangoon audience with some success. Her audiences at the Empire Theatre in Calcutta greeted the *Nautch* with roars for an encore and in India it became the most popular dance in the Denishawn repertoire, along with *Black and Gold Sari*. Just why the *Nautch* struck such a responsive chord with Indian audiences is connected with the politics of colonialism and nationalism. [...]

He [Ted Shawn] reasoned that their enthusiasm was a natural response to Ruth's superiority to the native nautch dancers, her 'having a richness and purity beyond the conception of these native women and having a beauty and charm of person not possessed by them...' Other onlookers suggested, a trace more cynically, that the natives may have been merely titillated by the spectacle of a Western woman in Indian dress performing a dance done only by harlots, but

Nala Najan, an Indian dancer born in America, supported Shawn's view. 'She opened the door,' he said. 'The Indians saw that a woman could dance and be respectable at the same time. Indian dance was looked down upon by the upper class and was relegated to a certain class of women. This changed after Miss Ruth went there.' (Shelton 1981: 198–99)

After her performance in Calcutta, Rabindranath Tagore came backstage and asked if St Denis would stay in India to teach at his Viswa Bharati (World University). An early Indian intellectual to stress the importance of dance, Tagore produced in the same year *Natir Puja—The Worship of the Danseuse*, idealizing and deifying devadasi dance (Meduri 1996: 160). A male dancer from Tamil Nadu, C.N. Vasudevan, is also known to have performed a dance on Nataraja while at Viswa Bharati in the late 1920s, leading Abanindranath Tagore to remark, 'It was as though the Southern bronze had come alive!' (Srinivasa Ayyangar 1986: 48). Though St Denis did not join the faculty at Viswa Bharati, she and Tagore did present one joint recital in New York in 1930 (Shelton 1981: 198). The Denishawn troupe finished the Indian segment of their tour with a week of performances in Madras in May 1926. There is no evidence that Rukmini Devi or any of the Theosophical coterie there saw Ruth St Denis perform (they may have been in Europe at the time) or what their reactions to her *Nautch* may have been. I suspect, however, that had they been in attendance they might have felt it less than edifying, given the reaction of the 'other onlookers' quoted above as well as the description of St Denis's *Nautch* by Jane Sherman, who witnessed it many times as a member of the Denishawn troupe during the 1920s:

This encomium [from the critic of the Rangoon *Daily News*] reflected the triumph of research and artistic instinct over the lack of concrete evidence, since there were few teachers to whom RSD could turn for help in realizing her vision of what a nautch dance must be. She knew from her reading that nautches were founded on a religious basis: they usually embodied some aspect of Krishna the god of love, and his goddess wife Radha, who was the symbol of the human soul. She knew that they told the story of their meeting and their love for each other. But she also recognized that nautch dancers were entertainers who danced to earn money. Somehow, she reconciled these contradictory elements into a convincing whole. The result was heavily weighted in favor of earth versus heaven.[...]

In a bright spotlight against a plain backdrop, this seductive creature enters upstage right. Her headsheet is wrapped half across her face, only her large, kohl-blackened eyes showing. She moves forward with a slow, voluptuous, swinging walk that flares out the folds of her skirt and causes the bells of her anklets to tinkle. She pauses a moment, removes one end of the headsheet from her face, and puts it on her left hip as she reveals a wide smile. Holding the other end of the gleaming material out in her right hand, she stands with pelvis thrust forward toward her extended left foot. Then she continues her wide walk-steps with a hip swagger as she makes a big salaam with both hands at her forehead, to the right, then to the left, then to the front, saucily greeting her audience. [...] Throughout most of the dance, RSD babbles her special, coquettish Hindi double-talk, thus creating a stage full of people where she is the center of attention. [...]

At one point, she bunches up the huge skirt in both hands and again advances directly toward the audience, this time with strong stamps of feet and bells as she grins ingratiatingly if with a touch of contempt. She drops the skirt, swaggers downstage left, and holds out a hand, pointing to its palm and demanding, aloud, 'Baksheesh!' When refused money, she turns away with disdain to repeat the demand on the right. (1979: 35, 37)

In this passage we perceive that St Denis was aware of some of the basic moves of Indian dance, such as the repetition of gestures right, left, and center; however, her template for nautch dance was essentially conjured up from a pastiche of Orientalist readings, photos in the New York Public Library, and her exposure to sideshow entertainers in the 'Streets of Delhi' at Coney Island, long before she reached India. The reception of this dance 'weighted towards earth versus heaven' among some of the more discriminating Indian connoisseurs of the day was decidedly mixed—a situation that I find somewhat puzzling, but which may reflect the fact that most English-educated Indians in the early 20th century learned from a young age to avoid rather than seek out opportunities to see Indian dance. Perhaps, therefore, a normative standard by which to judge Indian dance was known only by dancers and their teachers, not by the larger public, however erudite or educated. In the past few years the question of just how St Denis and her dancers were received has drawn the attention of dance scholars such as Uttara Asha Coorlawala, who confirms a 'split verdict' among Indian connoisseurs:

In Europe and the United States, St Denis's dances had drawn accolades from the artistic and cultivated Indians who traveled, including the musician Inayat Khan, the philosopher Ananda Coomaraswamy, the political activist and poet Sarojini Naidu, and the Maharajas of Kapurthala and Cooch-Bihar. However, the noted patron of the arts, Jamshed Bhabha, recalls that when as a little boy he was taken to see the Denishawn dancers at the Excelsior Theatre in Bombay, the show was vaudevillian, inconsequential kitsch—and in this opinion he is not alone. (1992: 124)

During the India segment of their Asia tour in the spring of 1926, Ted Shawn created his *Cosmic Dance of Siva* (Fig. 26). Shawn's 1929 book *Gods who Dance* attests to the fact that he was a voracious reader, of Coomaraswamy and his circle, of Nietzsche, of materials relating to

Fig. 26 Ted Shawn as Nataraja. From Ted Shawn, 1929, *Gods Who Dance*, New York: E.P. Dutton

religion, mythology, and the arts in many cultures (see his bibliography, 1929: 207–08), so it is no surprise that he settled on Nataraja as the subject for one of his dances. As the troupe moved through India, Shawn consulted with various dancers and scholars, commissioned a score, and built an elaborate costume through purchases from various shops and bazaars:

Early in the Indian tour I began to prepare myself for the creation of the *Cosmic Dance of Siva*. I read books on the theology of Siva, talked at length about the subject with scholarly men, and studied painting and sculpture representing the deity. The preparation for the final production was long and thorough.

Lily Strickland, whose published music we already had used for dances, was living in Calcutta where we met and discussed the Siva score which I commissioned her to write. I searched everywhere for proper accoutrements. At the Cawnpore bazaar I bought the first silver pieces of a two hundred-dollar collection of virgin silver that was assembled into the Siva costume I designed. [...]

Boshi Sen was a disciple of the Vedanta cult and took me to Allahabad where he asked a swami to tell me about Siva. The swami spoke lyric English and his words soared and burst into rockets of glory, sparkled and spouted like fountains in the sky. My previous studies of Siva and the swami's exposition convinced me that I had taken on quite a nifty subject for a solo in which I would try to dance the creation, preservation, destruction, reincarnation, an ultimate salvation of the universe. I turned to Boshi and said, 'What an awful fool I've been. Who am I that I should dare attempt this task that's beyond human doing?'

'You don't have to do it,' Boshi answered. 'Make your body an instrument and remove your petty self from it, and Siva will use your body to dance through. You will not be dancing, you, the little personal Ted Shawn, but Siva will dance—if you ask him to.' And so it was, and I never gave a performance of that dance without consciously asking Siva to take possession of my body to use as an expression of the power and the beauty and the rhythm of his being, and the dance never failed to reach its audience with power. (Shawn [1960] 1979: 197–8)

The piece premiered after the Denishawn company left India, at the Grand Opera House in Manila on 17 September 1926. Like St Denis's *Nautch*, it became a mainstay of their repertoire for decades to come, equally popular in 'legit' and vaudeville houses across the United States:

Ted scored a major triumph with his *Cosmic Dance of Siva*, which electrified his American audiences as it had in the Orient. As the Hindu sculpture of Nataraja or the dancing Siva, he wore only body paint, brief trunks, and a towering crown and stood on a pedestal within a huge upright metal ring that haloed his entire body. Moving in plastique, he mimed five cosmic stages: creation, preservation, destruction, reincarnation, and salvation. The dynamics of the solo ranged from still balances on half-toe to violent twists of the torso and furious stamping of the feet, all confined within the hoop that represented the container of the universe. At thirty-six, Ted was more agile than Ruth and more virtuosic, and critics devoted almost as much space to his dancing as to Ruth's. (Shelton 1981: 213)

While chroniclers of the Denishawn company's history are substantially in agreement that these intrepid American dancers 'scored a major triumph' in India and America with their dances on Indian themes, the curious fact remains that, in India at least, their legacy seems to have been short-lived, a splash rather than a deep penetration into the soil:

Apparently Ruth St Denis' nonauthentic impressions of Indian dance were indeed a great triumph in India. She was hailed by *The Times of India* with 'rapturous applause and genuine enthusiasm.' *Her Dance of the Black and Gold Sari* provoked virtual riots. Yet today, most dancers in India are unfamiliar with her name, whereas Pavlova, who also visited India within a year of St Denis, is recalled in reverential tones. (Coorlawala 1992: 124)

Though not acknowledged as an influence of any consequence by Rukmini Devi (or any other major South Indian dancer, to my knowledge), Ruth St Denis and Ted Shawn have a place in the revival, especially when we allow our focus to include not just South India but North India (especially Bengal), the United States, and Europe. In their youth, the three were consumers of the same international intellectual and cultural Orientalism that coloured events in South India: while St Denis and Shawn discovered Coomaraswamy's *Dance of Shiva* in New Jersey and Denver, Rukmini Devi (and George Arundale) turned its pages in India (or Europe), and, as noted earlier, St Denis and Rukmini Devi both loved Orientalist literature like *The Light of Asia*. They all shared the basic concept of dance as divine, a path to unity with god. Perhaps the most telling suggestion of St Denis's influence in India remains that no less a personage than Rabindranath Tagore asked St Denis to join his faculty. In her thoughtful evaluation of St Denis's impact on Indian dance, Coorlawala argues a significant historical importance for her Indian-ish dances, preceding as they did Pavlova's collaborations with Uday Shankar (considered below) by almost two decades. She also says that Pavlova created a series of dances based on themes originally choreographed by St Denis: 'That Pavlova admired St Denis' dances can be deduced from the fact that she included them in her own concert program, presented around England' (1992: 144). Finally, through the work of St Denis and Shawn, an awareness of Indian dance (however drastically mediated) was awakened in audiences throughout the United States and Europe and in the minds of young aspirants creating the new field of modern dance.

I want to dance for everybody in the world.

—Anna Pavlova (in Franks 1956: 40)

The beloved ballerina of her time, and a woman who continues to cast long shadows in the world of dance today, Anna Pavlova (1881–1931) logged as many miles as Ruth St Denis and Ted Shawn during her career as a professional dancer. She regularly performed at the world's leading opera houses, to be sure, but she also wanted to take ballet where it had never been. In the course of her travels Pavlova took a keen interest in, and studied whenever possible, the national dance traditions of the countries she visited.[20]

At age 10, she was accepted for ballet training at the Tsar's Imperial School of Ballet in St Petersburg, and upon graduation she rose steadily through the ranks of the Imperial Russian Ballet to become prima ballerina in 1906 or 1907 (Franks 1956: 17). This status allowed her to begin touring internationally; she performed in Paris in 1909, New York and London in 1910, and in 1911 she formed her own company. During World War I she toured North and South America for five years, and from the end of the war up until her death kept a home in London while touring the world with her company.

As early as 1909 at the Imperial Ballet, Pavlova danced the lead role in *La Bayadère*, a high-Orientalist period ballet of 1877 'set in the India of the rajahs' (Anderson 1992: 106); then on her first trip to India in 1922, she witnessed a Hindu wedding and became interested in creating dances based on more authentically Indian movements. Back in London, she was introduced to a young art student, Uday Shankar, who had 'produced brief dances for his father's shows [variety fundraisers for Indian veterans], including a successful garden party program in 1922 where King George V congratulated him' (Erdman 1987: 71). Pavlova invited him to choreograph two pieces, *A Hindu Wedding* (a piece for 22 dancers) and *Radha-Krishna* (with Pavlova and Shankar as principals, plus eight *gopis*, maidens). Shankar toured the United States with Pavlova in 1923/24. However, Joan Erdman reports that, as he was only appearing in *Radha-Krishna*, he was quite bored. Shankar asked to be cast in other dances as well, but Pavlova said no: 'Pavlova refused to use him as an extra. She suggested instead that he go to India and bring "something to show us. There are such wonders in your country and you want to try our things Never, never, never"' (1987: 73).

Bringing the focus back to the local events of revival in South India, Pavlova—like St Denis and Shawn—found it extremely difficult to see actual Indian dancers dancing in India and issued these young Indian artists a challenge. Her charge to Uday Shankar was essentially the same charge Rukmini Devi has said that she received from Pavlova: to find and resuscitate India's dance.

Together with her husband, Rukmini Devi first saw Pavlova in 1924 at London's Covent Garden, an experience she remembers as her 'first glimpse into the fairy tale world of ballet' (Ramnarayan 1984a: 28). Four years later Pavlova's troupe and Rukmini Devi's Theosophical entourage crossed paths at various places in Southeast Asia. During this time the two became friends. Rukmini Devi wanted to study ballet, and while Pavlova arranged for Devi to study with Cleo Nordi, a member of her troupe, she was intent on directing Rukmini's interests closer to home:

In 1928, Society work took the Arundales to Australia and the East Indies. Dr Arundale lectured in city after city. To their surprise and delight, the couple found that the Pavlova Company was also touring the same cities simultaneously. [...] Finally, at Surabaya, when she and Dr Arundale got into a boat sailing to Australia, whom should they see but Pavlova and her troupe of forty dancers! [...]

While sitting on the deck one day, Rukmini Devi said to her: 'I wish I could dance like you but I know I never can.' Pavlova was quick to reply: 'No, no. You must never say that. You don't have to dance, for if you just walk across the stage it will be enough. People will come to watch you do just that.' [...]

Rukmini Devi sighs and concludes her recapitulation: 'Incidentally Pavlova once said to me *you CAN learn ballet but I think that everyone must try to revive the art of his own country*. Pavlova herself stated that she had said the same thing to Uday Shankar who danced with her as Krishna.' (Ramnarayan 1984a: 28–29)

Pavlova was the model—and ballet the style—most highly privileged by Rukmini Devi in this retrospective interview and confirmed in other sources, such as the following letter written to her ballet instructor Cleo Nordi:

Anna Pavlova was certainly one of the most beautiful and inspiring artists I have ever seen. We believe in India that art is the language of the Devas, the Angels and Gods. If there was anyone who positively proved this theory and showed to the world the high worth of Art, Anna Pavlova was that one.

Anna Pavlova was the exemplification of the Indian conception of the dance of Siva and the sublimation of the body so that dance becomes the music of the body and the body is transcended till it is no more the physical but is only the vehicle of spiritual expression. When she appeared on the stage, she electrified the audience and it was impossible to look at anyone else. It is to her that I owe the inspiration to serve as an artist and to assist in the cultural revival of this country of mine. (in Franks 1956: 87)

I think the high-classical, fine-art resonances of ballet must have conjured up an aura Rukmini Devi felt appropriate for dance (more than, for example, the work of St Denis or Shawn). In the coming revival, this view of dance would be perfectly counterpointed, supported, and legitimated by the installation of Nataraja (appropriately referenced in Devi's testimonial to Pavlova above) both as a patron deity for dance and as central character in a revised repertoire of compositions. These compositions themselves would be interpreted by a new community of dancers, in an equally new setting.

Bharata Natyam awoke one morning to find itself great.

—T. Sankaran (1973: n.p.)

A remarkable transformation occurred in dance practice earlier this century in South India. From the time of 'Devi the Dancer' (Fig. 24) to 'Let Your Children Dance to the Rhythm' (Fig. 25), two snapshots framing 13 years of South Indian history, dance underwent a profound metamorphosis from nautch to bharata natyam, from 'untouchable' activity to national artform and finishing-school desideratum for young women of marriageable age. This transformation enfolded and was nurtured in the Indian nationalist movement, which was deeply influenced by European Orientalist thought and Victorian morality. Nataraja was a key agent in the transformation; his unsuitabilities from the point of view of previous dance practice became precisely the stellar qualities, of his revised résumé as applicant for nayaka-hero in the new dance. Through his work substantially grounded in late 19th-century European and Bengali intellectual currents, Ananda Coomaraswamy groomed Nataraja, brought him to the attention of artists like Rukmini Devi, Ruth St Denis and Ted Shawn, and Orientalist-spiritualists like Annie Besant and George Arundale. Nataraja was then moved center stage in Madras by Rukmini Devi and by the international set of people and ideas that educated, inspired, manipulated her. This, finally, must be my way of provisionally resolving the question of Rukmini Devi and agency: I see her as both an independent actor and as heavily conditioned by a set of people and ideas.

It is my hope that this study will contribute not only to our understanding of the dance 'revival' in South India—hitherto considered as primarily, or even exclusively, an internal artistic and social affair—but also to our understanding of other contemporary 'revivals' in and outside South Asia, of transnational aspects of cultural communication, and, finally, of the phenomenon itself of 'revival.' I've tried to crack open and take apart this term, to illustrate how it essentializes and masks a many-faceted historical process; I've tried to refine the very nebulous idea of 'influence' by articulating the conceptual threads connecting various actors in this drama; and while critiquing them I've tried to honour the imperfect but deeply committed actors who each in their own way worked toward a vision of truth and beauty.

NOTES

1. This essay grew through presentations for the exhibition 'The Cosmic Dancer: Shiva Nataraja' at the Yale University Art Gallery, the Social Science

Research Council seminar 'Sangit: Studies in the Performing Arts of South Asia' at the University of Pennsylvania, and an Ethnomusicology colloquium at the University of Illinois. Great support was given by my teacher T. Viswanathan of Wesleyan University, the American Institute of Indian Studies doctoral dissertation fellowship which supported me in India during 1989–90, and the University of Oklahoma Junior Faculty Research Grant which supported the revision of this article during the summer of 1996.

2. The Theosophical Society emerged within the general milieu of Spiritualism, a 19th century fascination with occult occurrences dating from the 'Rochester Knockings' of 1848 (Cranston 1993: 120). Spiritualism quickly attracted many influential followers on both sides of the Atlantic: in the 1860s, for example, séances were held in the Lincoln White House (Cranston 1993: 120). The immediate stimulus for the founding of the Theosophical Society was a lecture of the subject of the Kabbalah in the New York City home of the Russian émigré Helena Blavatsky in September 1875. Together with her American friend Colonel Henry Steel Olcott (a lawyer who had served on the panel investigating Lincoln's assassination), Blavatsky founded the Society two months later. The founders hoped to wean the more intelligent among the Spiritualists away from sheer fascination with occult phenomena towards a rational philosophy which could explain larger life questions. For the name, the founders invoked the composite term *theos* (god) plus *sophia* (wisdom)—a notion which dated back to Neoplatonism and had been used by early Christian mystics. Blavatsky glossed the term as 'divine wisdom such as that possessed by the Gods' (Cranston 1993: 145) and aligned her movement firmly in the tradition of Spiritualism, which she opposed diametrically to Materialism. Due to its impassioned embrace and defense of Asian religions, notably Buddhism and Hinduism, the Theosophical Society eventually gained a large following among Indian intellectuals and political leaders. This list included Jawaharlal Nehru, the first Prime Minister of Independent India, as well as Mohandas Gandhi, who stated that it was at the invitation of Theosophist friends—non-Indians—that he first read the Bhagavad Gita (while studying law in London) and came to a respect for his own ancestral culture (Cranston 1993: 195).

3. Before the 1930s the dance form was known variously as *nautch, cinna melam, dasi attam,* or *sadir.* One strategic move of the revival, for which credit has been claimed by several parties (see Arudra 1987: 21), was its renaming in the mid-1930s as *bharata natyam,* literally the complete dramatic presentation (*natyam:* dance, drama, and music) of Bharata. Bharata is a polysemic term referring to India itself, also to the legendary sage believe to have composed (ca. second century CE) the *Natya Sastra,* a comprehensive treatise dealing with all aspects of natyam form aesthetics to details of staging.

4. The South Indian cultural historian Theodore Baskaran writes that another Brahmin woman danced in public at least a year before Rukmini Devi Arundale: 'The public performance of Bharatanatyam was done even before Mrs Arundale, by one Mrs Balachandra at Kumbakonam sometime in 1934' (1996). While it is on record that this woman (known professionally as Kumbakonam Balachandra) danced at the Music Academy in December 1938 (Arudra 1987:

21), I do not have corroboration from another source of an earlier date for her dance.

5. A brief note is necessary to situate myself as a student of one of the hereditary families of non-Brahmin musicians and dancers. As a graduate student at Wesleyan University in Connecticut, I studied Karnataka music with Dr T. Viswanathan (b. 1926), brother of the dancer T. Balasaraswati. Balasaraswati's profound influence on 20th-century dance—in and outside India—was of a different order than that of Rukmini Devi, whom I characterize here as being preoccupied with 'rewriting the script' for dance. Balasaraswati, simultaneously conservative and a revolutionary, on the one hand did her utmost to preserve the heart of the scripts (musical, choreographic, spiritual) for dance as handed down by her female community ancestors and by the lineage of male nattuvanar teachers dating from the Tanjavur Quartette (first half of the 19th century), while she also defended the honour of hereditary dancers and their families against the attacks of Rukmini Devi and others on their character and artistic creativity. At the same time, she saw that Indian dance was heading into a radically altered world of performance and patronage and, as a brilliant creative dancer and musician (blessed with a visionary *guru*, Sri Kandappa Pillai), was able to survive into the new era. That Rukmini Devi was an intimate participant in the disenfranchisement of a community of artists to which my teacher's family belongs must not blind me as a scholar to the fact that she was simultaneously a dedicated artist and organizer who inspired many thousands of young people to study and respect the artistic traditions of India.

6. See Srinivasan (1984) and Kersenboom-Story (1987) for extensive accounts of the devadasi heritage in South India.

7. For summaries of the career of T. Balasaraswati, see Narayana Menon (1963) and Pattabhiraman and Ramachandran (1984a, 1984b).

8. See Sruti Foundation (1989) for an account of a recent seminar in their honour.

9. For an illustration of the changing relations between a nattuvanar from the traditional community and his Brahmin dance students as their careers developed, see Pattabhiraman (1987: 38) on Vazhuvoor Ramiah Pillai.

10. Dikshitar's *Sangita Sampradaya Pradarsini* included *svara* (Indian solfège) notation for hundreds of his grandfather Muttusvami Dikshitar's compositions; in some places he added European notational symbols to describe details of *gamaka*, ornamentation. In this he followed in the steps of his colleague Cinnasvami Mudaliar, publisher of *Oriental Music in Staff Notation* (1893), the first publication attempting to render Karnataka music in European notation.

11. Nationalist renaissances freighted with Orientalist overtones occurred not only in South Asia but in the Middle East and other regions of the world during the same time period. See discussions of the First International Conference of Arab Music in Cairo, 1932, in Ali Jihad Racy (1993), and of the founding of the Rashidiya Institute in Tunisia, 1934, in Ruth Davis (1989: 53).

12. Nethercot, who records numerous examples of internecine warfare within the mystical-political structure of this most unusual organization, feels

that this apparent favouritism did not please other Theosophical leaders back in New York.

13. Here, Nethercot drily observes the skepticism with which Besant's critics greeted her pronouncements. Invocation of the legendary *rishi* (sage) Agastya in Indian political discourse would be comparable to a claim by an American politician that God directed him or her to pursue a particular policy.

14. For her part, Rukmini Devi states that it was the influence of Mylapore Gowri Ammal as well as 'some friends' that 'persuaded her' to dance at the Diamond jubilee, a performance which she didn't consider a formal arangerram (Ramnarayan 1984b: 20). The most remarkable explanation I have come across for Rukmini Devi's early arangerram comes from a fellow dancer, Ram Gopal:

The western reader may find it strange that after only six months of training Rukmini dared give a recital that took a traditional dancer six years to perfect. The answer is simple. Rukmini Devi had assiduously studied Russian ballet technique and was an adept at barre work, also a rigid follower of the purest style of that great tradition (1956: 107).

15. Javali, like padam, is a dance-music genre of bharata natyam. Javalis are by most observers considered 'lighter' than padams, due to their textual content, relatively fast tempo, and to the custom of singers' taking occasional liberties with the structure of their ragas.

16. Padams on Murugan sometimes achieve a romantic tension by alluding to a rivalry between his two wives: his Tamil, southern sweetheart Valli, and his Aryan, northern wife Devayani (see Clothey 1978: 65; Zvelebil 1991: 81; Allen 1992, vol. 1: 227–32).

17. Some scholars hold that 'Padari' is a composition of Vaidisvarankoil Subbarama Ayyar, another 19th-century Tamil padam composer (see Allen 1992, vol. 1: 2080).

18. *Laya*, rhythm, is specifically located by K. Chandrasekharan at the foundation of Rukmini Devi's program:'I think she become convinced that only through discipline and control—through laya—could the regeneration of the art be effected, its excesses sheared' (in Ramnarayan 1984b: 24).

19. Meduri notes the complementary influence of the 1926 revival of the publication of Abhinavagupta's 11th century CE commentary on the *Natya Sastra*, which 'intellectualized, spiritualized and transcendentalized the theatrical tenets' of the *Natya Sastra* through a monotheistic Saivite lens (1996: 160).

20. A.H. Franks contrasts Pavlova's desire to 'dance for everybody' with her countryman Sergei Diaghilev's belief that 'the longer a work of genius remains hidden from the enthusiasm of the multitude the more complete and more intact it will remain for the lovers of true art' (1956: 40).

REFERENCES

Allen, Mathew, 1992, *The Tamil Padam: A Dance Music Genre of South India*, 2 Vols, Ann Arbor: University Microfilms.
Anderson, Jack, 1992, *Ballet and Modern Dance: A Concise History*, 2nd edn, Princeton, NJ: Princeton Book Company.

Arudra, 1986, 'Thodaya Mangalam—2', *Sruti*, 22-S (May), pp. 11–12.

———, 1987, 'The Transfiguration of a Traditional Dance', *Sruti*, 27/28 (January), pp. 17–36.

Baskaran, S. Theodore, 1996, E-mail correspondence with author, 18 April.

Capra, Fritjof, 1977, *The Tao of Physics: An Exploration of the Parallels between Modern Physics and Eastern Mysticism*, New York: Bantam Books.

Clothey, Fred W., 1978, *The Many Faces of Murukan: The History and Meaning of a South Indian God*, The Hague: Mouton Publishers.

Coomaraswamy, Ananda Kentish, 1957 [1918], *The Dance of Shiva: On Indian Art and Culture*, New York: The Noonday Press.

Coorlawala, Uttara Asha, 1992, 'Ruth St Denis and India's Dance Renaissance', *Dance Chronicle*, 15, 2, pp. 123–52.

Cranston, Sylvia, 1993, *HPB: The Extraordinary Life and Influence of Helena Blavatsky, Founder of the Modern Theosophical Movement*, New York: G.P. Putnam's Sons.

Davis, Ruth, 1989, 'Links between the Baron Rodolphe D'Erlanger and the Notation of Tunisian Art Music', in Margot Philipp (ed.), 1986, *Ethnomusicology and the Historical Dimension: Papers Presented at the European Seminar in Ethnomusicology*, Ludwigsburg: Philipp Verlag, pp. 47–57.

Desmond, Jane, 1991, 'Dancing out the Difference: Cultural Imperialism and Ruth St Denis's "Radha" of 1906', *Signs: Journal of Women in Culture and Society*, 17, 1, pp. 28–49.

Dikshitar, Subbarama, 1904, *Sangita Sampradaya Pradarsini*. Ettayapuram: n.a.

Dunlop, Geoff, and Jane Alexander (producers), 1993, 'Lord of the Dance', from *Dancing*, eight-part Public Television Series, New York: Thirteen/WNET in association with RM Arts and BBC TV.

Erdman, Joan, 1987, 'Uday Shankar in the West', *TDR* 31, 1 (T113), pp. 64–88.

Franks, A.H. (ed.), 1987, *Pavlova: A Biography*, London: Burke Publishing Company.

Gopal, Ram, 1956, 'Pavlova and the Indian Dance', in A.H. Franks (ed.), *Pavlova: A Biography*, London: Burke Publishing Company, pp. 98–110.

Guha-Thakurta, Tapati, 1992, *The Making of a New 'Indian' Art: Artists, Aesthetics and Nationalism in Bengal, c. 1850–1920*, Cambridge: Cambridge University Press.

Higgins, Jon B., 1993, *The Music of Bharata Natyam*, Delhi: American Institute of Indian Studies and Oxford/IBH Publishing Company.

Jeyaraman, Vanaja and T.A. Sundarambal, 1990, Personal communication with author, 14 May.

Kasson, John, 1978, *Amusing the Million: Coney Island at the Turn of the Century*, New York: Hill and Wang.

Kersenboom-Story, Saskia C., 1987, *Nityasumangali: Devadasi Tradition in South India*, Delhi: Motilal Banarsidass.

Lipsey, Roger, 1977, *Coomaraswamy: His Life and Work* (Bollingen Series LXXXIX, Vol. 3), Princeton, NJ: Princeton University Press.

Meduri, Avanthi, 1988, 'Bharatha Natyam: What Are You?' *Asian Theatre Journal*, 5, 1, pp. 1–22.

_____, 1996, 'Nation, Woman, Representation: The Sutured History of the Devadasi and Her Dance', PhD dissertation, Tisch School of Arts/NYU.

Mitter, Partha, 1984, 'Indian Artists, Western Art and Tradition', in Kenneth Ballhatchet and David Taylor (eds), *Changing South Asia: Vol. III, City and Culture*, Hong Kong: Asian Research Service (for the Centre of South Asian Studies, SOAS), pp. 77–89.

Mudaliar, Cinnasvami, 1893, *Oriental Music in Staff Nation*, Madras: Ave Maria Press.

Narayanan, Kalanidhi, 1990, Personal communication with author, 5 August.

Narayana Menon, V.K., 1963, *Balasaraswati*, New Delhi: Inter-National Cultural Centre.

Nethercot, Arthur H., 1963, *The Last Four Lives of Annie Besant*, Chicago: University of Chicago Press.

Pattabhiraman, N., 1987, 'Natyacharya Vazhuvoor Ramiah Pillai: A Creative Master in Traditional Mould, Part II' *Sruti*, 27/28 (January), pp. 38–48.

_____, 1988, 'The Trinity of Bharatanatyam: Bala, Rukmini Devi and Kamala', *Sruti*, 48 (September), pp. 23–4.

Pattabhiraman, N. and Anandhi Ramachandran, 1984a, 'T. Balasaraswati: The Whole World in Her Hands', Part 1, *Sruti*, 4 (January/February), pp. 17–31.

_____, 1984b, 'T. Balasaraswati: The Whole World in Her Hands', Part 2, *Sruti*, 5 (March), pp. 17–32

Post, Jennifer, 1989, 'Professional Women in Indian Music: The Death of the Courtesan Tradition', in Ellen Koskoff (ed.), *Women and Music in Cross-Cultural Perspective*, Urbana: University of Illinois Press, pp. 97–110.

Qureshi, Regula, 1991, 'Whose Music? Sources and Contexts in Indic Musicology', in Bruno Nettl and Philip Bohlman (ed.), *Comparative Musicology and the Anthropology of Music*, Chicago: University of Chicago Press, pp. 152–68.

Racy, Ali Jihad, 1993, 'Historical Worldviews of Early Ethnomusicologists: An East-West Encounter in Cairo, 1932,' in Stephen Blum, et al. (eds), *Ethnomusicology and Modern Music History*, Urbana: University of Illinois Press, pp. 68–91.

Ramanujan, A.K., 1985, *Poems of Love and War: From the Eight Anthologies and the Ten Long Poems of Classical Tamil*, New York: Columbia University Press.

Ramnarayan, Gowri, 1984a, 'Rukmini Devi: A Quest for Beauty, a Profile', Part 1, *Sruti*, 8 (June), pp. 17–29.

_____, 1984b, 'Rukmini Devi: Dancer and Reformer, A Profile', Part 2, *Sruti*, 9 (July), pp. 17–29.

_____, 1984c, 'Rukmini Devi: Restoration and Creation, A Profile', Part 3, *Sruti*, 10 (August), pp. 26–38.

Ratanjankar, S.N., 1967, *Pandit Bhatkande*, New Delhi: National Book Trust.

Sankaran, T. ('Dhanikan'), 1973, 'From Kamatchi to Bala', in *The Music Academy of Madras, Forty-Seventh Conference Souvenir*, Madras: The Music Academy of Madras.

Sarada, S., 1985, *Kalakshetra Rukmini Devi: Reminiscences by S. Sarada*, Madras: Kala Mandir Trust.

Schechner, Richard, 1985, *Between Theater and Anthropology*, Philadelphia: University of Pennsylvania Press.

Shawn, Ted, 1929, *Gods Who Dance*. New York: E.P. Dutton.

Shawn, Ted, with Gray Poole, 1979 [1960], *One Thousand and One Night Stands*. New York: Da Capo.

Shelton, Suzanne, 1981, *Divine Dancer: A Biography of Ruth St Denis*, New York: Doubleday.

Sherman, Jane, 1979, *The Drama of Denishawn Dance*, Middletown, CT: Wesleyan University Press.

Singer, Milton, 1972, *When a Great Tradition Modernizes: An Anthropological Approach to Indian Civilization*, New York: Praeger.

Sloss, Radha Rajagopal, 1991, *Lives in the Shadow with J. Krishnamurti*, Reading, MA: Addison-Wesley Publishing Company.

Srinivasa Ayyangar, K.R., 1986, Review of *Life and Art of C.N. Vasudevan: The Tamil Dancer and Tagore*, by V. Isvarmurti, Sahibabad, U.P.: Vikas Publishing House; *Sruti*, 21 (February), pp. 48–9.

Srinivasan, Amrit, 1984, 'Temple "Prostitution" and Community Reform: An Examination of the Ethnographic, Historical and Textual Context of the Devadasi of Tamil Nadu, South India'. PhD dissertation, Cambridge University.

Sruti Foundation, 1989, *National Seminar on Bharathanatyam Dance Traditions*, 8–14 Dec. 1989, Madras: Sruti Foundation.

St Denis, Ruth, 1939, *An Unfinished Life: An Autobiography*, New York: Harper & Brothers.

Subramaniam, V., 1980, *The Sacred and the Secular in India's Performing Arts: Ananda K. Coomaraswamy Centenary Essays*, New Delhi: Ashish Publishing House.

Terry, Walter, 1969, *Miss Ruth: The 'More Living Life' of Ruth St Denis*, New York: Dodd, Mead and Company.

Thapar, Romila, et al., 1977, *Communalism and the Writing of History*, New Delhi: People's Publishing House.

Vijayaraghavan, Sujatha, 1988, 'Kamala the Dancer: A Lotus that Sprouted a Thousand Petals', *Sruti*, 45/46 (June/July), pp. 19–46.

Zvelebil, Kamil, 1991, *Tamil Traditions on Subrahmanya-Murugan*, Madras: Institute of Asian Studies.

Avanthi Meduri

Bharatanatyam as World Historical Form

Rukmini Devi Arundale (1904–86), the celebrated revivalist of twentieth-century Bharatanatyam and founder of Kalakshetra, envisioned an international, portable, concert stage setting for the dance in the formative years of what is known as the Indian dance revival of the 1930s. Although Rukmini Devi worked within the political and cultural worldview of Indian nationalism, her vision was selfconsciously international because of her association with the worldview of the Theosophical Society, which had its international headquarters in India (Meduri 2005a: 3–29). Not only was Rukmini Devi married to Englishman George Sydney Arundale, who served as the Third President of the Theosophical Society, but her Kalakshetra institution was housed within the huge estate property of the Society, from which it received active patronage (Meduri 2005a: 3–29).

International dance scholars are aware of Rukmini Devi's association with the transnational worldview of the Theosophical Society. But they have preferred to selectively gloss over this history by describing Rukmini Devi's work within a national perspective (Meduri 2004b: 11–29). I have objected to this selective placement of Rukmini Devi within the Indian national perspective because it developed out of recycled, secondary interpretations and without examining primary sources, specifically the *Young Theosophist* and or *The Young Citizen* journals that Rukmini Devi edited between 1930–50 (Meduri 2004). These documents are not housed in Rukmini Devi's Kalakshetra institution but in the international archives of the Theosophical Society, with branches all over the world. In these primary sources, Rukmini Devi described how she constituted an international spiritual, traditional and classical aesthetic for Bharatanatyam and put the dance on the world map as early as the 1930s. Drawing on these unexamined sources, this essay will describe how Rukmini Devi developed her stage setting in the first five years of the dance revival between 1935 and 1940.

RE-SITUATING THE INDIAN NATIONAL REVIVAL IN AN INTERCULTURAL TRANSNATIONAL TEMPORALITY

Rukmini Devi was born into a traditional, Tamil Brahmin family living in Madurai, Tamilnadu. Her father, Nilakanta Sastri, was both a Sanskrit scholar and a theosophist. Her mother, Seshammal, on the other hand, was a traditional woman with a great love for music. Young Rukmini thus grew up in the two worlds of theosophy and Tamil culture simultaneously. After the sudden and unexpected demise of her father, young Rukmini met Dr George Sydney Arundale, an eminent theosophist, educationalist and protégé of Dr Annie Besant and married him in 1920 (Ransom 1938; Meduri 2005a: 3–29). Annie Besant was a British writer, theosophist and feminist who took part in the workers struggle before becoming a member of the Theosophical Society and becoming part of the Indian national movement for Independence in India in the late nineteenth century.

After her marriage, Rukmini became daughter, pupil and helper to Dr Besant and Dr Arundale, followed them on their world travels, and was made President of the All India Federation of Young Theosophists in 1923 and of the World Federation of Young Theosophists in 1925.[1] While the intercultural marriage enabled Rukmini Devi to travel the world and work in the field of theosophical education, she had no training in classical Indian dance in the 1920s, and presented herself more like an intercultural dancer, having studied modern Greek dancing from Eleanor Elder, a student of Isadora Duncan, and classical Ballet from Anna Pavlova.[2] Recognizing the creative potential in young Rukmini, Dr Annie Besant, who served as the second President of the Theosophical Society and as first woman President of the Indian National Congress, nurtured her as her own spiritual daughter and made her the leader of the World Mother Movement, conceived as a parallel movement to the World Teacher Movement, embodied by J. Krishnamurti (Besant 1928: 4).[3]

In the 1930s, when Rukmini Devi returned to India after her world travels, a huge controversy about the appropriateness of reviving the *sadir* dance performed by *devadasi* women, misnamed as temple prostitutes, was being debated in the press. The resistance to the proposed dance revival was immense because of the propaganda generated by the Anti-Nautch Social Reform movement of the 1890s, which motivated the British government to ban temple dancing in 1911 (Srinivasan 1985: 1873–5).[4] Respectable members of Madras society had taken public oaths not to patronize sadir at the turn of the century, because of its alleged association with prostitution. But newly founded national institutions like the Madras Music Academy, actively sponsored the national revival of the dance by renaming the dance as Bharatanatyam and urging urban women to learn the dance hitherto performed by devadasis and lend something of the dignity of their own social standing to the dance.[5]

The story of Rukmini Devi's visit to the Madras Music Academy in 1933 to witness the historic recital given by two devadasi dancers, how she fell in love with the dance, saw the luminous classical origins of the dance and decided to learn it from traditional male teachers, and devadasi dancers, has received numerous iterations and revisions in recent dance scholarship.[6] What has gone completely unremarked, however, is that Rukmini Devi did not just watch the dance on the national platform, but that she also heard and read English language textual commentaries provided by scholars like Raghavan, working in the employ of the Madras Music Academy in the 1930s.

Raghavan, India's distinguished Sanskrit scholar did not just rename sadir as Bharatanatyam but he also composed his inaugural English-language *Natyasastra*—inspired historiography by collaborating with traditional dance teachers and devadasi dancers, including the legendary T. Balasaraswati (Meduri 2004; Meduri 2008b). While Raghavan admitted to renaming the dance, he downplayed its significance in this way

The form now called Bharata Natya was long popularly known as Sadir, Nautch, and Dasi Attam; attam or adal and kuttu in literature; and Cinnamelam and *Bharatam* in music and dance circles. The name Natyam was used both in writings and in musical parlance. Thus when some time back after a period of disfavor caused by the anti nautch crusade, the art was being brought out again by enthusiasts and I started calling it Bharata Natya, there was nothing very much new or incorrect about it. The new name which became settled invested it with the requisite status, which was needed in the circumstances of its revival, and served to underlie its classical moorings. The name at once established the form in a historical continuity, which went up to Mohenjo-Daro and *Rig Veda*. (Raghavan 1958: 25–31)

V. Raghavan explained that while Bharata referred the dance to Bharata, the author of the Sanskrit theatrical text known as *Natyasastra*, the name Bharatam also referred the dance or *natyam* to the 'Bharatam' Tamil and Telugu dance teachers who taught sadir to traditional devadasi temple dancers in the nineteenth century. By choosing the Bharatam name from the repertoire of many names by which the dance was known in the nineteenth century, V. Raghavan was able to constitute a double-reed Sanskrit and Tamil, classical and anthropological historiography for sadir-Bharatanatyam. He did more in that he also underscored the spiritual aspects of the dance by contextualizing it within the historical context of temple ritual and worship, where the dance had been performed, prior to the articulation of the Anti Nautch Social Reform movement of the 1890s mentioned above (Srinivasan 1985: 1873–5; Meduri 1996a).

Rukmini Devi was enamored with Raghavan's double-reed historiography, as she was with the sadir dance itself, re-telling religious stories of god, creation, myth, and legend, with the help of stylized hand gestures (*mudras*). She thus decided to collaborate with Sanskrit scholars, Tamil dance teachers, and devadasi dancers to envision her dance revival, albeit within the transnational worldview of the Theosophical Society.

TWO REVIVALS IN THE 1930S

Two revivals were articulated synchronously in the 1930s: an Indian national revival sponsored by scholars in the Madras Music Academy, featuring traditional devadasi dancers, and dance gurus known as *nattuvanars*, and a trans-national revival sponsored by the Theosophical Society. While the national revival featured devadasi dancers, the Theosophical Society featured Rukmini Devi Arundale as the first upper class Brahmin woman or heroine to come forward to learn the stigmatized dance of devadasis.

To legitimize the dance, both revivals idealized sadir in the new name of Bharatanatyam, referred the dance to the textual history of the *Natyasastra*, affirmed the devotional and spiritual aspects of the dance, and prioritized male teachers over and above devadasi dancers. Both were desirous of reviving the dance, as a classical dance freed from the taint of temple prostitution that had become associated with the dance during the second half of the nineteenth century.[7]

Although the two revivals were similar, they were also very different because the Music Academy presented itself primarily as a public culture institution interested only in spearheading the revival of sadir and disseminating academic and historical knowledge about the representation. Rukmini Devi, on her part, did not see herself either as an academic historian or scholar, but rather as a theosophist dancer charged with a mission to revive sadir historically and give back to the art form its lost dignity and status as an ancient art form.

To establish visual similarities between devadasis and herself, Rukmini Devi transformed herself theatrically from an intercultural dancer, who had studied Ballet and Greek dancing, into a proxy devadasi, and wore, on her own intercultural/Brahmin body, all the jewelry and ornaments associated with the temple dancer, including her bangles, hair and ear ornaments, pendants, waist belts, and ankle bells.

But Rukmini Devi also internationalized the look of the devadasi dancer by designing new costumes in collaboration with an Italian seamstress working in the Theosophical Society and with lighting technologies imported from British stagecraft. In the process, she both contemporized and internationalized the image of the devadasi dancer and urged Theosophists and Indian national spectators watching her revival to think about sadir-Bharatanatyam from the local standpoint of the historic devadasi, presented on the platform of the Madras Music Academy and also from the perspective of the new urban Indian/Asian dancer—herself in this case—working within the global worldview of the Theosophical Society.

STAGING DANCE HISTORIOGRAPHY

Rukmini Devi's Bharatanatyam debut, presented on the occasion of the Diamond Jubilee Celebrations of the Theosophical Society in 1935, began with a few introductory remarks by Dr Arundale, who underscored the importance of reviving sadir as Bharatanatyam, *the* spiritual and classical dance of India. Reproduced below is an eyewitness account of the historic recital:

Nearly a thousand people were seated under the great rain tree, through whose giant branches glimpses could be caught of the stars in an almost purple sky. The stage was at first in semi-darkness: *on one side the ensemble of musicians, including her guru, were seated on rugs, with their picturesque instruments; on the other a group of young men appeared chanting in unison a most impressive dedication of the dance recital Bharata Natya to Nataraja, that aspect of Divine life.* The music grew stronger, and the lights came on and against the green curtains of the background, Rukmini appeared in her archaic white and gold dress, looking like some *temple carving*, full of arrested movement...For more than two hours she danced with scarcely a pause and all the time the audience sat spellbound absorbed by the beauty of movement, no less by the telling of beloved stories in voice, gesture, and expression (Ramnarayan 1984b: 21). [Italics mine]

If we read this description carefully we note that Devi began her debut by dedicating her dance to *Nataraja*, the cosmic dancer, and Lord of the dance, She invoked this presence theatrically by having a group of young men chant Sanskrit verses in praise of the cosmic dancer. The metaphoric invocation was effective in that it associated Devi's Bharatanatyam dance recital with Bharata's Sanskrit *Natyasastra*, as also with Nataraja, the presiding deity of the *Natyasastra*, both at once.

Rukmini Devi's doubling devices—which juxtaposed the ideal teacher (sage Bharata) with the actual teacher (Meenakshi Sundaram Pillai) and the cosmic dance (Nataraja's Dance) with the actual sadir–Bharatanatyam embodied by her—might appear facile. Yet the theatricalizing techniques proved effective because they poeticized the cultural and aesthetic historiography of Bharatanatyam, and transformed it into poetic or semiotic history. Thrilled by these new associations, which linked historical pasts with living presents, and forged with the help of dramatic techniques, including the projection of voice and choral effects, critic after critic described Devi's debut as conveying an otherworldly experience 'a sacramental and spiritual experience, such as the dance-dramas in their original purity were intended to convey.'[8]

By staging Bharatanatyam historically, with the help of three symbols including *Natyasastra*, guru, and temple, Rukmini created a historical stage setting that drew attention to its own theatricality while also referring to Raghavan's conceptual and constructed message in such a way as to appeal to the eye and mind of the urban spectator simultaneously.

STAGING THE GURU

For her next performance in Madras city, Rukmini Devi developed her stage setting by paying greater attention to her staging conventions. She seated her nattuvanar-*guru* and his ensemble along the wings of the Western proscenium and explained her actions in this way:

The musicians would follow the dancer with their music and drumming as she moved about the stage...I wanted to change all that. I made the musicians sit on the side of the stage. I also stopped having the Harmonium and the Clarionet as accompaniments, choosing instead the softer musical instruments *Mukhaveenai*, Flute, etc. I designed my own costumes, Madame Cazan who was good at tailoring and Mary Elmore helped me put my ideas into proper shape. Conrad Worldring, a remarkable young musician, who was a wonderful technician on stage, Alex Elmore who was a lighting expert, all of them did a marvelous job even with the limited equipment we had. All these things made a profound impact and presented the despised *Sadir* in an entirely new way. (Ramani 2003: 45)

The legendary Balasaraswati, a dancer hailing from the devadasi lineage of performers, explained why the teachers stood behind the devadasi dancers and moved with them as they danced. In Balasaraswati's own words:

You must understand why in the old days the *nattuvanar* and the musician used to walk behind the dancer in a performance. The audience used to be positioned on all sides of the performer. There was no power amplification and the dancer couldn't hear the musicians properly. Since the song and the rhythm must be heard by the dancer, the supporting cast used to move back and forth along with the dancer. It may present an amusing picture to you today, but we shouldn't laugh at it. Our elders didn't do anything foolishly. (Raman and Ramachandran 1984b: 21)

But Rukmini Devi changed the older model of presentation because she was working within the proscenium context of stage presentation in twentieth century India, and using Western theatre technology, including microphones, and moving spotlights which electrified the dance and enhanced its aura.

The staging decision was innovative in its time because it rejected the primacy of sight and seeing, structured by the Western proscenium, and encouraged a more inclusive look that would account for the authorial significance of the male dance teacher in the Bharatanatyam performance. Devi desired to keep the male teacher in the frame of the proscenium performance because he gave the dancer the gift of the dancing bells, which she ceremoniously wore around her ankles in each and every act of public performance.

STAGING THE HINDU TEMPLE

For her next public recital at the Madras Museum theatre in 1937, Rukmini Devi endeavoured to give depth to her two dimensional stage by designing a temple stage:

The stage was set to suggest a South Indian Temple with four large granite pillars and a temple tower in the background. Into this setting came Rukmini Devi in an exquisite red and gold costume with jewels and a beautiful gold and jeweled belt which gave her the appearance of an ancient bronze statue come to life and color. This effect was never lost and in fact gained when she danced...One was made happy and taken into a world where happiness and divinity were in the very air one breathed. (Elmore 1937: 58)[9]

C.T. Nachiappan, who had worked with Rukmini Devi as her stage manager and archivist from the 1940s, explained that Rukmini Devi designed numerous adaptable and portable temple stages that could be used contextually in rural towns, urban cities, and international contexts all at once. In his book entitled *Bharatanatya*, he features two temple stages constructed with dried bamboo leaves, and explains that such stages were used primarily when performing in the interior towns in south India, and also in Rukmini Devi's own theatre in Adyar (Nachiappan 2001: 27–9). Ramanarayan has described how Rukmini Devi used 'columns made of cloth on the cyclorama at the back of the stage,' and created another version of the temple stage by painting the mount of Nandi (the vehicle of Siva), as projection on the front curtain (Ramanarayan 1984b: 29). Those of us who have seen her dance dramas in India have also noted that she created temple backdrops with flowers and with simple cloth hangings reconfigured as domes and hung them on the back curtains of the Western proscenium.

STAGING SIVA-NATARAJA

After returning from her international tours in 1936 and 1937, Rukmini Devi traveled to the famous Chidambaram temple in South India to dedicate her dance to Siva-Nataraja, the presiding deity of Bharatanatyam, and danced in the courtyard of the temple. Much has been written about her dedication ritual, and how it was interrupted by huge mobs that gathered to witness her performance.[10] Soon thereafter, she pioneered the practice of mounting the icon on a pedestal and placed Siva-Nataraja in one corner of her temple stage. She was, in fact, the first dancer to stage the icon of Siva-Nataraja, in his manifestation as the Cosmic dancer, on the urban stage. In this iteration, Siva was not just a religious symbol associated with temple worship, but also a classical icon of high art embodying principles of Indian abstraction and classicism, described so eloquently by Ananda Kentish Commaraswamy in his *Dance of Shiva* (1918). Elsewhere, I have described how Coomaraswamy's publication of the *Dance of Shiva* mobilized international awareness of Indian dance, and inspired dancers like Ted Shawn and Ruth St Denis to travel to India in search of the dance.[11]

By ceremoniously placing the icon of Siva-Nataraja on her temple stage, Devi did two things: she reclaimed Siva-Nataraja as inspiration for classical Bharatanatyam.[12] In her own words, 'Bharata's *Natyasastra*, for instance, can be traced to the great Rishi Bharata, and even before him we can trace it back to the splendor of Nataraja himself' (1938: 223). She then enlarged the dance repertoire by choreographing new songs like *Natanam Adinar* that extolled the beauty and grandeur of Siva-Nataraja's cosmic dance and danced it herself on the temple stage.[13] In my doctoral thesis (1996a), I described how the iconic incorporation of the Siva-Nataraja on the temple stage, while forging visual associations with Raghavan's dance historiography, also emphasized the uniqueness of Indian dance history—one in which gods danced. She explained

In India we have this magnificent conception of the Divine One who Himself is a Dancer, a Flute-Player, a cosmic dancer...The great Being, Lord Nataraja, Himself is a dancer and so is Parvati and the Lord Sri Krishna, who danced in Brindavan. Nowhere except in India is there such a cosmic conception of art. (1942: 118)

What is important to note is that Rukmini Devi did not simply assign the Siva-Nataraja icon a specific stage placement on the modern stage, but ceremoniously mounted him on a small pedestal, and illumined him with oil lanterns and brass lamps, evoking links again to Kathakali performances. Thanks to Devi, two different lights, one belonging to the

devotional and spiritual history of the Indian temple, and the other to the objectified history of the moving spotlight, imported from British stagecraft, were forced to co-exist on the Bharatanatyam stage, without denying the legitimacy of the other. I want to suggest, that in this small action involving the juxtapositioning of the traditional oil lamp with the moving spotlight, was contained the embattled struggle of Indian tradition and modernism. Can god-light and stage light co-exist? Can spiritualism co-exist with Indian aesthetic modernism? This was Rukmini Devi's question and also her daring experiment.

Rukmini Devi politicized her temple stage and used it to articulate East/West differences. In her speech entitled 'The Culture of India,' recorded in Hollywood in 1938, Devi forged connections with Isadora Duncan's Divine Dancer aesthetic, which she was familiar with because of her training in Greek dancing mentioned above, while also pointing to her own different realization of divinity within the epistemological structure of the 'religious ceremonial.' She explained that 'In India, religion and classical dance are combined because both express the idea of creation, of rhythmic movement, of the influence of spirit upon matter...Religion, is Divinity expressed inwardly; Art is Divinity expressed outwardly' (1938: 220–3).

If Duncan was the Divine Dancer of the West, Devi presented herself as the Divine Dancer of the East. While Duncan celebrated Greek sculpture and Greek antiquity, Devi affirmed what she called the religious ceremonial, realized within the context of the Hindu temple. If the Western divine dancer claimed individuality and originality as a modern dancer by rejecting the stylized movement of Ballet, the Eastern dancer claimed agency by effacing her individuality as a modern dancer and reverentially reviving and reforming the stylized movement vocabulary of classical Bharatanatyam. Rukmini Devi encapsulated this East/West difference in this way: 'In my own dancing there are certain expressions which I have changed—I have attempted to create a costume and stage setting which is both simple and direct ... But I have tried to do this in the spirit of India and her glorious traditions, so that I could go further along that road towards which the great signpost of ancient India has ever pointed' (1941: 159).

RUKMINI DEVI'S SEMIOTIC PRACTICE

Rukmini Devi's temple stage setting took on a life of its own after the declaration of Indian Independence in 1947, and the formation of the Indian Republic in 1950 (Meduri 2000a: 138–40; Meduri 2008c: 230–4).

The newly formed state assumed patronage of the arts and established national Akademies to foster the development of Indian performing arts on a pan-Indian scale in the 1950s (Meduri 2008c: 230–4). In this time Rukmini Devi was celebrated as foremost Indian dancer and feted with numerous national awards.[14] At the first national dance seminar held in New Delhi in 1958, Rukmini Devi collaborated with both V. Raghavan and Kapila Vatsyayan, India's most revered scholar of the performing arts, and together they constituted the second state-sponsored Natyasastric-historiography for Indian performing arts (Meduri 2008c: 230–4).

Rukmini Devi was invited to speak about the dance revival on this historic occasion and describe what she had realized in her Kalakshetra institution. Not surprisingly, Rukmini Devi decided to speak about the new beginnings that she had constituted for the solo dance of Bharatanatyam in the 1930s. She read from her paper entitled 'Bharatanatya Shastra in Practice,' proceeded to describe her training with traditional teachers, and then spoke anecdotally about the presentational changes that she introduced into the dance practice, including the designing of new costumes (1958: 27–8).

Kapila Vatsyayan, returning to India after completing her dance and English studies education in the US (Coorlawala 2000: 103–09), presented a paper at the seminar, and witnessed this historic conversation. She rapidly took up bureaucratic positions within the Ministry of Culture and Education and took charge of India's international cultural relations programmes with foreign countries 'and gave direction to it for some three decades' (Erdman 1984: 77–98; Meduri 2008c: 230–4). Vatsyayan was responsible for creating bilateral and multi-lateral cultural exchange programs with 'over seventy countries in the fields of humanities, arts, fundamental sciences and social sciences.' She was also instrumental in sending both T. Balasaraswati and Rukmini Devi on international cultural exchange programs that India negotiated with UK, France, Germany, Russia and the US in the 1960s.

As a scholar, Vatsyayan, who collaborated with both Raghavan and Rukmini Devi, drew on Raghavan's literary historiography and Rukmini Devi's technique-based replication of his textual historiography, combined the two approaches with her own interest in sculpture and constituted a new, pan-Indian 'nationalist' historiography for Indian dance which was both similar to and different from Raghavan's in the 1960s. Vatsyayan's two most well-known books entitled, *Indian Classical Dance in Literature and the Arts* (1968/1977), and *Indian Classical Dance* (1974/1992), were published by the Publications Division, Ministry of Information and

Broadcasting, Government of India, and also the Sangeet Natak Akademi (Meduri 2008a: 150–2; Meduri 2008c: 230–4).

She carefully historicized Bharatanatyam as the 'Classical Dance of India', and provided an inclusive and sheltering pan-Indian historiography that was open to both traditional dancers like T. Balasaraswati, and also to urban dancers including Rukmini Devi, Shanta Rao, and Yamini Krishnamurthy among others (1974: 13–25). Vatsyayan's two Government sponsored publications manifested themselves as seminal text books for the post 1970s generation of urban dancers, and were used as such by Bharatanatyam dancers.

While this second historiography legitimized the dance in new ways, sociological issues revolving round the construction of the temple stage were not discussed in this official historiography. Was the Western proscenium, a bequeathal of British colonialism, an appropriate stage for a temple dance linked to rituals of worship? Did concert Bharatanatyam need a temple stage? Why did Rukmini Devi create this temple stage?

One could argue that the temple stage setting that Rukmini Devi had created was useful in that it heterogenized Raghavan's literary historiography and opened it up to multiple perspectives (Meduri 2008a: 147–50). Many styles of Bharatanatyam—known as Pandanallur-Bharatanatyam, Tanjore-Bharatanatyam, Kalakshetra-Bharatanatyam, Vazhuvoor-Bharatanatyam or Balasaraswati-Bharatanatyam, to mention just a few—were presented from within Rukmini Devi's temple stage setting. The stage convention was beneficial in that it enabled the public celebration of Indian tradition, encapsulated in the figure of the male dance-teacher, and facilitated the plotting of patrilineal genealogies for twentieth-century Bharatanatyam.[15] Spectators could see the dialogical interrelationships between teachers and students in each and every concert performance.

The temple was transformed into a second stage prop for Bharatanatyam as early as the 1950s. Dancers carry Devi's portable temple stage in their travelling suitcases, as part of the stage property associated with the Bharatanatyam dance recital, including dancing bells, costumes and ornaments. On the eventful day of an evening performance, the Bharatanatyam dancer irons out the creases in the temple curtains and hangs them ceremoniously on the back curtains of the Western proscenium with the help of push up pins, needles, duck tape, and safety pins. Made with paper, real flowers, and bamboo leaves, cloth curtains, dome hangings, and banners, Rukmini Devi's temple stage manifested itself as nothing more than a provisional, Third-World stage, reflecting the limited technological means available to Third-World dancers of classical Bharatanatyam. We need only contrast this poor stage with the spectacular stages constructed by American modern dancers Loie Fuller and Isadora Duncan (Thomas 1995: 53–60) to grasp the technological inequities defining First-World and Third-World dance performances.

The Siva-Nataraja icon, made of paper-maché and/or bronze metal, and including silver or brass lamps was similarly transformed into a third stage prop and absorbed into the mainstream practice of the dance. Bharatanatyam dancers carry this icon, along with lamps, oils, matchboxes, and cotton wicks, in their travelling suitcases. They place him/it in the same place that Devi had assigned, and light him/it in exactly the same way as he had been lit in the 1930s, that is, by striking a match to the match box. Devi thus transformed God, guru, and temple into theatrical stage props for Bharatanatyam, and three generations of urban dancers used them as such through the fifty-year period of the dance revival, continuing into the present.

Spectators in any part of the globe today can see the classical Bharatanatyam dancer, dressed in traditional costume with ankle bells tied to her feet, appear dramatically on the proscenium. She carries an imaginary bouquet of flowers in her hand. Rhythmically she dances her way to the icon and places her offering of flowers at the feet of Siva-Nataraja, then she glides gracefully towards her guru and pays her homage to him. After the two primary salutations, the dancer is free to take centrestage. Then she performs an elaborate performative salutation to the temple stage itself, sacralizes the Western proscenium theatrically, and transforms it into a three-dimensional temple stage. Splendidly, she performs sadir as Bharatanatyam, and stages herself theatrically as a dancer-historian in the manner of Devi.

In my doctoral thesis (1996a), I described how a large, regional, national and international community gathered around the semiotic signs of the dancing bells, icons of Siva-Nataraja, figure of the guru, temple backdrops, and dance costumes, and enabled the articulation of what Benedict Anderson has described as an imagined national community for the dance (1983: 30). This imagined community did not just comprise middle-class urban dancers, dance teachers, musicians, percussionists, dance scholars, dance anthropologists, dance historians and spectators, but interpellated a larger invisible community from the service sector including tailors, sculptors, cobblers, jewelers, flower vendors, electricians, cameramen, make up artists, and dramaturges who were called upon to serve the growing aesthetic needs of the new dance community as early as the 1940s (Meduri 1996a: 335–46).

Any sociological study of the practice of Bharatanatyam must recognize that it was the mechanical reproduction of the theatrical props associated with Bharatanatyam, prefigured by temporal coincidence, and measured by clock and calendar, that in fact provided the economic infrastructure structure that knit the dance community into an imagined ideological inter-national community in the 1940s. It was also this social and economic reproduction that inserted the dance work into the age of mechanical reproduction articulated so famously by Walter Benjamin in his essay of that title (1969: 217–51).

RETURN/RESCUE INITIATIVES IN THE 1980S

The 1980s were difficult years for Rukmini Devi as she was very ill and dying of cancer. She was fully aware in this time that the temple stage aesthetic that she had upheld, against all odds, had no exchange value in the new world of globalization and that very few even understood its historical provenance.

Chandralekha, the famous contemporary dancer, arrived on the dance scene in the 1980s. She mercilessly stripped down Devi's temple stage constellation, and spoke out against the religiosity of this stage. Shobana Jeyasingh, the renowned contemporary dancer in the UK, questioned the cultural assumptions in Devi's reconstruction of Bharatanatyam, and articulated an alternative postmodern aesthetic for Bharatanatyam. The 1980s represented a new moment in local and international dance practice as Bharatanatyam finally broke out of the dominant frame of Indian nationalism, Indian tradition, and Indian dance historiography in which it had been defined for over seventy years (Meduri 2008b: 298–328; Meduri 2005a: 5–8).

Yet, it was also in this moment when the Indian state opened up to the economic flows and pressures of globalization by sponsoring India festivals abroad that Vatsyayan, India's long standing bureaucrat, intervened in the social production of the classical arts by offering temples as new site-specific and tourist performance venues for Bharatanatyam.[16] If the temple stage was sustained as a concert stage setting through the 1980s, Bharatanatyam was performed both within the theatrical allegory of the temple stage and also within the actual precincts of the Hindu temple in the 1980s. From temple to temple stage, to temple again, the practice history of the sadir-Bharatanatyam had come full circle in the 1980s.

Rukmini Devi rebutted what I describe as the 'return initiative.' Vatsyayan explains that she felt it was time 'to relocate the dance in the precincts of the temple, to have dancers dance in the hall of the Chidambaram temple. When I spoke about my intention to Rukmini Devi she was mad at me. Is this what I taught you all these years, Kapila?...Was this what the struggle was all about, to return the dance to the temple?... You happen to be the Vice President of Sangeet Natak Akademi and you can do it. But I shall not be seen dead anywhere near it' (2005: 58).

Devi did not just speak against the 'return' initiative, but rebutted it in action by building a magnificent, site-specific temple theatre for Bharatanatyam. Known as Bharata Kalakshetra, Rukmini Devi's theatre stands on the hundred acre campus of Kalakshetra. Devi explained that although her theatre was conceived along the lines of the Kerala-style Koothambalam, it would also have a temple atmosphere. She averred that 'dance was really the art of the temple and that her temple theatre was built with that purpose in mind. It has many features of the temple, and we have adopted as much as possible all the ideals enshrined in the *Natyashastra*' (Kalakshetra brochure).

Why did Devi construct this temple theatre in the final stage of the Bharatanatyam dance revival? Did she desire to rescue her temple stage aesthetic from historical oblivion, or was she memorializing the collective history of the temple stage in which three generations of urban dancers had danced through the fifty-year period history of the dance revival?

In characteristic manner, Rukmini Devi did not explain herself but doubled her repudiation of the Indian State by turning down the Government's offer to grant Deemed University status to Kalakshetra. She declined the offer by telling Government officials that Government rules are diametrically opposed to the ideals of Kalakshetra where teachers (gurus) teach beyond the age of seventy because they are exemplary artists. 'Your modernization, she said, has no direction. In the name of modernization, I do not want to lose my soul. I would like to run this institution in our own traditional methods, suited to our own modern genius' (Nagaswamy 2005: 78). Devi thus spoke out for the last time, albeit in the age of globalization, not on behalf of either the urban dancer or Bharatanatyam, but her temple stage, comprising the three historical symbols of god, guru, and temple.

Will there be another Bharatanatyam dancer who will be called upon to grapple with the large questions of god, guru, history, historiography, and modernity on the local/global stage in the same way again? This was the question that haunted me during the time of my post doctoral research in India in 2001, when I began re-conceptualizing Rukmini Devi's aesthetic legacy within the transnational perspective of global modernities.[17]

The Bharatanatyam stage, neatly arranged with historical symbols, manifests itself as a haunted space. It is haunted not just by the ghostly iteration of dance history, but also by the absence/presence of the icon of Siva-Nataraja lit with traditional lamps. Can god-light and stage-light co-exist? This question, intricately linked to Indian modernity, impelled me to embrace Indian dance studies in the USA in the 1980s (Meduri 1996a: xliii-liv). Yet, it is this same question that still lingers in the post 1980s practice and is one that classical dancers worry about even as they light the god-lamp and perform Bharatanatyam on the global stage today.

CONCLUSION

Rukmini Devi is no more. So why should we worry about her temple stage? I think we need to take her inaugural temple stage setting seriously because it manifested itself as a historical stage setting and continues to inform the theory, history and practice of classical Bharatanatyam, both locally and globally. The allegorical structure lingers in the practice because Devi constituted it by engaging with the totality of Raghavan's cultural historiography, what Raymond Williams describes as the 'whole cultural process,' including 'traditions, institutions and social formations' (1977: 121–8).

I think it is imperative for those of us still engaged in writing the modern, social history of Bharatanatyam, albeit in the age of globalization, to move beyond the ideological framework of Indian nationalism in which we have hitherto conducted our critical investigations of Bharatanatyam and explore trans-cultural questions revolving around vision, history, divinity, spirituality, bodily writing, and visuality in modernism. To do this, we will have to cease thinking about the form of Bharatanatyam from within anthropological frameworks of the 'local,' or as a dialectical struggle between devadasi and urban dancers. We need to enlarge our historical perspective and articulate comparative critiques that will put twentieth-century Bharatanatyam in conversation with Duncan's modern theories of spiritualism. Intercultural scholarship such as what I am proposing will help us historicize aesthetic modernism with a global modernities perspective. To do this we need to think of Bharatanatyam as a double-sited world historical form in conversation with Western aesthetic modernisim and global politics from the moment of its constitution as a historical form in the 1930s continuing into the present.

Rukmini Devi's aesthetic legacy yields itself to a comparative, global modernities perspective because she was not a local but a global Indian thinking about the revival within a world perspective from the moment of its enunciation in the 1930s. Her aesthetic legacy interests me today because her preoccupation with history and historiography were uniquely postcolonial concerns, inspiring her to construct an allegorical temple stage, comprising historical symbols, which, she hoped, would enable the production of a modern, corporeal, and historical practice for Bharatanatyam, while also constituting a modern visual and spectatorial epistemology for classical Bharatanatyam in the world at large.

NOTES

1. Radha Burnier, the present President of the Theosophical Society, and first student of Kalakshetra, explains that Rukmini Devi, leader of the Young Theosophist movement, inspired young recruits by asserting that to be 'truly Indian one had to be truly inter-national, exhorting them to honor the best in all civilizations and to live it in their daily lives' (2005: 63).

2. For a summary description of Rukmini Devi's work within the Theosophical Society in the 1930s, see my essay (2004b: pp. 14–16); and (2005a: pp. 3–29).

3. See Annie Besant (1925); Josephine Ransom (1928: pp. 467–72); Meduri (1996a: pp. 177–295; 2005a: p. 29); and Allen (1997: pp. 70–4).

4. See Srinivasan (1985: pp. 1873–5); and Meduri (1996a: 56–61; 2004b: 11–29) for different discussions about the Anti Nautch Social Reform movement of the 1890s, and its impact on the life and artistic practices of devadasis.

5. See Arudra (1987: 17–36); Meduri (1996a: 219–41).

6. See Arudra (1986/87); Ramnarayan (1984a: 17–29); Meduri (1996a; 2005b: 201–03); and Allen (1997: 70–4) for different accounts of Rukmini Devi's visit to the Madras Music Academy.

7. See Srinivasan (1984, 1869–76); and Meduri (1996a: 49–110; 2004a: 435–48). All three essays describe the marginalization of devadasis from the nineteenth- and twentieth-century practices of the dance revival.

8. Quoted in *Kalakshetra Report 1936–1961*. Adyar: Kalakshetra Publications.

9. Alex Elmore's reviewed Rukmini Devi's 1937 performance in *The Young Theosophist*. Rukmini Devi edited this journal, which was renamed as *The Young Citizen* in the 1940s.

10. See Ramnarayan (1984b: 23) and Ramani (2003: 46).

11. See Meduri (1996a: 183–211); also see Allen (1997: 83–94).

12. For a selective but interesting analysis which explains how Siva-Nataraja became a national icon of the dance revival, see Allen's essay (1997: 79–83).

13. For a fuller explication of the dance work, and its choreography see Allen (1997: 74–9).

14. The Government of India nominated Rukmini Devi to lead cultural delegations to foreign countries and to chair national committees established for the incorporation of art and culture into higher education. The state also

honored her with numerous national awards including the Padma Bhushan and the Sangeet Natak Akademi award in the 1950s. In 1952, Rukmini Devi was nominated to serve as a legislative member in the upper house of the Indian parliament. She completed two terms in parliament, moved a bill for the Prevention of Cruelty to Animals, and received the *Prani Mitra*, or Animal Lover Award in 1968. The Royal Society for the Prevention of Cruelty to Animals, London also awarded Rukmini Devi with the Queen Victoria Silver Medal in 1958, and the Council of the World Federation for the Protection of Animals, the Hague, added her name to their Roll of Honor in 1959. Wayne State University awarded her an honorary Doctorate in Humanities, and the County and City of Los Angeles bestowed her with Scrolls of Honor in the 1960s (see *Kalakshetra Quarterly* 1986: 118–19).

15. In my essay, I discuss the phenomenon of improvisation in classical Bharatanatyam and focus on Balasaraswati's improvisation of *Krishna Nee Begane Baro*. I argue that improvisation and innovation within classical dance and music is always realized within the classical tradition and not outside it. See Meduri (2003a: 141–50).

16. For a brief discussion describing some media issues involved in the staging of Bharatanatyam dance recitals within the precincts of the Hindu temple in the 1980s, see Meduri (1996b: 53–7).

17. I dramatized the politics and the poetics of Rukmini Devi's temple stage in my theatrical productions featuring her local/global aesthetic vision in 2003/2004. The production was staged as part of the Centenary Celebrations and was featured in India, the US and the UK.

REFERENCES

Allen, Matthew Harp, 1997, 'Rewriting the Script for South Indian Dance', *The Drama Review* 41(3), pp. 63–100.

Arundale, George, 1936, 'The International Academy of the Arts', Adyar Pamphlet, No. 208, Madras: The Theosophical Publishing House, 1936.

Anderson, Benedict, 1983, *Imagined Communities: Reflections on the Origins and Spread of Nationalism*, London: Verso Editions, 1983.

Arudra, 1986/87a, 'The Transfiguration of a Traditional Dance: The Academy and the Dance Events of the First Decade', *Sruti* 27/28, pp. 17–21.

_____, 1986/87b, 'Dancers of the First Decade', *Sruti* 27/28, pp. 17–21.

_____, 1986/1987c, 'The Renaming of an Old Dance: A Whodunit Tale of Mystery', *Sruti* 27/28: pp. 30–1.

_____, 'E. Krishna Iyer (1897–1968): Savior of a Dance in Distress', *Sruti* 27/28: 1986/87d, pp. 32–6.

Balasarawati, T., 1988, 'The Art of Bharatanatyam: Reflections of Balasaraswati', *Sruti*, 50: pp. 37–40.

_____, 1991, 'Bala on *Bharata Natyam*', translated by S. Guhan, Madras: the Sruti Foundation.

Benjamin, Walter, 1969, *Illuminations: Walter Benjamin, Essays and Reflections*, translated by Harry Zone, London New York: Schoken Books.

Besant, Annie, 1925, *Star Congress at Ommen*, Adyar: Theosophical Publishing House.

———, 'The New Annunication', Adyar: Theosophical Publishing House, pp. 1–4.

Burnier, Radha, 2005, 'Rukmini Devi as a Theosophist', in *Rukmini Devi Arundale: A Visionary Architect of Indian Culture and the Performing Arts*, Avanthi Meduri (ed.), New Delhi: Motilal Banarsidass Publishers.

Coomaraswamy, Ananda. K., 1957 [1918], *The Dance of Shiva: On Indian Art and Culture*, New York: The Noonday Press.

Coorlawala, Uttara, 2005, 'The Birth of Bharatanatyam and the Sanskritized Body', in *Rukmini Devi Arundale: A Visionary Architect of Indian Culture and the Performing Arts*, Avanthi Meduri (ed.), New Delhi: Motilal Banarsidass Publishers.

———, 2000, 'Kapila Vatsyayan: Formative Years', *Dance Research Journal*, 32/1 (Summer), pp. 103–09.

Daly, Ann, 1995, *Done Into Dance: Isadora Duncan in America*, Bloomington and Indianapolis: Indiana University Press.

Devi, Rukmini, 1938, 'The Culture of India: A Radio Broadcast', *The Young Theosophist* (October), pp. 220–3.

———, 1941, 'Signpost of Ancient India', *The Young Citizen*, Vol. 18, No. 9, (September) pp. 158–9.

———, 1942, 'The Dance Art', *The Young Citizen*, Vol. 17, No. 7, (July), pp. 118–20.

———, 1958, 'The Dance Seminar: A Brief Day to Day Account', in *Report 1953–1958*, New Delhi: Sangeet Natak Akademi.

Elmore, Alex, 1937, 'Srimati Rukmini Devi in Bharatanatya', *The Young Theosophist* (March), Vol. 12(2), p. 58.

Erdman, Joan, 1984, 'Who Should Speak for the Performing Arts? The Case of the Delhi Dancers', in *Cultural Policy in India*, Llyod Rudolph (ed.), New Delhi: Chanakya Publications, pp. 77–104.

Gaston, Annie-Marie, 1996, *From Temple to Theatre*, New Delhi: Manohar.

Jordon, Kay, 2003, *From Sacred Servant to Profane Prostitution: A History of the Changing Legal Status of the Devadasis in India, 1857–1947*, New Delhi: Manohar.

Kristeva, Julia, 1980, *Desire In Language: A Semiotic Approach to Literature and Art*, New York: Columbia University Press.

———, 1984, *Revolution in Poetic Language*, translated by Margaret Waller, New York: New York University Press.

Meduri, Avanthi, 1988, '*Bharatanatyam*: What Are You?' in *Asian Theatre Journal* 5(1), pp. 1–22.

———, 1996a, Nation, Woman, Representation: The Sutured History of the Devadasi and Her Dance. PhD dissertation, New York University.

———, 1996b, 'Modern History of *Bharatanatyam*: Vibrant Form or Export Commodity', *Voices*, 1(3), pp. 53–7.

———, 2003a, 'Multiple Pleasures: Improvization in Bharatanatyam', in *Taken by Surprise: A Dance Improvisation Reader*, Ann Cooper Albright and David Gere (eds), Middletown, CT: Wesleyan University Press.

Meduri, Avanthi, 2003b, 'Western Feminist Theory, Asian Indian Performance and a Notion of Agency', in *Performance: Critical Concepts in Literary and Cultural Studies*, Philip Auslander (ed.), London, New York: Routledge.

_____, 2004b, 'Bharatanatyam as a Global Dance: Some Issues in Teaching, Research and Practice', *Dance Research Journal*, 36/2 (Winter), pp. 11–29.

_____, 2005a, 'Introduction: A Critical Overview', in *Rukmini Devi: A Visionary Architect of Indian Culture and the Performing Arts*, Avanthi Meduri (ed.). New Delhi: Motilal Banarasidass.

_____, 2005b, 'Rukmini Devi and Sanskritization: A Performance Perspective', in *Rukmini Devi: A Visionary Architect of Indian Culture and the Performing Arts*, Avanthi Meduri (ed.), New Delhi: Motilal Banarasidass.

_____, 2008a, 'Temple Stage as Historical Allegory: Rukmini Devi as Dancer-Historian', in *Performing Pasts: Reinventing the Arts in South India*, Indira Peterson and Davesh Soneji (eds), New Delhi: Oxford University Press.

_____, 2008b, 'The Transfiguration of Indian/Asian Dance in the UK: Bharatanatyam in Global Contexts', *Asian Theatre Journal*, Vol. 25, No. 2 (Fall), pp. 298–329

_____, 2008c, 'Labels, Histories, Politics: South Asian Dance on the Global Stage', *Dance Research*, Vol. 26, No. 2 (Winter), pp. 223–44.

Meduri, Avanthi and Jeffrey Spear, 2004a, 'Knowing the Dancer: East meets West', *Victorian Literature and Culture*, 32(2), pp. 435–48.

Nachiappan, C., 2001, *Rukmini Devi: Bharatanatya*, Chennai: Kalakshetra Publications.

Nagaswamy, R., 2005, 'Rukmini Devi as Divine Dancer', in *Rukmini Devi Arundale: A Visionary Architect of Indian Culture and the Performing Arts*, Avanthi Meduri (ed.), New Delhi: Motilal Banarasidass.

Owens, Craig, 1992, *Beyond Recognition: Representation, Power and Culture*, Berkeley: University of California Press.

O'Shea, Janet, 1998, 'Traditional Indian Dance and the Making of Interpretive Communities', *Asian Theatre Journal* 15, 1 (Spring), pp. 45–63.

_____, 2001, *At Home in the World: Bharata Natyam's Transnational Traditions*, PhD dissertation, University of California, Riverside.

Tejaswini, Niranjana, P. Sudhir, and V. Dhareshwar (eds), 1993, *Interrogating Modernity: Culture and Colonialism in India*, Calcutta: Seagull Books.

Pattabhiraman, N., and Anandhi Ramachandran, 1984, 'The Whole World in Her Hands: Part 1', *Sruti*, 4 (January/February), pp. 17–31.

_____, 1984b, 'The Whole World in Her Hands: Part 2', *Sruti*, 5 (March), pp. 17–32.

Raghavan, V., 1945, 'Her Infinite Variety', *Journal of the Music Academy Madras*, XXXIV, pp. 124–31.

_____, 1956, 'Variety and Integration in the Pattern of Indian Culture', *The Far Eastern Quarterly Review*, Vol. XV, 4 (August), pp. 497–505.

_____, 1958, 'The Dance Seminar: A Brief Day to Day Account', in *Report 1953–1958*, New Delhi: Sangeet Natak Akademi.

_____, 1974, 'Bharata Natya', *Journal of the Music Academy Madras* XLV, pp. 233–62.

272   Bharatanatyam

Ramanarayan, Gowri, 1984a, 'Rukmini Devi: A Quest for Beauty, A Profile', *Sruti*, 8 (June), pp. 17–29.

———, 1984b, 'Rukmini Devi: Dancer and Reformer, A Profile', *Sruti*, 9 (July), pp. 17–29.

———, 1984c, 'Rukmini Devi: Restoration and Creation, A Profile', *Sruti*, 10 (August), pp. 26–38.

Ramani, Shakuntala, 2003, *Rukmini Devi Birth Centenary Volume*. Chennai: Kalakshetra Foundation.

———, 2003, Shraddhanjali: Brief Pen Portraits of Great People who laid the Foundation of Kalakshetra, Chennai: Kalakshetra Foundation.

Ransom, Josephine, 1938, *A Short History of the Theosophical Society*, Madras: The Theosophical Publishing House.

Rokem, Freddie, 2000, *Performing History: Theatrical Representations of the Past in Contemporary Theatre*, Iowa City: University of Iowa Press.

Sarada, S., 1985, *Kalakshetra Rukmini Devi: Reminiscences*, Madras: Kala Mandir Trust.

Schechner, Richard, 1985, *Between Theatre and Anthropology*, Philadelphia: University of Pennsylvania Press.

Srinivasan, Amrit, 1983, 'The Hindu Temple Dancer: Prostitute or Nun?' *Cambridge Anthopology* 8, 1, pp. 73–99.

———, 1985, 'Reform and Revival: The Devadasi and Her Dance', *Economic and Political Weekly* 20, No. 44 (November), pp. 1869–76.

Thomas, Helen, 1995, *Dance, Modernity and Culture: Explorations in the Sociology of Dance*, London, New York: Routledge.

Vatsyayan, Kapila, 1968 [reprint1977], *Classical Indian Dance in Literature and the Arts*, New Delhi: Sangeet Natak Akademi.

———, 1974 [reprint 1992], *Indian Classical Dance*. New Delhi: Ministry of Information and Broadcasting.

———, 2005, 'Rukmini Devi as Teacher, Guide and Mother', in *Rukmini Devi Arundale: A Visionary Architect of Indian Culture and the Performing Arts*, Avanthi Meduri (ed.), New Delhi: Motilal Banarsidass.

Williams, Raymond, 1997, *Marxism and Literature*, Oxford and New York: Oxford University Press.

Anne-Marie Gaston

Dance and the Hindu Woman

*Bharatanatyam Re-ritualized**

INTRODUCTION

Bharatanatyam is one of the contemporary styles of classical Indian dance that are frequently performed, on both stage and television, in India and abroad. Since it boasts more students and more performances than any other, it can claim to be the most popular style today. Outside India, it is synonymous with traditional Indian culture and is a skill highly sought after among expatriate Indian communities. More important for the purpose of this chapter, Bharatanatyam is recognizably the same dance that previously formed an important part of both religious and secular celebrations in South India. According to Khokar, 'the founding of a new Bharatanatyam that had been lifted bodily from the sacred temple precincts and without ado transplanted on the lowly professional stage' took place in 1933 (1987: 41, 46).

In its modern manifestation, Bharatanatyam appears to occupy the same niche in Indian society that ballet occupied in the West in the last century. Both are classical art forms which could be regarded as museum pieces from another other era. In contrast to folk forms, both can be judged by recognized standards. Some knowledge of technique is necessary before either can be fully appreciated. Both are patronized by the élite, and performed on the concert stage. In both cases, there is usually a fee

* This chapter is based on interviews conducted with dancers, teachers, musicians, critics and connoisseurs (*rasika*), over a period of nine years up to and including 1989, in Delhi, Madras, Kumbakonam, Thanjavur, Bangalore, Baroda, Ahmedabad and Bombay. It forms part of a wider study of the sociology of Indian dance. I wish to thank all those consulted for their generous assistance in sharing with me their perception of an art we all love. Unless otherwise specified, all Indian-language terms are given either in Sanskrit or in the Tamilized Sanskrit peculiar to Bharatanatyam (see Kersenboom, this volume).

for entry into the concerts; dancers are paid; and they perform only after many years of training.

However, the recent origin of Bharatanatyam from a religious ritual gives it a dimension entirely lacking in Western ballet. Moreover, the temple tradition from which it developed was the preserve of a particular group: the *devadasis*. These hereditary dancers not only studied and taught dance; they also fulfilled other roles in traditional South Indian society, including that of the courtesan (see Carmichael 1904, 1910). The wave of puritanism which swept Hindu society during the British period led to the prohibition of the institution of the devadasi and the disapproval of those associated with it (see Srinivasan 1984, 1985). Consequently, while the originators of modern Bharatanatyam retained many of the earlier elements of the dance, they also sought to suppress those aspects which linked it most firmly with the person of the devadasi. In those early days, therefore, many of the rituals and ceremonies associated with the devadasi dance tradition were not performed because of the stigma still attached to it.

More recent trends form an interesting contrast. For example, in the context of the devadasi tradition, the validation ceremonies conferred the rights and obligations associated with being a hereditary dancer. Some of these ceremonies, adapted to the needs of modern Bharatanatyam, are now firmly established as traditional. Other innovations of a quasi-religious type have also appeared. As a result, Bharatanatyam has more ritual attached to it today than it had during the period of its revival when strenuous efforts were made to dissociate the modern form (Bharatanatyam) from the original (*catir kacceri*).[1] In this chapter, I describe some of these recent changes. I also examine the role of religious ritual in modern Bharatanatyam, and discuss how the increasing religiosity in the dance relates to social changes affecting both dancers and dance audiences.

Another recent development concerns caste and socio-economic status. Judging by the number of performances and the degree of participation, the importance of Bharatanatyam for the middle and upper classes in India far surpasses that of classical ballet training for girls in the West. In Madras alone, there are literally hundreds of performances each year. A high proportion of young girls from 'good families' (particularly high-caste or brahmin families) undertakes dance training. There is also considerable activity in Delhi, Bombay, Bangalore and other cities. This was not always the case. The involvement of the higher castes with Bharatanatyam began during the freedom struggle when the needs of nationalism took precedence over the prejudices of the past (Srinivasan 1984). Their participation gained momentum with Indian independence in 1947, and is now a major force behind the spate of public recitals throughout India and abroad. To quote T. Shankaran (cousin of the famous devadasi, T. Balasaraswati),[2] 'it is not a boom, it is an epidemic'.[3]

In the context of this take-over of the dance by non-traditional groups, it is important to remember that many dancers and teachers who were part of the hereditary tradition of the devadasi are still alive.[4] Kersenboom focuses on one such family in her chapter for this volume.[5] Many of the changes in the dance have therefore taken place within the experience of living people. Yet there continues to be disagreement about which elements are recent accretions and which, as part of the temple legacy, are hallowed by tradition. For while the majority of dancers, teachers and critics associated with Bharatanatyam are aware of the origins of the dance, many of them (including most of the top performers and many teachers) have never seen it in its original setting. Moreover, despite the fact that the older form is now believed to be purer and better, only some of the devadasis who formed part of that tradition have been consulted or emulated.[6] A great deal of filtering and selecting has taken place. This in turn has led to differences of opinion concerning the proper way to present Bharatanatyam (Chatterjee 1979: X, 16). The result, still in the process of creation, is a dance style considered acceptable for women of a higher social class to perform.

In this chapter, I show that some rituals and symbols now associated with Bharatanatyam can be traced to earlier practices, while others are recent creations. My concern is to examine this process of change. Since 1947 (the year of Indian independence, and the year in which dance as part of temple ritual was banned), many people have been active in defining the tradition that is accepted today as Bharatanatyam. My information is based on personal interviews and participant observation in the belief that a living tradition is best recorded by those actively involved in creating it.[7] I am concerned with opinions and experiences as reflections of what the dance means to different individuals. Where people maintain different views of what is historical or traditional within the dance, I am more interested in what such differences tell us about the current perceptions of the dance, and how these have developed, than in which view is closer to the truth.

The transition from temple ritual and its secular counterpart (*catir*)[8] to the dance style now called Bharatanatyam is marked by several changes. In particular, the hereditary component that determined how dancers were selected is no longer applicable. The widely acknowledged repertoire of the traditional secular component still forms the basis for present-day Bharatanatyam; indeed, most students today learn the full traditional programme before progressing to newer material (*Marg* 1979). In particular, the introduction of new themes and stage presentation has transformed the dance. Some of these innovations, developed since the dance moved away from the temples, are now accepted as part of its religious legacy. In fact, there has been a general attempt to validate the antiquity of the dance by emphasizing the religious rather that the secular elements.

To exemplify the changes taking place, I shall explore the attitudes of dancers, teachers and critics towards a range of phenomena. First, I examine the reintroduction of two of the validation ceremonies for the devadasi (the début recital and the worship of the ankle-bells) as not only acceptable but necessary to assert artistic credibility. Then I discuss the presence of an icon on the concert stage, in particular that of Nataraja throughout the début recital. I also consider the performance of acts of worship (puja) in front of that icon as part of the dance recital, and the use of hand signs similar to those used by the devadasi when dance was part of temple ritual. Finally, I explore the significance of menstruation for performers and teachers of dance.

THE TEMPLE TRADITION
Until 1920, temple dancing in South India was the almost exclusive preserve of the devadasi, who also belonged to the larger *icai vellala* community (Srinivasan 1985: 1876; Kersenboom 1987: 184). Until recently, this community included the majority of performers and teachers of dance. I refer to them below as 'traditional practitioners'. Historical accounts of the dance and personal interviews with older dancers and teachers reveal that some individuals danced predominantly in temples, some danced mainly on secular occasions, and some combined both activities. Dance was their profession, with specific duties, obligations and rewards. Entry into this profession was strictly regulated, and each stage in a dancer's professional life was marked with well-defined ceremonies. There was also a code of acceptable conduct intended to govern interactions with colleagues and patrons, the latter usually found among the upper classes, the learned and the privileged (Lakhia 1987: 53).

THE PRESENT STATE OF BHARATANATYAM
The cultural life which once centred on the great temples and major festivals of most South Indian towns, and on the palaces of local rulers,

has now largely shifted to urban centres such as Delhi, Bombay, Madras and Calcutta.[9] It is here, in a completely new context, that many young middle- and upper-class girls, particularly brahmins, study and perform Bharatanatyam. For most of these girls, the primary goal is not that of becoming self-supporting professionals. While in the past being a dancer was both a way of life and a profession, neither is the case for the majority of girls who study it today. More often, the dance serves as a social accomplishment, and as a means of learning about and expressing traditional Hindu social and artistic values. In this context, Bharatanatyam has become an integral part of the education of the upper and middle classes in most cities and towns. The most striking example of this change is the fact that, among the educated middle class, dance training culminating in the first public performance has become the social accomplishment *par excellence*.

Indian dance consists of aesthetic movement and theatrical dances, the latter drawn largely from Hindu mythology. Thus for many Indian girls both in India and abroad, the dance is regarded as an important vehicle for becoming familiar with Hindu myths, in particular, those myths which embody the ideal role they are to emulate as women. The function of the dance thus transcends the artistic, providing instead the medium for acquiring cultural identity and examples of female role models. As the Westernization and secularization of Indian society increases, this role has strengthened; it is particularly noticeable among expatriate Indians.

While attitudes towards both the person and the dance of the devadasi remain ambiguous, several devadasi rituals have appeared in modified form within modern Bharatanatyam. For example, four ceremonies[10] were considered essential for the devadasi whether her function was secular or religious: first, the ritual first dance lesson; second, the presentation of ankle-bells (*gajjai puja*; *gajjai*, Tamil) after the completion of the first item from the concert repertoire (*alarippu*, Tamil); third, the début recital (*arangetram*) after the completion of dance training; and fourth, the selection of a patron.

With regard to the first of these, the aspiring devadasi usually took her ritual first steps on pounded paddy with the teacher lifting her ankle and striking her foot on the ground. While this particular ritual is not performed today, on the occasion of the dancer's first lesson, when the dance class in conducted in the teacher's home, offerings of fruit, flowers, incense and money are arranged on a round plate and presented first, to the teacher's household deity and then to the teacher.

I consider the worship of the ankle-bells (gajjai puja) and the first public performance (arangetram) in detail below.

The ceremony for the selection of a patron is no longer relevant because it is now legally possible[11] and acceptable for dancers to marry. However, since accomplishment in dance often attracts a suitable husband, some have interpreted this as not entirely unlike the case of the devadasi. In some ways, the husband (or even the father) of the contemporary dancer can be said to serve the same function as the patron of the devadasi: his influence, and sometimes his financial backing, help to secure performances for his wife (or daughter). For while teaching Bharatanatyam has become a lucrative profession, there are few dancers who can support themselves as performers alone.

The First Public Performance

The début recital (arangetram) was perhaps that first devadasi ritual to be adapted into modern Bharatanatyam. The importance of this ceremony has increased to such an extent that other dance styles without this tradition, such as Odissi and Kuchipudi, have also adopted the practice. As dance becomes more and more popular, no expense is spared in preparing a daughter's first recital.

In the period of the dance revival, during the 1930s and 1940s,[12] dancers from non-devadasi (or non-traditional) families gave solo public dance recitals but did not usually refer to their first one as an arangetram. The connection with the temple tradition was evidently still too close and high-caste families did not wish to be associated with devadasi traditions. For this reason, Kalanidhi Narayan, a brahmin dancer who first performed in the 1930s, was adamant that her début recital was not an arangetram.

This attitude was not shared by all brahmins performing at that time, however. For example, the late Rukmini Devi, also a brahmin, acknowledged that her first recital was an arangetram on the grounds that she was dedicating her dance to God. Her earliest students report that, for them too, the first recital constituted an arangetram. Rukmini Devi's decision probably contributed to the gradual acceptance of the term. Yet it took another twenty years for both the ritual and the term to become an unquestionable part of modern Bharatanatyam. Today, some dancers still prefer not to give a formal début recital but the reason given is more likely to be that of the expense (Gaston 1983: 299–300).

Worshipping the Ankle-Bells

This ceremony was intended to mark the conclusion of the dancer's mastery over the first dance piece from the concert repertoire (alarippu).

In some instances, where it was intended to mark the completion of her dance training as a whole, worshipping the ankle-bells appears to have been included in the ceremonies of the début recital. The incorporation of a mini-recital known as gajjai puja into modern Bharatanatyam training was unknown until recently. Present-day celebrations of it include several dances: at least alarippu, *jatisvaram* and *sabdam*, and sometimes *varnam* and *tillana* as well, leaving only the descriptive dances (*padam; javali*, Telugu)[13] to be mastered before the first full-length recital. The rationale for such a mini-recital is that it constitutes an intermediate stage, thereby allowing the dance student to have the experience of performing before the taxing full programme required for a formal début recital. Another less charitable explanation is that it allows the teacher to receive the customary gifts (*gurudaksina*) that are otherwise given at the time of the first official performance. Not all teachers present their students in this mini-recital, but one thing is certain: this custom is an innovation that has taken root in the past five years.

The Presence of an Icon on the Concert Stage

A bronze image placed at stage left is a common feature of public recitals of Bharatanatyam today (Gaston 1983: 305). The image is usually that of *Nataraja*.[14] From both oral and pictorial accounts, the introduction of icons onto the concert stage is an innovation of the 1940s. Once again, the late Rukmini Devi bears some responsibility for the change which she accounts for in the following way:

People have Nataraja on the stage because I started it. People copy what I do. Dance is a form of worship. Why not have Nataraja? I am a person with devotion and a religious person, it is not just there as decoration.

For Rukmini Devi, the dance was a form of worship. She introduced the Nataraja image in order to create a temple on the stage.

This opinion is diametrically opposed to that held by devadasis who were performing Bharatanatyam on the concert stage during the same period. T. Balasaraswati, the most famous traditional dancer (see note 2), falls into this group. Her recitals are remembered by Nirmala Ramachandran, an early brahmin performer who also worked with T. Balasaraswati professionally:[15]

Bala never had a Nataraja on the stage. She did not believe in that sort of thing, bringing the temple to the stage. She was opposed to this. She said, it is in the mind.

Certainly, none of T. Balasaraswati's recitals that I saw from 1964 onwards included a Nataraja image, nor did her home have a large one on display as many dancers have today. She preferred to create a devotional atmosphere for what she regarded as a stage art by using artistic elements such as suggestion and gesture rather than by resorting to ritual elements used as stage props.

Similarly, no Nataraja image was present when Bala's daughter, Lakshmi Shanmugam-Knight, performed at the Mylapore Fine Arts Sabha (performing art centre) in Madras in August 1989. Nor was there a prominent image of Nataraja in Lakshmi's home when I visited the next day. She explained: 'It is not in our tradition to have Nataraja. I am carrying on my mother's tradition.' T.S. Parthasarathy, a brahmin secretary of the Madras Music Academy and dance critic of the *Indian Express*, confirms this:

The older dancers like Bala never had a Nataraja or started with a puja.[16] Now it is a stunt to attract the audience. When they see the Nataraja idol garlanded with coloured lights, it sort of inspires some devotion in the audience. A true artist does not start the recital with a devotional thing. Bala was an artist in the true sense.

Two brahmin dancers active in the same period agree. Chandralekha, who began performing in the 1950s, comments: 'No, if I feel worshipful I will not make a stagey thing out of my religiosity. It is totally phoney to put Nataraja on the stage.' Shanta Rao, who started her career before 1947, declares: 'No, I have a plain stage. It is a dance show not a puja.' Further evidence that an icon on stage is a recent innovation and was once not considered necessary is provided by three brahmin women who were also performing in the 1940s: Hema, Vijaya, and C.V.S. Vasanta. They did not have Nataraja on the stage or 'even own our own Nataraja image', an almost inconceivable situation today.

However, Nirmala Ramachandran remembers otherwise, despite her recollection (see above) that T. Balasaraswati did not follow the practice. As she says, 'it was fashionable even then'. This is confirmed by two other brahmin dancers, Yogam and Mangalam, who had active careers in the late 1940s and early 1950s:

Yes, we had Nataraja on the stage. We still have the one we used. This is because it is the cosmic dance of Shiva. He is the symbol of our dance. It is also decorative and it shows others that you are artistic.

Their attitude contrasts with that of a dancer from the non-brahmin *mudaliar* community who began to dance in the late 1930s while still very young. She has never had a Nataraja image on stage and condemns the modern practice of doing so: dancers today, she maintains, 'make fools of themselves with Nataraja'.

R. Nagaswamy (see note 9) bases his views on a reading of the texts (for example, *Natyasastra* III. 1–101). He concludes that 'Nataraja on the stage is a totally modern innovation. No text prescribes this. As a dancer you try to create the image.' This reinforces T. Balasaraswati's comment that religious devotion 'is in the mind'.

In general, dance critics are also strongly opposed to the idea of icons and acts of worship on stage. Only one critic, Subbudu from *The Statesman* (New Delhi), was willing to be charitable towards the presence on the stage of a Nataraja image. All the others share T.S. Parthasarathy's view quoted above. For example, Mohan Khokar, a well-known authority on the dance, comments:

I cannot stand those icons. Worship is your own personal business. I do not believe in having anything on stage which will distract. Often the Nataraja is so small no one knows what it is anyway. Nor do I agree to the practice of worshipping the image on stage. Worship is a private affair. Do it backstage before you go on. The worst is a dancer who prostrates herself in front of the image on the stage.

His remarks reveal an objection not only to public worship but also to elaborate declarations of devotion. Here his words echo those of another dance critic, Shanta Sherbjeet Singh of *The Hindustan Times* (New Delhi), in which she remarks on the difficulties encountered when the religious and the secular meet:

Nataraja is put on the stage to remind the audience and the dancer that the dance came out of the temple. It is so embarrassing to see the chief guest walk on the stage with shoes on, something one should not do near a religious icon. Worshipping Nataraja should be private and should not be part of the show. The presence of Nataraja shows the confused state of mind of the dancers.

It thus appears that most critics, as well as many of the dancers who began their careers at the beginning of the revival, are opposed to having an image on Nataraja on the stage.

In contrast, a considerable number of the more recent dancers and dance teachers that I interviewed consider the presence of an icon, usually Nataraja, to be highly desirable. Some dancers feel that a photograph of their dance teacher (if he or she has died) should be placed at the feet of the Nataraja image. The use of an icon on stage is insisted upon despite the fact that some of these dancers admit that the practice was not followed by their own teacher, or that it has not been part of their family tradition or even considered necessary. S. Umamaheswari (T. Balasaraswati's niece and therefore from the devadasi community, but born well after the dance was banned from the temples) exemplifies this tendency. 'Yes, I have a Nataraja on the stage', she explains, 'because my guru says that I must do it. I don't know why. My relation, Bala, never had one on stage. We do the puja to Nataraja before the curtain is opened.' She is clearly well aware that the practice is an innovation.

However, some brahmin practitioners believe that the presence of the Nataraja image, or of other images, sanctifies the place where they teach. For one female brahmin teacher, the image clearly has spiritual significance. 'When I or my students dance, I carry Nataraja with me,' she explains. 'I think of him when I dance and take his blessings. I think I am dancing in Chidambaram, the temple of Nataraja in Tamilnad.' Kamala Lakshman, one of the most important brahmin dancers from the revival period, and currently working in the United States of America, reports:

I carry a small Nataraja and Ganesha [Ganeśa][17] around to the various centres where I teach and place them in the classroom. I always keep Nataraja on the stage. This is because I feel that this dance is for him. It is not for human beings. We are born and we die, but we want some celestial power, something that is supreme. It is music and dance that has been given to us. It has all been given to us by him, so it is an offering to him.

This idea of creating the appropriate atmosphere for teaching the dance is considered particularly important by those who teach or dance abroad. As I noted earlier, expatriate communities consistently place a greater emphasis on the religious or devotional elements of the dance.

The Nataraja Image as a Component of the Début Recital

Although the presence of a Nataraja image during a performance is not universal, it is a common feature today, especially when the performance in question is a début recital. This too does not appear to have been part of the earlier tradition.

Mythali Kalyansundaram (of the icai vellala community) recalls that there was no Nataraja image at her début recital in the home of P. Ponnaiya Pillai in Thanjavur in 1947.[18] Nor was there one for the first performance given by the brahmin dancer Chandrabhagadevi and her (brahmin) husband U.S. Krishna Rao, both of whom now teach dance in Bangalore. He remembers the period when he was performing in the 1940s:[19]

... there was no Nataraja on the stage. This must have started fifteen years ago. Now they make an entrance and drop flowers, we never did that. We just came to the stage, touched the feet of the teacher, and started.

However, he believes that it is appropriate to have an image of Nataraja on stage during a début recital today, a belief he shares with many other teachers and dancers. The *arangetram* is the first stage. At that time you worship. At other times, you just feel the presence.' Most dancers today do have a Nataraja image on stage, although they rationalize its presence in different ways. For example, Mythili Kalyansundaram (like some other members of her community, such as another female dance teacher, Indira Rajan) believes that an icon suggests that the stage is a place of worship and therefore sacred. Perhaps these teachers consider a visible link with religion important because they are teaching and living in large urban centres.

Others consider the image to be purely decorative. This is reflected in the frequent absence of an image while on tour, a point made by several dancers. Most of them find it impractical to carry an image with them; they instal one only for performances in their home city. However, they usually worship privately before the performance. For the brahmin dancer, Usha Srinivasan, the image is a combination of talisman and stage prop:

I like a nice one, it looks nice on the stage, but I have also danced without one ... in Japan for three months we did not have a Nataraja, nor did we do puja, and nothing happened. I do not do puja in the green room.

This notion of the image as a talisman is reiterated by Subbudu, dance critic of *The Statesman* (New Delhi):

It is just a symbol, it looks nice. It is a shield or good luck charm to help one not make mistakes. Worshipping the image is just an outward show. It is the same as breaking champagne over the bow of a boat when it is launched.

Forms of Worship on the Concert Stage
Some dance teachers believe that, on entering the stage the dancer should first drop flowers at the feet of the Nataraja image.[20] She should then greet her seated teacher in the proper reverential way by touching the floor in front of him or her (*namaskaram*) and then placing her hands in a folded position (*añjalihasta*).[21] Some teachers include touching the teacher's feet as part of the reverential greeting. Others are shocked that a girl, in particular a brahmin girl, should be expected to touch the feet of anyone other than her husband (cf. Leslie 1989: 156 ff.). But for the brahmin dancer, C.V.S. Vasanta, it was simply not the practice in the

1940s (when she was performing) for dancers to pay homage to their teachers on stage:

In addition to the elaborate puja, the dancers come on stage and do namaskaram [namaskaram, Tamil] to the teacher. We never did either on the stage. Instead, we used to do namaskaram and puja at home before we set out.

According to her account, therefore, paying homage to one's teacher on stage is a recent innovation.

Although some dancers do not express the need to worship the Nataraja image on stage, they often regard the image itself as an important element of the dance. The presence of the image allows them to direct their spiritual energy towards it, which in turn gives them confidence. The brahmin dancer, Gita Ramakrishnan, elaborates:

Of course, it is very essential. I have a big Nataraja. First I do a big namaskaram to Nataraja, then to my gurus. Only then start. It sets the mood and gives me a lot of confidence. The curtains are open when this happens. I then feel that the stage has become benevolent. It promotes bhaktirasa [a feeling of devotion] which is the basis [of the dance].

There is an implication in Gita's comments that the icon is in some sense necessary to counterbalance other changes in the dance. However, her attitude makes a striking contrast to that expressed by T. Balasaraswati.

Most of my informants who are in favour of icons are not particular about which one that should be. Some feel that it should relate to the themes of the items to be performed. The brahmin dancer, Jayalakshmi Iswaran, explains:

When I did a show on Murugan, I had an image of Murugan on the stage. When I travel, I have an image of Ganesha that I put on the stage. I do a puja backstage before the performance, not on stage. At Kalakshetra, we have been trained to start with alarippu. We did namaskaram to the stage, to Rukmini Devi if she was there. Other schools [of Bharatanatyam] go and touch the cymbals and feet of the gurus.

The variety of icons chosen is increasing. Indira Rajan, from a traditional icai vellala family, explains why she includes an image of Jesus:

Because the dance items are based on God, the stage must be like a temple. Any god can be there: Nataraja, Ganesha. I have seen a Christian give her arangetram. I composed a varnam for her on Jesus. For a Christian student, we had a Nataraja and Jesus on the stage.

Mary, the mother of Jesus, is also considered appropriate.[22]

The testimony of my informants suggests that the importance of icons, and in particular that of Nataraja, is increasing. On the occasion of a dancer's first public performance, it is now an almost universally accepted practice to have an image of Nataraja on stage and to offer homage to him there. As I have shown, these début recitals are relics of the devadasi tradition that have taken new forms (Gaston 1983). We have thus moved from a time when the presence on stage of icons such as that of Nataraja was unusual, through an era in which the icon was increasingly prominent (partly as a prop, partly as an object for the expression of overt religiosity), to reach a third stage. Now two of the more recent brahmin dancers can claim:

> It is the tradition to have Nataraja on stage. We are keeping up the tradition. We have Nataraja on stage as he is the god of the dance. If we have another idol, such as Krishna [Krsna], it just means that we are doing the recital on that theme, in his presence.

This is the current situation.

The Use of Hand Signs

Once an icon was firmly established on the stage, new dance pieces were choreographed to include it. This new choreography, relating to the introductory portions of many modern dance recitals, recalls the ritual activities of the devadasi inside the temple.[23] For example, it was the custom for traditional temple dancers to enact many of the same rituals as the priests, using hand gestures (*mudra*) to mimic the implements used by the priests, such as the fly-whisk (*camara*) and lamp (*dipa*). The most important function of the devadasi was to circle the image in a clockwise direction while holding a pot (*kumbharati*). According to Kersenboom, 'being a devadasi was synonymous with waving the pot-lamp' (see this volume). By the late 1960s, however, a similar activity was introduced onto the concert stage: the hands are held so that they touch at the wrist (*alapadmahasta*; see note 21) and circled in front of the image. It is now more the rule than the exception, particularly for younger dancers (who are mainly brahmins; see Gaston 1983), to include this symbolic representation.

The offering of flowers (*puspanjali*) at the beginning of a dance recital is another devadasi ritual recently introduced, with some modification, into Bharatanatyam. Whereas the devadasi offering was a symbolic one, many dancers today offer real flowers. But both use the hand gesture appropriate for holding flowers (*puspaputa*; see n. 21). Nirmala Ramachandran's comments reveal her awareness that this is an innovation:

> When I started with Chokkalingam[24] the first piece was alarippu. This was right after the orchestra sang a stotra to Ganesha. We never brought flowers etc. as

they do now. If I had Nataraja on the stage it was just there, I never did puja to Nataraja on the stage.

Later, however, she altered her repertoire: she began with the invocation called puspanjali and dropped flowers in front of the Nataraja image. Other dancers who were performing in the 1940s (Shanta Rao, U.S. Krishna Rao) and the 1950s (Yamini Krishnamurthy, Indrani Rehman) have not followed this trend.

This ritual offering of flowers precedes the first dance item (generally an alarippu). But while alarippu on its own was accepted as part of the traditional concert repertoire, no mention is made in that context of a flower offering. Kersenboom describes it as part of the temple ritual, but not as part of the court tradition. T. Balasaraswati did not include it in her repertoire which was the court tradition (1980: 98–108). Today, however, this ritual offering of flowers has even been choreographed as a dance piece to be presented alone or in conjunction with the first dance item.

With the presence on stage of an icon, and the ritual offering of flowers (either as an invocation or as a dance piece), the first ten minutes of a modern Bharatanatyam recital thus encapsulates the earlier temple tradition, exemplifying the transformation of the secular into the religious. In 1964, when I was taught alarippu by K. Ellappa Pillai (a male dance teacher from the traditional community), the dancer began by simply standing centre stage. There was no elaborate entry with flowers in hand. Until his death in 1976, K. Ellappa Pillai (who also conducted the orchestra for T. Balasaraswati) did not include any suggestion of rituals. In 1970, when I was taught alarippu by K.N. Dakshinamurthy (also from a traditional family), he prefaced it with hand signs which mimicked various rituals in worship. For example, both hands were held in the gesture signifying the pot, then the right hand indicated the lamp being circled or the fly-whisk being shaken (alapadma, kapittha; see n. 21). This elaborate imitation had begun by 1964. By the 1980s, many although not all dancers followed this practice.

Should a Menstruating Dancer Dance?

According to Hindu social custom, menstruating women are impure and inauspicious (Altekar 1962: 194 ff.; Marglin 1985: 60–3; Leslie 1989: 283–90). In orthodox households, their activities are restricted. Regarded as extremely impure and temporarily untouchable, they are forbidden to enter temples, to cook, or to come into contact with others. According to Altekar, even the sight of their person and the sound of their voice were to be avoided' (1962: 195). In the context of the traditional dance, the devadasi had to be in a ritually pure state when she performed as part of temple worship.[25]

During my interviews, I explored the question of what activities associated with dance (teaching, studying and performing) were allowed during the menstrual period. The responses I received indicate that dancers are aware of being impure while menstruating: only one of my informants claims that she has never heard of such a taboo. The limits that this awareness puts on their dance activities varies with each individual. There appear to be two reasons for not performing: because of the perceived impurity ('We were impure on those days and we could not dance') and for reasons of health ('God does not enter into it').[26]

All the younger dancers I interviewed admit that they perform publicly when menstruating, and none either declines an invitation or cancels a public recital on that account. One brahmin dancer comments:

Because you are already committed you must perform, but there was an idea of pollution so I kept some distance from the cymbals and the musicians. You will pollute them if you touch them. We would not drop flowers in front of the image, or bow down in front of the icon on the stage.

Well aware of the potential she has to pollute, this dancer avoids all contact with sacred objects, in particular the flowers that would normally be offered to the image. The cymbals too are regarded as sacred. For example, a male non-brahmin teacher explains how he changed his former liberal views after an event which he interpreted as inauspicious:

I made them dance when I had a dance troupe but when it comes to a Bharatanatyam recital, I try to avoid having them dance. This is both for health reasons and religious reasons. Once my cymbals broke in my hand.

For him, there is a greater potential for inauspicious divine intervention when the dance being performed during menstruation is Bharatanatyam (a solo style) than when it is a group dance. In the group dance, the effect of one ritually impure dancer is presumably diluted by the presence of others not in that state.

The rhythmic accompaniment for Bharatanatyam is essential. The percussion instruments vary according to the situation: during a dance class, the teacher strikes a block of wood with a wooden stick (*tattukali*, Tamil); during recitals, metal cymbals (*talam*) are struck. Both the block of wood and the cymbals serve the same purpose: they guide the rhythmic beating of the dancer's feet. In this context, a male teacher from the icai vellala community explains:

No, one must not touch the talam. The monthly course is impure and the talam is holy. Now the girls take class and dance on those days, but they really should not. Just as one should not do puja on those days, so one should not dance.

The importance of the rhythmic instrument is underlined when we appreciate that consistently, whether in class or on the stage, restrictions are imposed on dancers touching it when they are menstruating.

Some teachers prefer their students to stay away when they are menstruating but are unable to enforce their preference. 'They used to be strict in the olden days,' laments one female brahmin teacher. 'Now we can't stop them from coming.' Some of the dance teachers appear to have the situation under control. 'They are not allowed in the teaching hall,' insists a male teacher in his early fifties from an icai vellala family.

One female teacher from a family with a previous devadasi connection is equally strict in relation to herself as a teacher as she is to her students dancing. 'I will not allow my students to come into the dance hall. On those days I will not dance, and when I teach I will not touch the tattikal [tattukali].' Before becoming a dance teacher, during her dance training, she remembers having to 'eat and sleep outside'. Others (but not all) from the same community also report that they had to avoid all contact with people while menstruating. Despite their own experiences, however, several women teachers from the icai vellala community do not recognize that their menstruating students have the same potential to pollute. A male teacher from the icai vellala community believes that dancers who did not dance while they were menstruating 'showed respect for the art'. Another male teacher from the icai vellala community expresses his reservations more forcefully. 'No,' he says, 'it is wrong. It pollutes if the student comes into the hall'. But while several teachers abstain from dancing because they see dance as the personification of God, others see nothing wrong in it. They also have no objection to their students coming to class when menstruating, although many students choose to stop of their own accord.

The choice is not always left to the individual. One brahmin performer in her thirties feels that the pressure to conform came from her female classmates. She explains:

We were just sort of told. It was hushed talk. If a girl came all days, then the tongues would wag as maybe she is polluting the classroom. This was only in the group classes, not in my private classes. My teacher never said anything ... He had a huge Nataraja in the classroom and it was a sort of temple-cum-classroom. While I myself did not see the logic or reason in this, I had no right to interfere with other people's beliefs, so I just stayed away on those days. It was out of deference to that rather than my own acceptance of this.

Another dancer, torn by her commitment to give a public recital yet conscious of her impurity, agonizes: 'When we have to give a public recital we must do it, but we apologize to God.' Sometimes the dancer is encouraged by her teacher to overlook the taboo, in particular, during a short condensed dance course. During the three short months in the 1940s that a brahmin woman, U.S. Chandrabhagadevi, studied with P.S. Minakshisundaram, he insisted that she dance daily in preparation for those occasions when she would have a professional engagement while menstruating. 'Try to dance,' he said. 'It is only by dancing that you will get over your headaches at this time.'[27] A male teacher from the icai vellala community is also willing to compromise when necessary. 'If they have to give a programme they must do it, but they must not go to the Nataraja, touch the talam, or the guru [dance teacher].' This view seems to be the most common. A brahmin dancer, now in her forties, remembers that previously not only performances but also dance classes were stopped. 'There was no question about it. We would not dance, nor would we touch the stick and block of wood that the teacher beats in the class.'

Thus the majority of dancers are willing to disregard 'pollution' when it comes to performances, but are reluctant to attend class. Most refrain from going to the puja room, lighting the lamp, going to temples, touching or going near others, and from personal religious practices such as meditation. Whereas cooking was once also forbidden to the menstruating woman, the decline of the joint family and the inability to find servants has forced many dancers to ignore this taboo.

In general, it appears that (in keeping with the current decline in religious taboos) abstention from dancing during the menstrual period is no longer as widely practised as it was twenty years ago. This decline in the religious observance of a private function is in marked contrast to the increasingly overt demonstrations of religiosity on stage. The impure state during menstruation and the potential for polluting a religious place or religious activity is still observed with regard to temples. Elsewhere, pragmatism has taken over. While dancers, teachers, and all those connected with the dance recognize that a menstruating woman is unclean, a new set of rules has been devised. These rules are open to a variety of interpretations and may be relaxed for a variety of reasons. For some, dance class is possible, for others, not; but for all concerned a performance must be honoured. The dancer isolates herself simply by keeping her distance and by not touching religious objects or other people. This suggests that the dance itself is regarded as less than holy, but is the dance that she performs in her impure state religious? It appears that it is separate from her body and above pollution.

CONCLUSIONS

During the period before the modern revival of Bharatanatyam, some elements of the dance were regarded as appropriate for the temple, and others for secular occasions. Today, some dancers are re-ritualizing the dance by introducing into the concert repertoire dance pieces and ritual movements that were originally intended to be danced only in temples. While the original stage performances of Bharatanatyam derived mainly from the court tradition, the incorporation of hand signs once used in rituals, the performance of a début recital, and the presence of an icon on stage emphasize the temple heritage of the dance. This trend removes Bharatanatyam from the realm of the strictly theatrical making it an increasingly religious phenomenon. At the same time, the religious element in the dance is becoming more formalized. The dance acts out the precise rituals of worship while the audience watches passively, very much as puja is performed in a temple.

For some, introducing rituals to the concert stage confirms that the dance is a religious experience, while for others this religiosity is phoney. In both cases, the attitude displayed appears rather different from that of, for example, the Tiruttani devadasi whose approach to her dance was 'respectful but matter of fact' (see Kersenboom, this volume). Non-hereditary dancers who began performing in the early period of the revival generally tried to avoid association with devadasi rituals because of the general disapproval of the institution of the devadasi. The more recent reintroduction of devadasi rituals seems to signify that the dance has distanced itself sufficiently from the devadasi tradition to be immune from that stigma.

Among dancers, it appears that while private ritual observances (for example, the menstrual taboo) are declining, public displays of religion are on the increase. This apparently contradictory development can be rationalized when we consider that most of the young women practising dance today have had a Western education. Outside their life as dancers, they have moved far from the traditional ways of their community. To obtain credibility as Bharatanatyam dancers, they therefore need to establish their religious credentials. This can be done by public expressions such as acts of worship on stage and the presence of a visible icon. No such practice was followed by the devadasi in relation to the Nataraja image. However, it is now taken so much for granted in Bharatanatyam that many dancers regard the presence of the Nataraja image as stemming from the devadasi heritage. Hence, when such displays of ritual are referred to as 'traditional', we should not take the description at face value. Rather, we should interpret this to mean 'affirming adherence to traditional values in the context of a dancing society'. This is surely one of the major functions that Bharatanatyam performs for Indian society today.

Because the dance is an extremely competitive field, and the competition is increasing, the apparent need for religious credentials may have led to an escalation of these tendencies. Many of the dancers whose careers extended from the 1930s to the 1960s included only the simplest show of religiosity, if any. In contrast, some of the more recent dancers today make a conscious effort to accentuate the religious spectacle. Even if a dancer is happy to exclude religious rituals, her teacher or, more important, her audience may encourage it. Consequently, as time passes, dancers, dance teachers and audiences seem increasingly to require that concert recitals include religious elements in the form of rituals and symbolic gestures.

Bharatanatyam is a living dance tradition, hence practices and perceptions of what is correct are in constant flux. At present, it appears that there is a trend to re-ritualize and romanticize the dance of the devadasi; but there is also a parallel tendency to question what is presently regarded as tradition and to call for new forms and new dances. Of all the arts (including painting, sculpture and music), it appears that dance has been the least affected either by outside influences or by innovation. For that reason, recent developments in the dance provide an excellent insight into the tensions and contradictions created by the impact of the twentieth century on traditional Indian culture. Only time will tell the extent to which Bharatanatyam will be re-ritualized, and what role this might play in the reinforcement of traditional role models for women.

NOTES

1. For the purposes of this volume, I have used the Tamil lexicon spelling, catir kacceri (see Kersenboom, this volume). My informants prefer the more popular form, 'sadir kacheri'.

2. T. Balasaraswati, who was celebrated for her traditional renditions of Bharatanatyam, continued both to dance and to teach until her death in 1984. She was affectionately known as Bala.

3. Unless otherwise specified, all quotations are taken from statements made by informants during interviews conducted in English. Informants' names are

spelled according to the preference of each individual. In order to remain faithful to the original speech, Indian-language terms incorporated into the English-language quotation are given the spelling current in Indian English.

4. While it is clear that much of the impetus behind this take-over has come from higher-caste, mainly brahmin, groups, I have avoided the terms 'high caste' and 'low caste' in favour of 'non-traditional'/'traditional', 'non-hereditary'/'hereditary', and even 'brahmin'/'non-brahmin'.

5. Kersenboom's chapter is based on interviews with P. Ranganayaki, a former devadasi from the Tiruttani tradition of the Subrahmanyasvami Temple, and on the diary kept by Ranganayaki's grandmother. Both women served as dancers in that temple, and performed both in the temple and in the palace. Their repertoire, and the way that they executed it, bear only marginal resemblance to what we see today on the concert stage. According to Kersenboom's informants, there was little attempt to achieve an 'aesthetic effect'. As Kersenboom comments, even the secular recitals of the devadasi were without the 'sweep and flourish' of present-day Bharatanatyam. For the emphasis of the devadasi tradition was on the ritual component. Just what this ritual component was, and how it reappears and relates to Bharatanatyam as we see it today, I discuss in this chapter. Where appropriate, I draw parallels with Kersenboom's chapter.

6. There are conflicting opinions about the pubic acceptance of the dance of the devadasis. According to Khokar, 'the dasis took the fullest advantage of the sudden buoyant interest in their art: a number of dancers in the community, Balasaraswati, Swarnasaraswati, Gauri ... took to the stage and became public idols' (1987: 47). According to Kersenboom, although the devadasis wanted to teach, 'public opinion did not encourage true devadasi art, and preferred on the whole the new generation of non-devadasi artists' (1987: 191). Amrit Srinivasan also claims that the dance traditions of the devadasis in her study have been overlooked (personal communication, September 1989).

7. For the most part, I have given the names of my informants because attitudes and opinions in the dance are weighted according to the background of the speaker. Moreover, since all my informants are used to giving interviews to the media, anonymity is unnecessary. However, I have omitted names where the issue is sensitive. Since opinions are often shaped by a person's social or caste group, this information is also given. For instance, being a professional dancer does not have the same social implications for a non-hereditary practitioner as it does for a hereditary (icai vellala) practitioner, for whom dance would once have been pre-ordained, together with all the stigma that such a calling entailed. (My informants prefer the more popular form 'isai vellala' to the Tamil lexicon spelling icai vellala.) Some individuals are frequently cited. For example, the late T. Balasaraswati was widely regarded as the doyen of the devadasi style and so her views are often invoked as exemplifying the tradition (sampradaya). Another important dancer was Rukmini Devi, a brahmin woman who was very active during the revival period, and whom I interviewed before her death in 1986.

8. See note 1; and Kersenboom, this volume.

9. In contrast to this trend, R. Nagaswamy, former head of the Archaeological Survey of India (Southern Circle), initiated and continues to be active in

organizing the annual dance festival in the Nataraja Temple in Chidambaram. The festival takes place over a period of ten days and most regional styles are represented. Nagaswamy has also introduced dance performances to the Chola temple of Gangaikondacolapuram. In addition, the Government of India Tourist Office has organized dance festivals at several sites of archaeological interest such as Khajuraho, Konarak and Halebid.

10. The devadasi who was involved in religious rituals was required to take part in two additional ceremonies: marriage to a deity or ritual object (*kalyanam*), and dedication to a temple (*muttirai*, Tamil). These are now illegal.

11. 'Any custom or usage prevailing in any Hindu community such as the Bogum, Kalavanthulu, Sani, Nagavasulu, Devadasi and Kurmapulu, that a woman of that community who gives or takes part in any melam (nautch), dancing or music performance in the course of any procession or otherwise is thereby regarded as having adopted a life of prostitution and becomes incapable of entering into a valid marriage ...' (the Devadasi Act of 1947; see Government of Madras Archives, 26 January 1948). See also Kersenboom 1987: xxi; Srinivasan 1984: 102–6.

12. The revival began in the early 1900s, gaining momentum in the late 1920s.

13. Alarippu, jatisvaram, śabdam, varnam, tillana, padam, javali: these are all names of musical pieces to which Bharatanatyam dances are set (Balasaraswati 1980: 101; see also Kersenboom, this volume).

14. That is, an image of Siva dancing in the pose called 'the wild dance of bliss' (*anandatandava*; Gaston 1982: 47, 114–32).

15. Nirmala Ramachandran danced in the temple dance drama that was revived and choreographed by T. Balasaraswati in the 1950s. The occasion marked a major event in which brahmin and devadasi dancers performed together. A photograph of this event is wrongly identified by Srinivasan as 'a group of dasis, early 20th century' (1984: iii).

16. The incorporation of worship into the dance perhaps stems from *Natyasastra* 1.125: 'He who will hold a dramatic spectacle without offering the Puja will find his knowledge [of the art] useless' (Ghosh 1967: 1.125).

17. Worshipping Ganesa, the elephant-headed son the god Siva, is believed to remove obstacles.

18. Mythali married into the T.P. Kuppaiya Pillai family which founded the Sri Raja Rajesvari Mandir dance school, so called 'because for us art is God, work is God, so we call our school a temple'. P. Ponnaiya Pillai belongs to the Tanjore Quartet. One of his relatives, P.S. Minakshisundaram Pillai, taught Rukmini Devi so the fact that Rukmini Devi had a Nataraja indicates that it was on her own initiative.

19. It was unusual for a brahmin man (that is, one for whom dance was not his hereditary profession) to dance Bharatanatyam at that time. For examples of brahmin men who were professional dancers, see the sections on Kuchipudi and Bhagavata Mela in *Marg* 1963.

20. Cf. *Natyasastra* 1.93–4: 'Thus for the destruction of the Vighnas, gods were placed in different parts of the Jarjara, and Brahma himself occupied the

middle of the stage. It is for this reason that flowers are scattered there [at the beginning of the performance]' (Ghosh 1967: 1.99).

21. For textual references to hand signs (hasta, mudra), see the *Abhinayadarpana* (Ghosh 1957: 53–3; kapittha, 55; alapadma, 56; anjali, puspaputa, 60). For illustrations of these signs, and additional textual references, see Gaston 1982: 36–43.

22. For Christian themes in Bharatanatyam, see Barboza 1985: 29–32.

23. A recent example is *mallari* (Tamil, Telugu), a piece of temple music played on a reed instrument and adapted for the dance (cf. Kersenboom-Story 1987: 77–8, note 181). Another example is the 'kowthwum' (*kautvam*, from the Sanskrit *kavitva*, 'a poem'; Kersenboom 1987: 44; Visveshvaran 1985).

24. A.P. Chokkalingam Pillai is a dance teacher who married into the Tanjore Quartet family, and is related to both P. Ponnaiya Pillai and P.S. Minakshisundaram Pillai.

25. As Kersenboom also mentions (see this volume), the auspicious presence of a devadasi was important at life-cycle events (*samskara*). According to some of my informants, the onset of menstruation is still celebrated by non-brahmins in South India. In earlier times, however, the ceremony included dance as an auspicious offering. For Example, M. Gopalkrishna (a dance teacher from the icai vellala community) notes that 'dance was a part of the festivities around the first menstrual period celebration'. The dancer herself would not, of course, be menstruating.

26. '... there can be no doubt that the complete isolation of women that was insisted upon during this period was partly due to the desire of ensuring complete rest which is so desirable for them during this period' (Altekar 1962: 195).

27. Her husband, U.S. Krishna Rao, who was also training at the same time, assures me that P.S. Minakshisundaram did not allow his female students to dance when they were menstruating.

PART III

Contemporary Extensions

Janet O'Shea

At Home in the World?

The Bharatanatyam Dancer as Transnational Interpreter

The stage lights come up gradually as a bharatanatyam dancer, costumed in a tailored silk sari and beautifully adorned in jewelry, walks out from backstage. In a manner neither formal nor completely relaxed, she walks downstage to a point beyond the normal performing space but still removed from the audience. She begins to explain the key features of this South Indian classical dance form. More specifically, she extracts, for decoding, the symbolic hand gestures known as *mudras* from bharatanatyam's semiotic lexicon. Standing in one place and without musical accompaniment, she performs mudras fluidly and gracefully. Meanwhile, she also translates into English the *sahitya*, or lyrics, of the song that the gestures will accompany. Demonstrating her skill in elegantly balancing the competing tasks of speaking and rendering gestural movement, she alerts the audience to the linguistic nature of the *abhinaya*, or dramatic dance.[1]

At the end of the synopsis, the dancer retreats backstage. A musical interlude signals the beginning of the 'actual' performance. The dancer reappears, walking crisply. When she launches into the performance of the piece, her gestures flow easily as in the explanation, but now she augments them with evocative facial expressions and a directed use of her gaze.

Bharatanatyam, a highly technical, primarily solo South Indian classical dance form, consists of a repertoire and vocabulary that bifurcates into *nritta*, abstract rhythmic choreography, and *nritya* or abhinaya, dramatic dance. Its nonthematic sections consist of explosions of virtuoso footwork, performed with legs rotated outward into a bent-knee position that exemplifies the form's characteristically grounded use of weight. An erect torso floats gracefully above the dynamic feet. The abhinaya component, by contrast, organizes itself around lyrical, leisurely phrases of gestural movement traced by articulated fingers, hands, and arms. In these segments, the dancer walks in time to the music, her body position almost quotidian in comparison with the sharply delineated positions of the more staccato phrases.

Preperformance explanations have characterized bharatanatyam performances over the course of the 20th century. In the mid-1920s, when *brahman* lawyer E. Krishna Iyer initiated his mission to resurrect bharatanatyam as a cultural treasure, he did so through lecture demonstrations as well as performances, which he offered in cities and towns of Southern India (Arudra 1986/87b: 33). Jewish-American dancer Ragini Devi's first international tours of classical Indian dance forms in 1937 and 1938 consisted of lecture demonstrations as well as concerts (*The Civil and Military Gazette* 1938).[2] In the mid-1940s, Ram Gopal introduced to his tightly designed series of short, classical Indian dances brief verbal explanations, which preceded each dance with a sketch of its overall theme (David 2001: 35–6). The specific practice of executing mudras while offering a verbal interpretation of sung poetic texts rose in popularity in the 1980s and early 1990s. During the early 1990s, the practice became so prevalent that dancers imported explanation into Indian performance contexts, including into bharatanatyam's home city of Chennai, formerly Madras.[3]

The demand for translation signals bharatanatyam's 20th-century history of recontextualization and its long-standing international circulation. The practice of interlocution both responds to and obscures the dance form's participation in a global culture market. It reveals the kind of historical double binds[4] with which the late-20th-century bharatanatyam dancer contended. The practice of verbal explanation thus speaks to the 20th-century predicament of bharatanatyam in which the dance form appears internationally as both an emblem of national and diasporic identity and as a 'high art' that transcends national and linguistic boundaries.

At the same time, however, verbal translation paradoxically accords the choreography an inscrutability while also demonstrating its translatability. This kind of preperformance synopsis lines up two thought systems: an English verbal framework and a South Indian choreographic one. The explanation of mudras in succession interprets the 'Eastern' choreography through the 'Western' linguistic system. The English-language epistemology thereby emerges as the means through which the audience finds the choreography intelligible. Thus, this style of translation relies upon a problematic[5] that treats the English-language framework as a mere explanatory device without its own cultural coding.

A spoken interlocution thus risks representing bharatanatyam more as a means of entry into a cultural field of reference,[6] than as a set of choreographic choices and compositional devices.[7]

ORIENTALISM AND GLOBALITY

When a dancer, viewer, or promoter presents bharatanatyam as both requiring and evading translation and treats the English-language explanation as culturally 'neutral,' s/he revisits the central premise of the 18th- and 19th-century orientalist treatment of Indian literary and scholarly texts.[8] The orientalist model of translation rested on the assumption that the 'Eastern' text required the intervention of an interlocutor who, through his[9] specialist knowledge, could unlock its mysteries for 'the West.' The public who received this information, within the orientalist paradigm, inhabited the position of subject rather than object of knowledge. The representation of 'foreign' texts and practices within 19th-century European society thus did not encourage viewers/readers to examine their own cultural investments but rather reinforced the presumed objectivity of their own social and political position.[10]

Preperformance translations, like the textual material of the colonial orientalist period, characterize bharatanatyam as an object of knowledge, to be uncovered and explained by an expert interlocutor. Nonetheless, they invert an orientalist division of labour by conflating the roles of 'native informant' and translator-author. As such, the translating dancer generalizes her own subject position by interlocuting for the dance form. The act of translation, then, marginalizes the dance form for its international viewership, designating it as that which requires explication; but at the same time, this translation universalizes the dancer's status as she adopts the position of the agent of information.

The very appearance of verbal translation, however, complicates even this dichotomy between subjects and objects of knowledge. While a preperformance synopsis foregrounds the dance's 'foreignness,' its standardized mode of delivery reveals the dance form's history of international circulation. Bharatanatyam, as well as *sadir* before it,[11] circulated internationally and responded to global discourses on dance. This transnational circulation dates back to, and, in some instances, anticipated the bharatanatyam 'revival' of the 1930s and 1940s.[12]

The international performance careers of both Indian and non-Indian dancers inflected the refiguration of the previously marginal sadir as the respectable concert form bharatanatyam.[13] Modern dance forerunner Ruth St Denis (Coorlawala 1992; Allen 1997),[14] ballerina and choreographer Anna Pavlova,[15] and Indian modernist Uday Shankar (Erdman 1987)[16] all played a role in the bharatanatyam revival, encouraging the return of audience members' and dancers' attention to Indian classical arts. Conversely, Balasaraswati's emphasis on expressivity won admirers among pre- and early modern dancers such as Ted Shawn and Martha Graham (Cowdery 1995: 51; La Meri 1985: 12; Pattabhi Raman and Ramachandran 1984: 26) who found in her claim that interior experience articulated universal themes (Balasaraswati 1988) a corroboration of their own views on artistry. The early 20th-century refiguration of bharatanatyam as a stage practice likewise intersected with a global, modernist concern with the reinvention of dance as a serious 'high' art. Revival period practitioners like Rukmini Devi and Balasaraswati both invoked discourses of individual creativity in their representation and legitimation of bharatanatyam.[17]

In the 1980s and 1990s, bharatanatyam circulated through ever-more global trajectories. The dance form operates as, in Arjun Appadurai's (1996) terms, intentional cultural reproduction for nonresident Indians in places as divergent as Los Angeles, Singapore, and Manchester. Bharatanatyam likewise provides a means of maintaining nationalist sentiment in exile for Sri Lankan Tamils in Canada, Germany, and the U.K.[18] Practitioners of this dance form have brought it to such disparate locales as Japan and Argentina. Iconic representations of bharatanatyam appear in advertisements and travel guides; bharatanatyam dancers formed the back-up routine for Madonna's performance for the 1999 MTV music video awards. The practice of this dance form likewise offers the successful performer international travel opportunities[19] and acclaim, and requires a global orientation to achieve this level of success. Dancers who strive to maintain professional lives in Chennai perform internationally in order to attain a level of financial reimbursement that offsets the generally low honoraria offered by Chennai venues and to generate the credibility needed to maintain the interest of Chennai promoters.[20] This state of transnational circulation, like the bharatanatyam revival's relationship to international discourses of dance, marks the concert art form as 'always-already' global.[21]

Translation not only operated as a method for negotiating this international circulation of dancers and choreographies, but also provided dancers with a strategy for marketing their performance work in transnational dance milieus. By the late 20th century, bharatanatyam's reputation as a reclaimed and respectable tradition produced a proliferation of trained and accomplished dancers. Chennai, for much of the last century, housed a surplus of bharatanatyam dancers in relation to its viewing public (Coorlawala 1996: 71; Gaston 1996: 119–21; Meduri 1996: xl)[22] as did other Indian and international metropolises. In order to develop a career as a performer, a dancer, facing such a surfeit, can contend with her competition by cultivating new audiences. This task presents obstacles as the complex coding of bharatanatyam requires specialized skills on the part of audience members for full comprehension. When a dancer translates a piece before performing it, she bridges a perceived gap between content and perception, thereby enabling a broader range of spectators to access the piece.[23]

Although verbal interlocution reiterates an orientalist problematic, the factors that foster the appearance of interlocution unsettle orientalist notions of a static tradition. The 20th-century's translating bharatanatyam dancer, rather than representing an ancient, unchanged culture, grappled with numerous, contemporary paradoxes. While some practitioners of the 1980s and early 1990s used verbal interlocution to contend with competing pressures upon the dance form, choreographers of the mid- to late 1990s, especially those working internationally,[24] developed projects that 'translate' (Erdman 1987) epistemologies, choreographic devices, and poetic texts, foregrounding rather than masking their transnational position.[25] These projects align different linguistic, movement, and musical vocabularies in such a way that they subvert a tendency to place European thought systems as the primary framework of interpretation.

TACTICS OF GLOBALITY: ALTERNATIVES TO ORIENTALISM

Toronto-based choreographer Hari Krishnan's composition *When God Is a Customer* (1999)[26] relies upon verbal translation but uses Telugu songs and their English translation, each as an accompaniment to different kinds of choreography. The piece counterposes sections that feature short, Telugu-language songs, which Krishnan[27] interprets through bharatanatyam's stylized gestures, with phrases of either quotidian gesture or abstract expressionist, contemporary dance-derived movement. The latter is accompanied by a spoken English translation of the poetic text projected over the sound system. This strategy retains bharatanatyam's characteristic relationship of dance to text. The piece de-exoticizes the mudra system for its Canadian audience, however, by treating it as equivalent to expressionist and pedestrian movement vocabularies.

As the poems begin, the lights come up slightly and Krishnan materializes out of the shadows. Barely visible in silhouette, he suggests, through stylized gestures, an intimate encounter between a courtesan and her god-lover. In silence, seated on a pedestal, Krishnan mimes the heroine's awakening the following day, stretching his arms, throwing back his head, and using small delicate movements to suggest the lady's ablutions. He holds a dignified, feminine pose, with a straight arm propped on a raised knee, accompanied by the voice-over of an English phrase that expresses the courtesan's joy: 'Today is a good day.'

Krishnan stands, descends from the pedestal, and, in conjunction with the sung Telugu lyrics, uses mudras and facial expressions to convey the mood of the song. He traverses the stage in a stately manner, walking in time to the music. In the role of the heroine, Krishnan extends his hands and draws them back, indicating the request 'ask him to come.' Subsequently, he raises a hand to his forehead and extends it forward, bowing slightly, conveying the promise 'I will give him a royal welcome.' He develops this mood of joyous anticipation, tracing his articulate hands and arms through improvised elaborations that invoke the regal status of the absent lover. At the end of the Telugu song, Krishnan resumes a more quotidian pose as he represents the woman patiently awaiting the paramour's arrival.

The piece proceeds in this manner as stylized mudras sculpt the particular images referred to in the Telugu refrains, the tone of which Krishnan conveys through semirealistic facial expression. During the English translation, however, his countenance remains neutral and he either holds a suggestive pose or extracts one word from the line of poetry, the connotations of which he invokes through the expansion of a symbolic gesture. For other phrases of English text, he suggests emotional overtones through full-body positioning rather than through facial expression and gestures with a specific linguistic meaning. For example, in one section, as the poetry describes the heroine's anxiety, he contracts his torso, bringing his hands to the center of his chest. He follows this sinking of the chest with a counteracting arch of the spine, led by the hands. He reaches his arms out from his center, pulling his entire torso into an open flexion and creates a vulnerable look that supplements the straining arms.

In creating the piece, Krishnan aligned the Telugu songs so that they formed a linear narrative (1999). As a result, the non-Telugu speaking audience member can anticipate the development of the theme as it unfolds, aided not only by English translation but also by the momentum of the storyline as evoked by Krishnan's gestures. Rather than dwell on a process of decoding, the non-Telugu speaking viewer's attention can focus on the choreographic priorities of the bharatanatyam-derived movement as well as the more expressionist ones. Krishnan's alternation between stylized gesture for Telugu songs and a more abstracted vocabulary for their English translation therefore speaks directly to the problematic of interpretation for an international audience.[28]

In *When God Is a Customer*, Krishnan provides an alternate solution to a preperformance explanation by situating verbal interpretation within the work itself. Instead of mystifying the bharatanatyam text by providing a synopsis of the presumably cryptic mudras, Krishnan accompanies both English and Telugu sections with movement. He therefore equates the languages by treating both as dance accompaniment rather than presenting one as the explanatory device for the other.

By contrast, *Triple Hymn* (2000) by Angika, a British dance company consisting of dancer-choreographers Mayuri Boonham and Subathra Subramaniam, translates not linguistic but melodic, choreographic, and rhythmic components into one another. The choreography interweaves bharatanatyam and carnatic music with European classical music. To the sounds of a European operatic melodic structure based on the words of the Sanskrit *Gayatri Mantra* and on a recitation of various names of Hindu goddesses, two dancers in classical costume render lyrical gestures from the bharatanatyam movement vocabulary. During the Gayatri Mantra section, they perform symbolic mudras, suggesting worship, prayer, and other ritual actions. They subsequently depict the various forms of the goddess through characteristic iconographic poses.

Rather than treat bharatanatyam as a cultural icon that depends on a European vocabulary for clarification, *Triple Hymn* places two signifiers of classicism-bharatanatyam and European classical music—alongside each other. Boonham and Subramaniam intertwine two traditional forms instead of interpreting one through the other. The choreographers thereby make explicit the cross-cultural exchange that fostered the project. The piece speaks to the dynamic, cosmopolitan London environment in which it was performed and, by pointing to such an ongoing interculturality, queries the need for explication.

Canadian choreographer Lata Pada's *Cosmos* (1999), like *Triple Hymn*, finds similarities in two different epistemological systems. As its name implies, the work concerns itself with theories of universal creation. *Cosmos* opens on a semidarkened, empty stage. A narrator, invisible but audible over the sound system, translates into English a quote from the Creation Hymn, of the *Rig Veda*. The stanza reflects on the paradox of universal creation: 'In the beginning there was nothing and there was not nothing.' The unoccupied stage space reinforces the mysteriousness of the quote. An ensemble of dancers bursts forth from the wings, perforating the charged vacuum with their interjections of dynamic, rhythmic phrases. The dancers career through the space, pursuing one another into an increasingly tighter spiral.

They wind their way into a close circle. They pause for a moment, tense in their stillness, before launching a phrase of staccato footwork. Each dancer takes a wide stance with legs rotated out and knees bent, hands at her waist. Their alternating pattern of footwork impels their bodies across the stage as the center appears to eject them outward. Their trajectories, linear at first, curve and cross, becoming increasingly chaotic. The ensemble, initially united, fractures into a collection of individual dancers, each tracing her own divergent spatial pathway after a 'big bang' of explosive footwork.

In the next scene, the dancers condense their traveling movements into parallel paths that follow specific orbits. Their routes widen and flatten elliptically so that they cross one another without pushing each other off course. While the first scene traced a transition from disorder to equilibrium, this scene moves from order to disruption. The dancers' set orbits waver as they deviate from their clear routes. The performers succumb to the pull of a black hole, resuming a pulsating phrase that indicates their increasing momentum as they catapult toward center stage.

The closing sections evince the harmony of the solar system. The dancers now develop cooperative relationships with one another, again interweaving without colliding or disrupting one another's trajectories. They break off into duets. Back to back, the dancers exchange weight, arms and hands articulating themselves into classical bharatanatyam mudras as bodies remain taut and straight even in tilted positions. The stylized gestures and the dancers' verticality reinforce the image of stability and balance in the relationships between the relatively proximate heavenly bodies.

Pada's piece depicts the creation of the universe by tracking the transition from the churning of nebulous, protoplasmic energy, its explosion into defined pieces of matter, and its ultimate condensation into the specific orbits of heavenly bodies. The choreography thereby blends the theories of creation put forth by European rationalist, scientific traditions, and by Vedic philosophy. As such, *Cosmos* explains the two epistemological systems through one another. The work, by placing the Vedic hymn at the beginning of a depiction of the 'big bang,' highlights the contradiction at the center of both the Vedic and scientific explanations of creation in that each hypothesis suggests that matter arose from an undefined primordial energy. Although Pada uses an English translation of the hymn, she nonetheless foregrounds the South Asian text as she uses it to demonstrate the paradox imbedded in the 'big bang' theory rather than using the cosmological hypothesis to argue for the rationality of the philosophical tract. In contrast to an orientalist project of translation, therefore, her composition does not treat the European scientific model as an objective explanation but rather foregrounds how its contradictions echo the concerns of the Vedic philosophical tract. Thus, the South Asian knowledge system frames the scientific paradigm, a maneuver that reverses the premise of orientalist translation practices.

Each of these late-century projects offers bharatanatyam an active role in a cosmopolitan urban environment by deploying methods of exchange between epistemologies that circumvent or reverse an orientalist problematic. Krishnan retains the translation paradigm but de-exoticizes the relationship between text and gesture by using English and Telugu in an equivalent manner. Boonham and Subramaniam create a harmonious fusion of classical disciplines and symbols that highlights the hybrid positioning of performers and viewers alike and, therefore, questions the need for translation at all. Pada, like Krishnan, examines different thought systems through one another and inverts an orientalist frame by interpreting the European epistemology through the Vedic philosophical one rather than vice versa. Each of these projects treats bharatanatyam as an entity that responds to the hybridity of its immediate, urban environment rather than as a discrete entity that requires explanation.

I began this essay with the image of the translating bharatanatyam dancer in order to query the historical legacy of this practice and, in doing so, to demonstrate what kinds of cultural and political dilemmas the late 20th-century bharatanatyam practitioner faced. I suggested that verbal interlocutions retain orientalist frames but also that they emerge out of factors that belie orientalist narratives of unchanging tradition. The late-century experiments that I discuss here engage explicitly with bharatanatyam's transnational position and offer the possibility that choreographic translations can move beyond orientalist models of interpretation. These choreographies, rather than representing isolated experiments, speak to the dance form's history of strategic negotiation with globality and hybridity as well as with the staging of local, regional, and national affiliations. In offering an alternative to orientalist paradigms, these projects present the possibility that practitioners can contend with the dance form's complex historical legacy while also challenging viewer expectations. As such, they level the choreographic field so that the dance form can truly be at home in the world.

NOTES

1. This essay is based on presentations given at the Association for Asian Studies (2000) and Dance Under Construction (2001) conferences.

2. Ragini Devi performed bharatanatyam and *kathakali*. She was among the first foreigners to perform Indian classical dance forms, the first nonhereditary dancers of both forms, and the first female kathakali dancers.

3. The city of Madras was officially renamed Chennai in the late 1990s, a shift that reinstated the Tamil name of the metropolis.

I base this observation of the relative prevalence of preperformance translation on my experience viewing international bharatanatyam concerts from 1988 to the present and in comparison between concerts in Chennai in 1989, 1995 to 1996, and 1999.

By using the phrase 'home city', I do not mean to suggest that the relationship between bharatanatyam and Madras/Chennai is organic and unself-conscious. Bharatanatyam established itself in Madras at the time of the bharatanatyam revival of the 1930s. This relationship did not go uncontested nor did it merely fix bharatanatyam in this city. The relationship between bharatanatyam, urbanization, and transnationalism requires more attention than I can give it here. For more information, see my discussion of bharatanatyam's production of locality (2001: 155–213).

4. I borrow this idea of the historical double binds of bharatanatyam from scholar and choreographer Avanthi Meduri who has designed a series of lectures in which she represents the tensions of gender, subjectivity, modernity, and nationhood through a performed limp.

5. I borrow this notion of a problematic of orientalism from Partha Chatterjee (1986). Chatterjee argues that postcolonial nations inverted the problematic of colonialism—independence rather than continued subjugation—but relied upon the same thematic, that of a binary difference between 'East' and 'West'. Here, I reverse Chatterjee's argument in order to draw out a shared problematic between 18th- and 19th-century scholarly and 20th-century preperformance translations.

6. British choreographer Shobana Jeyasingh comments on the assumption that contemporary dance derived from Indian movement vocabularies serves a function more 'cultural' than artistic and links this premise to the practice of offering word-for-gesture translations (1995: 192). Jeyasingh commences her *Making of Maps* (1991) with a deconstruction of the preperformance synopsis. Dancers' voices, projected over the sound system, intersect and interrupt one another with phrases like '*vanakkam*; good evening' and 'the *tillana* is a dance of joy'. Meanwhile, the ensemble moves slowly and decisively into and out of postures derived from bharatanatyam nritta choreography. Their impassive facial expressions contrast with the sunny voices of the verbal accompaniment.

7. Jeyasingh also identifies an over-emphasis on literal meaning in the British reception of Indian performance forms (Jeyasingh 1982: 4).

8. Edward Said cites the scholarship of Sir William Jones in the late 18th century as the inception of orientalist scholarship in India (1979: 75).

9. Here, I use the masculine pronoun intentionally in order to emphasize the gendered investments of orientalist thought. See Koritz (1997) for more on the gendered underpinnings of Orientalism.

10. A classic example of this phenomenon is the 19th-century colonial exhibitions in Europe (Mitchell 1992).

11. 'Bayaderes' (temple dancers) from South India appeared in Europe for the first time in 1838.

12. 'Revival' is the most commonly used term for the reformulation of sadir as the concert art form bharatanatyam. As Matthew Allen suggests, however, this term is 'drastically reductive' because this shift also consisted of a 're-population,' 're-construction,' 're-naming,' 're-situation,' and 're-storation' (1997: 63).

13. The bharatanatyam revival—including its politics and its historical investments—has already received much scholarly attention and therefore I only gesture to it here. I refer to, for instance, Allen (1997), Coorlawala (1992, 1996), Gaston (1992, 1996), Meduri (1988, 1996), and Srinivasan (1983, 1985), as well as my own essay on the contrasting perspectives of Balasaraswati and Rukmini Devi (1998).

14. St Denis performed her Nautch Dance and Radha before Indian audiences in 1926. Uttara Asha Coorlawala (1992) maintains that her performances encouraged Indian viewers to seek out the dance forms on which St Denis based her choreography. Allen likewise notes this influence but also emphasizes that the direct impact of the Denishawn company on India was 'short-lived' (1997: 91).

15. Anna Pavlova, who brought ballet to the status of 'autonomous art,' encouraged Rukmini Devi to seek out the art form of '[her] own country' (in Ramnarayan 1984a: 29). Joan Erdman discusses in some detail the influence that Pavlova had on Uday Shankar (1987: 71–73) who, in turn, was a 'catalyst to the renaissance in Indian classical dance' (69).

16. Shankar influenced the revival of classical Indian arts in several ways. First, as Erdman indicates, Shankar participated in the institutionalization processes that supported the classical Indian dance revivals by providing his students with training in bharatanatyam, kathakali, and manipuri alongside his own technique and improvisation classes (1987: 84). He also helped to spark the career of legendary devadasi dancer T. Balasaraswati. At Balasaraswati's first concert at the Music Academy in 1933, Shankar, as a member of the audience, was so captivated by her dancing that he requested a repeat performance. Haren Ghosh, a friend of Shankar and an impresario, who also attended the performance arranged Balasaraswati's first concert outside of southern India, which led to other concerts in north India and, ultimately, internationally (Arudra 1986/87a: 25, 1986/87c: 20).

17. Both Balasaraswati and Rukmini Devi located in bharatanatyam opportunities for creativity and individual expression. While Rukmini Devi found creative expression in the composition of new dances which, she maintained, sprang from traditional aesthetics (Ramnarayan1984b: 32), Balasaraswati found

opportunities for imaginative work in improvised sections of the inherited repertoire (Balasaraswati 1988: 39).

18. I am indebted to Jeyanthy Siva for first calling my attention to the use of bharatanatyam in the production of Tamil nationalist sentiment.

19. For instance, Gaston states that younger generations of icai vellala (the caste group that largely constituted devadasi communities) dancers have pursued professional performance in recent years because of the possibility it provides for international travel (1996: 129).

20. I base this observation on personal correspondence (1995–6, 1999) with Chennai-based dancers who are at different levels of renown and seniority.

21. I borrow the application of this Derridean phrase from Meduri (1996: 400). Meduri uses this phrase to query the gendered implications of the air of respectability that bharatanatyam acquired in the mid- to late 20th century.

22. Senior dancer and teacher Kalanidhi Narayanan describes this surfeit through reference to 'supply and demand' (1999). She suggests that Madras simply cannot provide solo concerts for all of its dancers as the number of dancers outweighs the number of performance slots. Gaston likewise identifies a 'dance boom' that occurred in the 1970s and 1980s (1996: 119–20).

23. Performers use other methods of bridging a gap in comprehension, including the provision of libretti and, more rarely, the use of supratitles.

24. Translation experiments are not, however, exclusive to performances in non-Indian contexts. Chennai-based choreographer Gitanjali Kolanad's What She Said (1993), for example, deploys scholar A.K. Ramanujan's English translations of Tamil Sangam poetry. Maharashtrian bharatanatyam dancer Sucheta Chapekar has reconstructed 17th- and 18th-century Marathi-language dance compositions and has integrated Hindustani (North Indian classical) music with bharatanatyam (Sethuraman 1985: 46).

25. Experiments with cross-cultural interpretation are not unique to the late 20th century. For instance, as Joan Erdman (1987) argues, modernist Uday Shankar's work translated Indian aesthetic components into European compositional frameworks.

26. Named after a scholarly text of the same title (Ramanujan, Narayana Rao, and Shulman 1994).

27. Here, in the interest of consistency and in capitulation to European and American conventions of nomenclature, I identify dancers and choreographers by their second names. This creates an awkward fit with Indian, and especially South Indian, naming conventions. However, I do this to avoid a situation in which scholars appear by last name and dancers by first name, an approach which might suggest that choreography is a less serious enterprise than writing.

28. The piece would have a different, although not necessarily predictable, effect in Chennai. The majority of dance viewers in Chennai speak Tamil with a significant minority speaking Telugu as their first language. Dance compositions until recently used a number of different languages, primarily Tamil, Telugu, and Sanskrit. In Chennai, as elsewhere, an emphasis on the comprehensibility of poetic texts has increased. Dancers, choreographers, and promoters have responded to

this concern by presenting more pieces in the Tamil language (Nandini Ramani 1999).

REFERENCES

Allen, Matthew, 1997, 'Rewriting the Script for South Indian Dance', *TDR* 41, 3 (T155), pp. 63–100.

Appadurai, Arjun, 1996, *Modernity at Large: Cultural Dimensions of Globalization*, Minneapolis: University of Minnesota Press.

Arudra, 1986/87a, 'Dancers of the First Decade', *Sruti*, 27/28, pp. 23–8.

———, 1986/87b, 'E. Krishna Iyer (1897–1968): Saviour of a Dance in Distress', *Sruti*, 27/28, pp. 32–6.

———, 1986/87c, 'The Transfiguration of a Traditional Dance: The Academy and the Dance, Events of the First Decade', *Sruti*, 27/28, pp. 17–21.

Balasaraswati, T., 1988, 'The Art of Bharatanatyam: Reflections of Balasaraswati', *Sruti*, 50, pp. 37–40.

Chatterjee, Partha, 1986, *Nationalist Thought and the Colonial World: A Derivative Discourse*, Minneapolis: University of Minnesota Press.

The Civil and Military Gazette, 1938, 'The Dance in Indian Sagas', 17 February: n.p.

Coorlawala, Uttara Asha, 1992, 'Ruth St Denis and India's Dance Renaissance', *Dance Chronicle* 15, 2, pp. 123–52.

Congress on Research in Dance, 1996, 'The Birth of Bharatanatyam and the Sanskritized Body', in *The Body in Dance: Modes of Inquiry*, Conference proceedings, The Congress on Research in Dance.

Cowdery, James R., 1995, 'The American Students of Balasaraswati', *UCLA Journal of Dance Ethnology*, 19, pp. 50–7.

David, Ann, 2001, *Perceptions and Misconceptions: Ram Gopal's Challenge to Orientalism*, MA thesis, University of Surrey, School of Performing Arts.

Erdman, Joan L., 1987, 'Performance as Translation: Uday Shankar in the West', *TDR* 31, 1 (T113), pp. 64–88.

Gaston, Anne-Marie, 1992, 'Dance and the Hindu Woman: Bharatanatyam Re-ritualized', in Julia Leslie (ed.), *Roles and Rituals for Hindu Women*, Delhi: Motilal Banarsidass Publishers, pp. 149–71.

———, 1996, *Bharatanatyam: From Temple to Theatre*, New Delhi: Manohar.

Jeyasingh, Shobana, 1982, 'Bharatha Natyam: Understanding Indian Classical Dance', *New Dance*, 23, pp. 3–5.

———, 1995, 'Imaginary Homelands: Creating a New Dance Language', in *Border Tensions*, Conference proceedings, Guildford: Department of Dance Studies, University of Surrey.

Koritz, Amy, 1997, 'Dancing the Orient for England: Maud Allan's *The Vision of Salome*', in Jane Desmond (ed.), *Meaning in Motion: New Cultural Studies of Dance*, Durham: Duke University Press, pp. 133–52.

Krishnan, Hari, 1999, Personal correspondence with author, July.

Meduri, Avanthi, 1988, 'Bharatha Natyam: What Are You?' *Asian Theatre Journal*, 5, 1, pp. 1–22.

Meduri, Avanthi, 1996. 'Nation, Woman, Representation: The Sutured History of the Devadasi and Her Dance', PhD dissertation, New York University.

La Meri, 1985, 'Encounters with Dance Immortals: Balasaraswati and Ragini Devi', *Arabesque* 11, 4, pp. 12–13, 25.

Mitchell, Timothy, 1992, 'Orientalism and the Exhibitionary Order', in Nicholas B. Dirks (ed.), *Colonialism and Culture*, Ann Arbor: University of Michigan Press, pp. 289–317.

Narayanan, Kalanidhi, 1999, Personal correspondence with author, September.

O'Shea, Janet M., 1998, '"Traditional" Indian Dance and the Making of Interpretative Communities', *Asian Theatre Journal*, 15, 1, pp. 45–63.

——, 2001, 'At Home in the World: Bharatanatyam's Transnational Traditions', PhD dissertation, University of California, Riverside.

Pattabhi Raman, N. and Anandhi Ramachandran, 1984, 'Balasaraswati: The Whole World in Her Hands' (Part Two), *Sruti*, 5, pp. 17–31.

Ramani, Nandini, 1999, Personal correspondence with author, September.

Ramanujan, A.K., Velcheru Narayana Rao, and David Shulman (trans and eds), 1994, *When God is a Customer: Telugu Courtesan Songs*, Berkeley: University of California Press.

Ramnarayan, Gowri, 1984a, 'Rukmini Devi: A Quest for Beauty', *Sruti*, 8, pp. 17–29.

——, 1984b, 'Rukmini Devi: Restoration and Creation', *Sruti*, 10, pp. 26–38.

Said, Edward W., 1979, *Orientalism*, New York: Vintage Books.

Sethuraman, R., 1985, 'Sucheta Chapekar's Experiment: Synthesis of Bharatanatyam and Hindustani Music', *Sruti*, 20 and 20-S, pp. 43–6.

Srinivasan, Amrit, 1983, 'The Hindu Temple-Dancer: Prostitute or Nun?' *Cambridge Anthropology*, 8, 1, pp. 73–99.

——, 1985, 'Reform and Revival: The Devadasi and Her Dance', *Economic and Political Weekly*, 20, 44, pp. 1869–76.

Andrée Grau

Political Activism and South Asian Dance

The Case of Mallika Sarabhai

INTRODUCTION

This article is part of a bigger research project, 'New Directions in South Asian Dance: Postcolonial Identity Construction', executed under the auspices of the Arts and Humanities Research Council's (AHRC) Centre for Cross-Cultural Music and Dance Performance in London. Much of the work I have carried out for the Centre has focused around two issues, which as a social anthropologist specialising in the study of dance, I am particularly interested in: (i) the study of institutions which promote dance and the kind of impact they have on the dance genres they promote; (ii) a focus on artists who see themselves as political/social activists and use their artistic practice to encourage people's awareness and understanding of different contemporary issues, such as gender discrimination, homosexuality, AIDS, world debt, domestic violence, or ecological issues.

The research I draw from for this article straddles both interests, focusing on dancer/choreographer Dr Mallika Sarabhai, director of the Darpana Academy for Performing Arts, an institution started by her parents Vikram and Mrinalini Sarabhai in 1949 in Ahmedabad, Gujarat. In the winter of 2001–02, I was able to do fieldwork at Darpana and in May 2004, Mallika,[1] together with a few members of her company, The Darpana Performance Group, were performers-in-residence at Roehampton under the auspices of the AHRC Centre, re-working aspects of *Colours of the Heart*, a human rights piece they had created earlier in the year, and working with local performers.

In this article I examine two issues in particular detail: I consider those aspects of Mallika's repertoire which deal with conflict and violence, and I address the issue of her position as a politically committed artist during a period in India which saw the rise of *Hindutva* (literally 'Hinduness'). A more detailed discussion of the politics and ethics of dance generally, of the Sarabhais' vision of the role of art in helping make the world a better place, and their implications for the dance scenes of both India and the diaspora, will be found in my forthcoming book *Dance, Politics and Ethics: Conversations with South Asian Dance.*

HINDUTVA IN POLITICS AND THE ARTS

Hindutva, a term coined by the Hindu nationalist Vinayak Damodar Savarkar (1883–1966) in his 1923 pamphlet entitled *Hindutva: Who is a Hindu?* promoted ideas regarded at the time as 'rather marginal at that stage of Indian nationalism' (Thapar 2000: 596). This built over the century into 'localized movements towards Hindu nationalism and nationalized Hinduism' (Appadurai 2000: 645) and was somewhat crystallised in the rise to power of the Bharatiya Janata Party (BJP, literally 'Indian People's Party') in the 1990s.[2] The promotion of 'Hinduness' is all-pervasive and found in many guises within Indian society and throughout the Indian diaspora. It is closely linked to modern mass media (Rajagopal 2001). It can be extremely subtle as in the representation of musicians and dancers in film, or much more blatant as in BJP propaganda, with which this article is not directly concerned.

The ethnomusicologist Greg Booth (2005: 62), for example, has shown that whilst Indian cinema's approach to communal tension generally 'appeals to a pan-community and pan-religious brotherhood', a number of films, through their representations of Indian music and dance, 'betray an unspoken and perhaps unconscious political agenda vis-à-vis the identities of Indian classical music'. The presence of similar ambivalence in other aspects of films has been discussed in some detail in a number of works, such as the collection of essays edited by Pfleiderer and Lutze (1985), and in Prasad (1998), Dwyer and Pinney (2001), Mishra (2002), Virdi (2003) and Desai (2004). Whilst he is careful to note that the film director V. Shantaram has produced films that are both explicitly anti-communal and often have a socialist content, Booth (2005: 62) also observes that the depiction of the contest between the two Kathak dancers in a film like *Jhanak Jhanak Payal Baje* (1955) is worth examining:

Intentionally or otherwise, the contest pits Ghirdar of Varanasi, the ultimate Hindu city, against Ram Prasad of Agra, the former Mughal capital. Ghirdar's dancing, moreover, is accompanied by *pakhawaj*, the pre-Muslim classical barrel drum of northern India, whilst his opponent is accompanied by *tabla*, an instrument whose name and morphology connect it directly to the arrival of

Turko-Persian culture in India. [...] Even the costumes of the two dancers [...] appear to reinforce a cultural dichotomy expressible in terms of traditional/non-traditional but also and respectively in terms of Hindu/Muslim.

Such representations might be read as reinforcing a feeling of Hindu superiority and reclaiming Kathak as a Hindu dance form by downplaying its Mughal influence. This could then become water to the mill of the BJP's appropriation of the past, through the creation of 'a Hindu linear identity from the very foundation of Indian history until now' (Thapar 2000: 597), which 'excludes other groups that are said to have entered India at various times whether as invaders, or traders and intruders, and interacted with Indian civilization', including Muslims, Christians and Communists (Thapar 2000: 597).

As the historian Romila Thapar has argued, and others too have observed, the diaspora has been significant to the rise of Hindutva, not only in aiding it financially, but also in constructing a climate where its ideology can flourish. This is why the study of South Asian Dance and its political and ethical entanglements has to take a 'global' perspective, though this article focuses mainly on one artist within India. Thapar (2000: 607) has commented that she was 'intrigued by the fact that the Hindutva ideology keeps on talking about the danger to the majority from the minority', that 'Hinduism was and is said to be in danger', and that 'people were called upon to stand up and proudly declare themselves as being Hindu' (Thapar 2000: 607). Considering that Hindus make up some 80 per cent of the Indian population, this is indeed puzzling. If one, however, takes a global perspective which incorporates the diaspora, and especially the diasporas of Europe and America, one finds that 'the Hindu constitutes a minority, surrounded by societies that are not Hindu. He can develop a mentality of the ghetto and a minority consciousness, and see his identity in those terms' (Thapar 2000: 607). In her view, then, 'the biggest carrier of the Hindutva approach has been among those Indians of the diaspora who accept these ideas and they influence the creating of a minority identity of the Hindu within India' (Thapar 2000: 608). The diasporic Indian, or the NRIs (Non-Resident Indians) as they are often referred to—especially those based in the USA—are undoubtedly role models for the Indian middle classes, and one could argue that this is why the Hindu nationalists have chosen models, which 'rather than characterize Hinduism as ancient, nonmodern, or traditional, [have] embraced capitalism, Western science, and technology as element of a modern, Hindu nation [... returning] to Hindu values, while incorporating Western and Vedic sciences' (Subramaniam 2000: 73–4).

In this way, the fact that Mallika has chosen in recent years to perform more in the USA than in Europe can be seen as a way of offering a contrasting vision of dance in India to that promoted by the hundreds of schools which have flourished in the USA, and which often reiterate in their presentations the myth of an unbroken lineage of dance from the *Nātyaśastra*—the monumental Sanskrit treatise on the dramatic arts written around 200 AD—to today, even though this simplistic vision, perpetuated by dancers and scholars from the 1930s, has been discredited in the past thirty years or so.

Indeed, both dancers and researchers from the 1930s to the 1980s seem to have been fairly unanimous in presenting this vision of dance history. In the early 1980s, however, some writing came out referring to the 1920s and 1930s as a period of revival, for example, the writing of Srinivasan (1985). To my knowledge, however, it is only in 1988 that the doyenne of Indian dance scholarship, Kapila Vatsyayan, started a discussion which explicitly questioned the revival movement (Vatsyayan 1988). A new generation of scholars has taken a much more nuanced approach to the reconstruction of the past in Indian dance.[3]

MALLIKA SARABHAI, THE FEMINIST ARTIST

Mallika is especially interesting for anyone concerned with the interdisciplinary and intercultural issues involved in South Asian dance, as she exemplifies both in a number of ways. She is an academic, an artist, as well as a businesswoman, and she does not make a distinction between the three roles in her own life. She has a Master of Business Administration (MBA, 1974) from the Indian Institute of Management and a PhD in Organisation Behaviour from Gujarat University (1976), with the thesis *Psychological Maturity and the Power Motive: Dynamics and Development*. This is a work she put in practice to manage Darpana when she took over the running of the institution in the 1990s. She is deeply committed to India generally and Gujarat specifically, but she is also a cosmopolitan artist working in Europe and the United States as well. She was awarded a D. Litt (1998) from the University of East Anglia in the UK for her contribution to the arts and was knighted by the French government, which made her a *Chevalier des Arts et des Lettres* (*Knight of the Order of Arts and Letters*),[4] describing her as having a 'myriad of talents in the field of culture' and being 'an activist espousing causes for changing lives of people for the better'.[5] In 2005, she and her mother were also among 1,000 women nominated for the Nobel Peace Prize. Although generally labelled as a 'dancer', she works in both dance and theatre, refusing to see a division between the two (she is also an accomplished singer), because they 'are all different strings to the same instrument' (Sarabhai 2004d). Similarly, choreographically her work explores both so-called 'pure classical styles' and 'fusion' work, always bringing a questioning twist to whatever she does.

In short, like many artists, she refuses to be categorised. Unlike many artists, however, she belongs to a cosmopolitan elite and has always been able to do what she felt was right for her, rather than follow artistic trends or bow to the social norms belonging to the women of her social class. Furthermore she has never been shy of controversy, whether in her private or artistic life. A key moment and turning point in her career has undoubtedly been her highly acclaimed performance as Draupadi in Peter Brook's *The Mahabharata*, which premiered at the 1985 Theatre Festival in Avignon, France. As she put it: 'When I ended my work in the *Mahābhārata*, I was no longer a dancer and an activist, but I had become a performer who used activism and performance together'.[6]

Mallika then developed new kinds of works, more politically and socially focused, such as *Shakti, Sita's Daughters*, and *V is for Violence*, often in collaboration with theatre director John Martin. Dance critic Reginald Massey (1991: 354) wrote in the *Dancing Time* at the time:

So far, I must confess I have seen very little experimental work from India or, more precisely, experimental work based on Indian techniques that has moved me. Now, thanks to Mallika Sarabhai, John Martin, and their musicians Adrian Lee (who composed the music), Dawson Benhassine-Miller and Tiken Singh I see a light at the end of the tunnel.

When discussing her work, Mallika describes it as being often 'womencentric', and *Colours of the Heart*, like many of her productions, is centred on women. It has been described in the following way by Sunderlal (2004):

The singer and dancers weave personal narratives into a universal one, and focus on issues that impact women allover the world. This production talks about the loss of innocence and the shackling of women by customs and traditions.

When asked if she was a feminist, Mallika replied (cited in Devik 2004):

I think I was born one. I can remember being so for a long time. In my earlier days I drew inspiration from my mother. Women's issues are human rights issues. Women constitute 51% of the world population. Women are not a minority. To me 'feminist' is not a dirty word. It's an honest fight against injustice.

As scholar-performer Ananya Chatterjea (2004: 104) puts it, 'Sarabhai has continuously performed critiques of patriarchal politics and repressive state action'. Furthermore, as Mallika said in her International Women's Day statement for the *Times of India* in 2004: 'Empowering women also means empowering men to allow them to be what they want to be' (Sarabhai 2004b). As she argued in a talk during her London visit: 'What is anti-Muslim today will be anti-Dalit tomorrow and is anti-women all the time' (Sarabhai 2004c).

There is no doubt that Mallika's political engagement and her artistic life are totally intermingled and she will use every platform for her cause. Whilst she graciously accepted the Woman of the Year Award for 2003, she also used the occasion to criticise corporate India (cited in Maluste 2004):

I feel strongly that corporate India has shown its frailty over ethical and moral issues in the aftermath of the Gujarat genocide. This segment of society was the only one powerful enough to stand for truth against political leaders who backed violence. But they did not, because the bottom line was more important to them. Money is the only god. By giving me this award, one segment of this society is saying 'Mallika, we believe in you, we may not have the courage to say it aloud but by giving you this award we support what you stand for, for this country'. That gives me a lot of warmth.

It is this spirit that pervades her artistic production, and whilst she certainly wants her works to be judged on artistic merit, they do not exist for her separately from their social and political message. Hers is a kind of war waged against social injustice and the financial apartheid so common in India, where, as Appadurai (2000: 637) puts it, 'one wants the poor near at hand as servants but far away as humans'. It is through the aesthetic dimension of her work that Mallika believes her message will gain potency, so that militancy and art are not separate domains.

She was trained by her mother Mrinalini in Bharatanatyam, the classical genre originally from Tamil Nadu, but now very much pan-Indian, and by the renowned guru C.R. Acharyalu in Kuchipudi,[7] the dance form from Andhra Pradesh. Mallika uses the movement material of both genres as part of her choreographic work. She comments, however, that for her, Kuchipudi has a softer quality, which is less suited to her more politically abrasive work. She prefers the sharpness of Bharatanatyam or the strength of martial art forms from both North and South India, which she also practises, as well as movements derived from folk dances, which Janavak, the folk company she directs, performs.

For her, every movement is potentially a choreographic movement, from those derived from yoga, which is part of the daily training of the Darpana Performance Group, to everyday movements which she likes exploring, to movements borrowed from many genres of dance she is learning from the variety of artists who spend time in Darpana. Observing her work both in India and in London revealed how the abstract rhythmic structures of Carnatic music underpin her compositional methods and add an intensity of emotion which helps give her dancers a strong performance presence to create—as the choreographer Carol Brown put it when she took part in the workshop led by Mallika at Roehampton University, 'a powerful alchemy which transforms choreography into social and political agency'.

'VALUES', 'TRUTH' AND THE SARABHAIS

Mallika was born into a family committed to science, the arts and a modern India rooted in its heritage, a family that 'always stood for value and truth' (Maluste 2004). Her father, the late Vikram Sarabhai, was a 'pioneering scientist, educationist, and industrialist, highly respected in diverse circles' (Chatterjea 2004: 103). Talking about him, Mallika commented that his 'greatest commitment was to India—an India where each individual citizen prospered and was nurtured and cared for' (Sarabhai 1992: 35). Mallika's mother, Mrinalini, was similarly strong-minded. As she put it to me when I interviewed her: 'I came from a family where women were never downtrodden', adding emphatically: 'I have never felt unequal as a woman in my life, ever!' Mallika sees herself as 'the inheritor of the mantle of two families who have given their all to nation building and to spreading truth and love, fearlessness and pride in being Indian' (Sarabhai 2004a). This is very much the ideology that has underpinned Darpana right from its inception, and throughout its existence Darpana has followed quite closely a Nehruvian philosophy of modernity, salient features of which include: national unity, parliamentary democracy, industrialism, socialism, scientific temper and secularism. Darpana is an institution committed to diversity and to social justice, and one could say that the key belief of its ideology is that the performing arts can be an effective medium to bring about social change.

As a privately funded institution, Darpana has been able to set its own agenda, having the dual role of housing artists as well as patrons of the arts through Natarani, the theatre which is part of Darpana and other artistic ventures it sponsors. This gives those at Darpana a somewhat privileged position. As any other artists, however, their work can be censored and these days, when the family fortune is not anymore what it was, the institution needs corporate sponsorship with all the problems this entails, as we will see later. Nevertheless in a country where people often feel they should not pay for art, and few artists can count on box office income to sustain their artistic production, they have enjoyed a freedom that many both within India and in the diaspora have envied. Unlike many artist-activists who have to privilege solo performances because of financial limitations (see Burns 2005), they regularly present large-scale works with complex staging. As a result there is undoubtedly a certain amount of professional resentment leading to a great deal of gossip about the supposed arrogance of the Sarabhais. Indeed, presenting my work, I have encountered what, to me, is a surprising degree of hostility towards them. Whilst it is true that the Sarabhais are in a privileged position, and when one is in a prominent position for a long time it is easy to become somewhat autocratic, it is also true nevertheless that many artists with similar social positions choose not to speak up. Neither do they spend the amount of time and energy, let alone money, the Sarabhais do to sustain a complex institution employing a large number of people and paying them a decent wage. I am sure there must have been times when Mrinalini and Mallika must have felt that their lives would be a lot easier if they concentrated on their careers as solo artists.

MALLIKA SARABHAI, THE POLITICAL ARTIST

As the political situation changed in India in the last quarter of the twentieth century, the Congress Party becoming increasingly corrupt and complacent after so many years in power and the nationalist parties gaining more support throughout the country, Darpana's position changed. Although critical of the Congress, Darpana these days has remained loyal to it. because it still sees the party as the best bet for a liberal democracy. Therefore, when the BJP came into power at the centre, Darpana became part of the 'opposition'.

Whilst Mallika's activism remained primarily social and confined within her artistic practice, it was largely only tolerated, if not necessarily valued or supported. Although 'her dancing body on the stages of New York, Brazil, and Delhi signalled a particular image of Indian women, one directly contradictory to the image preferred by the fundamentalist camp' (Chatterjea 2004: 106), it was only marginally threatening. As the BJP's power increased, however, and its lack of respect for human rights became apparent, Mallika became more actively political. A turning point was undoubtedly the traumatic destruction of the Babri Masjid in Ayodhya in 1992, when Hindus destroyed the mosque and murdered Muslims in horrific acts of violence to reclaim the supposed birthplace of Ram, as part of what Appadurai (2000: 645) argued was 'one form of [the] politicized Hinduism [which] took as its major program the liberation of Hindu temples from what were argued to be their illegitimate Muslim superstructures'. Watching on the news government ministers in jubilation over such acts deeply shocked Mallika. This led her to set up the Centre for Non-violence Through the Arts, under Darpana's auspices and to become more directly involved politically. As she put it: 'As a dancer, it made more sense to me to dance the horrors of caste violence than of bhakti and the love for Shiva' (Sarabhai 2004a).

Mallika's political campaign was paralleled by a government harassment campaign. Whenever Darpana engaged in building work, for example, government officials would find all sorts of problems about planning permission, health and safety, or anything else that would delay the work. In a similar fashion, Darpana's accounts were regularly scrutinised, even though nothing out of order was ever found. Darpana's paperwork and accounts had to be immaculate with full documentation for every transaction in the knowledge that government officials, who were constantly on the lookout for anything that they could use to get the institution in trouble, would pounce upon the slightest irregularity.

THE STATE VERSUS THE ARTIST-ACTIVIST

Another turning point came with the Godhra massacre and its aftermath in February–March 2002, when 58 people were burned to death in a train returning from a Hindu pilgrimage, and this led to communal violence. Communal violence was certainly not new to Gujarat. There had been serious communal riots in 1969 and 1992–3, but the government at the time had not been publicly partisan. There had been a public disapproval of the violence and the government had pleaded for communal harmony. In 2002, however, according to Lord Bhikhu Parekh (2002) and many others, any pretence of neutrality disappeared and the government openly encouraged Hindu violence against Muslims. Most of the Gujarati media were pro-government, provocative and grossly biased.

With the violence so close to home, Mallika became immediately involved, publishing an article on 5 March 2002 in *The Times of India* entitled—after Zola and the Dreyfus affair in the nineteenth century—'I Accuse'. Personal threats started that night. Yet she continued, and on 1 April 2002 she filed, with two other persons (Digant Oza and Indu Kumar), a public interest litigation (PIL) in the Supreme Court of India against the government of Gujarat for its involvement in the anti-Muslim pogrom. As with other advocates of inter-communal harmony, the government tried to terrorise her into silence, in the hope that she would withdraw the litigation.

Despite ongoing threats, Mallika continued both her litigation against the government and her work with Darpana, planning overseas tours, as obviously the institution needed to earn money in order to pay its staff. It was on one of these tours that the government latched on to try to cow her into silence by accusing her of illegal human trafficking. I cannot go into details of the whole affair here, as it is rather convoluted.[8] Suffice it to say here that Darpana comprises a number of organisations, including the folk dance ensemble Janavak mentioned earlier, which often performs at folk festivals worldwide. Janavak is made up of permanent professional dancers from Darpana and of dance students trained by Darpana. The latter have to pay for the trip, generally having to cover their fare and other expenses, whilst the organisations hosting the festival generally house and feed the dancers. Students are interested despite the cost involved because it gives them an exposure to international dance, allows them to travel outside India within a context approved by their families and, in a few instances, because it is believed that it may allow them easier access to a visa in the future. I was told, for example, that some felt that if they had been given a US visa for one of these tours, and had returned to India as planned, it would be easier for them to apply independently in the future. Whether this is true or not is debatable, but some certainly believed it. Not all students selected for intensive training—a training they pay for—however, will necessarily be taken on tour, as clearly they have to be of a professional dance standard and fit in with the rest of the company. This undoubtedly creates disappointment. It appears that a student in such a predicament, encouraged by the government, filed a complaint. Mallika was accused of human trafficking (under sections 14, 34, and 420 of the Indian Penal Code of 1860), for allegedly using Janavak's tour for smuggling Indian nationals into the USA.

Although it was immediately obvious that the claim was spurious and civil liberties groups throughout the country and overseas came to Mallika's support, Mallika had to surrender her passport and was not allowed to travel outside Gujarat without permission. November through January are important months for an Indian artist, as it is the season when the major festivals take place. Mallika was forced to apply for permission to travel for every performance. Giving permission for short periods only, and sometimes awarding it only a few days before the event, the government deliberately jeopardised her work, as sponsors organising the tours, especially the foreign ones, were not always willing or able to wait till the last moment. Whilst following legal regulations, the government was in effect undermining the very livelihood of Darpana, as all Mallika's dance earnings go into the running of the institution. Further, as the campaign against her grew—with headlines screaming 'the traitor of Gujarat', 'the whore of the Muslim' and so on—Darpana lost all its corporate sponsorship. Needless to say, this was a complete disaster.

As Mallika (2004c) stated in London: 'From being the most celebrated daughter of the state I would walk into a place and nobody would meet my eyes'. She also commented, when asked about the Congress returning to power in Delhi after the election that had just happened then, on how this would affect her situation: 'I will go back to a country where I am no longer a fugitive, but I am not sure I am going to a state where I am no longer a fugitive'.

THE AFTERMATH: CAN DANCE BE UNPOLITICAL?

On 12 December 2004, *The Gujarat Age* ran the headline 'State drops the case against Mallika'. The saga had lasted from 18 October 2003 to 12 December 2004. These had been fourteen months of state harassment to drown the voice of an artist to no avail. Yet what has been achieved? Although enquiries into the massacres are still taking place and Amnesty International filed a report in May 2004, the process is slow. The BJP is still in power in Gujarat and according to human right activists, four years after the massacre, victimisation and terrorisation of Muslims in the state continues. The goal of reducing Muslims to second-class citizens seems thus to have been accomplished in Gujarat and many believe that the Hinduist regime of Narendra Modi, Gujarat's Chief Minister,[9] 'taught a lesson to Muslims'. Innocent people are regularly detained illegally before being charged under the Prevention of Terrorism Act (POTA), and individuals criticising government officials can be charged with 'anti-national activities'. The human rights group *Counter Current* noted on 6 September 2006, that after a journalist had criticised a number of BJP ministers for mishandling a recent crisis, he was arrested (Gatade 2006). Committed activists like Mallika continue to be needed to remind everyone that the fight for securing justice has not been won. Mallika may have won her battle, but she certainly has not won the war.

NOTES

1. From now on, when referring to Mallika Sarabhai, I will refer to her as Mallika. This follows the Indian practice and will be useful when distinguishing the different members of the Sarabhai family referred to in this paper.

2. The BJP was created in 1980, as the main opponent to the Indian National Congress, the party of Indian independence, which dominated central government for the first four decades. The BJP led the Government of India between 1998 and 2004, and is still in power in the state of Gujarat, where Ahmedabad, the home of Mallika Sarabhai, is situated.

3. See for example the work of scholars such as Pallabi Chakravorty (2000, 2001), Uttara Coorlawala (1992), Alessandra Iyer (1996), Avanthi Meduri (1996, 2001) or Janet O'Shea (2001, 2003), to cite but a few.

4. She was awarded both the title of Knight and Officer, respectively, in 1999 and 2002. However, she 'physically' received the order on 14 July 2005. The other recipients at the ceremony were the dancer Alarmel Valli, the writer Nirmal Varma and the artist Naresh Kapuria.

5. See www.france-in-india.org

6. Cited from Darpana's website, accessed on 8 September 2005.

7. It is worth noting that she co-wrote *Understanding Kuchipudi* (1995) with him. See Sarabhai and Acharyalu (1995).

8. See the discussion in Chatterjea (2004) for further details.

9. Narendra Modi has been extremely important in the rise of the political dominance of the BJP in Gujarat. According to the biography on his website, he joined the BJP in 1987. Within a year, he was elevated to the level of General Secretary of the Gujarat unit and in 1995 he was made its National Secretary. He became Chief Minister of Gujarat in 2001 (http://www.narendramodi.org/bio.htm).

REFERENCES

Anonymous, 15 January 2004, 'The Sensibility Index is Dropping Rapidly', *The Times of India Online* (*City Supplement Kanpur Times*), (consulted 8 August 2004 from http://timesofindia.indiatimes.com/articleshow/msid-425195, prtpage-l.cms)

Appadurai, Arjun, 2000, 'Spectral Housing and Urban Cleansing: Notes on Millennial Mumbai', *Public Culture*, 12(3), pp. 627–51.

Booth, Greg, 2005, 'Pandit in the Movies: Contesting the Identity of Hindustani Classical Music and Musicians in the Hindi Popular Cinema', *Asian Music* (Winter/Spring), pp. 60–86.

Burns, Lucy Mae San Pablo, 2005, 'Woman and the Changing World on Alternative Global Stage: Sixth Women Playwrights International Conference', *Asian Theatre Journal*, 22(2), pp. 324–33.

Chakravorty, Pallabi, 2000, 'Choreographing Modernity: Kathak Dance, Public Culture, and Women's Identity in India', Unpublished PhD dissertation, Philadelphia, PA: Temple University.

———, 2001, 'From Interculturalism to Historicism: Reflections on Classical Indian Dance', *Dance Research Journal*, 32(1), pp. 108–19.

Chatterjea, Ananya, 2004, 'In Search of a Secular in Contemporary Indian Dance: A Continuing Journey', *Dance Research Journal*, 36(2), pp. 102–16.

Coorlawala, Uttara Asha, 1992, 'Ruth St Denis and India's Dance Renaissance', *Dance Chronicle*, 15(2), pp. 123–52.

Datta, Jyotirmo, 14 March 2003, 'Actor-Activist: Mallika Sarabhai in Citigroup's *Women of Asia* Series', *News India-Times*, http://desitalk.newsindiatimes.com/2003/03/14/women-actor.html (accessed on 23 March 2004).

Desai, Jigna, 2004, *Beyond Bollywood: The Cultural Politics of South Asian Diasporic Film*, London: Routledge.

Devik, Sangeetha, 8 August 2004, 'Mallika of All She Surveys', *The Times of India*, http://timesofindia.indiatimes.com/articleshow/msid-806898,prtpage-l.cms (accessed on 8 August 2004).

Dwyer, Rachel and Christopher Pinney (eds), 2001, *Pleasure and the Nation: The History, Politics and Consumption of Popular Culture in India*, New York: Oxford University Press.

Gatade, Subash, 6 September 2006, 'Writing a Sedition', *Countercurrent.org*, http://www.countercurrent.org (accessed on 12 September 2006).

Iyer, Alessandra (ed.), 1996, *South Asian Dance: The British Experience*, Choreography and Dance Series, London: Harwood Academic Publishers.

Joshi, Padmanabh K. (ed.), 1992, *Vikram Sarabhai: The Man and his Vision*, Ahmedabad: Mapin Publishing.

Maluste, Avanti, 19 April 2004, 'Dancer in the Dark', *The Times of India*, http://timesofindia.indiatimes.com/articleshow/msid-624073prtpage-l.cms (accessed on 8 August 2004).

Massey, Reginald, 1991, 'Mallika Sarabhai'. *The Dancing Time*, (January), p. 354.

Meduri, Avanthi, 1996, 'Nation, Woman, Representation: The Sutured History of the Devadasi and Her Dance', Unpublished PhD dissertation, New York: New York University.

Meduri, Avanthi, 2001, 'Bharatha Natyam—What are You?', in Ann Dils and Ann C. Albright (eds), *Moving History/Dancing Cultures*, Middletown, Connecticut: Wesleyan University Press, pp. 103–13.

Mishra, Vijay, 2002, *Bollywood Cinema: Temples of Desire*, London: Routledge.

O'Shea, Janet, 2001, 'At Home in the World: Bharata Natyam's Transnational Traditions', unpublished PhD dissertation, Riverside, CA: University of California.

———, 2003, 'At Home in the World? The Bhatatanatyam Dancer as a Transnational Interpreter', *The Drama Review*, 47(1), pp. 176–86.

Parekh, Bhikhu, 2002, 'Making Sense of Gujarat', http://www.india-seminar.com (accessed on 18 March 2004)

Pathak, Avijit, 1998, *Indian Modernity: Contradictions, Paradoxes and Possibilities*, New Delhi: Gyan Publishing House.

Pfleiderer, Beatrix and Lothar Lutze (eds), 1985, *The Hindi Film: Agent and Re-agent of Cultural Change*, New Delhi: Manohar.

Prasad, M. Madhava, 1998, *Ideology of the Hindi Film: A Historical Construction*, New Delhi: Oxford University Press.

Rajagopal, Arvind, 2001, *Politics After Television. Religious Nationalism and the Reshaping of the Indian Public*, Cambridge: Cambridge University Press.

Sarabhai, Mallika, 1992, 'My Father Vikram', in Padmanabh K. Joshi (ed.), *Vikram Sarabhai: The Man and his Vision*, Ahmedabad: Mapin Publishing, pp. 32–7.

_____, 2004a, 'Email letter to her friends and supporters on Wednesday 11 February, after the High Court rejected her appeal'.

_____, 2004b, 'Straight Answers: Mallika Sarabhai, Danseuse, on International Women's Day', *The Times of India*, 6 March, http://timesofindia.indiatimes.com/articleshow/msid-541139,prtpage-l.cms (accessed on 8 August 2004).

_____, 2004c, 'Public Talk at Hampstead Town Hall', 20 May.

_____, 2004d, 'We Voice What is Wrong', *The Hindu*, 17 August, http://www.hinduonnet.comlthehindulthscrip/print.pl?file=2004081700650100.htm&date=2004/08/171 &prd=mp& (accessed on 21 December 2005).

Sarabhai, Mallika and C.R. Acharyulu, 1995, *Understanding Kuchipudi*, Ahmedabad: Mapin Publishing.

Srinavasan, Amrit, 1985, 'Reform and Revival: The Devadasi and Her Dance', *Economic and Political Weekly*, 3 November, 20(44), pp. 1869–76.

Subramaniam, Banu, 2000, 'Archaic Modernities: Science, Secularism, and Religion in Modern India', *Social Text*, 18(3), pp. 67–86.

Sunderlal, Aruna, 29 July 2004, 'Straight Answers: Aruna Sunderlal, Director, Bangalore School of Music, on Presenting *The Colours of the Heart* by Mallika Sarabhai', *The Times of India*, http://timesofindia.indiatimes.com/articleshow/msid-794410,prtpage-l.cms (accessed on 8 August 2003).

Thapar, Romila, 2000, 'On Historical Scholarship and the Uses of the Past: Interview with Parita Mukta', *Ethnic and Racial Studies*, 23(3), pp. 594–616.

Vatsyayan, Kapila, 1988, 'Dance Scholarship: The Complex Indian Situation', in *Beyond Performance: Dance Scholarship Today*, Proceedings of the Essen Congress, Berlin: International Theatre Institute, pp. 114–23.

Virdi, Jyotika, 2003, *The Cinematic Imagination*, New Brunswick, NJ: Rutgers University Press.

Anita Kumar

What's the Matter?

Shakti's (Re)Collection of Race, Nationhood, and Gender

OCTOBER 1985

Norwalk, California

Indian Summer—thick, dry, smothering heat. The kind of heat where the sun's rays pierce just under the skin, with a slow, simmering burn; the kind of heat that sears the leather car interior and stings the skin, unassuming. This is what we were dealing with that Saturday afternoon.

My family and I are driving in circles, in search of the Norwalk community centre—one big room in the middle of a huge park. It is in this room that I, along with four other seven-year-old girls, will nervously demonstrate whatever dance knowledge we have gathered in the past year. This repertoire consists of five basic dance steps.

We are already a half hour late. There is a crown of orange and white flowers encircling my head, held up by at least a hundred bobby pins. The flowers seem to attract the sun's unrelenting rays, and the top of my head is as hot as a griddle. The braid mom has made stretches the hair on each side of my head so tightly that my temples throb from the stiffness.

I really can't take it anymore. I guess neither can my dad because he finally pulls over to call information for the center's phone number. He parks the car, and turns around to my aunt and I. *Deepa, Anita, why don't you get out and ask those people over there where this center is.*

A wave of heat washes over me. Did he seriously expect me to get out of the car looking like *this*—with my 10 layers of mascara, eyeliner, lipstick, and rouge; dripping from head to toe in gold jewellery? Of course I don't let on and dutifully join my aunt outside the car.

We are halfway to the group. The laughter, shouting, and din of playing are getting louder, more *real*. I stop. I cannot go any further. My aunt turns around. *C'mon, Anita. What are you doing?* I silently shake

FIG. 27   Anita Kumar at age six. (Photo by Vasanth Kumar)

my head no. She continues, and then, I am all by myself. And that is when it happens.

She has blonde, curly hair and is short and hefty, if I remember correctly. For some reason, red stands out. There's a boyfriend attached to her. They are walking towards me. She lets out a peal of laughter. They're getting closer. My right foot is tracing circles in the dirt. Closer. I can hear her voice now. Her left hand grips his right. Closer. They are now walking past me. And why I did it, I don't know, but I smiled—a timid, seven-year-old smile.

Honey, look at that big red dot on her forehead, and that red stuff on her hand. Why didn't you tell me Halloween came early this year?! A huge peal of laughter completes the statement. *Who Knew?* is the boyfriend's response. More laughter. There is a ringing in my ears. Were they talking about me? My eyes fixate on their backs; follow their disappearing figures. The joke sinks in. I am the joke.

JANUARY 2003

Culver City, Los Angeles—Viji's House

The faint smell of incense hangs in the air. I sit on the floor, next to Viji Aunty, watching as they stagger themselves throughout the tiny garage space. Krushit, Iman, Vaishnavi, and Aisha make up the back row, with Sasha and little Sandhya in the front. They all wear the standard uniform—the traditional salwar kameez—although Vaishnavi stands out in her bright orange and green half-sari. Because she is older than the rest, the dance sari is her required uniform.

Backs straight. Chins lifted. Eyes wide and looking straight ahead. Knees turned out. Bodies are poised, ready to do the opening prayer, *namaskara,* a homage to Lord Shiva. Six feet are poised, prepared to lift on the beat, when Jahnavi rushes through the door, struggling to undo the laces of her pink Converse in order to join the group in time. No shoes while dancing is the first rule engrained in a dancer.

I am taken by surprise. Jahnavi is Latina. In that instant, my own naïve constructions of nationhood were laid bare; what Homi K. Bhabha has referred to as 'the splitting of the national subject' (1994: 148). Under the assumption that the South Asian diaspora primarily uses dance as a cultural link to the homeland, as a symbol of national identity, what significance did the dance play for Jahnavi? Yes, it was a link to the homeland, but here 'home' becomes a slippery and contested position, reconfigured as part of the social imaginary.

Even more striking was my own astonishment at seeing Jahnavi, a fellow 'Other,' participating in this dance. Why was I so taken aback by Jahnavi's 'Latinaness' in this *bharatanatyam* dance class? Why would it have been less fascinating if she were white? As Marta Savigliano so aptly writes in her research on the transnational tango circuit, it was a case of 'exotics facing other exotics, fascinated by the processes of autoexoticism, carried away into re-exoticizing that already exotic Other' (1995: 179).

Viji Aunty cracks a beat on her wood block, and her students scramble into posture once again. Namaskara is officially completed once they have touched Viji's feet, a sign of humility, of giving up one's ego to the God Almighty.

'Okay girls. Let's get ready for leg stretches! L.A. to Bombay!' exclaims Viji.

In 'Dissemination: Time, Narrative and the Margins of the Modern Nation' (1994), Bhabha depicts the narrative for the contemporary nationstate as a shuttling back and forth between the performative and pedagogical:

It is precisely in reading between these borderlines of the nationspace that we can see how the concept of the 'people' emerges within a range of discourses as a double narrative movement. The people are not simply historical events or parts of a patriotic body politic. They are also a complex rhetorical strategy of social reference [...]. We then have a contested conceptual territory where the nation's people must be thought in doubletime; *the people are the historical 'objects' of a nationalist pedagogy*, giving the discourse an authority that is based on the pre-given or constituted historical origin in the past; the people are also the *'subjects' of a process of signification* that must erase any prior or originary presence of the nation-people to demonstrate the prodigious, living principles of the people as contemporaneity: as the sign of the present through which national life is redeemed and iterated as a reproductive process. (1994: 145; emphasis added)

The pedagogical representation of the nation-state treats 'a people' as a timeless and essential object. Simultaneously, the nation is conceptualized as a reiterative process of signification, constantly in flux as it is enacted in the present—the performative. This double narrative is what Bhabha refers to as 'splitting of the national subject' (145–6), characterized by perpetual movement between a time of the past (the pedagogical) and the present (the performative). It is this state of liminality that Bhabha claims as the narrative space of the contemporary nation-state.

My account of bharatanatyam, a South Indian classical dance, reflects such a trajectory, emerging from a space that plays on the very tension the performative and pedagogical. I follow the dance's performative rendering of race, nationhood, and gender within a South Asian diasporic community situated in Los Angeles. This process has emerged as a direct result of the migration of a South Indian woman, Viji Prakash, to Los Angeles from Bombay in 1975, and her and her husband's subsequent establishment of the Shakti Dance School.

The performative necessarily operates in and through the pedagogical. In fact, the very success of bharatanatyam's signification of race, nation, and gender rests in its dialectic relationship with the ahistorical and originary narrative of nationhood, disclosing itself in the actual learning and practice of the dance. When Viji teaches her students, she propagates an ideological construct of the dance whose foundation rests upon a master narrative of India. This construct is necessarily restorative and ahistorical, assuming a premodern, romantic narrative of the nation. Though bharatanatyam is originally a *South* Indian dance, within the South Asian diaspora, Gujarati (North Indian), South Indian, Bengali, and Pakistani families all learn the form as a classical *Indian* dance. In its transmigration, bharatanatyam has become one of the quintessential vehicles for the inculcation of various values, particularly for girls. Some of these values are identified as discipline, spirituality, focus, respect, and the ability to discern right from wrong. Thus, over the course of 15 or 20 years, the dance not only serves as a signifying practice, but functions as a corporeal disciplining of the body in these various traits, collectively identified as 'Indianness'. The students literally 'perform India', to play with Paulla Ebron's phrase (2002).

Here, my larger objective is to juxtapose representation with embodiment. While I trace the construction of racialized, nationalized, and gendered bodies, I ultimately posit the question of *how* processes of signification actualize and serve as productive forces (Foucault 1977). From its repeated movements to the larger social rituals required of a dancer, how does the dancer materialize particular constructions of race, nation, and gender through bharatanatyam?[1] As Judith Butler asserts, it is 'in conducting a critical genealogy of [materiality's] formulation' (1993: 32) through its repeated figurations, and hence its performance, that we can see how the body and its multiple identities come to be perceived as 'natural.'

The discursive and the experiential encircle each other in their own dance, and it is precisely within this encompassing that I attempt a narrative of the nation-state, of South Asian diasporic identity and collectivity. I want to emphasize that I do not take the sedimentation of identity to imply that identity is whole, unified and transparent. Rather, it is my contention at all times that multiple identities comprise the self, which at best is fragmentary and precarious (see Butler 1993, 1999; Kondo 1990, 1997).

RE(MEMBER)ING INDIA

One Tuesday in the middle of class, Viji Aunty has each of her students say a prayer in their native language. Sasha, Aisha, and Iman recite a Muslim prayer in Urdu; Krushit, a Zoroastrian prayer in Avista, Jahnavi does not speak in Spanish, but in Hindi. Finally, Sandhya, the only South Indian, sings a verse of *Karnatak* music. Again, I am fascinated and yet utterly perplexed that Viji Aunty has Muslim students learning bharatanatyam, a South Indian classical dance based on Hindu philosophy that reenacts the mythology of the Hindu gods. The politics of nationhood's performance deepens.

What about the millions of people massacred during the Hindu-Muslim riots of the 1947 Partition? What of the profound violence and hatred, rapes and pillage that ravage India to this day, such as in 1992 when Hindus attacked the 16th-century Babri mosque in Ayodhya, killing more than 3,000? Or 10 years later, in 2002 when Hindus expressed a desire to build a temple in the same space as the mosque and Muslims retaliated by setting a train on fire, killing 50 Hindu activists?

At a subsequent meeting one afternoon with Viji, I broach the subject.

PRAKASH: Dance is a universal form that transcends one's cultural identity, religious identity, and so on. Just because it comes from one geographical region doesn't mean that it must be passed on to those from the same region. For example, Parvathi—do you know who Parvathi is?

KUMAR: (*It's a rhetorical question and so I remain silent.*)

PRAKASH: Because you are Hindu, do you know more than another person who is not Hindu? Parvathi takes on whomever, whatever you want her to be. (2003a)

There is something quite beautiful in this response, one of the more positive possibilities of the transnational space and the migratory experience. Ironically, Viji's re-imagining of nation, community, and solidarity in this statement reflects a prominent slogan of the Indian nationalist movement, 'Unity in Diversity' (Pandey 1992: 28). However, this reconstruction is also based on a forgetting of national history, of 'the violence involved in establishing the nation's writ' (Bhabha 1994: 160). The justifications for forgetting or silencing are not hard to find: Why open up old wounds? How does one even begin to describe, to bring justice to the profound violence and tragedy that have been endured in

FIG. 28   Left to right: Manesha Parik, Uma Kadekodi, Maya Kadekodi, and Sai Patil of the Shakti Dance School in *Bhaav Chaturang* (Four Seasons of Emotion), James Armstrong Theatre, Torrance, CA, 4 September 2005. (Photo by Surendra Prakash)

these struggles, particularly since the very nature of the Partition draws so much debate (Pandey 1992)?

For transnational ethnic identities, the process of travel and resettlement generates a tension between the desire for belonging and longing, memory and the now, sameness and difference:

In general, the migratory experience can lead to more embracing identifications on the margin of the host society: Those who do not think of themselves as Indians before migration become Indians in the diaspora. The element of romanticization which is present in every nationalism is even stronger among nostalgic migrants, who often form a rosy picture of the country they have left and are able to imagine the nation where it did not exist before. (van der Veer 1995: 7)

The activity of *becoming Indian* at once highlights the performativity of nationhood and ethnicity. Simultaneously, it reveals the self-objectification of identity necessary when an individual moves into a larger structure where constructs such as race, ethnicity, and nationality are threatened. Becoming Indian is constituted by the larger hegemonic practice of *becoming American* (here, of course, I am assuming the migratory destination to be the United States). The state apparatus concurrently enforces this dialectic. It is essential to its own survival. Its power structures enforce the construction of the immigrant and ethnic minority as just that—a minority, perpetually incomplete, a member of an inassimilable ethnic culture, a construction 'imposed from the outside and encountered by ethnic subjects in the transition from the community into dominant culture' (Lloyd 1994: 229). Difference is perceived as a threat, yet necessary for the maintenance of a regime of power. At the same time, the state generates institutions and policies predicated on the molding of the minority subject into a generic and homogenous citizen (Rosaldo 1994: 241–2). A *successful* outcome is the continual and incomplete transfer of the minority's primary identification with their particular community to that of the dominant culture.[2]

Thus, there is a double formation, contradictory and fluctuating, in the constitution of the ethnic minority (therefore of the state as well), a plural belonging, 'of becoming American while staying somehow diasporic' (Appadurai 1996: 170). Questions of allegiance arise as the commitment to the country of origin and the country of settlement becomes a tension that continually defines the immigrant and ethnic minority. The diasporic community undermines the spatially and temporally bounded nation as it remains in constant dialogue with its homeland, whether through the real and imagined traveling back and forth or the channeling of finances, resources, and capital.[3] This deterritorialization lends itself to the production of locality more as multiple nodes of conjunctural and context-specfic interaction (see Gupta and Ferguson 1992). Ironically, it is also an integral force in the development of a number of national revivalist projects and religious fundamentalist movements (e.g., Hindu and Islamic fundamentalism, war in the Middle East, ethnic tensions in Eastern Europe), as people all over the globe find the traditional cohesion that accompanies community, solidarity, and allegiance challenged (see Bhatt 2001).

Theoretically, the traditional conceptions of the territorial nation-state might be coming undone. Yet in all practicality, it would be far too presumptuous to claim it is on its way out, or for that matter, if an 'out' can ever be claimed. For those who do not migrate out of choice and/ or those who find themselves on the margins of society, the erasure of race, nationality, and ethnicity may not necessarily be desired. As Dorinne Kondo reminds us, we cannot ignore 'the historically, culturally specific power relations that constitute and inscribe that difference' (1997: 178) of the diasporic subject. Consequently, it is in addition to deterritorialization that a reterritorialization of space, home, and identity is perpetually negotiated (178).

Once again, the double narrative of the performative and pedagogical arises. The very act of reconstitution implies an original or authentic locale from which the process of migration and the subsequent diasporic identity operates as its derivative or copy.[4] And yet, it is because the diasporic identity is continually in the process of replication that its performance is revealed:

> [R]epetition never fully accomplishes identity. That there is a need for repetition at all is a sign that identity is not self-identical. It requires to be instituted again and again, which is to say that it runs the risk of becoming de-instituted at every interval. (Butler 1997: 309)

The parents of first generation South Asian Americans are quite aware of this construction of Indianness. This plays itself out in the heightened cultural and social significance that bharatanatyam (as well as other cultural practices such as regularly attending temple and *balavihar*, attending social functions such as *ras* or *bhangra*,[5] learning Karnatak music, etc.) has assumed within the South Asian American community.

I return to this question of Muslims pursuing a Hindu art form. I ask myself: Do I know who Parvathi is? Because I am Hindu, do I know anymore than another person who is not Hindu? Moreover, because I do not actively engage in my 'Hindu-ness' through regular activities—such as attending temple, daily prayer, reading Hindu mythology—are Aisha,

Iman, and Sasha more 'Hindu' than I am, given that their knowledge of the Hindu gods, stories, and prayers are enacted on a regular basis through engagement with the dance? I turn to Henna and Sana Zaidi to explore these questions in greater depth.

Henna and Sana Zaidi are sisters. They are the first Muslims in the Shakti school to perform their solo dance debut, the *arangetram*.[6] The Zaidi family is Shi'a Muslim. Their mother, Azra, and father, Asad, migrated to Los Angeles from Pakistan in the early 1970s. Their own parents are from Utter Pradesh, a northern state of India, but relocated to Pakistan because of the Partition. Asad formulates these various movements into what he identifies as an integrated identity:

KUMAR: So, Uncle, we were talking about Hindu nationalism and equating Hindu nationalism with India, which is the predominant view in the country right now. There's a kind of coming together of secularism ... of secular India with the religious India. And your parents who were born and raised in India, who had to move to Pakistan, were forced to move to Pakistan after the Partition, what is their conception of India, knowing that they're Muslim, and their conception of India is very marginalized?

ZAIDI: Yeah. I would say, taking the liberty of talking about my parents, or let's say elders who migrated to Pakistan. I think their conception is sort of frozen in time, where they would just think of their old days when India was really an integrated India. And, if you talk to them, they will go back into their history, and they would talk about how good it was that they were able to mix and match, and talk to people, and not have to really worry about any distinction between Hindus and Muslims at that time.

My father dearly tells me stories that he felt so special because he was invited into this *rasoi*, or kitchen, of one of their Hindu neighbors, and he felt as if he was part of that family. So, especially for *us*, even from my parents' points of view, we are carrying on an image of our immigrant identity as an integrated identity, rather than an identity that is based on separation.

KUMAR: Can you explain that more, an integrated identity?

ZAIDI: Well, what I mean by integrated identity is that for us it really doesn't matter. We are all from the same part of the world, or same part of our ethnic identity. A South Asian means either India or Pakistan. And our upbringing, especially you know, ours—mine and Azra's and obviously, the kids'—is a reflection of an integrated identity, which means there is no separation based on either culture or language or you know, or religion, okay.

So talking about my parents originating from U.P. [Utter Pradesh], migrating to Pakistan during this political division, me and Azra growing up in Karachi, which is part of Sindh, coming over here and having our kids learn a *South* Indian tradition, rather than a North Indian tradition. I think that is what we call developing an integrated identity.

KUMAR: In a way, would you say then, that you are equating your father to this sort of timeless India. In that sense would you say, you and your wife as well as your kids, are also sort of working in that—

ZAIDI: —from that kind of image. Exactly. (Zaidi et al. 2004)

Operating here is a certain ahistoricism, the forgetting of historical context, which opens a new performative space for identities and interactions in ways that were not possible before, 'those contested spaces through which particular unities are sought to be constituted and others broken up' (Pandey 1992: 50). In fact, such sites ultimately instill in us a sense of hope, promise, and empowerment. It isn't because of the dance's 'Hindu-ness' or national significance that the Zaidi family participates in this art form. It is for its aestheticism. Certainly, this is Viji's strong conviction, and what she tries vigorously to instill in her students. She asserts during one of our midday conversations:

So for me culture is like ... bharatanatyam is like ... it's just good art. And you get from it, what you get from it. And I think once you get into that field of dance and music, it should not be, 'I am black, I am white, I am Hindu, or I am Muslim.' Or, you know, it *should* not be there, so that's what *really* art does. You know, just binds us all together. And we all know that. (2004a)

This is reinforced by Sana. When asked her friends' response to her sister and her learning bharatanatyam, she states,

We'd always just explain to them that you know, it's something that we have a passion for. It's something we enjoy even through the blood, sweat, and tears. It was just something that we always loved. And it was an *art form*, and that's how we viewed it. We viewed it as an art form with the backdrop of Hindu mythology. (Zaidi et al. 2004)

And yet, such a perspective easily falls prey to the reification (and thus simplification) of culture and tradition, a reaffirmation of an essentialized and timeless India. This is clearly stated in Asad's elaboration of what he means by an integrated identity and exemplified in the decision to have his daughters learn bharatanatyam.

Initially, the Pakistani community did not consider Henna and Sana's decision to study bharatanatyam appropriate. Henna recounts a story from her childhood:

HENNA ZAIDI: So my mosque friends, they were always like, 'Whoa, you're kind of weird 'cos you're doing something like that.' When we were young, when we were like ten, we really didn't bring it up to them because we knew that they really didn't *care*. They were just like, 'Whatever. That's something really weird.'

And I think there's this one incident where I think we had a program or something like that, and my dad took a picture of me when I was all in my like bharatanatyam costume and everything. And, I think I was eight or something like that, eight or nine. And somehow that picture got around to the whole community, the whole mosque community, and everybody was like, 'Oh, what is this!' Just people started talking crap, like, 'Oh yeah! They're turning into Hindus.' And my parents have always taught me, you know, that stuff doesn't matter. That's not going to help you. It's not going to hurt you. Just sidetrack it. Do what you want to do, you know.

Now, I've noticed that they've [friends] kind of been more curious towards it. Like, 'Oh, hey. I wanna come see your program. I wanna see what you're doing.' Like for example last night, I went to a friend's birthday party, and I met one of my friends there from the mosque. And she was very like, 'Wow! You guys are going to be dancing for three hours!' And so, slowly, slowly, there's a handful of people, a handful of our friends that we've known for a really long time that have become more supportive. [...] They're a little more open-minded to it. But then yeah there's always gonna be those people that are like, 'Ugh, whatever! Like they're so Hindu. They're so bad!' So it's like, always you see a mix of people. (Zaidi et al. 2004)

As an interesting corollary, when I asked Asad and Azra what the Pakistani community's reaction was to their daughters' performing their arangetram, a process that is incredibly intensive in terms of the family's expectations, time and finances, the following discussion ensued:

AZRA ZAIDI: Learning dance or any kind of artistic expression is very important [to us]. But for most of the Pakistanis, as you said, I mean because of this religious time or whatever, they think it's not important at all. I mean, that's just like a waste of time, waste of money.

KUMAR: So, in other words, if they were still learning ballet and they had a huge solo debut—

AZRA ZAIDI: —Yeah, that's Americanized.

ASAD ZAIDI: They [the Pakistani community] would be more, they would be more inclined, there would be more acceptance because it is again a class issue. Ballet is associated with Europeanization or Americanization of your class, or the culture, or upper-middle class. When I tell them that the girls are going to [perform at] Lincoln Center, their ears perk up. But when I tell them that they're going to perform bharatanatyam, then they're, you know, then they're *totally* confused.

AZRA ZAIDI: You know, most of the people understand Lincoln Center. This is Pakistani upper class I'm talking about. They know what Lincoln Center is, they know CalArts, and going to CalArts is a *big* deal. They know, they understand all these American or Western phenomena, you know. But they don't understand Indian phenomena, like bharatanatyam. They don't understand. I mean, they do. Probably they block their mind because they just don't want to think about it.

ASAD ZAIDI: See again, the whole question comes around ... is that, is you know—why *this*? And that's why I'm trying to say that the question in itself is, trying to tell us that we have to justify our actions because they do not necessarily fit the mold.

KUMAR: Have you felt like that? Have you felt like you've had to justify this whole process?

ASAD ZAIDI: No, not at all, not at all. They're ... first they are amazed. Second, they have a chance to actually see something new, okay. And the third thing is, it's like, 'Wow! Can it, can [this] actually happen?' But the other thing is that we (*turns to Azra*)—

AZRA ZAIDI: They are very supportive.

ASAD ZAIDI: No, no, no. They are very supportive. But at the same time we have covered our tracks.

KUMAR: Can you explain?

ASAD ZAIDI: This is why this whole *incriminating* question comes into the picture. If we were to tell the community what we are doing, that the girls are going to do this arangetram, bharatanatyam, a Hindu dance. And, if we had not gone through and [taught] them the Koran and having both of those two things, you know ... So they [the community] already have known that these girls have gone through their required fundamental religious traditions. *And* they're doing this [arangetram]. So their criticism perhaps is muted. But at the same time ... but that shouldn't really be the issue. It should never be the issue. (Zaidi et al. 2004)

Asad and Azra are very aware of the construction of identity. *We have covered our tracks*. The community's approval is predicated on the belief that the girls first and foremost are Muslim. Because the girls have performed all the normative activities necessary to firmly establishing this identity, it is okay for Henna and Sana to participate in bharatanatyam. *Their criticism perhaps is muted*. Interestingly, this assumption reveals the performative and pedagogical narrative at work—while 'Muslim religion' identifies who they *are*, the *being-ness* of this identity comes undone once the girls start learning bharatanatyam, at once highlighting its performativity.

Secondly, the Pakistani community's response to the girls learning bharatanatyam as opposed to their continued training in ballet is revealing. Ballet and Lincoln Center are both Western markers of class, utilized by ethnic minorities as racial markers. That is, as Kondo points out in her exposé on the appearance of Japanese avantgarde fashion designers on the international scene, 'For racialized, non-Western subjects, existence commences from the time of introduction to the West' (1997: 127). Engaging in activities such as ballet would presume an acceptance into mainstream upper-middle-class identity, and would be looked upon favorably since this would imply that the girls have 'made it' in U.S. society. Whereas in relation to learning bharatanatyam, Muslim identity is taken as the originary or authentic being of the girls, here, American or mainstream society is the originary source, which the ethnic minority (in this case, Henna and Sana) is expected to imitate. However, this notion falls apart once the girls' parents explain that Henna and Sana are going to Lincoln Center to perform bharatanatyam, not ballet. The *appropriate* ethnic minority identity is destabilized because the replication is not fulfilled in the expected manner.

Replication marks identity at risk Butler asks: '[W]hat if [identity] fails to repeat, or if the very exercise of repetition is redeployed for a very different performative purpose?' (1997: 309). This is clearly depicted in Henna and Sana Zaidi's engagement with the dance.

RE(VIEW)ING INDIA

In many ways, bharatanatyam within the South Asian diaspora parallels the nationalist project that Partha Chatterjee describes in India under British colonial rule (1993). The South Asian bourgeois immigrant readily concedes to the technological superiority of the West, what Chatterjee refers to as 'the material [...,] the domain of the "outside," of the economy and of statecraft, of science and technology' (1993: 6). In fact, such a concession is fundamental to the second wave of South Asian immigrants after the 1960s, since many came to the United States with the hope of actualizing the material promises of the American dream.[7] Yet, while modernization is crucial to the formation of bourgeois identity, there is also an active effort on the part of the conventional South Asian immigrant to resist *complete* Westernization, in this case Americanization, which represents sex, drugs, and rock and roll. In fact, the high value placed on individuality and defiance of authority, customs, and traditions, lends to the perception among South Asians that Americans suffer from a *lack* of culture and spirituality (6).

It is this spiritual realm—characterized by the arts, drama, and literature—that balances out the material acquisitions of the West, that serves to preserve cultural difference, an Indian 'essence' impervious to the dominant culture (this is most evident with Lila Kamhout, a subject to be taken up in the final section). For fear of complete acculturation, immigrant parents see the arts as the standard vehicle for the cultural training of subsequent generations of South Asian American youth whose ties to the homeland are even more tenuous. Why else has bharatanatyam come to serve as *the* quintessential rite of passage among the South Asian bourgeoisie, particularly females, within the diaspora?

For both the immigrant South Asian and the subsequent generations of South Asian Americans born and raised in the United States, bharatanatyam figures crucially in the construction of 'Indianness.' However, it carries different significations for both. That is, for the South Asian immigrant, identity conflict lies more in the development of an 'American' identity since it is not seen as 'natural' as their 'Indian' culture. Bharatanatyam simply strengthens South Asian customs and values that are already present. Yet for the South Asian immigrant's children, who are South Asian *and* American, the struggle lies in building 'Indianness.' In this context, bharatanatyam does not serve to reinforce, but rather to build cultural traditions and traits that are in danger of 'extinction.'

This distinction between the modern (West) and cultural (East) is necessarily gendered. The South Asian female immigrants and South Asian American females who have taken an activist stance within the South Asian community are likely to be considered more 'modern,' thus more Western and anti-South Asian by the community itself (Bhattacharjee 1992; Dasgupta and Dasgupta 1996). This response is not reciprocated in the behavior of the South Asian male immigrant and South Asian American male. In fact, the reverse seems to hold true, where the South Asian male is encouraged to be more assertive and vocal ('modern'), so as to demystify the stereotype of the emasculated Asian man (Dasgupta and Dasgupta 1996).

While in various ways this gendered nationalized discourse holds true within the Shakti Dance School, there are other discursive strands that run counter to and challenge this image of the feminized East and masculine West. This is most evident in the fact that Viji is the primary financial provider for the Prakash household since the dance school and company serve as its sole source of subsistence. However, more than this, Viji's character is quite strong, her presence commanding attention, as one of her students, Sai Patil, remarked. Additionally, Viji's own development of the art form in the United States presents a blurring of the gendered dichotomy between East and West. Her choreography and training is known for its rigour, speed, and intricacy.

I arrived at Viji Aunty's home in Cheviot Hills after I had just returned from a month-long trip to Europe. I had a lot of catching up to do. Summer was Viji Aunty's busiest season. This is when the orchestra from India as well as Ajit, her dance collaborator from Malaysia, visit for three to four months. So she tries to pack in as many programs as possible.

FIG. 29 Viji Prakash (left) as Meera and Lila Kamhour, Viji's first student, as Krishna in *Meera*. Choreographed by Viji Prakash, Long Beach Terrace Theatre, Long Beach, CA, 30 March 1991. (Photo by Kikkeri Prakash)

This summer, of 2003, was particularly intense. *Bhagavad Gita* (2002) was still touring nationally, and the big performance at Lincoln Center was right around the corner. *Prince to Buddha* (2003) was in the works, to be debuted at the Los Angeles County Museum of Art (LACMA) in September. And the weekend I arrived, Viji was taking another production, *Meera* (1988), to Houston. As if this was not enough, she had organized four dance camps for her students, and six students were delivering their arangetrams.

Earlier in the day, while I was on the phone with Viji, trying to get a sense of her schedule, she exclaimed, 'I wake up six in the morning to cook for all the musicians, Ajit, the family, and the students. By ten o'clock I am in the studio and I work until midnight!'

'Don't you think that's insane, Aunty?' I retort.

'No! I love it. I don't consider it work, since it's what I love to do. It's the cooking that I hate. I wish I didn't have to do it.' A typical Viji response.

So there I was in her kitchen, watching as she fixed a quick bite in between rehearsals. Somehow the conversation turned to the topic of kids, and I asked her, 'Aunty, did you ever think of *not* having kids?'

'Never. Once I was married, not having children was not an option. I had to be a mother' (Prakash 2003b).

Little did she know that she'd become the surrogate mother for 200 kids.

Similar to its role in India, bharatanatyam within the South Asian diaspora reproduces a recurring theme within Indian nationalism. That is, it serves as a superior vehicle for the transmission of Indian bourgeois traditions and values. The Indian woman serves as the central figure in this depiction of Indianness (Chatterjea 1993; Mani 1989). 'The woman becomes a metaphor for the purity, the chastity, and the sanctity of the Ancient Spirit that in India [...;] the mythical Indian women' (Bhattacharjee 1992: 30–1). In fact, for the South Asian bourgeois immigrant community, the South Asian American female, trained and cultured in bharatanatyam, becomes the symbol of the community, the mythic model minority.[8] As Anannya Bhattacharjee affirms:

The compelling, and approving image of model minority can be an inducement for building an image of a model India that is commensurate with this minority standing. [...] This is the model that must be constructed and reconstructed. At each moment it is externalized, preserved and celebrated as one might eulogize an ancient artifact. (32)

The model minority is itself a regulatory regime, constructed by the larger dominant culture and internalized by the South Asian bourgeois community. Employed by both parties to govern and construct South Asian identity, it becomes a pedagogical tool, presenting a timeless and homogenous image.

While the South Asian American female dancer is able to successfully utilize the economic opportunities that secure her materially in the American mainstream bourgeois culture, her uniqueness is demonstrated by her ability to resist complete absorption. The cultural domain remains intact (Chatterjea 1993: 130); traditions and spiritual values are reaffirmed by way of her dance training. Through the dancer, Indian identity is preserved, and in her lies the responsibility of passing this identity, complete and timeless, to subsequent generations.

What I find most poignant in the above vignette is Viji's response to marriage and motherhood. A fiercely independent and strong woman, Viji, still firmly gives credence to the traditional roles of wife and mother. According to Viji, an Indian woman will *naturally* get married at some point in her life, and once married, she *must* have children. There is no getting around it. While Viji's response seems at first to be contradictory, Sayanthani Dasgupta, writing on the gendered aspect of the Indian migratory experience to America and the generation of an Indian American community, points out that this is not necessarily the case. Historically, women have played an active, and moreover, integral role within social movements in India, while at the same time fulfilling their traditional duties as wife and mother (Dasgupta and Dasgupta 1996). Chatterjea (1993) analyses how such a construction of Indian middle-class womanhood—strong, educated, activist-oriented, and yet able to maintain the traditional roles of wife and mother—came to be. This fabrication of Indian middle-class womanhood went hand in hand with the intense Indian nationalist projects underway during the late 19th century. In fact, this is the reason why Chatterjea avows that there is a relative absence of gender discrimination in middle-class occupations, or why independent India gave women the right to vote without any major struggle, unlike what is encountered in British or American feminist movements.

Additionally, Dipesh Chakrabarty's discussion of the bourgeois domestic sphere in colonial India (1992: 13) provides helpful insights into understanding this seeming incongruity. In the national elite's understanding and subsequent desire for the construction of a modern self, based on European ideals, 'freedom' because a highly contentious term in the rhetoric for independence and its regulation of the 'modern Indian woman.' That is, freedom became an abstraction that ascertained an 'Indian' self, separate from its colonial oppressor. At the same time, for an Indian woman to be completely free like her British counterpart, she was labeled a *memsahib*, European woman, 'selfish and shameless' (13). Freedom, within the discourse of the Indian national elite, takes on a metaphysical nature, where it figured as freedom from the ego, as fulfillment of one's dharma, or one's moral duty.

Sayanthani Dasgupta recounts her experience:

My upbringing, although quite traditional in many ways, never convinced me that being wife and mother and a social-change agent were oppositional to each other. Although my parents had arranged my marriage when I was sixteen, they had not emphasized only the traditional 'good wife' role to me. I was raised on Mahatma Gandhi's proclamation, 'A woman who does not raise her voice against social injustices is committing injustices herself.' (1996: 387)

Similarly, Dasgupta's daughter Shamita (coauthor of the article), an Indian American born and raised in the United States, writes:

[A]ctivism was not something 'American' to me, nor was it something unique to my mother. I had grown up seeing a strong tradition of women's strength in India: from the mythical ferocity of the warrior goddess Durga to the very formidable presence of the women in my family. While I grew up hearing stories about my great-aunts, who fought and died in the Indian Independence Movement,

I was able to meet in person my grandmother's friends: elderly white-sari-clad ladies who turned out to be Black Belts in Judo, double PhDs, and international language experts. (387)

Both mother and daughter reference Hindu goddesses as one source for role models in their lives, identifying in particular the powerful goddess Shakti (also the name of Viji's dance school and company), the embodiment of female strength and energy.[9] In real life, the *virangana*, or brave warrior woman, reflects this image, personified in woman leaders such as the late Indira Gandhi. In India, viranganas do not occupy a marginal place in society, but instead are regarded with high esteem. However, in the process of migrating to the United States, Dasgupta and Dasgupta argue, the Indian bourgeois immigrant community has silenced such characters in the rewriting of their history and reconstruction of community to bolster the monolithic public image of the model minority:

As second-generation women are expected to be 'chaste' and 'pure', so too are they expected to be 'docile' and 'obedient'. Indeed, most 'second-generation' community members are taught to believe that Indian culture and political activism do not go together. Young women are raised to believe feminism and ultimately, perhaps, women's strength, is anti-Indian. (1996: 386)

While this view might hold some legitimacy, it also runs into the same pitfalls as the generalizing constructions of South Asian American female identity. In other words, in learning bharatanatyam the Shakti dancers are training themselves in the Indian national bourgeois discourse. Yes, they promote an essential and ahistorical notion of India and the model minority, yet, at the same time, they are anything but docile and submissive.

This is most evident in Viji's choreography, which through the years has only increased in pace to an incredible speed and complexity. It is not uncommon for dancers to walk out of class gasping for air and panting for water, tendrils of hair clinging to the sides of their faces and enormous circles of sweat staining the backs of their saris. The *gethu*, a signature piece of Shakti, is 10 minutes of continuous footwork, a choreographic 'conversation' between the dancer's feet and the *mridangam* (percussion) player, the beat increasing in speed and intricacy. Most of her students have attributed Viji's challenging choreography and rigorous training to the development of their own strong and very vocal personalities. One such student is Sai Patil.

Sai is a recent graduate of Stanford University. Through the course of her four years there, she successfully established and led the bharatanatyam dance team, Nupur. The group consists of girls from cities all over the country, each bringing her own unique training and background. While this is exciting because it opens up a space for different interpretations and choreographies, it can also be challenging since a certain level of cohesiveness is also necessary. In order for this to occur, somebody needed to take the lead. Given that Sai initiated the group, it was not surprising that she would assume this role. However, her explanation for this is interesting:

PATIL: At Stanford, I helped organize a bharatanatyam dance group. And though, we didn't mean for it to be this way, it just sort of happened. The Shakti dancers became the leaders. We started to lead the classes, the choreography. The students that didn't learn with Viji Aunty didn't produce exciting choreography. They were slower and couldn't keep up with us. They got tired faster. So we just kind of just took over, though we didn't mean to. (Patil 2003)

When probed further as to why the group dynamics allowed Sai and the other Shakti dancers (Manesha Parik and Asha) to become the leaders, given they had been dancing just as long as the other girls on the team, this was Manesha's and Sai's response:

PARIK: Viji Aunty does a really good job of making us perform a lot. So, we've done annual shows since we were five. And then, recently after finishing our arangetrams we've traveled more and done more shows and tours and stuff like that. And I don't think that everyone here [referring to Nupur] has had that same sort of experience.

PATIL: I think Shakti also has a very forward kind of take-charge attitude in general. [...] Even with a person with a quieter personality everybody is pushed to sort of like speak her mind. Everybody is pushed to do her best, ask questions, say when you don't get something. You know, tell each other when they're doing something wrong, and not take it personally. (Parik and Patel 2004)

Sai is quite emphatic in asserting that Viji and the dance school in particular played a crucial role in developing her identity as a strong, independent, and assertive South Asian American female:

PATIL: When she [Viji] walks into a room, she has no inhibitions. And I think when I was younger I was always intimidated a lot by different situations, where I didn't feel comfortable. I didn't feel like I fit in. And Viji Aunty just has this presence where she walks in, and she's who she is. And you know, if you can't handle that, then that's too bad! (*Sai and Manesha start laughing.*) But I mean, most people love it. Most people admire that, and that's what I try to strive for.
    [...] I think having the leadership be very open, and be very encouraging of open-mindedness, and just speaking your mind, knowing yourself, being blunt, and having opinions—I think that's really important. And that, that played into

the dance a lot because that was a huge forum for us growing up. That was where we developed those skills, you know, because in public schools you're not learning that. I mean, you have to raise your hand. And sometimes the teacher will call on you, and sometimes she won't. Sometimes you get embarrassed if you say the wrong thing.

KUMAR: Do you think that's also growing up Indian? I mean, part of your South Asian identity?

PATIL: Yeah. (*says this immediately and in a very matter-of-fact-tone*) Yeah, yeah, yeah. I think South Asian American girls somehow, in some way are encouraged to be kind of quiet. And encouraged to sort of be the, the modest, soft-spoken girls. And maybe that's a cultural thing. Maybe that's from watching Hindi movies where the girls are like, 'Ha, ha, ha. I don't like you. Ha, ha, ha.' (*The girls laugh.*) They're like all shy. Or, maybe it's just from our moms you know, teaching us don't ... like my mom used to tell me, 'Don't speak in such a deep, loud voice.' Or 'Crunch your cereal less.'

And, it's just little cultural conditioning. I think that having a forum for Indian women who can get together, speak their minds, be blunt with each other, talk about anything, raise their voices if they want to, you know, and still get stuff done, and still learn about their culture, and learn about the past, and learn about themselves. I think that has been extremely meaningful for me. (Parik and Patel 2004)

This dialogue reveals the multiple disciplinary discourses that choreograph Sai's identity as a South Asian American female—the school system (an institution of the dominant social structure), visual media, the South Asian family, and finally, the dance. While the school moulds Sai into an appropriate citizen of the state, Bollywood films and the family are sites for the partial construction of a South Asian female identity. That is, she learns that she must be gentle, docile, and coy—'feminine'. And yet, the practice of bharatanatyam, specifically through Shakti, has cultivated another construction of femininity—poise, independence, assertiveness—that takes after the paradigm of the virangana.

It is evident from these discussions that Viji serves as a prominent role model of strength and assertiveness in many of these girls' lives. Through the course of 15 or more years that a student develops a relationship with her, Viji is no longer simply a teacher. She is a second mother.

Viji and her husband's life history also breaks with the normative South Asian American discourse of 'family,' 'mother,' and 'father' ascribed by the mainstream Indian bourgeois community. Her husband, Kikkeri, attests to this during an interview. 'We just do whatever is necessary for something to get done, whether I do it, or Viji does it, it doesn't matter who does it. That's the philosophy that we have' (Prakash 2004). If their son needs to be picked up from school and Viji is rushing off to teach her class, Kikkeri will perform the task, bringing Adithya home and making sure that he has eaten something, is doing his homework, and practicing his music. While traditionally the man is the 'breadwinner' of the family (or both the man and woman have careers), for the Prakash household, Viji assumes this role and Kikkeri plays a supporting role. More importantly, for a community that primarily establishes its model minority status through the migration of men and women who are highly educated, highly skilled professionals from urban, centres, Viji has achieved material success as an artist. She might uphold Indian immigrant bourgeois ideals and maintain the fable of the model minority of one level, but in other ways Viji distinctly counters such constructions through her own life history as well as through her rendering of bharatanatyam.

Herein lies the *pleasure* in this particular disciplining of the body, the productivity of power (Foucault 1977, 1978). That is, bharatanatyam's scripting of the body inscribes a certain discourse around race, nation, and gender. Yet the highly complex choreography and incredible intensity of Viji's training, her proclivity to perpetually push the limits of what is possible with the dance, herself, and the students, constructs yet another narrative of nation and gender that does not lend itself as easily to the predominant portrayals of South Asian American females. That perhaps, contrary to what Dasgupta and Dasgupta contend, the South Asian bourgeois diaspora has not completely forgotten its strong female characters in its migration to the United States—and its writing of nation, history, and community.

UP(ROOT)ING INDIA

I walk in to NDM Dance Studios,[10] and I am struck by the image in front of me. Viji Aunty sits with her back to a movie poster, most likely a Hindi classic. Her right arm is raised up and her eyes are closed as though she is hailing the Higher Power from above. Her pose beautifully reflects that of the actress in the poster, whose right arm, strapped to a wood pole, is lifted in strength. Her head is thrown back, eyes shut tight. *Mother India* is the film title; the irony is not wasted on me.

Tonight's class is a special treat because Lila will be joining the group. Lila Kamhout is Viji's first student of the Shakti School. They met in 1977 at the Hare Krishna Temple in Venice Beach, where Viji first performed. Enthralled by Viji and the movements, Lila insisted that her dad convince Viji to teach her. Thus the seeds of teaching were planted and today, Viji attributes Lila's persistence as the reason why the Shakti Dance School exists.

Blonde and blue-eyed, Lila disrupts the traditional portrait of the South Indian classical dancer. In fact, one afternoon while reminiscing about the old days, Viji Aunty and Lila laugh over how hard it was to find hair that matched the color of Lila's, which was light brown at the time (a dancer's long hair was achieved by braiding a lengthy piece of fake hair into the dancer's real hair). Back in the '70s, the only fake hair available was jet black to match that of a typical South Asian. Lila had to resort to wearing a wig.

This Tuesday night in January 2004, Lila's two sons are also sitting in on the class. Delighted, Viji Aunty introduces the younger son to the other students, while Lila changes into her dance sari. 'That's Ganasham, you girls. That's Lila's younger son.'

'What's his name?' calls out one of the girls in the group.

'Ganasham, right? They can call you Ganasham?'

His large blue eyes timidly stare back at Viji as his tiny head slowly bobs up and down in approval.

'What's his brother's name?' asks another student.

'Karthakaya ... yeah.' A low murmur of whispers and chuckling makes its way through the group.

'All Indian names,' remarks yet another girl.

Viji replies, 'Oh Lila is more Indian than me or you, included. It's just ... that's how she is.' Just then, Lila emerges from the bathroom, ready in her bright blue sari. She quickly does namaskara and joins the girls on the floor in leg stretches.

In his book, *The Nation and Its Fragments* (1993), Chatterjee critiques the emergence of an Indian nationalist identity and discourse in resistance to colonial rule, which came to affirm the old binaries of the West versus East, modernity and materialism versus the spiritual and mystical. He explicates that it is within the cultural, spiritual domain that creativity reigned; the 'inner' realm was the site where the anticolonial nationalists 'imagined its community'—a "modern" national culture, that is nevertheless not Western' (6). In other words, in matters of material development, the East readily relinquished its agency. However, when it came to cultural traditions and the arts, the East acquired a variety of quite powerful means to preserve its 'inner essence.' The significance of such a project was that it came to form the basis of an Orientalist discourse. However, it the dichotomy between modern and premodern, material and spiritual, West and East that transparent?

The unraveling of these binaries occurs in Kondo's *About Face* (1997), as she teases apart the multiple and concurrent modes of Western

FIG. 30   Lila Kamhout as Drona blessing Viji Prakash, who plays Arjuna, in
Sons of Kunti, L.A. Festival, Wadsworth Theatre, Los Angeles, CA,
September 1990. (Photo by Kikkeri Prakash)

Orientalism, self-Orientalizing and counter-Orientalisms appropriated
by Japanese fashion magazine editors as they construct gendered and
nationalized narratives of Southeast Asia, Kondo poignantly points out
how one particular issue of the fashion magizne, *Ryuko Tsushin*, employs
Western Orientalist discourse in its women's edition, configuring Japanese
identity as female. However, in the edition for men, the counterpart article
reappropriates the East/West binary in Japan's relationship to Southeast
Asia. In other words, 'The men's magazine creates Southeast Asia as the
feminine, exotic Orient submissive to Japan's masculine and [material]
dominance' (85).

Similarly, Savigliano's tracings of the tango in the transnational circuit
paint an intricate nexus of the tango, but more specifically of passion,

repackaged by the first world in the form of 'Exotic Culture' (1995: 2) She traces the tango's global trajectory from its *rioplatense* roots to the Paris cabarets, and finally to Japan. This economy frames the relationship between the colonizer and colonized (in the form of imperialism and neocolonialism), first and third world, core and periphery. Thus, it becomes apparent that even the 'cultural' sphere is not immune to the (neo)colonizer's gaze.

Both of these examples point to how Orientalist discourses continue to circulate and inform geopolitical, transnational, and capitalist mass-consumerist endeavors and identities. At the same time, they also call into question the very binary of the feminized East and masculinized West, blurring the division between an 'inner' and 'outer' domain. Or, what even constitutes an 'inner' and 'outer' domain.

In a transnational context, what happens when Western hegemonic institutions attempt to integrate such aesthetic forms into their very structure? Is not the very dissemination and proliferation of bharatanatyam, an artistic and spiritual expression, mediated through the Western lens? Viji has been a faculty member of the World Arts and Cultures department at UCLA since January 1999. Through the years, South Asians have increasingly become a minority in the racial and ethnic composition of her classes. Her dance company gave a sold-out performance at the prestigious Alice Tully Hall at Lincoln Center in New York City, and she was invited by LACMA to debut to debut her latest production, *Prince to Buddha*, as part of their exhibition The Circle of Bliss: Buddhist Meditational Art (2003). Finally, what about Viji's Caucasian students, such as Lila? Viji proclaims Lila as her best dancer throughout the 25 years of running the Shakti Dance School: 'I have yet to see a dancer perform as well as Lila. To this day I have not seen anyone come even near to her level.' Viji reiterates this time and time again in her classes.

These questions point to the possibility of a blurring between the material and spiritual. In posing the boundaries as more porous, my objective is to collapse the gendered and romanticized image of the masculinized West and the feminized East that Chatterjee's argument ultimately upholds. In other words, if the task is to 'provincialize "Europe"' then, 'It cannot originate from the stance that the reason/science/ universals which help define Europe as the modern are simply "culture-specific" and therefore only belong to the European cultures' (Chatterjee 1993: 20).

The survival of the dominant culture relies on a discourse of difference, constructed through the very consumption and circulation of aesthetic forms from ethnic communities. The label 'classical Indian dance' cements the construction of the ethnic minority through the processes of exoticization and autoexoticization. Both parties objectify the dance, upholding it as a timeless symbol of Indian national identity and tradition. In doing so, the 'material' West and 'spiritual' East dance with one another, each dependent upon the other in defining itself and in assuring the maintenance of power.

This afternoon finds us in the back room of the Dunleer home (Viji's residence), amidst towers of costumes, ornaments, bells and other bharatanatyam 'stuff.' Viji cannot stand these conversations. 'Too much talking. I'll just be rambling.' She likes to *do*. So, Viji folds, unfolds, hangs, rehangs costumes while we chat. Lila and her two sons to her students in the dance class. *Lila is more Indian than me or you.*

KUMAR: What did you mean by that?
(*Viji takes a seat. I can tell she is intrigued. I finally have something interesting for her to talk about. I find myself emboldened.*)

PRAKASH: That's what I mean. She's ... her deference to the art, to the teacher, her respect, her attitude towards learning, to adults to teaching ... very, very respectful, always willing to learn. You know, she would never, she will never, sit down when I'm standing. She'd always make sure there'd be a seat for me, always make sure that some of these little gestures that for us are normal ... Her going to the temple, praying, reading so much about Hindu culture, knowing the stories, so many of the things even I may not know about Krishna, about ... just different things. The innate curiosity, the curiosity about the music, the eating habits, just her natural state of being, being somebody without pretending to be, or making an effort to be. It just comes naturally to her.

[... B]ut I think a lot of it largely has to do with her *samskaras*, her past life. It's a gift, it's a gift that cannot be nurtured in the course of 10, 20, 30 years. I strongly believe these are things that have come from the past. You know, it's a connection from the past, and her step into the future. I feel that. (Prakesh 2004b)

Viji's response epitomizes Orientalist binaries. To be 'Indian' is to acquire deference to the arts, to be spiritually inclined, and uphold characteristics of humility and respect for authority. Thus, there exists an inner being that is exclusive to an essentialized and racialized Indian identity. In fact, the successful personification of an 'Indian' being requires cultivation from past lives, transcending the materiality of an individual's life. The soul remains eternal and permanent; the body is immaterial and performative. This is why Lila, while Caucasian, can be more Indian than Viji or I. Her soul dictates her Indian identity and disciplines the body into 'Indianness.'

Viji's husband Kikkeri's response to my question of 'roots' reveals a similar binary between the material West and spiritual East:

PRAKASH: Roots has nothing to do with the color of your skin. It has everything to do with the beliefs, the thoughts, the ... what your parents have left you [with], and what your environment has given you. Root does not mean you know, an Indian root or an American root. But it means that you're well centered within yourself. So a person is confident about himself, wherever he goes. Whether he's in America, he's in Europe, or he's in the Middle East. He feels well grounded. He feels that he's a person of substance. That's what I mean by roots. Take for an example an Indo-American who doesn't have this background [bharatanatyam training] ... a lot of them get taken up by the so-called 'material' things that the West has to offer, and might get trapped into it much more so than a Westerner might because the Westerner would have some sort of a root, you know, given their religion, church, or this or that background. But an Indian who doesn't connect in this fashion, you know, might get lost. So that's why it's very important to the Indo-American community for their children to be exposed to some kind of art that takes them back to their culture, to where there forefathers came from. So I think in that way, Shakti plays an important role. (Prakash 2004)

Kikkeri sees bharatanatyam as providing the spiritual grounding for those who do not possess such means in their life. Particularly for the South Asian American youth: If they are not actively engaged in the temple or learning Hinduism, then exposure to the arts is absolutely critical. Otherwise, that child will easily fall into the material 'traps' of Westernization. But before we quickly assign Kikkeri's reply as a direct corroboration of the East/West binary, it's a statement that resists such oversimplification; it simultaneously deessentializes an 'Indian root' to race or nationality. *It has nothing to do with the color of your skin. Root does not mean you know, an Indian root or an American root. But it means that you're well-centered within yourself.* And this, he says, is how a Westerner who is more attentive and participatory in the cultural and spiritual activities of Indian culture (as in the case of Lila) can be much more 'rooted' than an Indo-American. The boundaries between the East/West, spiritual/ material, inner/outer, feminine/masculine become more opaque. Kikkeri does not let us off that easily.

APRIL 2003
I arrive at UCLA 15 minutes early this Monday afternoon. I am here to video-record Viji's World Arts and Cultures dance class, where 50 bodies

will pack the dance studio, decked out in their dance saris—a kaleidoscope of bright blues, greens, oranges, reds, and pinks. Under Viji's watchful eye and rigorous orders, they will spend the next two hours twisting, turning, bending, stomping, and of course, sweating.

I enter Studio 304. I am not alone. Meena is already busy wrapping her yellow sari around her waist. I smile, throw out a friendly hello, and quietly assume my seat on the floor in the back of the room. My eyes cannot help but make their way to Meena's corner. She is struggling with her sari.

'One-two-three.'

In and out she folds the cloth, but somehow when she tucks the pleats in the front, the cloth unravels.

'Ugh! How the hell do you do this?!' Meena looks up at me. With a guilty laugh, I immediately respond. 'I am so sorry, but I can't help you. The one time I wore a sari, it was 10 years ago, and my mom did everything for me.'

She smiles in complicity. She knows. We are the 'coconuts' of the community—Indian on the outside, but white on the inside.

Just then, two students enter. I recognize them from our conversation last week—Caitlin and Jessica. Without a moment's pause, I ask the girls, 'Can you guys help Meena because I have absolutely no clue how to wear a sari?'

'Oh sure!' The girls immediately take charge, rewrapping the cloth around Meena's waist. 'This is how you wrap it. And again. This is where you begin the count. Then you tuck in the pleats and wrap it around your shoulder. And, there you are!'

'Ohhhhh, that's how it goes.' Meena exclaims. All three break into laughter. Saved once again, I slip back into my seat on the floor, watching Caitlin as she quickly slips into her own dance sari. Its siren red color sets off the blue of her eyes.

CONCLUSION

While the dance might constitute a primary vehicle for ethnic identification (real and imagined), this narrative reveals that the production of community is anything but cohesive, homogenous, and pure. Rather, my contention is that group identity is founded upon a discourse of difference and divergence that is at all times seeking renegotiation based on its precarious positionings. At time, the stances seem to ply toward totalization and uniformity. Certainly this is one deployment of community. Yet, cultural and social signification is never that easy. These are processes that are derivative of the present; whose very beauty rests in the fleetingness and unpredictability of the moment and the ephemeral boundaries of inclusion versus exclusion. Numerous times, members of this community aggravate and challenge any normative order, and in doing so, elude naturalization of cultural identity (Bhabha 1994). Thus, this is a narrative that also speaks to the choreographing of marginality. It is a project very much invested in 'the creativity of making difference matter' (Tsing 1993: 15). It is a dance.

And it is quite literally the matter of difference that I wish to draw attention to. That is, at the same time that I trace the construction of racialized, nationalized, and gendered bodies through bharatanatyam, I also wish to highlight the dance's sculpting of race, nation, and gender on and within the body. This is a process that requires reiteration and persistence over time, for it is in its fidelity to 'stylized repetition of acts' (Butler 1999: 179) that race, nation, and gender eventually come to be seen as essential and ahistorical—pedagogical. Insofar as such constructs are an idealization—something that by definition can never be reached—and thus are in constant need of repetition, identities remain performative. Subsequently, it is the space between, the liminality of representation and the material, the 'performative and pedagogical' (Bhabha 1994), that characterizes the formation of contemporary identities, identities fraught with partiality, tension, and contradictory movements.

The performance is most transparent among students such as Lila, who stand in stark contrast to the traditional image of the 4,000-year-old South Indian temple dancer with her brown, almond-shaped eyes and long, black hair. Or Aisha and Sasha, who enact the *Ganesha Kautuvam*, the homage to the Hindu elephant god, even though their faith, Islam, proscribes the religious use of ritual figures and choreographed dancing.[11] Through bharatanatyam, each of these students maintains a particular understanding of the narrative of India.

The performative operates more subtly with South Asian American women, who in fact do constitute the majority of Shakti. These women, myself included, are quite emphatic about our identity as South Asian American females, born and raised in the U.S. How and to what degree each individual chooses to engage in her 'South Asian-ness,' 'Indian-ness,' and 'American-ness' varies. For instance, Sai identifies very much with her 'Indianess,' responsible for establishing a bharatanatyam dance team as well as actively engaging in a Hindi (Bollywood) film dance team as an undergraduate at Stanford University. Many weekends are spent watching the latest Bollywood films. Some Sundays, Sai leads a children's discussion group at the local (Hindu) balavihar.

There are others like Viji's daughter, Mythili, who, although she still distinguishes herself as South Asian American, finds the two labels increasingly blurred as she travels back and forth between India and the United States each year. Finally, there are those such as myself, also a first-generation South Asian American, like Sai and Mythili, for whom a sharp demarcation between Indian and American was deeply embedded early on as a child; for whom learning bharatanatyam was punctuated by traumatic moments where I was left feeling alienated and objectified. *The joke sinks in. I am the joke.*

As a result, dissociation from the 'home' land was vigorously sought out and created. Over the course of 18 years, the psychological 'othering' that set in after having been poked fun at manifests itself in the subsequent materialization of a self-inflicted 'othering' from the South Asian diasporic community through a number of embodied practices. In a way, the two scenes can be loosely viewed in a causal manner. That is, in its most simplistic rendering, the second event serves as the consequence of the first event. Almost two decades later, at 25, I am confronted with this self-othering through an event such as what transpired that afternoon at UCLA's Studio 304.

While I am here highlighting the performativity of identity, I am also speaking to dance's *bodily* inscription of race, nation, and gender. Perhaps within the 'nation split within itself,' punctuated by hetereogeneity and multiplicity, an element of the modern must be retained within the postmodern era. For those people who are struggling to claim a voice within the myriad of 'global ethnoscapes' (Appadurai 1996), or for those who have managed to finally etch some kind of footing within the dominant institutions that manage to find ever more creative and subtle means of maintaining its hegemony, the 'strategic' (Spivak 1988) use of the pedagogical might be necessary, in fact essential, to survival.

I return to the dance—movement, flux, exchange, bending, blurring, erratic. Dance loathes stagnation. Like identity. Dance is in the doing, the acting, the *experiencing*. Like identity. So the dance continues, as does identity, shuffling between past and present, performance and pedagogy, signification and corporeality. One does not take precedence over the other, but rather they work with one another, engrossed in their own dance, improvising as they go along.

NOTES

1. For purposes of length, the question of embodiment is not one that I take up in this paper, but explore further in 'Dancing with Shakti; Bharatanatyam and Embodied Performativity within the South Asian Diaspora' (Kumar 2005).

2. See Berlant (1996) in her critical look at what constitutes successful naturalization and 'Americanization' of the immigrant into the proper and law-abiding citizen. Here the state maintains power through a popular discourse centered around desire and longing:

[I]mmigration discourse is a central technology for the reproduction of patriotic nationalism; not just because the immigrant is seen as without a nation or resources and thus is deserving of pity or contempt, but because the immigrant is defined as *someone who desires America*. (413)

Also refer to Rosaldo (1994), where he looks to alternative configurations of the national community 'whose solidarity emerges more from diversity than from homogeneity' (240).

3. See Singh (2000), where she discusses the popular Gadar party (Party of Rebellion), organized and led by Har Dayal in 1913. An overseas, nationlist organization based in San Francisco, the Gadar movement actively worked to mobilize various Indian ethnic groups via widespread publications and armed sedition, against the British rulers in India. It quickly gained momentum among mainstream Asian Indian immigrants along the West Coast of the United States, eventually having strong political impact in India.

Some of Viji's earlier dance events were community benefits that raised money for particular tragedies back in India. For example, she remembers the first big production that she organized was a benefit to raise money for the 1989 Union Carbide tragedy in Bhopal, India.

4. I am applying Judith Butler's discussion of originality versus imitation within the regulatory regime of heterosexuality. However, I am using the dialectic of the nation and ethnic diasporic Identity as the structure of regulation. By arguing that imitation never presents an exact copy of the original, but is rather *parodic*, Butler highlights the very construction of an 'original' (1997: 308–10).

5. Balavihar would be akin to a Hindu Sunday School. Like the dance, balavehar serves as a connection to the homeland. It is primary institution within the diasporic community for the inculcation of Indian culture, spirituality, and strong values. Ras and bhangra are two North Indian popular dance styles. The latter has found incredible pop culture success as a result of its rhythmic incorporation by various hip-hop artists such as Jay-Z and Dr Dre into their songs.

6. Arangetram is the first solo performance by a bharatanatyam, dancer, typically lasting about three hours. Under the *devadasi* system, the arangetram established her as a professional dancer, and officially initiated her into ritual service and performance. In contrast, the arangetram has come to signal the termination of a young girl's or woman's dancing career. It is more to exhibit the many years of rigorous training (O'Shea 2001: 187). For the South Asian female

in the diaspora, the arangetram has in many ways come to be looked at as her rite of passage into the community, her embodiment of traditional Indian culture.

7. South Asian immigration to the United States occurred primarily in two waves, each of which took place in very different contexts and were of different compositions (Leonard 1997). The first phase lasted from the mid-19th century until 1914. Ironically, it consisted of uneducated peasant farmers, primarily males, form the North Indian province of Punjab who settled along the West Coast of the United States. The Immigration Act of 1917, prohibiting the entrance of people from Asia, effectively put an end to the first wave of South Asians to America.

Fifty years later, the Immigration and Naturalization Act of 1965 generated the second wave of immigrants, which continues today. The number of South Asians immigrating to the U.S. continues to increase, with India sending the largest number of immigrants from the region. Immigrants come from all over South Asia (India, Bangladesh, Pakistan, Sri Lanka, Afghanistan, and Nepal), and settle throughout the U.S., though primarily in metropolitan areas. However, unlike their predecessors, the second wave of immigrants is highly educated; highly skilled professionals from urban centers are employed primarily as scientists, engineers, and health professional. The reversal of discriminatory U.S. immigration policies toward Asians was largely driven by the desire to access and commoditize such intellectual capital. On the contrary, the most recent immigrants to the United States, whose arrival began in the early 1990s, are of a lower socioeconomic class. Employed as blue-collar workers in the service and industrial sector, they are having a harder time in the United States.

8. The label 'model minority' has been given to South Asians, as well as other Asian communities living in the United States, to characterize their high educational status and financial prosperity. The implication is that the ideal Asian immigrants and Asian Americans are those who have managed to successfully integrate themselves into a white, mainstream, and bourgeois culture without posing a significant threat to this dominant structure.

9. See Chatterjee (1993) and his discussion of the construction of the middle-class Indian woman by the nationalist project during British colonial rule. As a result of the nationalist elites' new relegation to the middle, questions emerged as how best to safeguard the sanctity of the bourgeoisie Indian woman and at the same time confront the inevitable changes modernity was bringing to the home and family. In response, a new patriarchy developed, legitimized by a discourse that elevated the role of woman as goddess or mother.

10. In response to the explosive success of Bollywood filmmaking as well as a more general interest in South Asian culture (evidenced by a surge of interest in henna art, Indian-inspired jewelry, fabrics, and designs by pop stars such as Madonna and Gwen Stefani, and subsequently by the fashion industry; as well as in mysticism and spirituality, evident in the Indian tone of Madonna's 1998 album, *Ray of Light*), NDM Studios was created specifically for the teaching and practice of a variety of South Asian dance forms, from the classical forms such as bharatanatyam to the more popular *bhangra* style.

11. The Whirling Dervishes are an exception because in this rendering of movement, the dancing is not choreographed. Rather, its purpose is to reach a higher spiritual level through trance.

REFERENCES

Appadurai, Arjun, 1996, *Modernity at Large: Cultural Dimensions of Globalization.* Minneapolis: University of Minnesota Press.

Berlant, Lauren, 1996, 'The Face of America and the State of Emergency', in Cary Nelson and Dilip Parameshwar Gaonkar (eds), *Disciplinarity and Dissent in Cultural Studies*, New York: Routledge, pp. 397–439.

Bhabha, Homi K., 1994, *The Location of Culture*, New York: Routledge.

Bhatt, Chetan, 2001, *Hindu Nationalism: Origins, Ideologies and Modern Myths*, New York: Berg.

Bhattacharjee, Anannya, 1992, 'The Habit of Ex-Nomination: Nation, Woman, and the Indian Immigrant Bourgeoisie', *Public Culture*, 7, 1, pp. 19–43.

Butler, Judith, 1993, *Bodies That Matter: On the Discursive Limits of 'Sex'*, New York: Routledge.

_____, 1997, 'Imitation and Gender Insubordination', in Linda Nicholson (ed.), *The Second Wave: A Reader In Feminist Theory*, New York: Routledge, pp. 300–15.

_____, 1999, *Gender Trouble: Feminism and the Subversion of Identity*, New York: Routledge.

Chakarbarty, Dipesh, 1992, 'Postcoloniality and the Artifice of History: Who Speaks for "Indian" Pasts?' *Representations*, 37, pp. 1–26.

Chakarbarty, Partha, 1993, *The Nation and Its Fragments*, Princeton: Princeton University Press.

Dasgupta, Sayanthani and Shamita D. Dasgupta, 1996, 'Women in Exile: Gender Relations in the Asian Indian Community', in Sunaina Maira and Rajini Srikanth (eds), *Contours of the Heart: South Asians Map North America*, New York: Asian Americans Writers' Workshop, pp. 381–400.

Ebron, Paulla, 2002, *Performing Africa*, Princeton: Princeton University Press.

Foucault, Michel, 1977, *Discipline and Punish: The Birth of the Prison*, New York: Random House.

_____, 1978, *The History of Sexuality: An Introduction, vol. 1*, Robert Hurley (trans.), New York: Random House.

Gupta, Akhil and James Ferguson, 1992, 'Beyond "Culture": Space, Identity, and the Politics of Difference', *Cultural Anthropology*, 7, 1, pp. 6–23

Kondo, Dorinne, 1990, *Crafting Selves: Power, Gender, and Discourses of Identity in a Japanese Workplace*, Chicago: University of Chicago Press.

_____, 1997, *About Face: Performing Race in Fashion and Theater*, New York: Routledge.

Kumar, Anita, 2005, 'Dancing with Shakti: Bharatanatyam and Embodied Performativity within the South Asian Diaspora', MA thesis, University of Southern California.

Leonard, Karen Isaksen, 1997, *The New Americans: The South Asian Americans.* Westport: Greenwood Press.

Lloyd, David, 1994, 'Ethnic Cultures, Minority discourses and the State', in Francis Braker, Peter Hulme, and Margaret Iversen (eds), *Colonial Discourse/Postcolonial Theory*, New York: Manchester University Press, pp. 221–38.

Mani, Lata, 1989, 'Contentious Traditions: The Debate on Sati in Colonial India', in Kumkum Sangari and Sudesh Vaid (eds), *Recasting Women: Essays in Colonial History*, New Delhi: Kali for Women, pp. 88–126.

O'Shea, Janet, 2001, 'At Home in the World: Bharata Natyam's Transnational Traditions', PhD dissertation, University of California, Riverside.

Pandey, Gyanendra, 1992, 'In Defense of the fragment: Writing about Hindu', *Representation*, 37, pp. 27–55.

Parik, Manesha and Sai Patil, 2004, Interview with author, Stanford, CA, 29 May.

Patil, Sai, 28 December 2003, Interview with author, Los Angeles, CA.

Prakash, Kikkeri, 21 October 2004, Interview with author. Los Angeles, CA.

Prakash, Viji, 4 March 2003a, Interview with author. Los Angeles, CA.

_____, 24 July 2003b, Personal conversation with author, Los Angeles, CA.

_____, 16 November 2004a, Interview with author, Los Angeles, CA.

_____, 23 November 2004b, Interview with author, Los Angeles, CA.

Rasaldo, Renato, 1994, 'Social Injustice and National Communities', in Francis Barker, Peter Hulme, and Margaret Iversen (eds), *Colonial Disourse/Postolonial Theory*, New York: Manchester University Press, pp. 239–52.

Savigliano, Marta E., 1995, *Tango and the Political Economy of Passion*, Boulder: Westview Press.

Singh, Jane, 2000, 'The Gadar Party: Political Expression in an Immigrant Community', in Jean Yu-Wen Shen Wu and Min Song (eds), *A Reader: Asian American Studies*, New Brunswick: Rutgers University Press, pp. 35–46.

Spivak, Gayatri C., 1988, 'Can the Subaltern Speak?' in Cary Nelson and Lawrence Grossberg (eds), *Marxism and the Interpretation of Culture*, Urbana: University of Illinois Press, pp. 271–313.

Tsing, Anna Lowenhaupt, 1993, *In the Realm of the Diamond queen: Marginality in an Out-of-the-Way Place*, Princeton: Princeton University Press.

van der Veer, Peter, 1995, 'Introduction: The Diasporic Imagination', in Peter van der Veer (ed.), *Nation and Migration: The Politics of Space in the South Asian Diaspora*, Philadelphia: University of Pennsylvania Press, pp. 1–16.

Zaidi, Asad, Henna Azra, and Sana Zaidi, 28 August 2004, Interview with author, Cerritos, CA.

Part IV

Dancers Speak:
Personal Journeys to and
from Bharatanatyam

Mrinalini Sarabhai

Creations

FOREWORD

Mrinalini Sarabhai, at the opening of *Creations*, writes of the necessity for the dancer to be trained in the body and the mind so the movement itself 'tells the story,' is the conveyor of the wisdom. She adds, it is not enough to merely imitate the technique but that the dancer must experience it, so the dance comes alive through that particular dancer and it becomes a 'living tradition.'

We are all concerned at this time in our ways of working to find an affirmation in life, not to be left with this desolation that pervades so much these days. And in dance, it is the gift of the individual dancer to be submerged into the dance, to give it that unmistakable quality of life that has certainly made the dance in India one of its life-lines, and is, in a small way, beginning to be just that in other parts of the world.

Mrinalini Sarabhai is to be thanked for her perseverance and continuous efforts in its behalf.

Merce Cunningham

MANUSHYA

Creative activity is a presentation in understandable terms of what we are, a picture of man's inner aspirations, joys and sorrows. Artists register not only the world outside in their work, but the deep unknown world inside, farther perhaps than those outer spaces which have already been reached. That is why much of the art today, especially in the Western world, is so frightening that the human being is scared to look. Why is he so scared? Because he sees in it the whole threatening universe around him, the chaos, the cruelty, the desolation that he himself has induced. He seems afraid to look at himself. It is the artist who is the courageous one, who paints what he sees and feels. Yet, if truly creative, he is able to transcend that terrible chaos. Artists have to face challenges with integrity, using every vestige of knowledge, of technique to translate what they perceive into a meaningful entity. They have to see the chaos not only in the context of our times but in a completeness of universal meaning, and to bring to that desolation some affirmation of life.

I can best explain this through my own dance drama *Manushya*, man. It was a child playing with his own reflection, suddenly conscious of the power of his limbs, discovering the 'I' of himself, that struck a deep chord within me. It made me ponder upon life and death, the inner meaning of existence. But life and art are two very different things. They do not use the same vocabulary. The choreographer has to know, to endure, to realize the emotions, yet present them in the language of art.

One begins with basic technique. Each component of a movement has to be analysed in relation to the whole and made purposeful in its particular situation. Then the movement has to be studied in relation to space. A visual impact becomes a contemplative experience and has then to be transformed into a kinetic composition. For example, the first scene in 'Man' is the birth of the child. It is not enough to think of birth in itself, but the meaning of birth in its eternal totality. Man springs from the womb, the centre of the mother, the comfort, the security, the enclosed space. Then there is the detachment when the child is born and the cry of the newly born babe resenting the separation from its home. The cry of the human being for some wholeness in life. Here there is a positive and a negative aspect. All these thoughts must communicate in movement not merely the content but the experience. While preserving an external unity there has to be an internal comprehension, and with the realization, a universal communication in dance.

What are the tools the dancer works with? Primarily, the body. The intellect contemplates, the body expresses. The body has to be perfectly trained in order that the mind can use it whichever way it will. The choreographer evaluates each movement and finds its unique quality, the '*sat*' or essence. Apart from the design, the movement has to integrate an intellectual, physical, emotional response and have a definite motivation. We are familiar with old movements, and most of us unquestioningly accept them. The choreographer does not merely accept a movement but tries to understand and analyse the 'why' of it. It is because teachers have not understood their technique but merely imitated their teachers, mistakes and all, that much of the dance forms in India have lost their purity. Purity is not necessarily 'old' or 'new'. It is a comprehension of the basic vocabulary, an identity with the source, an intuitive wisdom. An incident when I was studying in Tanjavur with Meenakshi Sundaram Pillai, that great doyen of gurus, comes to my mind. A particular step he taught me, my body refused to do. My mind also rejected the 'adavu' as ugly. Finally I requested him to change it, which he did. Three days later he made me sit beside him and asked, 'why did you not like that adavu?' 'I really don't know' I replied. 'My body and mind rejected it strongly.' He looked at me strangely and then chuckled. 'You are a dancer from your last birth' he said. 'That adavu was not for you. I took it from a film I saw. It is not really Bharata Natyam.

Today, students are beginning to enquire into the meaning of each stance and we who teach must be willing to explain. This questioning should be constantly encouraged, for only then is progress based on understanding and knowledge, and not on mere imitation. To explain the 'feel' of the movement and the relation of the limbs to each other from the very first steps of the technique, makes for a conscious rapport, an emotional rhythmic knowledge of the mind and body, in relation to the basic stance. Once the dancer identifies the body with his or her own movement experience, the form becomes an intrinsic part of one's being. From that stability built up in all the years of training is the body controlled. Once the body is mastered, the spiritual energy flows into the movement in an indescribable way, and the dance becomes a living tradition.

When the Rig-Vedic poem, an abstract composition, was presented in Bombay and in Delhi, it created quite a good deal of controversy. I was glad that it had made people think. When Manushya, my first composition, was danced in Delhi, very few understood what it was all about. Today, after more than two thousand performances, it is 'popular' and in great demand. This means that audiences are slowly reacting and understanding.

In a new creation, the choreographer may pick up a small incident, but he expresses it in the unmeasurable qualities of the soul. It has to be given a shape and form that is communicable. If a group of dancers are utilised, then again the design in space has to be consciously symmetrical even when it appears to be disordered. If there is a demand for a positive thought to be brought home, repetition may be used, sometimes symmetry may express meaningfully the ugliness of life. In the last scene of Manushya, man dies and is taken to the burial ground. The lifting, the pacing, the deliberate slowness of movement, the even steps with minute pauses, accentuated the feeling of the death and the peacefulness of it. The soul goes back to where it came from, this time not with the leap and cry of the unborn child as in the opening sequence, but the solemn almost peaceful return of the soul to its own home.

There were several significant experiences that led me to create the dance drama *Manushya*, man. I had mainly been a solo dancer, but the desire to create, to free myself from the basic structure of traditional movements and to present something other than ancient stories, was overwhelming.

The birth of my son Kartikeya made me aware of the magic of the human body and mind, and its constant unfolding. It was he, at five months, who gave me the first inspiration for the dance drama. By this time I had gathered around me a small group of dancers, and was eager to free the highly masculine *Kathakali* technique from its burdensome costume, which, though ornamental and exciting, did not really show the strong beauty of this powerful technique. The dance drama took two years to create, and even after that, underwent many changes.

Dancing is the dancer's search for a true identity through body, mind, and imagination. But in order to dance significantly, the instrument, in this case the human body, has to be trained to perfection. For this, discipline and dedication are absolutely essential, for technique is a means to an end and is used to release the body in order that it might move in perfect harmony.

Composition in dance, as in poetry or music, has to be an inner passion and literally burst out of one's being. While the creation is a mere spark in one's imagination there is a joy and anguish that is hard to describe. It is not like the serenity of waiting for the child to be born, where there is a wonderfully calm acceptance that everything is being taken care of. I can best describe this process of creating a dance drama in the words of young Gujarati poet who said, 'The poem has to write me.'

The outer world during this period seems to have no significance, and communication with others is a burden and a disturbance, even completely superficial. One has to destroy oneself in order to leave room for the knowledge to be made visible. It is a process of opening out one's inner being and searching for the source of the idea to be expressed in movement.

Behind all this, the body is already conditioned with the severe training it has had for years, involving fatigue and frustration, till the moment of complete integration of movement and mind.

The presenting of a new dance drama means not only dancing the theme with dramatic clarity and meaningful simplicity but coping with classical tradition in which the dancer has been nurtured, with philosophy which is part of one's inheritance, symbols which cannot be discarded, with music and with costumes.

The artist has to present an image that can be contemplated for the sheer delight of movement, can be a deep spiritual experience to audience and dancer alike, and suggest endlessly in a rapid succession of changing images the content of the story, in this case, contemporary man and his problems.

MEMORY IS A RAGGED FRAGMENT OF ETERNITY

From villages, from cities, came gruesome accounts of wife burning, women's suicides, and their horrible harassment. Every morning the newspapers highlighted these incidents. I could not sleep or eat. When I shut my eyes, I saw pictures of innumerable women, with empty eyes, beseeching me to tell their stories. The village well, so beautiful a symbol of gay chatting togetherness, was now an invitation of death.

Deep within me voices murmured demanding an answer. There was an anguish within me, devouring me, and only dance could set it free. Patterns trembled in the skyspace wanting to be born, but too much grief is not part of creativity so I waited till the sadness passed and a detachment was made possible. Suddenly the patterns became clear and the women of Saurashtra whose death haunted me, became women of the world.

A woman gets married. From that moment, she is in an alien country, uprooted, alienated from her family, filled with a loneliness that cannot be told, surrounded by strange faces, often, faces of hostility. No man ever fully understands this situation, however kind or loving he is. All these thoughts flowed through my mind and then slowly *Memory is a ragged fragment of Eternity* came alive.

The design begins with the childhood of a young girl. The classical elements of Bharata Natyam remain, like the playing of ball, the flying of kites, the innocence of childhood joy. The music in basic ragas stresses the beginning of life. The wedding scene is danced by the two characters who portray the friends of the girl, and later, her in-laws and society in general. The girl, is snatched away in the midst of her games and play, to be married. She is excited and delighted with the man and her new home. But he leaves her to go to work in the fields and the disrupting forces ignite the sparks of violence. The *sollukathu*s of Bharata Natyam, the rhythmic syllables, became alive for I infused them with expressiveness and stressed the powerful rhythm of each beat. The hatred, the greed, the jealousy are brought out in forceful movement and desperation and sorrow in the accented syllables.

The young woman realises her plight. She gives away her ornaments, everything she wears, but she is still an outsider, whatever she does is suspect. Closer and closer come the crowds. She tries to flee but they are in pursuit. Once they even entice her by drawing her into their circle, but this is only to catch her unawares. Finally she can bear it no longer and kills herself, jumping into the well with her tiny child. The crowd shrugs, smiles and moves away.

Dancing *Memory* I was overwhelmed by my own loneliness and the loneliness of all people everywhere, all over the world. While the idea started as an obsession—and all my obsessions come out in dance—the theme was really a cry from the heart for understanding.

Every stranger since has become my own.

Every sorrow mine.

Every hardship I feel with my own self.

Yet it is joy that I want to give in dance.

Shobana Jeyasingh

Getting Off the Orient Express

An important part of the history of Bharatha Natyam in the west is the methods and avenues through which the westerner has striven to understand and respond to it. During the time of Uday Shankar and Ram Gopal in the earlier decades of this century, the general public, with some notable exceptions, flocked to see them as exponents of oriental or Hindu dancing and both these dancers were commercial successes presented by leading impresarios in big theatres. In the case of Uday Shankar, a young art student in London, Anna Pavlova had a greater influence on him as a dancer than any classical Indian technique and yet he was seen as 'the authentic voice of India speaking directly and immediately to us from 5000 centuries of civilisation'.

The irony was, of course, that five thousand centuries of civilisation notwithstanding a few hundred years of colonial rule had, with other factors, brought about the demise of the classical technique through the alienation of the educated Indian from his fine arts and through the gradual erosion of the traditional sources of patronage—the court and the temple. And even as this review of Shankar was written in 1934 the fate of the dance in India seemed to be in the balance. It was still to be finally decided whether the Victorian social reformers (both Indian and English), who wanted the traditional community of dancers attached to the temples to be disbanded, would triumph or whether the dance was to be rescued from its old setting and rehabilitated in the new centres of power, the cities of India. The two sides had locked horns in the press and a great war of words was in progress. The classical technique was largely available only through a few members of the old world of dancers and their teacher/choreographers who had to be systematically sought out. The dance itself waited to be given the stamp of general social approbation including a change of name. In this process of rehabilitation Rukmini Devi, the Indian wife of a leading English theosophist, was to play a dramatic part. In 1934 she was yet to see the Bharatha Natyam recital that would take her away from performing bits of *Swan Lake* under the banyan trees of the theosophical centre in Madras to becoming a dedicated pioneer in bringing about the large scale accessibility of the dance in India.

When the rehabilitation of the classical technique finally got underway it judged Shankar harshly: 'Uday Shankar's dance, considered as some king of dance, was tolerable. But considered as Indian dance, as Bharatha Natya ... it was absolutely unconvincing except for the costume, the décor and the music' (K. Seshagiri in *Sound and Shadow*). 'Were Uday Shankar to stay in India for a few years and put himself to systematic training under a master ... (he) would not have striven in vain' (Ganadasa in the *Journal of Indian Renaissance*).

What K. Seshagiri failed to appreciate, apart from Shankar's genius for innovation and contemporary truth, was that in that magical place 'the Orient', a place invented by the west for its own amusement, costume, décor and music were very much of the essence. Here, 'virtuosity was in the tremor of an eyelid' (*New York Herald Tribune*) and 'where there was nothing more arduous than gathering flowers, nothing more troublesome than bees, nothing more frightening than the "the sound of approaching footsteps"' (*The Sunday Times*). Indeed a journey through its enchanted terrain provides countless diversions as in this description of its dance: 'The movement of the oriental dance is concentric. The knees almost instinctively come together and bend, the curved arms embrace the body. Everything is pulled together. Everything converges'. (Andre Levinson quoted by Alistair Macaulay in *Dance Theatre Journal*). This movement is noteworthy for its striking contrast to the turned out openness of Bharatha Natyam, and the stateliness of Kathak.

The post war immigration of Asian people into Britain was the earliest death knell for 'The Orient'. When the doe-eyed damsel moves into the semi next door she loses that most exotic of qualities—distance. And as the natives pondered on how best to assimilate these 'natives', Bharatha Natyam, through a semantic somersault, became one of the 'ethnic' dances of Britain. Its separateness became the key to its understanding. 'Orientalist' gave way to the incessant clamour of 'What does it mean?' of the ethnicists, as Indian classical dance, forsaken by the impresarios of the Shankar/Gopal era, did its round of the smaller regional arts centres. Bharatha Natyam came to be valued chiefly as an example of its culture and religion and Bharatha Natyam dancers came to be valued as race relation officers, cultural ambassadors, experts in multiculturalism, anthropological exhibits—everything save as dance technicians. The general belief was that the dance itself could not be appreciated without a detailed study of the Hindu pantheon together with the proper decoding of the innumerable hieroglyphic hand gestures and eye-movements. Here they were probably helped along the road by those who saw the parading of seemingly obscure cultural and religious appendages as a measure of the dance's complexity and richness of heritage.

While it is undoubtedly true that a major influence in the formation of the dance was temple ritual (the others were court life and secular theatre), what is often overlooked is the totally different definition of religious activity that the west has. Here religious dance is strictly liturgical dancing where integrity of emotion takes dominance over exhibition of technique. In India, where to be religious in no way presupposes a rejection of the secular or indeed the sensual (as exemplified in Khajuraho), religious dance has no limitations. In Britain, however, the same term denies the dance not only the lively debate, the abundance of new choreography, the backstage rivalries that characterise the dance scene in India but, more importantly, it denies the central role that technique plays in the dance and it obscures the fact that for the best part of the last sixty years, Bharatha Natyam has been seen, like any other performance art, on the theatre stage.

The other danger that the ethnicists court in the constant quest for explanations is to make the dance nothing more than the sum of its literal meaning. As any opera-goer would agree, an ignorance of the language is no impediment to the enjoyment of the music. Similarly, the 'meaning' of the ballet *Swan Lake* does not rest with the acting out of the story nor is that the ultimate aim of the production. What is more significant is that the choice of stories from myth and legend illuminate the kind of truth that the dance addresses and which its technique serves. What motivates the ballet-goer is not the blow-by-blow account of the plot nor the literal understanding of its mime but, quite simply, the dance itself.

Similarly, Bharatha Natyam is about dance, and the most pertinent quality of that dance is its classicism. This seemingly simple truth is yet one of the hardest to convey. The word itself has to be divested of its total Eurocentric bias before one can go along this more fruitful avenue of understanding. The *Oxford English Dictionary* firmly points towards Greece and Rome in its definitions of classicism. The organisation of material in dance books, the thinking behind the dance syllabus in educations institutions, the programming of dance festivals and the presentation of dance in the media, all derive from a categorisation that sees Dance with a capital D divided into classical (ballet), contemporary (western), social, folk and ethnic. This is tantamount to dividing mankind under the headings European urban, European rural, Travellers and World Tribes. Internationalism in dance matters, more often than not, is a nod across the Atlantic. This subconscious evaluation was tellingly brought home to me in an interview for an important dance appointment where I was a member of the interviewing panel. Asked how the candidate regarded South Asian dance, his reply was that he himself had the highest regard for central European folk dance. Pressed further on classical dance he felt that the basis of all dance was ballet. As for classical dances from another culture the idea seemed to cause him genuine puzzlement.

The word 'classical' first and foremost implies a particular relationship with the past. It is a gracious acceptance of the past as a refining process and though one can in the present carry on that process, it is done essentially in reference and in deference to what has gone on before. Classicism is often associated with certain golden periods of history where the ground rules were laid down, its aesthetic principles, manners and style are still associated with that art form. In ballet it is possible to see not only the Greek and Roman ideal of the human form but also the manners of the great European courts. Similarly, Bharatha Natyam is the product of both the pan-Indian, Sanskrit culture which produced the *Natya Sastra*. (The handbook for theatrical productions in AD 400) and the cultural achievements of the court at Tanjore in South India in the eighteenth and nineteenth centuries.

BHARATHA NATYAM TECHNIQUE

One of the features of the past history of Bharatha Natyam was the careful recording of it for future use in teaching and performance. The carvings of the dance poses in the great social and academic centres of those times, the temples, recorded in great detail the technical features of the dance. The numerous books and treatises dedicated to analysis of form, to the creation of an appropriate terminology, and to methodical codification of steps bear witness to the high esteem in which the correct rendering of technique was held. Indeed, a major role of the dance was to display the technique for its own sake as *Nritta*. *Nritya* on the other hand was the technique, together with stylised facial mime, in the service of drama.

The basis for the Bharatha Natyam technique is the perception of the human body as a geometric ideal both in its static position (pictured as the straight axis around which a circle could be drawn) and its articulation through the dance (which explores all the harmonious geometric shapes possible from the central axis within the circle). Kapila Vatsyayan in her admirable book *The Square and the Circle of the Indian Arts* discusses fully how this geometric ideal not only connects all the classical Indian art forms from music to architecture, but in fact is the expression of the fundamental belief in Hinduism regarding the relationship of man to the universe.

The *Natya-arambha* (the beginning of dance) position shows the body lowered along the central axis of the circle and divided along it through the *arai mandi* or demi plié. By so doing it creates a series of three equilateral triangles in space. (See diagram.)

To create this image the dancer has to centre the body by pulling in the stomach and pulling up the upper torso. There is a feeling of growing taller and expanding: this forms the base line of triangle 1. To create triangle 2, turn out from the hips is essential since without this the base line of the second triangle will not be legible. The depth of the plié is crucial if there is to be harmony between triangles 2 and 3. These three triangles form the Bharatha Natyam body picture and are the ideal that the dancing body aims for and which the classical sculptures show us. In post-colonial times the achievement of this uncompromising ideal is made harder by the fact that while the dance itself has been successfully rejuvenated, we still need to retrieve that systematic body training which alone could have made those athletic temple poses possible.

When the body moves from the natya-arambha position it does so through four foot positions. Unlike ballet, the demi plié of Bharatha Natyam is not an intermediary position from which the body moves. The

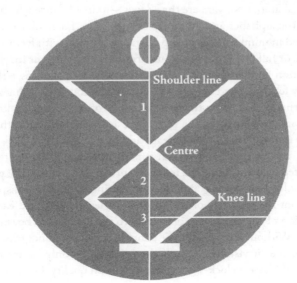

Indian technique demands a muscular consolidation of this position by allowing the weight of the lower body to 'earth' it. The arms in Natya-arambha in a semicircular shape peculiar to Bharatha Nataym create a three-dimensional effect to the circle and trace its curve.

A discussion of this primary position of the dance will not be complete without some indication of the philosophy or emotion that this technique implies. The placing of the body with the turnout and pulled up torso has the quality of openness and extreme stylisation in movement. Its relations to space is confident and secure and by virtue of its abstract quality it engenders a feeling of objective pleasure. There is a special quality to the pleasure that comes from technical achievements governed by strict rules where the achievements are ends in themselves. The rules of Bharatha Natyam Nritta, by referring to purely geometric ideals, make it also a totally objective dance.

As befits a dance where expression equals the physical expression of the technique, the training process is devoted to shaping the body to suit the dance. One could almost call it an indoctrination. This may sound mechanical and uncreative but what Arnold Haskell says about the pirouette and the fouetté could equally well be applied to the steps of Bharatha Natyam. 'These ... are the musical notes, limited in number, in themselves nothing. The effect depends on how they are combined and executed. It is this classicism that is helping the dancer to express herself, that leaves her so gloriously free, if only she is big enough'. The 'musical notes' in Bharatha Natyam are the *adavus*—units of dance which contain in them the alphabet and grammar of the dance. Each adavu (and they are limited in number) is made up of stance (vertical with feet in parallel, demi plié or full plié), foot positions, arm lines and patterns for the hand. In execution an adavu usually spans 6 or 8 beats, produces a rhythmic phrase by footbeats and requires the eyes to give focus to the lines created by the arms by following them. The corpus of adavus deal with all the movements possible including those that are static and those that allow the body to travel together with leaps and turns.

The nature of Bharatha Natyam Nritta can be understood and appreciated by considering the following principles; *Clarity*. The principle of '*angasuddha*' or correct and clean rendering of line is indispensable. Apart from the legibility of the three triangles as discussed earlier, the progression of the arms from one shape to the next has to be committed and firm. Without angasuddha the dance literally would not exist for that is what makes it visible. *Grace*. If there was to be only clarity then the dance would have a clock-work and mechanical quality. *Lasya* or grace is the vehicle through which Bharatha Natyam's obsession with strong line is presented to the audience and the tension between the abstract and the physical is resolved. *Vigour.* As a dynamic, lasya is seen as a complement to *tandava* or vigour. It points towards the strength and speed especially of footwork in the execution of the characteristic fast rhythms of the dance. *Precision*, or *tala suddha.* This principle is linked to the special relationship that Bharatha Natyam has to time. Through footwork it is possible to pattern time in such a minute and detailed way that on one level the dance is the percussive structure of the music. It is no accident that even the smallest joint in the body contributes to the movement; the neck joint and the wrist are all used to add percussive detail. Precision is at its most exciting when linked to speed and all adavus are therefore practised in three tempos. Speed is also a test of centredness because while the limbs move, angasuddha or clarity can only be maintained if equilibrium and control is there in the centre. This quality of effortlessness, which is the communication of the quiet centre, is much sought after.

The choreographer of Bharatha Natyam Nritta approaches his/her material very much as a ballet choreographer does. His or her artistry is seen in the imaginative combining of the adavus into *korvai*s (literally an enchantment) and the changes he can ring within the received corpus of steps. The choreography is governed by principles of symmetry (for example, movements started on the right followed by movements to the left) and harmony (the arithmetical progression of rhythm). The fact that it follows the compositional rules of classical music heightens the formal and abstract quality of its structure. The display of virtuosity is often a built-in feature and traditional choreography gives ample scope for polished articulation of the technique at speed. Such passages are recognised and applauded by the audience just as happens in a ballet performance.

A rigorous definition of the salient features of Bharatha Natyam Nritta (and for the purposes of this article I have not dealt with nritya or mime) does not necessarily consign it to a dance museum. Periods of conservation such as that immediately preceding and following India's independence are just as necessary as periods of development. The greatest strength of a classical dance lies in its objectivity when faced with the continuous flux of historical change. It alone has the tenacity to speak with confidence to the present without turning its back on the past.

Chandralekha

Reflections on New Directions in Indian Dance

One of the crucial experiences that shaped my response and attitude to dance was during my very first public dance recital (*arangetram*) in 1952. It was a charity programme in aid of the Rayalseema Drought Relief Fund. I was dancing 'Mathura Nagarilo', depicting the river Yamuna, the water-play of *sakhi*s, the sensuality, the luxuriance, and abundance of water. Suddenly, I froze, with the realization that I was portraying all this profusion of water in the context of a drought. I remembered photographs in the newspapers of cracked earth, of long, winding queues of people waiting for water with little tins in hand. Here, Guru Ellappa was singing 'Mathura Nagarilo'. Art and life seemed to be in conflict. The paradox was stunning. For that split second I was divided, fragmented into two people.

Through the years this experience has lived with me and I have not been able to resolve the contradiction which, of course, is a social one. On the one hand, a great love for all that is rich and nourishing in our culture and, on the other, the need to contribute positive energies towards changing the harsh realities of life. For me, to be able to respond to the realities of life is as crucial as to remain alive and tuned to sensuality and cultural wealth. I have struggled to harmonize, to integrate these diverging directions in order to remain sensitive and whole.

Being inheritors of colonial structures and institutions of education, language, liberal values, and maybe even notions of aesthetics, we cannot overlook the mediation of the West in shaping our approach to our traditional arts. Problems of revivalism, nostalgia, purity, exclusiveness, conservation, preservation, need to be examined. There is a tendency to swing between the polarities of rejecting the West to seek the security of our little islands, or of accepting the West at the cost of a wealth of traditions and without any attempt to try and listen to what they have to tell us.

Such conflict stems from a lack of consciousness and an inability to comprehend the central and basic issues which, ultimately, are connected with integrated and humanized existence on our planet. The East in order to be 'contemporary' would have to understand and express the East in its own terms; to explore to the full the linkages generated by valid interdisciplinary principles common to all arts and central to the creative concept of *rasa*; to extend the frontiers of the loaded cultural language of our soil.

I see dance as a visual, tactile, and sensual language, structured with a specific vocabulary and idiom, with a space/time, with organic bind, principles, and most importantly, related to the dynamics of energy and flow with a capacity to recharge human beings. The internal relation between the dance and the dancer and the external relation between dance and society are questions that cannot be taken lightly.

First of all, dance is an expression of physicality. In the course of human evolution, for a long time, physicality was a communal possession to be collectively expressed. The remnants of tribal societies show the basic unity of material life and physical expression. So we start from the fundamental premise that dance does not originate from heaven, that it has a material base, that it is rooted in the soil, the region, the community, in usages, work rhythms, habits and behaviour, food patterns, and social relations and in racial characteristics like nose, skin, eyes, hair—a whole lot of accumulations that go by the name of culture, and intimately related to body attitudes, physiognomy, and to work and tools. Even in its most stylized form, dance retains a certain universality of idiom and is an extension of and a supplement to spoken language.

The history of dance, then, cannot be separated from the history of the various stages of society. The variations in form are like variations in soil, climate, trees, vegetation. Over a long period of time, however, dance along with other arts and social functions, became integrated into the evolving hierarchical structures of society effecting a transformation in its role—from communal participation to communal consumption.

The codification of dance in a society that admitted a hierarchical structure introduced a process of rigidification in the roles of the performer and the spectator, propelling classical dance and dancers towards limiting, though exotic, specialisation and to a fossilisation of the form. Increasingly, the dances became a class preserve expressing an ideological content.

However, through all the distortions of the medieval period, the body retained a certain primacy and sensuality and played a vital role in maintaining human dignity in spite of much privation. It is when we come

FIG. 31   In *Sri*, Chandralekha choreographs a vision for the future. An iconic
vision of woman who is auspicious, beautiful, luminous, and empowered;
with multiple hands, multiple capacities, energies; a *dashabhuja*—
with ten hands—who can change all space, who can charge all space.
Photograph: Dashrath Patel

to contemporary times and an industrial/urban society that a sudden and harsh break occurs. The vital link, between body and nature, body and work, body and ritual, snaps. Dance becomes, almost totally, a spectacle.

A reversal too, takes place. While traditional thought conceptualises the human body as a unique centre, a centre of the universe, expanding outwards into the cosmos, industrial society converts the human body into the prime target of attack: as citizen, attacked by the political system; as consumer, attacked by the economic system; as individual, bombarded by the media, denied contact with nature, incapable of self-renewal, suffocated by poisons in air and water, isolated and deprived of directions for change.

The question then arises: What role can dance play in such a society? Can it recuperate energies? Can it initiate a living flow between individual and community? Can it integrate human perspectives? Can it infuse people with joy for life, radical optimism, hope, courage, and vision to negate all that is ugly, unjust, and hurtful? If our life is alienated, can our dances and arts help to transcend that alienation?

I have experienced dance as a sensual language of beauty and of essential freedom; a language of coordination as against alienation; a movement towards the human essence, the sap, the vitality, the *rasa*. It is this aspect of classical dance and its unflagging potential to regenerate the human spirit that constitutes for me its *contemporaneity* and the reason why we need to work with the form. Any human mode with a capacity to touch, to energise, to transform is potent. Otherwise art is primarily to be lived. It is nothing but the quality of all that is made.

Besides several negative features in the prevailing dance situation like spectacular mindlessness, archaic social values, faked religiosity, idealisation leading to mortification of the form, numbing sentimentality, literalism, verbalism, dependence on *sahitya*, on word, mystification and dollification, perpetuation of anti-women values, cynicism within the solo dance situation and its senseless competitiveness, there are also more serious questions: Why have classical Indian dance become so insular and unresponsive to the dramatic social, historical, scientific, human changes that have occurred in the world around us over the past forty years? What blocks and complexes prevent classical dancers from initiating basic changes? What makes them resistant to contemporary progressive social values? Why is it that even purely formal exercises and experiments have eluded these forms? Why have not attempts been encouraged to explore the power and strength of these forms, as for example, their links with martial arts?

At the same time, the criteria the parameters, the references, the directions for what constitutes 'new' and 'contemporary' in the realm of classical dance is a sensitive area and there can be no easy formulae and solutions. I believe one can make only one small step at a time with feeling and sincerity. The principles of wholeness and relatedness that form the core of traditional thought are the most relevant for us today. Through these we get some idea of the directions for a fresh search, questions of perceptual and creative levels, exchange and transmission, movement and control, art and experience, tradition and modernity, inner and outer, space and time, individual and collective, integrity and rupture, quantity and quality.

With my root and training in a classical dance form like Bharata Natyam, with its ancient lineage and formal purity, I had to contend with several contradictions inherent in working within 'traditional' form in a contemporary context.

I have increasingly been disturbed by current Western critical opinion which so effortlessly glamorises and valorizes Eastern 'traditions' in an uncritical manner entirely from an 'orientalist' and patronizing perspective. For us, in our Eastern contexts, both our 'traditionality' and our 'modernity' are complex and problematic areas which are not abstract theoretical categories but real every day concerns—both of life and of performing arts.

If our so-called 'traditions' are largely superficial post-colonial 'inventions' which subsume genuine experience and accumulation of the past, with its treasure-house of complex and holistic concepts of body/energy/aesthetics, then our so-called 'modernity' has turned out to be a movement that privileged the 'bourgeois' self, enabling an elite aesthetic to distort and de-eroticize the real and the liberating energies of the body. Those of us engaged in a battle for 'recovery' in several artistic and intellectual fields, therefore, find ourselves simultaneously battling on two fronts, often tending to get isolated and marginalized by national and international markets, by official state policy, and dominant cultural constructs.

If someone like me battles on regardless, it is entirely because of the pleasure I derive on the one hand from knocking the narrow-mindedness and vested interests, both at the national and international level and, on the other, from a real vision of the full blooming of a form that, I am convinced, can make a difference to the way we are looking at ourselves.

FIG. 32   A sequence from *Angika* choreographed by Chandralekha. This work grew out of a concern for what is happening to the human body in our times. Through this work Chandralekha explored the physical traditions like Kalaripayattu, the martial art of Kerala and its relation with the dance, revealing integral relationships between principles of work, ritual, performing, eating, and healing practices, indicating the tight unity of their dynamic structures and common origins. Photograph: Dashrath Patel

In our contexts, I believe dance is a 'project' that would enable a recovery of the body, of our spine, which for me, is a metaphor for freedom. Dance, for me, is not spectacle, or entertainment, or virtuosity.

It is not about seduction or titillation or loaded effects or exotic representations. For me, it is all about evoking human energy and dignity in an increasingly brutalising environment. Working with—and making a departure from—the exclusive classicism of Bharata Natyam, therefore, the questions before me have been: how to explore, expand, universalize the form; how to comprehend its inherent energy content; how to see it in relation to other allied physical disciplines in India—like yoga, ancient

FIG. 33   A sequence from *Mahakal*, choreographed by Chandralekha. She observes: The dance of Time danced by Timelessness, Mahakal goes beyond linear notions of time, linked to tea, to clock and calendars and ultimate countdown to death. It celebrates the multiple and cyclic notions of time in indigenous cultures. Photograph: Rafeeq Ellias

martial arts, and allied life activity with its investment in physical labour; how to interpret the purity of the Bharata Natyam line; its principles of balance and flexion; its body geometry of squares, circles, triangles, coils, curves; how to visualize this body-geometry in terms of space-geometry— the inner/outer correspondence; how to slash across the dead weight of the 'past' suffocating dance in the name of 'tradition'; how to pare dance of its feudal and religious acculturations, sticking like unhealthy patinas to the form, as also from the increasing pressure on it of the demands of the commercial market.

There are more questions: how to understand dance as a language in its own right, self-sufficient and with a vocabulary of its own—so as to free it from the tedious god/goddess narratives and staged religiosity, to give it a secular space of its own; how to demystify its content, which reinforces nostalgia and revivalism, promotes esoteric self-indulgence, and idealizes a deep woman content; how to recover and celebrate its abstract content of space and time; how to initiate and consolidate the conjunctions between our traditional forms and our contemporary concerns.

Any work with dance, therefore, in my context, involves engaging with the body and its primitive accumulations, its social complexes, its cultural stratifications. The 'content' of the body is vast and complex. There are no limited or fragmented concepts of the body in indigenous cultures. Here, the body is seen as a unity—with respect to itself as well as the society and the cosmos. Neither specific parts of the body nor physical systems are seen in isolation. For example, the traditional martial art form Kalaripayattu, with its swift leaps and spinal stretches, is integral with a scientific understanding of secretive points in the body—such as *marmas* and *chakras*. An ability to hurt presumes an ability to heal.

In this cosmology, the arts and sciences, too, are interdependent and richly cross-referenced. Dance, music, architecture, sculpture, yoga, medicine, martial arts, linguistics, grammar, are not isolated and mutually exclusive. This is the larger meaning of 'tradition'—to be integral, to be whole. Once this is understood, it is not 'tradition' we will need to break as much as the conditions that create isolation, exclusivity, specialization, competition. It is binary categories which promote narrow beliefs and linearity, against the joys of a world-view and curvature, that we need to break.

So, with all its contradictions, conflicts, tensions, splits, and ruptures, tradition, for me, is not a museum piece or fossil form, hermetically sealed forever, which precludes ideation, commentary, questioning, critique. I see tradition as open and fluid in terms of our times, in interactive relation with the past, accepting as well as foregrounding the tensions and disjunctions. This is the only way to locate tradition here and now—as a prerequisite for renewal of our energies at the level of our everyday life.

The issue, for me, is not 'tradition' versus 'modernity'. I do not see them as two different things. The task of the artist is to modernize the tradition through the creative process.

Not transplanting, borrowing, imitating, or becoming a 'shadow culture' of some other culture. It has to be an inward journey into one's own self; a journey constantly relating, refining the reality of the in-between area; to enable tradition to flow free in our contemporary life.

Ananya Chatterjea

Raga and Sloka

Troubling Femininity

The anti-terrorism bill has just been passed, exposing the violent authoritarian premises of the democratic regime we live in, with its sanctioned systems of surveillance and punishment. Meanwhile, women's groups like RAWA have warned us repeatedly that life under a government formed by the Northern Alliance or any other political group, may not be that different for the women in Afghanistan unless models of power and governance are changed dramatically. Yet, despite many claims of 'saving' the Afghan women, one of the justifications of the war, no attention has been or will be paid to their needs as articulated by them, or to their resistances. This is entirely logical: very similar notions of power are at work here; power is entirely identified with military aggression and assault.

The events of 11 September 2001, burned into our consciousnesses the realisation that notions of power are more than ever inalienably entangled in notions of masculinity. In its incarnation in a context riddled with fundamentalisms, terrorism, and counter-attack agendas, masculinity is all about brutish notions of maleness, and it is articulated through shows of military strength, threats to 'pulverize' and 'crush,' and exhortations to blood revenge. Here, the paradigm of maleness is almost exclusively bloodthirsty and destructive, and almost eclipses other ways of conceiving powerful behaviour. Concomitantly, femininity has come to occupy a space signifying weakness, at the receiving end of male use, just like the women in Taliban-ruled areas of Afghanistan are, in ignorance, supposed to be: veiled and submissive. Recall, for instance, this statement by an army general from Pakistan, published in an interview by Tariq Ali in *The Nation*: 'Pakistan was the condom the American needed to enter Afghanistan ... We've served our purpose and they think we can be just flushed down the toilet.' Of course, the outrage and anger the speaker feels at being used and discarded by the United States makes him see both

Pakistan, facilitating male, or American, penetration, and Afghanistan, the site of entry, as trapped in a helplessly feminine position, penetrated and perhaps raped. These mappings of volatile political situations in gendered and sexualized terms are dangerous in many ways: I draw attention to them only to point to the widespread crass and polarized understandings of masculinity and femininity generated by such rhetoric.

It is in this context I have come to value Chandralekha's work even more, especially the alternative notion of femininity that has long been a central concern in her work. *Raga* and *Sloka* in particular focus on a complex notion of femininity, and envision a world beyond compartmentalized gender distinctions that dominate contemporary configurations of identity and identification. In *Raga*, subtitled 'In Search of Femininity,' and where femininity is explored primarily by and in the bodies of men, and in *Sloka* as well, where the feminine is danced as the power of fertility and play, Chandralekha seems to be urging more complicated and less reified conceptualizations of masculine and feminine as energies and principles, not necessarily coincident with bodies marked male and female. In these two pieces, specifically, she wanted to explore the potential richness of the concept of femininity without ever romanticizing or sentimentalizing the experience of womanhood. Interestingly, while these works were often misread as emanating from 'Western influence' and as being explorations of homoeroticism only, research will show that for her, this notion of femininity stems from beliefs and practices indigenous to her cultural context, and has been a long-standing concern with her. However, while this is a theme running through most of her work, it is with *Raga* that she names it explicitly as the principle of femininity, and focuses primarily on its articulations through bodies marked as male.

Interestingly, *Raga*, and to a lesser extent *Sloka*, have attracted the most criticism from the media and audiences in recent years. That notions of femininity have been hijacked by crass commercialization—whether it comes in the form of anatomically incorrect Barbie dolls, or the smiles on the faces of women who, in airline advertisements, welcome us to luxurious vacations in 'exotic' lands—is obvious. So, no doubt, Chandralekha's revisioning of femininity as powerful life-energy would shift the frame of reference. But when I attended the U.S. premiere of this piece at Brooklyn Academy of Music in November 1998, for instance, I was taken aback at what seemed to be the very different reaction of a normally appreciative and progressive audience at this left-oriented space. After talking to several audience members picked randomly, I could only attribute the fact that several individuals had walked out during the performance of *Raga* to a central premise in this book: that Western audiences and critics often reject in the context of 'other' cultures what seems 'radical' in white/Western performance contexts, whether in terms of 'excess' or as replicating what seems to be the exclusive possession of the Western avant-garde.

Chandralekha's focus was on femininity, but her work read as homoerotic. Further, neither did it create strong images of woman-power/ Shakti, nor could it be read primarily as innovations in Bharatanatyam, which seemed to have been a prime expectation of the audience, and both of which have some popular currency in the world now. This of course within the limits approved by a hegemony-driven marketplace. Indeed, critics here who had applauded her previous works, and appreciated the manipulations of the Bharatanatyam form and the powerful female imagery in the context of South Asian cultural traditions, found this work problematic. Of course, critics in India too misread the work, because of its plethora of homoerotic images, as being Western influenced. Interestingly, *Sloka*, which reverses the arrangement of scenes in *Raga* and flanks the no doubt shorter sections of homoeroticism with women-centered sections, was much more widely accepted. Certainly, it was applauded widely in a performance in Bangalore, India (2000), which I attended. It also ran to packed houses in Osaka, Japan (2000), where the work was presented as a collaborative piece with sets created by celebrated visual artist, Hiroshi Teshigahara.

In surveying these different reactions, one has to wonder about expectations specific sets of audiences have about specific artists, expectations that are obviously affected by racial, ethnic, or national identities. Performance that reads as homoerotic and associates men with femininity is likely to be problematic with mainly conservative audiences. This is obviously not the case with audiences in New York or most other North American metropolises, where there is a history of performance work focusing on alternative sexualities, the kind of work still rare in contemporary India. Detested by mainstream critics as the 'gay Kamasutra,' *Raga* still sparked lively audience debates in India. On the other hand, progressive audiences at BAM, who were somewhat familiar with Chandralekha's work, found it difficult to fit *Raga* within the realm of their expectations. Anna Kisselgoff, for instance, who reviewed the work for the *New York Times*, deplored the work and its 'bare-chested' male dancers: in particular, she was offended by the lack of 'poetry' when 'one man hugs the other's rump.' Had she thought about is, though, she might have realized that this image was an exploration in profile of the *lingam-yoni* theme that recurs in Chandralekha's work, one that brilliantly resituated the erotic symbol. And of course, male bare-chestedness is no novelty, either in the American dance scene or the Indian one, so one wonders what the objection was about.

In this context, it is interesting that many scholars and activists from the third world have critiqued their Western/white counterparts for claiming homosexuality as *their* radical resistance to the institutionalization of sexuality, and as a movement spearheaded and led by Euro-Americans. At any rate, while the images in these pieces can be read indubitably as homoerotic, they cannot be separated from the avowed intention of the choreographer, or from the entire fabric of the piece: the question, for instance, that is more meaningful to ask in this context seems to me to be, how do these images of homoeroticism read in the context of and in relation to the performance of femininity and fertility? It is interesting that a most progressive colleague, whom I respect a great deal, remarked to me that it was probably the slow unfolding of the piece that was difficult for audiences, not the homoeroticism. Of course, I had pointed out already that the slow unfolding, a typical feature of Chandralekha's work, had been acceptable to North American audiences in other pieces like *Sri*, *Yantra*, and *Mahakal* (1995). But the slow elaboration of movement that read as homoerotic on the bodies of two South Asian men, the physical intimacy of movements drawn from Kalari massage sessions blending into erotic explorations, seemed too much.

In another rather problematic statement by Kisselgoff she faults the two men with not seeming professional dancers like the rest of the cast. It has precisely been the point of Chandralekha's work for a long time that physical disciplines like Kalari and yoga are deeply and historically connected to the dance and share understanding of the body and principles of movement. So while the two men are not indeed professional dancers, they are well-known practitioners of Kalari, no less professional than the dancers, and why that differentiation would matter so much in a nontraditional performance space such as BAM is still baffling to me. It is because of the widespread misreadings of the piece and problematic commentaries on it by leading dance critics that I want to offer another perspective on these works.

As a prologue to *Raga*, Chandralekha quotes the tenth-century poet from South India, Devara Dasamayya: 'If they see breasts and long hair coming, they call it woman, and if they see beard and whiskers, they call it man. But look, the sprit that hovers in between is neither man, nor woman.' Interestingly, the choreography inspired by this comment about superficial ways of marking gender through overt bodily characteristics alone seems to invoke a power that is not-neither-man-nor-woman, but rather, that is man and woman at once. This both-ness, this refusal to subscribe to sharp binaries, creates a productive ambivalence that, by virtue of allowing for multiple locations, makes for greater agency. Possibilities and choices, with their associations of openings and new spaces, are integral to this concept of femininity.

At any rate, for Chandralekha, one of the most adequate ways to metaphorise her concept of femininity is through the principle of curvature, both in movement line and energy. She refers, for instance, to the Hindu concept of *pradakshina* that characterizes the moment of a devotee's encounter with the symbol of divinity. The devotee's line of vision is important here because, of course, the devotee is always inscribed in the feminine space, constantly reaching toward what she desires. It is never enough to view the image of the deity frontally only: one must walk around the shrine several times, encounter the image from various angles and perceive different aspects of the same symbol as that circular pathway is traced and retraced. Curvature is also intimately connected to life, for it rounds away to make room for itself. This concept is juxtaposed with the enduring and basic concept of the 'geometry of the body' in her work, and her idea that the dancing body in the cultural traditions of India is primarily a 'continuous sequence of squares, circles, triangles, forming, dissolving, and blending ...' In this exploration of femininity through the geometric articulation of curvature and circularity, clarity of line is interwoven with its mobility. Both *Raga* and *Sloka* are marked by dancers creating overlapping curves through footwork, weaving in and out among each other, or perhaps standing in a circle and learning their torsos sideways toward each other and then curving them back up toward the other side, marking figures-of-eight with the chest.

Interestingly, Chandralekha's concept of femininity is resonant with tantric beliefs and even pre- and early Vedic practices of goddess worship. Talking about the varied ways in which feminine energy has been conceptualized in early Indian rural cultures, Pupul Jayakar writes about the concept of the goddess, the symbol of ultimate and ideal femininity:

The body of the goddess was a geometric abstraction as well as color. The appearance of the circle, the double-spiral, the cross, the square, the triangle, the svastika and the mystical diagram, constructed of an amalgam of mathematical figures, at the site of the Indus Valley and in the cave art of India, establishes an ancient worship of the female divinity in the form of hieroglyphs and simple geometric forms. Associations of the sacred feminine principle with pictorial abstraction are so deeply embedded in the Indian unconscious that the anthropomorphic form of the goddess never replaces the diagram, but continues to co-exist with it through the centuries.

This is similar to the way the goddess-sign is conceptualized in Tantra: through the alchemy of colour, sound, and geometric form that Jayakar also talks about. Indeed, the iconic imaging of the feminine principle in terms of verisimilitude with the human female body is certainly a later and often problematic development, deployed often to support the heteropatriarchal structuring of society. The setting up of a tradition of goddess-worship where goddess is invariably mother, and where feminine energy comes to be equated with nurturing, caring, and protecting, often functions in reactionary ways to subvert the very feminine energy that was to be adored, conflating women's sexualities with reproduction and their inevitable roles as self-sacrificing mothers.

At any rate, there is also evidence of other perspectives, that the overt symbols of such feminine power, female bodies, in fact often emanate this life force. Several ancient Hindu, and specifically tantric, texts such as the *Soundarya Lahari* tell us about the life-giving touch of different parts of the woman's body: the touch of her heel is supposed to send the Asoka tree into blossom, for instance. Vidya Dehejia, talking about the rich and erotic female iconography on the walls of temple sculptures in much traditional Hindu art, points out how female bodies and feminine energy had traditionally been regarded as markers of auspiciousness and hence necessarily present in places of public worship, not as objects of the male artist's and patron's gaze, but as an integral part of a symbolic and aesthetic framework. There is no doubt that there are associations of the female body and energy with possibilities of growth and fertility in traditional literature and art. In *Raga* and *Sloka*, however, Chandralekha avoids a dangerous coalescence of femininity with energies 'naturally' found in female bodies. Instead, she works through abstract ideals of femininity as the creative principle that is necessary to energize the world to emphasize its deeply spiritual moving force. It is in the translation of early abstract notions of feminine power and its representative forms, from ideas to real bodies, from stilled images to moving and living articulations, extending and reformulating ideas that she had explored in *Yantra* for instance, that Chandralekha renegotiates their contemporary relevance, and both secularizes and broadens current understandings of femininity.

In *Raga* the first two scenes are almost exclusively danced by women. In fact, the long middle section of the piece is bracketed off by shorter segments where the women, almost as if earth spirits, move with slow deliberation along the surface of the ground. As lights come up to the tapping of stones, pattering time in clear measures, we see three women sitting cross-legged on the floor, their heads bent over. In slow time, they come to sit straight up, then reach their spines down to the floor and curve their butts over, extending the legs beyond their heads, their toes touching the ground, in *halasana*, continuously in canon. As their legs move outward and then back in, they begin to raise themselves to sitting once again. The backdrop now begins to come alive—a large cylinder of bright red light, created by visual artist Anish Kapoor—illuminating the women before it in a different hue. As the piece progresses, this seemingly phallic shape is resymbolized through its association with colour, light, and the performance of a feminine sensibility. Having thus set the tone for this search for femininity, the women now herald its awakening.

Three women run in, diagonally to the upstage left corner, their hands in *alapadma*, arms stretched out in front as if in beckoning, gazes fixed in the direction of the corner at which they have arrived. The music of the flute, long strains as if eking out the melody, fills the space as one woman enters from that corner which they have charged into life, bearing a long dry leaf flaming at one end, wide and deep *mandalas* carrying her into the space. The flame is in front of her as she turns with it, performs a series of kalarippayattu leg swings and extensions, and leans forward charging the flame to coax into life energies that are as yet beyond the realm of the visible. The three women emphasize this invocation with flat step-forced arch foot rhythms, *tei tei didi tei*, remarking that diagonal line they had etched on the stage earlier. The mobile flame, carried by the woman, infuses the space with palpable forces as she dances with it, reminding us of the intimate relationship of heat with energy and flow. The moving flame in the hands of the woman who seems as if to coax life into being with the long sweeping lines of her arms, is in fact sensuous, as it undercuts the neat lines of her movement with its waving and somewhat unruly existence. Here fire, too is resignified: its associations with sanctifying functions, celebrated in Indian rituals, specifically in Vedic and Hindu religious or cultural practices, are undercut and overlaid with more secular notions of energy and moving force.

One man runs in, carrying another across his chest and shoulders in the wake of their exit. Gently, he lowers this other man down in a bridge position on the floor. They fold into each other and end up lying in a long line across the front surface of the stage, parallel to the audience, head to head. Their chests arch up to look at each other, one leg swirls up and then around, below the other leg, dipping the body close to the floor and up. This series of movements, repeated in different ways, establishes their presence on stage, two bodies interacting, recognising, focused on each other. For the first time, they now come to look directly at each other, and the space is filled with a woman's voice weaving classical melodies, and intensifying the concentration on stage. As the men turn their heads, look at the audience, and then return their gazes to each other, the women enter from the upstage right corner. Their goddess-like presence is heightened by the *varabhaya mudra*, images of blessedness, as they look at the men, turn and turn again, and then leave whence they had come. The articulation of femininity is now foregrounded as these two men move slowly across each other's bodies, exploring lines and energy circuits intersected occasionally with a different look of femininity as the women enter, comment on the men absorbed in their discovery of self and other.

From this moment until the end of the piece, the men never leave the stage, intent on weaving their own world. At one point, one, Sunny, stands facing the side, feet and hips parallel, knees bent, and elbows folding in from above his shoulders to hold his head. His partner Shaji stands before him and with calm purpose, flattened palms, traces the contours of his body, the curve in the spine, the long line of the torso, then he turns around and traces the rounded line of his butt, all the way down his legs to his feet. His hands now flatten on the floor, and from this squatting position, Shaji quickly flips his body up to hook his feet onto Sunny's shoulders, while his hands grip Sunny's ankles. The latter then encircles the other's hips with his arms, and curves down his upper body to behold Shaji's face, while the latter curves up his head and torso as if to catch and return that look. As Shaji returns to verticality, they stand facing each other. With a quick flick of one leg typical to the Kalarippayattu style, they sit with their butts resting slightly on their upraised heels, legs turned out, one knee touching the ground, the other up, arms out to rest the palms on the knees. From here they slip their legs under themselves easily so that they lie on the floor on their fronts, their torsos arching up close against each other, supported by their arms. They take a moment to look intently at each other before they raise their butts high off the ground and loop their sloping legs in and out to weave a network of energies linking floor to air, as they move their bodies together, in perfect harmony and ease.

Into this self-focused world, where the one and the other draw cocooning movements around themselves, which dissolve even as they are being formed to mark overlapping circles, of exploration, there are occasional interruptive possibilities, specifically in the form of the entry of the women. They run into spaces demarcated by the men, intercutting them with sharp rhythmic footwork patterns, often jumping in between the two male bodies on the floor as they travel diagonally across the space. They pause in the downstage left corner to look at the men, who are undeterred in their focus on each other, and fixing their gazes on the men, they step downstage, leaning over the bodies of the men as they pass by them. At one point, Meera runs in, easing herself in between the men. She jumps into the square made by their intertwined shins, beating a quick succession of steps *digi-digi-digi-digi* on the balls of her feet, and then quickly folds her knees under to sit, inserting herself into that space between. From this space, she reaches out to relate to both men, leaning her head on one's shoulders to gaze at the other, even while they continue to move in relation to each other. At times, she is integrated into their world, such as this where their interactions create intersecting lines and relationships, and there are other moments of non-absorption, where her quick-moving, playful and naughty energy is oppositional and antithetical to their slowly curving movement.

Thus, even while the main focus of this piece is on the exploration of feminine energy through the curvilinear and un-bound yet precise lines of kalarippayattu, embodied by the men, there are constant reminders that femininity, which to Chandralekha is in fact about sensuality and the flow of life-energy, is also not a fixed 'look' or form, but about many manifestations of the same force. There are also moments when the men take on the sharper, faster, occasionally more martial movements of Kalarippayattu, chasing Meera with the crocodile walk, which is a series of jumps with the horizontal body held in a close parallel to the ground with the toes and palms in a push-up position, so much so that she ultimately leaves the space. This aggressive accent is also seen momentarily in the last moments of the men's movement sequence, where they simulate the attack and defense movement patterns of Kalarippayattu. And what seems impossible to absorb into the idea of femininity so long explored, acts as foil to make stronger by contrast.

What is significant here is the unlatching of philosophy from biology in a necessary and concomitant relationship, the de-essentialised understanding of femininity. If femininity signifies life force, that which enables creativity, the philosophy of curvature, the energy of play, it is not anchored to female bodies, but inherent in all bodies. Neither is it articulated through movements typically indicative of female behaviour, but rather through a wide range of movement qualitatively invoking these characteristics. What is also then integral to this understanding of femininity is fertility, understood as creative life force, not to be associated with ovarian or reproductive fertility. The intertwining of femininity with fertility in fact comes to signify the movement of life-energies toward the fulfillment of their own potential. Thus, while *Sloka* continues to explore femininity through male bodies, extending the thematic concerns of *Raga*, it also links it immediately to themes of fertility and the awakening of vital forces in female bodies. Moreover, *Sloka* continues in different ways to interweave the sense of play inaugurated in *Raga* with the auspicious energy of the feminine principle.

I want to refer briefly to the version of *Sloka* reworked by Chandralekha in a collaborative venture with visual artist, Hiroshi Teshigahara, and performed primarily in Japan. The artist created an uniquely beautiful set with green bamboo: a bamboo curtain downstage, running from stage left to the middle, another upstage, running from stage right corner to center, and a tunnel made from filings of the bark of the bamboo center stage. The pre-performance lighting scheme, created by Sadanand Menon, lit the bamboo tunnel set in center stage in rotating looks of ice and fire: one emphasized the cool green of the bamboo with an emphasis on blue, the other emphasized the full roundness of the tunnel shape with an emphasis on the ambers. The dancers and musicians interacted with the set constantly, weaving in and out of the bamboo curtains, running through the tunnel, highlighting both the theme of play and the theme of fertility and life-energies. The bamboo stalks swayed as the dancers moved through them and musicians tapped on them with their drumsticks, the loose ends of bamboo sheaves on the tunnel trembled with the wind caused by dancers' quick entrances and exits. The greenness of the bamboo, the inherent mobility of the set on stage, the suggestion of birthing in the shape of the tunnel, all emphasized the themes of Chandralekha's work.

Sloka begins with a half-hour-long scene mesmerising in its slow and deliberate performance of eroticism if we understand the erotic in the sense of Audre Lorde, as power, as that movement which facilitates the realization of our sensuous potential. Chandralekha's allusion to 'hidden secrets in our bodies' in her introduction to the piece is no doubt somewhat problematic in the way it mystifies and renders esoteric the concepts that inspire the piece. Perhaps it is more helpful to read the statements as referring to ideas that were once important in the cultural framework but have been suppressed as an increasingly intense patriarchal organization of society became systemic. Certainly the poetic and metaphoric conceptualizations of the body as in yogic and tantric visualizations of nerve centers as spiraled chakras and of life force as *kundalini shakti*, the coiled snake, seem to exist primarily as specialized knowledge that has to be discovered, though their piecemeal and commercialized popularity as exotic Eastern kitsch in the Western cultural marketplace might suggest otherwise. That such references to the tremendous creative potential of feminine energy and sexuality should come to be suppressed in patriarchal contexts that seek inevitably to weaken the inherent power of our sensuous and sexual processes and render out bodies docile is of course not surprising. This first act of *Sloka* then recalls such ideas through movement rich in metaphoric images and tensile energy, incredibly patient in phrasing, seeming to stretch the very boundaries of time and space without large overt physicalities.

Against a soundscape of Caranatic Ragas sung intermittently by Soundaram Krishnan, we see a woman, Padmini Chettur, sitting on the ground. Silhouetted in the dark, the soles of her feet are together, her head bent close to the floor. The increasing lights discover her slowly raising her head and upper body. Rising onto the balls of her feet, sitting on her haunches, she turns in her hips parallel to each other. As one knee places itself on the ground before her, the other lengthens out behind her and curves up behind her head. A series of quick swings in and out with that leg. Ultimately she comes to sit, her butt on the floor, legs in parallel, feet in front of her. Slowly, her arms reach out and her fingers clasp the big toes of either foot, raise from the floor to bring her body to a V-shape on the floor, and then open the legs outward to either side. As the arms lower to the floor, the legs come down as well to seat the body in a wide 'second position.' Now, hands in *pataka*, the arms circle around the body and create a series of *lingam-yoni mudras*, gestures signifying creativity and fertility, close to the chest. Now the pataka hands join above the head to open into alapadma, that symbol of the thousand-petalled lotus, the *sahasrara chakra*, that lies dormant as the topmost *chakra* in our nervous system, waiting to be energized into blossom and ultimate knowledge by the kundalini shakti, the lowest energy center lying at the bottom of the spinal column, in the sacral area. The alapadma rotates around itself so that the turning wrist ultimately pulls the left elbow in, flexing in front of the face. The movements flow in an uncompromising *vilambit laya*, committed to fulfilling every line in the time and space that it seems to ask for. The slowness of the energy evokes curvature, but though the process of performing the movement has only roundedness, the consummation of moving lines marks itself through geometricized positions that often have angular edges.

Now, the hands are in pataka, and one slides in front of the other as the figures open wide creating the image of an opening, as a prologue for an awakening of potent spaces within the body, particularly those energy centers lying along the spine. The left elbow flexes up to face the hand, in pataka, forward. The right hand in *mukula*, symbol of a bud, rich in potential, rises from the ground along the surface of the body, and finding itself before the left palm, sprouts energetically into alapadma. The hands now come to the eyes, invoking vision, as the fingers cross into *kartarimukha* and trace the line of the open eyes. The eyes respond: the irises shift, carrying the gaze to the right, then to the left, up and then down; they flutter like the flame of a lamp that heralds are arousal of the goddess spirit; they circle around, energizing all direction within the lines of sight. Now the palms are together in the *matsya mudra*, the gesture of the fish, a traditional symbol of female sexuality, swimming down the chest to curve up. Now the arms, lifted above the head, curve the head, curve backward to arch the torso and head to the floor. The arms come up, the hands in *yoni mudra*, to mark the chest, the stomach, and then dissolve into another sequence.

As she dances, this woman remarks the body through images that unravel the porous, sensory body: the salutation to the sun, the bow, the opening flower, the trident with the first and third fingers on the two eyes, and the middle finger on the 'third' eye, that center of nervous and spiritual energy. This scene reads interestingly against the traditional representation of sexual play in much Indian classical performance, where the woman often describes the nail and teeth marks left on her body by her lover. Interestingly, the inversion of this also exists in some rare instances in folk and devotional literature, where the woman, in the intensity of her passion and desire, marks her lover's body. In the first scene of *Sloka*, however, the erotic marking of the woman's body is performed very differently, rewriting notions of eroticism, sensuality, desire, and pleasure as they are inscribed in the process of mapping the flow of feminine forces. Here, the autoerotic modality of this self-focused exploration in the search for femininity casts the body as the realm of energies that, once tapped, will generate pleasure, sexual and sensual power, life, and more energy. Further, in this search, the common hierarchical encoding of the body, where the feet are regarded as lower than the rest of the body, closest to the dust, is destabilized, for the erotic energy stretches from the toes to the brain and travels through the pores of the body as it extends, rotates, and encircles it. sexuality, in this understanding, is integral to the flowing energy of femininity that energizes the entire body as erogenous zones, instead of being understood only in relationship to the sex act and specific related body parts.

As she rises slowly and comes to stand in a wide mandala, her hands now curve around on her breasts in alapadma gestures, and open out to either side of her body. Two men run in from either side swiftly and place themselves close beside her, standing in the 'fish-tail' balance where the raised leg extends out sideways from the now composite image of the three bodies: the woman in center, her arms out to the side, her hands in *alapadma*; the men on either side, their bodies partly behind her, their chins in the hands that cup up and out wards as they open into the *mudra*, as if sprouting from her. As her arms extend out, the heads travel along to mark a semicircular pathway around them. She turns her head to return the look of the each of the men one by one, deliberate in their mutual beholding. Then lowering her arms, she circles her wrists and drops them into *dolahasta*, the gesture that is often seen on the image of Siva Nataraja as he dancers in bliss or *ananda*, and then raises her arms above her head. Meanwhile the men ritually mark the four directions of the space with the typical sequence of movements that are used to invoke the sacred energies of a space in which Kalarippayattu is to be practiced. With a jump, Padmini widens her stance to stand in a deep and wide mandala facing back this time, her arms out to either side, her hands in *shikhara mudra*, signifying, among other things, the *lingam* or the phallus. Now the men mobilized by the momentum of the large torso circles they have just drawn, slide their bodies onto the floor smoothly. Through the folds of her sari, from between her legs, we see the heads of the men emerge as they arch their torsos up from the floor. This image reminds of Chandralekha's idea in *Yantra* that 'Men come from women's bodies,' but as in that context, it invokes neither associations of motherhood nor sentimental notions of woman as prime reproductive force. Rather, in this context, we sense the immediate association of life force with the feminine principle, energies, movements, lines that confirm the flow of life, and metaphors of its tremendous power to generate life. We also see the mobilising of the inner space of the mandala as it is intersected by these bodies that emerge from it.

The scene ends as the men lock arms under Padmini's mandala as if to form a seat on which she can sit. They lift her up to carry her forward, then back, and then finally run off the stage with her. Padmini is certainly here the operative sign of the feminine. The image reminds of the cultural practice of *bhashan*, common in the state of Bengal, where the goddess-spirit is called into an image created of clay and straw at the auspicious time of her worship. The goddess is invoked and adored, and then, at the end of the festival season, her image is immersed in water, where the sign of the divine dissolves into its constituent materialities and the stuff of our myths, and is washed along by the waters of the river. This kind of practice is much more typical of ceremonies of goddess worship than in the worship of male deities, though of course, Bengal is well-known for its strong tradition of *devi-puja* or goddess worship. This journey, carrying the goddess, is most significant: it is a time when the 'feminine energy' is deeply manifest as much in the devotees, who participate in this recycling of energy and life-energy, as in the goddess-spirit.

There is also another moment of significance here. While devotees generally circumambulate the spaces where the deities are installed, these icons themselves sometimes repeat this gesture of the mobilized gaze. Local traditions often decree that deities be carried in procession from their seat in the temple or shrine to specific locations, generally within city limits. These processions, occasions of great sociocultural significance, are also mostly associated with the periodic reenactments of specific mythologies, more often than not linked to the ritual death and rebirth of the divinity. The dynamism of the deity allows for openings in the apparently structured space of the temple. Moreover, it mobilises the gaze that beholds the devotee and, in the beholding, blesses many at the same time. Journeys and processionals, then, are of deep ritual significance in this cultural framework. Disallowing the ossification of sacredness in defined spaces, and replaying the endless drama of life, death, and rebirth ritualistically, they can be argued as suggesting understandings of divinity as feminised, characterised by movement and, unlike immanent godheads, subject to the cyclical energies of life.

In charting images for a viable contemporary vision of femininity, Chandralekha repeatedly refers to local customs and ideas that surround religious practice or operate in the realm of, or invoke dimensions of life that are larger-than-the-ordinary. Interestingly, she has always referred to alternative or at least lesser-known practices in her cultural framework, those that stand at a distance from what has been endorsed as Tradition. But it is in translating these images from a divine context to a human one, placing primacy on the female principle, and negotiating their relevance in contemporary notion of femininity, which is routed through the body in all its sexual and sensual richness, that she secularizes and radicalizes them. Briefly tracing the genealogy of this idea of femininity ultimately helps to illuminate the specific context and relevance of pieces like *Raga* and *Sloka*.

For Chandralekha, the linking of this search for femininity with the process of self-realisation, and its conceptualization as the force that invigorates the realisation of the full potential of the self, has been part of a long search. Years ago, she collaborated with filmmaker G. Aravindan in making a film entitled *Sahaja* to be shown at the Women's Exhibition in Moscow in 1986. In particular, Chandralekha created the script for the film and also played an important role in the process of making it. The term *Sahaja* thought refers to the particular philosophy of the Bauls, followers of a wandering folk-religious group, known to advocate their philosophy through singing and dancing. In Sahaja and some other schools of thought in India, such as Tantra, the principle of femininity is revered as the ultimate route to salvation. Discussing this idea in the context of several Bhakti or devotional texts in India, Chandralekha emphasised that this is not to be understood as an advocacy of the equality of the two sexes, but rather as the primacy of the feminine mode of being, historically understood as the primary principle found in nature, humanity, and all manifestations of life: 'The man prays to god to reveal the feminine in him so that be can be the undifferentiated, undivided being. He prays to god to take away the maleness from him so he can be *prakriti*, realise the principle of nature in himself.' In Tantra texts too, the man cries as he struggles to realise the nature of the female in him. Again, celebrating typical *bhakti* thought, Meerabai, the devotee queen, wrote many songs where all human beings are seen as Radha, forever yearning union with her lover-god, while divinity is seen as Krishna. In the Gaudiya and the Sakhi *bhava* sects of the Vaishnavaite devotional practice, male devotees identifying with the *gopinis*, cowherdesses who adore Krishna, is particularly common. Femininity is thus also a positioning, a force that carries the individual toward an embodied awakening and leads to an opening into self-realization.

To return to *Sahaja* the film: Here Chandralekha wanted to explore the ways in which the notion of femininity enriches traditional Indian performance, with particular reference to *abhinaya* or expressive modes of classical performance. Generally, in this mode, the performer focuses on becoming, as opposed to being, which might be understood as naturalistic and logistic verisimilitude, and the project offered Chandralekha opportunities of witnessing and documenting master performers and gurus, males taking on female roles in the course of narrating a particular story, a strong tradition in Indian classical performance. She linked this performance of femininity with the concept of the *ardhanarishwara*, the male-female Shiva-Shakti intertwined deity. This however, proved annoying to the then minister of culture, who felt his manhood threatened by these implications of femininity and insisted that the film be withdrawn from the exhibition. Interestingly, the ardhanarishwara figure, danced by an exponent of the Mayurbhanj Chhau style, occasionally marking his way across the stage with the typically curvilinear movements of this styles of dancing, had been part of *Raga* initially. But, by her own admission, Chandralekha felt ambiguous about his place in the highly metaphoric choreography and felt it was more a concession to her harsh critics rather than her own design, and edited these sections later.

It seems that while the feminine is generally celebrated in and as aspects of pre-colonial cultural production, the notion comes to be crystalised into a dominant characteristic inherent in some idea of Indianness, later, in contact with 'other' cultures, particularly from the West. It is in fact with Western theorisings of Indian culture and religion that we begin to see how femininity, used as a distinction governing the relationality of East and West, comes to stand in for difference. It is also when the philosophical and spiritual dimensions of femininity are eclipsed and it is collapsed into negative associations, where attributes previously celebrated are constructed in terms of lack. Here, femininity becomes the modus operandi of racialization and enables and structures relations of power in the colonial state. Annapurana Garimella, tracing the history of the reception in Indian art in the Western imagination, shows that with the beginning of Indology, we see a growing discomfort with this emphasis on the feminine, the necessarily embodied spirituality, and on the multiple centres of divine energy. Western scholars like Hegel, Mill, and Cunningham, seeking to comprehend Indian and specifically Hindu art and religion through the grand organizing concepts of western aesthetics and philosophy, found Hindu art to be predominantly effeminate, lacking the masculine categories of rational thought, and concluded that India's racial consciousness was essentially feminine.

The project of Indian nationalism took up this line of thinking, similarly choosing to be embarrassed by the lush female iconography and the feminized mode of knowing in Hindu thought, particularly with its emphasis on *maya* or play and illusion as creative principle. Earlier thought systems and practices came to be overwritten with the development of the virulent nationalism in the early twentieth century that exhort to 'manliness' as the only antidote to colonial rule. One such example is the nationalist ascetic, Swami Vivekananda, who, though a disciple of Ramakrishna Paramahansa, reconstituted Hinduism through the masculinist characteristics of aggression in order to counter the devastation of Hinduism. On the other hand, his guru, the Kali-devotee Ramakrishna, repeatedly situated himself though his songs and teachings as the feminine in this relationship of human and divine, even when understood through the dynamics of a mother-son relationship. The move to eradicate the 'effeminacy' of the Indian male, which had supposedly led 'others' to power in the country, while somewhat thwarted in the face of Gandhian philosophy, returned with redoubled strength in contemporary times with the development of religious fundamentalisms. This led to an overwhelming emphasis on *Advaita*, or non-dualist philosophy, as 'authentic' Hinduism, marginalizing the indigenous polytheistic traditions and revoking the centrality of the feminine principle. This does not mean that goddess worship and adoration of the feminine principle are not abundantly practiced in rural and tribal popular culture, but just that they are deliberately 'de-authenticated' as tradition.

In light of this history, Chandralekha's work reads as a move toward remaining submerged and marginalized traditions within the cultural context in which she is working, not in a vein of cultural revivalism and premodern nostalgia, but in terms of refiguring tradition to make the most sense of them in contemporary times. More importantly, her work reads as resistance to contemporary fundamentalist claimings of Hinduism, deliberately coextensive with Indianness, as characterized by a need to recover *purusharth* (valor, energy), lost through centuries of foreign domination that has resulted in such 'effeminacy' and 'impotency.' Culture and religion here come to be narrowly wrapped around a concept of masculinity that is constituted uniaxially, as social determinism. In this rhetoric a compulsorily aggressive action-orientedness and heterosexuality mark the ideal Hindu subject, who can effect a slippage to pass as the ideal Indian subject. It is the face of this heavy elitist embracing of Advaita philosophy, and the consequent contemporary masculinization of Hinduism in fundamentalist religious politics that Chandralekha's pieces must be read. Her exploration of femininity primarily through the bodies of men, her linking of it with abstract notions of fertility and her recasting of it as life force, is very largely about resisting what she sees as the masculinist drive of current global politics and economy in the age of capitalist neocolonialism.

Reviewing the context in which these pieces are created and initially performed highlights the resistive potential they are seeped in. Interestingly, while this is often read as rejection of 'tradition,' research also illuminates that it is indeed traditional cultural practices that are recalled and activated in the choreography to emphasize ideas of mobility and openness, the recycling of birthing and dying, creating and dissolving, in an ongoing process of life, to set in motion images of femininity that can revitalize us. *Raga* and *Sloka* bring into focus play, intimations of maya or *leela*, the illusory yet creative principle that brings the world, as humans know it, into being. The image of Meera running in to insert herself in between the two men in *Raga*, of Sunny suddenly running away from Shaji in *Sloka* as if tempting him to chase him, a game-like structure of catch between them, their torsos waving as they change direction running, the unstill shapes of the feminine life principle.

Such work also places in high relief the spiritual sensuality of bodies and spaces, and the vitalizing. Opening-up of spaces within and without bodies. Witness for instance, the last scene of *Raga*: the women run in and sit in a triangular formation of stage, folding their legs to one side, each woman marking the different tips of the triangle. With their eyes they begin to energize the farthest reaches of the space before them as their gazes, slow and unwavering, travel from one corner and crave arches through space to each the other corner. Suddenly, the light come up to illuminate the two men standing high up, atop two ladders that are barely lit, facing each other, their arms extended up, atop two ladders that are barely lit, facing each other, their arms extended up. As the women turn to sit facing them, the men move even closer to each other to stand, their legs crossing, intersecting the ground on which each man stands. Slowly, their arms descend and each man clasps the other around the waist. From their waists they bend backward, chests curving outward, pushing an opening out of the tip of the other vertical triangle they had at first seemed to mark with the women. The horizontal triangle of the women on the floor mobilizes itself simultaneously as they similarly curve their chests out and back, reminding one of the opening of the thousand-petalled lotus, the *sahasrarachakra*, that marks total spiritual awakening. The space darkens. As the lights come up one last time, we see the women once more on the floor, facing front, sitting calm and centered, earth women. Indeed, the dancers in *Raga* and *Sloka* are not divine beings. They are men and women intent in their search for feminine principle of life-movement, exploring dynamic realms of feminine energy, working constantly with movement to reframe principles of creativity and sexuality in secular terms, dancing to throw the carefully ordered fundamentalist universe, that insists on partitioned energies and controlled bodies, in disarray.

Contributors

MATTHEW HARP ALLEN teaches ethnomusicology at Wheaton College, Massachusetts, USA. He studied Karnatak music with flutist T. Viswanathan, with whom he wrote the book *Music in South India* (Oxford University Press), and for several years he sang in the ensemble accompanying Bharatanatyam dancer Lakshmi Shanmukham Knight (1943–2001), daughter of T. Balasaraswati.

RUKMINI DEVI ARUNDALE (1904–1986) was a highly influential figure in the history of Indian dance. Raised in the shadow of the Theosophical Society, in the 1930s she emerged as one of the first non-hereditary practitioners of Bharatanatyam. She founded Kalakshetra, one of the earliest institutions for the performing arts in the country. She introduced a number of innovations in the technique, form, repertoire, and presentation of Bharatanatyam. In the late 1950s and early 1960s, she served as a member of the Rajya Sabha. She was awarded the Padma Bhushan, the highest civilian honour in the country in 1956. In 1977, Morarji Desai offered to nominate her for the post of President of India, which she declined.

T. BALASARASWATI (1918–1984), granddaughter of the legendary Karnatak musician Veena Dhanammal (1867–1938), was recognized worldwide as one of the greatest dance artists of the last century. Trained primarily by Kandappa Pillai of Thanjavur (1899–1942), Balasaraswati ('Bala') was part of a hereditary artistic genealogy that reached back to the late eighteenth century. Bala's performances received acclaim throughout India, and her performances frequently took her to the United States. She taught Bharatanatyam at several prestigious universities including Wesleyan University and the University of California-Los Angeles. Dance practices in Bala's family are being continued by her grandson Aniruddha, son of her only daughter Lakshmi. A major biography on Bala, entitled *Balasaraswati: Her Art and Life* by Douglas M. Knight Jr., is forthcoming (Wesleyan University Press).

JOEP BOR is the founder of the World Music Academy at the Rotterdam Conservatory. In addition to numerous articles, he has written and edited six books on Indian music, including *The Voice of the Sarangi* (1987) and *The Raga Guide* (1999). At present he is a professor at Leiden University.

CHANDRALEKHA (1928–2006) was one of India's most innovative, radical, and controversial choreographers. Trained in Bharatanatyam by Kanchipuram Ellappa Pillai (1908–1974) in the 1950s, Chandralekha consciously opted out of the dance scene between 1972 and 1984, when she became involved in visual communication for activists in the non-government sector. In 1995, she began to create a series of revolutionary choreographies, beginning with *Angika*. Her new work eschewed the staged religiosity of modern Bharatanatyam, and explored the intersections between the body, erotic experience, movement, and the politics of representation. In addition to the scholarly analysis of Chandralekha's work in the writing of Ananya Chatterjee, a fascinating biography is Rustom Bharucha's *Chandralekha: Dance, Woman, Resistance* (Harper-Collins 1995).

ANANYA CHATTERJEA is Associate Professor and Director of Dance in the Department of Theater Arts and Dance, University of Minnesota. She is also Artistic Director of Ananya Dance Theatre (www. ananyadancetheatre.org). Her book, *Butting out! Reading Cultural Politics in the Work of Chandralekha and Jawole Willa Jo Zollar*, was published by Wesleyan University Press in 2004.

ANNE-MARIE GASTON (Anjali), internationally recognized Bharatanatyam and Odissi dancer, choreographer, scholar, and photographer, holds a doctorate in the Sociology of Indian Artistic Traditions from Oxford University. She is a member of the InterCulture Lab, University of Ottawa, and artistic director of Cultural Horizons (www.culturalhorizons.ca). Her major publications include *Siva in Dance, Myth and Iconography* (Oxford University Press), *Bharata Natyam from Temple to Theatre* (Manohar), and 'Dance and Religion/Spirituality' in Frank Burch Brown (ed.), *Handbook of Religion and the Arts* (Oxford University Press).

ANDRÉE GRAU is Professor at Roehampton University, London, where she holds a Chair in the Anthropology of Dance. She has published widely in numerous academic and professional journals, both on Tiwi and South Asian dance. Her children's book *Eyewitness Dance* (Dorling Kindersley 1998) has been translated into eight languages. She is currently writing a book focusing on the Sarabhais as three generations of performers involved in political activism.

TERESA HUBEL is an associate professor of English at Huron University College, the University of Western Ontario, in London, Ontario, Canada. She has written numerous essays on a variety of subjects, most of which have arisen out of her continuing captivation by the literature, dance, film, and history of India and which have been published in such journals as *Ariel*, *The Journal of Commonwealth Literature*, *Modern Asian Studies*, *Modern Fiction Studies*, *Dalhousie Review*, and *Kunapipi* as well as in diverse collections of essays. Duke University Press published her book, *Whose India? The Independence Struggle in British and Indian Fiction and History* in 1996. With Neil Brooks, she also edited a collection of essays entitled *Literature and Racial Ambiguity*. These days she is working on a new book about the white working classes of colonial India.

Born in Chennai, India and now living in London, UK, SHOBANA JEYASINGH has produced around 50 works for the stage, theatre, and camera. She has received numerous awards for her work, including two Time Out Dance awards and three Digital Dance awards. Shobana was awarded an MBE in January 1995. She also holds honorary degrees from Surrey University and De Montfort University, Leicester. In 2008 she was named an Asian Woman of Achievement in Britain.

In 1975, SASKIA C. KERSENBOOM saw the *ajapa natanam* of Shiva-Tyagaraja in the Tiruvarur temple as a student of Sanskrit, Tamil, and Bharata Natyam. This encounter triggered her PhD dissertation, *Nityasumangali: Devadasi Tradition in South India* (Utrecht University 1984; Motilal Banarsidass 1987) and her subsequent research, multimedial publications, including *Word, Sound, Image: The Life of the Tamil Text* (Berg Publishers 1995), and her artistic work as a dancer, teacher, and choreographer. At present she is Associate Professor of Theatre Studies at University of Amsterdam, and Director of the Paramparai Foundation.

HARI KRISHNAN is an internationally respected dancer, choreographer, teacher, and dance scholar. He specializes in traditional courtesan-style dance and contemporary abstractions of Bharatanatyam. His work has been presented throughout Canada, the USA, the UK, India, Malaysia, and Singapore. Krishnan is World Dance Artist in Residence in the Dance Department, Wesleyan University, Connecticut, USA and Artistic Director of inDANCE, Toronto, Canada. His research brings together several interpretive and theoretical approaches, and integrates the disciplines of performance studies, anthropology, history, and gender studies. Krishnan is on the board of directors of CORD (Congress of Research in Dance), and is the author of several important works on Bharatanatyam, the most recent being an essay entitled 'From Gynemimesis to Hypermasculinity: The Shifting Orientations of Male Performers of South Indian Court Dance' in Jennifer Fisher and Anthony Shay (eds), *When Men Dance: Choreographing Masculinities Across Borders* (Oxford University Press, 2009).

ANITA KUMAR is a doctoral candidate in Anthropology at the University of Southern California in Los Angeles. She was the 2005 winner of *The Drama Review* (TDR) 2005 Student Essay Competition, and is the film review editor of *Visual Anthropology Review*. 'Bharatanatyam and Identity Making in the South Asian Diaspora: Culture through the Lens of Occupation' is forthcoming (*Journal of Occupational Science*, Fall 2009). She lives in New York City, and conducting fieldwork on domestic violence in immigrant communities.

AVANTHI MEDURI is Reader in Dance/Performance Studies at Roehampton University, London, and Convener of the first graduate program in South Asian Dance Studies in the UK. Trained in Bharatanatyam and Kuchipudi since childhood, Meduri stepped out of a professional career in dance in the 1990s, and works in dance-theatre and arts education today. Meduri received her PhD from the Tisch School of Arts New York University in 1996, and taught at several universities in the United States. Her articles have appeared in various international journals, including *Asian Theatre Journal*, *Women and Performance*, *Dance Research*, *TDR*, and the *Dance Research Journal*. She is also editor of *Rukmini Devi Arundale: A Visionary Architect of Indian Culture and the Performing Arts* (Motilal Banarasidass 2005).

JANET O'SHEA is Associate Professor in the Department of World Arts and Cultures at the University of California, Los Angeles. Her previous publications include *At Home in the World: Bharata Natyam on the Global Stage* (Wesleyan University Press 2007) and 'Dancing through History and Ethnography: Indian Classical Dance and the Performance of the Past' in Theresa Buckland (ed.), *Dancing from Past to Present* (University of Wisconsin Press 2007). She is currently co-editing the second edition of the *Routledge Dance Studies Reader*.

P. (PARTHEPUTT) RAGAVIAH CHARRY (*c.* 1780–1840) was a 'native informant' for Holt Mackenzie's Mysore Survey Project. Holt Mackenzie (1787–1876) is best remembered for drafting a memorandum on land revenue in northern India which became the template for the revenue systems that were implemented by the British in northern and central

Acknowledgements

This project began in 2007, when I was approached by Ira Raja to edit an anthology on dance for Oxford University Press. This connection was made through Indira Viswanathan Peterson, and I would like to thank both Ira and Indira for initiating the dialogue that has resulted in this book.

I am deeply grateful to all my colleagues whose work appears in this volume for acquiescing to have their essays anthologized.

I owe particular thanks to B.M. Sundaram, Hari Krishnan, Leslie Orr, and Simon Reader for their support and encouragement. Victoria Gross, my assistant for this volume, has been tireless in her pursuit of permissions and other administrative correspondence. I would also like to thank Lisa Blake who also contributed to the administrative dimensions of the project in its later stages.

Finally I would like to thank the staff of Oxford University Press, New Delhi for their enthusiasm and support of this project.

The publisher and editor thank the following authors and copyright holders for their kind permission to reproduce material previously published elsewhere:

ABC-CLIO, Matthew Allen, Ashgate Publishing Limited, Joep Bor, The British Library, Ananya Chatterjea, Centre National de la Danse (Paris), Darpana Academy of Performing Arts, Saskia Kersenboom, Sunil Kothari, Hari Krishnan, Anita Kumar, The Laban Centre, Marg Publications, Avanthi Meduri, MIT Press Journals (The Drama Review), Motilal Banarsidass, A.C. Muthiah, Janet O'Shea, Sage Publications Ltd., Sangeet Natak Akademi, Mallika Sarabhai, Mrinalini Sarabhai, Shobana Jeyasingh Dance Company, Amrit Srinivasan, Tamil Isai Sangam, Vivekananda Kendra Patrika (Chennai), and Wesleyan University Press.

Every effort has been made to trace the copyright holders and obtain reproduction rights. The editor and publishers hereby state that should any inaccuracies or omissions be brought to notice, these will be rectified in future reprints of this volume.

1. Charry, P. Ragaviah, 'A short account of the dancing girls, treating concisely on the general principles of dancing and singing, with the translations of two Hindo songs'. This work was originally printed at the Gazette Press, Triplicane (1806). It survives in the form of a sole copy at the British Library in London (Shelfmark C.131.ff.11). Reproduced here with the permission of the British Library.

2. Bor, Joep, 'Mamia, Ammani and other Bayaderes: Europe's Portrayal of India's Temple Dancers', in Martin Clayton and Bennett Zon (eds), 2007, *Music and Orientalism in the British Empire*, London: Ashgate, pp. 39–70. Reproduced here with the permission of Ashgate Publishing Ltd.

3. Kersenboom, Saskia, 'The Traditional Repertoire of the Tiruttani Temple Dancers', in Julia Leslie (ed.), 1991, *Roles and Rituals for Hindu Women*, Delhi: Motilal Banarsidass, pp. 131–147. Reproduced here with the permission of Motilal Banarsidass.

4. Krishnan, Hari, 'Inscribing Practice: Reconfigurations and Textualizations of Devadasi Repertoire in Nineteenth and Early Twentieth Century South India', in Indira Viswanathan Peterson and Davesh Soneji (eds), 2008, *Performing Pasts: Reinventing the Arts in Modern South India*, Delhi: Oxford University Press.

5. Soneji, Davesh, 2009, 'Salon to Cinema: The Distinctly Modern Life of the Telugu *Javali*', Copyright © Davesh Soneji.

6. Reddi, Muthulakshmi, 'Why Should the Devadasi Institution in the Hindu Temples be Abolished?' This work was originally printed at the Central Co-operative Printing Works, Ltd., Chintadripet, Madras (1929).

7. 'The Humble Memorial of Devadasis of the Madras Presidency' by the Madras Devadasis Association. This memo was originally published in 1928, and is addressed to Sir C.P. Ramaswami Iyer, Law Member, Government of Madras. The memorandum is signed by eight members of the 'Madras Devadasi Association', including the famous vocalist Bangalore Nagaratnammal (1878–1952).

8. Srinivasan, Amrit, 'Reform or Continuity? Temple "Prostitution" and the Community in the Madras Presidency', in Bina Agarwal (ed.), 1988, *Structures of Patriarchy: State, Community and Household in Modernising Asia*, Delhi: Kali for Women, pp. 175–198. Reproduced here with the permission of the author.

9. Hubel, Teresa, 'The High Cost of Dancing: When the Indian Women's Movement Went After the Devadasis', in Laura B. Lengel (ed.), 2005, *Intercultural Communications and Creative Practice: Dance, Music and Women's Cultural Identity*, Westport, Conn. and London: Praeger, pp. 121–140. Copyright © 2005. Reproduced with permission of ABC-CLIO, LLC.

10. Raghavan, V. (Bhava Raga Tala), 'Bharata Natya Classic Indian Dance, The South Indian Sadir Nautch: The Recent Controversy Over the Art' in *Sound & Shadow* 2 (6) [1933]: 56–9.

11. Arundale, Rukmini Devi, 'The Spiritual Background of Indian Dance' in *Vivekananda Kendra Patrika*, X (2) [1981]: 9–12. Reproduced here with the permission of Vivekananda Kendra Patrika (Chennai).

12. Balasaraswati, T., 'Bharata Natyam'. This essay was originally written as the Presidential Address for the 33rd Annual Conference of the Tamil Isai Sangam, which took place on 21 December 1975. It was translated from Tamil to English by S. Guhan. Reproduced here with the permission of the Tamil Isai Sangam, Chennai.

13. Allen, Matthew Harp, 1997, 'Rewriting the Script for South Indian Dance', in *TDR: The Drama Review*, 41 (3) [Fall 1997]: 63–100. © MIT Press, Reproduced by permission of MIT Press.

14. Meduri, Avanthi, 'Bharatanatyam as World Historical Form'. Originally published in French as 'Le bharata natyam: une forme historique mondiale' in *Danses et identités: de Bombay à Tokyo*, ed. Claire Rousier, Pantin: Centre national de la danse, 2009, pp. 225–244. Reproduced here with the permission of the author and Centre National de la Danse (Paris).

15. Gaston, Anne-Marie, 'Dance and the Hindu Woman: Bharatanatyam Re-ritualized', in Julia Leslie (ed), 1991, *Roles and Rituals for Hindu Women*, Delhi: Motilal Banarsidass,

pp. 149–171. Reproduced here with the permission of Motilal Banarsidass.

16. O'Shea, Janet, 'At Home in the World? The Bharatanatyam Dancer as Transnational Interpreter' in *TDR: The Drama Review* 47, 1 (Spring 2003): 176–186. © MIT Press, 2003. Reproduced by permission of MIT Press.

17. Grau, Andre, 'Political Activism and South Asian Dance: The Case of Mallika Sarabhai', in *South Asia Research*, 27 (1) [2007]: 43–55. Reproduced by permission of SAGE Publications Ltd., London, Los Angeles, New Delhi, Singapore and Washington DC. Copyright © 2007

18. Kumar, Anita, 'What's the Matter? Shakti's (Re)Collection of Race, Nationhood and Gender' in *TDR: The Drama Review*, 50 (4) [Winter 2006]: 72–95. © MIT Press, 2006. Reproduced with the permission of MIT Press.

19. Sarabhai, Mrinalini, 1987, 'Creations', in *Creations*, Ahmedabad: Mapin Publishing. Reproduced here with the permission of the author.

20. Jeyasingh, Shobana, 'Getting Off the Orient Express' in *Dance Theatre Journal*, 8 (2) [1990]: 34–7. Reproduced here with the permission of the Shobana Jeyasingh Dance Company and the Laban Centre, UK.

21. Chandralekha, 'Reflections on New Directions in Indian Dance' in Sunil Kothari (ed), 2003, *New Directions in Indian Dance*, Mumbai: Marg Publications, pp. 50–8. Reproduced here with the permission of Sunil Kothari and Marg Publications.

22. Chatterjea, Ananya, '*Raga* (1998) and *Sloka* (1999): Troubling Femininity', in *Butting Out: Reading Resistive Choreographies Through Works by Jawole Willa Jo Zollar and Chandralekha*, Middletown, CT: Wesleyan University Press, 2004. Reproduced here with the permission of the author and Wesleyan University Press.